P9-DGX-304

The Ozarks

The Ozarks
Includes Branson, Springfield & Northwest Arkansas

Ron W. Marr

photographs by the author

The Countryman Press ✳ Woodstock, Vermont

FIRST EDITION

DEDICATION

This book is for Lori, who showed me that time ceases, and the finest journey begins, when you take your first walk together.

"The most important trip you may take in life is meeting people halfway."
—Henry Boye

"If you lived here, you'd be home now." —Anonymous

ISSN 1932-0655
ISBN-10: 0-88150-664-8
ISBN-13: 978-0-88150-664-8

Maps by Mapping Specialists Ltd., Madison, WI
Text and cover design by Bodenweber Design
Composition by PerfecType, Nashville, TN
Front cover photograph of the view of Ha Ha Tonka State Park
    © Lake of the Ozarks CVB

Published by The Countryman Press, P.O. Box 748, Woodstock, Vermont 05091

Distributed by W. W. Norton & Company, Inc., 500 Fifth Avenue, New York, NY 10110

Printed in the United States of America

10 9 8 7 6 5 4 3 2 1

EXPLORE WITH US!

Welcome to the first edition of *The Ozarks: An Explorer's Guide*. Kick off your boots, pull up a chair, and set a spell. This is intended to be the very first, very best, and most truly comprehensive wanderer's bible of the hills, hollers, sights, and spectacles that make up the Missouri and Arkansas Ozarks. Within this book you'll discover 50,000 square miles of sheer pretty, along with insights into the ways, traditions, history, and personalities of those who inhabit this ancient highland. In contrast with many such guides, this one is written by a local, someone who knows both the hot spots and back roads and has infused every page not just with in-depth and opinionated descriptions, but also with a hefty and happily readable dollop of Ozark anecdotes, philosophy, and humor.

During your travels you'll trip across informed commentary on the shows, lodgings, restaurants, and attractions in Branson, Mo., Live Country Music Capital of the World. You'll discover unsuspected urbanity, wining, and dining in upscale and eclectic spots such as Springfield, Mo., and the ever-growing quad-cities region of Northwest Arkansas (known locally as "Arkansopolis"). But that's just the beginning of the tale. You'll find tiny rib shacks and pie shops far off the beaten path and learn of the best roads for soaking in the glorious colors inherent to an Ozark fall. Throughout the book detailed listings are included for bed & breakfasts and resorts, restaurants, and shopping; state, local, and federal parks; attractions and festivals galore; and more than a few spots that are only known by those in the know. Just think of this book as a personal narrator, a guide whose services have been engaged to uncover the very best (and sometimes the very strangest) that the Ozarks region has to offer.

WHAT'S WHERE

The journey of 1,000 miles may begin with the first step, but in this case it also begins with the first page. At the beginning of this book is an A-to-Z listing of the basics, some highlights, and some tips that will be helpful while traveling the Ozarks. For a quick reference covering anything from apple festivals to float streams, BBQ joints to trout fishing, railroad trips to wineries, allow these pages to start you on your way.

LODGING

Most of the lodging options found in this guide are privately owned, with the lion's share of emphasis placed on bed & breakfasts, resorts, campgrounds, and private cabins (and one very cool, ultraluxurious cave). Franchise or chain operations are not included here, nor should they be. My goal is to lead you to the roads less traveled, to respites often hidden by the bright lights and golden arches lining the main drag.

RESTAURANTS

As with all *Explorer's Guides*, each chapter of this book includes separate sections for *Eating Out* and *Dining Out*. The former is normally intended to specify a sense of the casual, while the latter implies the putting on of the dog. In the Ozarks, however, the line between casual and fancy-pants is blurry, if not wholly nonexistent. In 99.9 percent of cases you really don't have to worry about dress codes in these parts. Generally speaking, as long as you're a paying customer, Ozark restaurateurs don't give a hoot what you wear. As long as you've got on clothes, and the folks at the next table don't start requesting a can of Lysol, you're fine.

PRICES AND TIMES

We're a happy bunch of capitalists in this great country, and therefore any of the prices and times listed in this *Explorer's Guide* are subject to change. Because this can happen so rapidly, most entries include present hours of operation and sample prices from current menus, rate cards, and attractions. This will give you a basic idea of what to expect, even if entrées, room charges, admission fees, or hours should suddenly alter.

KEY TO SYMBOLS

- ⓌⓌ **Weddings:** Listings including the wedding-ring symbol are a dandy place to get hitched. In the Ozarks. This can include not only certain B&Bs, resorts, and hotels, but also caves and outdoor chapels.

- ❦ **Special Value:** The ❦ symbol represents spots that perform above and beyond the call of duty in terms of quality, service, or unique offerings. In many cases the ❦ symbol refers to free admission, which we all know is the very best kind.

- 🐾 **Pets:** If a listing is accompanied by a tiny dog paw, you are free to bring along Fido or Tabby. On the other hand, there will be leash restrictions (both in private and public campgrounds). Common sense is the rule, and obviously you won't be the most popular person on the block if your pooch howls at the moon from dusk till dawn. Few B&Bs accept pets, and some establishments accept pets only with an extra charge. To date, no restaurants have been found that allow anything but Seeing Eye dogs . . . for that you have to go to either France or Montana.

- ✐ **Kid-Friendly:** The crayon symbol identifies spots that allow and/or welcome the younger crowd. In many cases you should note that bed & breakfasts tend to have restrictions on your progeny. Some specify certain age limits, and others ask you to call in advance.

- ♿ **Handicapped Accessible:** The wheelchair symbol is intended to note locales that either meet ADA (Americans with Disabilities Act) standards, or at least have ramps or paved paths. This is the Ozarks, remember, so a number of sights and establishments may not yet be up-to-date. Others may be "partially" handicapped accessible. As with all things, if this is a concern, it is best to call ahead for detailed information.

- ❄ **Off-Season:** This symbol, the snowflake, is highly subjective in the Ozarks and subject to change. Shows and businesses in outdoor- and entertainment-oriented areas—such as Branson, Mo.; Eureka Springs, Ark.; and the Lake of the Ozarks—often close for vaguely specified periods during winter months. This is due not to snow (we get very little) but to a lack of tourist trade. You should always call for information if traveling to such places between December and mid-March.

Ⓨ **Liquor:** The martini-glass icon is your key to "John Barleycorn's World of Hydraulic Amusement." That said, lounges and bars are not as prevalent in the Ozarks as they are in most other regions. This stems in large part from the number of small towns, and the accompanying local culture that doesn't promote getting a snoot-full. On the other hand, most little towns do have a bar hidden away someplace, and all the larger towns and cities are loaded (no pun intended) with restaurants offering award-winning wine lists and full bars. Areas such as Springfield, Mo., and Fayetteville, Ark., in particular offer numerous clubs with outstanding live music.

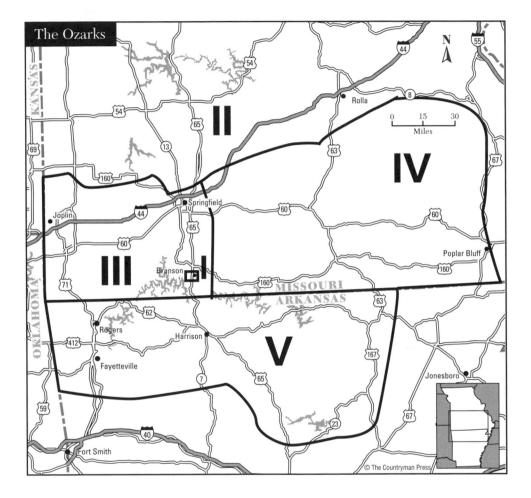

CONTENTS

ACKNOWLEDGMENTS

Compiling a book of this scope, length, and detail can at first glance be a bit daunting. At second glance it gets downright scary. Luckily I never experienced a drought in terms of folks who were ready, willing, and able to toss in hints, suggestions, tips, and advice. While it would be virtually impossible to list everyone who assisted with this travel tome—partially because of the sheer numbers and partially because I often have a hard enough time remembering my own name—thanks are warranted nonetheless. Therefore, I send my heartfelt appreciation to each business, chamber of commerce, convention bureau, and state or federal agency that contributed information, offered assistance, and answered my frequently silly questions.

On a more personal note, a few people should be recognized for duty above and beyond the call. My profound thanks go to Danita Allan Wood, editor and co-publisher of *Missouri Life* magazine, for recommending my work to The Countryman Press. Gratitude is also sent to my oldest friend (and renowned BBQ pitmaster), Edward T. Boys, for his incomparable insights into the location of the true Ozark borders and the inscrutable world of dandy rib shacks. Extra credit is awarded Edward T. for his encyclopedic knowledge of events involving horses, mules, and steam-powered machinery. Appreciation is happily sent to my parents, Bill and Ruth Marr, for providing me with their firsthand accounts of both the infinite sights of Branson and the equally infinite craft fairs of Northwest Arkansas. Of course, no acknowledgment page would be complete without recognition of the invaluable assistance of Henry Red-Dog, Boris Mahlemiut, and Jackie P. Russell.

The book would surely not have gone as smoothly as it did if not for a few other integral philosophical consultants. For starters, I send regards to Mike Hibbard, who vividly describes certain of his youthful days in Arkansas as "John Barleycorn's World of Hydraulic Amusement" (a phrase that I stole at my first opportunity). Next would be former "Beach Boys" associate, traveling troubadour, and skateboarder extraordinaire Baron Stuart. Baron supplied a plethora of witty commentary throughout the writing process and helped me recall that I'm really, really glad I escaped the utterly awful town of Elk City, Idaho, with both skin and sanity partially intact.

And as always, my eternal thanks to my girlfriend, Lori, for her loving support, research help, proofreading skills, and sense of humor. Lori consistently demonstrates incredible patience in putting up with my various moods, admittedly odd ways, and pitiful attempts to master the blues harp.

Thanks, y'all.

INTRODUCTION

When Herman Engelhardt immigrated to America in the late 1800s, it was with the prevailing illusion that the streets were paved with gold. Born in 1858 in Rubenau, Germany, a nail maker by trade, Herman's illusions were shaken when he first saw the 120 acres of government land he planned to homestead in Douglas County, Mo. Far from possessing glowing yellow pavement, this patch of Ozark ground near Ava, Mo., was covered with trees, rocks, snakes, and ravines. To Herman, however, the metaphorical gold was still there. He soon realized that superficial appearances are deceptive; to unearth a treasure, one must learn to dig.

And so he began, aided by his wife, Pertha, and their five children. During winters he felled trees and prepared the land for cultivation. Money could be made from the railroads in those days, at least by those who were accomplished with a broad-bladed ax, and the funds Herman acquired from hand cutting railroad ties kept food on the table. A barn was built long before thoughts of a house were a glimmer in the eye, and the Engelhardts shared quarters with the precious livestock that meant the difference between survival and bankruptcy.

Time passed, and after nearly two decades of backbreaking labor that entire 120 acres of trees, rocks, snakes, and ravines was under profitable cultivation. At least a small part of the Ozark wilderness had been tamed. Golden roads can appear in the most unexpected places.

I suppose I come by my love of the Ozarks naturally. My great-aunt Lena was born amid the cows, goats, and stacks of hay in that old barn. Framed photos of Herman and Pertha, my maternal great-grandparents, hang on a wall of the red Ozark cabin I call home. My grandmother Elsie taught me to fish and gave me my love of dogs, woods, rainbows, and simplicity. I've no doubt she learned these things by osmosis at the knee of her own parents, acquiring via a harsh and happy rural life the skills inherent to mining humor from adversity and joy from the commonplace. Perhaps that's why she lived to nearly 102. Life is mostly about perception and approach, after all. My grandmother was still chopping down trees, making pies, and aging sauerkraut at age 90 (though if I recall, she'd stopped cooking lye soap in the backyard some years earlier).

There are a thousand Ozark stories of similar vein. The personality of a rural region can usually be defined by observing the history of its settlers, and nowhere will you find a place with more personality (and personalities) than the Ozarks. Though modern culture is now a regular part of this hard and majestic place, modern amenities and conveniences share a lesser billing with well-established traditions and beliefs.

Quite simply, Ozarkers are a breed apart. To outsiders they often seem a contradiction, both shy and extroverted, quiet and boisterous, industrious and lazy. In truth, there are no contradictions at all. The Ozarker merely has a respect for priorities and a hefty dose of common sense. He rarely succumbs to the peer pressure or political correctness of the outside world (peer pressure within his own community is another story) and functions according to his own heart, rules, and genetically independent nature. Putting in the crops is important, but so is the first day of deer season. Fixing a leaky roof is vital, but if it's not raining, the roof doesn't leak (and if it is raining, it's too wet to fix the darned thing anyhow). Milking the cows, mowing the brush, and doing a fair day's work are essential; so are BBQ, fishing, and taking a nap.

Independence is the primary trait of the average Ozarker. That, and an outrageous sense of humor that encompasses the belly laugh, odd pun, practical joke, and graveyard genre. Both these characteristics were born of the population's predominant Scots-Irish ancestry and a generations-long sequestering from society at large. The Ozarker knew he had to get by with the help of only family members or perhaps a few neighbors. He also knew that if he wanted to be amused, he'd best amuse himself.

Though the infusion of modern culture has to a great degree homogenized the almost Elizabethan language of yesteryear Ozarks, you'll still find a fair amount of colloquial expressions in everyday use. All these maxims, metaphors, and similes appear tailor-made to elicit a grin. An Ozarker might casually inform you that his house is so small, he can't cuss the cat without getting hair in his mouth. He might say that a sleet-covered highway is slick as a wax snake on a glass floor. Those who contemplate purchase of a ridiculous item might be chastised with the wisdom that they "don't need that any more than a tomcat needs a marriage license." Ozarkers know that some individuals would rather climb a ladder to tell a lie than stand on the ground and tell the truth. They realize that the world is chock-full of long-winded types who will talk your leg off and then cuss you for being crippled. They know that intelligence is not a given, and that a sizable percentage of the populace may well be duller than a pound of wet leather.

OZARKS MAILBOX

Independence and humor are key ingredients to the makeup of an Ozarker, but the hill folks share one additional attribute. Put bluntly, they have streak of stubborn a mile wide. Ozarkers can be so bullheaded that they'll not only disagree on how their homeland got its name, they'll even disagree on its borders. The former dispute is a bit easier to tackle than the latter. The word *Ozarks* is likely a corruption of the phrase *Bois d'Arcs*, meaning "wood of bows" and referring to the hedge trees from which the Osage Indians fashioned their archery gear. Then again, it may be a corruption of *Aux Arcs*, meaning "with bows," referring either to the Quapaw Indians or a French trading post located in northern Arkansas. The literal truth will never be known, which is just fine as it gives us fodder for friendly arguments.

But a less convivial squabble involves the location of the actual borders of the Ozarks. Some say the region runs north and south between the Missouri River and the Arkansas River. Others (self included) say that such a claim is nuttier than a fruitcake. The eastern and western borders are even more dicey. You'll find people who say the Ozarks include parts of Kansas and Oklahoma (these people are typically either from Kansas or Oklahoma) and others who say the borders stop shy of Springfield, Mo. (long regarded as the Queen City of the Ozarks). A few deluded souls will go so far as to try to convince you that parts of the Ozarks lie in Illinois, which is a little like insisting parts of the Everglades are found in Wisconsin.

The only conclusion worth mentioning is that hardly anyone can agree on the borders and boundaries of the Ozarks. Ask a dozen different people—teachers, doctors, geologists, cartographers, fishing guides, or even your garden-variety Hillbilly—and you'll get a dozen different answers. Some will define the borders by geological formations and topography, others by cultural standards and ethnic heritage. For the purposes of this book, I tend to integrate the two, with greater emphasis placed on the latter. After all, while the lay of the land can shape the attitudes and actions of people, it is the people who bring texture and character. They are the spice the keeps the stew interesting.

You can tell when you're in the Ozarks because the people act like Ozarkers. When they behave differently, you're someplace else. Roughly speaking, the area covered in this book places the northern border in a curvy line from Sullivan, Mo., on the east, around the Lake of the Ozarks, and down to Harry Truman's birthplace in Lamar, Mo., toward the southwest. The western border follows the natural western state lines of Missouri and Arkansas, south to a point somewhere near Crawford County, Ark. On the east the Black River serves as a delineating landmark in Missouri; the border then travels past Mammoth Springs, Ark., on an angle to Heber Springs, Ark., and Greers Ferry Lake. From there it takes a turn to the northwest and more or less makes a wobbling trek toward the western border of Arkansas.

The Ozarks are a real place, but in a sense they are also a state of mind. And the pronouncements formed by those minds are wide and varied. There's not been (and never will be) any fast-and-firm method to assure that you're standing within the boundaries of the Ozarks. Unless, of course, you adopt our Hillbilly Zen attitude of "you either is . . . or you ain't."

OZARKS ARTIFACTS

Geologically, this is an ancient and enduring land; the rocks found around Taum Sauk Mountain and Elephant Rocks State Park in Missouri are a billion and a half years old. Scientists say that even millions of years ago, when seas still covered much of the Ozarks (and most of the rest of present-day America), this area formed a cluster of islands. The terrain of the Ozarks was shaped not by glaciers but rather by volcanic activity, eons of erosion, and the uplift of the Ozark Plateau. For visitors (even if they're not rockhounds), ancient lands translate to ancient critters and ancient people. As a result, the ground is a treasure trove of minerals, fossils, and (thanks to a host of ancient tribes) arrowheads and primitive stone tools.

The Ozark Plateau is a highland region consisting of approximately 50,000 square miles, the only highland region between the Appalachians and the Rockies. In reality it is three plateaus: the Springfield Plateau, the Salem Plateau, and the Boston Mountains. The Bostons are the tallest and roughest of these areas (reaching over 2,000 feet above sea level in spots), while the rest of the area is more rolling and deeply forested. It doesn't feel "rolling" if you're trying to walk it (the saying here is that while our mountains may not be that high, our valleys are mighty deep), so perhaps the allusion is more that of "rolling" down a steep hill than falling off a sheer cliff.

The Ozark topography is noted for its karst features, full of caves, springs, and sinkholes. To say there are a few caves and springs would be a gross understatement; we live among and above nearly 7,000 caves and at least that many springs. Big Spring, near Van Buren, Mo., and Mammoth Spring at Mammoth Springs, Ark., pump out 280 and 240 million gallons per day, respectively, and you can tour, ride, explore, dine, get married, or vacation in subterranean luxury in some our developed caverns. Also, the area is rich in minerals. The mining of lead, zinc, saltpeter and sulfur (for gunpowder), limestone, and charcoal have at one time or another all proven bonanzas in the Ozarks. The Joplin and Carthage, Mo., district at one time lived and died by mining, and the University of Missouri–Rolla is viewed as one of the country's finest schools for mining engineers. Timber also played a huge role in early industry. Visitors of today see our deep and mysterious forests and sometimes assume they are viewing stands of virgin growth. Nothing could be farther from the truth. The Ozarks have been basically denuded (by humans) several times since the early 1700s. That's the nice thing about trees: They grow back. Such should prove a lesson to those who believe forestry is a destructive industry. When managed properly, this renewable resource springs to life time and time again.

And then there are our rivers. The Ozarks are ruled by rivers. From the days of the Bluff Dwellers and Osage to the days of satellite TV and the Internet, our spring-fed crystal waters have served as a source of food, of transportation, of commerce, and of recreation. Today travelers arrive from around the world to float and fish the legendary White River and Buffalo National River of Arkansas. In Missouri they seek out the Current and Jacks Fork, two streams that make up the Ozark National Scenic Riverways, or the stunningly beautiful North Fork of the White. The Army Corps of Engineers dammed many of our rivers over the past century, both for flood control and to harness hydroelectric energy. Lakes such as Table Rock, Bull Shoals, Norfork, Greers Ferry, Beaver, Taneycomo, and the world-renowned Lake of the Ozarks are sources of fun, functionality, and free enterprise not just for the souls who reside near their banks but also for literally millions of visitors.

When viewed in their entirety, the Ozarks of today are a symbiotic relationship of new and old. The past is the present, and the present is the past. You will still find bluegrass, country, and gospel music played on many a town square on a summer's eve, just as they were 100 years ago. But you will also find them in the huge and luxurious theaters of Branson. The Live Country Music Capital of the World, Branson is now a first-tier vacation destination. The town welcomes more than 7 million visitors annually and boasts more than 57,000 theater seats (that's 12,000 more than Broadway). While the numbers seem to accelerate on a daily basis, you will also find 400 restaurants, 200 lodging facilities, 5,000 camping spaces, 9 golf courses, 45 theaters offering 80 shows per day, and countless shops, stores, amusement parks, and attractions.

Other Ozark cities boast a similar level of growth and development. The northwest corner of Arkansas—holding the towns of Springdale, Rogers, Bentonville, and Fayetteville—is fast becoming a major metropolis. Universities, industry, restaurants, and entertainment (which rivals the best of the coasts) are found in this exploding region. Perhaps explanation enough arrives with the knowledge that Bentonville is home to the corporate headquarters of Wal-Mart. Back in Missouri, Springfield has continued to live up to its moniker of Queen City of the Ozarks. Restaurants exist for any and all ethnic tastes; entertainment options range from baseball, major concerts, and collegiate athletics to opera, ballet, blues, live theater, and bluegrass. Springfield's growth is nothing short of astounding and can be attributed to wise planning, long-term vision, and excellent park and educational systems. This growing city is prosperous and clean, and more than a few residents have left major urban centers to spend their life within its comparably idyllic boundaries.

The real draw, however, is that all the major Ozark cities have one thing in common. It is the attitude of the people. Even our larger cities still feel like small towns. On a busy street drivers will still allow you to pull ahead in traffic; residents wave and say hello. Again, it's the mesh of new and old; a 21st-century lifestyle combined with 19th-century values, convictions, and attitude.

When looking at the Ozarks, it seems to always come back to that word. It's an attitude. The people here are attached to their land, sometimes fiercely so. Get out into the country and you will find that nearly every hill, creek branch, or sharp curve has a name. Ask directions, and you might well be told to "drive up to where Jimmy Bob Taylor used to live, then turn right where the old church burned down in '84." We don't operate by street numbers or highway signs. We live by landmark and memory. What seems to make the Ozarker unique is that he'll generally define himself as an Ozarker (or, as many of us tend to say, "just a Hillbilly") rather than as a resident of Missouri or Arkansas. Even when they are unacquainted, Ozarkers realize that they have more in common with one another than they do with most who reside outside their region.

With that thought in mind, it should come as no surprise that things are a little different here. Things are fun and gorgeous and interesting, but they're different. For starters, you can rest assured that the Ozarker is a genial host to strangers, unless the stranger happens to be rude or nosy. In that case the local fellow will just appear genial, silently wonder how a body could get so far along in life without learning any civilized manners, and offer the drawling question, "You ain't from around here, are ya?"

The average Ozarker is also seriously fond of his church, and if you're from one of the coasts, you may be surprised by just how many churches there are in these parts (not to mention the religious billboards found along major interstates). You'll see churches all over the place; they're thicker than june bugs on a new porch light. Quite a few may be of denominations you never knew existed, and contrary to popular media conceptions, most of them don't endorse snake handling. Churches can be old or new, built of frame, brick, or cinder block. Lately the church structure of choice seems to be the prefabricated steel building. In the warmer months you'll trip across a plethora of old-time tent revivals, which seem to magically transform into fireworks stands as Independence Day draws near.

That said, to clear up another erroneous media conception, residents of these hills are rarely pushy or overly evangelical about their religion. It's a private thing, as it should be. If you're interested and ask, the locals will gladly invite you to a service. If not, the subject will likely never arise. Hollywood portrayals and the malarkey of the evening news are far different from reality, and never the twain shall meet.

The goal of this Explorer's Guide to the Ozarks is to provide you, gentle reader, with a road map to many of the sights, sounds, tastes, and events of this quirky and beautiful hill country that so many of us love so deeply. The goal is not just to show you the popular high points and the traditional tourist spots, but to take you down the blacktops and gravel paths, to give you directions on the road less traveled. Within these pages you'll find five-star restaurants, elegant spas, and a town whose claim to fame is albino squirrels. You'll find live performances by major stars and drive far into the boondocks to a place where spectral balls of starlight (said to the be the spirits of long-dead Indians) dance to and fro under a midnight sky. You'll see the cairns, cave dwellings, and artifacts of the first inhabitants and follow your nose to the finest hickory-smoked ribs on the planet. You'll discover pie shops and Puccini; tour caves and castles; walk in the steps of Jesse James, Wyatt Earp, and Bill Hickock; and linger over the desk where Laura Ingalls Wilder wrote her *Little House* books. You'll ride at dude ranches, chase monster trout, and perhaps hunt a white-tailed deer (or even bag a buffalo, if such is your taste). You'll eat deep-fried catfish and hush puppies till you're fuller than a tick, then fall asleep in a Victorian bed & breakfast (no chain motels or restaurants are included in this guide; why go for carbon copies when you can have the real deal?). You'll paddle a canoe, ski behind a jet boat, and walk forest paths that seem untouched by time. You'll wander mills and museums and celebrate at festivals commemorating everything from frogs, sucker fish, and apple butter to kites, clowns, and hog calling. Heck, you can even catch an international piano competition.

And that's just the beginning. Welcome to the Ozarks.

The more they change, the more they stay the same.

WHAT'S WHERE IN THE OZARKS

ANTIQUES Nowhere in the world will you find more antiques shops than in the Ozarks. However, in this part of the world *antiques shop* is often synonymous with *junkyard*. A healthy sense of *caveat emptor* should be employed, for when it comes to dickering, the Ozarker will not tell you that the horse has only three legs; you'll have to count them for yourself. As a rule of thumb, antiques emporiums that appear too fancy are overpriced and full of reproductions. Those that appear too dumpy are loaded with rusty screwdrivers, broken can openers, and glass telephone insulators. Look for shops on the two-lane blacktops. For some reason, those sporting antiquated gas station signs and a preponderance of lounging dogs seem to hold the greatest treasures. On the other hand, trips to the massive **Heartland Antique Mall** (417-532-9350 or 1-800-532-9350; www.heartlandantiquemall.com) in Lebanon, Mo., have never disappointed. Plus, the **Russell Stover** candy store next door offers free samples.

APPLES Ozark residents will organize a festival at the drop of a hat, making merry over topics ranging from A to Z. At the start of that celebratory alphabet you will discover two excellent apple extravaganzas. The **Old Tyme Apple Festival** in Versailles, Mo. (573-378-4401), is held the first Saturday of every October. Drawing an average of 35,000 people, it features 400 vendors, a parade, apple pie and fiddlers' contests, a tractor show, a car cruise, a demolition derby, and a gospel-singing extravaganza. In Mount Vernon, Mo., **Apple Butter Makin' Days** (417-466-7654), also held in October, attracts 50,000 people. Not only will you taste apple butter, apple dumplings, and apple pies, but you can also enjoy live bluegrass, a nail-driving competition, a turtle race, a bubble-gum-blowing contest, and 400 craft vendors.

BBQ Texans brag to high heaven about theirs. North Carolinians

assume they serve up the ultimate. Down Memphis way the locals swear on a stack of Bibles that nothing can surpass their version. Of course, that's either a case of wishful thinking or delusions of grandeur. The only real BBQ is Ozark BBQ, and you'd be hard pressed to locate even the tiniest of towns that doesn't boast at least one purveyor of quality Q. We're talking hickory smoked, cooked slow, with sauce on the side. Though the dining possibilities are endless, you should strive mightily to visit **Homer's BBQ** (573-468-4393) in Sullivan, Mo. (he smokes over a hickory-and-sassafras mix), and the **Crosstown BBQ** (417-862-4646) in Springfield, Mo. If it gets any better than this, then you're up at the Pearly Gates, splitting a slab of ribs with St. Peter.

BLUEGRASS The heartbeat of the Ozarks is bluegrass. Mountain music is found on every corner in Branson, with the two oldest shows being the **Baldknobbers Jamboree Music Show** (417-334-4528; www.bald knobbers.com) and **Presleys' Country Jubilee** (417-334-4874; www .presleys.com). Down in West Fork, Ark., you'll find the classic local venue

known as the **Little O' Opry** (479-839-2992), and you won't want to miss the Harrison, Ark., annual **Bluegrass Festival**, held in mid-May. An all-time classic festival, renowned from coast to coast, is **Bluegrass Pickin' Time** (573-759-7716) in Dixon, Mo. This party is so good, they hold it twice each summer, on Memorial and Labor Day weekends.

BRIDGES Between the late 1800s and the 1930s more than two dozen swinging bridges were built in the Lake of the Ozarks region. Although most of these are long since gone, either succumbing to time or disappearing beneath the waters of the lake, a couple of examples still exist near the little town of **Brumley**. If you enjoy walking (or driving) across ancient, creaking, cracking suspension bridges, this is your cup of tea. North of Eureka Springs, Ark., on SR 187, the 1949 **Beaver Bridge** offers a suspension bridge measuring 554 feet in length with a 312-foot span. Just keep in mind that it's a one-way road. You don't want to have to back up.

CATFISH In terms of both prevalence and popularity, catfish joints place a close second to BBQ joints in the

Ozarks. These days, most places serve both. The favorite way to order catfish in the Ozarks is deep fried, and it usually arrives with hush puppies, french fries, coleslaw, and (at the really good places) a bowl of ham and beans. For a true catfish gorge-athon, simply visit either the **AQ Chicken House** (479-751-4633; www.aqchicken.com) in Springdale, Ark., or **Dowd's Catfish House** (417-532-1777) in Lebanon, Mo.

CAVES There are an estimated 5,500 caves in the Missouri Ozarks, and another 2,000 in Arkansas. Not a people to look a gift horse in the mouth, the local folks have for years utilized these caverns to earn a living. You can explore, dine, walk, ride, and even get married in various Ozark caves. **War Eagle Cavern** on Beaver Lake (479-789-2909; www.wareaglecavern.com) has been open to the public since 1978, and the famous **Meramec Caverns** (573-468-3166; www.americascave.com) has drawn tourists since 1935. As a bonus, it's just one of the hundreds of spots where Jesse James allegedly hid out.

CIVIL WAR Missouri is in fact third (behind Virginia and Tennessee) in numbers of Civil War actions fought on her soil, and blood flowed freely all over the Ozarks. One of the largest scrapes, which forced Missouri to remain in the Union, took place in Pea Ridge, Ark., in March 1862. The **Pea Ridge National Military Park** (479-451-8122; www.nps.gov/peri) is a 4,300-acre site that offers complete details of the day nearly 30,000 troops met in battle. Also, to the north in Republic, Mo., the **Wilson's Creek National Battlefield** (417-732-2662; www.nps.gov/wicr) provides an in-depth look at the day, in August 1861, when 2,300 combatants lost their lives.

DOGWOOD The dogwood tree is so beloved in the Ozarks that we have built entire festivals around it. (That said, we have also built entire festivals around frogs; a party is a party, after all.) In Siloam Springs, Ark., the **Dogwood Festival** draws 30,000 people annually and is held the last weekend in April. In Camdenton, Mo., the **Dogwood Festival** (1-800-769-1004; www.camdentonchamber.com), also taking place in April, features more than 100 floats and a variety of events. Plus, the town hands out more than 1,500 free dogwood saplings.

DRIVE-IN MOVIES The drive-in theater is alive and well in the Ozarks, complete with movies, concession stands, and playgrounds up front for the kids. In Aurora, Mo., you'll find the **Sunset Drive-In Theater** (417-678-6609; www.sunsetdriveinaurora.com). In Cuba, Mo., there's the **Highway 19 Drive-In** (573-885-7752). And right on the trail of the hallowed Route 66, in Carthage, Mo., you'll find the **66 Drive-In Theater** (417-359-5959; www.comevisit.com/66drivein). Just pull in, park the car, and feel like a 1960s teenager again.

ELEPHANT ROCKS The massive boulders found at **Elephant Rocks State Park** (573-546-3454; www.mostateparks.com/elephantrock.htm) are as much as 27 feet high and 680 tons. What's different about these hunks of stone is that they were not left by the glaciers. Rather, they are 1.5-billion-year-old pieces of granite that sheared off volcanic magma. The park itself is only 132 acres, but that's more than enough. Interactive in a prehistoric manner, Elephant Rocks offers a Braille Trail for the blind.

EQUESTRIANS It's an Ozark maxim that there's absolutely no reason why you should walk when you can ride. With that thought in mind, you'll discover myriad parks, resorts, and dude ranches that can provide you with a well-behaved horse. Take a look in Eminence, Mo., at either **Coldwater Ranch** (573-226-3723; www.cold waterranch.com) or **Cross Country Trail Ride** (573-226-3883; www.cross countrytrailride.com), and you'll see why Eminence is known as the Trail Riding Capital of the United States. Another excellent resort for the horsy sort is the **Meramec Farm Cabins and Trail** (573-732-4765; www .meramecfarm.com), in Bourbon, Mo. Last but not least, if you wish to look rather than ride, don't miss the **Missouri Foxtrotting Horse Breed Association Show** (417-683-2468; www.mfthba.com) in Ava, Mo. Shows and sales take place in both June and September.

FALL COLORS Fall in the Ozarks is no less than a riot of color, no matter your locale. The deep orange, red, and yellow hues are breathtaking. To see them up close and personal, one of the best drives you can take is the **Glade Top Trail**. In the third week of October, the **Glade Top Trail Flaming Fall Festival** (417-683-4594; www.avachamber.org/events) takes place in Ava, Mo. Not only can you prepare to go look at the trees, but you also can enjoy square dancing, a sausage-and-pancake breakfast, and a BBQ chicken dinner on Sunday. As a sidenote, don't forget to drive this trail

in spring. Our springtime colors are just as pretty as the fall version.

FESTIVALS As mentioned previously, in the Ozarks any excuse is reason enough for hold a festival. The options are nearly infinite, from **Frog Fest** in Waynesville, Mo., to **Dixon Cow Days** in Dixon, Mo., to the **Crawdad Days Music Festival** in Harrison, Ark. This is but the smallest of samples and doesn't even consider the fairs that are held annually in nearly every county. For those who like their arts and crafts and wish to peruse the handmade goods of local artisans, few events compare to the **War Eagle Fair** in Rogers, Ark. (479-789-5398; www.wareaglefair.com), or the **Applegate Farm Autumn Fair** (1-888-404-7478; www.oleapplegateplace .com) in Bentonville, Ark. Both of these events take place twice a year (October and May) and encompass literally thousands of booths and products. Of course there's plenty of food and music, too.

FISHING You're never far from water when you come to the Ozarks, which means you're never far from fine fishing on our innumerable lakes, creeks, ponds, and rivers. Most of us in these parts are handling a fishing pole by the time we can walk. A couple of personal recommendations here: If you're after bass, try the **Kings River** in Arkansas or the **Gasconade River** in Missouri. If you want trout, there is no place better than either the **White River** of Arkansas or the **North Fork of the White** in Missouri. And for catfish, if you can find a local who is willing to share a few secrets, you can on occasion catch some honking-big catfish from Missouri's **Bryant Creek**. Of course you do need the

"noodling" season. This involves the fine art of wading along riverbanks, blindly groping around under a hole or submerged log, tickling a catfish's belly to make him/her mellow, and then yanking the sucker out bare-handed. Less painful but no less unusual is the sport of gigging. This is the practice of running a well-lit, flat-bottomed boat up a river at midnight and spearing fish with sharp sticks (and yup, there's a legal season for it). **Bird's Nest Lodge** (573-775-2606 or 1-877-707-7238; www.birdsnestlodge .com) in Steelville, Mo., is the only place I've ever heard of that offers gigging tours and provides gigging guides. The fine folks at Bird's Nest will also clean your catch, set you up on a float trip that doesn't involve impaling carp, rent you a campsite or cabin, and feed you. What more could a body want?

proper licenses. The **Missouri Department of Conservation** provides all regulations and seasons, as well as online license purchase, at 1-800-392-4115 (https://wildlifelicense.com/mo). **Arkansas Fish and Game** also offers complete information and online purchases at 1-800-364-4263 (www.agfc .state.ar.us).

FLOATING Many people simply think of the Ozarks as a land of rugged hills and deep forests. Thus it often comes as a surprise to learn that, more than anything, we are a region ruled by water. Soon after, they learn that our creeks and rivers are the paddler's version of Nirvana. Many visitors like to bring their own canoe, kayak, or raft—though such is hardly a necessity. The areas bordering nearly every Ozark river hold outfitters aplenty. Virtually all offer both canoe rental and shuttle service, with many also providing the option of campgrounds, cabins, or motel rooms.

GIGGING Since fishing is second nature to an Ozarker, there should be little surprise that we have come up with a wide variety of methods with which to send our piscine friends to their reward. Missouri even has a

GOLF In an old episode of *The Beverly Hillbillies*, Jed and Jethro take to the golf course bearing rifles and shotguns. Their intention is to "shoot some golfs." Sadly, all they bag on their urban hunting trip are handfuls of little white "golf eggs." Times have changed; these days it seems the Ozarks have gone golf crazy. From the championship courses at the **Lake of the Ozarks** and **Branson**, to the private golf community of **Bella Vista, Ark.**, to the many 9- and 18-hole links found in virtually every town with more than 2,000 people, we can satisfy the inexplicable urge to drive, putt, and chip. Leave the shotgun at home. Golf eggs are mighty tough eating even after you boil them.

HARRY TRUMAN The 34th president of the United States, "Give 'Em Hell Harry," is one of but two Ozarkers who went on to become commander in chief (the other being that fellow who dated Monica Lewinsky). Harry was born in an 1884, 560-square-foot home in Lamar, Mo., and the **Harry S. Truman State Birthplace Historic Site** (417-682-2279; www .bartoncounty.com/truman.html) has been fully restored. The tour guides are especially friendly and knowledgeable here and will show you everything from HST's baby bed to the outhouse. This home is actually something of a double dip, as the Trumans sold it to relatives of **Wyatt Earp** (another Lamar native). Until the late 1950s the Earp clan ran the home as a memorial to the western lawman of OK Corral fame.

HIKING You can hike just about anywhere in the Ozarks. If you can handle the hungry ticks, chiggers, and mosquitoes that reside in the high weeds between late March and late October, then a hiking trail is normally no more than a stone's throw away. For those with stamina, perhaps the most interesting is the **Colosseum Trail** at **Ha Ha Tonka State Park** (573-346-2986; www.mostateparks .com/hahatonka.htm), near Camdenton, Mo. This trail can be as easy or as strenuous as you wish. If you decide to take the fork that ventures into **Whispering Dell Sink**, keep in

mind that you'll encounter 300 wooden steps. It's a beautiful part of the world, of that there's no doubt, but you'll have to work to get there.

HILLBILLIES It's probably not such a good idea to walk up to a Hillbilly and ask him if he's a Hillbilly. We call ourselves that (and are proud of it), but we don't like it when others use it as a pejorative. That said, you can see plenty of reasonable facsimiles of Hillbillies at the aptly named **Hillbilly Days** (417-588-3256; www.lebanon missouri.com). The festival, located at Bennett Spring State Park, just 11 miles north of Lebanon, Mo., has been held every June for more than three decades. It features a catfish fry, bluegrass music, and events such as finding a nickel in a haystack and cow-chip tossing. If you need more Hillbilly infusions, simply go to Branson and enjoy a performance of the **Baldknobbers**.

HOGS During football season it is not uncommon to see folks in Fayetteville, Ark., walking around wearing red plastic pig snouts. That's because Fayetteville is home to the University of Arkansas and its cherished **Arkansas Razorbacks**. It's fitting and proper that an Ozark college team should be named for our friend the swine, for we have tendency to consume the little porkers with gusto (with sauce on the side, thank you very much). Though political pork has little to do with the real deal, Fayetteville was also the home of newlyweds **President Bill** and **Senator Hillary Clinton**.

HUNTING Tracking and smacking the wily woodland creatures—whether they be of fur or feather—is an Ozark

tradition. The opening day of deer season is almost a national holiday for us, and you've never truly experienced tenacity and dedication till you've seen camo-clad folks heading out long before dawn to call in wild turkeys. We have hunting galore, and, as is true with fishing, you can find all the information you need in a couple of easily accessible locations. The **Missouri Department of Conservation** provides all regulations and seasons, as well as online license purchase, at 1-800-392-4115 (https://wildlifelicense .com/mo). **Arkansas Fish and Game** also offers complete information and online purchases at 1-800-364-4263 (www.agfc.state.ar.us).

INNS By design and intent, this Explorer's Guide does not concentrate on motel lodging or franchises. Anyone can locate such places; they dot the American landscape like acne on a teenager. Luckily, if you're traveling in this part of the world, you will find a treasure trove of resorts, ranches, campgrounds, and especially bed & breakfast inns. In addition to the numerous listings within each chapter, check out these locator sites for additional options. **Bed & Breakfast Inns of Missouri** (www.bbim.org) includes lengthy listings and descriptions of some of the best to be found in the Ozark region of the Show Me State. If seeking a B&B in Arkansas, the **Bed and Breakfast Association of Arkansas** (www.bedandbreakfast arkansas.com) will tell you everything you need to know.

IRISH WILDERNESS Located in the Missouri Ozarks' Oregon County, the 16,500-acre **Irish Wilderness** (573-996-2153; www.fs.fed.us/r9/forests/ marktwain/ranger_districts/doniphan)

lies deep within the **Mark Twain National Forest**. A bit eerie, a bit mysterious, and more than a bit incredible, this deep-woods haven was home to a group of impoverished Irish immigrants prior to the Civil War. When the battles raged, the isolation of the area made the Irish Wilderness the perfect hideout for Bushwhackers, thugs, and creeps of all shapes, sizes, colors, and denominations. What happened to the immigrants remains a mystery to this day. While you may not find that particular answer, you will find a wealth of streams, caves, sinkholes, and wildlife. When the fog clings close to the ground in the morning, you may just hear the lilting songs of long-gone settlers from the Emerald Isle.

JAM SESSIONS Back in the days when highways were sparse and isolation a constant (in other words, from time immemorial until about the 1970s), Ozarkers found ways to entertain themselves. One of the most popular pastimes was music, and the free jam session lives on today in a number of locales. Just drop by with an instrument or a lawn chair (depending on whether you want to play or listen) and have yourself a fine old time. **Pickin' in the Park** (479-636-8204; www.mainstreetrogers.com) happens every Saturday night from May through October in Frisco Park, Rogers, Ark. During the summer months in the beautiful town of Neosho, Mo., you can drop by the **Gatherin' on the Square** any Thursday evening for a taste of bluegrass, country, and gospel. **The Ozark Jamboree** in Doniphan, Mo. (573-593-4348), is held every Friday and Saturday night year-round. Just look for the cars downtown; they'll be parked in front of what used to be a Ben Franklin store. And of course in Salem, Mo., **Ozark Country Music** (573-729-4811) kicks into gear every Friday 7–10 PM in the Salem City Hall Auditorium.

JESSE JAMES Just a word of warning: 7 out of 10 attractions in the Ozarks will likely make the claim that Jesse James either slept there, hid there, ate there, or robbed there. Some of these tales are true, some of them aren't. Let's just say Jesse got around a lot, and we're right proud of his fame. Other than that, this guide makes no comment on the veracity of any allegation regarding the sleeping, hiding, eating, or robbing habits of the renowned outlaw.

KEWPIE DOLLS If you want to know the truth, they're scary-looking little imps, reminiscent of a Depression-era version of Chuckie the killer ventriloquist dummy. Nonetheless, Kewpie dolls were popular in their time, and they originated in the heart of the Ozarks. If you wish to see all things

Kewpie, visit the **Bonniebrook Historical Society and Kewpie Museum** (1-800-539-7437; www.kewpie-museum.com). The home was the residence of Kewpie creator Rose O'Neill. This "woman for all seasons" was the most highly paid illustrator in America, studied sculpture under Rodin, became a millionaire and lost it all, married a couple of times, and was considered one of the "five most beautiful women in the world."

LAKES Thanks to the Army Corps of Engineers, who get all giddy every time they spy a creek with enough water to dam, the Ozarks are full of lakes. In Arkansas you have bodies of water such as **Beaver Lake** and **Greers Ferry Lake**, with **Bull Shoals** and **Norfork lakes** straddling the border with Missouri. Also in Missouri are **Stockton**, **Pomme de Terre**, **Taneycomo**, **Table Rock**, **Clearwater**, and of course the massive **Lake of the Ozarks**. If water sports are what you seek, you need look no farther.

LITTLE HOUSES Without doubt the most famous "Little House" in the world belonged to author Laura Ingalls Wilder. You can tour her **Rocky Ridge Farm** at the **Laura Ingalls Wilder Museum and Home** (417-924-3626 or 1-877-924-7126; www.lauraingallswilderhome.com), in Mansfield, Mo.

MARK TWAIN NATIONAL FOREST Consisting of more than 1.5 million acres, the Mark Twain (www.fs.fed.us/r9/forests/marktwain/contact) is a superb wilderness dotted by rivers, streams, and some of the largest natural springs in America. Broken into nine different ranger districts, the forest includes hundreds of miles of hiking trails, numerous scenic drives, seven congressionally designated wilderness areas, 40 campgrounds (these can be reserved by calling 1-877-444-6777), and thousands of acres of primitive and semiprimitive areas.

MILLS The gristmill was often the center of life here, a place that not only ground the grain but also served as trading post and ground zero for the telling of tall tales. The **War Eagle Mill** (479-789-5343; www.wareagle mill.com) in Rogers, Ark., is one of the few that still work, doubling as store and restaurant. Others, such as the **Rainbow Trout and Game Ranch** (417-679-3619; www.rock bridgemo .com), **Zanoni Mill Inn** (417-679-4050 or 1-877-679-4050; www.bbim .org/zanoni), and **Dawt Mill** (417-284-3540 or 1-888-884-3540; www.dawtmill .com), have been transformed into bed & breakfasts and resorts.

MUSEUMS History and traditions rate highly in the Ozarks, and it's the rare small town that doesn't possess a local

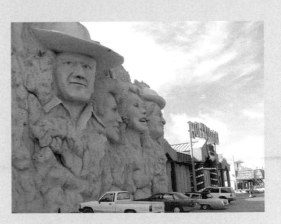

museum. The artifacts and subject matter encompassed by these bastions of the past are nearly infinite, but some of the best include the **Arkansas Air Museum** (479-521-4947; www.arkairmuseum.org) in Fayetteville, Ark., and the **Daisy Airgun Museum** (479-986-6873; www.daisy museum.com) in Rogers, Ark. Those interested in the Civil War will want to check out **General Sweeny's Museum** (417-732-1224; www.civil warmuseum.com) in Republic, Mo. However, perhaps the best museum in the Ozarks is the **Ralph Foster Museum** (417-334-6411; www .rfostermuseum.com), located in Lookout, Mo., on the campus of the College of the Ozarks. It features 40,000 square feet and three stories of displays, and you'll find everything from prehistoric Indian artifacts to the truck owned by Jed Clampett of *Beverly Hillbillies* fame.

NUTS Natives of this region will freely speculate that most urban folks likely think them a bit nuts. However, the festival held each year in Stockton, Mo., refers to a type of nut grown on trees, not the type of nut who braves subfreezing weather to spear fish from a Jon boat. The

Black Walnut Festival (417-276-5161; www.stocktonlake.com) is a four-day event held in late September that draws thousands of visitors from far and wide. Not so coincidentally, Stockton, Mo., is also the home of the **Hammons Products Company**, largest processor of black walnuts in the world.

OPERA Contrary to popular belief, not all opera in the Ozarks is of the horse or Grand Ol' variety. At **Opera in the Ozarks at Inspiration Point** (479-253-8595; www.opera.org), located in Eureka Springs, Ark., you can soak up all the Rossini, Verdi, or Puccini you'd like. And then of course you'll want to go have some catfish and catch a screaming bluegrass band.

OZARK NATIONAL FOREST Consisting of 1.2 million acres in Arkansas, the **Ozark National Forest** (479-968-2354; www.fs.fed.us/oonf/ozark) offers anything the outdoorsperson could desire. From hiking, biking, and horseback riding to floating, kayaking, picnicking, and camping, this sprawling and rugged forest is a cavalcade of bluffs, mountains, rivers, and trees.

PASSION PLAY The world's number one attended outdoor dramatic presentation (viewed by more than 7 million people and counting) is *The Great Passion Play* (479-253-9200; www.greatpassionplay.com) held in Eureka Springs, Ark. Chronicling the last week of Jesus Christ, performances are held from April through October. It goes without saying that this just wouldn't be the Ozarks if the venue for this performance wasn't also home to the **Passion Play All-You-Can-Eat Buffet**.

PIE Homemade pies are a staple in this part of the world, but the best of the best can be found in the tiny establishment known as **A Slice of Pie** (573-364-6203), located in Rolla, Mo. You can eat there, or pick up pies, cakes, and even slices to go. Just a tiny sample of choices includes apple and blackberry crumb, chocolate chip mint, and Tahitian cream. There's a "Toll House" pie, and of course such favorites as pecan, strawberry rhubarb, mincemeat, and mudslide. A favorite cheesecake is the white chocolate cappuccino. This place is so addictive, it should sport warning labels on the doors. Quite simply . . . there's none better.

QUILTS It's only when an Ozarker moves from the Ozarks that he learns not all womenfolk are expert quilters. It's the rare home indeed that doesn't have at least one or two quilts passed down from mothers and grandmothers. For those from parts yonder who sadly remain quiltless, a trip to the **Quilt Cottage** (417-339-3445) in Branson, Mo., is in order. Virtually everything in this store is handmade, and many of the intricate designs rate as true works of art. My mother, an expert quilter in her own right, gives this shop high marks.

RAILROADS For many years the only way to travel the Ozarks (with the exception of mule, foot, and canoe) was by railroad. You can still view the deep forest and rugged hills from restored passenger cars if you climb aboard the **Arkansas & Missouri Railroad** (479-751-8600 or 1-800-687-8600; www.arkmorr.com) or the **Eureka Springs & North Arkansas Railway** (479-253-9263; www.esnrailway.com) in Eureka Springs, Ark.

Both trains offer a variety of trips, historical narration, and food. The latter in particular is known for its fine dinners on the Eurekan Dining Car.

RELIGION When it comes to church-going, the Ozarks is a bit like Baskin-Robbins. The only difference is that we have far more than 31 flavors. This strong faith is exemplified by the giant *Christ of the Ozarks* (1-866-566-3565; www.greatpassionplay.com), located on the site of *The Great Passion Play* in Eureka Springs, Ark. The sculpture is over 250 feet tall and weighs more than 2 million pounds. When we say religion is big in these parts, we're not just whistlin' Dixie.

RIVERS If bluegrass is the heartbeat of the Ozarks, then our amazing rivers are the lifeblood. Many visitors choose to float the crystal-clear **Current** and **Jacks Fork**, the two streams protected under the auspices of the **Ozark National Scenic Riverways** (www.nps.gov/ozar). Pretty as they are,

however, that duo are but the tip of the proverbial iceberg. In Arkansas you can hook the massive trout that reside in the legendary **White** or take a trip back in time and float the awe-inspiring **Buffalo**. For bass fishing it's hard to beat the **Kings River**; for a leisurely float there is always **War Eagle Creek**. In Missouri it quickly becomes clear why so many settlers traveled via water, and why so many visitors continue to explore or rivers and creeks today. The **Niangua**, the **Meramec**, the **Big Piney**, and the **Gasconade** are all favorites of fishermen and floaters, as are smaller tributaries such as **Bryant Creek**, **Courtois Creek**, **Huzzah Creek**, and the **Bourbeuse River**. The choices just go on and on—**Elk River, Beaver Creek, Big** and **Little Sugar creeks**, the **James River**—but there's one stretch of water that everyone agrees is the best. That would be the **North Fork of the White River**. The North Fork has Missouri's largest population of wild rainbow and trophy-sized brown trout, and words simply do not do justice to the scenery you'll experience during a float. To enjoy the North Fork up close and personal, stay on its banks in one of the luxurious treehouse cabins at **River of Life Farm** (417-261-7777 or 1-888-824-2398; www.riveroflifefarm.com). Located on the North Fork in the heart of the Mark Twain National Forest, River of Life has been featured by NBC's *Today* show, the *Wall Street Journal*, the *St. Louis Post-Dispatch*, and *Missouri Life* magazine.

SPOOKY LIGHTS It is the understatement of the millennia to say that the Ozarks are a bit long in the tooth. Traveling back to the dawn of time itself, this country was high and dry when much of the rest of the continent was nothing but a deep puddle. When a place is that old, it should come as no surprise that inexplicable phenomena are a regular part of life. For one of the most popular unexplained mysteries, head south of Joplin, Mo., to the road known as the **Devil's Promenade** (any local will give you directions). If you're lucky, you'll be visited by the **Hornet Spook Lights**. These glowing, darting, and diving balls of orange and yellow flame (investigated but never explained by the Army Corps of Engineers) are thought by many to either be the disembodied spirits of a star-crossed Quapaw Indian couple or the ghost of a miner searching for his missing head. Tales abound, including the legend that many who see the lights discover only the next morning that their head is pounding and the back of their pickup truck is full of empty Budweiser cans. Amazing!

SPRINGS If you wonder why so many Ozark streams are icy cold and crystal clear, it's because many of them are fed by natural springs. Counting the springs found in the Ozarks would take a lifetime (the numbers literally run into the thousands), so just appreciate how pretty they are as you take a gander at the deep-blue waters. The biggest spring in the Ozarks (in fact, the biggest in the world) is creatively named **Big Spring** (573-323-4236; www.nps.gov/ozar). This giant, found in Carter County, Mo., pours forth 286 million gallons per day. Not far behind, just across the border in Arkansas, the average flow at **Mammoth Spring** (870-625-7364; www.arkansasstateparks.com/mammoth-spring) is nearly 240 million gallons per day. Many other springs push out nearly as much water; **Greer Spring**, which doubles the flow of Missouri's Eleven Point River, comes in at 220 million gallons per day. For high ratings on the Richter scale of drop-dead gorgeous, don't miss **Alley Spring** on the Jacks Fork River (314-323-4236; www.nps.gov/ozar) or **Blue Spring** (314-323-4236; www.nps.gov/ozar) on the Current. The latter sports one of the deepest blue colors imaginable.

SYMPHONIES The classics are alive and well in the Ozarks. Two symphonies demonstrate melodious proficiency: The **North Arkansas Symphony** (479-521-4166; www.nasymphony.org) has interpreted and performed the finest in musical interludes for more than half a century. Equal in expertise is the **Springfield Symphony**, which offers everything from Broadway's best to jazz jams to chamber groups. For more information on the Springfield Symphony, it is best to contact the **Juanita K. Ham-**

mons **Hall for the Performing Arts** (417-836-7678; www.hammons hall.com).

TRIGGER THE WONDER HORSE If you ever wondered what happened to Trigger, you can find him at the **Roy Rogers and Dale Evans Museum** (417-339-1900; www.royrogers.com) in Branson, Mo. Stuffed alongside Trigger are Buttermilk and Bullet, not to mention all the Roy and Dale memorabilia under the sun.

TROLLEYS The trolley still goes *clang, clang, clang* in Eureka Springs, Ark. The **Eureka Springs Transit System** (479-253-9572; www.eureka trolley.org) will take you to every location in this most hilly of towns, saving time and preventing wear and tear on shoe leather, legs, and lungs. The Eureka Springs Trolley is the past made modern, and an adult's all-day pass is just $4.

TROUT In a nationwide Trout Unlimited survey taken in 1998, the **White River** of Arkansas was named the 11th best trout stream in the nation. This is no small accomplishment, as it places the White in close proximity to such world-class streams as the Madison and Upper Yellowstone rivers in Montana and the Henry's Fork of the Snake River in Idaho. This river is particularly known for its rainbow and brown trout, and excellent fishing can be had below **Beaver Dam**, in **Lake Taneycomo**, and below **Bull Shoals Dam**. The latter choice alone provides close to 100 miles of trout water. Brown trout of more than 40 pounds have been taken from both the White and its tributaries. One of these, the **North Fork of the White** in Missouri, is esteemed for not only its great fishing but for its stunning scenery as well. The trout-fishing possibilities abound in the Ozarks. On March 1 of each year at **Bennett Spring State Park** north of Lebanon, Mo. (417-532-4338 or 417-532-4307; www.mostateparks.com/bennett.htm), more than 3,000 anglers line up shoulder-to-shoulder in anticipation of the bell that signals the start of the season.

UNDERGROUND WEDDINGS You've heard of underground newspapers and underground railroads, but near Camdenton, Mo., the underground wedding has been all the rage since 1948. **Bridal Cave** (573-346-2676; www.bridalcave.com) has been the site of more than 2,000 weddings, and varied packages offer such perks as recorded pipe-organ music and a lifetime pass to the cave. The cost to get hitched beneath the earth is in the $500 range, though an adult can tour the cave for a mere $13.50.

VERMIN Not the most pleasant of categories, granted, but in this case forewarned is forearmed. If you plan to do some hiking in the Ozarks between early spring and late fall, you should

know that an army of hungry little critters wish to tag along. Our hot temperatures and high humidity are the perfect climate for ticks, chiggers, mosquitoes, and even snakes (cottonmouths, copperheads, and the occasional rattler being the ones to watch out for). Make sure to bring along the Off, Cutter, Skin So Soft, and a big stick. Also, you would be well served to do just a bit of prehiking research into how to deal with tick bites. Lyme disease isn't a big fear factor here, but ticks can carry all sorts of crazy stuff, and more than a few people have skin reactions to the bite itself. If you know you're even somewhat allergic to chomping bugs, you might consider hiking during the colder months. The weather is generally quite mild, and you'll avoid all that pesky swatting, itching, and cursing.

VICTORIAN HOMES Some of the finest examples of Victorian architecture can be found in Carthage, Mo. At one time the home of more millionaires per capita than anywhere else in America, Carthage is loaded with well-preserved residences in the Classical Revival, Queen Anne, Georgian,

Italianate, and Romanesque styles. Free maps to a **Victorian Home Driving Tour** are available from the Carthage Convention & Visitors Bureau (417-359-8181; www.visitcarthage.com). Some other homes—such as **Leggett House** and **Phelps House**—offer public tours. Either way you'll come in contact with domiciles exemplifying just how high some of the other half used to live.

WAL-MART It's the world's largest retailer, but its humble beginnings go back to Sam Walton's five-and-dime in downtown Bentonville, Ark. The international headquarters of Wal-Mart is still located here, as is the **Wal-Mart Visitor's Center** (479-273-1329; www.walmartstores.com). The center is in fact found in that original shop from which Sam built an empire, and you'll receive a detailed history of both past and present. Best of all, admission is free.

WILDLIFE Drive down any two-lane blacktop or gravel road in the Ozarks and you'll see plenty of wildlife. In fall white-tailed deer tend to get a little more up close and personal than you'd prefer, often jumping in front of your car. That said, either a simple drive off the beaten path or a trip to any state park or conservation area will be rewarded with abundant wildlife sightings. If you prefer a more controlled environment (and this place is seriously great), take a tour through the **Wonders of Wildlife Museum and Zooquarium** (417-890-9453 or 1-877-245-9453; www.wondersofwildlife.org) in Springfield, Mo. In this 92,000-square-foot facility, affiliated with both the Smithsonian Institution and the American Association of Zoos and Aquariums, you will find more than

225 species of animals in live habitats. Interactive electronic displays are prevalent, and the exhibits are outstanding. One area is a treetop, free-flight aviary; another holds river otters and bobcats. Intended to re-create the habitat at the bottom of Table Rock Lake, a 140,000-gallon freshwater aquarium, viewable through huge windows, is the home of bass, gar, catfish, and spoonbill. Another 220,000-gallon saltwater aquarium houses sharks, eels, and rays. And of course you will not want to miss the reptile gallery, which at the time of this writing contains the world's oldest and largest albino alligator.

WINERIES Prior to Prohibition, the wine industry of the Ozarks (specifically Missouri) ranked second behind only New York. Many wineries still exist today, perfecting and selling award-winning vintages. Some of the more famous of the more than 50 vineyards include **Ferrigno Winery** (573-265-7742), **4M Vineyard and Rosati Winery** (573-265-6892 or 573-265-8147; www.mcc-llc.com/rosati winery), **Heinrichshaus Vineyard and Winery** (573-265-5000; www .heinrichshaus.com), **Meramec Vineyards** (573-265-7847 or 1-877-216-9463; www.meramecvineyards.com), **St. James Winery** (573-265-7912 or 1-800-280-9463; www.stonehillwinery .com), and the **Peaceful Bend Vineyard** (573-775-3000; www.peaceful bendvineyard.com). And here you thought we were all about moonshine.

X FILES If little green men are your thing, then you need to sign up for the annual **Ozark UFO Conference** (479-354-2558; www.ozarkufo.com) held in Eureka Springs, Ark., every April. Three days of speakers, discus-

sions, and presentations on all things otherworldly should provide plenty of fodder at the next meeting of your local alien abductee workshop.

ZOOS At the **Turpentine Creek Exotic Wildlife Refuge** (479-253-5841; www.turpentinecreek.org), near Eureka Springs, Ark., you can observe more than 100 lions and tigers that have been rescued from mistreatment. There are also plenty of bears, monkeys, deer, and birds on hand, and you may opt to rent a room or treehouse cabin on the refuge grounds. The **Wild Wilderness Drive-Thru Safari** (479-736-8383) in Gentry, Ark., offers a 6-mile drive through a 200-acre park that's home to rhinos, hippos, alligators, giraffes, bears, and leopards. At the Strafford, Mo., **Exotic Animal Paradise** (1-888-578-9898; www.exoticanimalparadise.com), you will find more than 400 acres of giraffes, camels, buffalo, ostriches, tigers, bears, and hundreds of species of birds. At this complex you may also ride a camel, or zip around on go-carts and paddle boats. Last but not least, the **Dickerson Park Zoo** (417-864-1800; www.dickersonparkzoo.org) in Springfield, Mo., is a first-class operation featuring more than 500 animals representing better than 170 species.

Texas

Les Brown's
Band Of Renown
Les Brown Jr. Presents
The Music Of Your Life!

UTTON
EAMILY THEATER

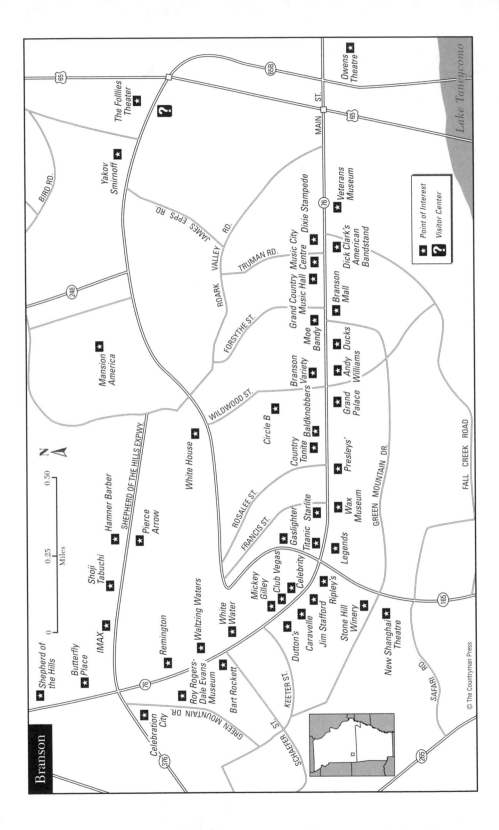

BRANSON, MISSOURI

I n the Ozarks they look at things a little different. What happens in Vegas may very well stay in Vegas. But what happens in Branson . . . now, that's something you're not ashamed to talk about in church.

In an era when flash, shock, and gratuitous thrills inundate the national entertainment scene, Branson, Mo., hit upon a lucrative formula for which the public was apparently starved. You will not find slot machines or scantily clad showgirls in Branson. You will find Andy Williams and Petula Clark singing standards of yesterday. You do not go to Branson to rave pretentious over Christo's latest surreal rendition of modern art. You go to laugh at corny jokes and visit the Ripley's Believe It or Not Museum. You do not go to Branson to wax eloquent over a tiny overpriced entrée that would fail to sate the appetite of a baby bird. Instead you belly up to the trough and gorge yourself silly on catfish and BBQ.

Simply put, people do not visit Branson to impress their friends, neighbors, and co-workers. They visit for the pure pleasure of simple fun. The town is the antithesis of highbrow and tony, and the visitor who expects quiet refinement will be sorely disappointed. Urban chic and Ozark humor are at least 1,000 light-years apart and, at least in Branson, never the twain shall meet.

Branson is admittedly something of an anomaly in a region whose main claim to fame is outdoor beauty; even locals seem a tad baffled by the town's rise to prominence. Ask native Ozarkers their opinion of Branson, and at first you'll notice a regional pride in the vein of "local boy makes good." That this once tiny village in the Ozark boonies has transformed itself into the Live Country Music Capital of the World is no small source of bragging rights.

Welcoming more than 7 million visitors annually and boasting more than 57,000 theater seats (that's 12,000 more than Broadway), the lofty designation is not without merit. Branson's 400 restaurants, 200 lodging facilities, 5,000 camping spaces, 9 golf courses, 45 theaters offering 80 shows per day, and countless shops, stores, amusement parks, and attractions have made it a first-tier vacation destination.

On the other hand, those same native Ozarkers will shake their heads and display the mildest trace of a frown over the bright lights and crowds that intrude upon the solitude of their beloved Ozark hills, rivers, and forests. The glitter and fame of Branson slightly rubs against the grain of rural locals who enjoy their isolation, folks who are genetically disposed to embarrassment by copious amounts of hoopla. The natives respect Branson for taking the national stage . . . they just wish it didn't carry on so.

Nevertheless, Branson is here to stay. To no small degree, the area's ever-growing popularity can be attributed to that fierce dedication toward providing wholesome family entertainment. As suggested earlier, Branson is the "anti-Vegas," a place where Mom, apple pie, and a celebration of the "good ol' USA" reign supreme. Perhaps a decade ago the town risked stereotyping itself as catering mostly to Grandpa and Grandma, NASCAR fans, and the Red State constituency who preferred *Walker, Texas Ranger* over *The West Wing*. Such is no longer the case.

Branson has adapted with the times, constantly expanding its selection of shows and attractions, all of which retain a squeaky-clean aura. It's now a top destination for people of all ages, and the Florida mouse should be very afraid: Branson is marketing heavily for younger families with small children. The new Branson Landing, a nearly half-billion-dollar project slated for completion in 2006, will occupy 95 acres with 1.5 miles of waterfront. Anchored by a Bass Pro Shop and Belk Department Store, the estimated 4.5 million annual visitors to Branson Landing will find a 220,000-square-foot convention center, a four-star 260-room hotel, a 100-room boutique hotel, 140 waterfront condos and pent-houses, and a full-service marina. The list of restaurants, entertainment venues, and shopping is longer than a tent revivalist's sermon, and a spectacular fountain (designed by the same folks who created the Bellagio's fountain in Las Vegas) will serve as the centerpiece for nightly music, light, and water shows.

Just down the road in Hollister, Mo., projects totaling more than $1.2 billion in investment money are scheduled for completion over the next several years. A 53-acre shopping center with 413,000 square feet slotted for retail space will feature both big-box stores and numerous small retail concerns. A $20 million development at Branson Creek will include 380 condos and 59 custom homes. Estimated at a price tag of $200 million, Landing View's 90 acres will bring 5- and 10-story buildings with 273 whole-ownership condos. The largest and most ambitious development, Sanctuary on the Green, will hold 2,100 condos, 1,700 homes, a marina, retail shops, a golf course, restaurants, and hotels. The price? A mere $1 billion.

Though it has only received international prominence as a country music mecca since the late 1980s, Branson's evolution as an entertainment center stretches back nearly a century. Rueben Branson opened his general store and post office near White River in the early 1880s. Though the first industry of the area revolved around timber and logging (homesteaders could purchase 160 acres for approximately $14), whispers of tourism were heard as early as 1907. In that year Harold Bell Wright published his novel *Shepherd of the Hills*.

Wright, afflicted with tuberculosis, spent 7 years enamored with the peace and serenity of the Ozarks. From his notes about real-life people and events (mixed with hefty side orders of fiction) he penned a book that became a publishing phenomenon, spawning eight movies and more than a dozen TV productions. In modern terms think *Bridges of Madison County*, a simplistic tome that somehow caught the collective imagination and achieved household-name status. As the years went by, thousands traveled to the Ozarks to view the land described by Wright.

But prior to Wright's book, fame of the long-lasting sort was already trickling from a hole in the ground. Before long that trickle would become a torrent.

The hole in question—originally called Marble Cave—was located roughly 6 miles from Branson and thought to contain a huge cache of Carthage marble. The Marble Cave Mining and Manufacturing Company was certain it had struck the mother lode at the onset of 1884 operations. It was only half wrong.

The bad news was that the "marble" turned out to be subpar. The good news was that the cave contained a treasure trove of bat guano, used as nitrate for gunpowder and fertilizer. While not as exotic sounding as marble in terms of dinner conversation, guano still fetched the princely sum (in mid-1880s prices) of $700 a ton.

Not all good things can last forever. The guano train ran out of steam in 1899, and since the bats refused to make more, the company sold "Marble Cave" to Canadian William Lynch. Lynch began developing the cave for tourism (changing the name to Marvel Cave), and though he died in 1927, his daughters kept the operation running until 1950.

In that year Marvel Cave was leased to frequent visitors Hugo and Mary Herschend of Wilmette, Ill. The couple, along with sons Jack and Pete, took over and expanded the cave tours, drawing 8,000 visitors in their first summer. Over the next few years they constructed an authentic 1880s Ozark village, initially to entertain and occupy those waiting to tour the cave. In 1960 Silver Dollar City was born, drawing 125,000 visitors in its inaugural season.

The expansion has been nonstop ever since. Today Silver Dollar City remains the primary draw of Branson—one of many entertainment properties owned by the Herschends.

Like smoking licks from a bluegrass banjo, things started happening fast. Hot on the heels of Silver Dollar City came the music and shows. The Baldknobbers Hillbilly Jamboree opened in 1959. In 1960 the Old Mill Theater began "organized" *Shepherd of the Hills* performances. In 1963 Table Rock Dam was completed, with Table Rock Lake joining Bull Shoals and Lake Taneycomo as a huge draw for boaters and fishermen.

In 1969 *The Beverly Hillbillies* filmed five episodes at Silver Dollar City, with Jed, Granny, and the rest of the Clampett clan giving Branson a priceless amount of national publicity. In the 1980s country stars such as Roy Clark, Boxcar Willie, and the Sons of the Pioneers rolled into town.

In 1991 *Time*, *People*, the *Wall Street Journal*, the *Los Angeles Times*, and *60 Minutes* all discovered Branson. Since then the area has virtually exploded, suffering some of the pangs of extreme growth but for the most part retaining a hometown atmosphere and a reputation for down-home fun and clean entertainment.

It's not Manhattan. It's not Chicago. It's not San Francisco.

It's just Branson . . . and proud of it.

AREA CODES The area code for Branson and surrounding communities is **417**.

GUIDANCE Branson/Lakes Area Chamber of Commerce (417-334-4084 or 1-800-214-3661; www.bransonchamber.com or www.explorebranson.com), 269 SR 248, Branson, Mo. This is the most complete source you will find for all things Branson. That said, a trip through the Internet, phone book, or tourist magazines will garner hundreds of spots willing to sell tickets for Branson shows, offer package deals for lodging, or inundate you with promotional legerdemain. Prices vary, and a little research could save you a few dollars here and there. Just make sure that your "bargain" doesn't involve a 3-hour presentation for the poor little time-share nobody wanted. An afternoon with a boring time-share salesman will not only put a damper on your trip, but might require alcohol abuse or years of intensive therapy.

By the same token, I doubt you could stop at a single chamber of commerce office or visitors center in the state of Missouri and not find a 7-foot-tall carousel loaded with Branson pamphlets. Such being the case, you might as well go to the source and speak with the Branson chamber. The folks here are extremely helpful (it's a well-funded outfit) and truly do offer a wealth of knowledge.

For the Table Rock Lake area, contact **Table Rock Lake Chamber of Commerce** (1-800-595-0393; www.tablerocklake.org), P.O. Box 495, Kimberling City, Mo.

GETTING THERE *By auto:* US 65 connects from Springfield, Mo., to the north, and from Harrison, Ark., to the south. Stretches of this road seem to exist in a state of perpetual construction, a result of ever-increasing traffic. Each year more and more of US 65 is four lane (it's already that way from Springfield to Branson), and hopefully the whole thing will be completed by the time this book sees print.

If you're arriving from either the east or west via I-44, simply watch for the US 65 exit at Springfield. Branson is a mere 35 miles south.

By air: **Springfield-Branson Regional Airport** (417-869-0300; www.sgf-branson-airport.com), located 40 miles north of Branson, is served by American Airlines, American Connection, American Eagle, Northwest Airlink, US Airways, United Express, and Allegiant. The airport offers facilities for buses, vans, rental cars, and hotel and hospitality limousines for groups en route to Branson (or other Ozark locations). A little more than 100 miles to the southwest of Branson is **Northwest Arkansas Regional Airport** (479-205-1000; www.nwara.com), 1 Airport Blvd., Bentonville, Ark. This new airport (completed in 1998) is serviced by American Eagle, Continental Express, Delta, Northwest Airlink, US Airways Express, and United.

MEDICAL EMERGENCIES All of the following hospitals operate satellite clinics in surrounding counties.

Skaggs Community Health Center (417-335-7000; www.skaggs.net), US Bus. 65 N. and Skaggs Rd., Branson, Mo., has been a part of the Branson community since 1950. The facility has 105 rooms, numerous specialties, 24-hour emergency care, and helicopter service.

Cox Medical Center North (417-269-3000; www.coxnet.org), 1423 N. Jefferson Ave., Springfield, Mo., and **Cox Medical Center South** (417-269-3000; www.coxnet.org), 3801 S. National Ave., Springfield, Mo., are part of the massive Cox network and include 274 and 562 beds, respectively.

St. John's Regional Health Center (417-885-2000; www.stjohns.net), 1235 E. Cherokee St., Springfield, Mo., is a 1,016-bed center.

✳ Wandering Around

EXPLORING BY CAR Once you arrive in Branson, expect to slow down and enjoy the scenery. For years SR 76 (aka **the Strip**: go west for all the theaters, eateries, shows, and motels; go east or take US Bus. 65 S. to visit downtown Branson itself) was not only the main drag, it was the only drag. Traffic would become so backed up that many visitors referred to the Strip as the "5-mile parking lot." Things are better now. City fathers realized that traffic snarls had to be eliminated, and an ambitious highway project was instituted in 1992. The first third of the time-saving loop around Branson opened in 2003. Drivers can now bypass much of the Strip if they so choose, by taking SR 465 (the **Ozark Mountain Highroad**) off US 65. It will pop you out right around the Shepherd of the Hills attraction and Silver Dollar City. You'll eventually want to cruise the Strip, but if it's your first trip to Branson, you might not want to tackle it right off. Be advised that the traffic, from folks coming from or going to shows, is worst in the early evening.

EXPLORING BY FOOT **Table Rock Lakeshore Trail** (417-334-4104), 4600 SR 165, Branson, Mo. A 2.2 mile trail (that would be one-way), this is a beautiful hike that runs from the Dewey Short Visitor Center to the Table Rock State Park Marina. If you should happen to visit in spring, you'll see an amazing array of wildflowers in bloom, not to mention redbud and serviceberry trees. If you come in fall, your jaw will drop open at foliage as multicolored as an earth-toned rainbow. At either time bring your camera, for there are also some great views out over Table Rock Lake itself. This is a smooth and easy trail, an easy trek for those who want to stop and smell the roses (or, more likely, the dogwood).

THE BRANSON STRIP

✳ To See

🐾 ✎ ♿ **Dewey Short Visitor Center** (417-334-4104), 4600 SR 165, Branson, Mo. Located just south of the Table Rock Dam, the Dewey Short Visitor Center is a cut above your usual informative stop-over. The center features a four-season exhibit that will give travelers a true sense of the Ozarks in all their glory (with sight and sound, but alas no olfactory nuances), and displays chronicling how life was in the hill country of olden days. In the facility's 176-seat theater various presentations are provided on Table Rock itself and the surrounding areas. Admission is free.

🐾 ✎ **Table Rock Dam Tour** (417-334-4104), 4600 SR 165, Branson, Mo. While at the Dewey Short Visitor Center, don't miss the chance to visit the Table Rock Dam and Powerhouse. Daily May–Oct., for the tiny fee of $3 (kids under 5 are free) you will travel to the depths of the dam and see how electricity is produced. Seriously, it's a lot more interesting than it sounds on paper. Tours are offered 9–11 AM and 1–4 PM.

🐾 ✎ ♿ **Shepherd of the Hills Trout Hatchery** (417-334-4865; www.mdc .mo.gov/areas/hatchery/shepherd), 483 Hatchery Rd., Branson, Mo. This hatchery, a massive facility with open-air tanks, is the largest in the state of Missouri. More than 400,000 trout are raised each year, with 80 percent of them released into nearby Lake Taneycomo. There is a free visitors center and trails, but should you visit in winter you'll encounter a little-seen natural attraction: For whatever reason—likely the sight of all those tasty fish—the area around the hatchery has turned into a winter roost for a huge number of turkey buzzards, great blue herons, bluebirds, blackbirds, and seagulls. The hatchery is 6 miles south of Branson, occupying 211 acres and hosting a quarter million visitors annually. On the grounds are four hiking trails, and guided hatchery tours are a tourist favorite. The tours are held (free of charge) Memorial Day–Labor Day, weekdays at 10 AM, 11 AM, 1 PM, and 2 PM.

SCENIC TOURS ✎ ♿ **Branson Scenic Railway** (417-334-6110 or 1-800-287-2462; www.bransontrain.com), 206 E. Main St., Branson, Mo. For a unique look at the Ozarks, climb aboard the Branson Scenic Railway. Departing at 9 AM, 11:30 AM, and 2 PM late Apr.–Dec., the 1¾-hour narrated trip takes visitors to places deep in the hills that are inaccessible via car. A regular boarding pass is $21.75 for adults and $11.75 for kids 3–12. May–Dec., each Saturday at 5 PM a dinner train departs from the station (the historic old depot in downtown Branson). For the price of $49.75 you will receive not only the full tour but also an elegant four-course candlelight dinner.

✎ ♿ **Ride the Ducks** (417-334-3825; www.bransonducks.com), 2320 W. SR 76, Branson, Mo. Departing approximately every 15 or 20 minutes 8–5, Mar.–Dec., these modified, World War II–era, amphibious vehicles take visitors down SR 76 and SR 165, past Table Rock Dam and the Shepherd of the Hills Fish Hatchery, and then cruise the waters of Table Rock itself. A trip on the Ducks is something of a Branson tradition, possibly because all riders receive a "wacky quacker." The yellow plastic noisemakers lose their adult appeal after about 2 minutes, but they will provide your kids with endless hours of amusement as the grating, pseudo-quacking sounds send you on a premature excursion to the insane asylum. A Duck tour takes about 80 minutes. $16.95 adults, $9.50 ages 3–12.

MUSEUMS 🐾 ♿ **Titanic: The Legend Continues** (417-334-9500 or 1-800-381-7670; www.titanicbranson .com), 3235 76 Country Blvd. and SR 165, Branson, Mo. Apr. 17–May 21, 9 –9; May 22–Dec. 16, 9 AM– 11 PM; Dec. 17–Jan. 1, 9–6. $16.95 adults, $9.95 ages 5–12; 4 and under free. Everyone who saw the much-ballyhooed movie with Leonardo DiCaprio knows how this show ends (the boat sank). However, as one of Branson's newest attractions, the

TOUR BRANSON ON AN AMPHIBIOUS DUCK

Titanic museum takes you behind the scenes and inside the hull of history's most celebrated shipwreck. More than 400 personal and private artifacts from the disaster are on display, and visitor tickets resemble the actual boarding pass given to passengers on the White Star Line. The exhibit includes an interactive area along with authentic renditions of staterooms, the bridge, and the Grand Staircase. For history buffs, *Titanic* aficionados, or simply those who want a slightly waterlogged trip back in time, this promises to be a novel experience.

THE NEW TITANIC MUSEUM

🐾 ♿ **57 Heaven Museum** (417-332-1957 or 1-800-LUV-1957; www.57 heaven.com), 1600 W. SR 76, Branson, Mo. $15 adults, $13 kids 12 and under. Located in the new Dick Clark American Bandstand Complex, 57 Heaven contains the finest automobiles, of all makes, from 1957. The 70 different vehicles are part of the Patch Collection (created by Glenn E. Patch), and the car museum itself includes numerous vignettes and re-creations of life in the 1950s (featuring homes, kitchens, living rooms, and beloved toys). For the car fan, there are plenty of convertibles, Corvettes, Chevy Bel Airs, and Thunderbirds. Even such names of the past as Hudson, Studebaker, and Nash are represented.

RIPLEY'S BELIEVE IT OR NOT MUSEUM

♂ & **Ripley's Believe It or Not Museum** (417-337-5300; www.ripleys branson.com), 3326 76 Country Blvd., Branson, Mo. Mar. 15–Dec. 15, 9 AM– 11 PM; Dec. 16–Mar. 14, 9–7. $14.95 adults, $7.95 ages 4–12. Kids under 4 are admitted free. You might as well go ahead and take a picture of it; everyone else does. The cracked, split, and broken-front facade (not to mention the foyer) of the Ripley's Museum is designed to resemble the aftermath of the great New Madrid, Mo., earthquake of 1812 (the worst earthquake in recorded history, making those California temblors pale in comparison, "believe it or not"). Such are just a sample of the oddities you will find in this latest cavalcade of the bizarre in the Ripley's franchise. You've got your two-headed calves, shrunken heads, and unicorn men. You've got your model of the USS *Forrestal* built out of 48,000 matchsticks, not to mention a miniature Roman Colosseum constructed of 1,971 playing cards. Take the self-guided tour through seven separate galleries and prepare to experience shock and awe.

♂ & **American Presidential Museum** (417-334-8683; www.american presidentialmuseum.com), 3107 W. SR 76 (Francis St.), Branson, Mo. Apr.– Jan., open Tue.–Sat. 9–5, Sun. 9–4. Winter hours are Tue.–Sat. 9–5. $10 adults, $9 seniors. Kids are admitted free. If you wish to sit behind the desk in the Oval Office, learn the seven roles of the president, or learn about first ladies. The American Presidential Museum is as complete a tour as you will find. The National Freedom Shrine offers 28 famous historic documents, and visits to *Air Force One* and the White House Christmas festivities are especially informative. A nice touch to this museum is the film of presidential bloopers, which allows viewers to actually see our distinguished (or nondistinguished, as the case may be) leaders as real people rather than all-powerful icons.

✍ ♿ **World's Largest Toy Museum** (417-332-1499; www.worldslargesttoy
museum.com), 3609 W. SR 76, Branson, Mo. Mon.–Sat. 9–7. $12.12 adults,
$9.97 ages 7–16. Kids 6 and under are admitted free. If you're feeling nostalgic
for a cherished toy, you will no doubt find it here. The range runs from toys of
the 1800s to Shirley Temple and Tom Mix memorabilia to Spider-Man and Star
Wars. Of course there's an on-site gift shop where you can purchase (what else?)
toys. Also located within the Toy Museum is the **Harold Bell Wright Museum**,
devoted to the acclaimed author of *Shepherd of the Hills*. Visitors can view
Wright's original manuscript, numerous artifacts, and a half-hour movie.

✍ ♿ **Veterans Memorial Museum** (417-336-2300; www.veteransmemorialbran-
son.com), 1210 76 Country Blvd., Branson, Mo. Daily 8 AM–9 PM. $12.25 adults,
$5 ages 6–12. Veterans receive a $2 discount. Sculptor Fred Hoppe has pulled off
a major accomplishment in creating his Veterans Memorial Museum, geared
toward honoring those who fought and died in both world wars, Korea, Vietnam,
and the Persian Gulf. Inside, you'll find the walls covered with more than half a
million names of veterans who have given their lives in time of war, as well as the
world's largest war memorial bronze sculpture. More than 70 feet long and weighing 15 tons, the piece features 50 life-sized soldiers storming a beach. Each soldier's face was modeled after an actual combat veteran; Hoppe's father, a World
War II hero, was the basis for the lead soldier. There are more than 2,000 military
artifacts in this museum (Hoppe personally wrote the description for each one),
and in front of the museum sits a full-sized P-51 Mustang fighter plane.

✍ ♿ **Hollywood Wax Museum** (417-337-8277; www.hollywoodwax.com), 3030
W. 76 Country Blvd., Branson, Mo. Open daily at 8 AM. $12.95 adults, $8.50 seniors, $6.95 ages 6–12. I like to keep this guide honest, so before describing the
Hollywood Wax Museum let me offer a disclaimer. I've always found celebrities
to be a bit fake, and thus have little desire to look at their wax counterparts.
Frankly, it's my opinion that the personalities and intellect of the real and the tal-
low are pretty similar. That said, if you want to spend $13 and view the visage of
your favorite talk-show host, professional wrestler, or movie star du jour in wax,
then go right ahead. You'll find about a zillion of them here. Some people like
such stuff—different strokes for different folks and all that. Still, if you really
want wax, for $13 you can probably
find a place in Branson to buy a couple of really nice scented candles.

✍ ♿ **Roy Rogers and Dale Evans
Museum** (417-339-1900; www.roy
rogers.com), 3950 Green Mountain
Dr., Branson, Mo. Hours for the
museum are 9–5:30. Performances
at the **Happy Trails Theater** are at
9 AM, 2 PM, and 8 PM. Days vary, so
call in advance. Admission for the
museum alone is $14.44 for adults
over 18, $8.86 for ages 12–17, $13.44
for AAA members, and $12.44 for

WORLD'S LARGEST TOY MUSEUM

military veterans. Admission for the Happy Trails Theater alone runs $22.47 for those over 65, $24.47 for ages 18–64, and $15.55 for ages 12–17. Combo packages are priced $22–35.

To answer your question, Trigger, Buttermilk, and Bullet are all stuffed and serve as museum displays. Luckily, Roy and Dale didn't receive the same treatment. If you enjoyed the King of the Cowboys and Queen of the West, you'll love this museum. There are pictures, saddles, family photos, fan mail, and every sort of artifact you might imagine. The museum features interactive displays, videos, a themed laser shooting gallery, and a kids' discovery area with roping steers and stick horses. At the 308-seat Happy Trails Theater, Roy "Dusty" Rogers Jr. (and the High Riders) performs his parents' most famous songs, shares the experiences of a lifetime, and takes questions from the audience. If you can get past the stuffed horse, this is a wonderful remembrance of a simpler time and a happy Saturday afternoon at the movies.

✐ **Bonniebrook Historical Society and Kewpie Museum** (1-800-539-7437; www.kewpie-museum.com), 485 Rose O'Neill Rd., Walnut Shade, Mo. Apr. 1–Nov. 30, Mon.–Sat. 9–4. $7 adults; kids under 12 admitted free. Born in the 1870s, Rose O'Neill was way ahead of her time. At one time the most highly paid illustrator in the United States (accomplishing this goal while still a teenager), she studied sculpture under Rodin, became a millionaire, lost her entire fortune, was divorced twice, and had homes across America and in Europe. She was called "the Queen of the Bohemians" and considered one of the world's five most beautiful women. Her greatest claim to fame, however, was the creation of the legendary Kewpie doll. Rose's most cherished residence, and the home in which she died, was Bonniebrook, located 10 miles north of Branson in the little town of Walnut Shade. Today visitors can not only tour the restored mansion (it burned to the ground in 1947) but also view original drawings and personal letters, photographs, copies of Rose's artwork, and various Kewpie items. On-site is a gift shop where you can purchase Bonniebrook trinkets and some of the Kewpie items that are still being manufactured today.

🍴 ✐ ♿ **Ralph Foster Museum** (417-334-6411; www.rfostermuseum.com), 685 Graham Clark Dr., Point Lookout, Mo. Mon.–Sat. 9–4:30. $4.50 adults, $3.50 ages 62-plus. High-school-aged kids and younger are admitted free. Located just 2 miles south of Branson in Point Lookout, on the College of the Ozarks campus, the Ralph Foster Museum is a stop that should not be missed. This is the mini Smithsonian of the Ozarks. Originating in the 1920s as a way to collect, preserve, and exhibit the history of the Ozarks, the museum really took off when Ralph Foster of Springfield took an interest during the 1960s. Contributing extensive collections of western and Native American artifacts, as well as a huge gun collection and financial assistance, Foster was instrumental in helping the facility thrive. Today it consists of three stories of exhibits, a total of 40,000 square feet of displays, and another 20,000 square feet dedicated to research areas and offices. Gallery topics within the structure include African and North American animals, firearms through the ages, Ozark history, natural history, and the minerals, birds, butterflies, and rocks of the Ozarks. As well, there are clocks, primitives, an area devoted to Rose O'Neill (the Kewpie doll creator), and the huge Ralph Foster gun collection. Last but not least, be sure to look over the original Clampett family truck featured on *The Beverly Hillbillies*.

GIANT BANJO ⚘ ✎ ♿ **The World's Largest Banjo** (417-335-3535 or 1-800-828-9068; www.grandcountry.com), Grand Country Square, 1945 SR 76, Branson, Mo. This giant re-creation of a collectible Gibson banjo, weighing in at more than 3,000 pounds and more than 47 feet long, can be found in the Grand Country Market, part of the Grand Country Square Complex. The neck holds five fiber-optic strings, and many visitors think it's right cool to have their photo taken next to it. I'm not sure of the reason for this, though the site is admittedly more interesting than the World's Largest Ball of Twine or the World's Largest Frying Pan.

✳ To Do

THEME PARKS ⚘ ✎ ♿ **Celebration City** (800-475-9370; www.celebrationcity .com), 1383 SR 376, Branson, Mo. A Silver Dollar City property, Celebration City is a 112-acre theme park that opened in 2003. Centering on the highlights of 20th-century America, it includes carousels, fountains, a boardwalk, and the Route 66 area. The perfect place to take younger kids, many of the park's rides are of the mellow sort—from carousels to flying carpets. However, there are rides for older kids and adults as well. The Ozark Wildcat is a wooden roller coaster that hits 45 mph; the boardwalk features a wealth of arcades and games such as those found on a state fair midway (without the toothless carnie workers). In total there are 30 rides and attractions at Celebration City, with the highlight of the park being the Kodak-sponsored **Evening Extravaganza**. Yes, it's yet another laser light show, but if you're into such things, it is a fairly good one. There are food and shows aplenty at Celebration City (absolutely no alcohol), as well as numerous shops. Open mid-Mar.–late Oct., 3–10 PM. It should be noted that the attraction is open only on weekends during Mar., Sep., and Oct. A one-day pass is $27 for those ages 12–61, $22 ages 4–11, and $25 ages 62 and up.

⚘ ✎ ♿ **Whitewater** (1-800-475-9370; www.bransonwhitewater.com), 3505 W. SR 76, Branson, Mo. Open May–Sep., daily 10–6. Whitewater at Branson (owned by Silver Dollar City) offers ample opportunity to get soaking wet. Rides include the Raging River Rapids and the Paradise Plunge, with its 207-foot drop. The Surfquake pool holds 500,000 gallons of water and allows for tube riding and bodysurfing, and throughout the park are dining spots featuring the expected ice cream, funnel cakes, hamburgers, and pizza. Alcohol is neither sold nor permitted, as is true with all Silver Dollar City properties, and revealing swimsuits or thongs are forbidden. One admission fee covers all the rides: $32.33 adults, $26.75 ages 4–11. Seniors (over 62) can buy a one-day pass for $14.49.

⚘ ✎ ♿ **Shepherd of the Hills** (417-334-4191 or 1-800-653-6288; www.the shepherdofthehills.com), 5586 W. SR 76, Branson, Mo. Author Harold Bell Wright completed *The Shepherd of the Hills* in 1907, and the publishing world has never been the same. This blockbuster, fictionally based upon the authentic characters Wright came to know and love in the Ozark hills, became the fourth most read book in history (no small feat when you consider that the number one

🦉 🔗 ♿ **Silver Dollar City** (417-266-7300 or 1-800-475-9370; www.silverdollarcity.com), 399 Indian Point Rd., Branson, Mo. The original Branson theme park, and without question the biggest draw in town, Silver Dollar City originally arose (in 1960) as a small 1880s Ozark village. Its purpose was to entertain travelers while they waited to tour Marvel Cave, the tourist attraction leased and operated by the Herschend family. You have to wonder if the Herschends ever suspected that Silver Dollar City would develop into one of America's favorite theme parks, or that they would expand and develop their company into a national entertainment powerhouse. Today the 61-acre Silver Dollar City complex includes five huge festivals, 20 state-of-the-art thrill rides, 60 specialty shops featuring handcrafted goods, live entertainment (more than 40 shows daily), literally hundreds of old-time craftsmen demonstrating skills and arts from eras past, and more than a dozen restaurants. For the kids, the rides include roller coasters such as Wildfire (five inversions and a 15-story drop), the Powder Keg (0–53 mph in 2.8 seconds), and Buzz Saw Falls (featuring a nine-story drop into a reservoir). Parents may more enjoy the **Frisco Silver Dollar Line Steam Train** or the guided tour through **Marvel Cave**. The latter is a 1-hour jaunt that descends 300 feet underground to the Cathedral Room,

spot is held by the Bible). The book still offers a relevant topic today, comparing the social structure of urban areas—with their anonymity and technology—against the unspoiled and regenerative purity of nature and those who reside there. A basic theme lies in the concept that having less equates to actually having more.

The original homestead of John and Anna Ross (the couple known in the book as Old Matt and Aunt Mollie, who allowed Wright to stay in their home during the eight summers it took to complete his tome) is now the site of tours, shows, and the famous dramatic performance of *Shepherd of the Hills*. The Ross cabin has been completely restored, and the 1901 Morgan County Church (which was

one of the largest cave entrance rooms in the United States. The tour continues downward for another 200 feet, where visitors can hop a cable train back to the surface.

The restaurants at Silver Dollar City are geared toward leaving you full, sometimes too much so, but there is a much-appreciated twist here: In contrast with many theme parks, the food is very good. The Herschend family has long prided itself on first-class operations, and whether you are indulging in fried chicken, BBQ, or one of the famous buffets, you will be surprised at the quality. The favorite here is the **Mine restaurant**, offering a BBQ buffet and side dishes, lit with lanterns and designed to resemble a working mine. Those who wish to imbibe should keep in mind that alcohol is neither served nor permitted in any Silver Dollar City property.

The craftsmen at Silver Dollar City tend to be native Ozarkers, folk who have learned their trades from birth. You'll find glassblowers, basket makers, blacksmiths, candy makers, wood-carvers, gun and knife experts, log hewers, lye soap makers, and much more. Most of these artisans sell their works in the Silver Dollar City stores, and again, the quality of the goods is what you would expect in fine city boutiques.

Music shows run the gamut from outdoor shoot-outs to Cajun singers, bluegrass experts, Hillbilly singers, and street comedians. The Silver Dollar City festivals are large-scale productions, not gimmicks just thrown together to make a few extra bucks. Few visitors ever go away dissatisfied.

A one-day pass to Silver Dollar City, which includes all rides and shows, runs $42 for those over 12, $40 for those over 62, and $32 for ages 4–11. Kids 3 and under are admitted free. The park is open from late March until the end of December. Hours vary depending on the month. Call for current times, but as a general rule you're safe if you assume 10–6 for rides, shops, and attractions. Music shows and dining run later in the evening.

moved to its current location) is a popular spot for weddings (417-332-4971). You can enjoy shops on the grounds, a homestead tour by jeep, a climb to the top of the 230-foot **Inspiration Tower**, the **Rockin' S Chuckwagon** music show and brunch, and a campfire dinner with the legendary **Sons of the Pioneers**.

For those who wish to see all that Shepherd of the Hills has to offer, the best deal is the Super Combo package. At $92 adults, $46 ages 4–16, and $84 for those over 55, you can enjoy music and brunch at the Rockin' S Chuckwagon Show, take a Homestead Tour, visit the Inspiration Tower, have dinner and enjoy tales and tunes with the Sons of the Pioneers, and then sit down for the outdoor

INSPIRATION TOWER AT SHEPHERD OF THE HILLS

drama. This latter involves a cast of 100 actors, 40 horses, a flock of sheep, innumerable firearms, and the actual burning of a log cabin (you should note that the performances are canceled should it happen to rain). For those who might not wish the full treatment, there are also separate prices for all these attractions. In addition, trail rides on horseback are available at $14 for adults (pony rides for kids 7 and under are $2).

The park itself is open late Apr.–Oct., and the outdoor drama is performed Mon.–Sat. at 8:30 PM (the preshow begins at 8). In late Aug. the show-time switches to 7:30, with preshow at 7. During Nov.–Jan. a special **Trail of Lights** tour is offered ($7 adults, $3 kids) when the park is decked out for Christmas. Also, the Inspiration Tower is open year-round.

GOLF Branson Creek Golf Club (417-339-4653 or 1-888-772-9900; www.bransoncreekgolf.com), 144 Branson Creek Dr., Branson, Mo. Designed by Tom Fazio, this 18-hole course has been rated the number one public course in Missouri. Fees, which include cart, bag tag, and range balls, are $48 in Jan.– Feb., $60 in Mar., $76 in Apr., $90 (Sun.–Thu.) and $94 (Fri.–Sat.) May–Oct., and $60 in Nov.–Dec. No T-shirts or denim are allowed, personal coolers are forbidden, and all food and beverages must be purchased on the property.

Top of the Rock Golf Course (417-339-5312; www.bigcedarlodge.com), 612 Devil's Pool Rd., Ridgedale, Mo. Part of the Big Cedar Lodge complex, Top of the Rock is a unique nine-hole, par-3 course designed by Jack Nicklaus. This beautiful little course set high above Table Rock Lake is open year-round. Greens fees for non–resort guests are $35 for 9 holes and $50 for 18. Electric cart rentals are $7 and $14 for 9 or 18 holes.

Holiday Hills Resort and Golf Club (417-334-4838; www.holidayhills.com), 630 E. Rockford Dr., Branson, Mo. This course, originally built in 1938, was completely overhauled in 1997. Not nearly as tough as Branson Creek, it is the perfect choice for those who prefer relaxation over fierce competition. Open year-round. $55 7–noon, $41 noon–3, and $29.50 after 3 PM.

Thousand Hills Golf Resort (1-800-864-4145; www.thousandhills.com), 245 S. Wildwood Dr., Branson, Mo. A local favorite, the 18-hole Thousand Hills offers a par-64 course. Small things matter, and if you tend to lose balls (as I do), you'll appreciate the fact that this facility provides a GPS free on every cart. As for awards, *Golf Digest* gave Thousand Hills a three-and-a-half-star rating. Greens fees are $62 and $36 (18 or 9 holes).

Ledgestone Golf Course and Country Club (417-335-8187; www.stone bridgenorth.com/g_ledgestone), 1600 Ledgestone Way, Reeds Spring, Mo. *Golf Digest* has described Ledgestone as "a masterpiece of mountain golf architecture." After one visit you'll see what that means: This is a stunningly beautiful course. Water comes into play on 10 of the 18 holes, but the par-3 hole 15 may bring your biggest challenge. From a cliffside tee box you shoot straight down into a valley. This one will test both your control and your distance perspective. Greens fees and cart are $72 for 18 holes during peak months. Winter rates (Oct.–Feb.) are $58.

Pointe Royale Golf Course (417-334-4477 or 1-866-334-4477; www.pointe royale.com), 142 Club House Dr., Branson, Mo. If you play Pointe Royale, keep an eye out for some of the country music stars who live alongside the course. Also, keep an eye out for the water hazards on 12 of the 18 holes. This is a challenging facility with narrow fairways, usually considered the original championship course of Branson. Greens fees are $65 for walk-on players not staying at Pointe Royale.

✳ Wild Places

Table Rock State Park (417-334-4704; www.mostateparks.com/tablerock.htm), 5722 SR 165, Branson, Mo. Created in 1959 and consisting of 356 acres, Table Rock Park is a very busy little place encompassing numerous campsites, a marina, a store, and trails. The marina itself is a major rental center for Waverunners, pontoon boats, ski boats, and fishing boats, and it also includes a well-stocked scuba shop. The store has all the supplies you could desire for a day messing around the lake or hanging out at the campsite, and visitors can even try their hand at parasailing.

Ruth and Paul Henning State Conservation Area (417-334-3324; www.bransonconnection.com/freestuf/ conserv.htm), Missouri Dept. of Conservation, Branson Forestry Office, US 65 N., Branson, Mo. Just past the end of the twinkling lights of the Branson Strip (SR 76) you'll come across a 1,534-acre area of steep hills and hickory trees. Paul Henning (producer of *The Beverly Hillbillies*) and his wife, Ruth, donated this land to the Missouri Conservation Department, thus protecting for perpetuity many of the areas described in Harold Bell Wright's *Shepherd of the Hills*. Locales such as Mutton Hollow, Little

HENNING STATE CONSERVATION AREA

Pete's Cave, and Sammy Lane's Lookout can all be viewed by visitors. Within the Henning Conservation Area (which is a nice break from Branson's nonstop shows and buffets) are trails, great views of the White River hills, and a blessed silence. The area is open 8 AM–dark, and neither fires nor camping is permitted.

Hercules Glade Wilderness Area (417-683-4428; www.fs.fed.us/r9/forests/ marktwain/ranger_districts/ava), Mark Twain National Forest, Ava/Cassville/ Willow Springs District Office, 1103 S. Jefferson St., Ava, Mo. Located 20 miles east of Branson, the 12,315-acre Hercules Glade is one of the seven wilderness areas falling within the Mark Twain National Forest. Loaded with springs, creeks, bald hills, and glades, the area's only access is via foot or astride a horse. Spring and fall are the best times to visit, due to the array of colors, but in summer you will likely see critters normally assumed to live primarily in the Southwestern deserts (armadillos, lizards, and roadrunners). Keep in mind that spring and summer in the Ozarks also feature a proliferation of ticks, mosquitoes, and all those other fun vermin that lead to itchy skin. You can camp anywhere in Hercules Glade, as long as you move 100 feet or more off a trail. Make sure your fire is dead-out before you leave.

✄ ⚄ **Dogwood Canyon Nature Park** (417-779-5983; www.dogwoodcanyon .com), 2038 W. SR 86, Lampe, Mo. A 10,000-acre private preserve, Dogwood Canyon was developed by Johnny Morris, founder of Bass Pro Shops, and is full of ridges, forests, and creeks. Visitors can view elk, buffalo, and Texas longhorn cattle. As well, there is a Civil War museum, an old lead mine, and a working general store. Located south of Branson (and 16 miles west of Big Cedar Lodge), Dogwood offers a 6-mile paved trail that visitors can hike for $7.95 adults, $3.95 ages 3–11. Bicyclists share this trail, and bikes can be rented for $16.95 adults, $7.95 kids. This is just the beginning. Although some activities are weather dependent, options are many. An open-air tram provides a 2-hour wildlife tour ($23.95 adults, $9.95 kids) through the depths of the Ozarks. A private, guided jeep tour is $50 adults, $35 ages 3–11. Self-guided catch-and-release trout fishing runs $20 adults, $10 kids (for the first hour); guided half-day fishing trips are $195 per person. Horseback-riding fees are $30 per person, or you can kayak on Table Rock Lake for $30 adults, $20 ages 6–11.

LAKES **Table Rock Lake** (417-334-4101, 877-691-0558; www.swl.usace.army .mil/parks/table rock/faq.htm), Army Corps of Engineers, P.O. Box 1109, Branson, Mo. 65616 The Table Rock Dam, one of the four dams used to control flooding on the White River and provide hydroelectric power, was completed in 1958. At 252 feet high and nearly 6,500 feet long, the dam holds in a reservoir comprising some 43,000 acres with 745 miles of shoreline. Located 6 miles south of Branson, this Army Corps of Engineers project offers all the amenities and activities you would imagine on most lakes and is also home to the 350-acre Table Rock State Park. For fishermen, much of the lake is suited to the pursuit of bass, crappie, and channel catfish. However, the tailwaters of Table Rock (which are also the headwaters of Lake Taneycomo) are very cold and provide some lunker brown and rainbow trout. If you want to have some fun, fish for largemouth bass after dark during mid- to late summer. Hit the banks south of the dam in the wee hours of the morning and try for smallmouth bass.

Lake Taneycomo (417-334-4101; www.branson.com/branson/lakes/table), Army Corps of Engineers, P.O. Box 1109, Branson, Mo. 65616 A trout fisherman's heaven, the cold waters of Taneycomo (at places they average 48 degrees) came about thanks to the building of Table Rock Dam 22 miles upstream. When Taneycomo was first constructed in 1913 it was a warm-water lake, but Table Rock gave it a physical southern boundary (1958), and the waters cooled dramatically. This was bad for such early resort towns as Rockaway Beach (who wants to swim in 48-degree water?) but good for those who wish to catch record-breaking brown and rainbow trout. At 2,080 acres, Taneycomo is the home of both the Shepherd of the Hills Trout Hatchery and the Powersite hydroelectric dam. If you stick your toe in the water you'll get a chill, but if you toss a line you'll likely get a trout.

CAVES **Talking Rocks Cavern** (417-272-3366 or 800-600-2283; www.talking rockscavern.com), 423 Fairy Cave Lane, Branson, Mo. Found 5 miles to the west of Branson, this cavern offers 45-minute tours daily 9:30–6. For cavers the crystal formations, stalactites, soda straws, and curtains offer innumerable photo opportunities. The tours are $13.95 for those 13 and up, $6.95 ages 4–12.

✱ Lodging

BED & BREAKFASTS For those who would prefer a bed & breakfast over one of the infinite numbers of franchise hotel rooms in town, you might check out the **Ozark Mountain Bed & Breakfast Service** (1-800-933-8529; www.ozarkbedand breakfast.com). Its web site provides many lodging options, complete with numerous pictures and prices.

Finding a room isn't tough in Branson; hotels and motels are thicker than cats at a fish fry, and vacancies are usually available even if you don't have reservations. Both the Strip and the entire surrounding area are lined with hotels and motels of varying price and quality. Almost all will have their prices shining from a huge, lighted sign, along with the omnipresent nonteaser in the genre of FREE HBO or CONTINENTAL BREAKFAST. In this guide I'm avoiding comment on the vast majority of the franchised Super 8/Comfort Inn/Best

Western offerings and their clones. You can find those on your own. Below are establishments that offer a bit more for your money.

& ✱ **Abbe Chimes Bed and Breakfast** (417-779-1630; www.abbechimes .com), 464 Pokeberry Lane, Lampe, Mo. Located to the south of Silver Dollar City, the Abbe Chimes is a new (built in 2003) contemporary home set on 46 acres above Table Rock Lake. The home features central air, an indoor swimming pool, and exceptionally large rooms with cable TV, VCR, fireplace, microwave, refrigerator, dataport-equipped phones, and double whirlpool bath. The three suites range in decor from contemporary to 19th century to South Pacific. A gourmet breakfast is served every morning at 9. Rates begin at $150 a night, and while neither pets, kids, nor smoking is permitted, there is a boarding kennel nearby for the former.

❅ **Aunt Sadie's Bed and Breakfast** (417-335-4063 or 1-800-944-42501; www.auntsadies.com), 163 Fountain St., Branson, Mo. Aunt Sadie's was voted one of the four most romantic inns in the United States by *Redbook* magazine. The four private cabins and two guest rooms offer amenities such as hot tub or whirlpool bath, TV/VCR, microwave, small refrigerator, and fireplace. It's a lovely setting, back in the midst of 7 acres of timber and only a few minutes from Branson. A huge country breakfast is included in the price, and on-site you'll find not only a day spa with three massage therapists but also a beautiful wedding chapel. Rates begin at $95 for a room and $115 for a cabin. Neither pets nor children are permitted, but smoking is okay on the outside decks.

Barger House Bed & Breakfast (417-335-2134 or 1-800-266-2134; www.bargerhouse.com), 621 Lakeshore Dr., Branson, Mo. A great rendition of an 18th-century colonial home, Barger House is located on the upper stretch of Lake Taneycomo. You can cast a line from the bank or take advantage of the private boat dock. Best of all, tackle and bait are provided if you don't have your own. Should you wish to take a dip, other than in the lake (and Taneycomo is cold, which is good for trout and bad for swimming), you can take advantage of either the large swimming pool or the hot tub. The home offers three guest rooms beginning at $95 per night with numerous amenities, and the breakfast will leave you happily stuffed. If biscuits and gravy aren't to your liking, opt for steak and eggs, grilled pork chops, or (the best) cream-cheese-stuffed French toast with strawberries and hot syrup. Pets are not permitted, smoking is allowed only outdoors, and you must call to discuss bringing the kids with you.

♿ ❅ **Bradford House** (417-334-4444 or 1-888-488-4445; www.bradford house.us), 296 Blue Meadows Rd., Branson, Mo. A gorgeous Victorian home built in 1994, the Bradford House borders on majestic as you are welcomed by the two-story spiral staircase, common room with 25-foot ceilings, and panorama of windows. One of several Bradford properties located in Branson, the home is more of a cross between hotel and inn than the typical B&B. However, it does a good job of holding on to a sense of class. Smaller rooms (15) begin at $89 per night; suites (five), at $109. A full breakfast is served, and amenities include an outdoor pool, Jacuzzi rooms, a 400-movie video library, free wireless Internet, and private hot tub or whirlpool bath. Pets and smoking are not permitted, but kids are considered on a case-by-case basis.

◯◯ 🦐 ❅ **Branson Hotel Bed and Breakfast** (417-335-6104 or 1-800-933-0651; www.bransonhotelbb.com), 214 W. Main St., Branson, Mo. Built in 1903 and restored in 1992 as a bed & breakfast, Branson Hotel's verandas (both upper and lower) are wide and deep, reminiscent of something you'd find in the Deep South. Located in downtown Branson, seven guest rooms beginning at $85 per night. One of these rooms, now named the Fox's Den, served as the residence of author Harold Bell Wright while he was writing *The Shepherd of the Hills* in 1906. Full of antiques and with a beautiful harvest table for breakfast, the hotel does not accept pets or permit smoking. Call to inquire about lodging with kids. Because of its lovely decor and history, the home is a favorite spot for small weddings.

⌀ ❧ **Cameron's Crag** (417-335-8134 or 1-800-933-8529; www.camerons -crag.com), 738 Acadia Club Rd., Point Lookout, Mo. If you want to enjoy the best views of both Lake Taneycomo and Branson, stay at Cameron's Crag. Perched high on a bluff above the lake, the contemporary home's four rooms offer king-sized bed, private entrance and bath, cable and VCR, microwave, coffee bar, and refrigerator. A private hot tub overlooking the lake is a perfect spot from which to enjoy the panoramic vista. Rooms run $95–135, and school-aged kids are accepted. As is the standard, smoking and pets are not allowed.

⬭ ❧ ✳ **Emory Creek Victorian Bed and Breakfast** (417-334-3805 or 1-800-362-7404; www.emorycreekbnb .com), 143 Arizona Dr., Branson, Mo. There's a reason Emory Creek is considered the most elegant bed & breakfast in Branson. The luxurious blue and white Victorian, built in 1993 and owned by Sammy and Beverly Gray Pagna, features five suites and a host of amenities. Breakfast is a four-course affair, with live music coming from Sammy on the piano. Fresh cookies are in your room upon arrival, and plush terry-cloth robes are in the bathrooms. A wildlife trail wanders through 7.5 acres, with a garden gazebo suspended over the forest floor. Furnishings inside are Victorian to the core, and a shining grand staircase rises from the home's main salon to the second story. Should you wish to read, a library offers both the classics and bestsellers. Rates run $95–150 a night, and lunch and dinner can be arranged for an additional fee. Kids over 13 are permitted; smoking and pets are not.

⌀ ✳ **Falls on the Lake Bed & Breakfast** (417-334-3833 or 1-866-448-9760; www.fallsonthelake.com), 417 Dale Ave., Hollister, Mo. Just minutes from Branson, this getaway on Table Rock Lake offers peace and quiet. The landscaping is impeccable, complete with flowing waterfall, and rates for the three suites range $100–165 per night. Amenities can include TV and VCR, central air, private spas, outdoor hot tub, private entrance, and fireplace. For breakfast make sure to sample (or more than sample . . . this stuff is good) the caramel walnut French toast. Kids of all ages are accepted at the Falls, but smoking is outside only, and pets are a no-no.

⬭ ❧ ⌀ ✳ **Gaines Landing** (417-334-2280 or 1-800-825-3145; www.gaines landing.com), 521 W. Atlantic St., Branson, Mo. Each of the three suites at Gaines Landing features a private hot tub right outside your door, but such is just the beginning of the nice touches provided by this small establishment located in "old" downtown Branson. The rooms feature king-sized bed, TV/VCR with free popcorn and movies, microwave, small refrigerator with complimentary refreshments, and (in one case) a wood-burning fireplace. Gaines is close to everything, but also situated back in a small stretch of woods. It's the best of both worlds, with restaurants and shows very close but peace and quiet awaiting back at your room. $85–145. Smoking and pets are out, but kids are accepted without restriction.

❧ ⌀ ✳ **Lakeshore Bed and Breakfast** (417-338-2698 or 1-800-285-9739; www.lakeshorebandb.com), 47 Elm Lane, Branson, Mo. Located right on Table Rock Lake and just 2 miles south of Silver Dollar City,

Lakeshore offers three rooms (one is a two-bedroom suite) that are close to all the attractions but also allow for the fun of splashing around in the water. Kids are welcome here, and at $60–95 per night, the lodgings are some of the most economical in Branson. You can bring your boat and moor it at Lakeshore's dock, pedal around in their boat, or simply sit outside and watch the sunset. Rooms come with queen beds, a full kitchen, and private bath (the suite also includes TV, VCR, refrigerator, coffee bar, and whirlpool tub and shower); a large breakfast is provided each morning. Pets are prohibited, and smoking is allowed outside only.

❋ **The Martindale Bed & Breakfast** (417-338-2588 or 1-888-338-6330; www.martindalebnb.com), 164 Martinda Lane, Branson West, Mo. Also on Table Rock Lake, the Martindale's two rooms, both elegantly furnished and running $70 per night, offer some great views of the lake and nearby woods. There are TVs in mirrored cherry armoires, VCRs, scroll beds, private baths, and a screened-in porch and deck. A big breakfast, featuring flickering candles and background music, is an example of the sort of hospitality provided by the native Ozark owners. Pets are not allowed, smoking is permitted on the screened porch, and kids are considered on a case-by-case basis.

❀ ✔ ❋ **Red Bud Cove** (417-334-7144 or 1-800-677-5525; www.redbudcove.com), 162 Lakewood Dr., Hollister, Mo. This is a nice place to visit in spring if you enjoy a gorgeous garden of flowers and the purple blossoms of the trees that are this inn's namesake. A renovated barn, Red Bud features eight suites (queens,

kings, honeymoon, and family). Located right on Table Rock Lake and only about 15 minutes from the Branson Strip, Red Bud's suites feature private entrance, a living room (some have working fireplace), private bath, a kitchenette, TV, and phone. Rates, which include breakfast, run $97–145 per night, and kids are accepted. Pets are not allowed, and if you wish to smoke, you will have to do it in the great outdoors.

❀ ❋ **Twin Hearts Bed & Breakfast** (417-334-7070; www.twinheartsbb .com), 148 Cypria Lane, Branson, Mo. It appears that countless hours have gone into the creation and maintenance of the landscaping and indoor water garden that grace this nice contemporary home. If you enjoy a peaceful chair on the porch, this is your type of place. The inn's three rooms range $75–100 per night and include such amenities as king-sized bed, cable TV, VCR, telephone, and private bath. The largest room features a fireplace and whirlpool bath. Pets, smoking, and children under 15 are not permitted.

RESORTS ⊗ ✔ ♿ ❋ ⛾ **Big Cedar Lodge** (417-335-2777; www.big cedarlodge.com), 612 Devil's Pool Rd., Ridgedale, Mo. For sheer beauty and luxury, the feel of the best lodge you could ever discover in either the Adirondacks or the Rockies, Big Cedar Lodge wins hands-down. Purchased in 1987 by John Morris (owner of Bass Pro Shops), the facility included and expanded greatly upon the palatial homes and grounds of several wealthy Missourians from generations past. Just 10 miles south of Branson, the 800-acre lodge offers lodging in the form of private log cabins ($169–

699 per night), Knotty Pine cabins ($89–319), or cabins in the 10,000-acre Dogwood Canyon Nature Park just a few minutes away ($149–299). Rooms in the Falls Lodge are priced $109–249, while rates in the Spring-view Lodge are $69–269. Last but not least is the Valley View Lodge, where lodging costs $79–1,499. The most elaborate room (for those who can afford to blow $1,500 per night) is the Governor's Suite. It consists of a four-bedroom, 2,500-square-foot suite with full kitchen, living area with fireplace, flat-screen TV, dining table for eight, and great views of Table Rock Lake.

Obviously the amenities and size of the rooms and cabins vary by price, but this resort lives up to its lofty reputation by providing the Top of the Rock Golf Course, a full-service marina on Table Rock, trails, fishing, horseback riding, a spa, massage, carriage rides, campfire chuckwagon tours, and much more. As to dining, the Devil's Pool restaurant (see *Dining Out*) is known for it, lunch and breakfast buffets, prime rib, and champagne Sunday brunch. The **Truman Smokehouse**, open for breakfast and lunch only, offers smoked ribs, brisket, sausage, and chicken (plus great pastries), and the **Worman House** restaurant (reservations only) provides its own champagne Sunday brunch. For casual dining there is the **Buzzard Bar**. Big Cedar is popular for groups, meetings, and weddings, capable of accommodating up to 350 guests for receptions and 225 guests for seated dinners.

∞ ♪ ♿ ❄ ♈ **Chateau on the Lake Resort, Spa, and Convention Center** (1-888-333-5253; www.chateauon thelakebranson.com), 415 N. SR 265, Branson, Mo. A John Q. Hammons

hotel, the Chateau prides itself on Old World charm and service. Given a Four Diamond rating by Triple Λ, this "Castle in the Ozarks" is situated on the peak of a forested hill over-looking Table Rock Lake. The hotel includes 301 rooms, divided into Standard, Traditional, Deluxe, over-sized Chateau Kings, and 57 elaborate suites. A 10-story lobby atrium greets visitors, who will enjoy a level of professionalism and courteous service more commonly associated with renowned urban establishments. Accommodations include such touches as tiled stone baths, hand-tooled iron lamps, and cherrywood beds. All rooms come standard with two phone lines with voice mail and dataports, iron and ironing board, wireless web TV, feather pillows, triple sheets, hair dryers, and lighted makeup mirrors. Room rates for a Standard are $89–169, and $109–199 for a Traditional. Deluxe rooms run $129–219, while the prices for the Chateau Kings are $149–249. Lake-view Ambassador Suites will set you back $189–309 per night, while a Vice Presidential Suite is $459–509. Last but far from least, the 1,000-square-foot Presidential Suite (one of two) offers every perk imaginable in the $559–609 range.

In terms of amenities and recreation, guests can enjoy indoor and outdoor pools, a 24-hour fitness area and salon, hot tubs, tennis courts, hiking and biking, and a full-service marina. The **Spa Chateau** is for those who wish to be pampered in style and has a lengthy menu of both spa and beauty treatments. The Chateau is also an increasingly popular wedding spot, boasting a 32,000-square-foot ballroom capable of hosting from 50 to

1,500 guests. For outdoor weddings, both the greenbelt Pavilion and Garden terrace can easily handle 50–250 guests, and full catering (small or large) is a regular service.

The Chateau Grille (see *Dining Out*) features accomplished chefs and is a *Wine Spectator* award-winning eatery, while the more casual **Atrium Cafe and Wine Bar** and **Steeple Lite Deli** allow for casual meals. You would also be remiss if you failed to stop in the **Sweete Shoppe**, with its pastries, ice cream, and classic soda fountain.

CAMPING Private campgrounds and RV parks in Branson are as prevalent as fleas on a fat dog. With more than 50 sites from which to choose, visitors can take their pick from simple tent spaces to full-service accommodations capable of handling the largest RVs. Public campgrounds at Table Rock Lake are largely managed by the Army Corps of Engineers.

🕷 ✑ ♿ ❄ **Compton Ridge Campground** (417-338-3911 or 1-800-233-8648; www.comptonridge.com), 5040 SR 265, Branson, Mo. The best time to hang your hat at Compton Ridge is in the middle of September, when fiddle players from across the country descend for the annual Ozarks Fiddler's Convention. What else would you expect from a facility whose family tree includes eight generations of native Ozarkers? Tent sites at the main campground begin at $23 ($26 with water and electric); full RV hookups (water, sewer, 30 amp, and cable TV) begin at $30. At the smaller, north campground, hookups begin at $28. Amenities include rest rooms, laundry facilities, Internet service, both an outdoor and an indoor pool, a

game room, hiking trails, tennis courts, basketball courts, and playgrounds. There are kitchen and pavilion shelters on the grounds, a 650-seat convention building, church services, and store. The Compton Ridge motel features standard motel rooms beginning at $43.95 (kitchenettes are also available), and rooms in the lodge building run $30–50. Cabins can be rented for $99–119 per night. Keep in mind that neither pets nor smoking is permitted in rooms, lodge, or cabins.

🕷 🐾 ✑ ♿ **Table Rock Lake** (1-877-444-6777; www.swl.usace.army.mil/parks/tablerock/campgroundpages.htm), 4600 SR 165, Suite A, Branson, Mo. With more than 1,200 individual campsites, the Army Corps of Engineers offers camping in 13 different campgrounds. Most of the areas are open from spring (generally Mar. or Ap.) until Sep. or Oct. Fees are $11–12 for a basic site, $15–17 for a site with electricity, $16–17 for sites with electricity and water, and $15–18 for sites with electric, water, and sewer. It should be noted that only two of the sites (Big M Park and Eagle Rock Park) have the full facilities. Sites can be reserved by phone (there is a $5 administration fee), and most come with picnic table, shower, toilet, fire ring, and parking space.

🕷 ✑ ♿ ❄ **The Wilderness at Silver Dollar City** (417-338-8189 or 1-800-477-5164; www.thewildernesslogcabins.com), 7347 W. SR 76, Branson, Mo. Located just a few minutes from all the theaters, the Wilderness offers cabins, 50-amp RV spots, rental RVs, and campsites. Though right in the thick of things, this lovely spot will make you feel you are out in the woods. Cabins come in various sizes (sleeping four comfortably or six if you don't mind a bit of crowding) and run $55–149 per night. RV trailer rentals begin at $75 per night; if you bring your own rig, 30-amp and 50-amp sites are $26 and $29, respectively. A basic tent site is $16, or $21 if you opt for water and electric. As to amenities, all cabins (with the exception of the rustic "pioneer cabin") come with heat, air, table and chairs, ceiling fans, bathroom, shower, microwave, cable TV, coffeepot, refrigerator, gas grill, and rocking chairs. Cabins with kitchens also include a sink, two-burner stovetop, linens, and towels. The RV rental trailers include heat and air, TV, refrigerator, stove, microwave, coffeepot, shower, toilet, and fire ring.

✳ Where to Eat
EATING OUT

All listings are in Branson, Mo.
🍴 🧺 ♿ **Branson Cafe** (417-331-3021), 120 W. Main St. Mon.–Sat. 5:30 AM–8 PM. This old café, located in the original part of Branson, was first opened in the early 1900s. From appearances, this is where the locals meet in the morning to hash around the latest gossip. They do this over coffee (as in java that costs less than a buck, not as in some fancy-schmancy high-dollar latte or cappuccino) and heaping plates of biscuits and gravy (which you can get for about $3). The Branson Cafe is known far and wide for its fried chicken, catfish, pancakes, and pies—it's a diner the way diners are supposed to be—but for one heck of a big sandwich you should opt for the breaded pork tenderloin. This must be an Ozark thing, but almost all diners in these parts offer the giant pork tenderloin. They taste great, and at $5.75 this one is a steal.

🍴 🧺 ♿ ♈ **Dockers** (417-332-0044), 3100 Green Mountain Dr. Open seven days a week, 7 AM–10 PM. Designed to look like a paddle-wheeler, Dockers is a popular tourist spot for breakfast, lunch, and dinner. The morning breakfast buffet runs $4, while lunch and dinner are $6 and $10, respectively. All of these smorgasbords are loaded with food—heavy on the fried and the meat, which is our normal diet in the Ozarks—but it is the wise and hungry traveler who spends a few bucks more and opts for the evening seafood buffet. For $14 you can make an absolute pig of yourself with unlimited crab legs, shrimp, rock lobster, catfish, trout, and much, much more. The restaurant also offers a full choice of liquor and a sports-bar motif.

🧺 ♿ **Gwin's Home Cannery** (417-334-5756), 1810 W. SR 76. Daily 7 AM–9 PM. The Home Cannery has been in Branson for nearly 20 years and is another one of the many Branson establishments that offer buffets for every meal. But there's a difference between Gwin's and many other stops. Here, everything is homemade (and yes, that means the mashed potatoes don't come out of a box). You can get breakfast in the $5 range, with dinner averaging out to just double that. Home Cannery also has a full menu (lots of sandwiches) and regular "blue plate specials" at every meal.

🍴 🧺 ♿ **McFarlain's** (417-336-4680), 562 Shepherd of the Hills Expwy. Mon.–Sat. 8 AM–10 PM, Sun. 9–9. Located in the Branson IMAX, McFarlain's has become one busy place due to good food that is also inexpensive. This establishment is something of a respite from other Branson eateries, as there is no buffet line full of folks who seek to pile their plates six stories high. It's all table service here, and the emphasis is on quality. Breakfast might be as simple as the $2.99 biscuits and gravy, or as decadent as berries-and-cream French toast. This latter, at $4.99, consists of French toast topped with cream cheese frosting, your choice of blueberries or strawberries, whipped cream, and powdered sugar. There are also numerous skillets and omelets in the $4–8 range. Appetizers for lunch or dinner could be either fried green tomatoes or fried sweet potatoes at $5.29 (you can order a sampler platter with a bit of each for the same price . . . and the sweet potatoes are outrageously good), and a host of burgers and sandwiches for $5–8. Dinner entrées encompass deep-fried catfish (the only way it should be cooked) at $8.99, chicken-fried steak ($8.49), and a 10-ounce rib-eye steak for $15.99. If you've got some time after the meal (and don't forget to order pie), catch the IMAX film *Ozark Legacy and Legend*. It chronicles six generations of the native Ozark McFarlain family and will give you a clear view of what the Ozarks both were and are.

🍲 🎣 ♿ ♈ **The Plantation** (417-334-7800), 3460 SR 76. Mon.–Thu. 7 AM–10 PM, Fri.–Sat. 7 AM–midnight, Sun. 9–9. The name alone will tell you what it looks like. This is a big, long eatery right on the Strip, and it's been voted Best Buffet in Town more times than I can count. Inside, you will find plants everywhere, as well as copious amounts of food. Many chickens gave their lives in the quest to make the Plantation a Branson icon, and diners show their appreciation by eating till they burst. With a drink, the dinner buffet costs in the $10 range. While chicken is the claim to fame (well-battered and tasty), you'll also find such regional favorites as catfish (usually with a choice of baked, breaded, or Cajun), hush puppies, and fried okra. There are buffets for breakfast and lunch as well, or you can order from the menu. The Plantation has a full bar to satisfy that mint julep craving.

🍲 🎣 ♿ **The Shack** (417-334-3490), 108 S. Commercial St. Mon.–Sat. 7–7; closed Sun. This is the second oldest place in Branson (just a tad younger than the Branson Cafe). While it originally was housed in nothing more than a shack (which flooded on a regular basis), new quarters were established in the early 1980s. Luckily the food is just as good as it was reputed to be in the 1940s. For breakfast, you can have the standard bacon, eggs, hotcakes, or biscuits and gravy. This is real cooking, pure Ozark food, and the pan-fried chicken, catfish, tenderloins, and pot roast are just as good (if not better) than the fare you would receive at many of its more expensive counterparts. Plus, the atmosphere is honest, no pretensions. The simple desserts (like raisin crème pie) will make you smile. Best of all, you would be very hard pressed to spend more than $10 per person. Credit cards are not accepted.

🍲 🎣 ♿ **Whipper Snappers** (417-334-3282), 236 Shepherd of the Hills Expwy. Located in the Branson Towers hotel; open for dinner daily 4–8. I once knew a fellow in Butte, Mont., name of Scott, with a severe crustacean addiction. With his black hole of an appetite, Scott actually ran a Red Lobster out of lobster during one of its "all-you-can-eat" specials. I look forward to the day he stumbles into

Whipper Snappers. For $24.99 this restaurant offers an all-you-can-eat lobster, crab leg, and seafood buffet. These are whole lobsters, not just claws or tails, with giant crab legs, peel-and-eat shrimp, fried shrimp, clam strips, crawdads, gumbo, and catfish. Toss in a salad bar and dessert bar and you end up with one of the best buffets imaginable. On the other hand, there are plenty of menu items for those who don't wish to take part in an oceanic version of gastronomic intensity. Fried chicken and country-fried steak are $8.99, and the Caribbean chicken pasta is $12.99. Whipper Snappers is very casual, totally non-smoking, and does not serve alcohol of any kind. A children's menu is available.

DINING OUT

Unless otherwise noted, all listings are in Branson, Mo.
♪ & ♈ **Buckingham's** (417-337-7777; www.clarionhotelbranson.com), 2820 W. SR 76. Daily 1–11 PM, with dinner served after 4:30. You could call the decor of Buckingham's (located in the Clarion Hotel) "early American African veldt." This place is amusing, and not only is the food good, but the outside patio is the perfect spot for a drink or three. There's a full lounge at Buckingham's, and at last count it served 20-plus types of martinis. The bartenders also invite you to make up your own. No matter how strange, they'll take a shot at creating it. In the realm of food, start with the hickory-smoked trout ($6.95) or the crab au gratin ($7.95). The list of appetizers is lengthy, but not as much so as the possible entrées. The Ozark staples are available; a 16-ounce fried catfish is $16.95. Or you could get into the

restaurant's theme and order either safari meat loaf (made from venison and boar sausage and costing $14.95) or the mixed game grill. The latter is a combination of ostrich, duck, and wild boar sausage served with a variety of sauces ($26.95). The restaurant offers numerous pasta, seafood, pork, and beef selections (the surf and turf, a 6-ounce filet mignon and 6 ounces of skewered lobster tails, is $28.95); unique desserts; and more than a few dishes prepared tableside. A free kids' menu is offered for children under 10. It's not fancy, with its grilled cheese, chicken fingers, and pasta with red sauce, but just that the restaurant thought to provide such a service shows impressive forethought and a dedication to customer service.

♪ & ♈ **Candlestick Inn Restaurant & Lounge** (417-334-3633; www.candlestickinn.com), 127 Taney St. Open for lunch Mon.–Fri. 11–3, for dinner Sun.–Thu. 5–9. On Fri.–Sat. the restaurant is open for dinner 5–10. With its ambience of linen and candlelight, and its romantic view of Lake Taneycomo, the Candlestick Inn is regarded as one of the finest dining establishments in Branson. True to the Branson atmosphere, Candlestick manages to offer well-prepared dishes and great service without coming off as snobbish. Some diners, those accustomed to the "fine-dining" offerings and rather snooty demeanor of chic urban restaurants, might be a bit disappointed. Such would be a mistake. What would seem formal in Branson would be defined as casual in other venues, but that's part of the beauty of the region. The Candlestick strives to make patrons comfortable, and those patrons can range from an elderly couple out for an anniversary dinner to a family with a passel of kids. *Comfort* is byword here, something provided by the view over Taneycomo, the wood-burning fireplace, and the nonhovering service that makes you feel at ease. Appetizers include such tried-and-true favorites as tequila-marinated shrimp skewers ($10) and crab-stuffed mushroom caps ($7). As for entrées, the trout amandine ($21—and the almonds are maple roasted) and roast rack of lamb ($29) are perennial favorites. Also on the extensive menu are traditional favorites such as grilled KC strip ($28), sautéed veal ($22), and the extremely popular fillet and lobster ($40). Desserts are creative and plentiful, with the Candlestick Cupcake—a chocolate confection prepared to order (note that it should be ordered in advance)—offered at a well-spent $8. The restaurant has smoking and nonsmoking sections and a full bar. Reservations are requested.

✐ ᕦ ᵞ **The Chateau Grille** (1-888-333-5253; www.chateauonthelake branson.com), 415 N. SR 265. Open daily for breakfast 6:30–10, for lunch 11–2, and for dinner 5–10. Located within the Chateau on the Lake, this restaurant offers a more formal dining atmosphere without being stuffy. Continuing the Old World look for which the Chateau is renowned, and featuring views of Table Rock Lake, the Grille specializes in American selections for breakfast, lunch, teatime, and dinner. The Sunday brunch, with more than 50 entrées, is a perennial favorite. Also, the Chateau Grille was named a 2001 Award of Excellence winner by *Wine Spectator* magazine. A children's menu is available (no need to leave the kids in the room), and guests may even reserve

the Chef's Table, enjoying their meal deep within the Grille kitchen and discussing techniques of preparation with the chef himself. For starters, try the Missouri wild mushroom tart ($9), rich caps sautéed with Portugal marsala cream and displayed in an herbed tartlet. The $39 fillet and lobster entrée includes a 6-ounce tenderloin and 6-ounce cold-water lobster tail, but the excellent Chateau chicken vanilla ($24) should be tried at least once. Jumbo shrimp, encased in scallop moussseline, spinach, and roasted red pepper, are stuffed into a chicken breast, wrapped in puff pastry, and covered with a sauce made from Madagascar vanilla beans. Dress is casual, and smoking is not allowed. The restaurant features a full bar; reservations are recommended.

✐ ᕦ ᵞ **The Devil's Pool** (417-335-5141; www.bigcedarlodge.com), 612 Devil's Pool Rd., Ridgedale, Mo. Open daily, 7–11 for breakfast, 11–2 for lunch, and 5–9:30 for dinner. Sunday brunch is held 10–2. Located in the luxurious Big Cedar Lodge, Devil's Pool offers "contemporary Ozark cuisine." In English, that means you can have hickory-smoked prime rib, pork ribs, or Mediterranean pasta. The servings are large here, and—as would be anticipated in a lodge setting (dark woods and stone fireplace)—all entrées come complete with salad, vegetable, and a choice of either baked potato, fries, mashed potatoes and gravy, or the ever-popular smoked bacon grits. For an appetizer, try the barbecue quesadilla at $7.75. A new twist on an old BBQ technique, it's a combination of smoked pulled pork; jalapeños; and provolone cheese. Popular entrées include the aforementioned hickory-smoked prime rib

($26.95 for a 16 ounce) and BBQ glazed country-style meat loaf. This ain't your momma's meat loaf: For $17.95 you'll receive a combination loaf of beef, pork, chicken, and local wild mushrooms. The Devil's Pool has a full bar and is entirely nonsmoking except on the patios. Reservations are recommended for dinner.

✳ Entertainment

BRANSON SHOWS All listings are located in Branson proper unless otherwise noted. Showtimes and prices change on a regular basis, and more than a few of the entertainers tend to move from theater to theater. Make sure to check web sites or call ahead for details. For a further note on prices, please be aware that the figures listed below are guidelines. Varying admission fees can range by several dollars depending upon where and when you purchase.

Acrobats of China Featuring the New Shanghai Circus (1-877-212-4462; www.acrobatsofchina.com), 645 SR 165. Shows at 3 and 8 PM, May 15–Dec. 15. $29 adults, $15 ages 13–17, $9 ages 6–12. If you want to see the definition of grace, art, and true athleticism, do not miss this show. Held in the New Shanghai Theater, this is the sort of performance that will leave you shaking your head in wonder. The acrobats, ranging in age from 13 to 45, have trained since they were young children, and many of the feats they demonstrate simply do not seem possible.

Act of God (1-866-339-1960; www.actofgodbranson.com), 2353 W. SR 248. Shows take place May 24–Dec. 10, Tue.–Sun. at 10 AM in the Musical Palace. $19 adults; children 13 and under are admitted free. This entire production is based upon religious themes (they call it the only "100% God-Centered Show in Branson") and features skits, music, and comedy revolving around biblical themes.

Andy Williams Moon River Theater (417-334-4500; www.andy williams.com), 2500 76 Country Blvd. Shows are held at 7 PM, Apr. 15–May 29 and Sep. 9–Oct. 26. Christmas Show is held Nov. 1–Dec. 11. $38 for ages 16 and up, $18 for children under 15. Admission for the Christmas Show is $40 adults, $18 children. Andy Williams is getting up there in years (we're talking the octogenarian realm), and times and shows change depending on his throat, schedule, and stamina. At the time of this writing his main performance is an evening show with Petula Clark; however, it would behoove the visitor to call ahead and check exact performers, performances, and ticket availability. The Moon River Theater itself is a warm and charming venue, shooting for sophistication via woodwork and selected pieces of fine art. The hall does offer a reasonable facsimile of Moon River in the form of a koi-stocked pond that runs along the side

ANDY WILLIAMS MOON RIVER THEATER

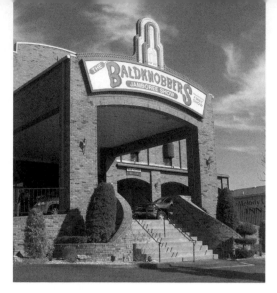

THE BALDKNOBBERS THEATER

of the building itself. Of course the legendary entertainer still sings his trademark song. Despite his age, you receive the impression that Andy Williams truly enjoys putting on a show, and his voice has held up surprisingly well. The typical presentation will include trademark hits, with comedy and dancing thrown in to offer a well-rounded performance reminiscent of Andy's TV variety show. The 11-member orchestra—featuring musicians from all over the world—is an extremely talented group that provides excellent backup. The annual **Christmas Show**, two shows daily, is very popular; reservations are necessary.

Baldknobbers Jamboree Music Show (417-334-4528; www.bald knobbers.com), 2835 W. SR 76. One show per day is offered Mon.–Sat. at 8 PM, Mar.–Dec. $25 adults, $13.50 children. The Baldknobbers are Branson's original country music show, having been in town since 1959. Their theater complex encompasses a motel, restaurant (which seats 230 and offers inexpensive meals and a country buffet), and theater. The entertainment

here is pure country—this troupe was doing *Hee Haw* long before *Hee Haw* was a glimmer in the eye of network TV programmers. Expect lots of country, gospel, and patriotic music, interspersed with rapid-fire jokes and an abundance of slapstick comedy.

Biggest Magic—Brett Daniels and Kirby Van Burch (417-336-1220; www.thegrandpalace.com), 2700 W. SR 76. Shows are held at 2 and 8 PM, May–Nov., in the Grand Palace Theater. Days vary. $29 adults, $17 ages 4–12. Brett Daniel and Kirby Van Burch, two of the hottest magicians going, have combined their shows to offer an extravaganza of illusion. These guys are not of the card-trick-and-rabbit-out-of-a-hat genre. They specialize in the big stage illusions à la Copperfield and appear with the requisite white Bengal tiger. Let's hope it behaves better than Siegfried and Roy's cat.

Bob Anderson (417-334-7535; www .bobanderson.tv), 3431 W. SR 76. Shows are Apr.–Dec. at 8 PM in the Club Vegas Theater. $49 adults (which includes dinner), $26 for the show only. $11 (dinner included) for those under 12. You likely have seen Bob Anderson on many of the popular talk shows of the 1970s and '80s. Known as the "singing impressionist," Anderson can imitate to near perfection most of the top vocalists of our times. If you enjoy the likes of Sinatra, Sammy Davis Jr., and Tony Bennett, you'll enjoy Bob Anderson. Though he is an impressionist, the production is really a highlight of superb musical talent. No amateurish Nixon impersonations here. Just good tunes.

Bobby Vinton in Concert (1-888-462-7267; www.bransonvarietytheatre .com), 2701 W. SR 76. Showtimes are at 10 AM, 2 PM, and 8 PM, Nov.–Dec., at the Branson Variety Theatre. Days vary. $35 adults, $13 children. Given that many of his songs are classics that stand the test of time—"Blue Velvet," "Mr. Lonely," and "Roses Are Red," to name just a few—it's really no surprise that Bobby Vinton has sold more than 75 million albums. His Branson show proves that some entertainers never lose their class, as Bobby is still spinning his cherished ballads, complete with a full orchestra and joined by members of his family. This is a show for all ages, both Vinton fans from back when and those who've only heard his famous songs on oldies stations.

Branson Follies (417-335-5543 or 1-888-236-5543; www.bransonfollies.com), 464 SR 248. Shows Sun. 2 PM, and Mon., Tue., Fri., and Sat. 2 and 8 PM, Sep.–Dec., at the Follies Theater. $36 adults, $20 ages 16 and younger. If you're starting to feel a creak in your back or a hitch in your get-along, the correct therapy might lie in taking in the performers at the Branson Follies. All of them are in their 60s, 70s, and 80s (in 2005 the headliner was Patti Page). The show is something of a tribute to the variety shows of decades past: The 1930s–1950s are the focus. If you're feeling that the roll around your middle is a lost cause, then take note of senior Ziegfeld girls as they perform high kicks and splits while wearing 15-pound feathered headgear.

Branson Showcase (417-335-2396 or 1-877-487-2386; www.bransonwhitehousetheatre.com), 755 Gretna Rd. Showtime is 7 PM, year-round, Mon.–Fri. in the White House Theatre. A special Showcase Jubilee is held Sat. at 7 PM. $28 adults (with dinner at

$10), $6 kids (dinner included). They call this the Magnificent 7 show, a high-energy attraction featuring more than 30 musical numbers and a staggering 150 costume changes. There are show tunes, standards, classics, Elvis impersonations, magic, and much more in this 2-hour production. The **Showcase Jubilee** presents a totally new act each week, which is televised every Saturday afternoon on Fox.

Braschler Music Show (417-334-4363; www.braschlermusicshow.com), 3044 Shepherd of the Hills Expwy. Showtimes are 3 PM, Mon.–Fri., and 8 PM Sun., Aug.–Dec., in the Hamner Barber Variety Theater. $24 adults; kids under 12 admitted free. Another one of Branson's long-running shows, the Braschlers have been performing around town for nearly 25 years. Most of the fare consists of bluegrass, gospel, country, and comedy, with the first entrée being especially entertaining. This is a true family affair, and the head of the clan, Cliff Braschler, is still singing tenor.

Breakfast with Mark Twain and Norman Rockwell (417-336-2112; www.bransonsuperstars.com), 205 S. Commercial St. Showtimes are at 10 AM (breakfast served at 9 AM) Mon., Wed., Fri., and Sat., Mar. 7–Dec. 31. $29 adults, $9.75 children. Mark Twain is practically synonymous with Missouri, and Norman Rockwell with the hometown values espoused by Branson. In this one-man show by Clem Samuels, held at the Owens Theater in "old" downtown Branson, you'll get plenty of both in a nice little show. The Twain character will regale you with the wit and wisdom for which the classic American author was noted. The backdrop consists of more than 100 of Rockwell's best-known prints.

Brett Family Morning Show (417-336-3100 or 1-877-252-7388; www .brettfamily.com), 3600 W. SR 76. Showtime is 10 AM, Mon.–Sat. at the Legends Family Theater, Apr.–Dec. $22 adults, $5.50 ages 4–16. A variety show in the old-fashioned sense, the Brett Family Morning Show has consistently been voted one of the best in Branson. Singing, dancing, comedy, and patriotic music (with some magic thrown in for good measure) are all a part of this fast-paced production. There is some major talent to be enjoyed at this event, especially the well-blended harmonies and a cappella solos.

Broadway! The Star-Spangled Celebration (417-334-2500 or 1-888-462-7267; www.bransonvarietytheatre .com), 2701 W. SR 76. Showtimes are at 2 and 8 PM, Tue.–Sun., at the Branson Variety Theatre, May–Dec. $32 adults, $10 children. Featuring the best of Broadway, this splashy music-and-dance show features selections from 50 hit productions, including *Cats*, *Oklahoma*, *Les Misérables*, *Chicago*, *Cabaret*, *My Fair Lady*, *A Chorus Line*, and *Grease*.

Buck Trent Morning Show (1-800-764-9324; www.bucktrent.com), 1945 W. SR 76. Showtime is 9:30 AM, Mon.–Sat., at the Grand Country Music Hall, Sep.–Dec. $26 adults ($30 with breakfast), $6.50 for kids under 12 (with breakfast). For 15 years Buck Trent's screaming five-string banjo has served as a wake-up call for Branson visitors. Buck is an all-around entertainer—tossing plenty of country comedy into his act—and is accompanied by a troupe of first-tier vocalists and fiddle players. If a cup of strong coffee and a big breakfast doesn't jump-start your heart in the early-morning hours, Buck Trent certainly will.

Celebrate America (1-866-707-4100; www.mansionamerica.com), 189 Expressway Lane. Showtime is 8 PM, Tue.–Sun., at the Mansion America Theater, Apr.–Dec. $29 adults, $15 children. Something of a history lesson set to music, the plot of the show revolves around a small town's Independence Day celebration. Via a narrator and music, a wise old grandfather explains to a small girl what makes America great. What follows is nearly 2 hours of song and dance portraying scenes and events from colonial times to the present. Celebrate America is a fine way to introduce kids to America's legacy in an entertaining manner, and adults will love both the message and the nostalgia.

Christmas Dreams (1-800-884-4536; www.thegrandpalace.com), 2700 W. SR 76. This is a limited-time show that plays Nov.–Dec. at the Grand Palace Theater. Call ahead for times, days, and prices. If you're tired of the same old *Nutcracker* but still want the elaborate costumes and pageantry, then by all means attend Christmas Dreams. This show was created especially for Branson and made its debut here a couple of years ago. The gist of the show is the Yuletide season as observed by Christmas ornaments, a production enhanced by placing six mini stages throughout the audience. On the main stage 30 professional actors, singers, and dancers portray the various ornaments. This is a colorful production, and those in the audience are literally surrounded with song and surprise.

Christmas on the Trail Dinner

Show (417-334-4191; www.the shepherdofthehills.com), 5586 W. SR 76. Showtime and dinner is at 5:30 PM, Mon.–Sat. at the Pavilion Theatre, Nov. 2–Dec. 17. $25 adults, $12 for kids under 12. Santa meets John Wayne at Christmas on the trail. Guests first receive dinner from an 1800s chuckwagon—the menu consisting of trail stew, corn bread, taters with honey, and a campfire cobbler— and then are invited to join in for cowboy Christmas carols. Later on comes a stop at the Holiday Gift Shop, complete with a St. Nick who is waiting to review Christmas lists from the kids. The finale of the event is a trip up the legendary Shepherd of the Hills Trail of Lights, which ends with an ascent of the 230-foot-tall Inspiration Tower.

Comedy Jamboree (417-335-2484; www.grandcountry.com), 1945 W. SR 76. Shows at 1 PM daily, year-round, in the Grand Country Music Hall. $26 adults; ages 12 and under are free. If you don't like being yanked from the audience and pulled on stage to participate, this might not be the show for you. On the other hand, the Comedy Jamboree offers machine-gun jokes, lots of music and dance, and the virtuosity of pianist Tracy Heaston. It's good for more than a few laughs, particularly if you're not the shy type.

Comedy Pet Theater (417-335-2484; www.grandcountry.com), 1945 W. SR 76. Showtime is at 10 AM daily, June–Aug., at the Grand Country Music Hall. $26 adults, $15 ages 4–17. Master juggler Gregory Popovich has created a show that is going to the dogs . . . literally. Popovich rescued 15 cats and eight dogs from the pound and has trained them to assist him in a number of odd and unusual tricks. The show was huge in Vegas, and you may have seen it on both Jay Leno and David Letterman. If you're traveling with kids, don't miss this stop on your Branson vacation. They'll be talking about it for months.

Country Tonite (417-337-9333 or 1-877-336-7827; www.starlite -entertainment.com), 2905 W. SR 76. Showtimes are 3 and 8 PM, Mar.– Dec., daily (except Wed.) in the Americana Theater. $26 adults, $10 kids. A straight song, dance, and comedy show, Country Tonite offers the gamut of country tunes from the classics of yesteryear to today's favorites.

Cowboy Church with Norma Jean (417-739-1378; www.prettymissnorma jean.com), Little Opry Theater at the IMAX Theater Complex, Shepherd of the Hills Expwy. Showtimes are 10:30 AM and 8 PM, year-round. Admission is $10. The performer known as Pretty Miss Norma Jean was a regular on the old *Porter Wagoner Show* and a favorite on Nashville's Grand Ol' Opry in the 1960s and '70s. Still going strong, she now can be found performing with the singing group "Norma Jean and the Cowboys."

HOME OF THE COMEDY JAMBOREE AND GRAND JUBILEE

The vast majority of the numbers are gospel and country.

Cruisin 57 Matinee (417-332-1960 or 1-877-588-1957; www.dickclarks branson.com), 1600 W. SR 76. Shows at 8 PM daily (call for times of upcoming matinees), Mar.–Dec., in Dick Clark's American Bandstand Theater. $29 adults, $15 kids. I've never really understood how Dick Clark became so famous. Does he sing? Does he dance? Does he tell jokes? Such confusion aside, Dick is somehow the icon for the 1950s, and—as would be expected—such is what this show is all about. It's '50s clothes, a '50s band, '50s songs, and a '50s feel. If you liked watching *Happy Days*, you'll enjoy this production.

Dalena Ditto Country Variety Show (417-338-4999; www.dalena ditto.com), 3455 W. SR 76. Showtimes are 10 AM, Wed.–Sun., Apr.–Dec. at the Mickey Gilley Theater. Call for admission prices. Dalena Ditto grew up in the world of country music and has performed all over the country with the likes of Willie Nelson and Faith Hill. This is a country show—both classic and modern—and Dalena is joined on stage by ventriloquist Patty Davidson.

Dino's Christmas Extravaganza (1-800-884-4536; www.dinoplayspiano .com), 2521 SR 248. Shows at 8 PM, Nov. 1–Dec. 9, every day but Sun. in the Tri-Lakes Center. $37. One of the best-attended Christmas shows in Branson. The piano virtuosity of Dino Kartsonakis has to be heard to be believed. It is recommended that those wanting to see Dino during his limited engagement reserve their tickets early.

Doug Gabriel Show (1-800-954-8554; www.douggabriel.com), 3440 W. SR 76. Shows at 10 AM, Mon.–Sat., Apr.–Dec. at the Jim Stafford Theatre. $25 adults, $8 kids. In addition to his regular morning gig, Doug Gabriel is also popular for his **Christmas Show** and the occasional appearance of the legendary Roy Clark. Doug is a superb piano and guitar player (he occasionally brings out the guitar he built from the muffler of an old Thunderbird); the show consists of not only music but also comedy and dancing. Also on stage are the Gabriel family, performing everything from gospel standards to the best of Elvis.

Dutton Family (417-332-2772; www .theduttons.com), 3454 W. SR 76. Showtimes are 2 and 8 PM, Tue.–Sat., Mar.–Dec in the Dutton Family Theater. $24 adults; kids under 12 are admitted free. If you want proof of the power of genetics, just take a gander at the Dutton family. There, up on the stage, are about 20 Duttons of various ages. All are playing different instruments, singing, and entertaining the crowd. From classical to bluegrass and country to swing (with plenty of rock thrown in for good measure), the family offers a fully loaded buffet of musical entertainment. Small wonder that Dutton performances are one of the favorites of Branson locals.

Elvis and the Superstars (417-336-2112 or 1-800-ELVIS-95; www.elvis inbranson.com), 205 S. Commercial St. Shows at 2 PM, Tue. and Sat., and 8 PM, Mon., Wed., and Fri. Shows take place every month but Feb. at the Owens Theater in downtown Branson. $26 adults, $7 kids. I'm a bit leery of tribute shows. It's not that some of them aren't good; it's that some of them are so bad. This one scared me a bit, at first, as it advertised with the line "Elvis the way you remembered him." Frankly, I remem-

Dolly Parton's Dixie Stampede (1-800-520-5544; www.dixiestampede.com), 1525 W. SR 76. Showtimes are 5:30 and 8 PM at the Dixie Stampede building. Call for exact months and days, as they can vary throughout the year. $42 adults, $23 ages 4–11. Quite simply, the Dixie Stampede defines Branson. Dolly Parton is not known for doing things in a small way, and this extravaganza fits her image like a glove. Those in attendance should be prepared for a good nap afterward, for the meal alone will leave you fat and happy. Where else will you be served not only a whole rotisserie chicken, but also a BBQ pork loin, soup, biscuit, corn on the cob, baked potato, dessert, and unlimited Pepsi, tea, or coffee? Always covering the bases, the show does offer a vegetarian meal, even though the sight of a vegetarian in Branson is on a par with seeing Mick Jagger at a Baptist picnic. The show itself is on an equally grand scale. Think of a full-scale re-creation of the Civil War, complete with buffalo stampedes, ostrich races, nearly two score of horses, pyrotechnics, and a huge cast. The Dixie Stampede is something you have to see in Branson, if for no other reason than to brag to your friends how much you ate.

DOLLY PARTON'S DIXIE STAMPEDE

ber Elvis being really fat and sweaty and taking a ton of drugs. But sometimes it's good to be proven wrong. Elvis and the Superstars, starring Dave Ehlert as the King of Rock and Roll (before he went on the 89,000-calorie-a-day diet), is a good way to spend the evening. It's not all about Elvis. There are also passing (and beyond) imitations of the likes of the Blues Brothers, Rod Stewart, Patsy Cline, Liberace, Sonny and Cher, Neil Diamond, Willie Nelson, and Aretha Franklin.

50's at the Hop (1-800-434-5412; www.50satthehop.com), 3440 W. SR 76. Shows at 2 PM, every day but Wed., Aug.–Dec. at the Jim Stafford Theatre. An 8 PM show is held on select Sundays. $26 adults, $9.50 ages 7–12. As you've likely noticed, the retro show is pretty big in Branson, a reflection of the current prevailing visitor demographic. At this version you will see all the poodle skirts, ducktails, and malt shops you might expect. The music is well performed, virtually every 1950s hit you can name is on the agenda, and the selections range from Motown to Elvis and doo-wop to rock.

Frederick in Concert (417-334-4144 or 1-800-276-728; www.waltzing waterstheatre.com), 3617 W SR 76. Showtimes are 10 AM and 1 PM, Jan.–Mar., and 10 AM, 1 PM, and 6 PM Apr.–Dec. at the Waltzing Waters Theatre. $12 adults, $6 kids. Piano virtuoso Frederick Antonio plays two (count 'em!) grand pianos at the same time as a huge, lighted multicolored fountain arrangement dances, pulses, and shimmies in time to the music. Frederick and the fountain share top billing, the former being truly a seasoned showman and the latter consisting of 40,000 gallons of water. At some point in their trip almost everyone makes it to Waltzing Waters; it's a Branson standard.

From Patsy to Present (417-339-3939 or 1-866-306-SHOW; www.patsy inbranson.net), 2206 W. SR 76. Shows are at 5 PM, year-round, in the Branson Mall Music Theater. $25 adults, $10 ages 6–12. A tribute show to the late Patsy Cline, starring Tracy Lynn, the production features classic country, bluegrass, rockabilly, and blues tunes. An exceptional aspect of the performance comes from Michael T. Hermsmeyer, who not only plays every instrument on stage, but plays them all to near perfection.

Goldwing Express (417-335-4382; www.bransonimax.com), 3562 Shepherd of the Hills Expwy. Shows at 2 PM, Mon.–Sat., May–Dec. at the Little Opry Theatre. $23 adults, free for kids under 12. Bluegrass music is the heart of the Ozarks, and of all the players in Branson you'll find few as accomplished as Goldwing Express. These three Native American brothers, as well as their father, will have your foot bouncing as you listen to their banjo, mandolin, guitar, and upright bass expertise. The family includes plenty of jokes in the act, but the music is the star of the show.

Grand Jubilee (417-335-2484; www .grandcountry.com), 1945 W. SR 76. Shows Apr.–Dec., Mon.–Sat. at 8 PM. $22 adults, $21 ages 55-plus; ages 0–12 are admitted free. A music and comedy show with a wide range. Visitors can enjoy the sounds of the Grand Jubilee's headliner band, New South. Both country hits and some excellent quartet vocals are the primary draw. Longtime Branson local Terry Sanders (portraying the character Homer Lee) will join in with his own brand of Hillbilly humor.

Grand Old Gospel Hour (1-888-840-1888; www.gospelhour.org), 2700 W. SR 76. Showtime every Sun. at 10 AM, year-round, at the Grand Palace Theater. Free. This honestly isn't a show, but more of a very large church service. On the other hand, there is plenty of gospel music. It's a bit fire-and-brimstony for my tastes, but some folks like their religion on the caffeinated side.

Hamner Barber Variety Show
(417-334-4363 or 1-888-335-2080;
www.bransonvariety.com), 3090 Shepherd of the Hills Expwy. Showtimes are at 3 and 8 PM, Mar.–Dec. in the Hamner Barber Variety Theatre. Call for exact days and times. $26 adults, $8 ages 6–15. A bit of author bias here: I never met a magician or ventriloquist I didn't like (if you exclude that stupid "Waylon and Madame" act). That said, the Hamner Barber show offers some great comedy and some right dandy illusions. The duo of Dave and Denise Hamner seem to have a thing for birds, and you'll be amazed by the appearance of these trained avians. Ventriloquist Jim Barber enjoys his work, judging by his grin, and manages to perform several different voices at virtually the same time. To top it all off, a nonfeathered flock of singers and dancers demonstrate their talents as accent points for the various illusions.

Hank & Patsy Together Again
(417-336-2112 or 1-800-358-4795;
www.bransonsuperstars.com), 205 S. Commercial St. Showtimes are Mar.–Dec. at 2 PM, Mon., Wed., and Fri., and 8 PM Sun. in the Owens Theater. $26 adults, $7 children. Randy Steffen portrays Hank Williams Sr. and Susan Hudson resurrects Patsy Cline in this tribute to the king and queen of that ol'-time country music. You'll hear famous Hank and Patsy songs such as "Crazy," "Your Cheatin' Heart," "Walkin' After Midnight," and "Honky Tonkin'."

Hank Williams Revisited (417-335-3533; www.bransonimax.com), 3562 Shepherd of the Hills Expwy. Shows at 5 PM, Mon.–Sat., year-round in the Little Opry Theatre. $20 adults; kids 12 and under are admitted free. In

THE HUGHES BROTHERS THEATER

this venue the venerable Mr. Williams (he sure gets around a lot for a dead guy) is portrayed by Nashville recording artist Tim Hadler. If you saw the classic George Clooney movie *O Brother Where Art Thou* and loved the Ry Cooder soundtrack, then this show is for you. Hadler has the old Hank tunes down pat and offers up his own tribute to June Carter and Johnny Cash as well.

The Haygoods (417-339-4663; www.haygoods.com), 1835 W SR 76. Shows at 8 PM, Tue.–Sat., Mar.–Dec. in the Music City Centre. $28 adults, $11 kids. Forget the Partridge Family; those clowns were nothing in comparison with the Haygoods. The eight Haygood siblings (seven brothers and one sister, ranging in age from 12 to 28) bounce back and forth between playing fiddle, sax, guitar, drums, harp, and piano. They sing, they dance, they tell jokes. This is a truly talented bunch, and for pure technical prowess, wait until they start belting out their a cappella numbers. Small wonder they have been in Branson for 13 years and entertained nearly 3 million visitors.

Hughes Brothers (1-800-635-3688; www.hughes-brothers.com), 3425 W. SR 76. Showtimes are 10 AM and 7:30 PM, Mon.–Sat., Mar.–Dec. in the Hughes Brothers Celebrity Theater. $25 adults, $12 ages 13–18, and $5 ages 3–12. If Branson ever goes the way of reality TV, the first act would no doubt be a wrestling match between the Haygoods and the Hughes Brothers. These five guys, who own their own theater, are known for singing in near-perfect harmony and for dancing like screamin' demons.

Their repertoire is massive, covering everything from old western standards to Broadway show tunes to gospel.

The Jim Owen Show (417-336-0884; www.jimowenmusic.com), 3115 W. SR 76. Shows at 10 AM, Tue.–Sat., Mar.–Dec. in the Country Tonite Theater. $19 adults, $5 ages 7–12. Jim

The Jim Stafford Show (417-335-8080; www.jimstafford.com), 3440 W. SR 76. Showtimes are at 3 and 7:30 PM, Mon.–Sat., Aug.–Dec. in the Jim Stafford Theatre. $29 adults, $8 kids. The talent hierarchy of Branson is measured in tiers. At the top level you have perhaps 5 or 10 shows that are known nationwide and will continue drawing huge crowds for as long as the artists wish to perform. One of these is the Jim Stafford Show. Jim, the man who gave us songs like "Spiders and Snakes" and had a major TV variety show in the 1970s, has now been hanging out in Branson for about 20 years. He's been voted Branson's Best Entertainer, and, more importantly, my father claims this is one of the two best shows in town. Visitors come to see Jim Stafford year after year after year. The reason? Stafford can't help being funny, even when he's telling the same old jokes. He has been called the "Victor Borge of Guitar," and there's more than a little truth in that label. Jim plays, and jokes, and sings some more, and jokes some more. To say he's merely "accomplished" at both would be the understatement of the decade. The show also includes a **3-D Virtual Thrill Ride** in what is arguably Branson's most comfortable theater. Sometimes joining Jim on stage is young son Sheaffer. Jim Stafford lives up to his reputation night after night.

THE JIM STAFFORD THEATRE

Owen is known in country music circles as not only a performer, but also an acclaimed songwriter (one of his biggest hits was "Louisiana Woman, Mississippi Man," recorded by Loretta Lynn and Conway Twitty). He has also portrayed Hank Williams Sr. in two TV movies. In Branson, Jim offers up a pure country show with lots of comedy and tributes to the likes of Williams and Grand Ol' Opry legend Ernest Tubb.

The John Tweed Show (417-332-2200; www.johntweedshow.com), 2215 W. SR 76. Shows at 3 PM, Tue.–Sat., Apr.–Dec. at the Moe Bandy Theater. $20 adults; free for ages 12 and under. For part of the show, John Tweed offers up a tribute to the crooners, delivering the music of Sinatra, Louis Armstrong, and Nat King Cole. In another segment you'll be regaled with show tunes. Interspersed between are the sounds of the 1950s and (of course) a whole lot of country.

Joseph and the Amazing Technicolor Dreamcoat (417-239-1333; www.mansionamerica.com), 189 Expressway Lane. Shows at 3 PM, Tue.–Sun., Apr.–Dec. in the Mansion America Theater. $29 adults, $15 children. Just when you thought Branson was all about Hank Williams and go-cart tracks, you trip across a full-scale Broadway show. This Andrew Lloyd Webber creation is produced in all its original glory in the magnificent Mansion America Theater. The show revolves around the biblical story of Joseph and his fancy duds, but does so by incorporating musical stylings from rock to calypso to country. This is a production perfect for all ages.

Ladies of Motown (417-336-2112 or 1-800-358-4795; www.bransonsuper stars.com), 205 S. Commercial St.

Shows at noon, Mon., Wed., Fri., and Sat., Mar.–Dec., at the Owens Theater in old downtown Branson. Free. It's not often you find something free in Branson, but for a rare treat particularly nonthreatening to the wallet, drop by and see the Ladies of Motown show. It stars Dee Dee Hamilton (formerly of the Platters) and offers up tribute to the likes of the Supremes, the Ronettes, Martha and the Vandellas, and the Shirelles.

Larry Gatlin & the Gatlin Brothers Co-starring Pam Tillis (1-800-734-5515; www.sullivanshows.com), 1984 SR 165. Showtimes are 2 and 8 PM, Tue.–Sat., Apr.–Dec. at the Welk Resort Theatre. $37.50. The legendary Gatlin Brothers have added some new shows to their schedule, now offering spring and summer performances in addition to their usual fall gig. Joining them in fall is Pam Tillis, a Country Music Association Vocalist of the Year with three platinum and two gold albums to her credit. The show features all the hits that these two headliners have recorded over the years. Over Christmas the Gatlins are joined on stage by the Lennon Sisters of Lawrence Welk fame.

Legends in Concert (417-332-1205 or 1-800-374-7469; www.legends branson.com), 3216 W. SR 76. Showtimes are at 3 and 8 PM, every day but Wed., Feb.–Dec. in the Legends Family Theater. $28 adults, $11 ages 4–12. They call this the World's Greatest Tribute Show, and the impersonators at Legends will make you think that the likes of Buddy Holly and Frank Sinatra have returned for one more performance. The list of stars imitated by the troupe includes Patsy Cline, Roy Orbison, the Blues Brothers,

THE LEGENDS FAMILY THEATER

Elvis, Marilyn Monroe, Judy Garland, Johnny Mathis, Shania Twain, and many more. You'll leave the theater wondering if it was live, or was it Memorex?

Les Brown's Band of Renown (1-866-4-RENOWN; www.bandof renown.com), 3455 W. SR 76. Showtime is at 2 PM (call for exact days), Apr.–May and Sep.–Dec. at the Mickey Gilley Theater. $28 adults; $5 for children under 13. Travel back to the days when swing was king with the ever-enduring Les Brown's Band of Renown. The group performs hits from the big band era, with the tunes of Glenn Miller, Tony Bennett, and Dean Martin figuring prominently. Between numbers visitors can expect comedy and dancing.

Lost in the 50's (417-337-9333; www .starlite-entertainment.com), 3115 W. SR 76. Shows at 8 PM daily, Mar.–Dec., in the Starlite Theater. $27 adults, $10 kids. To paraphrase a famous movie tagline: "Where were you in '52?" The answer might come during this show, which features a plethora of poodle skirts, biker jackets, and the nostalgia of your favorite TV shows of the 1950s and '60s. The writers of the production must have been particularly impressed with the character of Mayberry's wacky deputy Barney Fife, as he figures prominently.

Lowe Family of Utah (1-800-734-5515; www.thelowefamily.com), 1984 SR 165. Shows at 10 AM, Mon.–Sat., at the Welk Resort Theatre. $26 adults, $10 kids 4–15. In this 2-hour show the multitalented Lowe family of Utah sings, dances, and touches upon almost every musical genre imaginable. This group has toured the world and appeared on numerous network TV specials.

Mel Tillis (417-335-5715; www.tri lakescenter.com), 2527 SR 248. Shows at 2 and 8 PM Sept.–Oct. at the Tri-Lakes Center. Days vary. Call ahead for additional showtimes. $35 adults, $15 kids. The famous stuttering singer, Mel Tillis, still plays a limited number of engagements in Branson. To see him in person and enjoy his litany of country hits, it is advised that you make reservations early.

Mickey Gilley (417-334-3219 or 1-800-334-1936; www.gilleys.com), 3455 W. SR 76. Shows at 8 PM, Wed.–Sun., Mar.–Dec. in the Mickey Gilley Theater. A 10 AM Thu. show is also offered Sep.–Oct. $25 adults, $5 ages 12 and under. Mickey Gilley's nearly 40 major hits (17 of those went to number one) and honky-tonk piano fill the air as the country legend is backed by an eight-piece band. Mickey tells plenty of amusing stories in between tunes, many about his childhood in Louisiana and youthful adventures with his cousins Jerry Lee Lewis and TV preacher Jimmy Swaggart. Joining him on stage is comedian Joey Riley.

Moe Bandy Show (417-334-6802; www.moebandy.com), 2215 W. SR 76. Shows at 8 PM, Sun.–Fri., Apr.–Dec. in the Moe Bandy Theater. $26 adults, $5 ages 12 and under. If you're a fan of Moe Bandy hits such as "Good Ol'

Boys" and "It's a Cheatin' Situation," then this is the show for you. Performing with Moe are his wife, Teresa (a Missouri native), and the Americana Band.

Motown Downtown Starring Walter White (417-337-5233; www.motowndowntown.com), 1840 W. SR 76. Shows at 8 PM, Tue.–Sat., Mar.–Dec. in the Nova 4 Cinemas. $25 adults, $6 kids. If the name *Walter White* doesn't immediately jump to the front of your consciousness, then just think of the Platters. Walter was the former lead singer of that groundbreaking Motown group. In this show you will hear the very best of Motown classics by one of the men who created their initial and long-enduring fame.

Neil Goldberg's Cirque (417-336-1220 or 1-800-884-4536; www.remingtontheatre.com), 3701 W. SR 76. Showtimes are at 2 and 8 PM, Tue.–Sun., May–Dec. in the Remington Theatre. Call ahead for exact schedule. $40 adults, $19 for kids 12 and under. This is not your county fair circus. Cirque does feature creative trapeze artists and outstanding acrobats, but you will also enjoy giant ultraviolet puppets, stilt creations, and all the pomp and glitter of more than 100 different costumes. They might not shoot a guy out of a cannon or cram clowns into a tiny car, but this international cast will definitely give you your money's worth.

Number 1 Hits of the 60's (1-886-339-1960; www.1hitsofthe60s.com), 2353 W. SR 248. Shows at 8 PM, Mon.–Sat., Mar.–Dec. at the Musical Palace. $29 adults; kids under 13 are free. While there was some absolutely great music that came out of the 1960s, those who made the music

weren't exactly the epitome of squeaky clean or all-American. Frankly, it's a little surreal watching a show that portrays the 1960s as such a happy and peaceful era. No matter; the 16-member cast of this show does perform more than 100 of the best '60s hits (such as tunes from Ray Charles, the Beatles, the Beach Boys, Sonny and Cher, the Supremes, and the Mamas and the Papas). Just enjoy the music, and try and not to take a psychological detour into the fact that most of it was the result of a twisted youth culture that thrived on protests, drugs, and flag burning.

Ozark Mountain Jubilee (417-335-2484; www.grandcountry.com), 1945 W. SR 76. Shows at 7 PM, Sun. only, Feb.–Dec. in the Grand Country Music Hall. $22 adults; kids 13 and under admitted free. The show is pure country, both old and new, as performed by both local entertainers and the Max Bacon family. A bit of the corn fed style of comedy (and some great piano playing) is provided by Mike Patrick.

The Pierce Arrow Theatre (417-336-8742 or 1-877-687-4241; www.piercearrowtheater.com), 3069 Shepherd of the Hills Expwy. Showtimes are at 3 and 8 PM, Mon.–Sat., Feb.–Dec. in the Pierce Arrow Theater. $27 adults, $11 kids. The group known as Pierce Arrow features Dan Britton, who for 20 years was listed in the *Guinness Book of World Records* as having the planet's lowest bass singing voice. Dan and the rest of the quintet have some unbelievable harmonies and are particularly effective when they perform renditions made famous by stars such as the Oak Ridge Boys. Appearing on stage with Pierce Arrow is Kim Boyce, a former

Peter the Adequate Magic Show (800-358-4795; www.petertheadequate
.com), 205 S. Commercial St. Shows at 2 PM, Sun. only, Mar.–Dec. in the
Owens Theater. $28 adults, $7.25 ages 6–16. Because he's not flashy and
doesn't appear in a billion-dollar theater, Peter the Adequate may get some
of the least press in Branson. This is a shame, since he puts on one of the
best shows in the whole town. Both self-deprecating and funnier than a
crutch, Peter revels in the fact that he doesn't make airplanes or elephants
disappear. He also seems to like the fact that he's a one-man show (often
running back and forth to change music in the sound machine). You'll see
sleight of hand up close (real close, as in he might pull you on stage), mind
reading, escapes (as when he is lowered headfirst into an aquarium that fits
only his head), and much more. This man is a true performer. He doesn't
have all the glitz and glitter because he doesn't need it. Don't miss this one,
especially if you're traveling with the kids.

Miss Florida who has had 11 number one gospel hits, and comedian Jarrett Dougherty.

Presleys' Country Jubilee (417-334-4874; www.presleys.com), 2920 W. SR 76. Shows at 8 PM, Mon.–Sat., Mar.–Dec. in the Presleys' Theater. $23 adults, $11.50 kids. There is some debate as to who came first to Branson, the Baldknobbers or the Presleys. The one clear fact is that the Presley family was the first to have a music theater on the SR 76 Strip, this arriving after numerous years performing their musical comedy in any venue where people would pay to listen (including more than a few dripping Ozark caves). As the town of Branson exploded, the Presleys were right in the thick of the action, and their show continues today. You'll hear gospel (one of the family's patriarchs was a Pentecostal preacher), listen to Hillbilly comedy (the blacked-out teeth are a must), and also enjoy country standards and the hits of today. All this, accompanied by finger picking, strumming, and fiddle playing as can only be done by those who have grown up with a guitar, banjo, or bow in their hand.

Red, Hot and Blue (417-335-2484; www.grandcountry.com), 1945 W. SR 76. Shows at 10 AM Sun. at the Grand Country Music Hall—but days and times vary throughout the year. $26 adults; children 12 and under admitted free. With a cast of eight high-energy performers, Red, Hot and Blue is a nostalgic musical tour.

Red Skelton: A Tribute by Tom Mullica (417-336-1600; www
.skeltontribute.com), 1835 W. SR 76. Showtimes are at 10 AM and 5 PM, Sun.–Fri., Apr.–Dec. in the Music City Centre. $23 adults, $6 kids. Red Skelton was the gentle giant of comedy, making people laugh without the need for shock, obscenity, or vulgarity. In this tribute his admirer and friend Tom Mullica re-creates all of Red's great characters, such as Freddy the Freeloader, Clem Kadiddlehopper, Gertrude & Heathcliff, the Mean Widdle Kid, and George Applebee.

Righteous Brothers' Bill Medley and Paul Revere and the Raiders (417-332-1960 or 1-877-588-1957; www.dickclarksbranson.com), 1600 W. SR 76. Shows at 8 PM Apr.–Dec., but days vary greatly. $36 adults, $20 kids under 12. In Dick Clark's new American Bandstand Complex, the Righteous Brothers' Bill Medley joins Paul Revere and the Raiders for a compilation of their many number one hits.

Shepherd of the Hills Outdoor Drama (417-334-4191 or 1-800-653-6288; www.theshepherdofthehills.com), 5586 W. SR 76. Shows at 8:30 PM (7:30 PM after Aug. 23), Mon.–Sat., May–Oct. at the Shepherd of the Hills Outdoor Theater. $31 adults, $14 kids. *Shepherd of the Hills* has been performed at this theater well over 5,000 times, making it the longest-running outdoor drama in history. The story, based on the 1906 book of the same name by Harold Bell Wright (the fourth most widely read book in publishing history), brought the Ozarks to the attention of the world and predated the entertainment phenomenon that would become Branson by more than half a century. The tale, based partially on residents Bell met when he came to live in the Ozarks, is a broad-strokes epic centering on collective human traits—love, loss, power, and the meaning of life. No small production, each performance requires 80 actors, 40 horses, a flock of sheep, numerous guns and rifles, and the actual burning of a log cabin.

Showboat *Branson Belle* (1-800-475-9370; www.showboatbransonbelle.com), 4800 SR 165. Showtimes are at noon, 4, and 8 PM, Mar.–Dec. Call ahead for exact days. $54 adults, $23 kids. More than just a show, the *Branson Belle* offers a three-course meal and over 2 hours of entertainment as

PRESLEYS' COUNTRY JUBILEE

HOME OF SHOJI TABUCHI'S INCOMPARABLE SHOW

The Shoji Tabuchi Show (417-334-7469; www.shoji.com), 3260 Shepherd of the Hills Expwy. Showtimes are at 10:30 AM, 3 PM, and 7:30 PM, Mar.–Dec. in the Shoji Tabuchi Theatre. Call ahead for more information, as the days vary. $42 adults, $22 children. At this, arguably the most popular show in Branson,

you cruise slowly around Table Rock Lake. The boat itself is an 1890s-style paddle-wheeler, 78 feet wide, 265 feet long, and capable of handling more than 700 guests per cruise. Entertainment varies depending upon whether you take a noon, afternoon, or evening jaunt on the water, but the possibilities include everything from full-scale Vegas-style productions—musicals with all the special effects—to acrobats to live bands to comedy. The meals are very good on the *Belle*—likely on a par with, if not above, anything you find at the

restaurants in town, with children's meals, vegetarian offerings, and restricted diet requests gladly provided. This attraction is part of the Silver Dollar City family (the heaviest of the heavy hitters responsible for much of Branson's rise to fame), and they don't skimp on the quality.

Siegfried & Roy Present Darren Romeo: The Voice of Magic (1-800-734-5515; www.sullivanshows.com), 1984 SR 165. Showtimes are at 2 and 8 PM, Mar.–Dec. at the Welk Resort Theatre. Call for exact days. $30 adults, $15 ages 4–11. Siegfried and

Shoji Tabuchi takes "glitz" to a whole new level. For starters, his theater cannot be missed due to about 5 miles' worth of purple-neon lighting. Inside, things get even better. The men's room features black lion's-head sinks imported from Italy, black leather chairs, a marble fireplace, a burled walnut mirror circa 1868, and (best of all) a carved mahogany billiards table. Lest the ladies feel left out, their powder room comes complete with wainscoting and a ceiling reproduced from the 1890s Empire period. Live cut orchids are on all the granite and onyx pedestal sinks—which are of course set off by jeweled glass and elaborate chandeliers.

And you haven't even seen the show yet. Branson really doesn't get any better than this. Tabuchi is an Asian, violin-playing version of James Brown, without doubt the hardest-working Japanese fiddle player in Branson. He's an extremely talented musician blessed with boundless energy, his range encompassing a mix of soulful country, screaming bluegrass, and classical perfection. His band is equally talented, and it's a sign of a true professional that Tabuchi takes the time to introduce each one to the audience. Small touches of this nature are not lost on the crowds, and Tabuchi endears himself with a style nothing short of masterful. Dorothy Tabuchi, Shoji's wife, handles production numbers that can involve anything from cowboy choreography to the annual Sugar Plum Fairy dance at Christmas. Keeping with the family atmosphere, both of Branson and of this theater in particular, Christina Tabuchi, the couple's daughter, often makes an appearance. The Shoji Tabuchi Show runs near 2½ hours. In most cases that would be a bit long to sit in one spot, but this production is so fast paced and well done that patrons don't really seem to notice the time. Maybe they're still thinking about the bathrooms?

Roy may not be what they once were, thanks to the overbite of a large tiger, but their protégé Darren Romeo continues their legacy. In 2005 Darren was named International Magician of the Year at the Magic Castle Awards in Hollywood, and his Branson show features first-rate illusions, excellent effects, and fantastic music. The combination results in the most visually enchanting magic show in Branson.

Smoke on the Mountain (1-800-419-4832; www.smokeonthemt-branson .com), 3562 Shepherd of the Hills Expwy. Shows at 10 AM, Tue.–Sat., Apr.–Dec. at the Little Opry Theatre. $24 adults; kids under 12 are admitted free. A musical comedy that is drawing great reviews, the story is set in 1938 at the fictional Mount Pleasant Church. The event is the church's "first ever Saturday Night Sing." The audience is treated to such old-time gospel favorites as "Church in the Wildwood" and "I'll Fly Away." These are the gospel tunes of yesteryear that moved on to become folk classics.

Spirit of the Dance (1-888-462-7267; www.bransonvarietytheatre .com), 2701 W. SR 76. Showtimes are at 2 and 8 PM, generally on Sun. and Fri. (call for exact dates), Mar.–Oct. at the Branson Variety Theatre. $35 adults, $18 ages 12–17, $13 ages 3–11. In the beginning there was the acclaimed *Riverdance*. However, the creator of Spirit of the Dance wanted to move beyond merely the traditional foot stomping of Ireland, with the final product being a dance revue that covers all cultures and styles from salsa to rock and beyond. The dancers are from the Irish International Dance Company, and their energy and talent is surpassed only by the show's choreography, lighting, and costumes. How these folks keep it up their frenetic pace for 2 hours is an amazement in itself.

Stuck on the 70's (1-877-336-7827; www.starlite-entertainment.com), 3115 W. SR 76. Shows at 3 PM daily, Mar.–Oct. in the Starlite Theater. $27 adults, $10 kids. When I think of the 1970s, my foggy memories are generally of bands like Styx or Deep Purple or the ever-popular REO Speedwagon. This 1970s show remembers a different sort of era, a much more family-oriented, simple time that I must have missed. Think more in terms of *The Love Boat* and Barry Manilow, then mix in a bunch of dance numbers, and of course a dash of disco. Let's face it, many of the tunes that came out of the '70s weren't exactly the pinnacle of musical achievement. Which is perhaps why Stuck in the 70's also offers songs from the '60s and '80s.

Tall Timber Lumberjack Show (417-338-2957; www.talltimbershows .com), 681 Long Lonesome Trail. Shows at 5:30, Sat.–Thu., June–Oct. $32 adults, $22 ages 6–15. Quite sim-

ply, Branson needs more shows like this. While the town holds a plethora of music, dance, and magic revues, Tall Timber is one of the few productions that offer something you would never expect. Hands-down, it's the coolest attraction in town. Two crack teams of lumberjacks compete for the title of "Bull of the Woods" in 13 different events, ranging from log rolling and ax throwing to pole climbing and log cutting. You don't know just how neat this is until you see it first-hand. Better yet, you'll enjoy this presentation while chowing down on a lumberjack-sized meal of either a large rib-eye steak or a half-pound chicken breast, complete with a hearty soup, roll, potatoes, dessert, and bottomless drinks.

Tony Roi's Elvis Experience (417-336-1600; www.bransonelvis.com), 1835 W. SR 76. Showtimes are at 2 and 8 PM, Mon.–Sat., Mar.–Dec. at the Music City Centre. $25 adults, $10 kids. Cuban-born Tony Roi does look an awful lot like the King of Rock and Roll, and his singing and dancing prowess is self-evident. Though the Elvis imitation business has been overworked to the hilt, Tony's version is far better than most. For Graceland devotees, this is a well-done and genuine tribute.

Two Fluffy Women . . . Country Meets Broadway (417-336-2112 or 1-800-358-4795; www.2fluffywomen .com), 205 S. Commercial St. Shows at 5 PM Mon., Wed., Fri., and 8 PM Tue., Thu., and Sat. Performances take place Mar.–Dec. in the Owens Theater. $27 adults, $8 kids. The Two Fluffy Women in question bring you the songs of the Andrews Sisters, Doris Day, Patsy Cline, Dolly Parton,

Bette Midler, and more. Also a part of the show is the first-class magician Peter the Adequate.

World Famous Platters (417-337-9333; www.worldfamousplatters.com), 3115 W. SR 76. Shows at 10 AM Mon.–Sat., Mar.–Dec. in the Starlite Theater. $22 adults, $10 children. The Platters are still around, and with the assistance of a few additional backup singers they belt out such hits as "Only You," "The Great Pretender," and "Smoke Gets in Your Eyes."

Yakov Smirnoff (1-800-33-NO-KGB; www.yakov.com), 470 SR 248. Showtimes are at 9:30 AM, 3 PM, and 8 PM, Apr.–Dec. in the Yakov Smirnoff Theater. Call ahead for exact dates. $30 adults; kids 12 and under admitted free. Yakov Smirnoff defines Branson when he says, "Only in America can a Russian and a Japanese own theaters in the middle of the Ozarks." Yakov, who has starred in movies with Robin Williams, Tom Hanks, and Jack Nicholson (to name a few), has been pulling in crowds for years. As always, he performs at a high energy level, tells tales of his immigration to America, and lets everyone know without question that he loves his adopted country. The man is also very accessible to visitors, taking photos with many patrons after the show. On stage with Yakov is the juggler Slim Chance, who is probably good enough to have a theater of his own.

✳ Selective Shopping

MALLS AND COMPLEXES The **Branson Mall** (417-334-5412), 2206 W. SR 76, Branson, Mo. Also known as the home of **Wal-Mart**, this mall features roughly 25 shops. The other anchor store in the facility, the **Jubi-**lee Market**, is a large grocery store and likely the best place for the cheapest food and supplies if you're renting a condo or camping. I have always been amused by the store **Hicks in the Sticks** (full of wonderfully stupid Hillbilly and gag gifts), and if you're into country tunes, you will find ample stock at the **Ernest Tubb Record Shop**.

Factory Merchants of Branson (417-335-6686; www.bransonoutlets.com), 1000 Pat Nash Dr., Branson, Mo. Mon.–Sat. 9–9, Sun. 9–7. Just look for the big red roof with the white lettering reading 90 STORES. Though the number is actually one or two above 90, this two-level outlet facility features such names as Nautica, Van Heusen, Reebok, Samsonite, and Izod. From clothes to quilts to CorningWare, you can spend a few hours wandering around here—and munch on hot pretzels to boot.

Factory Shoppes at Branson Meadows (417-339-2580), 4562 Gretna Rd., Branson, Mo. Built in a Victorian design, the Factory Shoppes are anchored by an 11-screen theater complex and a 30,000-square-foot factory outlet store. Names represented include Lee, Wrangler, and Jantzen, as well as shops covering the gamut of jewelry and home decor. One shop of particular interest is **Foozies** (417-339-2424), which has a huge selection of books, many discounted up to 80 percent. Another is the **Mountain Man Nut and Fruit Company** (417-336-6200), which offers some of the best candy, dried fruits, jams, jellies, honey, and (of course) nuts available anywhere.

Grand Country Square (417-335-3535 or 1-800-828-9068; www.grand

country.com), 1945 W. SR 76, Branson, Mo. I've never quite known how to define Grand Country. It's part water park, part hotel, part arcade (with an indoor miniature golf course), part live country theater, part restaurant, and part shopping center. If you add all these together, the whole is greater than the sum of the parts. The Grand Country Market has gifts and novelties, and an adjacent 24,000-square-foot building offers two levels of shopping. The lower level is themed by area. Do you want statues of Indians? They've got a section. Do you want John Deere farming memorabilia? They've got a section. Do you want Elvis, Wizard of Oz, Betty Boop, and Franklin Mint selections? Of course, they've got a section. Branson souvenirs are prevalent, and, oddly, a rather large nautical area features everything from statues of sailors to home decor. Upstairs is something of a collectibles treasure chest, with everything from Scooby-Doo and Precious Moments to Beanie Babies and Christmas decorations. It's admittedly sort of an odd place, but odd in a good way. If you get tired you can drop into the **Grand Country Buffet** and consume enough food to feed the entire populations of your smaller third-world countries.

Tanger Factory Outlet (417-337-9328; www.tangeroutlet.com), 300 Tanger Blvd., Branson, Mo. Mon.–Sat. 9–9, Sun. 10–7. Another mega complex with nearly 100 shops, this outlet establishment includes Ralph Lauren, Tommy Hilfiger, Guess, J.Crew, and Larry and David. There are more of the currently popular brand names here than at some of the other spots in town (Big Dog and Eddie Bauer, to

name two), and the shopping possibilities aren't confined to clothing. An Oneida factory store, Book Warehouse, Kitchen Collection, and Bath & Body Works are representative of what is available at Tanger. After all the buffets and deep-fried catfish you've consumed on your trip, you might even drop by Vitamin World for some omega-3 fish oil. A trip to the Ozarks lowers the blood pressure, but it can play havoc with the cholesterol.

THE ENGLER BLOCK (417-335-2200; www.englerblock.com), 1335 W. SR 76, Branson, Mo. The Block is open Mar.–mid-Dec., 9–6; mid-Dec.–Mar. 1, 10–5. Noted Branson wood-carver Pete Engler took an abandoned warehouse and turned it into something far more than a collection of specialty shops. The Engler Block is as much a museum of local culture as it is a craft mall, with artisans ranging from glassblowers, potters, and jewelers to furniture makers, dulcimer luthiers, and watercolor artists. When you purchase an item here, you are usually buying it from the person who made it. Selected shops include:

Artfolk Music & Wood (417-334-2100; www.artfolkmusic.com). Walking into this store, you can expect to hear music, laughter, and the sounds of creation. It consists in part of the **Dulcimer Barn** (they'll show you how to play this ancient instrument before you take one home), **Handmade Country Furniture**, and **Ozark Mountain Toys**, and everyone here seems to be an artisan of some sort. You'll tap your toe when you walk past the "Pickin' Porch."

Goyne Candles (417-339-1912; www

.petalsandwaxart.com). The owners of this store pride themselves on their artistic, handmade candles. They should, for the results are beautiful. Also check out their line of "permanent water" silk botanicals.

Helwig Art Glass (417-335-2290). You really don't find too many glassblowers in your local mall, but you'll find one here. This is a true art form, and one that is becoming increasingly rare.

The Ozarks Mountaineer Book Shop (417-336-2665; www.ozarks mountaineer.com). For decades the *Ozarks Mountaineer* magazine has provided a great read, covering history, folklore, and places to visit here in the hills and hollers. For an additional treat, stop by its bookstore in the Engler Block, which carries numerous titles in the line of Ozarks history, how-to, cookbooks, gardening, humor, pioneer skills, and much more.

Reigning Cats and Dogs (417-335-3990). This shop deserves inclusion for its name, if nothing else. Its claim to fame lies in a wide array of products for both pets and pet lovers, including figurines, cat and dog jewelry, bowls, treats, pillows, purses, and stationery (for those dogs who like to send thank-you notes).

SPECIAL SHOPS **Alaska Down South** (417-339-2800; www.alaska downsouth.com), 1150 W. SR 76, Branson, Mo. In Branson for more than 10 years, Alaska Down South started by focusing on bringing all things Alaska to the Ozarks. Since that time it has expanded to include art and decor from the northern United States, Canada, and Africa. Shop for antler and ivory carvings, scrim-

shaw, and a wide variety of unique home decor.

Dick's Oldtime 5 and 10 (417-334-2410), 103 W. Main St., Branson, Mo. Dick's is almost as well known in Branson as the Baldknobbers or Silver Dollar City. In business since 1929, this store in the original part of town carries a bit of everything imaginable. It holds true to what it always was, a five-and-dime store, and in a lot of ways it feels like a museum. From A to Z, you'll no doubt find something you can't live without among Dick's 50,000 items.

Frontier Flags (417-334-1776; www .frontierflags.com), 1318 W. SR 76, Branson, Mo. No matter what kind of flag you seek, chances are you can find it here. U.S. flags, military flags, state flags, Confederate flags, and religious flags are just part of the offerings. You can also find plenty of wind socks, decals, magnetic ribbons, and flagpoles of all sizes.

The Quilt Cottage (417-339-3445), SR 165 S. (0.25 mile past the Welk Resort), Branson, Mo. There are several quilt stores in Branson, but this shop has the widest selection and features the most shapes, sizes, designs, and colors. Almost everything here is handmade, rather than the machine-made items found in chain stores. If you want a quilt that looks like it was painstakingly handcrafted by your great-grandmother, this is the place.

✷ Special Events

March–April **Family Spring Break Days** (417-266-7300 or 1-800-475-9370; www.silverdollarcity.com), 399 Indian Point Rd., Branson, Mo. Something of a preview for the season to come, this festival takes place in early spring. The rides and the shops are just opening for the year, and you will enjoy great music, food, comedy, and magic.

April–May **World Fest** (417-266-7300 or 1-800-475-9370; www.silver dollarcity.com), 399 Indian Point Rd., Branson, Mo. World Fest is a relatively new affair that features the very best of cultural delights from around the globe. An Irish celebration, German stilt jumpers, steel drums from Trinidad, and Scottish drum lines are just the beginning. As usual at Silver Dollar City, come hungry.

May–June **Bluegrass and BBQ Festival** (417-266-7300 or 1-800-475-9370; www.silverdollarcity.com), 399 Indian Point Rd., Branson, Mo. From late May until early June, Silver Dollar City begins to reflect the Ozarks the way they're meant to be. The Bluegrass and BBQ Festival brings in top bluegrass groups and solo acts from around the nation, and the BBQ buffet served up in the Frisco barn will leave you feeling fat and happy. All styles of Q are on hand, from the vinegar-based sauce ladled on a smoked North Carolina pulled-pork sandwich, to Memphis dry rub, to an ultraslow-cooked Texas brisket. When you combine those delectables with smoking bluegrass, there is simply no way to go wrong.

Red, White and Bluegrass Weekend (417-266-7300 or 1-800-475-9370; www.silverdollarcity.com), 399 Indian Point Rd., Branson, Mo. Toward the last week of May the bluegrass continues during a three-day festival featuring yet more of America's great bluegrass aficionados.

June **Mardi Gras in Branson** (417-335-8842; www.cajunzydecofestival .com), 1700 W. SR 76, Branson, Mo. Something just feels right about mixing the Ozarks with the sight, sounds, and tastes of Cajun country. After all, both of us will eat almost anything that slithers, crawls, or growls. Such being the case, early June's three-day Mardi Gras in Branson offers the best of both worlds. At the Ramada Inn's festival grounds you'll listen to numerous Cajun and zydeco players, tour arts and crafts booths, and eat yourself silly. After all, who could turn down the opportunity to compete in a crawdad-eating contest?

June–August ♪ **National Kid's Festival** (417-266-7300 or 1-800-475-9370; www.silverdollarcity.com), 399 Indian Point Rd., Branson, Mo. Running from early June till near the end of August, National Kid's Festival provides more than 100 hands-on activities. There's music, food, street entertainers, and a variety of special shows geared specifically for the younger set.

September **Compton Ridge Campground Fiddler's Convention** (417-338-2911; www.comptonridge.com), 5040 SR 265, Branson, Mo. For three straight days (usually Thu.–Sat.) in the middle of September, fiddlers from around America take the stage at Compton Ridge and compete for top honors. The jam sessions are nonstop during this annual celebration, taking place on an impromptu basis all over the park. You can't listen to fiddle music on an empty stomach, so there's a catfish fry Friday night and a pig roast on Saturday. Talk about cheap eats: You can attend both gorge-fests for $6 each.

September–October **Festival of American Music and Craftsmanship** (417-266-7300 or 1-800-475-9370; www.silverdollarcity.com), 399 Indian Point Rd., Branson, Mo. This is the festival that made Silver Dollar City famous, a shindig that has taken place since the park's inception. From early September till the end of October, craftsmen from all over the country are on hand to show, sell, and demonstrate how they make their fine handcrafted goods. There are juried art shows, the Tastes of America Food Fair, and more than 400 musicians who fill the air with the sounds of gospel, bluegrass, folk, country, western, swing, and big band music. If you're going to make plans to hit only one major festival in Branson, this would be first choice.

November–December **An Old Time Christmas** (417-266-7300 or 1-800-475-9370; www.silverdollarcity.com), 399 Indian Point Rd., Branson, Mo. Christmas comes early to Silver Dollar City—the park starts getting decked out in early November and stays that way till the end of Christmas. Offerings include a Dickens Christmas Show, a Holiday Lights Parade (Santa's sleigh alone boasts more than 3,000 lights), the tree-lighting celebration, carolers, and all the good feelings of the holidays. Weather permitting, certain rides and attractions are open during this celebration of Yuletide joy.

The Northern Border

2

ROUTE 66 COUNTRY

THE LAKE OF THE OZARKS

THE OSAGE LAKES DISTRICT

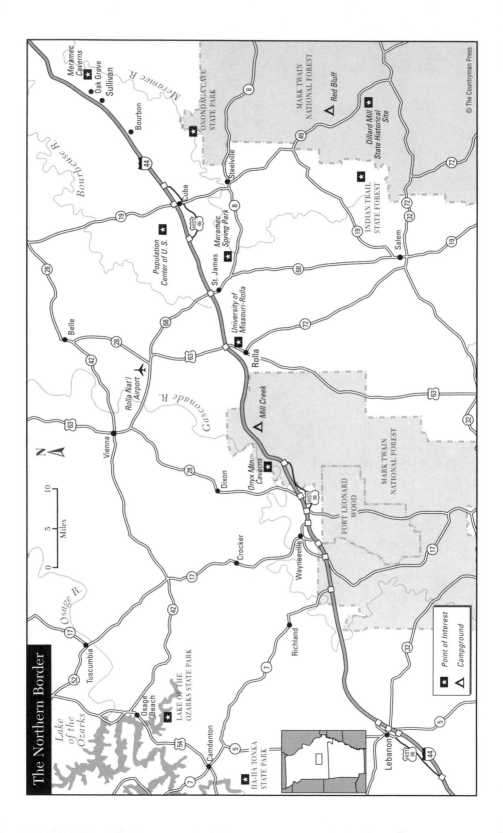

The Northern Border

ROUTE 66 COUNTRY

Though most people feel the need for speed, the desire to reach their destination as quickly as possible, such a preconception is unsuited for the Ozarks. Forget the normal expectations of modern life, and realize that you are traveling through a land older than time itself. The Ozarks are for dawdling, for wandering around, for taking the time to smell roses, wade creeks, and allow the mystical feel of this ancient region to seep into your soul. Remember that the joy is in the journey.

As with most parts of the country, the interstate highway system has taken all the fun out of travel. You zip along with the stampede, avoiding the big rigs as they blow past, viewing scenery that is hardly dramatic (unless you consider golden arches to be stunning or powerful). Highway designers are to travel what fast-food cooks are to eating. Their entrées will fill you up, and they might even keep you alive. But did you really enjoy it?

The northern border of the Missouri Ozarks is no different in this respect. I-44 stretches from St. Louis to Texas, a seemingly unbroken path of franchise operations and rolling countryside. In the northern Ozarks what would later become I-44 was originally an Indian trail, later becoming a wagon path for settlers and freighters. For a time it was known as the Wire Road, a bumpy and muddy track running alongside newfangled telegraph poles. During the Civil War both the Blue and the Gray used the thoroughfare to shuttle troops. Finally the earth that once felt only the hooves of spotted ponies and the step of tanned moccasins became "the Mother Road," the legendary Route 66 running 2,448 miles from Chicago, Ill., to Santa Monica, Calif. Built between 1927 and 1938, Route 66 was not a straight stretch of asphalt. Intentionally, it wandered and veered and connected the heartbeat of the small towns that dotted its entire length. Roadside attractions of every type, shape, color, and description became the rule of the day, unique stopping points that gave moments of lighthearted joy to travelers weary from the Depression and those heading west in the hope of a better life.

This section of the northern Ozark border (as is true for the Ozarks as a whole) has no definitive boundaries. Technically, a geologist would tell you that Sullivan, Mo., is included within the region. Then again, there are also those who claim that tomatoes are a fruit and that dogs can't smile. In short, to use the Ozark vernacular, what's true in theory "ain't necessarily so" in reality. The closer you get to St. Louis, the farther away you are from the real Ozarks. The speech is different; the attitudes and approach to life are different. Life is quicker and less traditional. The independent spirit that makes the Ozarks unique succumbs to the group-thought and influence of pop culture. Frankly, many of those living in the north and northeast border country would not identify themselves as Ozarkers (and neither would those of us who live in the midst of the real deal). They would prefer to be viewed as more urban and mainstream.

However, in deference to the geologists, and because of the fine examples of karst features (caves and sinkholes), state parks, fine rivers, and at least one BBQ joint in Sullivan, I'm blurring the lines and stretching the border to the northeast. Again, it's a rather subjective call. Sullivan doesn't feel like the Ozarks, but just down the road St. James and Cuba do. It's a matter of perspective and attitude.

AREA CODES There are two area codes over the Route 66 region. The Lebanon area to the southwest is covered by the **417** code. The rest of the region is under the **573** code.

GUIDANCE Pulaksi County Tourism Bureau (573-336-6355 or 1-877-858-8687; www.visitpulaskicounty.org), 137 St. Robert Blvd., St. Robert, Mo. This bureau is extremely helpful and covers a wide area. It is your best source of information for not only the Waynesville/Fort Leonard Wood vicinity, but regional lodging, dining, and various driving tours as well.

Lebanon Area Chamber of Commerce (417-588-3256; www.lebanonmissouri .com or www.lebanondowntown.com), 186 N. Adams, P.O. Box 505, Lebanon, Mo. The folks at the Lebanon chamber offer an excellent package, well worth ordering before beginning your trip. Just ask and they'll provide everything from phone books, brochures, and maps to directions and events calendars.

Two other chambers that offer helpful literature and information are the **Cuba Chamber of Commerce** (573-885-2531 or 1-877-212-8429; www.cubamo chamber.com), 71 Hwy P; and the **Rolla Area Chamber of Commerce** (573-364-3577 or 1-888-809-3817; www.rollachamber.org), 1301 Kingshighway, Rolla, Mo.

GETTING THERE As pointed out elsewhere in this *Explorer's Guide*, the Ozarks are not known for a plethora of major airports. Most travel is best accomplished by car (although there are options aplenty if you consider boat, canoe, foot, horse, or mule as viable conveyance).

By auto: From Sullivan to Lebanon, the most efficient path is I-44. However, the most efficient is not always the best or most scenic. If you're not in a tremendous rush, do your best to follow the historic road signs and wander the back roads on old Route 66.

By air: **Lambert–St. Louis International Airport** (314-426-8000; www .lambert-stlouis.com) is the closest major terminal to Route 66 country. Try to avoid taking I-270 S. between 4 and 6 PM (weekdays), or you may find yourself in a traffic jam.

When leaving the terminal, head toward the airport exit on Lambert International Blvd. You will travel 0.2 mile, at which point Lambert International Blvd. becomes Natural Bridge Rd. Drive 1 mile on Natural Bridge Rd. and turn left onto I-70 W. Travel 2.9 miles and take exit 232 onto I-270 S. (toward Memphis). After 14.4 miles, take exit 5B onto I-44 W. toward Tulsa. Sullivan, Mo., the eastern edge of the Route 66 Ozark journey, is 71 miles west on I-44.

You can also fly into **Springfield-Branson Regional Airport** (417-869-0300; www.sgf-branson-airport.com), 5000 W. Kearney, Springfield, Mo. This is a small airport with limited numbers of flights—though what you lose in size, you make up in low stress, easy access, and convenient parking. My personal experience at SCF/Branson is that the facility is extremely well kept and the staff (including TSA agents) very friendly.

MEDICAL EMERGENCIES Both these small regional hospitals offer a wide range of surgical and medical specialties, as well as 24/7 emergency room services: **Phelps County Regional Medical Center** (573-458-8899; www.pcrmc.com), 1000 W. 10th St., Rolla, Mo. **St. Johns Hospital/Lebanon** (417-533-6100; www.stjohnslebanon.com), 100 Hospital Dr., Lebanon, Mo.

✳ Wandering Around

EXPLORING BY CAR The construction of I-44 began in the late 1950s and lasted until the 1970s. By 1985 **Route 66** had been decommissioned, its meandering trek tossed to the wayside in the name of expediency. The Ozarks are a rugged country, even the northern border, but you couldn't really tell it if you stayed on the big highways. From Sullivan to Lebanon they were more or less created in the gentle drainage dividing the Meramec, Bourbeuse, and Gasconade rivers.

It is possible to take historic Route 66 southwest across the entire Ozarks. Just follow the small signs, generally located on the outer roads paralleling I-44. For a true taste of what this renowned thoroughfare used to be, however, leave the interstate at exit 169. Turn left onto CR J, cross over I-44, and immediately turn right onto CR Z. This portion of Route 66 was paved in 1943 and was one of the few stretches of the famous road that were four lanes. Proceeding ahead, you will pass through **Hooker Cut**, immortalized on many period postcards and at one time considered the deepest highway cut in the United States. Watch for the very first crossroads (the only indicator is a yellow house on your left) and turn left onto Teardrop Rd. Drive 0.25 mile and you will notice a bar and BBQ pit on your right. This is the **Elbow Inn**, a popular hangout (catering to locals, soldiers from Fort Leonard Wood, and motorcycle enthusiasts) that serves tasty BBQ on the outdoor deck during the summer months. Originally

THE ELBOW INN, JUST OFF ROUTE 66

WAYNESVILLE'S HISTORIC STAGECOACH STOP

known as the Munger-Moss sandwich shop, this spot has been in business on and off since the 1930s.

Just past the Elbow Inn turn left onto the gravel road with the street sign reading TEMPORAL ROAD. This scenic 5-mile drive takes you deep in the hills following the Big Piney River. Peering through foliage (which is thicker than cats at a fish fry in spring or summer), you will notice that the river bends in a sharp U. This is **Devil's Elbow**, for which the community in the vicinity of the Elbow Inn was named. Travel a few miles farther and you will drive underneath a 40-foot-high wooden railroad trestle bridge. It makes a fantastic photo opportunity, and you'll feel like you just stepped onto the set of an old John Wayne movie.

Turn around in the driveway of the first house on your left (it is at the foot of a steep grade) and return the way you came. Take a left at the intersection of Teardrop and Temporal roads (at the Elbow Inn) and cross the 1923 steel bridge over the Big Piney. You will now head toward the community of Devil's Elbow.

Pass through Devil's Elbow, with its many breathtaking views, and you'll arrive back on CR Z, the four-lane section of Route 66. You'll notice a "half curb" on this length that was originally designed to keep the cars on the highway (though quite often drivers ran up on it and tipped over). Continue straight ahead at the CR Z and SR 28 intersection. At the stoplight, the entrance to **Fort Leonard Wood** will be 2 miles to your left, home to several army museums, Stone Mill Spring, and Miller Cave. To continue on Route 66, drive straight ahead and down the hill into the town of Waynesville. Here there is a historic square containing an old stagecoach stop and courthouse museum. If you proceed straight ahead, watch for Superior Rd. on your left. A 0.25-mile drive down Superior will bring you to the small parking lot of Roubidoux Spring, which pumps out 30 million gallons of water per day. Trout can be caught in this creek as it flows 2 miles to the Gasconade River. Also, note a large pasture across from the spring. This was a resting spot for Cherokee Indians on the infamous forced march known as the Trail of Tears.

EXPLORING BY FOOT Those who enjoy hiking should keep in mind that the Ozarks tend to become hotter than a pistol during the summer months. And of course, at least in this part of the world, you can't have heat without skyrocketing humidity. In other words, the deep forests and trails provide the perfect breeding conditions for creepy crawlies such as ticks, mosquitoes, and chiggers (not to mention the occasional copperhead or cottonmouth snake). This information is not meant to deter the hiker, but rather to advise that bringing bug repellent is just as important as sturdy and comfortable shoes.

Walking the Ozarks is much more fun in the cooler months than at the height of summer, and during fall the colors are beyond vibrant. Still, though, a spring or

THE COLORFUL HISTORY OF HOOKER AND DEVIL'S ELBOW

In the 1890s the now barely existing hamlets of Hooker and Devil's Elbow were the home of sporting clubs for the wealthy. Primarily consisting of businessmen from St. Louis, these hunters and fishermen converged upon the stretches of the Big Piney and Gasconade rivers in search of near-guaranteed hauls of fish and wild game. More than that, though, the sportsmen's clubs were the site of major bragging sessions. It's easy to imagine the air was heavily scented with the acrid smell of Cuban stogies, and more than a few potent potables no doubt added detail to the tales of the "ones that got away." The most popular of the clubs—long since gone—was Hooker's Camp, named for local woodsman and guide John Hooker.

Devil's Elbow was named by tie-rafters, who would float railroad ties downriver to market. The ties were hand cut by the tie-hackers who worked the forests upstream and were a main source of income for many Ozark men both before the turn of the 20th century and through the Great Depression. The railroad ties were usually formed by deft strokes of a broad-bladed ax (more than a few toes and feet felt the bite of the blade), and the tie-rafts floated downstream were often more than a mile long. Alas, the rafts could never make the U-turn in the Big Piney, which led to horrendous jams. It's was said that the devil himself could not float ties through this portion of the river—hence the name *Devil's Elbow*.

summer hike has its own rewards. The woods are full of life, a symphony of sight, sound, and scent. Just remember your Boy Scout training and "be prepared."

All of the state parks feature a number of fine hikes, which arrive with varying degrees of difficulty.

Bennett Spring State Park has numerous trails that provide views of hardwood forests, crystal-clear streams, the spring itself, and the spring branch. All trails are limited to foot traffic and average a 7 percent grade. **Natural Tunnel Trail** is a 7.5-mile hike (allow 4 hours for the round trip) extending south along Spring Hollow to the Natural Tunnel. This unique geological feature is 15 feet wide and takes an S-shaped curve before ending 296 feet later. When you first notice the opening of Natural Tunnel, you may think it's a cave. Upon stepping in, you will see the exit and realize you are in a huge natural tube. Follow the blue arrows on either the east or west

BENNETT SPRING STATE PARK

side of Spring Hollow, then take the single trail to Natural Tunnel. Reliable sources claim that, at various times in the past century, one end of Natural Tunnel was boarded up and used as a cattle pen.

At **Meramec State Park** the only trail designated for anything other than hiking is the **Wilderness Trail**, which may also be used for overnight backpacking. It comprises a 6-mile southern loop and a 4-mile northern loop, the latter of which winds through the Meramec Upland Forest Natural Area and heads to Copper Hollow, where lead and copper were once mined. Copper Hollow Spring is a scenic flow that cascades down cliffs into the valley below; behind the spring you can find a conical sinkhole. Eight backpack camps are located along the trail, and overnighters must register near the trailhead. It's been reported in recent years that black bears have been spotted along the Wilderness Trail. Sightings, however, have been very infrequent.

If a more urban hike is to your liking (and if the convenience of being able to fish within the city limits is appealing), you'll enjoy the **Waynesville Walking Trail**, located right in the middle of Waynesville, Mo. At 1 mile, this trail winds along Roubidoux Creek from the Waynesville Park to Laughlin Park. Follow the path down a slight incline and you will come to the Roubidoux Bridge. Continue, and you'll soon wind up in Laughlin Park. Here you will find **Roubidoux Spring**, home of an underwater cave that draws scuba divers from around the country. A deck overlooks the spring, and Laughlin Park offers picnic tables, a large playing field, and easy-access fishing even for the handicapped. If you have a fishing license and remembered to bring your gear, you may cast a line into the Roubidoux.

EXPLORING BY RIVER The **Niangua River** is a slow and scenic stream that begins near the town of Marshfield in Webster County, Mo., and dumps into the Osage Arm of the Lake of the Ozarks. The river flows from south to north-northeast, and 114 miles of it are navigable by canoe. It's popular in fishing circles for brown and rainbow trout, bass, catfish, and a variety of panfish, and much of the land surrounding it is undeveloped. Access is good, and outfitters become plentiful as floaters approach the Bennett Spring State Park vicinity. The best time to float is spring to fall (Apr.–Sep. is prime season), when the river is consistently at navigable levels via both rains and numerous springs.

The **Big Piney River** begins in the south-central Missouri Ozarks (Texas County), flows northward through the Mark Twain National Forest in Phelps and Pulaski counties, and empties into the Gasconade River near St. Robert. Like most rivers in this region, it is a slow and tranquil stream, though floaters should note that deadfall can accumulate around bends during the higher water flows of spring. The Big Piney is almost always navigable and, thanks to the lack of development in surrounding areas, offers numerous photo opportunities.

The **Gasconade River** is reminiscent of the day Dolly Parton visited a pretzel factory; you've never seen so many curves in your life. At 265 miles this is the longest river lying wholly within the state of Missouri, and it's arguably in the competition for most crooked stretch of water in the world (by air, the length from end to end is only 120 miles). The Gasconade begins in Wright County near Hartville, Mo., finally flowing into the Missouri River near the town of Gasconade. The river is generally slow, except during high water, and flows to the northeast. That is to say, the Gasconade eventually ends northeast of where it started, for canoeists traveling this stream will literally find themselves, at one time or another, hitting every point on the compass. Don't let the curves discourage you; the Gasconade may be the best-kept secret in the Ozarks. The river runs through isolated areas—much ranchland and the Mark Twain National Forest— and floaters should not forget a camera. The tree-covered bluffs are stunning, pocked with caves both small and large, and wildlife is prevalent. The Gasconade is an excellent fishing river for smallmouth bass, goggle-eye (a member of the bass family), bluegill, crappie, and a variety of sucker fish (right tasty if deep fried, but then again what isn't?).

The **Meramec River** receives an awful lot of press, primarily because there are so many things along the northern Ozark border named *Meramec*. The river first rises near Salem, Mo., in Dent County, and pours into the Mississippi about 20 miles south of St. Louis. The entire river can be paddled year-round, but the most popular stretch is between Maramec Spring Park and Meramec State Park. There is a little more whitewater on this river than on the other streams in this region—some stretches can hit a Class II status—but it's all still easily handled by novice floaters. The Meramec offers good fishing and is very pretty unless you plan on going all the way to the Mississippi. The closer you get to St. Louis, the more development you'll see. As far as scenery, there is very little reason to proceed past the towns of St. Clair or Pacific. But, at 207 miles in length, the Meramec does provide plenty of awesome sights. The numerous outfitters that service the Meramec, and the proximity to the recreational possibilities of larger town and cities, consistently make it a tourist favorite.

Courtois Creek, a very fun, 21-mile length of water, has its headwaters in the Mark Twain National Forest of Washington County. The stream terminates when it flows into the Meramec River near the CR E bridge in Crawford County. The forests along the banks are dense, and wildlife viewing is plentiful. Floaters on the Courtois will feel they have traveled back in time, as most of the river is remote and secluded. Normally the Courtois is a shallow, flatwater river with very little current. Take note of the word *normally*. During high water the current can increase dramatically, resulting in crosscurrents and eddies. Plus, due to the proximity of overhanging limbs, floaters unaccustomed to hairpin turns can suddenly find themselves wet. That said, if you are a paddler of even intermediate skill, I highly recommend the Courtois at high water; it's perhaps my favorite Ozark float. While not dangerous in the least, the Courtois can offer some mild thrills when it runs swift.

Last but not least, don't try to pronounce *Courtois* with a French accent. If you do, the locals will look at you funny. It's pronounced *COTE-a-way* or sometimes *CODE-way*.

Huzzah Creek, like the Courtois, is another tributary of the Meramec; its 23 miles both begin and end in Crawford County. Anyone can normally float the

Huzzah; 9 days out of 10 it will be slow and tranquil. However, caution should be exercised on the 10th day. At high water this is a curvy stream that can become a nudge dangerous for the novice. One of the best things about the Huzzah (although this situation is changing due to St. Louis weekend traffic) is that it's uncrowded. Go on a weekday and you may well have the creek to yourself. The water is clear, the fishing is good, and outfitters are plentiful.

Yet another tributary of the Meramec, the **Bourbeuse River** gives the Gasconade a run for its money in terms of curves. The river itself measures 138 miles total, but that means nothing on the Bourbeuse. For example, the 107-mile stretch through Franklin County measures only 27 air miles! Still, that is no reason to avoid the Bourbeuse. Yes, you can travel long distances between access points (count on a minimum of 8 miles), but the bass fishing is excellent, and the scenery will distract you. The water isn't as clear as on some of the other Ozark rivers, but a plus of the Bourbeuse is that there are a few ripples here and there. Nobody in their right mind could call these "rapids," but it's still fun to see and hear some splashes of whitewater from time to time. You'll feel like you're going a heck of a lot faster than you really are.

✳ Villages

Bourbon, Mo. Bourbon prides itself on a small-town atmosphere, of being a community full of "plain folks." The 1,357 residents have little desire to be part of the big city and wisely enjoy their slower pace.

Although populated since the early 1800s, settlers didn't really begin arriving in the area until after the 1860 completion of the southern branch of the Frisco (then Pacific) Railroad to Rolla. Land was plentiful and cheap thanks to railroad right-of-way offerings and land grants promised to veterans of the War of 1812. The town was supposed to be called St. Cloud, and then Richard Turner set up a general store.

Turner was no fool, and he began selling a newfangled type of whiskey to the primarily Irish laborers who spent long days at work on the railroad. On the porch of his store, at all times, sat a large barrel of "Bourbon."

The rest is history.

MURAL IN DOWNTOWN CUBA

Crocker, Mo. In the late 1800s the Crocker depot was the heart of the Frisco Railroad line. Today the Crocker Festival of Railroad Days occurs each year the weekend before Labor Day.

Cuba, Mo. Considered one of the fastest-growing small towns in the Ozarks, Cuba boasts 3,500 residents, two industrial parks, and a small municipal airport. Incorporated in 1857, scenic Cuba is often referred to as the City of Murals. The town is dotted with many wall-sized paintings celebrating both the town's island namesake and local history. In 1928, for instance, mechanical problems once forced famed pilot Amelia Earhart to land outside town. Yes, there is a mural celebrating that event.

Dixon, Mo. The famous Bart Simpson line "Don't have a cow, man," is wholly inappropriate in Dixon. This is perhaps the only village in America where you can win your own bovine during the annual Dixon Cow Days, held the third weekend in September. A trip back in time, Dixon also offers visitors the chance to pick fresh fruits and vegetables from a variety of local berry, tree, and pumpkin farms. Not last and certainly not least, fishermen shouldn't miss an inexpensive (and usually productive) day of angling at the well-stocked Cardin's Lake.

Leasburg, Mo. A hamlet of but 336 people, Leasburg is graced with some exceptional natural wonders. Both Onondaga Cave and Huzzah State Forest are just a few miles from town; still, the most unusual attraction of the area is Snake Pit Cave, a 50-foot-wide sinkhole. You can peer over the rim and see an underground lake. A word of warning: They don't call it Snake Pit Cave for nothing. During the warmer months watch out for slithering reptiles that might well be working on their tans.

Lebanon, Mo. A jewel of a town, Lebanon's location halfway between Rolla and Springfield has led economic prognosticators to label it a "micropolis." Numerous predictions state that phenomenal growth is a certainty over the next decade.

Lebanon is lucky, for if appearances are any indicator, the 12,000 residents appear to have the sort of civic pride that will permit such an explosion to occur in a beneficial manner. In 1998 Lebanon opened the 120,000-square-foot Kenneth E. Cowan Civic Center (an unusual addition to a town of this size), and a variety of "clean" manufacturing industries have proven a huge boon to the local economy. Known as the Aluminum Boat Capital of the World, the town features a number of major watercraft manufacturers, as well as the world's largest producer of wooden barrels (the Independent Stave Company) for the aging of fine wines and bourbon. Floating and fishing are nearby on the Gasconade and Osage Fork rivers, and nearby Bennett Spring State Park draws trout fishermen by the thousands.

Rolla, Mo. No one is quite sure how Rolla got its name. One theory points to the suggestion that southern settlers meant to honor Raleigh, N.C., but lacked the spelling skills to appropriately complete the task. Yet another theory is that it was named by disgruntled citizens who had been ignored in picking the townsite. As payback, or so the legend goes, they chose to name the town for a very homely stray dog (named Rollo) who thrived on harassing the locals and creating general mischief.

No matter, Rolla is these days an eclectic town of 14,090 souls and home to one of the University of Missouri's four campuses. The college was initially founded in 1871 as the University of Missouri School of Mines and Metallurgy but was elevated to a higher status in 1964. The campus' primary focus is still engineering and mining, although full-course majors covering the spectrum of other fields are also offered.

St. James, Mo. There is an intangible something about St. James that personi-fies charm. The town of 3,700 is clean, well kept, and friendly. Visitors can enjoy the beautiful, 1,800-acre Maramec Spring Park, which not only pumps out more than 100 million gallons of water per day but also holds the remains of the fasci-nating Maramec Iron Works. If that's not enough, visitors can fish for trout or float nearby rivers such as the Courtois, Huzzah, and Meramec or enjoy the fruits of five local wineries.

St. Robert, Mo. The "Gateway to Fort Leonard Wood," St. Robert is a modern boomtown. Though the official population stands at 2,760, the daily transit work population is estimated to be 30,000 to 40,000. Within the town itself are more than 500 businesses and 1,200 hotel rooms. Until 1951 St. Robert was known as Gospel Ridge, and its location at the intersection of the legendary Route 66 and Fort Leonard Wood was famous for bars and other "personal services" popular among the troops. These days the town has calmed considerably, a well-kept and extremely busy bedroom community that continues to grow by leaps and bounds.

Steelville, Mo. Billing itself as the Floating Capital of the United States, Steelville's claim to fame can be found not only via the recreation of surrounding rivers, but also from its quaint and picturesque Main Street. Founded in 1835, Steelville is called home by an estimated 1,450 residents.

Sullivan, Mo. Though I really don't consider the Sullivan area as being in the Ozarks proper, a trip is more than worth your time. The reason would be Mer-amec State Park. Also, located in nearby Stanton, Mo.—and promoted by the billboards you've no doubt seen for 100 miles in either direction—is Meramec Caverns. The caverns opened as a tourist attraction in 1935 and were one of the infinite oddities found on old Route 66 during its glory days. Meramec is the most popular commercial cave in Missouri.

The best thing about Sullivan, however, is that it is the home of Homer's BBQ, a simple and simply incredible little eatery that should never be missed.

Waynesville, Mo. With more than 4,000 residents, Waynesville was named for Revolutionary War hero General "Mad Anthony" Wayne. The oldest town in Pulaski County, founded in 1833, it is also home to the U.S. Army's 65,000-acre Fort Leonard Wood Maneuver Support Center. Waynesville, Pulaski's county seat, is a town that likes its festivals, with Paw Paw Daze and Frog Fest being two area favorites.

✳ To See

MUSEUMS 🏛 ✿ ⚐ **The Mineral Museum** (573-341-4616), 125 McNutt Hall, UMR campus, Rolla, Mo. Open year-round, Mon.–Fri. 9–5. Free. Featuring many displays from both the 1893 Chicago and 1904 St. Louis World's Fairs, the museum boasts of more than 3,500 specimens of rocks and minerals from 47 states and 92 countries.

Memoryville, USA (573-364-1810; www.memoryvilleusa.com), 2220 N. Bishop Ave., Rolla, Mo. If vehicular nostalgia is your thing, then this collection of auto-mobiles from yesteryear and scenes from the early 1900s is well worth a stop. Memoryville is easy to find, located on US 63 N. off I-44 at exit 186.

ROLLA'S VERSION OF STONEHENGE

🐾 ✎ ♿ **Route 66 Museum and Research Center** (417-533-7667), 915 S. Jefferson, Lebanon, Mo. Mon.–Thu. 8–8, Fri.–Sat. 8–5. Free. Loaded with one-of-a-kind memorabilia from the heyday of "the Mother Road," this tribute to Route 66 is the result of thousands of hours of volunteer labor. Located in the same building as the **Lebanon–Laclede County Library,** the museum boasts of possessing the collection of renowned historian Jim Powell, founder and former president of the Missouri Route 66 Society. On-site is a themed diner and gift shop, the latter just because no one should ever be lacking a replica US 66 highway sign in their office, den, or bedroom.

CULTURAL SITES 🐾 ✎ ♿ **Stonehenge** (573-341-4111; http://web.umr.edu/~stonehenge), 14th St. and Bishop Ave., Rolla, Mo. Open year-round. Free. The famous English megalith of the Salisbury Plain, or at least a reasonable facsimile thereof, can be found on the northwest edge of the university campus. As is appropriate for a town with a renowned engineering school, the structure determines equinoxes, solstices, and dates and allows for a correct astronomical viewing of the North Star.

🐾 ✎ **Barrels of Fun** (417-532-7700 or 1-800-532-0733; www.barrelsoffunstore .com), 1100 S. Jefferson, Lebanon, Mo. The Independent Stave Company provides more than half of the world's output of barrels. Many are made of white oak, used to age fine wines and bourbons. Visitors to this plant can enjoy tours (during nice weather only, as much of the tour is outside) that begin every half hour 9:30–2:30. Three levels of retail shopping are offered, and handcrafted walnut and oak items are prevalent. On the top floor is a wine-tasting area featuring more than 500 wines and bourbons (this makes your visit worthwhile, right there) with wine accessories and a variety of specialty food items on sale.

WINERIES If popular media conceptions are to be believed, the garden-variety Ozarker is far more likely to take a tug off a jug of white lightning than to daintily sip a glass of white wine. A steaming still full of moonshine is a more common depiction than a lovingly tended vineyard.

The truth, however, is that the Missouri Ozarks have specialized in the art of growing grapes and making wine for more than a century. Prior to the Volstead Act of 1919, Missouri's wine industry ranked second behind New York. Though

Flying J Travel Plaza (573-860-8880), 825 N. Loop Dr., exit 226 off I-44, Sullivan, Mo. There is absolutely no logical reason why a truck stop should be included in this *Explorer's Guide*. I would fully adhere to such a premise if it wasn't for having dropped in at the Flying J. This is one of those strange places that tries to sell everything under the sun . . . and actually succeeds. There is a deli featuring a deep-fried menu encompassing mushrooms, chicken gizzards, hot wings, and more. There are cheeseburgers, hot dogs, baskets of fries, and cream cheese Danish. There is both Mexican and Japanese fast food, but the place is really most famous for its fried chicken. Most of these items are available at 6 AM, by the way.

The shelves of the Flying J contain an encyclopedic selection of items ranging from antacids to art deco sculpture to TVs to giant boom boxes. Clothing is everywhere (black leather jackets seem popular), and the book selection is interesting to say the least. Choices range from 1960s-era pamphlets of relationship advice, to local recipe collections, to (my personal favorite) "how to train your stock dog." Of course collections of CDs and cassettes—an amazing percentage of which have been recorded by musicians you've never heard of—are available for purchase.

THE FLYING J TRUCK STOP

production fell during the Depression and post-Depression years, in the 1960s many of the original wineries and vineyards experienced a renaissance.

Today Missouri has 51 wineries that rack up $26 million per year in wine sales. The rocky soil, sunny days, and a long growing season result in consistent bumper crops. In the St. James and Steelville area six different wineries offer tours, samples, and sales.

Ferrigno Winery (573-265-7742), 17301 SR B, St. James, Mo. Open Mon.–Sat. 10–6, Sun. noon–6. Open weekends only Jan.–Feb. Ferrigno offers 10 different wines, ranging in taste from dry to semisweet. Particularly good is the Vino Di

Famiglia, a mellow, light red wine best served chilled. The grounds provide a wooded wildflower trail for picnics or relaxation, and the **Winegarden Deli** sells a variety of sausages and Missouri cheeses. Ferrigno is located 4 miles north of the I-44 St. James exit on SR B.

4M Vineyard and Rosati Winery (573-265-6892 or 573-265-8147; www.mcc-llc.com/rosatiwinery), 22050 SR KK, St. James. Mo. Open Mon.–Sat. 9–dark, Sun. 11–dark. In 1997 Marvin and Donna Rippelmeyer purchased Rosati, which had stood idle for more than a decade. Originally built in 1933 by Italian immigrants, it was one of Missouri's first bonded wineries. Today Rosati sells a variety of wines, an award-winning Concord grape juice, and local crafts from its on-site store. A 1920s town house on the property has been converted to a bed & breakfast, and down the road just a mile is the **4M Vineyards Farmer's Market**. Do not pass up the jams, jellies, and local honey. The winery can be found between St. James and Cuba, 2 miles down the south service road at I-44 exit 203.

Heinrichshaus Vineyard and Winery (573-265-5000; www.heinrichshaus .com), 18500 SR U, St. James, Mo. Open most weekdays 9–6, Sun. noon–6. Closed every Wed. Call ahead. Heinrichshaus specializes in dry white wines produced from French hybrid and native American grapes. The winery also offers a very pretty terraced picnic area and sells a variety of wine accessories.

Meramec Vineyards (1-877-216-9463 or 573-265-7847; www.meramecvine yards.com). Open year-round, Mon.–Sat. 9–5, Sun. noon–5. One of the more well-known and well-visited vineyards, this facility's main lobby contains both the works of local artists and a gourmet gift shop stocked with food and wine-related items. Staff are friendly, full of information, and always willing to answer questions. Meramec's **Bistro d'Vine** serves light lunches and has even been mentioned in *Southern Living* magazine. The covered courtyard, gardens, and **Bocce Court** (now, there's something you don't often find in the Ozarks) make Meramec Vineyards well worth the stop. It's easily reached by taking exit 195 off I-44 and driving 0.75 mile east on the north outer road.

St. James Winery (573-265-7912 or 1-800-280-9463; www.stonehillwinery.com), 540 Sydney St., St. James, Mo. Open Mon.–Sat. 8–7, Sun. 11–7. Closes at 6 PM during winter. Since 1970 St. James has been producing wines (23 varieties) that have been award winners in both national and international categories. Justifiably proud of their operation, the folks here offer an extensive tour of the facilities and feature gourmet foods, wine accessories, and glassware in their gift shop. The winery is visible when taking the St. James exit off I-44.

Peaceful Bend Vineyard (573-775-3000; www.peacefulbendvineyard.com), 1942 SR T, Steelville, Mo. Open Tue.–Fri. 10–5, Sat. 10–6, Sun. noon–5. Take exit 208 off I-44 and drive south 8 miles on SR 19. Turn right onto SR 8 and drive 2 miles, turning right onto SR T. Peaceful Bend is 2 miles ahead on your left. This beautiful vineyard and cellar set on 72 acres is one of those well-kept secrets that is no longer a secret. Visitors can take a gentle stroll through the vineyards or walk along the banks of the Meramec River. Best of all, owners Katie and Clyde Gill offer a rustic guest cottage on the premises, with prices beginning at $75 per night (two-night minimum).

✳ To Do

✦ 🐾 ◊ **Meramec Farm Cabins and Trail** (573-732-4765; www.meramecfarm .com), 208 Thickety Ford Rd., Bourbon, Mo. It's been a bed & breakfast since 1982, but a working family farm since 1811 (10 years before Missouri was granted statehood). This is a full-scale farming and ranching operation, raising hay, cattle, horses, and a bit of anything else you could name. But it also makes for a unique vacation, one that has been touted in such magazines as *Travel and Leisure* and *American Cowboy*. Guests may stay in one of two well-equipped log cabins (rates begin at $75) and are encouraged to help around the ranch (or not), relax, enjoy the river, or hike about the 470 acres. The big draw here, however, is horses. Even the tenderfoot guest will enjoy sitting high in the saddle on one of the famed smooth-riding, gaited Missouri Foxtrotters. A variety of different riding/ lodging packages are offered. A three-day/two-night package for two is $450 and includes cabin, riding guide, and picnic. There are also weekday specials, a kayaking and riding special, or even rides by the hour ($20 per hour). Those who really want to get out and see the Ozarks up close can join an eight-day ride across Missouri, at prices starting at $1,195.

✦ ◊ **Meyer's Tree and Berry Farm** (573-759-7998), SR D, Dixon, Mo. Meyer's is just down SR D from Cardin's Lake (see *Wild Places*). Should you need some fresh blueberries to go with your catch, this U-pick farm can provide them in-season. It also has pumpkin patches and Christmas trees. Call ahead to make sure the goodies are ready. As any farmer will tell you, sometimes you can be picky and sometimes you can't.

✦ 🐾 ◊ **Clifty Natural Bridge** is also located north of Dixon. Drive north on SR 28 for 4 miles, turning onto SR W. After 3.9 miles you will see a CONSERVA-TION DEPARTMENT sign. The hike to this unique formation will take more than an hour, and because it involves wading through creeks and traversing rocks, heavy footwear is strongly recommended. If you make the hike in summer, also bring mosquito repellent.

✦ ◊ ♿ **Fort Leonard Wood** (573-596-8844 or 573-596-2666), corner of Nebraska St. and E. Dakota St. Mon.–Sat. 10–4; closed Sun., Christmas, and New Year's. Covering more than 100 square miles of territory, Fort Leonard Wood is larger than some eastern states. The home of the military police school, chemical school, and army engineer school, the complex is the Maneuver Support Center for the army. A complex of three museums represent the contributions of the Military Police, Chemical Warfare, and Engineering Divisions to the armed forces throughout history. There are both static and interactive displays.

Having been carved out of rugged Ozark terrain, Fort Leonard Wood is the home to more than a few natural wonders. **Stone Mill Spring**, with a flow of 18 million gallons of water a day, is stocked with more than 3,000 pounds of rainbow trout per year and offers some very good fishing. Caves abound in the area, with **Miller Cave** being the largest. Archaeological evidence from the cave has proven that the area was inhabited from 8000 BC to AD 1300. The mouth of the cave overlooks a scenic view of the valley and Big Piney River, and it can be reached via a difficult hiking trail.

PARKS AND PRESERVES Mark Twain National Forest (www.fs.fed.us/r9/mark twain). Comprised of more than 1.5 million acres, the Mark Twain is a superb wilderness dotted by rivers, streams, and some of the largest natural springs in America. Broken into nine different ranger districts, the forest includes hundreds of miles of hiking trails, numerous scenic drives, seven congressionally designated wilderness areas, 40 campgrounds (these can be reserved by calling 1-877-444-6777), and thousands of acres of primitive and semiprimitive areas. The Mark Twain is a true playground for hunters, fishermen, hikers, equestrians, and campers.

✐ ☕ ♿ ✳ **Bennett Spring State Park** (417-532-4338 or 417-532-4307; www .mostateparks.com/bennett.htm), 26250 SR 64A, Lebanon, Mo. Each year, on the first day of March, upward of 3,000 fishermen will line the banks of the 1.5-mile spring branch creek of Bennett Spring State Park. In that there is little surprise, because in the weeks leading up to opening day of trout season more than 8,000 trout will have been stocked in the meandering spring branch. Missouri fishing licenses and a daily trout tag can be purchased at the park store.

Pumping out more than 100 million gallons of water per day, Bennett is Missouri's third largest spring. The park itself consists of more than 3,200 acres (general admission is free) and offers a nature center, swimming pool, dining lodge, trout hatchery, seven different trails, rental cabins, float trips, fly-fishing lessons, picnic areas, and playgrounds. Five different campgrounds provide a total of 189 individual sites and can be reserved anywhere from six months to two days in advance (1-877-422-6766, or online at www.mostateparks.com).

Lodging and camping is plentiful in commercial concerns adjacent to and near the park. Many of these have access to the Niangua River, into which the spring branch flows. The Niangua, only 1.5 miles downstream, is a slow river of the Class I genre serviced by numerous outfitters.

A word of advice to prospective floaters: The Niangua is a very pretty river, but lately it seems to attract a younger crowd. On fine summer weekends those out for laid-back paddling or bird-watching might note a number of boisterous 20-somethings on the river, performing with the hyperactivity for which 20-somethings are known. While this is a good thing in and of itself, it should be noted that those with small children (or old fogies, a category in which I voluntarily accept membership) might better enjoy a calmer float.

⌾ ♨ ☕ ✐ ♿ ✳ **Maramec Spring Park** (573-265-7124 or 573-265-7387; www .tigernet.missouri.org/~tjf/maramec.html), 21880 Maramec Spring Dr., St. James, Mo. Open morning till dusk (usually till 9 PM in summer). $3 per car, $10 per bus. Unlimited season pass for $20. One of the most peaceful, gorgeous, and well-kept parks you will ever find is this gem, located just 6 miles southeast of St. James on SR 8, privately owned and operated by the not-for-profit James Foundation.

More than 96 million gallons of water per day burst forth from the spring. However, that's just the beginning of the sights in this off-the-beaten-path discovery. More than 200,000 trout are stocked annually into the Meramec River, which seems a bit odd since *Meramec* is the Algonquian word for "catfish." Also on the

THE SPRING BRANCH AT MARAMEC SPRING PARK

subject of names, sharp-eyed readers will notice that Maramec Spring Park insists on spelling its name differently from either the Meramec River or Meramec State Park. The reason is that the privately owned Maramec Spring Park retains the original Algonquian spelling, while Meramec State Park and Meramec River do not.

Maramec Spring Park contains 1,860 acres of forest and fields, and the public-use portions include amenities such as a café, store, campsites, fish feeding, picnicking, shelters, and fishing. You can even get married in Maramec, assuming you want to and somebody has asked.

Several trails are located within Maramec, with the prettiest being the **Spring Branch Trail**. This 1.5-mile trek meanders around both the spring and spring branch. Visitors will also wish to visit the fascinating and imposing remains of the old **Maramec Iron Works**. Founded by the James Family in the early 1800s (that would be the James family whose foundation owns the park and for whom the town of St. James is named . . . not the Jesse James family), Maramec was the first successful ironworks west of the Mississippi. The Meramec River, a clear, calm Ozark stream, flows through the park, providing excellent fishing and floating. You just don't find a better day trip than this park.

RUINS OF THE MARAMEC IRON WORKS

🎖 🐾 ✎ ♿ ❄ **Meramec State Park** (573-468-6072 or 573-468-6519; www.mostateparks.com/meramec .htm), 115 Meramec Park Dr., Sullivan, Mo. Its proximity to the greater metropolitan St. Louis area makes Meramec State Park a busy place. If you seek a quiet trip, I suggest that you try to hit this spot on a weekday rather than a height-of-summer weekend. On the other hand, should your timing not be so precise, Meramec's 6,896 acres will normally allow you to find a corner away from the madding crowd. Open since 1927, the park holds more than 40 caves. Tours of **Fisher Cave**, the largest, are offered for a nominal charge on a seasonal basis. Swimming, fishing, rafting, and canoeing in the Meramec River are the major appeals of this very popular area. The park store offers raft and canoe rentals, campsites (including three group sites), rental cabins, motel rooms, and a conference center. A rustic dining lodge provides hearty and decent food, but don't expect anything too fancy (if you're looking for Wolfgang Puck, you took a wrong turn at Los Angeles).

LAKE 🐟 ✏️ **Cardin's Lake** (573-759-6664), 14200 Colorado Rd., Dixon, Mo. You'll need to pick up a Missouri fishing license, but this local lake stocked with perch, catfish, and crappie is an area favorite. Take exit 163 off I-44 and then travel 10 miles north on SR 28 to SR D. Turn right onto SR D for 0.25 mile, then take another right onto Colorado Rd. Cardin's Lake is 0.75 mile ahead. The lake is well enough stocked that the fish generally bite with enthusiasm.

CAVES 🐟 🐾 ✏️ ♿ ❄️ **Onondaga Cave** (573-245-6576 or 573-245-6600; www .mostateparks.com/onondaga/geninfo.htm), 7556 CR H, Leasburg, Mo. In addition to the Show Me State, Missouri is also known as the Cave State. More than 5,500 caves go far to prove that beauty is more than skin deep. One of the most popular of these underground wonders is Onondaga Cave, located in **Onondaga Cave State Park**, 7 miles southeast of the I-44 Leasburg exit, on SR H in Crawford County.

A 75-minute, 1-mile cave tour is led by a naturalist over concrete walkways (with lights and handrails). Onondaga is a highly scenic cave, with many stalactites, stalagmites, cave corals, and massive draperies. A more strenuous. 0.25-mile tour can also be had on weekends (or by special arrangement) in **Cathedral Cave**, the park's other cavern. However, the attractions of this park are not merely subterranean; you'll also find plenty of activity on the surface. The park's campground offers both basic and electric/water campsites, and **Vilander Bluff Natural Area** provides a panoramic view of the Meramec River. The river valley offers many opportunities for fishing, canoeing, or a relaxed picnic, and a park visitors center is loaded with historical tidbits and exhibits.

Onondaga's hours vary throughout the year. Cave tours are not offered Nov.–Feb. In Mar.–Oct., the visitors center is open daily 9–5. Park gates are closed 11 PM– 7 AM. Cathedral Cave tours are given every Sat. and Sun. at 1 PM (Memorial Day–Labor Day) and by special arrangement. $10 adults, $8 seniors (above age 65), $5 ages 6–12; free admission is granted for kids under 6.

✏️ ♿ **Meramec Caverns** (573-468-3166; www.americascave.com), I-44 and SR W, exit 230, Stanton, Mo. Open every day except Thanksgiving and Christmas. Opens at 9 AM most months. $7–14. Consisting of seven levels and 26 miles of underground passages, Meramec Caverns was opened as a tourist attraction in 1935. Now, topside, visitors can enjoy a motel, campgrounds, canoe floats, riverboat rides, a gift shop, a restaurant, and a mid-1800s mining village. The largest commercial cave in Missouri, Meramec also wins the award for the most billboards on I-44. It features an amazing array of stalactites, fossils, limestone formations, and an underground river, and over the years it has played host to Indians, European miners, ballroom dances, and Civil War engagements. A Confederate gang once blew up a Federal powder mill here, and local legend insists that Jesse James and his gang later used the caverns as a hideout during their outlaw days. As you'll quickly learn in the Ozarks, Jesse James is still a drawing card. In the eastern states, hotels and inns like to boast that "Washington slept here." In the Ozarks, it's "Jesse James and his gang hid here." That kind of tells you where we Ozarkers place our priorities.

✔ **Onyx Mountain Caverns** (573-762-3341; www.pulaskicountyweb.com/onyx cave), 14705 PD 8541, Newburg, Mo. From St. Robert, Mo., go east on I-44 to exit 169. Cross over I-44 and travel east on the outer road for 1 mile. Spring and fall 8–5; summer 8–6; winter 9–4. Dec.–Feb., closed Mon.–Wed. $7.75 adults, $3.75 for children younger than 12. This cavern, placed on the National Register of Historic Places in 1999, was used for thousands of years as a shelter by numerous Ozark Indian tribes. You can view artifacts pulled from the ashes of firepits and take a tour featuring unusual onyx formations and an underground river (which is yet to be fully mapped).

✳ Lodging

BED & BREAKFASTS

Bourbon, Mo.
🦌 🐾 ✔ **Meramec Farm Cabins and Trail** (573-732-4765; www.meramec farm.com), 208 Thickety Ford Rd. See *To Do*.

Steelville, Mo.
🐾 ✔ **The Cottage at Peaceful Bend** (573-775-3000; www.peaceful bendvineyard.com), 1942 SR T. Those seeking privacy or the perfect site for a romantic getaway will not be disappointed with the Cottage at Peaceful Bend. Found on the grounds of the Peaceful Bend Vineyard, the single, simple cottage includes a kitchen, full bath, two bedrooms, and a small living room. There is easy access to the Meramec River right there on the property, and with 72 acres of ground there are plenty of chances for hiking, birding, or a sunset picnic. The owners of Peaceful Bend don't provide meals (guests are given a basket of treats and wine upon arrival), but they do stock the fridge. Rates at begin at $75 per night for one to two people, or $100 per night for three or four. Smoking is permitted, and pets are permitted with an extra $10-per-night charge.

St. James, Mo.
Crutiques Bed and Breakfast (573-265-7931; www.crutiquesbedand breakfast.com), 18790 CR 3480. Located 2 miles south of St. James on SR 3480, Crutiques is a relatively new home (built in 1981) that makes up in amenities what it lacks in age. The wraparound porch and patio are relaxing (the latter even has a woodstove should the morning be chilly), and the screened porch features a 7-foot wicker porch swing. The small touches are what make Crutiques special. Primitive antiques are everywhere, and cut flowers and freshly baked cookies are present upon arrival. The home overlooks the Meramec River Valley, and a lake (complete with Jon boat) is avail-

able for use by guests. A full breakfast is served on china, crystal, and linen. Right next to the kitchen and dining room is a hearth room with a homey brick fireplace. Three guest rooms are available (all of which contain feather bed and ceiling fan); rates range $80–120 per night. The inn is open year-round (closed Thanksgiving and Christmas), and neither children nor pets are allowed. Smoking is not permitted inside the home itself.

∞ ♪ **The Painted Lady Bed and Breakfast and Guest House** (573-265-5008; www.paintedladybandb .com), 1127 S. Jefferson. Luxury amenities are the standard here (such as turndown services and chocolates on the pillow), and the goal of innkeepers Sandy and Wanda Ziff is that guests finish their stay feeling pampered and relaxed. Built in 1990 and opened in 1995, the Painted Lady features six guest rooms with showers or tubs (one has a Jacuzzi); the iron and brass beds range from double to queen to king. A full breakfast is served (an all-you-can-eat affair), and guests may dine either in a formal dining room, at the informal harvest table, or on an outside deck—or receive a "breakfast in a basket." The grounds surrounding the home comprise 60 acres of grass and woods.

Accommodations run $85–175 per night. Reservations are recommended, and smoking is permitted only in designated areas. Pets are not allowed. The Painted Lady welcomes children but prefers that families with children under 12 stay in the property's detached guest house. The Painted Lady also welcomes both honeymooners and those who wish to hold their wedding on the grounds. The latest addition to the property is a small private

cottage (named **Little Tara**) adjacent to the main home, perfect for those seeking a bit more privacy.

🍷 **Rosati Bed and Breakfast Retreat** (573-265-6892 or 573-265-6880; www.mcc-llc.com/rosatiwinery), 22050 SR KK. In addition to being a vineyard, winery, and farmer's market, the Rosati also encompasses a bed & breakfast. A 1920s-era Colonial town house greets visitors, and each of its four large bedrooms holds a private bath. In the main parlor is a fireplace and adjoining sunporch. Rates at Rosati are in the $70–75 range, and special weekend packages (which include dinner) are frequently offered. Upon check-in guests are presented with snacks and a bottle of the award-winning Concord grape juice from 4M Vineyards. Neither children under 12 nor pets (of any age) are allowed at Rosati. However, the home does contain both smoking and nonsmoking rooms.

Rolla, Mo.
A Miner Indulgence Bed & Breakfast (573-364-0680), 13750 Martin Spring Dr. A large, modern, brick Colonial home, A Miner Indulgence offers elegance, spacious rooms,

THE PAINTED LADY B&B

and a unique antique decor (as in a corn shucker, invalid chair, and newspaper delivery wagon, to name just a few items). Guests can enjoy an in-ground heated pool, hot tub, and well-stocked library, but they will especially enjoy the food. The attention some B&Bs afford to dining places a distant second to appearance and physical surroundings. Not this one. The menu varies, but guests are guaranteed a full country breakfast typically consisting of fresh orange juice, a fruit cup, an egg dish, waffles, French toast, or pancakes. Each has a flavor unique to A Miner Indulgence. Bacon or sausage complements the meal, along with a never-ending supply of coffee, tea, or milk. Let's put it this way: You won't start the day hungry.

Set on 4 acres that were once a Civil War campground, the inn offers two spacious rooms. Both have a private bath and sitting area, and both come complete with a coffeemaker and a variety of teas, coffees, and hot chocolate. Those acquainted with the heat and humidity of an Ozark summer will be happy to hear that A Miner Indulgence has central air-conditioning. Rates are currently $75 per night (double occupancy, with a $10 charge for each additional person). Special meals are available, and dietary restrictions can be accommodated. Children over age 12 are welcomed; critters, smoking, and smoking critters are not (smoking is allowed on the porches or in the pool area). As an aside, there is a meaning behind the name A Miner Indulgence: The inn is owned by Barb and Ron Kohser, and Ron is a professor and chair of the Metallurgical Department at the University of Missouri–Rolla.

Dixon, Mo.

⊗ 🐾 ❦ ✧ **Rock Eddy Bluff Farm** (573-759-6081 or 1-800-335-5921; www.rockeddy.com), 10245 Maries Rd. 511. When Tom and Kathy Corey decided to forgo city life and move back to the Ozarks, they did so with a firm philosophy in mind. They sought to escape the frenzy of racing rats, but more than that they wished to share what they love with guests. As those who stay at their Rock Eddy Bluff Farm will attest, the Coreys have not faltered in that goal. A small, scenic inn surrounded by 150 acres of lush Ozark landscape, Rock Eddy looks down upon the one-of-a-kind Gasconade River Valley. Visitors can hike, canoe (canoes are provided for guest use), fish, swim, or take an Amish wagon tour. The point of this retreat, however, is simple relaxation. Accommodations include the Treehouse Suite, with three delightfully furnished rooms and an outdoor hot tub. The Turkey Ridge Cottage is but a brief stroll from the river and has three bedrooms and a foldout couch. Those who want to rough it can choose the Line Camp Cabin, with heat from a woodstove, lights from oil lamps, and water from a pitcher pump. Rates at Rock Eddy run $100–155 per night, and it's open all year (except when the Coreys take a vacation themselves). Smoking is only permitted outdoors or on porches. Children are welcomed, as are well-behaved pets. A full country breakfast is part of the Treehouse Suite's package (in the cabins, the "fixin's" for breakfast are provided, and guests do their own cooking). Also, the farm hosts small, intimate weddings.

❦ ✧ **Blue Jay Farm** (573-759-2400; www.bluejayfarm.net), 10500 Circle Dr. Situated on 360 acres, complete with a 7-acre, spring-fed lake, Blue Jay Farm was established in the early 1900s by Frank Wielandy, one of the original founders of the Missouri Department of Conservation. The present owners, the Goodman family, have lived on the property for five decades. At this relaxing and tranquil escape, with lovingly restored log cabins, guests have the option of either taking part in numerous activities or doing nothing at all. Four cabins are found at Blue Jay Farm, and guests will not be disappointed by any of them. Rates run $65–195 per night (double occupancy, with a $15 charge for each additional adult), and weekly rates are available. Smoking is not permitted, but (one of the rare places that really boast of this) the farm is extremely pet-friendly.

CANOE OUTFITTERS AND CAMPING
Even the less popular rivers of the Ozarks are serviced by numerous outfitters, most of which offer their own campgrounds and shuttles. Prices for canoe rentals run approximately $25–40 per day. Camping can range from the primitive (some outfitters offer free tent camping; most charge a minimum of $5) to RV hookups to cabins and motel-style rooms. Canoe rental rates quoted in the following listings generally refer to a single craft for one or two people, and rates often drop a bit if several canoes are rented. Most outfitters also rent kayaks, rafts, Jon boats, and float tubes. Camping and accommodation rates listed are for adults (across the board, the charge is lower for children), usually per person per day.

The following firms have all exhibited staying power (smaller outfitters come and go) and offer something a bit different from the standard campground. Because many of the outfitters advertise floats on several rivers, I've listed them under the primary area to which they provide service. Travelers should call the individual establishments or check web sites prior to embarking. Reservations are heavily recommended, and in most cases a deposit is required. Outfitters and campgrounds more times than not accept pets, on the provision that the pet is leashed (and no, you can't take Fido along in the canoe or raft). Also, by very wise Missouri law, no glass containers are allowed on the river.

Niangua River
🐾 🛶 **Adventures Float Trip** (417-588-7238; www.mo-adventures.com), 13550 SR 64, Lebanon, Mo. Tent camping $10, RV sites $17, sleeper units $59. Canoes rent for $35.

🐾 🛶 ♿ **Bennett Spring State Park** (417-532-4338 or 417-532-4307; www.mostateparks.com/bennett.htm), 26250 SR 64A, Lebanon, Mo. Cabins include a kitchen and one or two bedrooms and begin at $104 per night. Motel rooms start at $78. A single canoe is $35.

🐾 🛶 **Circle J Campground Canoe Rental and Cafe** (417-532-4430; www.circlejcampground.com), 10221 SR 64, Lebanon, Mo. RV spots start at $20; cabins, $50. Canoe rental starts at $35, and guided fishing trips are available.

🛶 **Fort Niangua River Resort** (417-532-4377 or 1-866-532-4377; www.fortniangua.com), 84 Cat Hollow Trail, Lebanon, Mo. Fort Niangua offers a choice of air-conditioned and heated cabins, trailers, an RV park, and primitive campgrounds. Recreational facilities include a lighted basketball and volleyball court, swimming pool, and fully equipped game room. A convenience store, laundry, and showers are located in the main building. Cabins begin at $50, RV hookups start at $20, and tent camping is $4.50 per person per night. Canoe rental is $35.

🐾 ✤ Maggard's Canoe & Corkery Camp (417-532-7616 or 1-888-546-9788; www.nianguariver.com), 15750 SR 64, Lebanon, Mo. Most of the campsites are shaded, with picnic tables and flush toilets close by. Camping is free all year (Sun.–Thu. nights, holidays not included) with canoe rental. On weekends, camping is $5 per person the first night, and the second night is free with canoe rental (which runs $32–40). Pets are not allowed.

🐾 ✤ Niangua River Oasis Canoe Rental (417-532-6333 or 1-800-748-7249; www.nrocanoe.com), 171 NRO Rd., Lebanon, Mo. Cabins run $65–250 per night (the latter does sleep 15 people). Canoes are $35. Two nights of free camping are provided (when available) with canoe rental. This campground has security personnel, and loud noise isn't tolerated after 11 PM. Dogs are permitted only on a leash and only in the campground. They are not permitted in the cabins.

🐾 ✤ Redbeard's Ranch (417-588-7337; www.redbeardsranch.com), 30075 Marigold Dr., Lebanon, Mo. Owned and operated by Jane and Bud Meador, Redbeard's is located on 295 acres with more than a mile of Niangua River frontage. In winter, open most weekends from 6 PM Fri. to 3 PM Sun. Open daily Memorial Day–Labor Day. This is a very family-oriented environment, and the owners do not tolerate wild parties or foul language. Though cabins are expected to be built in the future, at present only primitive camping spots (there are showers and flush toilets) are available. The cost is $5 per person per night. Canoe rental starts at $30. You can rent a tepee at Redbeard's for $50 per night (two-night minimum); for $10 per person you can camp with your horse and enjoy area trails.

🐾 ✤ Riverfront Campground & Canoe Rental (417-588-3386 or 1-888-673-7668; www.riverfrontcamp canoe.com), 13 Riverfront Trail, Lebanon, Mo. A family-owned facility, the premises consist of 200 acres fronting on the Niangua. Primitive campsites are $5 per person per night; RV sites are $6 (in addition to the regular camp fee). Security is provided on the grounds, and breakfast and lunch can be purchased at the camp cookshack. For groups of more than 30, dinners can be catered on request. Riverfront enforces a quiet environment after 11 PM, and a convenience store is stocked with minor provisions.

✤ Sand Spring Resort (417-532-5857 or 1-800-543-3474; www.river frontcampcanoe.com), 1996 SR 64, Lebanon, Mo. Reservations only. This is a more upscale facility with above-average accommodations. Prices run from $42 for a single sleeper to $89 for a suite. Canoe rental starts at $35. A full-service restaurant with weekend and breakfast buffet is located within the confines of the resort, and fly-fishing tips and seminars are regularly available.

Big Piney and Gasconade Rivers
✤ 🐾 Boiling Spring Campground (573-759-7294; www.dixoncamping .com), 18500 Cliff Rd., Dixon, Mo. Floats are available on both the Big

Piney and Gasconade rivers, with the campground open Apr. 15–Nov. 15. Camping begins at $10, canoe rental at $30. This is a simple campground, but one that is kept up. The facilities include tent camping sites, RV hookups, rest rooms and showers, a lighted boat ramp, camp grills, picnic tables, volleyball nets, and horseshoe pits.

🦞 🐾 🛶 **Rich's Last Resort** (573-435-6669; www.richslastresort.com), 3401 Windsor Lane, Duke, Mo. Rich's has provided camping, canoes, and cabins since 1972. It's been a home to so many campers and floaters that the owners are actually compiling a book from the memories and anecdotes of the regulars. The campground offers tent sites beginning at $6 per person, with electrical hookup for RVs costing an additional $7 per night. For scout, church, and youth groups, tent sites are $4 per night. Cabins begin at $55, and while pets are allowed, there is a $5 nightly charge for dogs. Canoe rental for Big Piney floats runs in the $40 vicinity, and rafts and kayaks are available. Rich's is open from the beginning of turkey season in April till end of deer season in November.

🐾 🛶 **Lay Z Day Canoes and Camping** (573-336-8630; www.layzday.com), 23417 Teak Lane, St. Robert, Mo. Located 3 miles south of I-44 off exit 163, the Lay Z Day offers several **Full Moon Floats** on the Big Piney per summer (whenever there is a full moon, more or less). The trip begins at 7:30 PM and ends at midnight and features a huge hot dog and marshmallow roast underneath an old railroad trestle bridge. Prices for this trip should be obtained by calling in advance. Regular canoe rental starts at $45, and campsites begin at $6.

🦞 🐾 🛶 **Gasconade Hills Resort** (573-765-3044 or 1-800-869-6861; www.canoemissouri.com), 28425 Spring Rd., Richland, Mo. Gasconade Hills offers nine cabins and a lodge for nightly or weekly rental. Two cabins front on the river, and six allow dogs inside. Charges run from $85 (for cabins) to $195 (for the lodge) per night. Canoes, kayaks, Jon boats (nice on the Gasconade), rafts, and tubes are available, with canoe rental beginning at $38. Primitive campsites start at $5; RV sites, $16. Hot showers and a store are on the premises, and for a small charge the resort holds a fantastic Saturday-night BBQ. This is a true family retreat, situated in a drop-dead-gorgeous location on the Gasconade. No boom boxes, loud music, foul language, or obnoxious behavior is permitted, and public intoxication results in expulsion from the premises with no refund. Gasconade Hills is the place for campers with kids, or simply those who don't wish to put up with screaming yahoos.

Courtois Creek, Huzzah Creek, Meramec River

🐾 🛶 **Ozark Outdoors** (573-245-6437 or 1-800-888-0023; www.ozarkoutdoors.net), 200 Ozark Outdoor Lane, Leasburg, Mo. The amenities offered by outfitters tend to increase when you move up to the Meramec River and its tributaries. Ozark Outdoors is no exception, offering floating, camping, and cabins on the Meramec, Huzzah, and Courtois. There are many options here for trips and groups, but daily canoe rental starts at $20 on weekends ($17.50 weekdays). No children under 12 are allowed without parental supervision. Campsites are either on or near the banks of the Meramec River; most are shaded and include picnic tables and grills. Amenities at the campground include a 30-by-50-foot swimming pool, full-service shower house, fishing, swimming, kids' area, hiking trails, volleyball, and horseshoes. Campsites start at $7.50 per night for adults, $4 for children under 12. Full hookups are $10 per night for RVs. For those who don't feel like truly roughing it or seek a bit more privacy, Ozark Outdoors has a number of small log cabins. They come complete with kitchenette, refrigerator, microwave, air-conditioning/heat, rest room, shower, and one bedroom with bunk beds and a full-sized bed. Weekend rates start at $65 per night. Also on the premises is a 10-unit motel.

🐾 🛶 **Bass' River Resort** (573-786-8517 or 1-800-392-3700; www.bass resort.com), P.O. Box BB, Steelville, Mo. 65565. This resort offers everything from canoeing and rafting to steak dinners and log cabins. Numerous trip plans to fit most needs are offered on the Meramec, Huzzah, and Courtois. Primitive campsites, cabins, A-frames, a "hideaway house," and more are the lodging options at Bass' River Resort. Prices run from $7.50 for a campsite to nearly $200 per night for a house. Canoe rental starts at $40 per canoe (or $20 per person). A nice touch here is that the resort can provide a number of different horseback adventures, most in the $20–40 range.

🛶 **Huzzah Valley Resort** (573-786-8412 or 1-800-367-4516; www.huzzah valley.com), 970 E. Hwy. 8, Steelville, Mo. Huzzah bills itself as "Missouri's Most Complete Resort." While that claim is the expected Ozark exaggeration, the resort does make a considerable effort to provide a large variety

of options and services. Lodging at Huzzah comes in a number of forms. Campsites start at $7.95 and come with an outdoor table and fire ring with BBQ grill. All the campsites are near the beaches, swimming, and playgrounds. RVers can get full hookups, including 30- or 50-amp electric, and never fret about hitting slideouts with their neighbors. Pull-through sites are also available for big rigs. A motel room starts at $74, and cabins start at $105. If you have a large group, you can rent one of several renovated farmhouses for $750 per night. That sounds steep until you realize there is a 20-person minimum and the houses have six bedrooms capable of sleeping four to six people each. Keep in mind that neither smoking nor pets is permitted in the cabins or farmhouses. Canoe rental starts at $20, as do horseback rides (there is a "kiddie ride" offered for around $5). Huzzah also provides hiking trails, volleyball, hayrides, and a well-stocked store. Best of all—and more campgrounds should do this—there is an area for families and a "loud" area.

🐟 🐾 🛶 **Garrison's Canoe Rental RV Park and Resort** (573-775-2410, 1-800-367-8945, or 1-800-235-2232; www.timeon.com/garrisons), P.O. Box 1069, Steelville, Mo. 65565. Garrison's is yet another one of the resorts offering a massive menu. Floats are available on the Meramec, Huzzah, and Courtois, with canoe rental beginning at $32. Horseback trail rides come in a gamut of packages and choices. The campgrounds focus on families and groups, and lodging choices are infinite. You can rent a $6 tent site or spring for a $400-per-night river bluff lodge. In between is every size and shape of cabin, ranch house, RV spot, and cottage imaginable. You can even rent a tent, in the event you left yours lying back home in the driveway. All services are available between Memorial Day and Labor Day; if you're vacationing in winter, call to see what is available and open. Garrison's holds a number of festivals throughout the year. Independence Day is big, as is the annual bluegrass festival. The resort has a store on-site, as well as a rustic diner serving weekend meals cafeteria-style.

❧ ✐ **Bird's Nest Lodge** (573-775-2606 or 1-877-707-7238; www.birds nestlodge.com), P.O. Box 1385, Birds Nest Rd., Steelville, Mo. 65565. Bird's Nest Lodge is the only place I've ever seen that offers gigging tours and provides gigging guides. Gigging, if you've never done it or heard of it (and most people haven't if they aren't from the Ozarks), basically involves killing fish with sharp sticks. In short, you spear the little devils from boats. It's pretty popular in these parts—so popular, in fact, that it has its own legal season. The staff at Bird's Nest will not only take you out for a day of gigging but also clean and cook your catch later on. It's doubtful you will find this service anywhere else in the country. For more traditional fun (but seriously, you should go gigging sometime just to say you've done it), float trips begin at $23 per canoe. Lodging starts at $7 for a campsite and runs up to $26 for a modern cabin. Many package plans are offered on these 29 acres of riverfront. The lodge's dining hall is rustic but good, with a large outdoor deck (with tables) overlooking the Meramec River.

EATING OUT A Slice of Pie (573-364-6203), 601 Kingshighway, Rolla, Mo. It's a little cubbyhole of a place, marked with a small sign and painted arrow next to a Laundromat. The parking lot holds only a few cars, but it probably sees more auto traffic than I-44. The comings and going at A Slice of Pie are nonstop. Whether you're eating in or grabbing pie to go, this little shop is a local tradition. The reputation is justified, for the pie, cakes, and cheesecakes offered here will remind you of the kind Grandma used to make (assuming, of course, that Grandma came from the Ozarks and made pies with crusts as tasty as their filling). The choices are endless, from apple and blackberry crumb to chocolate chip mint to Tahitian cream. There is a "Toll House" pie, pecan pie, strawberry rhubarb, mincemeat, and mudslide. A favorite cheesecake is the white chocolate cappuccino, and the apple walnut cake is a work of art. It should be noted that not all pies are offered on all days—the current menu is on a blackboard behind the counter—but at any given moment you'll have enough selections that decision making will become difficult. Prices start at around $3.77 for a half slice ($4.50 for a whole slice . . . which is huge), $14.95 for a whole pie, and $8.50 for a half pie. Hours are 10–10, seven days a week. There's always a pie of the month, and special orders can be provided with a couple of days' notice.

The Missouri Hick Bar-B-Q (573-885-6791), 913 E. Washington, Cuba, Mo. The most basic rule of thumb when seeking out a BBQ joint is this: You should smell it long before you

THE WORLD'S GREATEST BBQ JOINT

Homer's Bar-B-Q (573-468-4393), 693 Fisher Dr., Sullivan, Mo. Open Thu.–Fri. 10:30–8, Sat. 10:30–10. Simply put, Homer's is one of the two best BBQ restaurants in the world (in my opinion it ties Arthur Bryant's in Kansas City). You may see the big ARE U READY? sign from I-44, hand painted on a piece of plywood. When you find the restaurant, located in a small strip mall with potholes in the asphalt, you will see what used to be an old drive-in (the ice

HOMER'S: IT DOESN'T GET ANY BETTER THAN THIS.

see it. If the scent of hickory reaches you inside the car, the place is usually worth a try. The Missouri Hick Bar-B-Q, located on Washington Street in Cuba, passes this initial litmus test

THE MISSOURI HICK BAR-B-Q

with flying colors. The restaurant is housed in a relatively new, two-story building purposefully rustic in appearance, and the staff are very friendly and happy. Smoking all the meat over wood (as is the only true way to BBQ), the Hick features brisket, ribs (pork), chicken, and sausage. Combo platters, a large number of side dishes, family packs, and catering are also available. Prices run from $4.49 for a pulled-pork sandwich to $15.95 for a full slab and all the fixin's. There is a children's menu, and for those who really want something different, a house specialty is "Ory's Spud." This is a monster-

cream cone is still on the original sign). Inside are a few well-worn booths, some with a book, magazine, or Bible lying atop. A weathered plastic menu board hangs over the ordering counter.

Owner Homer Britton is not much on decor. He is busy focusing on the food. All his selections are slow-smoked (ribs are on the

PITMASTER HOMER BRITTON SLOW-SMOKES ALL HIS MEATS.

pit for 4 hours) over a combination of hickory and sassafras wood. The result is nothing short of perfection; you can taste this deep and sweet combination of smoldering hardwoods, but it isn't overwhelming. The choices include ribs (a full rack is $15.91), a half chicken for $7.62, chicken wings at $6.44, and pork tips for $8.37. An unexpected choice is blackened tuna or salmon for $7.62. Under no circumstances should you miss the specialty of the house: Homer takes a simple pork steak (again, $7.62) and turns it into something you didn't know existed. Served on a bun, the boneless steak is so tender that it literally falls apart when you take the first bite.

sized baked potato full of baked beans and pulled pork, covered with cheddar and Monterey Jack cheese ($5.49). The ribs are first-rate here; the pitmaster at the Hick has applied a dry rub prior to cooking that is tasty without being overpowering. It seems to hold traces of pepper and paprika, but there is also a slight sweetness. No matter the ingredients, the rub creates a light crust that adds character without numbing the taste buds.

Zeno's Steakhouse (573-364-1301; www.zenos.biz), 1621 Martin Springs Dr., Rolla, Mo. Serving the Rolla area for more than 40 years, Zeno's has long been a local tradition for breakfast, lunch, and dinner. Located at the 184 exit off I-44 (a quick 0.25-mile drive down Martin Springs Dr.), the entire facility encompasses not only the restaurant itself, but also a motel and **Scheffer's Lounge**. For an appetizer, many people choose the "Madisonion"—a giant, blooming onion served with a special sauce ($5.50). "Center of the Plate" steaks are this restaurant's primary claim to fame, with prices ranging upward from $15.95. "Zeno's Pride," a 20-ounce slab of prime beef, is $21.95. A number of traditional Italian dishes are on the menu, and seafood offerings include an entire channel catfish ($11.35), walleyed pike ($14.20), and either broiled or batter-fried lobster (market price). If you've never had a batter-fried lobster, you should try it. In the Ozarks deep frying is considered a fine art, and this is one tasty crustacean.

Johnny's Smoke Stak BBQ (573-364-4838), 201 W. SR 72, Rolla, Mo. According to many folks, Johnny's is the *only* place in the northern Ozarks for BBQ. It's been a consistent winner in the *Rural Missouri* magazine readers' poll, and at $10.75, its evening BBQ buffet (Wed.–Sat. after 5, and all day Sun.) draws a huge crowd. A lunch buffet is available weekdays at $6.50 and includes potato, bread, entrée, and salad bar. A full-slab rib dinner at Johnny's (it easily feeds two people) costs $24, a little more pricey than other places. Also on the menu are steaks and catfish. Although I wouldn't give this restaurant nearly the accolades others do, it is a good choice while in the Rolla area. The interior is comfortable, and the portions are hearty.

Dowd's Catfish House (417-532-1777), 1760 W. Elm (old Route 66), Lebanon, Mo. Open Sun.–Thu. 9–9, Fri.–Sat. 11–10. Located at exit 127 off I-44 on old Route 66, Dowd's has only been in its present location for 5 years. In that brief span, however, it has quickly become a local favorite. As the name says, the specialty is catfish. These fillets are all boneless and come either deep fried or broiled. The four-fillet meal (the smallest) goes for $7.49 and comes with hush puppies; choice of potato, a side salad, or pinto beans; tomato relish; and coleslaw. You'd think that this would

fill up even the most ravenous customer, but you'd be wrong. Dowd's is famous for its all-you-can-eat dinners, and it offers more than a few. Catfish, of course, is part of every dinner. At $11.49 it features the same sides as the regular dinner, but with the addition of fried okra after 4 PM. From there, though, the choices multiply. You can get an all-you-can-eat catfish, shrimp, or ribs version for $12.99 (or get all three—ribs, shrimp, *and* catfish for $13.99). The catfish, shrimp, and crab legs selection is $19.99. Even children get an all-you-can-eat option. The prices start at $1 for each year up to 11 years of age. Dowd's is also a fine BBQ smokehouse, and (as if you didn't expect this) all-you-can-eat BBQ entrées (brisket, ribs, or chicken) begin at $8.99.

Caveman Bar-BQ & Steak House (573-765-4554), 26880 Rochester Rd., Richland, Mo. Owner David Hughes smashed, drilled, shoveled, and carted more than 160 tons of rock to create his Caveman Bar-BQ. This isn't surprising when you consider that the establishment is located inside a cave, on a bluff 100 feet above the Gasconade River. Eleven years after the excavating was finished, the restaurant remains a huge hit not only with locals, but with patrons from around the world. They first come to see this most unusual of BBQ joints. They come back again for the food. Full of waterfalls and fountains and sporting a carpeted floor (easier on the feet than rocks), the Caveman's humidifiers remove 9 pounds of water from the air per hour. The resulting atmosphere is comfortable, with the temperature remaining a constant 69 degrees. Visitors park in a gravel lot, are driven to an elevator, and then are lifted the 100 feet to the restaurant by elevator.

The Caveman is known for its hickory-smoked ribs, pork, brisket, and chicken, but the menu also features steaks, seafood, cheesecake, homemade pies, and a huge salad bar. This is just part of the story. Though the specialty of the house is the baby back ribs, you can also order frog legs, gator tail, and crawdads. Prices range $5.99–30. Visitors should note that this is a non-smoking, no-alcohol restaurant. In addition, it only accepts cash—no checks or credit cards. The restaurant is closed Nov.–Mar., and hours and days vary during spring, summer, and fall. Memorial Day–Labor Day, the hours are Wed.–Fri. 5–8:45 for dinner, Sat. noon–8:45, and Sun. noon–7. Calling ahead is a good idea.

The Bell Restaurant (417-588-2587), City Rt. 66 E. (Elm St.), Lebanon, Mo. It's just a simple diner, a throwback to a simpler time. There are the vinyl booths, the Formica-topped lunch counter with spinning black stools, and uniformed waitresses rushing to serve the never-ending trail of hungry customers. But this is no modern-day rendition of what a proprietor thinks a diner should be. This is not an attempt at retro chic. The Bell Restaurant is just doing what it's done since the 1950s, providing a big meal—breakfast, lunch, and dinner—at a fair price. Specials at the Bell might include a big plate of biscuits and gravy for $2.99, or omelets from $3.95. For lunch you will find the usual suspects of burgers and a wide variety of sandwiches. If you're hungry, go for the breaded pork tenderloin (it's a whopper) for $3.25. A side of curly fries, only $1.75, will satisfy any appetite. Evening meals feature BBQ ribs from $9.95 or catfish fillets from $9.95. Slices of either fruit pie, cream pie, or pecan pie begin at $1.75.

LEBANON'S BELL RESTAURANT

Bennett Spring Dining Lodge (417-532-4547), 26250 SR 64A, Lebanon, Mo. The Bennett Spring Dining Lodge was built by Franklin Roosevelt's Civilian Conservation Corps in 1933. Costing $14,000 at that time, it still reflects that great rustic look with plenty of stone and dark wood. Today the dining lodge remains a favorite with the thousands of visitors who descend upon Bennett Spring each year. Open daily from 7 AM to 1 hour past the whistle (during trout season, which signifies the end of the day's fishing), the lodge is open for breakfast, lunch, and dinner. Breakfast and dinner buffets are offered Saturday and Sunday mornings and Friday and Saturday nights. While not a fancy place, Bennett Spring Dining Lodge does offer a few twists along with traditional favorites. You can order sandwiches from a long list (a BLT is $4.99), and a soup and salad bar runs $5.99. Dinner prices range from fried chicken at $8.99 to deep-fried shrimp at $12.99. For $6.99 the lodge will cook your fresh trout to order (you have to catch it and clean it), and the meal comes with soup, salad bar, and two side dishes. Friday's evening buffet is catfish and fried chicken ($11.49), while

Saturday's features BBQ ribs and fried chicken. Both are a good deal—again nothing fancy, but well worth the price. Children 10 and under can eat at the buffet for half price.

✳ Entertainment

🔊 ♿ **Meramec Music Theater** (573-775-5999; www.mrun.com/mmt), SR 8 W., Steelville, Mo. $15 adults, $14 seniors, $7.50 ages 12 and under. A truly excellent facility for such a small town, the Meramec Music Theater's Christmas show is considered a very big deal. Still, quality entertainment can be found in this venue every month save January (not because awful music is performed in January, but rather because the theater is closed). Shows generally take place once per week, and the normal starting time is 7 PM. Performances tend to be in the genre of classic country, gospel, bluegrass, or cowboy music, but you'll occasionally find a headliner such as Ricky Skaggs or Ralph Stanley. If you get a chance, make sure to catch the Meramec Quartet. This foursome has some unexpected talent.

🍴 🔊 ♿ **Highway 19 Drive-in** (573-885-7752). The drive-in movie is often thought of as a thing of the past, but somehow the legacy of Route 66 has allowed a few of these American treasures to hang on. In Cuba, Mo., it seems the drive-in is alive and well. For more than 50 years the Highway 19's solo silver screen has stood tall over a grassy parking lot. Holding 250 cars, this bit of nostalgia even still has some of the old-style car speakers (though radio sound is available, too). This memory of simpler times can be found just north of the I-44 and SR 19 intersection.

SPECTATOR SPORTS 🔊 ♿ **Lebanon I-44 Speedway** (417-532-2060), 24069 SR 66, Lebanon, Mo. Auto racing has moved into the first tier of spectator sports, and nowhere is this trend more evident than at the I-44 Speedway. A new high-banked clay oval track was built in 2004, and races take place every Saturday between April and mid-September. Divisions include late models, modifieds, factory stocks, and bombers. Special events drawing huge crowds are the Independence Day celebrations (with dandy pyrotechnics) and the **Bill Willard Memorial**, which awards a $10,000 first prize.

✳ Selective Shopping

Heartland Antique Mall (417-532-9350 or 1-800-532-9350; www.heart landantiquemall.com), 2500 Industrial Dr., Lebanon, Mo. Open 8–8, seven days a week. With 40,000 square feet and 250 individual dealers, Heartland is an antiques lover's dream come true. There are countless aisles of antiques, and staff are both knowledgable and courteous. Found inside the mall is **Knife Country**, which features a nice selection of blades, and a **Wisconsin Cheese** outlet boasting 130 varieties. Next door (and this place is worth it just for the free samples) is a 5,000-square-foot **Russell Stover** candy outlet. The complex is located off I-44 at exit 127.

Lebanon Books (417-532-2500), 1116 Lynn St., Lebanon, Mo. You'll find a bit of everything in Lebanon Books, the largest bookstore in town. Aside from the latest best-selling tomes, the store carries magazines, toys, games, gifts, and even some sporting goods.

Shepherd Hills Factory Outlet
(417-532-7000 or 1-800-727-4643;
www.shephills.com), just north of
I-44, exit 127, Lebanon, Mo. Open
8–8, seven days a week. Most factory
outlets are pretty much the same,
offering little of unique value. Such
cannot be said of the Shepherd Hills
Factory Outlet. It's ranked as the
world's largest dealer of Case pock-
etknives, but wandering the aisles of
this huge store will result in much
greater finds. There is Mikasa china,
Denby pottery, Hummel figurines,
and a large selection of walnut bowls
and carvings. You will find massive
amounts of pictures, candles, baskets,
artificial flowers, and wind chimes.
Best of all is an unbelievable number
of Zippo lighters and Swiss Army
knives. Until you've seen some of the
ones for sale here, you wouldn't have
believed so many blades and tools
could fit into a single implement.

Nancy Ballhagen's Puzzles (417-
286-3837; www.missouripuzzle.com),
25211 Garden Crest Rd., Lebanon,
Mo. (exit 135 off I-44 east of Lebanon). Open Wed.–Sat. 11–5, Sun.
noon–5, Mon. 11–5. Closed on Tue.,
most major holidays, the last Sun. in
June, and the first 2 weeks in Jan.
Nancy Ballhagen likes her puzzles.
She likes them so much that she
keeps more than 3,200 different jig-
saw puzzles in stock at her store.
Obtained from more than 50 American and European companies, the
puzzles range in size from 100 to
18,000 pieces. From clown puzzles
and Civil War puzzles to covered
bridge puzzles and Colorado ski
resort puzzles, the puzzling topics run
from A to Z (obviously, I stopped looking at C). They might be constructed

of wood or metal. They might be two
dimensional or three dimensional (the
four-dimensional puzzle, which allows
you to travel through time, is not yet
on the market). When completed,
they might appear in holograph form
or as a photomosaic.

The Book Addict (573-265-5665),
116 N. Jefferson St., Saint James, Mo.
Those who enjoy the written word
should make a point of stopping into
the Book Addict, a nice little store on
the main drag of St. James. Not only
does this surprising shop have more
than 20,000 used volumes for sale
(surely you can find something to
read with this many choices), but it
also features locally made stained-
glass art pieces.

✳ Special Events

May **Frog Fest**. Held annually on the
first weekend in May, Waynesville's
two-day Frog Fest offers bluegrass,
food vendors, frog jumping, frog
kissing, and a three-legged race (for
humans, not frogs). The festival began
when the Missouri Department of
Transportation was widening the road
into Waynesville. An outcropping
seemed to have a familiar shape, and
enterprising locals painted it into the
likeness of a frog.

Bluegrass Pickin' Time (573-759-
7716), Carol's Memorial Bluegrass
Park, N. SR 133, Dixon, Mo. For
nearly three decades, on their farm
just north of Dixon, the Bill Jones
family has played host to one of the
best bluegrass festivals in the country.
Though the event takes place twice
per summer—on Memorial and Labor
Day weekends—it is usually best to
arrive a couple of days before the
actual performances start. There is

parking for more than 1,000 cars and electricity for 400 RVs, and most of the folks camping out will be having their own impromptu concerts. Everyone is welcome (bring an instrument, no matter what it may be)—this is a real family event. Drugs and alcohol are forbidden. There's an admission charge ($8–12, or three- and four-day passes for $28 and $30, respectively), and you'll more than get your money's worth. The music is great, and you never know who will turn up. One year former U.S. attorney general John Ashcroft (also a former Missouri governor and senator) ended up on stage. He has an excellent voice, by the way.

June **Hillbilly Days** (417-588-3256; www.lebanonmissouri.com). Hillbilly Days began more than 30 years ago at Bennett Spring State Park, intended to be a onetime event celebrating the 50th anniversary of Missouri's state park system. The event was such a hit that it's still going strong, now sponsored by the Missouri Department of Natural Resources and the Lebanon Area Chamber of Commerce. Friday night features a catfish fry and bluegrass music, while Saturday's happenings include bobbing for apples, searching for nickels in a haystack, and cow-chip tossing. Sunday brings gospel music and an antique car and tractor exhibit. Of course Hillbilly Days offers an endless supply of food and more than 100 craftsmen exhibiting and selling their wares.

Pulaski County Regional Fair, St. Robert City Park. Taking place each year in early June, Pulaski County puts on a fair featuring crafts, a carnival, a livestock show, and bull riding. If you want to see a real fair, this is a good one.

July **Laclede County Fair** (417-588-9607), Laclede County Fairgrounds, Lebanon, Mo. Laclede County's fair has been a tradition since 1910. Livestock displays are numerous, and evenings feature a demolition derby, horse pulls, and truck pulls. A full midway lights up the grounds with the sights and sounds of carnie games (and of course carnie workers).

August **Central Missouri Regional Fair**. Drawing nearly 15,000 people, Rolla's fair is a four-day event that occurs in early August. It's a large-scale version of the smaller county fairs—you can easily spend several days at this event and not feel you've seen it all.

September **Dixon Cow Days**. In 1929 merchants in Dixon, Mo., hoped to attract Depression-era shoppers to town. For several months the hook was a drawing for a free cow. Not only did thousands of people come to town, but they stayed for dancing, dining, and discounted retail items. The tradition soon died off, but Dixon merchants of the 1980s reincarnated it. Thus was born Cow Days, a two-day event held annually the third weekend in September. You can enter the drawing to win your own cow as well as enjoy crafts, street dances, live music, parades, and a beauty pageant. Really, who could pass up the chance to play "Cow Patty Bingo"?

Paw Paw Daze. The Waynesville Planter's Club spends a Saturday in late September celebrating the pawpaw tree. Held annually at the Waynesville City Park, this event offers a your chance to dig into some pawpaw pie and pawpaw jam.

Bluegrass Pickin' Time (see *May*).

THE LAKE OF THE OZARKS

As is true with many rural residents of south Missouri, I have mixed feelings about the Lake of the Ozarks. On the one hand, there are fond childhood memories of family visits to our cousin Junior's primitive fishing resort and marina near Gravois Mills. On the other, crossing to the east side of the lake and viewing the perpetual development on US 54, I am reminded of the frenzy for dollars that transformed Florida from bucolic wonderland to a close encounter of the hyped kind. Progress has its price, and the bargain struck by the Lake of the Ozarks included trading a bucket of tradition for a barrel of tourism.

But beauty is in the eye. For many, the lake—which covers 57,000 acres and includes 1,375 miles of shoreline—is known as the Midwest Coast. The entire area is a cross between upscale trendy and downscale day trip, with only a lingering hint of the old-time Ozarks remaining. Nationally regarded golf courses, luxurious resorts, and restaurants with $500 bottles of wine share space with go-cart tracks, burger joints, water parks, and T-shirt shacks. The pace (as well as the shopping possibilities) is literally nonstop. Boats by the thousands cruise the 129-mile main channel and its tributaries, and those seeking an outdoor vacation with an urban flair will not be disappointed.

The Lake of the Ozarks originally sought to distance itself from its locale. Union Electric Light and Power of St. Louis, the firm that built Bagnell Dam, first called it the Osage Reservoir. In 1931, when the lake was bank-full, members of the Missouri Congress thought it deserved more respect. After all, at the time this was the largest human-made lake in the world. Their idea was to honor a famous (and long-dead) Missouri politician. For a brief time the Lake of the Ozarks was known as Lake Benton. Ad executives and promoters usually win the day in these matters, and by 1932 virtually every piece of ad copy to reach the public extolled the virtues of Lake of the Ozarks. It sounded better, in a *build-it-and-they-will-come* sort of way.

The history of the lake reaches back to the Osage Indians, who traditionally wintered in the area. French fur trappers may have been the first white residents (leading to communities such as Gravois Mills and Versailles), and Zebulon Pike and his gang of intrepid explorers passed close by. It is known that just after 1800 both Daniel Boone and his son Nathan trapped beaver on Ha Ha Tonka Lake. By the early 1800s white settlers were moving in, and in 1825 the Osage

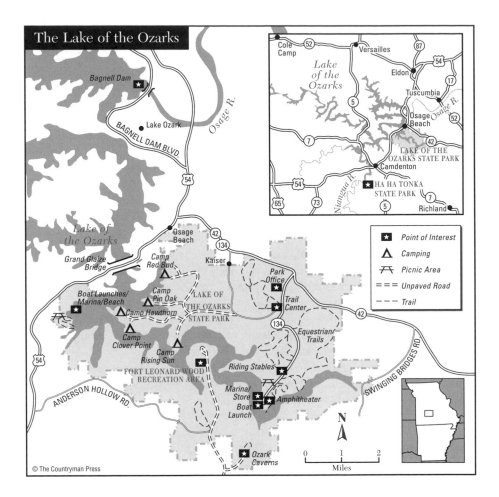

ceded all their lands and were moved west. Up until the early 1900s the lake region was just like the rest of the Ozarks. Those who settled here were fond of isolation and independence (though the majority were of German descent, in contrast with the Scots-Irish who adopted the Ozark lands to the south). The Civil War brought regional conflicts, Bushwhackers, and outlaws. People lived off the land, making the necessities themselves and making money from outside sources as required.

The idea of damming the Osage River, and by extension the tributaries of Gravois Creek, the Grand Auglaize River, and the Niangua River, came about shortly after the turn of the 20th century. When Union Electric picked up the reins of the project, the idea became a reality. Construction of Bagnell Dam began in 1929, privately financed to the tune of $30 million (the last privately financed dam in America). More than 20,000 workers flocked to the massive undertaking, hungry for the Depression-era jobs. Not so happy were those who lived in towns such as Linn Creek, which was to be inundated. Providing the luxury of electric lights to St. Louis city folks didn't strike the insular locals as a particularly rational or convincing reason for the bum's rush, but the end result was predictable. More than 500 Linn Creek residents were dislodged from the simple farmsteads they had treasured for generations (the government had given Union Electric the power to condemn homes and farms), 32 cemeteries were relocated, countless buildings were destroyed, and 30,000 acres of timber were cleared. Bagnell Dam, 2,500 feet long and 150 feet high, was completed in record time. By May 1931 there was boat traffic on the lake, and production of electricity began the following December.

Today, as mentioned, the production of power shares prominence with the tourist industry. The Lake of the Ozarks falls into the category of prepackaged fun in that you will not find any unpleasant surprises here. You can enjoy a fine meal, hear popular music, hire a guide, spend the day waterskiing, shop till you drop, and retire in a sumptuous suite featuring turndown service and chocolates on your pillow. The bad news is that such homogenized and utterly safe conformity makes for few happy surprises. I'm not saying it isn't fun; for millions the lake is the personification of a good time. I am saying it is fun in the amusement park fashion, with sensory overload and a predictable plot being a given.

After 75 years, natives of the predominantly rural Ozarks will still freely expound that the big lake and its environs don't reflect their heritage or lifestyle. In the geographic sense they are wrong, but in the cultural sense they could not be more on the money. Perhaps better stated, the lake region resides in a different type of Ozarks from that which "real" Ozarkers know and love.

AREA CODES The Lake of the Ozarks is a huge body of water, and if taken in its entirety (with connecting lakes and river tributaries to the north and west included) would encompass several area codes. All the towns and attractions covered in this chapter, however, are found in the **573** prefix.

GUIDANCE Long known as the Midwest's summer playground, the Lake of the Ozarks is adept at promoting its infinite recreational opportunities, events, and businesses. Six different chambers and visitors bureaus offer extensive web sites and will gladly answer questions and mail vacation guides.

Lake of the Ozarks Convention and Visitor Bureau (573-348-1599 or 1-800-FUN-LAKE; www.funlake.com), P.O. Box 1498, Osage Beach, Mo. 65065, This should be your first stop, as it will tell you everything you wanted to know about the Lake of the Ozarks but were afraid to ask. Contact the bureau via phone or web site and request its free guide, which runs more than 150 pages and is packed with details pertaining to lodging, dining, boating, golf, and area history.

Lake of the Ozarks West Chamber of Commerce (573-374-5500 or 1-877-227-4086; www.lakewestchamber.com), Lake Rd. 5-35, P.O. Box 340, Sunrise Beach, Mo. 65079. This chamber includes the towns of Gravois Mills, Laurie, Sunrise Beach, and Greenview. The visitors center can be found on SR 5 in Sunrise Beach.

Camdenton Chamber of Commerce (573-346-2227 or 1-800-769-1004; www .camdentonchamber.com), 611 N. SR 5, Ryland Center, Camdenton, Mo. Serving the communities of Camdenton and Linn Creek, the Camdenton Chamber also provides data on both the Big and Little Arms of the Niangua River.

Lake Area Chamber of Commerce (573-964-1008 or 1-800-451-4117; www .lakeareachamber.com), 1 Willmore Lane, Lake Ozark, Mo. Specializing in the east side of the lake, this chamber can provide you with details on Lake Ozark, Osage Beach, Horseshoe Bend, North Shore, Linn Creek, and Kaiser. It's located in the historic Willmore Lodge, just north of Bagnell Dam.

Eldon Chamber of Commerce (573-392-3752; www.eldonchamber.com), 203 E. First St., Eldon, Mo. To the north and east of the lake proper, Eldon offers a respite from the heaviest of the tourist traffic.

Versailles Chamber of Commerce (573-378-4401; www.versailleschamber .com), 101 N. Monroe, Versailles, Mo. Versailles is a historic town that predates the building of the lake. Its chamber can provide guidance on water activities, dining, and the local Mennonite community.

GETTING THERE *By auto:* Whether driving in from Springfield or St. Louis, the simplest way to the Lake of the Ozarks is via I-44. Take the 130 exit at Lebanon, Mo., and head north on SR 5 for 25 miles to Camdenton. From there, either continue on SR 5 to visit the western side of the lake or turn right onto US 54 to reach the eastern. If traveling from Kansas City, Mo., take I-70 E. to Columbia, Mo., and turn right onto US 63 S. At Jefferson City, Mo., turn onto US 54 S., which will take you directly to the lake.

By air: The closest major airports to the lake itself are **Lambert–St. Louis International Airport** (314-426-8000; www.lambert-stlouis.com), **Kansas City International** (816-243-3000; www.flykci.com), and **Springfield-Branson Regional Airport** (417-869-0300; www.sgf-branson-airport.com). Of these, the latter is the most convenient, only 75 miles southwest of Camdenton, Mo. However, the lake region does offer five commuter airports for those who might be arriving by small plane.

Lee C. Fine Airport (573-348-5251) offers an asphalt 6,500-by-100-foot runway. It is located on SR 134 in Osage Beach.

Grand Glaize Airport (573-348-4469) is also located in Osage Beach (at the intersection of US 54 and SR KK). Its asphalt runway is 3,205 by 60 feet.

Camdenton Memorial Airport (573-346-0300) is on SR 5 S. in Camdenton. The airport's asphalt runway is 4,000 by 75 feet.

Eldon Model Airpark (573-392-2291) is situated at the intersection of Airport Rd. and US 54 in Eldon. The runway is concrete and measures 3,330 by 75 feet.

Versailles Airport (573-378-6373) has a concrete runway of 2,800 by 40 feet. The address is 10998 SR 52 in Versailles.

MEDICAL EMERGENCIES **Lake Regional Hospital** (573-348-8000; www .lakeregional.com), 54 Hospital Dr., Osage Beach, Mo. Lake Regional is a

300,000-square-foot, 140-bed hospital offering comprehensive services such as cardiac, oncology, orthopedic, and OB-GYN. The facility is state of the art, with 75 doctors and more than 1,000 employees on staff. The Emergency Department is first-rate, having been designated a Level III Trauma Center by the Bureau of Emergency Medical Services, and the Lake Regional System provides services and clinic in 13 locations in surrounding counties.

✳ Wandering Around

EXPLORING BY CAR When you wish to escape the frenzy of the Osage Beach area and have a relaxing picnic, don't forget the "other dam" on the Lake of the Ozarks. **Tunnel Dam**, located 20 miles west of Camdenton, is 3 miles long and crosses the **Big Niangua River**. The drive to Tunnel Dam is outstanding, running through hills and deep forests, crossing low water and one-lane bridges. Many times you will find yourself on old gravel roads that will make you feel as if you've slipped 50 years back in time.

Take US 54 west out of Camdenton for 8.4 miles, to the junction of SR J and SR U. Turn left onto SR U, and then immediately turn right, heading 2.5 miles to Edith. Turn right onto Whistle Rd. (gravel), travel 1 mile, and cross the small bridge. This is **Tunnel Dam Road** (in local lingo, the area is known as "the Whistle"). You will probably find no better place for a picnic in the Lake of the Ozarks vicinity. The water is cool and clear, shallow enough that kids can wade and play to their heart's content. This is not a speedboat place (you'll understand when you see it), but it could be the ultimate spot to splash around in an inner tube, canoe, or kayak.

Past the Whistle, you can travel on up (and up, and up, and up) Tunnel Dam Rd. to the top of some very large hills. Make sure to stop and look around, for the scenic vista brings meaning to the term *photo opportunity*. You will be looking down on the dam and powerhouse, not to mention green-forested hills. This area has neither the urban pace nor the dining/dancing/shopping experiences prevalent on the Bagnell Dam strip, but it is one of the few places in the Lake of the Ozarks region that will remind you that you're in the Ozarks. This drive offers the perfect contrast between old and new, what is and what was.

EXPLORING BY FOOT **Colosseum Trail/Ha Ha Tonka State Park** (573-346-2986; www.mostateparks .com/hahatonka.htm), 1491 SR D, Camdenton, Mo. If you want a relatively short hike (0.5 mile) with splendid sights, Colosseum Trail will

TUNNEL DAM

THE "WHISTLE"

gladly fill the bill. Beginning at the Natural Bridge parking lot, you will pass underneath the 70-foot-wide, 60-foot-long, 100-foot-high natural bridge. Continue following the trail and you may venture to the Colosseum, a sinkhole 500 feet long and 300 feet wide. The history and legend behind this area is unsurpassed. Within the Colosseum is Whispering Dell Sink—more than 150 foot deep—and both Counterfeiter's and Robber's Caves. These shelters were used by outlaws in the 1830s (true to the name, one of the caves held the printing press of a gang of counterfeiters). It should be noted that while parts of the Colosseum Trail are ranked as moderately difficult, the trek down Whispering Dell Sink to the spring should only be attempted by those in very good shape. There are more than 300 steep wooden steps, enough to test the calves, knees, and lungs of seasoned hikers (it about killed me).

EXPLORING BY WATER The Missouri Department of Natural Resources came up with a novel twist when it floated the idea (pun intended) of creating the **Aquatic Trail** at **Lake of the Ozarks State Park**. It's a 9-mile trek (requiring about 2 hours) running between Grand Glaize Beach on the northwest and Public Beach #1 at the lake's east end. A total of 14 stops, each brightly marked with an orange and white buoy, highlight unique geological features, plant life, shelters used by Indians, caves, and glades. One of the best sights is the **Lumberman's Logging Chute**. Before the lake was created (covering Grand Glaize Creek), hill residents often made money by hand cutting railroad ties and floating them to market. The bluff shown on the tour is where—well over a century ago—these pioneers pushed the ties down into the creek's current. You'll need to bring a boat (or rent one) to take this trip, but a detailed map and booklet of the tour is available at the park office (573-348-2694).

Camdenton, Mo. Camdenton is one of the newest county seats in the state of Missouri, established in 1931. When Union Electric Light and Power Company of St. Louis dammed the Osage River, the body of water held captive by Bagnell Dam forced the relocation of more than a few towns. One of these was Linn Creek, the original Camden County seat. Some residents moved to a "new" Linn Creek while others moved to the freshly minted Camdenton, being platted at the intersections of SR 5 and US 54. Camdenton is home to Bridal Cave, which holds the world's record for most underground weddings (to my knowledge there are no records kept for underground divorces). During the third week of April the famous Dogwood Festival brings visitors from around the world. Just a few miles outside town you'll find the not-to-be-missed Ha Ha Tonka State Park, and the ruins of what was to have been the opulent 20th-century castle and estate of a wealthy Kansas City businessman.

Gravois Mills, Mo. Before the town was platted in 1884, early Missourians had congregated around a local gristmill (built in approximately 1835). These days the economy of this village of roughly 200 souls centers on the lake. As is true with its neighbor up the road (Versailles), Gravois Mills steers clear of the fancy-sounding French pronunciation (the local name is pronounced *grav-OYS* or sometimes *grav-OY*). A few miles north of Gravois Mills is Jacob's Cave. The largest commercialized cave in the lake area, Jacob's boasts of possessing the world's largest geode. It's also the only walk-through cave in Missouri completely accessible to the disabled.

Lake Ozark, Mo. Located on what locals often call the "St. Louis side of the lake," Lake Ozark will never be accused of ignoring the tourists. It's a cornucopia of T-shirt joints, arcades, psychics, tattoo parlors, boutiques, restaurants, and shops, not to mention high-end resorts, homes, golf courses, and condos. This first mile or so of US 54 (south of Bagnell Dam) is referred to as "the Strip," and those seeking go-cart rides (a novelty here are "bumper boats"—basically motorized inner tubes) or ashtrays boasting Hillbilly caricatures won't be disappointed. Neither, however, will those seeking world-class dining or in-hotel Pilates classes. Bagnell Dam Blvd. (US Bus. 54) turns off US 54 and winds into the aforementioned upscale district of eating and lodging. Because the Lake of the Ozarks was privately financed (not an Army Corps of Engineers lake, as are most in the Ozarks), homes can be built right down to the waterfront. Many visitors love Lake Ozark, which offers the traditional tourist venues and infinite preplanned vacation packages. Two events are truly noteworthy. Eagle Days takes place in early January, and thousands come to view the bald eagles that winter around the lake. On the third weekend of September, the three-day Annual Osage Mountain Man Rendezvous is a fantastic chance to see buckskin-clad latter-day Jeremiah Johnsons test their frontier skills.

Laurie, Mo. The town of Laurie didn't officially come into existence until after the state began construction of SR 5 in the mid-1920s, at which time area residents built a general store, gas station, and church (*Laurie* was the surname of the store's original owners). Though today it is full of resorts, marinas, restaurants, and stores, Laurie still manages to hold on to its unique and friendly personality.

A worthwhile stop in Laurie is St. Patrick's Church, Cemetery, and Museum, which dates from 1868. Also, mid-September brings the annual Hillbilly Fair, featuring carnival rides, music, food, a beer garden, and a Hillbilly dress contest.

Osage Beach, Mo. Immediately south of Lake Ozark on US 54 is Osage Beach, the tourism epicenter for the Lake of the Ozarks. The community stretches for 8 miles, a testament to consumerism on steroids. You'll find malls and shops of all shapes, creeds, colors, and descriptions. The largest of these is the Osage Beach Premium Outlet, which alone holds 110 top-name manufacturers. You'll also find more golf courses, resorts, restaurants, and nightclubs than you can shake a platinum card at, and each year the options seem to become larger and more luxurious. The majority of these venues are well planned and well staffed, offering fine fare and anything your heart desires. Osage Beach is the main entry to the massive Lake of the Ozarks State Park. As well, the powers that be hold numerous festivals and regionally oriented extravaganzas. In early June the Midwestcoast Summerfest offers bands, a BMX bicycle stunt team, and more than 100 competing wakeboarders.

Versailles, Mo. The Morgan County seat, Versailles was named for either (a) the palace in France or (b) a town in Kentucky. Conventional wisdom points to the latter, and those who insist upon pronouncing the town as *ver-SIGH* will immediately be pegged as pretentious tourists. The name is *ver-SALES*. With a population of 2,565, Versailles is an old town (platted in 1835) that seems a laidback rural contrast to the hectic and increasingly upscale west side of the lake. Numerous Mennonite farms are located in the surrounding area, and drivers should be aware of horse-drawn buggies traveling down the road. Versailles is also the home of the Morgan County Museum, a pre–Civil War hotel that allegedly played host to the likes of Jesse James (one of the 10,000 places Jesse slept) and P. T. Barnum. Not to be outdone in terms of townwide celebrations, the Old Tyme Apple Festival begins the first Saturday of each October.

✳ To See

MUSEUMS 🕯 ⌀ ♿ **Old St. Patrick's Church, Cemetery, and Museum** (573-374-6279; www.mothersshrine.org), 176 Marian Dr., Laurie, Mo. French traders were the first non-Native people to settle in this area, and by 1822 several of the Osage chiefs had converted to Catholicism (in large part because the first priest allowed the Indians to inject aspects of their culture into traditional rituals). The original St. Patrick's Church was completed in 1868, and much of the original look and feel remain intact. Thanks to a massive renovation, St. Pat's was placed on the National Register of Historic Places in 1979. Inside the church is a museum that was once the living quarters of the circuit-riding priest. Tours of the church and grounds take place 10–noon each Sunday, Memorial Day–Labor Day.

🕯 ⌀ ♿ **Mother's Wall of Life** (573-374-6279; www.mothersshrine.org), 176 Marian Dr., Laurie, Mo. Open to the public 24 hours a day. Paying tribute to all mothers and the Virgin Mary, this shrine features 25,000 flowers, a waterfall, fountains, and a 14-foot-tall stainless-steel rendition of Mary. A black granite wall contains the inscribed names of more than 2,300 mothers (the first person to place his mother's name on the wall was the late Pope John Paul II), and 102 flags set off this 80 acres of peace and tranquillity. At Christmas thousands of lights replace the flowers. Anyone can have a name inscribed on the shrine—all that is required is that you have a mother and $325.

THE MOTHER'S WALL OF LIFE

🌸 ✐ **Camden County Museum** (573-346-7191), Linn Creek, Mo. Apr.–Oct., open Mon.–Fri. 10–4; open on a limited basis Nov.–Mar. The Camden County Museum can be found on SR V (just off US 54) in Linn Creek, the former county seat that was relocated upon the construction of Bagnell Dam. The building is in fact the old Linn Creek school, and each classroom revolves around a different historical theme. One of the best exhibits is the weaving room, where local residents weave rugs that are available for purchase.

🌸 ✐ **Miller County Museum** (573-793-6998), Tuscumbia, Mo. Open mid-May–mid-Sep., Mon., Wed., and Fri. 10–4. This museum is of the "folk life" variety and contains all sorts of antique machinery and crafts. Its main focus is to offer a glimpse into the Miller County lifestyle of yesteryear, and it also concentrates on the area's Indian heritage. Located on W. SR 52 outside Tuscumbia, the museum is situated in the old Anchor Mill building.

🌸 ✐ **Morgan County Historical Museum** (573-378-5530), 120 N. Monroe St., Versailles, Mo. Open Tue.–Fri. noon–5, Sat. 9–noon. The best-known landmark in Versailles is the Martin Hotel, which predates the Civil War and was regularly used by troops of both sides (legend has it that both Old Glory and the Stars and Bars were on the hotel's flagpole, depending upon who was in residence). Now the home of the Morgan County Historical Museum, the hotel's 28 rooms have each been decorated with a different historical theme. When walking into the main lobby, be sure to note the eight-day Seth Thomas wall clock, as well as the original hotel desk.

HISTORIC SITES 🌸 ✐ ♿ **Willmore Lodge** (573-964-1008 or 1-800-451-4117; www.willmorelodge.com), 1 Willmore Lane, Lake Ozark, Mo. Open year-round, Mon.–Sat., this onetime lodge is home to the Lake Area Chamber Visitor Center and Museum. Upon its completion in 1930 it was known as Egan Lodge, allegedly an administrative building named for the president of Union Electric. Of course, things are not

MORGAN COUNTY HISTORICAL MUSEUM

always as they seem, and the 6,500-square-foot, 29-room Adirondack log building included an oil-burning furnace, the 1930 version of an air conditioner, a huge kitchen, servant quarters, a bar with an ice-making machine, and a primitive intercom system wired to each guest room. In other words, it was a party pad.

There was a scandal involved with the Egan Lodge (what a surprise), and in 1945 the lodge was sold to Cyrus Willmore, a prominent St. Louis developer who saw that the lake was going to be a major destination for wealthy St. Louisans. He paid $320,000 for not just the lodge but also a Union Electric–owned hotel, pleasure boats, 40,000 acres of lakefront property, and 800 miles of shoreline. Union Electric reacquired the building and adjoining property in 1996, purchasing the lodge and 30 acres of undeveloped shorefront property for $1.06 million. During that same year Union Electric offered use of the building—now listed on the National Register of Historic Places—to the Lake Area Chamber of Commerce for its offices, a visitors center, and a museum of lake history.

The swinging bridges. Between the late 1800s and the 1930s more than two dozen swinging bridges were built in the Lake of the Ozarks region. Although most of these are long since gone, either succumbing to time or disappearing beneath the waters of the lake, a couple of examples still exist near the little town of Brumley. Locals still drive over these bridges, but both appear as if they could collapse in a strong wind. The smaller, metal-floored bridge has holes and cracks. The wood-planked bridge crossing Auglaize Creek has many loose boards that bounce and squeal. (If you're walking across it, watch for gaps between the old boards. You could easily break a leg or ankle if you're not careful.)

From Osage Beach, take SR 42 for 11 miles to the southeast. If you go past the CITY LIMITS sign, you've gone too far—the turnoff is just before the sign. Take a left onto Swinging Bridges Rd., and you will soon come to the smaller of the swinging bridges, now part of the Lake of the Ozarks State Park. Cross over, take a right, and you will be met by the 400-foot plank bridge. It was built in 1930 by Union Electric after the waters backed up by Bagnell Dam covered the roads. There are few better picnic spots than along the banks of this creek (the fishing is pretty good when the water is up), and fires are allowed in specified areas. Also, camping is permitted (an honor box on a post will accept the small charge), and there are outdoor rest rooms on-site.

BRUMLEY SWINGING BRIDGE

✳ To Do

GOLF Golf has always been a drawing card at the Lake of the Ozarks, but over the past 10 or 15 years the region has gone crazy over the addictive allure inherent in whacking the little white ball. With all the waterfront resorts, amenities, and championship courses from which to choose, you might think you took the wrong exit at St. Louis and wandered down to south

DAMMED IF YOU DO, DAMMED IF YOU DON'T

The Great Osage River Project, started in 1929, provided jobs for thousands during the Great Depression. The price tag was $30 million (a heap of coin in modern terms, a fortune of inconceivable proportions in Depression-era economics), and Bagnell was the last and largest major dam to be built in the United States entirely with private capital. It's 2,543 feet long and supports a 20-foot-wide roadway (about wide enough for two Model Ts) and 3-foot-wide sidewalk. The power station is 511 feet long; the flood-control spillway section, 520 feet. The power plant produces 215,000 kilowatts. Most of this juice goes to eastern Missouri, particularly the St. Louis area. The dam was what led to the creation of the Lake of the Ozarks, which covers 57,000 acres, stretches 92 miles, and encompasses more coastline than the state of California (1,375 miles). For further historical information, or to inquire about scenic overlooks or tour possibilities of Bagnell, stop by the Lake Area Chamber Visitor Center and Museum at the Willmore Lodge.

BAGNELL DAM IS 2,543 FEET LONG

Florida. More than 15 golf clubs, with designs by the likes of Robert Trent Jones, Arnold Palmer, and Tom Weiskopf, make the lake region a golfer's paradise.

The rates provided here are for greens fee, cart, and a round of 18 holes and represent weekday and weekend costs in-season. In most cases off-season rates run $10–15 less per round. Also, many of the lake's hotels and resorts provide "golf-a-round" packages via which you can sample a variety of area links. The most comprehensive list of participating resorts (which also provides details on each particular course) can be found at **www.golfingmissouri.com**. Most courses accept reservations for tee times far in advance of daily play (and tee time reservations are recommended).

Bay View Golf Club (573-346-6617), 32 Sylvan Bay, Linn Creek, Mo. Open since 1991, Bayview is a nine-hole, par-35 public course overlooking the lake. Open year-round; tee times are advised but not mandatory. $30–35.

Bear Creek Valley Golf Club (573-302-1000; www.bearcreekvalley.com), 910 SR 42, Lake Ozark, Mo. Bear Creek opened in 2001 and is known for its beautiful scenery. An 18-hole, par-72 public course, its facilities include a full-service bar and restaurant. $45–49.

The Golf Club at Deer Chase (573-346-6117; www.deerchasegolf.com), 770 Deer Chase Rd., Linn Creek, Mo. Deer Chase is an 18-hole, par-71 public course that is open year-round. Both duffers and experienced golfers will appreciate the scenery, as the fairways wind through the hills surrounding the Auxglaize River Valley. $36–42.

Dogwood Hills Golf Club (573-348-3153; www.dogwoodhillsresort.com), 1252 SR KK, Osage Beach, Mo. One of the original courses in the region, Dogwood Hills has been around since 1962. Open year-round, this 18-hole, par-70 public course (part of the Dogwood Hills Resort Inn) is a local favorite. $32–49.

Eldon Country Club (573-392-4172; www.eldoncc.com), 35 Golf Course Rd., Eldon, Mo. Heading north from Osage Beach on US 54, you will come to the small town of Eldon. Here, the Eldon Country Club features an 18-hole, par-70 semiprivate course. In 2001 the zoysia fairways and bunker system were upgraded. For $35–38 per round, this course offers fewer crowds and a good value.

Indian Rock Golf Club (573-372-3023; www.indianrockgolf.com), 100 Indian Lake Ave., Gravois Mills, Mo. Hole 17 at Indian Rock, a par 3, is known for a deep lake in front and a large rock outcrop in the rear. The 18-hole, par-72 semiprivate course is set among the homes that are a part of this golf/retirement community.

Lake Valley Country Club (573-346-7218; www.lakevalleygolf.com), Lake Rd. 54-79, Camdenton, Mo. With six par 3s, six par 4s, and six par 5s, Lake Valley features large and fast greens. Open year-round, the course is an 18-hole, par-72 challenge. Greens fees are $56 for both weekdays and weekends.

Lodge of the Four Seasons (573-365-3000; www.4seasonsresort.com), 3.0 miles down SR HH (Horseshoe Bend Pkwy.) off US Bus 54, Lake Ozark, Mo. One of the most prestigious resorts at the Lake of the Ozarks, the Lodge of the Four Seasons has long been known for its golf possibilities. The 18-hole, par-71 **Witch's Cove** course was built in 1971 and was designed by Robert Trent Jones. In 1996 *Golf Digest* rated it as the second best public course in Missouri. $69–79.

The **Seasons Ridge** course opened in 1991 and consists of 18 holes at par 72. In 1996 *Golf Digest* ranked it as one of Missouri's top 10. As is true with the courses at the Four Seasons, scenic features such as rock outcrops, spring-fed lakes, and considerable elevation changes are a given. $60–79.

For seriously devoted golf aficionados (with deep pockets), Four Seasons offers the **Private Quarter's Club**, a luxury villa time-share option that includes membership at the **Club at Porta Cima Jack Nicholas Signature Course**.

Old Kinderhook (573-346-4444; www.oldkinderhook.com), SR 54-80, Camdenton, Mo. The 18-hole, par-71 semiprivate Tom Weiskopf course is nicely set off by rolling fairways, flowering trees, and rock waterfalls. $65–75.

Osage National Golf Club (573-365-1950 or 1-866-365-1950; www.osage national.com), 400 Osage Hills Rd., Lake Ozark, Mo. The original 18 holes at Osage National were designed in 1992 by golfing legend Arnold Palmer. Since then another 9 holes have been added, leading to a wide variety of play (three different 18-hole combinations, all of which are par 72 and public). The motto of Osage National is "The must-play course at the lake." $68–78.

Rolling Hills Country Club (573-378-5109; www.golfrollinghillscc.com), 13986 Country Club Rd., Versailles, Mo. The oldest course in the lake area, Rolling Hills was established in 1957. A member-owned course, it is far enough away from the lake proper to allow a sense of quiet and tranquillity. The 18-hole, par-71 Rolling Hills is open year-round and costs a mere $42 (weekends and weekdays).

Sycamore Creek Golf Club (573-348-9593; www.sycamorecreekgolfclub.com), 1270 Nichols Rd., Osage Beach, Mo. Sycamore Creek may be the only golf course in the United States that is built around an operating fish hatchery. It is an 18-hole, par-72 public course known for exquisitely manicured greens and fairways. According to surveys by local media, Sycamore Creek has been the favorite of area residents for the past 7 years. See the fish and whack the ball for $42–45.

Tan-Tar-A (573-348-8522; www.tan-tar-a.com), SR KK, Osage Beach, Mo. Tan-Tar-A (along with Lodge of the Four Seasons) is arguably the most famous resort at the Lake of the Ozarks. **The Oaks** course, a public, 18-hole par 71, features water hazards on 11 holes and more than 60 white-sand bunkers. This was the site for the 1994 PGA Club Pro Championship, and fees are $59–79. The nine-hole, par-35 **Hidden Lakes** course is also part of Tan-Tar-A's offerings. Play 9 holes for $29, or 18 holes for $39.

✳ Wild Places

PARKS 🐾 ✐ ⅙ ✳ **Lake of the Ozarks State Park** (573-348-2694; marina 573-348-1233; stables 573-348-2694; www.mostateparks.com/lakeozark.htm), P.O. Box 170, Kaiser, Mo. 65047. Open from sunrise to half an hour after sunset. The park office is open Mon.–Fri. 8–4:30; the visitors center, daily 9–5 Apr.–Oct. With 17,441 acres and 85 miles of shoreline, Lake of the Ozarks is the largest state park in Missouri. Though the main roads can become very crowded in summer (as can side roads), its size alone makes it a fine respite from the nonstop pace of the area's commercial frenzy. There are 10 different trails stretching a total of 23 miles, all of which are open to hikers. Backpackers are permitted on the **Woodland Trail**, all-terrain bicycling is popular on **Trail of the Four Winds**, and horseback riding is allowed on both Four Winds and **Squaw's Revenge Trail**.

THE SNYDER CASTLE RUINS AT HA HA TONKA STATE PARK

LAUGHING WATERS GET THE LAST LAUGH

🐾 🦮 ♿ ❄ **Ha Ha Tonka State Park** (573-346-2986; www.mostateparks.com/
hahatonka.htm), 1491 SR D, Camdenton, Mo. Nov.–Mar., open at 8 AM; Apr.–
Oct., open at 9 AM. Park gates are closed at sunset. Park office is open
Mon.–Fri. 8:30–3 in winter; 9–5, summer. The visitors center area is open
8–sunset. Ha Ha Tonka was proposed as Missouri's first state park in 1909.
Government moves slowly, and 69 years later that proposal became reality.
This is one of the most unusual parks not only in the Ozarks, but in the entire
United States. It's in keeping with the odd history of the place that it's not
better known. Full of caves, springs, sinkholes, natural bridges, springs, and
creeks, Ha Ha Tonka even features its own haunted castle.

The name is said to mean "laughing waters," although the etymology is
fairly dubious. Somehow it seems an inside settlers' joke that the Osage
Indians would use the phrase *ha ha* for laughter. No matter; it does seem
true that the Osage used the huge open areas and natural amphitheaters
(the result of collapsed cave systems) as meeting places. There is no doubt
at all that Daniel Boone and son Nathan trapped here around 1801, or that
Meriwether Lewis wrote to Thomas Jefferson of the spot in 1805, or that the
area was a favorite of a notorious band of counterfeiters and robbers in the
1830s (who minted fake Mexican dollars in one of the caves).

But what most people want to know about is the castle. Wealthy
Kansas City businessman Robert Snyder was enamored with the area,
which he first encountered on a 1903 hunting trip. Buying up 2,500 acres (in

60 different tracts), he imported stonemasons from Scotland and began work on a 9,000-square-foot castle (not including stable houses, greenhouses, or the 80-foot water tower). Alas, Snyder would never see the structure completed. He was not only one of the first auto owners in Kansas City, but also one of the first people killed in an auto accident in Kansas City. Sometimes being a trendsetter is painful, and by 1906 Robert Snyder had shed this mortal coil.

Snyder's sons finished the castle, though not with the grandeur their father intended, and used it as a summer home. When Bagnell Dam was built by Union Electric in 1931, the lake waters backed into the Niangua River's spring branch and flooded some of the most beautiful parts of Ha Ha Tonka. The sons sued the power company; after a long fight, Union Electric eventually settled out of court.

The Snyder boys used the castle less and less; eventually, as changing times and the Great Depression shrank the family fortune, they leased it out as a hotel. It was supposedly unburnable, and yet, in 1942, the wooden shingles caught on fire and the entire interior was gutted by flame. Over the next 35 years numerous private owners acquired the property. Most had great designs for commercial success, with success remaining consistently elusive. In 1978 the state of Missouri acquired the land. Thanks to a grant from the Federal Land and Water Conservation Fund, and the desire of the 1978 owners to acquire a tax write-off on a white-elephant property, the sale price of Ha Ha Tonka was only $160,000. Ironically, that was the exact same amount Governor Herbert Hadley had requested that the 1909 legislature provide for the acquisition (the expenditure failed to carry by a single vote).

VIEW FROM SNYDER CASTLE

Now consisting of more than 3,600 acres, Ha Ha Tonka offers a number of trails, courtesy docks for those who arrive by boat, picnic areas, and a deep and mysterious spring that spews out 49 million gallons of water per day. It's a beautiful place, full of wonders uncounted, a Hearst-like monument to fleeting wealth, and the only partially quiet ghosts of Indians, trappers, heroes, villains, and time.

Within the park are 230 campsites (ranging from the primitive to those with electric hookups) and eight rustic cabins. Also, guided cave tours are available at the wheelchair-accessible **Ozark Caverns**, which features the well-known Angels Showers. This formation, a combination of stalactites and waterfalls that drip into a natural basin, is a visitor favorite. Two swimming beaches are provided (Public Beach #1 is the most popular with locals and tourists alike), and marinas feature boat rentals.

Perhaps among the most unusual aspects of this park are the **Ozark Homestead Stables**, open daily from 9 AM till just before sunset. Both experts and novices can rent horses that suit their fancy; 1-hour, 2½-hour, and all-day rides, as well as pony rides, are offered. All are staff guided, and reservations are strongly suggested. The stables also give lessons, and by special arrangement will set up hayrides and overnight trips.

CAVES ✄ ☃ **Jacob's Cave** (573-378-4374; www.jacobscave.com), 23114 SR TT, Versailles, Mo. Located between Versailles and Gravois Mills on SR TT (off SR 5), the cave is open 9–5 from Memorial Day to Labor Day, 9–4 the rest of the year. $10 adults, $5 ages 4–12. Open to the public in 1932, Jacob's Cave was the first "show cave" at the Lake of the Ozarks. Taking the guided tour through the cavern (which holds a constant temperature of 53 degrees), you'll find pools, the obligatory stalactite columns and "soda straw" formations, the bones of mastodons and bears, and the much-advertised "world's largest geode." Also within the operation is a large rock shop where you can purchase any number of souvenirs or pieces of handcrafted silver jewelry.

∞ ✄ ☃ ❄ **Bridal Cave** (573-346-2676; www.bridalcave.com), 526 Bridal Cave Rd., Camdenton, Mo. Winter, 9–4; spring and fall, 9–5; summer, 9–6. $13.50 adults, $6.50 ages 5–12. The Lake of the Ozarks's answer to the wedding chapels of Las Vegas has to be Bridal Cave, located just north of Camdenton, Mo., on SR 5 and open to the public since 1948. To date close to 2,000 weddings have been performed in the underground bridal chapel. Two different packages are offered for the prospective bride and groom ($400 and $550), and both come standard with minister, recorded pipe-organ music, and of course a lifetime pass to the cave for the happy couple. Other options are available, and those wishing to get hitched in subterranean style may call the wedding reservations department at 573-346-2676. On the other hand, you aren't required to pledge undying love in order to experience the formations and interesting lake here: Tours leave every few minutes. On the surface are a 2,400-square-foot rock and gift shop, snack center, nature trails, and a boat dock (you can reach Bridal Cave by water; just dock up at mile marker 10 on the Big Niangua River).

✄ ☃ **Ozark Caverns** (see Lake of the Ozarks State Park, above).

❋ Lodging

If you're looking for a place to stay at the Lake of the Ozarks, you'll have plenty of options. In the immediate vicinity (I'm not counting outlying areas here) you'll discover more than 20 bed & breakfasts, 28 campgrounds and RV parks containing more than 1,500 campsites, and 165 resorts, condos, and motels. In addition, there are 26 marinas, many of which offer boat rentals—and one featuring houseboat rental. However, the plethora of choices does not mean you can safely wait till the last minute to make your decision. The lake is a very busy place between Memorial Day and Labor Day, and the wise traveler books a reservation early. This is particularly important in regard to the larger, upscale resorts, which have traditionally enjoyed a huge amount of repeat business. Keep in mind that the lake is the preferred summer weekend escape of St. Louis residents (only a couple of hours away), and they flock in droves to their favored spots.

The selections provided are intended to represent the western, northern, and eastern (Osage Beach) sections of the lake and are establishments offering something a bit above and beyond (golf courses, marinas with boat rental, restaurants and lounges on-site, or full handicapped access). Prices are per night and reflect summer rates. Most of these operations are open year-round, and off-season rates are considerably less.

BED & BREAKFASTS **Bass and Baskets Bed and Breakfast** (573-964-5028; www.bassandbaskets.com), 269 Dogwood Rd., Lake Ozark, Mo. Ed Franko is happily addicted to bass fishing. His wife, Debbie, both collects and sells **Longaberger Baskets**. Integrating their hobbies into the decor of their home, in 2001 the Frankos opened Bass and Baskets Bed and Breakfast (try saying that five times). From a boat hanging from the ceiling to fishing lures to family portraits to Debbie's mother's wedding dress, personal touches are everywhere. Each

of four guest rooms comes with a Jacuzzi tub, fireplace, TV, and VCR, not to mention views of the lake. A full breakfast is served each morning. As is true with the majority of B&Bs these days, smoking, pets, and young children are not permitted. Prices range $129–149 per night for both single and double occupancy.

Blackhawk Inn (573-365-3800; www.blackhawkinn.com), 25 Blackhawk Estates, Lake Ozark, Mo. According to the prestigious *Missouri Life* magazine, "Blackhawk Inn is so much more than a bed and breakfast. Really, it is a resort and breakfast." Many who have spent a few days at the 5,500-square-foot home, situated atop a bluff looking out over the lake, seem to agree. A three-level home with three outdoor decks, Blackhawk features five suites, all with private bath and lakeside views from a private balcony. Some include fireplace and TV/VCR, and a large hot tub is available on the main deck. Kids, pets, and smoking are not allowed. Rates run $125–165 per night.

3 B's Bed and Breakfast (573-346-9822 or 1-877-346-9822; www.3bs.org), 75 Sylvan Bay Dr., Linn Creek, Mo. Those who enjoy a golf vacation but prefer a bit more peace and quiet than is provided by the big resorts will like 3B's. This is a relatively new and modern home located on the seventh hole of the Bayview Golf Club, with all three suites coming complete with cable TV, VCR, fireplace, private bath, and whirlpool tub. Rates run $102–119 per night, and smoking, pets, and children under 12 are not permitted.

Buck Creek Bed and Breakfast (573-372-1212; www.buckcreekbb.com), 32907 Buck Creek Acres Rd., Gravois Mills, Mo. Over on the quiet side of the lake in Gravois Mill, Buck Creek is a peaceful B&B with a great front porch. Breakfast is a major attraction here, and though the menu varies, guests can count on homemade biscuits and gravy, eggs and sausage, fruit, and homemade pastries. Four guest rooms, most warm and homey with dark paneling and plush carpet, run $70–120 per night, making it one of the better values on the lake. Buck Creek does not allow smoking, alcohol, or pets.

Castleview Bed and Breakfast (573-346-9818 or 1-877-346-9818; www.lakelinks.com/castleview), SR D, Camdenton, Mo. Though most B&Bs tend to name their individual suites, Castleview's truly reflect the intended theme (the Hunter, the Sweetheart, the New Orleans, and the Vintage). All in all, this is the type of enterprise that allows you to feel at home. Best of all, this informal retreat is right next to Ha Ha Tonka State Park. The home's large living room features a fireplace, cable TV, and stereo, and all rooms include private bath, satellite TV, ceiling fan, and queen-sized bed. Smoking, kids under 12, and pets are not permitted (there is a resident dog named Max). $104–109. Castleview also offers a number of specials, a corporate rate, and a military rate.

Cliff House Inn (573-348-9726; www.lakecliffhouse.com), 2183 Carlson Ct., Osage Beach, Mo. You begin your day at Cliff House (which does sit high on a cliff; no false advertising here) with a full breakfast delivered to your room. Next, you look out over the main channel of the lake from your private deck. Serving visitors for over a decade, the B&B's landscaping is extensive, featuring flowers, trees, a goldfish pond, and a gazebo (with hot

tub). The four guest suites come complete with cable TV, CD player, clock radio, hair dryer, iron, and ironing board. Rates are $145–160 per night, and weekends and holidays require a two-night minimum. A popular lodging choice at Cliff House is the Garden House. With its fireplace and Queen Anne canopy bed, and located just a few steps from the outdoor hot tub, this is a favorite for a romantic weekend. The normal restrictions apply as to smoking, kids, and pets.

⋈ ♞ ♣ ♬ & **Inn at Harbour Ridge** (573-302-0411 or 1-877-744-6020; www.harbourridgeinn.com), 6334 Red Barn Rd. and SR KK, Osage Beach, Mo. Built in 1999, Harbour Ridge is designed for couples of any age. The romantic getaway is the house specialty (you can even get married, with up to 25 guests in attendance, at the wedding gazebo), and the innkeepers thrive on filling personal requests. They are more than happy to pick up flowers or champagne for your room, set your tee time for golf, or assist in discovering any of myriad lake activities. Four guest rooms are rented at $129–189 per night. The Inn at Harbour Ridge will accept kids and pets, but accommodations are limited. Pets must be crated and not left alone in rooms (there is a $50 deposit and $10-per-night fee) and leashed when in common areas. Kids do not need their own crate, though it would best if they were older and housebroken. You'd be wise to call ahead and discuss the matter with the innkeepers prior to making a reservation.

HOUSEBOATS Lake of the Ozarks Marina (573-873-3705 or 1-800-255-5561; www.lakeoftheozarksmarina .com), SR 5 N., Camdenton, Mo. You needn't stay in a resort, hotel, or B&B when visiting the Lake of the Ozarks. If you have a large family or group of friends, you can spend your entire vacation on the water. Lake of the Ozarks Marina rents houseboats ranging in length from 56 to 65 feet, sleeping 10 to 12. These luxurious cruisers come complete with everything from electronics (both personal and aquatic) to sheets, silverware, dishware, gas grills, microwaves, and much, much more. The 65-foot version has a large living area with ceiling fan, dining table and chairs, breakfast counter, fully equipped kitchen, and deluxe gas grill. There are five queen-sized beds and four large bedrooms, wet bar, sun canopy, hot tub, and two full baths. Rates vary from $1,195 (for a three-day weekend on a 56-foot boat off-season) to $5,695 (a full week on a 65-footer during the height of summer season).

RESORTS AND LODGES

Lake of the Ozarks West

🐟 🛥 ♿ ❄ **Lakeview Resort** (573-374-5555 or 1-800-936-5655; www.lakeview-resort.com), HCR 69, Box 505-L5, Sunrise Beach, Mo. It's fitting that a family-oriented resort is still owned by the family who founded it. St. Louis butcher Jake Drake first saw the Lake of the Ozarks in 1946. Today Lakeview, with its three peninsulas and more than a mile of shoreline, is owned and operated by son Dan and grandson Jake Jr. The resort offers 75 cottages or condos, containing one to eight bedrooms, priced in the $95–235 range. The only things you need to bring are towels and any special cooking gear (blenders, food processors, and such). Otherwise, all accommodations are fully equipped. On-site are indoor and outdoor swimming pools, swim docks, pebble beaches, a boat ramp, covered docks, tennis courts, a Laundromat, and a marina with boat rentals. The only thing you can't bring to Lakeview are pets.

🐟 🐾 🛥 **Rock Harbor Resort** (573-374-5586 or 1-877-203-4186; www.rockharborresort.com), 973 Rock Harbor Rd., Sunrise Beach, Mo. Located in a quiet cove, Rock Harbor is another family-owned and family-operated establishment with one-, two-, three-, and four-bedroom units. The choices range from a simple motel room to cottages, duplexes, and fourplexes. With the exception of the motel rooms, all accommodations come with living and dining area and furnished kitchen, and both daily and weekly rates are available ($65–220 per night; $455–1,540 per week). Pets are accepted here with prior approval and an extra fee, but the resort really prefers you leave Fido or Lassie in a kennel or with friends. Activities are plentiful, with a pool, playground, launch ramp, and boat rentals. A canoe or a fishing boat (without motor) go for $20 per day. A fishing boat with a 9.9-horsepower motor is $45 per hour, a bass boat with a 30-horsepower motor is $70 per hour, and pontoon boats rent for $200–250 per hour, depending on size.

North Lake

🐟 🛥 🛥 ♿ ❄ 🍸 **Alhonna Resort** (573-365-2634; www.alhonna.com), 1237 Outer Dr., Lake Ozark, Mo. Those who enjoy boating will not be disappointed with Alhonna, built in the 1950s by Al and Honna Vilmin. The resort offers 25 different rentals, with choice of boats ranging 16–30 feet. Rates vary, with a 16-foot fishing boat renting for $50 for 2 hours, a 23-foot ski boat costing $115 for 2 hours, and a 30-foot pontoon boat going for $100 for 2 hours. Skis and ski tubes can also be rented. The resort, which started out as eight cabins with rustic knotty-pine interior, now boasts of 60 lake-front and lakeview units. There are motel rooms, deluxe four-bedroom condos, and even a private house, with prices stretching $65–257 per night. All accommodations (with the exception of the motel) are equipped with a BBQ grill and picnic table, basic kitchen supplies, microwave, coffeepot, and toaster. Small pets are accepted, with an extra charge of $7 per night and a $25 deposit. Other amenities include an indoor pool with sauna and hot tubs, a heated outdoor pool, and a full-service gas dock at the marina (which also sells bait and licenses).

Also at Alhonna is **Bobber's Restaurant and Lounge**, featuring breakfast and lunch daily (well under $10) and dinners served on Fri., Sat., and Sun. The Sunday breakfast buffet ($6.95) is of the all-you-can-eat genre.

✎ ⚕ ✳ ⅄ **The Resort at Port Arrowhead** (573-365-2334 or 1-800-532-3575; www.lakeoftheozarksgetaway.com), US Bus. 54 (2 miles south of Bagnell Dam), Lake Ozark, Mo. The Resort at Port Arrowhead went through a major renovation in 2002 and now features 207 rooms and suites, not to mention a full-service restaurant and lounge with live entertainment. It is as renowned for weekend vacations and family trips as it is for being a conference center. The facility includes two outdoor pools (one heated), one indoor pool, a children's wading pool with a waterfall, two hot tubs, miniature golf, seasonal supervised children's activities, a chil-

dren's playground, a fitness room, an arcade, shuffleboard, boat slips, a boat ramp, and a gift shop. Your vacation becomes more pricey on this side of the lake: A standard room in-season begins in the $169 area.

⊙ ✎ ⚕ ✳ ⅄ **Country Club Hotel and Spa** (573-964-2200 or 1-800-964-6698; www.countryclubhotel.com), SR HH and Carol Lane, Lake Ozark, Mo. With 12 outdoor and four indoor tennis courts, racquetball courts, indoor and outdoor swimming pools, a fitness center, and close to area golf courses, the Country Club Hotel is aimed at those who enjoy physical activity. However, thanks to health spa services, spa treatments, personal training, and exercise classes, it also caters to the guest who enjoys a degree of pampering. The variety of accommodations include deluxe rooms, suites, and villas, with nightly rates of $180–370. Serving breakfast, lunch, and dinner is the Bourbon Street Grill (see *Dining Out*). Last but not least, the resort is adept at weddings and wedding receptions and has a skilled staff of professional event planners.

✎ ⚕ ✳ ⅄ **The Lodge of the Four Seasons Resort and Spa** (573-365-3000 or 1-800-THE-LAKE; www.4seasonsresort.com), Horseshoe Bend Pkwy., Lake Ozark, Mo. Arguably the most famous resort at the lake, Four Seasons's 350 rooms are both spacious and luxurious. Rates at the height of the season run anywhere from $159 to $500 per night. The resort is the home of the lake's largest and most complete marina, and golf is a huge draw here. The Seasons's Ridge and Witch's Cove courses are regularly named as two of the best in the state. As well, the Lodge houses one of the Midwest's largest resort spas, **Spa Shiki**, which has been nationally recognized by NBC's *Today* show and *Self* magazine. The 15,000-square-foot facility offers massages, body treatments, facials, and salon treatments, as well as a fully equipped Pilates studio, steam, sauna, and whirlpool.

The dining options at this resort are numerous. Included are **Breeze's Cafe**, **Soleil** (for breakfast and lunch), and the **Seasons Ridge Grill**. For dinner, **HK's** restaurant (named for Four Seasons founder Harold Koplar) is a lake tradition. In terms of thirst quenching, **Breezes Sports Bar**, the **Lobby Bar**, and the **Parrot Bar** provide a casual and laid-back atmosphere. For after-dinner entertainment, the **Blue Moon** is a martini bar featuring music and dancing.

Osage Beach

🦐 🛥 ♿ ❄ 🍸 **The Inn at Grand Glaize** (573-348-4731 or 1-800-348-4731; www.innatgrandglaize.com) 5142 US 54, Osage Beach, Mo. If you want something that is right in the thick of things but offers good value as well, the Inn at Grand Glaize is a fine choice. The facility has been recently remodeled and is located 0.25 mile west of the Grand Glaize Bridge on a secluded cove. Rooms (147 standard rooms, 2 luxury suites, 2 boardroom suites, and 2 junior suites) run $89–199. On-site are a restaurant and lounge, a marina with boat and WaveRunner rental, an outdoor pool, a fitness room, and a game room. You can also take advantage of the services of an on-call massage therapist or hire a fishing guide (though not at the same time).

⚭ 🦐 🛥 ♿ ❄ 🍸 **Tan-Tar-A Resort, Golf Club and Spa** (573-348-3131 or 1-800-826-8272; www.tan-tar-a.com), SR KK, Osage Beach, Mo.

This is the big kahuna of all the lake resorts, the only one more famous than Lodge of the Four Seasons. A Triple A Three Diamond establishment, Tan-Tar-A was ranked one of the three midwestern resorts "families would love most" by *Midwest Living* magazine. A huge place situated on 420 acres, it offers 27 holes of championship-level golf, one indoor and two outdoor pools, bowling, tennis, horseback riding, a health club, a spa and salon, an arcade, and the recently completed (three stories tall) **Timber Falls Indoor Waterpark**. Also on-site is a full-service marina with boat rental and fishing guides. Food and drink are plentiful here. The **Black Bear Lodge** features causal fare and a rustic decor, while **Windrose on the Water** provides fine dining with a lake view. The **Oaks** bar and grill overlooks the golf course of the same name, and for the kids there is also a **Burger King** and pizza.

Accommodations are a bit different here, and there are a number of options amid the 950 total rooms. The complex consists of five interconnecting buildings, all of which are within walking distance of restaurants and activities. A few minutes away is Tan-Tar-A's **Estates Complex**. These buildings (set on 200 acres surrounding a nine-hole golf course) appear from the outside to be private homes. In reality, they contain two to four guest rooms or full suites. Midsummer prices range from $154 per night for a room to $419 for the largest suite. Tan-Tar-A is also known for its weddings; a very quaint stone chapel is on the grounds. A full staff of wedding planners can put together an affair for anywhere from 10 to 200 guests.

CAMPGROUNDS 🐟 🐾 🐕 **Cross Creek RV Park and Campground** (573-365-1211 or 1-888-250-3885; www.crosscreekrvpark.com), Lake Ozark, Mo. Located 3.5 miles north of the dam, and then another mile off SR W, the 40 acres of Cross Creek make for a natural lake vacation. Open Mar.–Nov., the campground features a stocked, 10-acre fishing lake, petting zoo, playground, store, showers, Laundromat, and paddle boat rental. Moreover, pets are welcome here for a minimal extra charge. Lodging includes tent sites (from $15), RV sites (from $20 for full hookup), and either rustic, deluxe, or tree-house cabins from $39. For something different, you can even cross the water and sleep on your own small island. For $49 you achieve privacy, and the site includes electricity, water, toilet, and BBQ grill.

🐟 🐾 🐕 Ⓨ **Deer Valley RV Park and Campground** (573-374-5277; www.deervalleypark.com), Lake Rd. 5-41, Sunrise Beach, Mo. Sunrise Beach, on the west side of the lake, is not known for having a beach. The Deer Valley Campground changes that each year between Apr. 15 and Nov. 1, when the 100 tons of sand it hauls in sports palm trees and happy campers. Containing 203 campsites, the park offers both tent camping and full RV hookups (beginning at $12 and $18, respectively). **Franky and Louie's Bar and Grill** faces the beach, and a full marina with gas pumps, new docks, and boat rental is on-site. A 24-foot pontoon boat runs $325 per day, and canoes are a mere $2.50 per hour. Pets are welcome as long as they are on a leash.

🐾 🐕 **Osage Beach RV Park** (573-348-3445 or 1-800-562-7343; www.osagebeachrvpark.com), 3949 Campground Lane, Osage Beach, Mo. Just 0.33 mile off US 54 in Osage Beach, this park includes five air-conditioned cabins and 74 CATV full-hookup RV sites. Summer rates for cabins (one to four people) are $39.95, and the fee for hookups is $24.50. Pets on leash are allowed at the latter (for 50¢ per day per animal, maximum of two dogs), but neither pets nor smoking is permitted in the cabins. Open Mar. 24–Nov. 1. Note that the cabins are for sleeping only; they do not have kitchens or rest rooms. However, the park does have rest rooms and showers on-site, as well as a swimming pool, playground, meeting room and pavilion, shuffleboard, Sunday church services, and free Wi-Fi and dial-up connections (located in the main office if you just can't survive without your e-mail).

✳ Where to Eat

EATING OUT 🐕 ⅛ Ⓨ **On the Rise Bakery & Bistro** (573-348-4224; www.ontherisebakery.com), 5439 US 54, Osage Beach, Mo. Open Wed.–Sun., 7:30–noon for breakfast and noon–3 for lunch. Owner-chef Mike Castle knows the Lake of the Ozarks better than most. He spent summers working at area restaurants in his high school days, prior to attending the Culinary Institute of America. After graduation he returned, first performing as a sous chef at the near-legendary Blue Heron and later managing the Heron's sister restaurant, the Potted Steer. In 1995 he and wife Cheryl struck out on their own, the result being the On the Rise Bakery & Bistro. The establishment was named a "Top 10 Taste" in 1999 by *Southern Living* magazine. The interior is sort of a courtyard style, complete with striped awnings, bronze tables, wicker chairs, and clouds painted on the ceiling. There is also a small outdoor courtyard should you wish for the real thing. The array of breads, muffins, cookies, pastries, and flatbreads will convince even the most hard-core Atkins dieter to fall off the wagon. Lunch offers specialty soups, salads, and sandwiches, with all meats smoked over dried applewood. Semi-potent potables are offered, and choices range from a $2.50 glass of ale to a $100 bottle of wine.

✨ ❖ **The Fish and Co.** (573-873-0022; www.thefishandco.com), 268 Wego Fish (mile marker 31; Lake Rd. 5-89U), Camdenton, Mo. Mon.–Sat. 11 AM–1:30 AM, Sun. 11 AM–midnight. You get the impression, upon walking into Fish and Co., that this is truly a local place. You're half right. Lots of locals do congregate here, but there's also a fair amount of visitors arriving both by land and water. What the heck, a place that still has an air hockey table in the game room has to be okay. The menu has the usual burgers and tenderloins, but also available are fried dill pickles ($5.75), baked potato soup ($4.25), and a catfish dinner ($13.95). Live entertainment is provided most Thu.–Sun. nights during summer months, and the bar serves beer, wine, and mixed drinks.

✨ ❖ ❖ **The Ozark Bar-B-Que** (573-374-7769; www.ozarkbar-b-que.com), SR TT (mile marker 10.5 by water), Sunrise Beach, Mo. Is it a BBQ joint, a marina, or a gift shop? Truth be known, it's all three. From swimwear to kids' toys to wakeboards to skis and ski ropes, the boutique, marine store, and marine market (where you can purchase food, soda, and packaged

liquor and beer) has quite an impressive selection. There are gas pumps at the dock and the smell of hickory smoke in the air. The Ozark features all-hickory-smoked meats, as well as salads, sandwiches, and burgers. A slab of ribs runs $18.99, but those who wish to make a gastronomic statement might choose the $9.59 Ozark Burger. This is the ultimate cheeseburger in paradise, and it weighs in at a full pound. Aside from some tasty BBQ, the signature item here seems to be the onion rings. For $8.29 you receive a huge pile (feeding several people), all hand breaded and made to order. Open 11–10 weekdays and 8–10 weekends in-season, the Ozark is a nice, casual diversion after a hard afternoon of water sports. Enjoy the Q, look at the goldfish in the pond, or view the numerous carp that congregate at the dock (hoping for a free meal, no doubt).

DINING OUT ✨ ❖ ❖ **The Brass Door** (573-348-9229; www.the-brass-door.com), 5167 US 54, Osage Beach, Mo. A feeling of comfortable warmth arrives after you step through the entrance of the Brass Door. The interior, warm and woody with stone fireplaces (and of course brass), somehow just feels like home. The servers are friendly, and the lack of pretense allows for a relaxing meal. Open in the evening only (5 PM, with early-bird specials 5–6 PM), the restaurant is known for both steak and seafood. The steak Jack Daniels ($24.99, pan fried and arriving with onions, tomatoes, and peppers) is a fine twist on the traditional KC strip. The crabcakes ($15.99) are of a recipe that appears to be unique to the Brass Door. However, for a pure change of pace, try the fried lasagna. It's a traditional lasagna, deep fried and served with marinara sauce. Ozarkers like deep frying anything they can (it's something of a regional obsession), and after you've seen a fried lasagna, the very tasty batter-fried lobster appetizer ($9.99) should come as no surprise. Wine, cocktails, and beer are plentiful, and live entertainment is featured Friday and Saturday nights. Also, a kids' menu is offered for the younger set.

✍ ☕ ⅋ **The Duck Restaurant** (573-365-9973; www.theduckrestaurant .com), 67 Cherokee Court, Lake Ozark, Mo. As is true with a number of eateries at the lake, the Duck is a recipient of *Wine Spectator* magazine's Award of Excellence. A wide variety of wines are available, but connoisseurs will appreciate the selection of vintage ports. Opening at 5 PM Wed.–Sun. during the summer season, the Duck is appropriately located right on the water. The front balcony is inviting, the perfect spot for a cocktail and a relaxing view of the lake. Prices range around $17–36, and though the menu is not huge, it seems to go for quality over quantity. Diners might enjoy the lobster and shrimp ravioli or the veal chop *au poivre* (it comes with a rich green peppercorn and brandy cream). Dessert should not be forgotten: The name *molten chocolate cake* says it all. A final reason to appreciate the Duck is that it's serious about its embargo on cell phone usage (the place should get a medal just for that).

✍ ☕ ⅋ **Andre's Restaurant** (573-365-2800), 1.75 miles down SR HH, Lake Ozark, Mo. Open daily 5–10 PM; Sunday brunch 9:30–1. Things start to get a little creative at Andre's, owned and operated by certified chief executive chef Andre Torres. For one thing, you just don't find that many places serving sushi in the Ozarks. Andre's does, Friday and Saturday in the bar, with many choices, including a salmon roll for $2, a California roll for $4.50, and a six-piece sashimi for $11. But such is just the beginning. A Brie en croute appetizer (Brie wrapped in a crisp shell sided with roasted garlic and apricot marmalade) is $6.50, while the grilled pork tenderloin entrée is $19.50. Another novel variation, the tenderloin is marinated with a dry rub and olive oil before being lightly glazed with a habanero mustard sauce. The veal escallope ($23.50) is served with ever-elusive morel mushrooms and a glaze of cream sauce. The extensive wine list provides both French and American vintages, beginning by the glass at $5 and by the bottle from under $20 up to $175. Last but not least, if you have some spare time on your trip and seek something different, check into the times and dates of Andre's cooking classes.

✍ ☕ ⅋ **Bourbon Street Grill** (573-964-2222; www.countryclubhotel .com), SR HH and Carol Lane, Lake Ozark, Mo. Breakfast is served 7–11, lunch 11–2, daily. Dinner is served 5–9 Sun.–Thu. and 5–11 Fri.–Sat. Located inside the Country Club Hotel, Bourbon Street has managed to create a reasonable facsimile of the sights, sounds, and tastes of the Big Easy the way it was pre-sinking. As you would expect in bayou country (but as you would not expect at the lake), you can start your meal with such tidbits as oysters on the half shell ($7 per half dozen), crawfish pie ($7), or Mississippi catfish bites ($8). Though you can get a regular ol' steak if you like, you'd be better advised to try the crawfish étouffée ($13.75), delta catfish ($12), or pecan-crusted chicken ($14). And of course, for dessert, the praline bread pudding is only $5. The look and feel of Bourbon Street have been effectively captured with parquet floors, wrought iron, ferns, and brass. And do not miss dropping by when Lynn Zimmer is performing with his jazz band. Zimmer is a world-renowned clarinetist (he's played with just about anyone who is anyone) who fires up the tunes four nights a week.

✍ ♿ ☿ **The Potted Steer** (573-365-5743; www.thepottedsteer.com), 5085 US 54, Osage Beach, Mo. Open Tue.–Thu. 5:30–10 PM, Fri.–Sat. 5–10 PM. Two restaurants at the Lake of the Ozarks are renowned above all others, both founded by Dutch immigrant Joseph H. Boer. The first of these, the Potted Steer, opened at its present location in 1972 and is the first building west of the Grand Glaize Bridge. This restaurant is regarded as "the place to be" for fine dining and romance. It has a full bar and huge wine list (bottles run $32–650), and numerous return diners feel the food is nothing short of perfection. Appetizers can include such selections as salmon roulade ($12.95) and pan-fried quail ($8.85). For dinner a traditional favorite is the batter-fried lobster ($38.95; legend has it that Boer was the first to bring this dish to the area), baby beef liver ($22.95), veal Oscar ($27.85), or morel chicken ($23.45). For dessert, both the ice cream and cheesecake are homemade. The Potted Steer is obviously not the most inexpensive of spots. However, if you have a thick wallet or feel like splurging for a special occasion, it's the perfect choice.

✍ ♿ ☿ **The Blue Heron Restaurant** (573-365-4646; www.blueheron.the pottedsteer.com), SR HH, Lake Ozark, Mo. Located high on a bluff overlooking the lake (it's the first driveway on your left after you turn onto SR HH off US 54); open Tue.–Sat. 5–10 PM. The second of Joseph Boer's superb restaurants, the Blue Heron is . . . well . . . blue. Diners can enjoy cocktails at the outdoor gazebo (yup, it's blue too) and soak in some spectacular views. The Heron has held a *Wine Spectator* magazine Award of Excellence almost since its opening in 1984. With more than 350 selections and many limited vintages, this is no surprise. Prices run $30–500 per bottle. Additionally, you can enjoy numerous cordials and cognacs, or for $5 go for a 1.5-ounce Calvados apple juice, distilled, fermented, and aged many years in oak casks. The Heron has a more casual feel than its sister restaurant, but the food is just as good (if not better) than that found at the Potted Steer. For starters, the restaurant offers Kobe beef, which comes from Wagyu cattle in the Kobe province of Japan. Free of antibiotics and

THE BLUE HERON RESTAURANT

hormones, these cattle are fed beer and massaged by a geisha and are no doubt the envy of overly hormonal cattle raised in the American West, who chug tetracycline at the first sniffle, drink too much whiskey, and rarely get a date. A Kamado Wagyu Kobe fillet goes for $62, although you can also order a KC strip for $34.50. The menu here is as long as your arm, loaded with excellent lamb, veal, seafood, poultry, and beef entrées. In addition, some of the appetizers provide a unique taste. For something different, try the steamed mussels in hazelnut beer ($15) or a lobster bisque supreme soup ($13.50).

✳ Selective Shopping

Osage Beach Premium Outlet (573-348-2065; www.premiumoutlets .com), 4540 US 54, Osage Beach, Mo. Mon.–Sat. 9–9, Sun. 9–6. A regional draw that attracts shoppers from far beyond the Lake of the Ozarks, the Osage Beach Premium Outlet features more than 110 shops and stores in the vein of Brooks Brothers, Eddie Bauer, Gap, and Reebok. More than just clothing, the center also offers ample selections of housewares, home furnishings, gifts, and specialty items.

The Rabbit Patch Gift Shop (573-317-1990; www.rabbitpatch.com), 323 E. US 54, Camdenton, Mo. They call the Rabbit Patch a "warm and fuzzy shopping experience," which is an apt description for a place full of rabbits and bears. However, those concerned with contracting tularemia should rest assured that these critters are of the collectible variety. There's a bunch of them—all styles and shapes and sizes—as well as a wide array of candles, charms and bracelets, linens, and stained-glass lamps.

Wood'n Ya Wanit and Art Gallery (573-348-6300), 5497 US 54, Osage Beach, Mo. With two locations in Osage Beach (a second one is found at the Tan-Tar-A Resort), this gallery represents more than 140 American artists. The good thing is that it's not your typical gallery. Yes, there are the obligatory limited-edition prints, but what you should really check out are the wood carvings, glass fish, and metal wall scenes.

The Dogpatch Store (573-365-6344), 1482 Bagnell Dam Blvd., Lake Ozark, Mo. The Lake of the Ozarks is built around tourists. Thus it is almost demanded that you take a stroll through the oldest tourist shop around. The Dogpatch Store, located right on the Strip, has been here since 1947. You've got your magnets and T-shirts, your Route 66 stuff, your water pistols, your live hermit crabs, and your saltwater taffy. When it comes to souvenir shops at the lake, Dogpatch stands head and shoulders above the rest.

✳ Special Events

January **Eagle Days** (573-526-5545 or 573-964-1008), Willmore Lodge, 1 Willmore Lane, Lake Ozark, Mo. The American bald eagle is a regular at the Lake of the Ozarks—Missouri has become one of the leading states where the big birds winter—and eagle-watching has become the thing to do when the water is too cold for water-skiing, swimming, or fishing. The event takes place the first week of every January, and high-powered telescopes are provided on the deck of the Willmore Lodge. However, the eagles can be viewed all the way from the lodge down the Osage River to the town of Tuscumbia. The World Bird Sanctuary in St. Louis provides naturalists to answer questions, brings live eagles in captivity, and offers interactive displays. The event is free and open to everyone.

February **Polar Bear Plunge** (1-800-846-2682), Osage Beach, Mo. Some things are admittedly more fun to watch than they are to do. Still, if you want to brave the elements and help raise money for the Special Olympics, the Polar Bear Plunge might be your cup of iced tea. In late February at Public Beach #2 (Lake of the Ozarks State Park), hundreds of participants don odd costumes, hold a parade, and go splashing neck deep into the 38-degree water. For those who aren't crazy about freezing themselves silly, a 3.1-mile Polar Bear Strut (walk/run) is also available. Afterward, a huge party is held at the Tan-Tar-A Resort. It's free for the plungers, but anyone can join the fun for a low admission price.

April **Annual Dogwood Festival** (1-800-769-1004; www.camdenton chamber.com), Camdenton, Mo. The flowering dogwood is the state tree of Missouri, and nowhere do they celebrate this white-blossomed beauty more than in Camdenton. Having taken place in mid-April for more than 50 years, the Dogwood Festival begins on a Thursday evening with a ham-and-bean dinner, carnival, and live music. On Friday evening you can enjoy an art show, fish fry, talent show, and the Miss Dogwood Pageant. Saturday brings the famed Dogwood Parade, featuring more than 100 floats (more than 1,500 dogwood saplings are given away to those in attendance). Hammered dulcimer music, an art show, and a lawn tractor pull are all part of the fun. Live music can be heard noon–10 PM. A dogwood

festival just wouldn't be complete without dog contests, and you can enter yours in a variety of categories ranging from cutest to ugliest (as if there were any ugly dogs).

June **Midwestcoast Summerfest II** (573-348-1599 or 1-800-386-5253; www.midwestcoastsummerfest.com), Lake of the Ozarks State Park, Osage Beach, Mo. With its 1,000-plus miles of shoreline, Lake of the Ozarks is sometimes (usually by chamber of commerce folks) referred to as the Midwest Coast. Hence the long moniker of the Midwestcoast Summerfest II, which takes place in early June. Both professional and amateur wakeboarders (more than 100) compete for cash, prizes, and acclaim. Numerous exhibits offer plenty of things to buy, and food and drink are plentiful. Live bands keep toes tapping and visitors dancing, and a BMX bicycle stunt team performs some amazing acrobatic feats. The younger crowd loves this festival.

Osage River Pow Wow (573-369-2710), Miller County Fairgrounds, Eldon, Mo. For a celebration of all things Native American, the annual Osage River Pow Wow features authentic dances, arts, period and ceremonial dress, and food (lots of it). The drummers and dancers are the big draw here, though you will also find many booths and activities for both kids and adults. The Pow Wow kicks off in mid-June.

August **Lake Rescue "Shoot Out" Benefit** (573-348-1221; www.lake shootout.com), 21 Mile Marker, Shooter's 21 Restaurant and Club, Osage Beach, Mo. This is the largest unsanctioned boat race in the Midwest, if not the United States, and it's been taking place for nearly two decades. Some of the fastest boats in the world (they must be more than 22 feet in length) compete in a variety of classes for the fastest 1-mile time (some top 200 mph!). The event is sponsored in part by all the fire departments in and around the Lake of the Ozarks (not to mention such folks as *Powerboat* magazine and Budweiser); all the proceeds benefit local fire and rescue teams.

Laurie Hillbilly BBQ Cook-Off (573-216-9358 or 573-374-8776), Laurie Fairgrounds, Laurie, Mo. This two-day BBQ extravaganza, sanctioned by the Kansas City BBQ Society, just gets bigger and better each year. It's now expanded to offer a "Kid's Q," a separate competition for those ages 5–15. The winner of the cook-off instantly earns an invitation to one of the greatest of all BBQ events, the American Royal Livestock, Horse Show and Rodeo in Kansas City. In Laurie itself, however, the cash prize for first place is a cool $1,000.

Make sure to get in on the free BBQ chicken wing samples that are provided (only at certain hours). And don't miss touring the grounds and looking at the competitors and their rigs. As you might imagine, the food is great. On-site, as is only fitting and proper at a BBQ competition, is live music, dancing, and a beer garden.

September **Hillbilly Fair** (573-374-4871), Laurie Fairgrounds, Laurie, Mo. Held over three days in mid-September, locals and visitors dress in Hillbilly attire, hold a parade, and enjoy all the carnival rides and food that make any fair a raving success (and this one has been going on for almost 40 years). Friday and Saturday nights offer dancing, live music, a beer garden, and bingo. This of course just wouldn't be the Ozarks unless, come Sunday morning, worship services were offered. The arts and crafts booths are also a good chance to view and buy some unique items.

Osage River Rendezvous and Mountain Man Festival (573-964-1008 or 1-800-451-4117), American Legion Campground, Lake Ozark, Mo. Always taking place the third weekend in September, the Mountain Man Rendezvous is without doubt one of the best times to be had in the lake region. It's a three-day affair held at the foot of Bagnell Dam (open to the public Fri.–Sat. 9–5, Sun. 9–3), with a theme of pre-1840 Ozark life. Although little discussed in popular fiction, the Ozarks were heavily influenced by the fur trade from the 1600s up to the mid-1800s. This modern shindig is a re-creation of the same festivals held by the early pioneers, who would meet on occasion to socialize, barter, trade, and restock on provisions. You'll see living history via black powder and anvil shoots, tomahawk and knife throwing, fire starting, and of course the telling of tales beyond tall. Shopping is plentiful on Trader's Row, but you won't find stuffed toys or Lake of the Ozarks shot glasses. You *will* find anything that might have been crafted more than 150 years ago. Handmade items, folk art, and widgets from the past are the stock in trade here. The founders of this event are sticklers for accuracy, and Trader's Row is monitored for authenticity. As well, you can stay at the Rendezvous in a primitive camp-site, but with the requirement of dressing in period attire and utilizing only those things available at the time. In short . . . be prepared to start your own fire, tote your own water, and live without air-conditioning and MTV. $5 adults; free for ages 12 and under. In one of the few instances when the 21st century encroaches on the celebration, real money is preferred over beads, pelts, or wampum.

October **Eldon Turkey Festival** (573-392-3752; www.eldonchamber .com), Eldon, Mo. Miller County, Mo., is one of the country's top producers of domestic turkeys. The first Saturday in October, the town of Eldon pays homage to this distinction with its annual Turkey Festival. This is one of those attractions that, for pure fun and quirkiness, should not be passed by. Activities include a turkey egg toss, turkey trot, and (my personal favorite) frozen turkey bowling. However, the games are just the beginning of the fowl goings-on. Vendors, music, a quilt show, live music, and an old-time steam-operated farm machinery exhibit all contribute to the carnival atmosphere. And as for food, you just haven't lived till you've had some turkey fingers or made like King Henry VIII and strolled around chomping on your giant smoked turkey leg.

Old Tyme Apple Festival (573-378-4401), Versailles, Mo. If an apple a day keeps the doctor away, then the physicians of Versailles must be hard up for work. The first Old Tyme Apple Festival took place in 1980, and today the event boasts more than 400 vendors, a parade, apple pie and fiddlers' contests, a tractor show, a car cruise, a demolition derby, and a gospel-singing extravaganza. Held the first Saturday

in October—the car cruise is held Friday night—this local festival now draws more than 35,000 locals and visitors. Small wonder it is consistently voted one of the best festivals in the state by the readers of *Rural Missouri* magazine.

Mid-November–New Year's Day **Annual Lake Lights Festival**. The lake is not shy about celebrating the holidays, and from just before Thanksgiving to the first of the year both land and water are alive with sights, sounds, and twinkling lights. The festival begins when businesses along the major thoroughfares (US 54, SR 42, SR KK, and SR HH) turn on all the bright Yuletide displays. Parades generally begin the next day, when Ameren UE (the company that bought out Union Electric, builders of the lake) flips the switch at Bagnell Dam. As the season progresses visitors can enjoy the **Annual Enchanted Village of Lights** at Laurie. Held at the Laurie Fairgrounds, on SR O off SR 5, more than 27 acres feature nearly 200 lighted Christmas scenes, decorated trees, 4-by-8-foot "greeting cards," and other displays (admission is free). Sights of the season are also dramatic at Tan-Tar-A Resort in Osage Beach and St. Patrick's Church (again in Laurie). A favorite, for those who enjoy the simpler times, is the annual Versailles **Old Fashioned Christmas** held in front of the Morgan County Historical Society Museum and the Versailles Area Chamber of Commerce office. Those in attendance can revel in caroling, watch the big bonfire, and sip on free hot cider or hot chocolate. Horse-drawn buggies and wagons are available to view the various light displays around town.

THE OSAGE LAKES DISTRICT

You might call the Osage Lakes District the "anti–Lake of the Ozarks." This is a quiet area, the lakes of relatively recent (less than 50 years old) construction. In many ways the surrounding region consists of small towns that have changed little over the years, places that treasure traditional rural ways but are coincidentally located next to a lake. While many vacation homes overlook both Stockton and Pomme de Terre lakes, they could in most instances be regarded as simple weekend vacation cabins. Both lakes are creations of the Army Corps of Engineers, and building down to the water's edge is prohibited. This has limited rampant development, such as that found at the Lake of the Ozarks, and kept boating, fishing, and camping possibilities as pristine as possible.

This is not a part of the world where you will find five-star restaurants, glitzy nightclubs, go-cart tracks, luxurious resorts, cute boutiques, or antique-bedecked bed & breakfasts. It is a locale where you will find peace and quiet, family fun, and beautiful scenery. The pace is slow, a fact to which many travelers will attest if they've come up behind a tractor on the two-lane blacktops, following a farmer on the way to his fields. Urban magazines and newspapers often write of "the heartland," but quite frankly few have visited, and fewer yet have any idea where it's truly located. It is here, one of countless rural regions dotted about the Midwest, villages where the Friday-night football game draws packed bleachers and the Sonic Drive-In is still part of the strip cruised endlessly by local teens in pickup trucks.

This is not to say that the region is without amenities or history. In the latter case, it is reputed that the French explorer LaSalle gave the Pomme de Terre River its name ("apple of the earth," referring to the potato bean that grew wild and was an Indian staple) when he crossed the Ozarks in 1682. This was Osage Indian country, home to the proud and legendary tribe that inhabited the Ozarks for hundreds of years prior to the arrival of Europeans and the largely forced infiltration of southeastern tribes such as the Choctaw, Chickasaw, and Cherokee. To the west, in Lamar, you will find the birthplace of Harry Truman, Missouri's only president. Though small motels and numerous franchise food operations are prevalent on the main drags of the larger towns, equally as evident are family-owned restaurants, pretty parks, fairs, and festivals.

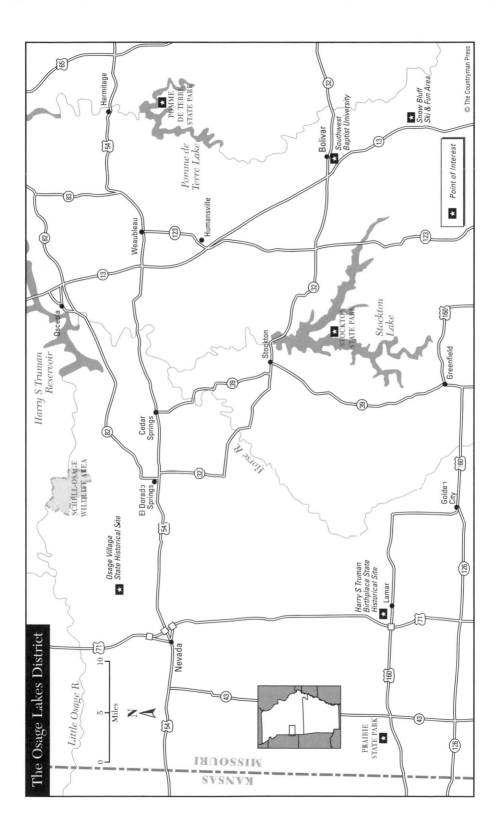

The Osage Lakes District

The Osage Lakes District is one of those increasingly rare parts of America where the words *neighborhood* and *community* still hold deep meaning. This is not a region that time forgot, but it is an oasis where the more objectionable, frenetic facets of modern life have been relegated to the back burner. Luckily, visitors are welcomed.

AREA CODES All of the towns and cities in the Osage Lakes District fall under the **417** area code.

GUIDANCE When traveling in the Osage Lakes District, several area chambers of commerce provide complete information on events, dining, lodging, lake activities, and area history. The **Pomme de Terre Lake Area Chamber of Commerce** (417-745-2299 or 1-800-235-9519; www.lakepommedeterre.com) is located in Hermitage, Mo. To the southwest, everything you wish to learn about Stockton Lake can be acquired from the **Stockton Lake Association** (417-276-5161; www.stocktonlake.com). Many visitors choose to stay in Bolivar, Mo., the largest town in the area. The **Bolivar Area Chamber of Commerce** (417-326-4118; www.bolivarchamber.com or www.bolivarmo.com) offers a wealth of advice and history. If your goal is to visit the birthplace of Harry Truman, contact the **Barton County Chamber of Commerce** (417-682-3505; www.bartoncounty .com), 110 W. 10th St., Lamar, Mo., or check out www.lamarmo.com.

GETTING THERE *By auto:* From the south, the area is easily accessible by several major highways that branch off I-44. From Springfield, both SR 13 and US 65 will put you, respectively, in the vicinity of Bolivar and Pomme de Terre Lake. Lamar, Mo., is on US 71, approximately 20 miles north of Carthage, Mo. To reach Stockton Lake and Greenfield, drive north on SR 39 off I-44. If arriving from Kansas City, take US 71 S. to US 54 E. Then turn south onto SR 39.

By air: Less than an hour from most of Osage Lakes District, the **Springfield-Branson Regional Airport** (417-869-0300; www.sgf-branson-airport.com) is the most convenient choice for air travelers. **Lambert–St. Louis International Airport** (314-426-8000; www.lambert-stlouis.com) and **Kansas City International** (816-243-3000; www.flykci.com) are located within a half day's drive.

MEDICAL EMERGENCIES Citizens Memorial Hospital (417-326-6000; www .citizenmemorial.com), 1500 N. Oakland Ave., Bolivar, Mo. Citizens Memorial is a 74-bed hospital with 23 physicians and dentists offering a range of services from outpatient to emergency care.

Barton County Memorial Hospital (417-681-5100; www.bcmh.net), 2nd and Gulf streets, Lamar, Mo. A 49-bed hospital with emergency services, Barton County has provided health care to area residents since 1949. In addition to its full range of offerings, the hospital features a sports injury clinic.

✴ Wandering Around

EXPLORING BY FOOT For a look at some relatively unmolested remnants of the Osage Indians who first inhabited the area, take a walk on the 3-mile **Indian**

Point Trail at **Pomme de Terre State Park**. Located on the south (Pittsburg) side of the park, the trailhead for Indian Point is across from the campground entrance. Follow the signs for just shy of 1.5 miles and you will encounter the first of the Osage cairns, used as burial markers, monuments, and topographic signposts. Continue straight ahead and in just a few minutes (about 0.1 mile) you will reach Indian Point Overlook, which offers fantastic views of Pomme de Terre. After peeking out at the lake from the overlook, return to the trail and turn left. At roughly the 2.5-mile mark you will find a second cairn and may ponder the lives and times of those who built it. Continue to walk straight, and in 0.5 mile you will return to the trailhead and parking lot.

✳ Towns and Villages

Bolivar, Mo. In July 1948 President Harry Truman and Venezuelan president Romulo Gallegos came to town. In order to thank the residents of Bolivar, Mo., for celebrating the man who had liberated their country, Venezuela had donated a large statue of Simon Bolívar, leader of the 1817–1825 South American revolution. Truman and Gallegos performed the unveiling of the sculpture, and the locals applauded with gusto. The two dignitaries apparently never realized that Bolivar, Mo., was in fact named for a town in Hardeman County, Tennessee.

Founded in 1835, Bolivar (pronounced *BALL-uh-ver*) is now the home to 9,143 residents, not to mention Southwest Baptist University. The North Ward School Museum and the Ella Carothers Dunnegan Gallery of Art are also found here, but the area holds true to its Ozark roots. The annual **Country Days Rodeo** is held the second weekend of every July, followed by the **Diamond S Bull Blast** the first weekend of August.

SIMON BOLÍVAR

Greenfield, Mo. Established in 1842, the county seat of Dade County is called home by 1,358 citizens. In town you'll find an 1888 opera house (restored in 1986 and the site of local theater productions)—but the real reason to visit Greenfield is the **Buffalo Days festival**. Held annually for more than 30 years, the fair features all the best of small-town festivals. There is a midway, quilt contests, townwide BBQ, cakes, pies, and food galore. The Buffalo Chip-Chucking Contest is a highlight: Those with a good throwing arm compete to see who can toss hunks of dried buffalo dung the farthest.

Hermitage, Mo. Hickory County was named in honor of Andrew Jackson, nicknamed "Old Hickory." Thus it is fitting that the county seat, Hermitage, is named for the plantation owned by the seventh president of the United States. With a population of less than 500, and located just north of Pomme de Terre Lake, Hermitage boasts of several popular festivals. The annual Ozark Market Day, held on the Saturday closest to July 4, finds the town square transformed into an old-time marketplace. Literally hundreds of Ozark craftsmen show up to both display and sell their creations. On the first Saturday after Labor Day, the Pomme de Terre Fall Festival kicks into gear. Again, the regional artisans descend with their unique, handmade products. Last but not least, the Pomme de Terre Black Powder Rendezvous is held just south of town each May. Also found in Hermitage is the Hickory County Historical Society Museum, housed in an 1855 antebellum home.

Lamar, Mo. Harry Truman only lived in Lamar for the first 11 months of his life, but such was long enough to give the town bragging rights as his birthplace. Lamar is an interesting little town of 4,435 residents, and the Truman birthplace might be the least interesting stop. Held in late August, the Lamar Free Fair/ Lamar Farm & Industrial Expo is Missouri's largest free fair event (there are no gate fees). The downtown square is transformed into a festival grounds, and the number of contests, events, activities, and displays held at the fairground proper is truly impressive. The square is something to see in and of itself, being the second largest downtown square shopping district in the state of Missouri. There you will find the Barton County Historical Society and Museum, the county courthouse, a Civil War cannon, a 1913 bandstand, a 16-foot-tall replica of the Statue of Liberty, and a memorial to Harry Truman. Yet one more unusual attribute of Lamar is its Stilabower Public Observatory, designed to allow accessibility to both the handicapped and small children.

LADY LIBERTY GUARDS THE LAMAR SQUARE.

A little-reported historical tidbit of Lamar is that, at age 22, lawman Wyatt Earp was the town's first constable (he departed after the death of his wife, Urilla; the couple had been married hardly a year). Also, the town was literally ripped apart by the Civil War, as the sympathies of the residents were equally divided between North and South. It was only in 1910 that veterans of the opposing sides met on the courthouse lawn, shaking hands over the barrel of the cannon.

Stockton, Mo. With just under 2,000 residents, the county seat of Cedar County is the gateway to both Stockton Lake and Stockton State Park.

The Corps of Engineers lake is well known for fishing and scuba, but surprisingly it is one of the most popular lakes for sailing in the state of Missouri. There is even a Stockton Yacht Club, which holds various races and regattas throughout the year. Though not many towns pride themselves on being nuts, Stockton has good reason to crow over such an attribute. It is the home of the Hammons Products Company, the world's premier processor and supplier of American eastern black walnuts for both food and industrial uses.

✳ To See

MUSEUMS ✾ ✐ **North Ward Schoolhouse Museum** (417-326-6850; www .rootsweb.com/~mohspcm/museum.htm), 201 W. Locust, Bolivar, Mo. Open May 15–mid-Sep., 1–4. $2 adults, $1 ages 6–12. Built in 1903, this former school features exhibits in 13 different rooms covering three floors. Local Indian artifacts, farm implements, and toys from years past are featured. As proof of local pride, one room is dedicated to a teacher who instructed area children for nearly 50 years. On the museum grounds you can examine a two-story log cabin that dates from 1867.

✾ ✐ ♿ **Hickory County Historical Society Museum** (417-852-4333), Museum St. on the town square, Hermitage, Mo. The threat of a stay in the primitive 1871 stone jail in Hermitage was no doubt an effective deterrent for more than a few 19th-century chicken thieves. Today both the jail and other historical buildings can be found on the northeast corner of the town's courthouse square (the 1896 courthouse is still in use). The Hickory County Museum, which resides inside an 1855 antebellum home, is a treasure trove for those who seek a trip to the past. To keep the theme complete, an antiques and gift shop is found in a building constructed the same year as the home.

✾ ✐ ♿ **Barton County Historical Society and Museum** (417-682-4141), basement level, Barton County Courthouse, Constitution Square, Lamar, Mo. Open Mon.–Fri., 12:30–4:30. As is true with the county seats of many Ozark towns, the Barton County Courthouse dates from the late 1800s. While the Barton County Museum (lower level of the courthouse) is interesting in and of itself, the entire courthouse grounds offer a glimpse into the textured history of the area. A Civil War cannon, a bandstand built in 1913, and a 16-foot-high replica of the Statue of Liberty surround the edifice. Plus, the shopping and dining choices found around the well-designed square will give you plenty to do when it's time to return to the present.

HERMITAGE'S 1871 STONE JAIL

CULTURAL SITES ✾ ✐ ♿ **Simon Bolívar statue**, College St. and SR Bus. 13, Bolivar, Mo. Bolivar is allegedly the largest town in the

United States named for the leader of the South American revolution. Thus it is fitting that the country of Venezuela presented local citizens with a statue of the heroic leader. Technically, Bolivar was named for the village of Bolivar, Tenn. However, since Bolivar, Tenn., was in fact named for the "Great Liberator," the gift was graciously accepted.

✿ ✐ ♿ **Ella Carothers Dunnegan Gallery of Art** (417-326-3438), 511 N. Pike St., Bolivar, Mo. Open Mon., Wed., Fri., 1–4. Free admission. Right across the street from the North Ward School Museum is this fine art gallery, a true prize for a town of this size. Displaying a wide range of styles and subjects, the gallery features the works of artists indigenous to Missouri as well as those known around the world. Special exhibits are held during the year (call for more information), and the gallery is the permanent home of both the Dunnegan and Wainscott art collections.

✿ ✐ ♿ **Stilabower Observatory** (417-682-3384), Sixth and Maple Sts., Lamar, Mo. There are very few public observatories in the nation, but you'll find one in Lamar. The Stilabower Public Observatory features a 14-inch telescope, digital imaging, and computerized tracking. Better yet, it has been specially designed to accommodate both young children and handicapped individuals. Call ahead for viewing times, but the observatory (located right across from Lamar High School, adjacent to the football field) is open to the public on Tue., Thu., and Sat. nights.

HISTORIC SITE ✿ ✐ ♿ **Harry S. Truman State Birthplace Historic Site** (417-682-2279; www.bartoncounty.com/truman.htm), 1009 Truman St., Lamar, Mo. Open Mon.–Sat. 10–4, Sun. noon–4. One of America's most famous presidents, and the only one born in Missouri, Harry Truman was born in the back bedroom of this tiny 1884 frame home. The 560-square-foot house, which young Harry's parents purchased for $685, has been re-created with period authenticity. Four downstairs and two upstairs rooms feature modest furnishings and lack both electricity and plumbing. Thus it was good that the grounds included a water well and outhouse. A little-known bit of historical trivia is that the Trumans sold this home to the Earp family. Relatives of the famous western marshal lived there till the late 1950s.

THE STILABOWER OBSERVATORY

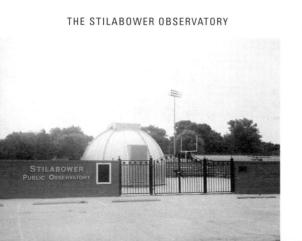

✴ Wild Places

✿ 🐾 ✐ ♿ **Prairie State Park** (417-843-6711; www.mostateparks.com/prairie.htm), 128 N.W. 150th Lane, Liberal, Mo. Open Apr.–Oct., Tue.–Sun. 9–5, Sat. 1–5; Nov.–Mar., Tue.–Sun. 9–3, Sat. 1–4. Much of Missouri was once native prairie, but the changes that came with settlers, farming, and development have reduced the tallgrass from 13 million to 65,000 acres. Prairie State Park, at nearly

4,000 acres, is the largest remaining tallgrass prairie in the state. Full of wandering buffalo, prairie chickens, tallgrass (some of which can reach heights of 8 feet), and wildflowers, the park offers three hiking trails, picnicking, and an excellent visitors center. Camping is allowed with approval of the park naturalist. To reach this unique area from Lamar, drive 16 miles west on US 160. Turn right onto SR NN for 1 mile, then turn left onto the gravel Central Rd. for 3 miles. Turn right onto 150th Lane and head 1.3 miles to the park visitors center.

🐾 🐛 ✎ ♿ **Pomme de Terre State Park/Pomme de Terre Lake** (417-852-4291; www.mostateparks.com/pommedeterre/geninfo.htm), HC 77, Box 890, Pittsburg, Mo. In the late 1950s the U.S. Army Corps of Engineers dammed the Pomme de Terre River as part of the flood-control plan for the Missouri River Basin. The result was the 7,800-acre Pomme de Terre Lake (113 miles of shoreline) and the accompanying 734-acre Pomme de Terre State Park. Much more quiet and peaceful than many of the more publicized parks in the Ozarks, Pomme de Terre is a near-perfect choice for a quiet weekend of camping and fishing. Split into two parcels (one on the Hermitage side of the lake, the other on the Pittsburg side), the park features more than 250 campsites, four paved boat launches, marinas, numerous picnic sites, a playground, several hiking trails, and two public beaches. But the best part of Pomme de Terre is the fishing; this is an angler's paradise. A very cool and clear lake, Pomme de Terre holds the usual Ozark species such as bass, catfish, bluegill, and carp. The addition of two other species, however, has made Pomme de Terre a favorite with the hook-and-line set. For starters, fine-tasting walleye have been introduced into the lake, and they're thriving thanks to the coolness and clarity of the waters (the Pomme de Terre River—which forms the lake—is spring fed). The true prizes, though, are the lake's northern muskies. These are large, hard-fighting, hard-to-catch fish, and this is the only lake in Missouri that has them. Anyone who has ever hooked a muskie will attest that the wait is worth it; the fish is so aggressive that, when it does decide to take a lure, you'll think you have a Volkswagen on the end of the line.

🐾 🐛 ✎ ♿ **Stockton State Park/Stockton Lake** (417-276-4259; www.mostate parks.com/stockton.htm), Stockton, Mo. You don't normally think of the Ozarks as a mecca for sailboats, but the 25,000-acre Stockton Lake is that and more. The open topography and prevailing southwest winds of Stockton have made this body of water so popular with sailors that it not only has its own yacht club but is the home of numerous regattas and contests as well. Formed when the U.S. Army Corps of Engineers dammed the Sac River in the early 1970s, Stockton's 298 miles of shoreline and 12 parks (one state owned, the rest operated by the Corps of Engineers) provide

STOCKTON LAKE

ample opportunities for boating, fishing, scuba, camping, and sailing. The 2,175-acre Stockton State Park encompasses 29 basic and 45 electric campsites (there are many more spots in the other areas as well), picnic areas, a full-service marina, a dining lodge, and a small motel. Just shy of an hour north of Springfield, Mo., this is another lake that has not suffered the pangs and perils of excess development. The pace of Stockton is slow and relaxing, stressing simple fun and a back-to-nature approach over five-star hotels, T-shirt shacks, and neon lights.

❋ Lodging

RESORTS AND LODGES ✍ ♿ ❋

Eagle's Nest (417-852-4301 or 1-800-259-6936; www.eaglenests.com), HC 76, Box 2690, Pittsburg, Mo. Located 2 miles west of Pittsburg on SR J, Eagle's Nest offers five different rustic (but well-appointed) log cabins ranging $85–95 per night. All come with full kitchens and bath and include a propane grill on the deck for evening BBQ. For those on a budget, or who seek only a clean room and soft bed while on a blast-and-cast expedition, five "Fish and Hunt" cabins run $49–57 per night. All the cabins are nonsmoking, and pets are not accepted. The rates are based on a two-night stay with double occupancy, but the fee for additional guests is only $6 per person. Eagle's Nest offers a couple of options not found in many small resorts. Fishing and duck hunting guides are available, and—most unusual of all—on-site is the **Eagle's Nest Art Gallery**. In between catching muskies (or rather, trying to catch muskies) you can view the works of numerous local artists.

🐾 ✍ ♿ ❋ **Stillwater Resort** (417-282-6241; www.stillwaterresort.com), Rt. 2, Box 1616, Wheatland, Mo. With its blue and white housekeeping cabins, Stillwater is a bit reminiscent of an early-1960s resort. This is a good thing, as the atmosphere is relaxed and peaceful. The 10 cabins rent for $55–110 per night (three-night minimum between Memorial Day and Labor Day, double occupancy), with a $6 charge for each additional person. Pets are accepted here for $7 per night. All the cabins include color TV, bed linens and towels, microwave, refrigerator, coffeemaker, dishes, utensils, and pots and pans; three have ovens. Also, all have decks with furniture and a BBQ grill, and a kids' playground is located at the edge of the lake. Each cabin has its own covered boat slip (bring your own craft; the charge for the slip is $6 per day). Fishing guide services are available, and for the RV enthusiast there are numerous camping spots with full hookups.

✍ ♿ ❋ **Sunflower Resort** (417-282-6235 or 1-800-258-5260; www.sunflowerresort.com), Rt. 2, Box 2681, Wheatland, Mo. The Sunflower offers numerous kitchenette-equipped rooms running $50–95 per night. Very family-friendly, the facility includes a playground; rentals of boats, motors, and paddleboats; horseshoe pits; volleyball; tetherball; and indoor Ping-Pong. The individual lodging units appear clean and modern, and again are priced for those on a budget.

✍ **The Old Country House** (417-276-5822; www.stocktonsoldcountryhouse.com), 14411 S. SR 32, Stockton, Mo. Within walking distance of Stockton Dam, this century-old home comes equipped with linens, dishes, silverware, and all the usual amenities (TV, VCR/DVD, microwave, full kitchen, dishwasher, and air-conditioning). Smoking and pets are not allowed, but the home is a very good choice for the large family. Prices per night begin at $75, depending upon the number of people staying, which makes it extremely affordable (compare this with the average economy room at a Holiday Inn). This is just a nice, much-loved home, and a few of the owners' commonsense restrictions accentuate the rural character of the area. For instance, they ask that you not clean fish or game in the house or climb over their neighbor's fence to play with the donkeys.

✂ ⚠ ❊ ⵙ **Orleans Trail Resort and Marina** (417-276-3566 or 417-276-5161; 1-800-826-0230 or 1-877-525-3886; www.orleanstrail.com), 15857 S. 1525 Rd., Stockton, Mo. Open year-round, the Orleans has recently completed a large construction project and now offers 80 rooms (smoking, non-smoking, kitchenettes, regular guest rooms, and suites). Prices run $50–200 per night, and children under 8 stay free. A full-service marina provides sailboat slips, covered slips, fuel dock with pumpout, boat rentals, and a bait-and-tackle shop. Also on-site is the Orleans Trail Restaurant (see *Eating Out*).

CAMPGROUNDS

🎗 🐾 ✂ ♿ ❊ **Pomme de Terre State Park** (417-852-4291 or 1-877-422-6766; www.mostateparks.com). Camping is available at 250 spots located on both the Pittsburg and Hermitage sides of the park. Each camping area includes rest rooms, showers, picnic areas, and laundry. Some sites are open year-round, while others are closed Nov–Mar. During the summer season prices are $8 for a basic campsite, $14 for an electric campsite, $15 for a campsite with electricity and water, and $17 for a site with electric, water, and sewer. Pets are okay but must be kept on a leash.

🎗 🐾 ✂ ♿ ❊ **Stockton State Park** (417-276-4259 or 1-800-334-6946; www.mostateparks.com). Stockton has fewer campsites than its sister lake, Pomme de Terre, but prices and services are virtually the same. The best campsites at Stockton are available through the park areas operated by the Army Corps of Engineers.

🎗 🐾 ✂ ♿ ❊ **Pomme de Terre/U.S. Army Corp of Engineers** (417-745-6411; www.nwk.usace.army.mil/pommedeterre/pomme_home.htm), Rt. 2, Box 2160, Hermitage, Mo. The Army Corps has six campgrounds located around Pomme de Terre: Nemo Landing, Damsite, Outlet, Wheatland, Lightfoot Landing, and Pittsburg Landing. All are affordable and feature level sites, posts for lanterns, picnic areas, and fire rings. A number also include electricity, showers, dump stations, and playgrounds. Although prices vary per campground, the average is $10–14 for a nonelectric site, $14–20 for one with plug-ins. A single, day-use fee of $3 is charged for launching boats, and there is a $1 charge (for those over 12) for swimming at corps beaches.

🎗 🐾 ✂ ♿ ❊ **Stockton Lake/Army Corps of Engineers** (417-276-3113, 417-276-3114, or 1-877-444-6777; www.nwk.usace.army.mil/stockton/stockton_home.htm), Stockton Project Office, 16435 E. Stockton Lake Dr., Stockton, Mo. Eight of Stockton's

11 campgrounds (Cedar Ridge, Crabtree Cove, Hawker Point, Masters, Orleans Trail North, Orleans Trail South, Ruark Bluff East, and Ruark Bluff West) are managed by the corps. Consisting of nearly 4,000 total acres and nearly 600 total sites (400 nonelectric, 181 electric, and some group areas), amenities include showers, dump stations, picnic areas, shelters, boat launches, and swimming beaches. Regular-season camping fees are $12 for nonelectric basic sites and $14 for nonelectric prime sites (better lake views and access). The electric basic sites are $16, and the electric primes are $18. As is also true at the corps facilities at Pomme de Terre, the day-use fee for boat launching is $3, and the beach fee is $1 for those over 12 (up to a maximum of $4 per car).

✳ Where to Eat

EATING OUT Orleans Trail Restaurant (417-276-3566 or 417-276-5161; 1-800-826-0230 or 1-877-525-3886; www.orleanstrail.com), 15857 S. 1525 Rd., Stockton, Mo. Open for lunch and dinner. A simple but nice restaurant located at the Orleans Trail

ORLEANS TRAIL RESORT HOSTS A MARINA AND RESTAURANT.

Resort and Marina, the Orleans Trail offers some choices different from what you'll find at the local diners and franchise options more common to the area. You can order a hickory-smoked pulled-pork sandwich for $4.95. For just a buck more, however, you can opt for the chicken peanut wrap, a grilled chicken breast filled with peanuts, rice noodles, vegetables, and a medium-spicy sauce, all wrapped in a spinach tortilla. The menu is large here, stretching from the down-home breaded pork tenderloin sandwich to the more refined Cobb salad. For dinner, a 16-ounce T-bone runs $19.95, and a number of fish and pasta dishes are available as well. Actually, one reason to like this place is that it still offers liver and onions (with a salad bar trip) for only $6.50.

Tea Garden Cafe (417-326-3568; www.thecountryhearth.com), 113 N. Main Ave., Bolivar, Mo. When driving around Bolivar you will see every fast-food franchise known to humankind, as well as the obligatory local diners and family restaurants. Therefore, it is something of a shock to trip across the Tea Garden Cafe. Open Mon.– Sat. 11–4, Sun. 11–3, this little oasis on the west side of the town square sits on the upper floor of the **Country Hearth Gift Shop**. A nonsmoking establishment, its bill of fare lists numerous specialty teas, chai, cappuccino, espresso, and flavored coffees. A menu of lighter foods is a far cry from the typical Ozark catfish and BBQ stop. A provolone and pastrami sandwich is $5.50, and salads are in the $7 range. A huge stuffed potato (with ham, turkey, bacon, cheese, onion, sour cream, and butter) is a mere $6. "Tea Time" is 3–4 daily (good to know if you've traded the London fog for the Ozark hills) and features scones, crumpets, and desserts. Not to be left behind in our present cyber-society, the Tea Garden even has high-speed Internet access.

The Java Mule Espresso and Tea Bistro (417-682-6853; www.javamule.com), 206 West 10th St., Lamar, Mo. You can just forget about your Starbucks when visiting the rural towns of the Ozarks. Nine times out of 10, asking for a cappuccino at the place with the EAT sign will only mark you as a city slicker. On the other hand, drive through Lamar and you will find a small shop that has combined urban coffee desires with a pride in local equine life. The Java Mule, open Mon.–Fri. 6:30–6 (lunch is served 11:30–1:30, Mon.–Fri.), is just off the northwest corner of the town square. Drinks run from $1.50 for a coffee of the day to $3.95 for a specialty espresso. You can learn some mule trivia while having a sip of your "Nevertheless Bess," a concoction consisting of espresso, caramel, and vanilla, topped with whipped cream and more caramel. Of course, it is named in honor of former first lady Bess Truman, whose husband's birthplace is right down the road. Lunch at the Java Mule is of the healthy and light variety, with a "Mulie the Greek" salad (a pasta dish with feta cheese) going for $4. For dessert, don't forget the delicious "oatmule" cookies.

The Blue Top Cafe (417-682-5080), US 71 and US 160, Lamar, Mo. The Blue Top has been in Lamar since 1941 (I first ate here when I was a kid nearly four decades back) and is the quintessential small-town gathering spot. It's where the farmers and local working folks come to drink coffee, swap stories, and load up on biscuits

THE LEGENDARY BLUE TOP CAFE

and gravy in the morning. If the Java Mule is the future, then the Blue Top is the past. It's a tradition, and that alone is reason enough to stop. Breakfast is good and lunches are hearty, with your usual menu of pancakes, omelets, and sandwiches. At night you can order a 12-ounce T-bone for $8.95, a 16-ounce hamburger steak for $6.95, or chicken-fried steak for $5.95. The Blue Top prides itself on its fried chicken (three pieces for $6.25), which comes with a salad, choice of potato, homemade rolls, and honey. Longevity is worthy of respect, and the traveler should always take a chance on the Blue Top. You'll see the old weathered sign (reading FOOD) from US 71. Where else could you get a big pile of fried chicken livers for $2.85?

✳ Entertainment

Barco Drive-In Theatre (417-682-2434), E. US 160, Lamar, Mo. Open Apr.–Oct., and with space for 400 cars, the Barco Drive-In has brought the outdoor silver screen to Lamar area residents for more than 50 years. There are very few drive-in theaters left in America. A living rendition of a simpler time, the Barco is one of the best, offering stereo sound and first-run movies. It's located 1.5 miles east of the Lamar town square.

✳ **Special Events**

Also see Towns and Villages.

May **Pomme de Terre Rendezvous** (417-282-5845), Below Lake Dam, SR 254, Hermitage, Mo. Over the first weekend in May the 1840s come alive as latter-day mountain men demonstrate their skills in such events as black powder shooting and knife and tomahawk throwing. There are craft and food booths galore, as well as live music and old-time machinery exhibits. In the past, even a French colonial artillery brigade has shown up for the fun. Best of all, admission is only $1 for those 12 and older.

Truman Day Celebration (417-682-2279), 11th St., Lamar, Mo. The Truman Day Celebration was for years held in June on the Lamar town square. Recently the event has been moved to early May and takes place on Lamar's 11th Street near the president's birthplace (we're guessing Harry didn't mind). The staff of the historic site offers refreshments and informative programs, and booths stretching both east and west of the Truman home are full of food and drink, as well as historical and handmade crafts.

July **Ozark Market Day** (1-800-235-9519), Hermitage, Mo. A free event held on the Saturday closest to Independence Day, Ozark Market Day finds the town square of Hermitage filled with literally hundreds of local artisans. Craftspeople from all over the Ozarks show up at this festival to show off (and hopefully sell) their creations.

August **Lamar Free Fair/Lamar Farm & Industrial Expo** (417-682-3687), downtown square, Lamar, Mo.

A fair in the old-time tradition, the Free Fair lives up to its name. In fact, it's the largest free fair (there is no gate admission) in the state. Visit this event and you can enjoy parades, a carnival midway, live music, an antique-car show, livestock exhibits, and 4-H displays. Contests are prevalent, as they are at all the best fairs, in the vein of fair queen, prettiest baby, and ugliest truck. If you want a taste of what the rural Ozark fairs used to be (and sometimes still are), this is your prime choice.

September **Pomme de Terre Fall Festival**, Hermitage, Mo. Taking place the first Saturday after Labor Day on the courthouse lawn in Hermitage, the Fall Festival features a plethora of craftsman booths, art, food, and music.

Black Walnut Festival (417-276-5161; www.stocktonlake.com), Stockton, Mo. The largest processor of black walnuts in the world—the Hammons Products Company—is locally owned in Stockton, Mo. Such being the case, the biggest festival of the year celebrates this profitable nut. Held near the end of September (usually the third weekend of the month), it's a nearly 50-year-old, four-day event that the entire town takes part in. You'll find a parade, hordes of artisans and food booths, a horseshoe-pitching contest, live music, and carriage rides. Contests can include anything from the typical beautiful baby competition to talent contests, turtle racing, and pedal tractor pulls. Although the Hammons company doesn't usually give tours, it does offer guided explorations of all things walnut during the festival days (starting at 2 PM Wed.–Fri. and after the parade on Sat.).

The Southwest Missouri Ozarks

3

THE OZARK MINING REGION

SPRINGFIELD, MISSOURI

THE OZARK MINING REGION

Despite their beauty, the Ozarks have always been a hard land. For early settlers particularly, the rugged and rarely forgiving country demanded fortitude, independence, and pioneer spirit. Perhaps nowhere in the Ozarks were these qualities more required and more apparent than in the southwest section of Missouri. This was and is a territory shaped by extremes. In terms of topography you need but look to see the contrast. The rolling Springfield Plateau, as found in the Joplin, Neosho, and Carthage areas, is far different from the bluffs, ravines, and wild scenery you experience as you drop down into the White River Valley near Cassville, Noel, and Roaring River State Park. In terms of wealth, the history of the region is a contest between flat broke and fabulously wealthy, a gulf between eking sparse stocks of corn from thin, rocky soil and the fortunes that emerged from lead, zinc, and limestone mines.

During the Civil War (and both before and after . . . it is often said that the War Between the States lasted 10 years in Missouri, and 4 years everywhere else) the southwestern Missouri Ozarks experienced nonstop battles and skirmishes. Missouri is actually third behind Virginia and Tennessee in numbers of battles fought, and many of them took place on the Kansas-Missouri border. Residents of that time leaned toward the Southern cause, more out of a sense of independence and pride (the hill residents hated any government telling them what to do) than out of sympathies with slaveholders. Frankly, most people here didn't have the money to own slaves. Had they been left alone, the isolationist Ozarkers would more likely than not have been content to live their lives away from the internecine battle.

But such was not to be the case. Though the Civil War officially began on April 12, 1861, and ended April 9, 1865, the unofficial fights between pro-slavery Missourians and free-state Kansans had long before exceeded the boiling point. The elected government of Missouri had actually voted to secede from the Union, but Federal troops had other ideas. They wished not only to hold control of the Missouri and Mississippi rivers, but also to possess the valuable lead reserves that had been discovered in the southwest Missouri Ozarks. Ousted governor Clairborne Fox and members of the Missouri General Assembly (11 senators and 44 representatives), on the run from Union forces, met in Cassville

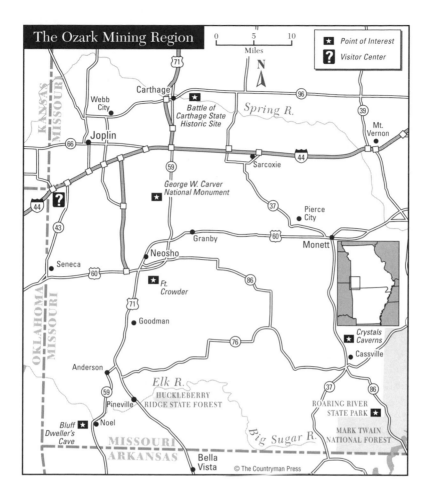

The Ozark Mining Region

0 5 10
Miles

N

★ Point of Interest
? Visitor Center

KANSAS
MISSOURI

Webb City
Carthage
Battle of Carthage State Historic Site

Spring R.

Joplin

Sarcoxie

George W. Carver National Monument

Mt. Vernon

Pierce City

Granby
Neosho

Monett

Seneca

Ft. Crowder

Goodman

Crystals Caverns

Cassville

Anderson

Elk R.
HUCKLEBERRY RIDGE STATE FOREST

ROARING RIVER STATE PARK

Pineville

Bluff Dweller's Cave

Noel

Big Sugar R.

MARK TWAIN NATIONAL FOREST

OKLAHOMA
MISSOURI

MISSOURI
ARKANSAS

Bella Vista

© The Countryman Press

and declared it the Confederate capital of Missouri. Soon thereafter, they went to Neosho and ratified the Articles of Secession.

Left to their own devices, it could strongly be argued that residents of this region would have largely ignored the war and continued to live as they always had, keeping to themselves and remaining more concerned with family and community than with political turf wars. Their stance, as was true with all Ozarkers (and to a degree still is true), was initially one of opinionated neutrality. They had their views and were quick to air them, but the daily tasks of growing a crop and putting food on the table superseded fighting and dying over the squabbles of politicians.

A strategic mistake by the Union generals changed all that. Border Missourians, and especially Ozarkers in the precious mining region, were indiscriminately viewed by Federal forces as traitors and Rebels. Virtually all were treated with utter contempt. With the implicit blessings of the North, renegade Jayhawkers from Kansas (under the command of such men as Jim Lane and Jim Montgomery) rode through the borderlands, burning, pillaging, and plundering at will. The proud Ozarkers fought back with a vengeance, now supporting the Rebel cause against those who would destroy their homes. They gladly harbored equally violent Missouri Bushwhackers under the command of leaders such as William Quantrill and Bloody Bill Anderson (both the James and Younger boys perfected their future trade under the tutelage of these two men).

The ground ran red with blood, and before long, friend and foe were interchangeable. Justifiable paranoia and fear were rampant. The Union might show up at midnight to conscript troops, burn a barn, appropriate stock and valuables, or shoot suspected Rebels. The Bushwhackers might do much the same, simply to prevent their blue-coated opponents from acquiring provisions. A sizable number of deserters from both sides, harboring a criminal mentality, saw the potential of a fat harvest and tore through the land like a whirlwind, stealing what they could and murdering without hesitation.

Until the end of the war the fighting and carnage were unprecedented. In addition to the atrocities of Bushwhackers and partisans, the armies of North and South engaged in a deadly game of tug-of-war over mining region towns and settlements. Cassville was attacked time after time, sometimes held by the Gray and sometimes by the Blue. The Battle of Carthage saw that town burned to the ground, and by 1866 its population was nearly nonexistent. Two battles were fought at Newtonia. The village of Jollification, between Monett and Granby, was twice set to the torch. Oddly, or perhaps not, the Jolly Mill was spared on both occasions. This could be attributed to either luck or the fact that the Jolly Mill served as a whiskey distillery (it continued producing whiskey, illegally, until just before World War I).

The war eventually ended, as most wars do, and the rebuilding process began. Mining had taken place in the district since the early 1800s (Ozark explorer Henry Schoolcraft wrote in 1819 of how he had dug lead from a streambed, scratched out a shallow pit to melt it, and molded bullets on the spot). Concerted mining efforts had begun in earnest around 1850, and though the mining camps were deserted during the war years, by the 1870s the mines were in full production. Overnight Joplin transformed into a town of thousands (with nearly 80 saloons and bawdy houses for the footloose miners).

THE JASPER COUNTY COURTHOUSE IN CARTHAGE

Lead became a bonanza for mine owners, though not for the workers. The men who dug the ore were paid a pittance and suffered from mine cave-ins, black lung, and temporary blindness from acidic waters deep in the earth. When the miners discovered that the "black stuff" clinging to the lead was in fact zinc (at first they'd tossed the unknown substance into piles that sometimes reached hundreds of feet in height), the boom increased proportionately. By 1880 the mining region shipped out more zinc than lead. The mines were money pits in the finest sense of the term.

Carthage, which seemed doomed to die by the ravages of the war, experienced a resurgence in the late 1800s due to the discovery of Burlington limestone (known as Carthage White Marble). The population swelled to nearly 10,000, and in the 1900 census it was the wealthiest town in America per capita. The gracious mansions and homes of Carthage (not to mention the magnificent Jasper County Courthouse) still stand today, reflecting the town's sincere reverence for and devotion to its past.

And what became of native Ozarkers after the war? Used to hardship and sacrifice, they simply returned to their farms and started over. New settlers seeking elbow room moved in from Tennessee and Kentucky, but also from Europe. Holding similar values to the Ozarkers, desirous of cheap land, and hearing that the streets of America were paved with gold, these latter immigrants moved to the Ozarks and were assimilated into the isolated communities.

For good or ill, civilization and progress came to the mining region in the 20th century. As always, the new and the old still bubble in a single Ozark pot, and this unique section of southwest Missouri remains a study in contrast. When the mines petered out, agriculture took over. As agriculture suffered, the local economy received yet another blow. As recently as the 1980s, those driving into downtown Joplin would find a town in the grip of an ongoing recession.

However, with the rapid growth of the region—and the popularity and acclaim of nearby cities such as Branson and Springfield—the mining region has received yet another lease on life. Soft-manufacturing firms provide jobs to thousands without destroying the environment. The transportation industry—freight and trucking firms—is huge in the towns that border I-44. An influx of investment has allowed community pride to emerge anew, and when combined with a burgeoning tourist population, these once wealthy towns that had fallen on hard times are quickly returning to their earlier grandeur. Just a quick trip through Carthage, with its stately mansions, manicured lawns, numerous parks, and unique shops, will prove that time is a healer. A drive though Joplin, seeing the hustle and bustle, sampling the artistic venues, and walking the miles of greenway, will serve as testament to that town's endurance. A day at Roaring River State Park, experiencing the quaint and friendly hamlets of Cassville and Noel, will teach the lesson that old and new can live in harmony.

The Ozark Mining Region was a hard land of extremes and contrasts; you'll get no argument there. But more than that, it is a living example of the power of resiliency.

AREA CODES All of the cities and towns found in the Ozark Mining Region fall under the **417** area code.

GUIDANCE Numerous chambers of commerce and visitors centers serve the busy and growing Ozark Mining Region of southwest Missouri. For information on events, dining, lodging, and individual town services, the following are the most helpful.

Joplin Convention and Visitors Bureau (417-625-4789 or 1-800-657-2534; www.joplincvb.com), 602 S. Main St., Joplin, Mo.

Carthage Convention & Visitors Bureau (417-359-8181; www.visit-carthage .com), 402 S. Garrison St., Carthage, Mo.

Cassville Area Chamber of Commerce (417-847-2814; www.cassville.com), 504 Main St., Cassville, Mo.

Monett, Mo., Chamber of Commerce (417-235-7919; www.monett-mo.com), 705 E. Broadway, Monett, Mo.

Neosho Area Chamber of Commerce (417-451-1925; www.neoshocc.com), 308 W. Spring St., Neosho, Mo.

GETTING THERE *By auto:* From either the east or west, I-44 is the main route to the Ozark Mining Region. It passes directly through Joplin, with Carthage approximately 28 miles to the north on US 71. Following US 71 S., you will arrive at both Neosho, the "Flower Box City," and Noel, the "Christmas City." To experience the beginning of the White River Valley and Roaring River State Park at Cassville, take US 60 from Neosho to the town of Monett. From there, turn south onto SR 37. At Cassville, continue south on SR 112.

By air: Travel by air becomes simpler for Ozark visitors as they move toward this growing region. Just 42 miles south of Joplin on US 71 is **Northwest Arkansas Regional Airport** (479-205-1000; www.nwara.com), 1 Airport Blvd., Bentonville, Ark. This new airport (completed in 1998) is serviced by American Eagle, Continental Express, Delta, Northwest Airlink, US Airways Express, and United. The **Springfield-Branson Regional Airport** (417-869-0300; www.sgf-branson -airport.com), with all the conveniences and amenities of the greater Springfield area, is located less than 60 miles east of Joplin up I-44. **Joplin Regional Airport** (417-623-0262; www.jlnairport.com), SR 171 and Dennis Weaver Blvd., offers service via American Connection.

MEDICAL EMERGENCIES Feeling a tad under the weather is no problem in the Ozark Mining Region. The following six hospitals, all full service with 24-hour emergency rooms, are but a short hop from any location in the area.

Freeman Neosho Hospital (417-451-1234; www.freemanhealth.com/ About_Us/Freeman_Neosho.htm), 113 W. Hickory, Neosho, Mo. 67 beds.

St. Johns Regional Medical Center (417-625-2354; www.stj.com/default.asp), 2727 McClelland Blvd., Joplin, Mo. 367 beds.

Freeman West Hospital (417-347-1111; www.freemanhealth.com/About_Us/ Freeman_East.htm), 1102 W. 32nd St., Joplin, Mo. 389 beds.

Cox Monett Hospital (417-235-3144; www.coxhealth.com/hospitalsphysician clinics/CoxMonett/default.htm), 801 Lincoln Ave., Monett, Mo. 47 beds.

McCune Brooks Hospital (417-358-8121; www.mccune-brooks.org), 627 W. Centennial St., Carthage, Mo. At the time of this writing, McCune Brooks is in the process of replacing the existing hospital with a new 62-bed facility in Carthage. Construction is expected to be completed in late 2006–early 2007.

St. Johns Hospital (417-847-6000; www.southbarrycountyhospital.com), 94 Main St., Cassville, Mo. 18 beds.

✳ Wandering Around

EXPLORING BY CAR In the early part of the last century, the locals of southwest Missouri made a habit of tapping the sugar maple trees for their sweet syrup. Though you'll no longer see too many Ozark maple trees with spigots in their sides, you can still explore the beauty of the region via the 30-mile **Sugar Camp Scenic Byway**. Begin your trip on SR 112, just south of Cassville, Mo., and drive through Roaring River State Park. You'll be driving "down" into **Roaring River**, with the last mile falling away at a rapid 400-foot pace (in other words, go slow and shift down). There is plenty to do in Roaring River, and you might want to visit the fish hatchery, hike one of the numerous trails, tour the Chinquapin Nature Center, or take a stroll back to Roaring River Spring itself. As you prepare to leave the park, watch the road signs and turn onto Forest Road (FR) 197. Though this is a gravel road, it is in very good shape (surprisingly, most Forest Service roads are well maintained). This route travels 8 miles and eventually hooks up with SR 86. In between—and this especially applies if you're traveling in fall—be prepared for some jaw-dropping colors and breathtaking ridgetop vistas. For a brief stop, pull into the **Onyx Cave Picnic Area**. The adventurous (or those who don't mind getting a bit dirty) can crawl nearly 100 feet into this little hole in the wall. Continuing ahead a few miles, you will turn left onto FR 2275 and enter the community of Eagle Rock. Just ahead is the intersection of SR 86. Drive back north through the junction of or SR 76 and SR 86 and return to Cassville. If driven straight through, the whole loop requires a little more than an hour. Nobody does it that quick, though; you'll want to stop, see the sights, and click off lots of photos.

EXPLORING BY FOOT ✇ ✄ ♿ **Carver Trail** (417-325-4151; www.nps.gov/gwca), 5646 Carver Rd., Diamond, Mo. Because most visitors travel in summer, and because after April even the smallest Ozark weed patch transforms into a tick

ROARING RIVER SPRING

factory, it is wise to either (a) tuck your pant legs into your shoes and spray them heavily with deet, or (b) take short hikes that are well maintained and well beaten down. Thus, for both enjoyment and a lack of bloodsucking parasites, I recommend the 1-mile Carver Trail at the George Washington Carver National Monument in Diamond, Mo. Beginning at Carver's bust just outside the visitors center (you can press a button and hear Carver's own voice reciting a poem), you will walk ahead until you come across the tiny cabin where the brilliant man was born a slave. As you continue, you will follow the same paths that George played upon and explored as a boy. You will pass his statue, cross a small, arched bridge, and walk around a pretty little spring-fed pond. Soon you will approach a second home, built by George's kindly "owner," Moses Carver, in 1881. The house is open to visitors and contains bits and bobs of interpretive information. Moving forward, you'll cross a couple of tiny creeks, a prairie area, and the cemetery where both Moses Carver and his wife, Susan, are buried. The trail ends back at the visitors center.

EXPLORING BY RIVER Starting just north of Noel in Pineville, Mo., the **Elk River** forms at the intersection of the Big and Little Sugar creeks. Roughly 55 miles in length, the Elk is clear and pretty, and generally fairly slow. That said, the current can jump up to the Class II range after a heavy rain. The flow of the river is more or less north by northwest, and it eventually dumps into the Grand Lake of the Cherokees in Oklahoma. Until relatively recent times you could count on an unspoiled and quiet trip down the Elk. These days, though, as more and more visitors continue to discover southwest Missouri, things can get a bit busy on good-weather weekends. There's a reason for that: The Elk is a gorgeous float with good fishing. Numerous access points, campgrounds, and outfitters make for an easy and relaxing day (or days) on the river.

Big Sugar Creek, one of the tributaries of the Elk, encompasses about 25 miles that are easily navigable by kayak or canoe. Just behind the Elk in terms of popularity with floaters, it has a good current but no whitewater that would surpass the abilities of the beginner. The creek is locally famous for its clear water and fine fishing. The Big Sugar can be floated almost any time of year, except of course for those spells when the occasional Missouri drought pays a long visit.

If the Elk and Big Sugar are too busy for your tastes, you might want to sample the nearly 8 miles of **Little Sugar Creek** that are consistently floatable. There aren't a lot of folks who opt for the Little Sugar, but that's only because most people prefer a longer float. For a day trip, this creek is perfect. It's pretty and clear; birds, trees, and wildlife are plentiful. Little Sugar would actually be my first choice if my goal were a lazy day of floating with a full cooler and plenty of eats.

The best time to hit **Indian Creek** is in the months of early spring; the rest of the year, the water isn't deep enough to float. When the rains of March and April come down, however, you can almost always count on a fairly swift current. Almost 27 miles in length, the Indian flows southwest until it dumps into the Elk. It's a fairly remote river (this is a relative statement—the rivers of southwest Missouri are all close to numerous towns), and shutterbugs will find ample scenery to record for posterity. There are a couple of low-water bridges and drops on the Indian, so the inexperienced floater should watch carefully. Don't be ashamed to pull to the bank and portage around such obstacles if you believe they're beyond your skill level.

✳ Towns and Villages

Carthage, Mo. Still full of grand Victorian homes, Carthage was considered the wealthiest town (per capita) in America at the turn of the 20th century. Mining barons had made a killing with their lead and zinc operations, and Carthage White Marble was renowned around the country. For examples, just look at the Field Museum in Chicago or the Macy's building in New York City. Founded in 1841, Carthage was burned to the ground during the Civil War, and the July 5–6, 1861, Battle of Carthage and Battle of Wilson's Creek (at Springfield) were two of the first major conflicts in the War Between the States. Today this town of 12,688 is one of the prettiest stops in the Ozarks. At no time is the beauty more evident than in early October, when "the Maple Leaf City" holds its annual Maple Leaf Festival. In Carthage you can take a tour of Victorian homes, sample numerous restaurants and specialty shops, or visit Civil War battle sites and museums. The town is perhaps best known as the home of the famous Precious Moments Inspiration Park, but it should be equally well regarded as the birthplace of zoologist Marlin Perkins and outlaw queen Belle Starr.

Cassville, Mo. For about 5 minutes in 1861 (actually, it was Oct. 31–Nov. 7) Cassville served as the Confederate capital of Missouri. Obviously, the designation was short lived, as the Show Me State ended up remaining in the Union. Things are mellower these days, and Cassville is a popular stop for trout fishermen on their way to Roaring River State Park (only 7 miles away). The town is surrounded on two sides by the Mark Twain National Forest, and the 30-mile driving loop known as the Sugar Camp National Scenic Byway offers nature at its very best.

Diamond, Mo. The little town of Diamond made a major contribution to the world when it produced the genius of George Washington Carver. Born a slave, the humble Carver went on to become a scientist, teacher, philosopher, and inventor of all things peanut. The George Washington Carver National Monument in Diamond is a tribute to the great man. While there, make sure to check out the informative visitors center, walk the 1-mile Carver Trail, and view the bronze statue of Carver as a boy.

CARTHAGE IS FILLED WITH VICTORIAN HOMES.

Granby, Mo. Just south of Diamond lies Granby, the original lead and zinc town of the Ozarks. Around the year 1850, the Jolly Mill was established. The name apparently arose from the fact that the mill was used as a whiskey distillery until World War I. The mill has been restored by the Jolly Mill Park Foundation, and the grounds now include a peaceful park and good fishing in Capps Creek.

Joplin, Mo. Though settlements were formed in the Joplin area in the mid-1800s, it wasn't until after the Civil War that times became interesting. In 1870 lead was discovered in huge quantities, and the town was the center of an unprecedented mining boom. *Wild and woolly* is an understatement, as the population grew to the thousands and more than 80 saloons, gambling houses, and pleasure parlors kept the rough miners entertained. Production of lead and zinc continued unabated for years (close to a billion dollars' worth was shipped from the region between 1900 and 1940)—the mines only shut down in 1970. Economic depression followed, and by the 1980s many of the buildings in downtown Joplin boasted locked doors and plywood-covered windows. I happened to work there during that period, and on any given day I could be greeted by a collection of panhandlers, hobos, or one unfortunate fellow who seemed to wear a Santa Claus suit year-round.

That's the past. Now Joplin is a culturally diverse city of more than 45,000 that has pulled itself up by its bootstraps and created its own renaissance. It's clean, up-to-date, and growing at a remarkable pace. Theater, art, shopping, and restaurants have replaced the old saloons and inns of ill repute, and a downtown revitalization is in full swing. Local retail and national/regional firms employ more than 35,000 residents. Joplin boasts of beautiful parks, two regional health centers, an airport, colleges, and 40 separate trucking companies. Though it would come as a surprise to those who saw the town just a couple of decades ago, Joplin is now consistently listed as one of the most livable small cities in American. The Dorothea B. Hoover Historical Museum and the Everett J. Ritchie Tri-State Mineral Museum celebrate the past, and the Joplin Municipal Building features a mural by renowned artist Thomas Hart Benton. Just outside town on Riverside Drive you can view Grand Falls, the largest continuously running waterfall in Missouri. Of course, any discussion of Joplin would be incomplete without mention of the Hornet Spook Light, an unexplained dancing orange ball that appears almost any night (in the same spot) on an isolated road near the town.

Monett, Mo. Originally known as both Plymouth and Billings, Monett received its permanent name in 1887. The town of more than 7,000 residents now features a 75-acre city park and nearly 10 miles of greenway trails. The town's proximity to Springfield, Joplin, and Branson—it's less than an hour from each—has made it popular as a bedroom community for those who wish to enjoy a more rural lifestyle combined with city amenities.

Mount Vernon, Mo. The seat of Lawrence County, Mount Vernon's 4,000-plus residents are most proud of their nationally known festival, Apple Butter Makin' Days. A three-day extravaganza that has been held annually for nearly 40 years, the event consistently draws nearly 50,000 visitors. Music, food, contests, parades, and pageants all center on the preparation of apple butter, cooked in huge copper kettles over open fires. During the Civil War more than 100 different regiments camped in and around Mount Vernon, and the town flew either the Stars and Bars or Stars and Stripes depending on which uniform was in residence.

THE WORLD'S LARGEST FLOWER BOX

Neosho, Mo. When rated on a basis of sheer pretty, there are few small towns that can compare with Neosho. Nationally known as the Flower Box City, in the mid-1950s the town received a grant to experiment in city beautification. As a result, planters were placed in every location imaginable. Flower boxes can be found in front of virtually every business, church, school, and home in town. As if that weren't enough, Neosho's Morse Park holds the World's Largest Flower Box (formerly a 66-foot-long, 8-foot-wide railroad gondola car), filled with flowers, shrubs, and trees. Also in town is Big Spring Park (a popular site for weddings, set around the spring itself, which pumps out nearly 900,000 gallons daily) and the oldest national fish hatchery in the United States. Festivals are popular in Neosho; October brings Barnyard Days, which draws artisans and craftsmen from around the nation.

Noel, Mo. The Christmas City of the Ozarks, Noel is a pleasant little town of 1,480 situated on the Elk River. Canoeing is popular here, down the Elk, Big Sugar Creek, and Indian Creek. The Elk River bluffs literally reach out to create a ceiling above SR 59 between Noel and the small town of Lanagan. Just 2 miles south of Noel is the commercial Bluff Dweller's Cave and Browning Museum. As caves go this is a good one, featuring the 10-ton Balanced Rock (which can be moved by the pressure of a finger) and the Musical Chime formation (which produces a tone when thunked). As mentioned, however, Noel's big claim to fame is its designation as the Christmas City of the Ozarks. Since the 1930s the town has invited people from around the world to send their stamped, personal Christmas cards to the local post office to receive the red and green NOEL postmark. More than 100,000 cards a year are still received (town volunteers help out and affix the special mark). There is no charge for the service. Just package up your Christmas cards, make sure they are stamped, and send them to: Postmaster, Noel, Mo. 64854.

✳ To See

✎ ♿ ✳ **Neosho National Fish Hatchery** (417-451-0554; www.fws.gov/midwest/neosho), 520 E. Park St., Neosho, Mo. Free. Established in 1888, this is the oldest operating federal fish hatchery in the United States. The city of Neosho eventually grew around the hatchery, and today the facility attracts 45,000 visitors per year. Tours are offered Mon.–Fri. 8–4:30 by appointment. In addition, a 3-mile paved walking trail (very popular with joggers) meanders around and through the hatchery.

MUSEUMS ✐ ♿ ❄ **Newton County Historical Park and Museum** (417-451-4940; www.neoshocc.com/interest7.html), 121 N. Washington St., Neosho, Mo. Open Wed.–Sun. 12:30–4:30. Free. Originally the county jail and home of the sheriff, the Newton County Historical Society Museum holds, among other things, frontier-era farming equipment, tools, and household items. Also on the grounds are the restored **Newton County School 111**—an 1896 structure built by the county's Anti-Horse Thief Society—and an 1850s log cabin built by the great-grandfather of a Neosho businessman.

✐ ♿ ❄ **Longwell Museum** (417-451-3223; www.crowder.edu/index.html), 601 Laclede St., Neosho, Mo. Free. Located in the Elsie Plaster Community Center at Neosho's Crowder College, the Longwell Museum possesses many artifacts regarding Thomas Hart Benton and the Daisy Cook Collection. In addition, the museum displays 5,000 photos, manuscripts, and records from the days when Crowder College was Fort Crowder, a World War II Army Signal Corps training facility and POW camp for German and Japanese soldiers.

Granby Miner's Museum (417-472-3014), 218 N. Main St., Granby, Mo. The redbrick building on Granby's Main Street could easily be an old five-and-dime. If you spot the MINER'S MUSEUM sign and take a step through the doors, though, you'll soon find yourself journeying into the past. The little village of Granby is the oldest mining town in southwest Missouri, the locale where the bonanza of lead and zinc was first discovered. The photos, tools, and history found in the museum will leave no doubts that the pioneer miners were a tough and inventive lot.

GRANBY MINER'S MUSEUM

✐ ♿ ❄ **Joplin Museum Complex** (417-623-1180; www.joplinmuseum .org/about.htm), 7th St. and Schifferdecker Ave., Joplin, Mo. Tue. 10–7, Wed.–Sat. 10–5, and Sun. 2–5. $2 adults; children under 5 are admitted free. Located in Schifferdecker Park, the Joplin Museum Complex holds several different museums thoroughly detailing the history of both Joplin and the mining operations that built the town. The **Everett J. Ritchie Tri-State Mineral Museum**, founded in 1931, displays an impressive collection of lead and zinc ore. Also on hand are numerous mining tools and equipment, and histories exemplifying the rugged work and lives of the miners. **The Dorothea B. Hoover Historical Museum** puts its focus more on the town of Joplin itself. Geared heavily toward Victorian days, the collections include dolls, a circus room, a kids' playhouse, and an ancient American LaFrance fire engine. Various submuseums (larger displays) are located within the complex, such as the Empire District Electric Company Museum, the Joplin Sports Authority Sports Hall of Fame, and the National Historical Cookie Cutter Museum.

POWERS MUSEUM

❦ ♂ **Civil War Museum** (417-237-7060), 205 E. Grant St. Carthage, Mo. Mon.–Sat. 8:30–5, Sun. 1–5. Admission is free. This museum chronicles and celebrates the Civil War in the Ozarks, and one of its bragging points is a 7-by-15-foot mural detailing the Battle of Carthage. Also in the museum are many artifacts of the War Between the States. Visitors can purchase souvenirs and signed, numbered prints of the mural.

❦ ♂ ♿ **Powers Museum** (417-358-2667; www.powersmuseum.com), 1617 W. Oak St., Carthage, Mo. Tue.–Sat. 11–4, Sun. 10–5. Closed Mon. and Dec. 18–Mar. 9. Admission is free. Yet another jewel hidden away in a small town, the Powers Museum highlights a nearly complete history of Carthage during the 19th and 20th centuries. Opening in 1988, the museum resulted from a bequest left by lifelong Carthage resident Marian Powers Winchester. Housing an artifact collection of more than 10,000 items, Powers has more than four dozen main gallery exhibits and has hosted nearly 40 traveling exhibits and displays. It also features a gift shop, research library, and media presentations.

❦ ♂ **Lawrence County Historical Society Museum** (417-466-7654; www.mtvernonchamber.com), 11110 Lawrence (Farm Rd. 1137), Mount Vernon, Mo. Open Memorial Day–Oct., 1–4:30. Admission is free. Located inside the lovely **Jones Memorial and Chapel**, this museum offers far more than you might expect. Inside are an 1865 hearse and a statue of Lady Justice, removed from the top of the Lawrence County Courthouse. One area of the museum celebrates the involvement of locals in conflicts ranging from the Civil War to Desert Storm; another focuses on the Depression era. The Hall of Time is a fine vignette into life during the 1950s, '60s, and '70s (polish up those disco boots). There is a gift shop within the museum, and adjacent is the historic, fully restored **1845 Adamson Cabin**.

CULTURAL SITES ❦ ♂ ♿ **Neosho downtown square/murals**. Many of the buildings in downtown Neosho are listed on the National Register of Historic Places. Murals celebrating the town's heritage add to the charm of the Flower Box City. A five-panel mural chronologically depicting the history of Newton

PRAYING HANDS

County is located on the main floor of the Newton County Courthouse. The *Centennial Mural* is found in the Municipal Auditorium, and the *Skaggs Tile Mural* is on the Mills Park Centre Building in Big Spring Park.

🐾 🔊 ♿ **Webb City *Praying Hands*** (417-673-1154), Ball and McArthur streets, Webb City, Mo. More than 32 feet high and weighing 100 tons, *Praying Hands* was created in 1972 by local artist Jack Dawson. It serves as a symbol of spiritual growth for local residents and draws visitors from a four-state area. Admission is free.

🐾 🔊 ♿ ***The Kneeling Miner*** (417-673-1154), southern end of Main St., Webb City, Mo. Another creation of Webb City artist Jack Dawson, the 10-foot-tall *Kneeling Miner* commemorates Webb City's legacy as a lead-mining town.

🐾 🔊 **Red Oak II** (417-358-9018), 3 miles north of Carthage on SR 96, 1 mile on SR 12. Open Mar.–Dec. This little-known spot north of Carthage continues to grow both because of its unique sights and cheap ($1) admission. The abandoned town of Red Oak was moved 25 miles by Lowell Davis and preserved as a reasonable facsimile of a 1929 Ozarks town. There are Burma Shave signs, a Phillips 66 station, an operating general store, and a blacksmith's shop with penny arcade games. Also on the site is a café and a little museum detailing the life of Belle Starr (the Ozarks are proud of their outlaws).

GEORGE WASHINGTON CARVER NATIONAL MONUMENT

🐾 🔊 ♿ **George A. Spiva Center for the Arts** (417-623-0183; www.spivaarts.com), 222 W. Third St., Joplin, Mo. Tue.–Sat. 10–5, Sun. 1–5; free. With its two galleries, numerous classes, and extensive library, the Spiva Center offers regularly changing exhibits by local, regional, and national artists. The gift shop allows visitors the opportunity to purchase an infinite number of original works of art.

HISTORIC SITES 🔊 ♿ ✳ **George Washington Carver National Monument** (417-325-4151; www.nps.gov/gwca), 5646 Carver Rd., Diamond, Mo. Born a slave, kidnapped, orphaned, and nearly dying of whooping cough, George Washington Carver overcame all odds and mastered chemistry, botany, music, herbalism, art, cooking, and massage, eventually heading the Department of Agriculture at the Tuskegee Institute. His groundbreaking work with the peanut began in 1903, and he discovered more than 500 uses for the legume. Rather than seek profit, Carver spread his information for free, with the aim of helping African American farmers escape poverty. His monument in Diamond, Mo., the home of his birth, was the first such park to honor an African American scientist and educator. The visitors center features a film and exhibits and is open daily. The **Carver Discovery Center** offers interactive displays for both adults and kids, and the 1-mile **Carver Trail** wanders the woods Carver explored as a child and passes by his statue.

✦ & ❀ **Newtonia Civil War Battle Site** (417-592-0531), Newtonia, Mo. Free. Two major Civil War battles were fought in Newtonia, one on September 30, 1862, and the other on October 28, 1864. Approximately 20 acres of the battlefield, and the 1852 **Ritchey Mansion** and cemetery (built by early settler Colonel Matthew Ritchey and his wife, Polly), are now preserved by the Newtonia Battlefields Protection Association. The site is open to the public on a daily basis, and tours are by appointment. Legend has it that the ghost of Polly still roams the mansion on cold nights, covering guests with blankets. This a handy thing to know if you're prone to chills. Newtonia is approximately 25 miles east of Neosho on SR 86.

✦ & **Battle of Carthage State Historic Site** (417-682-2279; www.mostate parks.com/carthage.htm), E. Chestnut Rd., Carthage, Mo. Missouri originally seceded from the United States. On July 5, 1861, Missouri governor Clairborne Fox led 6,000 Confederate troops against a 1,000-member Union force commanded by Colonel Franz Seigel. The Rebels won the day in a 12-hour running battle that began 9 miles north of Carthage and was fought throughout the streets of the town. This 7.4-acre plot in Carthage is where Fox's troops camped after their victory. An interpretive shelter explains the history of the battle, and the area is little changed in nearly 150 years. As a sidenote, it is said that, after the battle, casualties were cared for in the Jasper County Courthouse. According to local lore, one of the nurses was Carthage resident Myra Belle Shirley, who later went on to be known as the infamous Belle Starr.

Phelps House (417-358-1776; www.visit-carthage.com), 1146 Grand Ave., Carthage, Mo. All that marble money pouring into Carthage led to some pretty nice shanties. Of those that

HISTORIC PHELPS HOUSE

remain, one of the best is Phelps House. A three-story Victorian constructed in 1895 of Carthage limestone, the home contains rare woodwork, original light fixtures, hand-painted wallpaper and mosaic tiles, a Shakespearean library, and 10 fireplaces. It's open for tours Apr.–Dec., Wed. 10–3:30. Admission $5.

∞ ✎ ♿ **Kendrick Place** (417-358-0636; www.kendrickplace.com), 131 Northwoods Rd., Carthage, Mo. Sold to the Kendrick family in 1860, this historic home was built by slaves in 1849. An old-style mansion in the true sense of the word, it was regarded at one time as one of the most opulent residences in Missouri. Apparently the Kendrick clan was of a diplomatic bent, as they managed to convince both Union and Confederate troops of their neutrality during the Civil War. The home was occupied by troops of both sides at one time or another (though one wonders what might have happened should they suddenly have arrived at the same time) and survived the conflict unscathed. This was no small feat, as most of the homes in the Carthage area were plundered, ravaged, and burned. It's a true museum of living history. Guided tours are available, and the home can be rented for weddings or other special occasions.

ZOOS ✎ **Reptile World Zoo** (417-206-4443; www.reptileworldzoo.com), 1733 Kodiak Rd., Joplin, Mo. Open daily 10–6. $8 adults, $4.50 for kids under 12. No vacation is complete (assuming you have a 12-year-old boy and a sister he wants to scare) unless you visit a reptile farm. Joplin has a good one in the Reptile World Zoo. From Ugandan black forest cobras to yellow anacondas to American alligators and Nile crocodiles, all things slimy and slithering are here under one roof.

✎ ♿ ❋ **Promised Land Animal Park** (417-271-4606 or 1-800-866-7173; www.promisedlandanimalpark.com), HCR 01, Box 1086, Eagle Rock, Mo. Located south of Cassville on SR 86, near the town of Eagle Rock and Table Rock Lake. $6.50. Not your typical zoo, the drive-through Promised Land was created for the breeding of rare and endangered species. You'll see everything from camels and zebras to monkeys and llamas. A petting zoo is provided so that both kids and adults may touch and feed the animals.

REPTILE WORLD ZOO IN JOPLIN, MO.

URBAN OASES ∞ ✎ ♿ ❋ **Big Spring Park** (417-451-1925; www.neoshocc.com), W. Spring St., Neosho, Mo. Just three blocks off the Neosho town square (across the street from the chamber of commerce), the 7-acre Big Spring Park offers lush gardens, a kids' wading pool, a gigantic floral clock, and numerous picnic areas. Of course the park's namesake is in residence at all times, gushing out nearly 900,000 gallons of frigid water per day. Big Spring is a must for the photographer, and weddings are a regular occurrence.

☞ ♿ ✳ **World's Largest Flower Box** (417-451-1925; www.neoshocc.com), corner of North and College streets, Neosho, Mo. I'm not sure if there is a Guinness record for flower boxes, but if there were, the box in Neosho's Morse Park would certainly be in the running. Residents took a former railroad gondola car (66 feet long, 8 feet wide, and 44 inches deep) and transformed it into a wonderland of flowers, trees, shrubs, and plants. These folks take the *Flower Box City* moniker very seriously, a lucky turn for those smart enough to stop and smell the flowers.

🏕 ☞ ♿ **Schifferdecker Park** (417-623-1180; www.joplinparks.org), 7th St. and Schifferdecker Ave., Joplin, Mo. There are 23 different parks in the city of Joplin, constituting a total area of nearly 1,000 acres. One of the finest is the 160-acre Schifferdecker, home of the Joplin Museum Complex. The park also features a swimming pool, 12 tennis courts, a picnic pavilion, a baseball diamond, and an 18-hole golf course.

✳ To Do

FOR FAMILIES Also see *Zoos*, above.

☞ ♿ **Route 66 Carousel Park** (417-626-7710; www.route66carouselpark.com), 3834 W. 7th, Joplin, Mo. Featuring go-carts, amusement rides, arcades and games, 36 holes of miniature golf, batting cages, picnic areas, and all sorts of food and refreshments, Route 66 is open Mar.–Nov. Admission itself is free, but you'll have to cough up a bit of cash for the individual rides and activities.

☞ ♿ **Crystal Springs Trout Farm** (417-847-2174), Rt. 3, Cassville, Mo. If either you or the kids want a stringer loaded with rainbow trout, do not miss a stop at Crystal Springs. Developed in the 1950s, the farm hatches trout for stocking operations. However, a sizable area is also reserved for private fishing. Simply put, you will catch fish. There's no fishing license required, no limit, and you only pay for what you catch. This is where potential anglers should take note. While free bait and tackle are gladly provided, and while the friendly Crystal Springs staff will clean and ice your catch, you are charged $3.95 per pound. The fish bite so quickly and easily here that if you don't watch it, you could easily end up with 20 pounds of trout in your cooler. Don't let that fact put you off. This is a fun spot, and kids love it. The farm is located on Partridge Lane off SR Y, and visitors would be well advised to call ahead for specific directions. The season for fishing here runs Feb. 15–Nov. 15.

☞ ♿ **Royal Oaks Arena** (417-548-7722; www.royaloaksarena.homestead.com), 9895 Cork Lane, Carthage, Mo. This is a massive indoor/outdoor facility that features numerous events throughout the year. In addition to bull riding and rodeos, you might be able to catch such attractions as the Ozark Quarter Horse Show, the Missouri Classic Team Penning Championships, the Equine Sales Fall Festival Horse Sale, the annual Four State All Breed Horse Show, or the Draft Horse and Mule Sale. If you've never been to a horse or mule sale, it is a highly recommended experience. Just remember, unless you plan on buying, to keep your hand down and your mouth closed. These auctioneers move fast.

ANGELS

⊂⊃ 🐾 ✏ ♿ **Precious Moments Inspiration Park** (1-800-543-7975; www
.preciousmoments.com), 4321 Chapel Rd., Carthage, Mo. The brainchild of
Samuel Butcher, creator of those cute little figurines and dolls treasured by
collectors, Precious Moments is an entertainment monument to ceramic
angels. You can visit the **Precious Moments Chapel** (featuring 52 biblical
murals), the **Fountain of Angels**, the **Pink Ribbons Crusade** (I'm not sure
how this figures in with ceramic angels, but it's a tribute to the late Princess
Diana), a visitors center, or the **Memory Makers Auto Experience**. The park
further offers numerous music shows, gift shops, and restaurants. Various
packages are available for weddings, groups, and lodging (the Precious

✏ ✳ **Medicine Hat Trading Company** (417-246-5889; www.everycowboys
dream.com/medicinehattradingco), 12724 SR 70, Carthage, Mo. Owner Brent
Erwin has required a reputation for running an operation particularly suited to
beginning riders, and even more particularly suited for kids. He offers a stable
full of gentle, well-trained horses and specializes in both trail rides and horseback birthday parties. Medicine Hat is open all year, and the price is a low $20
per hour per horse.

GOLF **Carthage Golf Course** (417-237-7030; www.carthage-mo.gov), 2000
Richard Webster Dr., Carthage, Mo. A small-town course with a big reputation,
this 18-hole facility was labeled one of the Top 10 Hidden Gems in Missouri by

PRECIOUS MOMENTS WEDDING CHAPEL

Moments Best Western and Cubby Bear's RV Park are nearby). A visit to the chapel itself is free, but most of Precious Moments requires a daily attractions pass. After all, this is a large operation that hosts 400,000 visitors annually and employs a staff of 250. Hours are Mar. 12–Apr. 23, 9–5; Apr. 24–Nov. 4, 9–6; Nov. 5–Dec. 31, Sun.–Thu. 9–6 and Fri.–Sat. 9–8. Winter hours are 9–5 for the chapel and gift shop only (all other attractions are closed). The cost of the attraction pass is $9 adults, $8 seniors (50-plus), and $4 ages 4–12. The Memory Makers Auto Experience is an additional $9 per person.

the *Kansas City Star*. The Carthage links feature two ponds, one with a fountain, more than 30 bunkers, and narrow fairways. Greens fees for 18 holes are $15 Mon.–Thu. and $17 Fri.–Sun. Cart rentals are $22 for 18 holes.

Cassville Golf Club (417-847-2399; www.cassvillegolfclub.com), SR 112 S., Cassville, Mo. Just a short distance from Roaring River State Park, the Cassville Golf Club was listed among the Top 10 Public Courses in Missouri by the *Kansas City Star*. Its 18 holes will provide a challenge, but perhaps the true joy of this course is the surrounding beauty of the deep-woods Ozarks. It's very affordable as well: Weekday greens fees are $19 for 18 holes ($12 for 9 holes), and weekend fees are $22 for 18 holes ($14 for 9 holes). Cart rental is $8 and $12.

UNEXPLAINED MYSTERIES

The Hornet Spook Light, Joplin, Mo. If you're up for a scary tale, wait until the night is dark and meander south of Joplin toward a little-used road (called the Devil's Promenade) on the Oklahoma border. If you're lucky, and literally thousands of people have been, you will catch a firsthand glimpse of the legendary Hornet Spook Light. Located near the ghost town of Hornet, the light is most often described as a yellow or orange ball that travels east at a high rate of speed. It dips, dives, throws off sparks, and may even land on your car hood. Approach it, however, and the Spook Light will disappear. It is alleged that in 1946 the Army Corps of Engineers attempted to study the flaming ball, finally giving up and labeling it a "mysterious light of unknown origin."

Theories abound as to the source of this friendly spook. Some say it is the ghost of a Quapaw Indian couple; others, that it's either a miner or an Osage Indian chief who is searching for his missing head. More scientific theories include marsh gas, minerals and gases arising from the earth, refracted headlights from I-44 (doubtful, as the light was first seen in the 1800s), subatomic disturbances from the New Madrid fault, and the ingestion of way too much beer. The most popular local explanation claims that the Devil's Promenade was at one time the site of an old wooden bridge. Those who walked across the bridge at midnight could summon up the devil, who would either ask three questions, grant three wishes, or kill you on the spot. Personally, I tend to believe the "too much beer" hypothesis.

To get to the Devil's Promenade and the Hornet Spook Light, head west on I-44 out of Joplin. Take the next-to-last exit before Oklahoma and drive south on SR 43. In approximately 4 miles a potholed, paved road crosses SR 43. This is Spooklight Road. Turn right and keep driving a mile or three till you find a convenient place to park. Or just look for the other cars. At times the road can get a tad crowded with Spook Light hunters.

Schifferdecker Memorial Golf Course (417-624-3533; www.joplinparks.org), 7th St. and Schifferdecker Ave., Joplin, Mo. An 18-hole, par-71 course, Schifferdecker's greens fees at are $11 on weekdays, $14 on weekends. Cart rentals are $10 and $20 for 9 and 18 holes. The course is open year-round, with hours being 7 AM–9 PM during June, July, and Aug.

✳ Wild Places

Grand Falls. The Ozarks are not known for waterfalls, but the largest continuously flowing one is located just south of Joplin. Though it only drops about 25 feet (and that's during the spring runoff), this spot is so pretty that's it's more than worth a look. Just head south on SR 86 from I-44. Drive 1 mile, cross the Shoal Creek bridge, and immediately turn right. Go straight ahead for approximately 3 miles and you'll see the falls on your right. It's just a short hike down to the water and a great photo opportunity.

PARKS ✿ ♂ ♿ Roaring River State Park (417-847-2539), Rt. 4 Cassville, Mo. Located 7 miles south of Cassville on SR 112 is one of the oldest state parks in Missouri. Donated to the state in 1928, Roaring River is extremely picturesque, and the spring that emerges from the base of the limestone bluff churns out 20 million gallons of water per day. Roaring River is basically cut out of a mountain valley—part of the rugged, White River section of the Ozarks—and trout fishermen flock here by the thousands. The 2.5-mile spring branch, fed by the creek, is divided into three separate fishing zones (the one that allows wading is catch-and-release only). Approaching nearly 3,400 acres in size, and adjacent to one of the southwest sections of the Mark Twain National Forest, the park features a trout hatchery, a beautiful blue-green spring pool, a swimming pool, picnic areas, and a store. Seven trails totaling more than 10 miles in length are prized by both hikers and bicyclists, and the **Chinquapin Nature Center** offers interpretative displays and programs by park naturalists. Accommodations are abundant here. There are 187 campsites (ranging from primitive to electric), and the **Roaring River Inn** is equipped with 26 guest rooms and a restaurant. In addition (make your reservations early if visiting in summer), 26 rustic cabins with full kitchens are available for rental.

✿ ♂ ♿ ❋ **Mark Twain National Forest** (Cassville Ranger District: 417-847-2144; www.fs.fed.us/r9/forests/marktwain), SR 248 E., Cassville, Mo. One of the nine districts of the 1.5-million-acre Mark Twain National Forest can be found adjacent to Roaring River State Park. More than 70,000 acres of the forest are found in Barry and Stone counties, with endless hiking, fishing, horseback riding, camping, and goofing-around possibilities. Some of the developed areas include **Big Bay Campground**, **Big Bay Picnic Ground and Boat Ramp**, and **Shell Knob Recreation Area**.

If you're seeking to tour by car (particularly in fall, when the colors are beyond outrageous), do not miss the Sugar Camp Scenic Drive (FR 197), Onyx Picnic Area, and **Piney Creek Wilderness**. The latter is of particular interest for hikers. Found 20 miles east of Cassville, Piney Creek encompasses 8,100 acres crisscrossed by 13 miles of trail. The north trailhead offers a parking area, bathroom facilities (as in "modern outhouse"—there isn't running water here), camping areas with fire rings, quite a few hitching posts for horses, and the Piney Lookout Tower.

GRAND FALLS

Big Sugar Creek State Park (417-847-2539; www.mostateparks.com/bigsugar .htm), Rt. 2, Cassville, Mo. Take US 71 south from Joplin to Pineville; get off at the SR W exit, and follow 8th St. east for 5 miles along Big Sugar Creek. Still in the developmental stages, the mission of 2,082-acre Big Sugar Creek State Park is to preserve in its pristine state a portion of the Elk River section of the Ozarks. Close to the Arkansas border as it is (you can hit Arkansas if you spit real hard), some of the park's flora and fauna take on a distinct southern bent. For instance, don't be surprised by the number of flattened armadillos (or "sail-cats," as we call them) that you might see on area roads. Hikers will want to try out Big Sugar Creek's **Chinquapin Trail**, a 3-mile loop that follows a stream through deep valleys. Walking this trail you'll understand the too-often repeated Missouri Ozarks adage that "our mountains ain't much for height . . . but our valleys are mighty deep."

CAVES ✐ **Bluff Dweller's Cave and Browning Museum** (417-475-3666; www.4noel.com/bluffd), 2 miles south of Noel, Mo. on SR 59. Open Mar.–Nov., 8–6. Discovered in 1925, this commercial cave is lighted and features a 45-minute guided tour. A tad more natural than some show caves, it takes its name from the discovery of the bones, tools, and relics of a flat-headed man who once inhabited the 56-degree hole (Fred Flintstone should be so lucky). Among the highlights of the tour are the **Musical Chimes**, a rock formation with a heavy iron content that elicits different tones when tapped by the guide. The cost to tour Bluff Dwellers Cave and the adjacent Browning Museum (full of rocks, mineral, antiques, spear points, and arrowheads) is $10 for ages 13 and up, and $5 for ages 5–12. Those under 5 are admitted free.

✳ Lodging

BED & BREAKFASTS

Neosho, Mo.
✐ ♿ ✳ **Old Jaeger Winery and Bed and Breakfast** (417-451-9463; www .oldjaegerwinerybnb.com), 19619 E. SR 86. It's a little-known fact (and one that France hates to admit these days) that the Ozarks saved the French wine industry. By the 1880s French vineyards were being destroyed by lice. Hermann Jaeger, a Neosho, Mo., vintner, noticed that while his grape vines were also infested, they stayed healthy. Hermann began exporting his rootstock to France. As a result, he was in 1889 awarded the French Cross of the Legion of Honor and the national Order of Knighthood. The site of old Hermann's operation is now a B&B

offering three different suites featuring such amenities as Jacuzzi, satellite TV, Internet access, and unlimited phone calls across the United States. Prices range from $49 to $139.50 per night. At the time of this writing, the winery and Hermann's original house and barn are being restored. Smoking and pets are not permitted at Jaeger Winery, but kids are welcomed.

Joplin, Mo.
⊙ ♞ ✐ ♿ ✳ **Creekside Cottage Bed and Breakfast** (417-782-1874; www.creeksidecottage.net), left on SR NN off SR 86 (just after Shoal Creek Bridge). This little cabin is hidden away in the woods on the edge of Shoal Creek. From its relaxing porch, the sounds of creek, woods, birds, and

critters will lull you to sleep and wake you gently. The cabin has all the amenities (no phone, though . . . on purpose) and is air-conditioned. This is a pure-relaxation sort of stay, and if the 10 acres of peaceful forest don't mellow you out, then you're in a heap of trouble. The hearty breakfast consists of muffins, yogurt, sweet breads, eggs, sausage, coffee, tea, and milk. Rates are $149 for one night, or $130 per night if you're staying for several days. A complete wedding package is offered for $595. Kids under 7 stay free. Smoking is not permitted inside.

⚭ 🦐 ❋ **Prosperity School Bed and Breakfast** (417-673-0833; www .prosperitybnb.com), 4788 SR 200. During the height of the mining boom, the little town of Prosperity boasted 5,000 residents. In 1907 the imposing two-story, redbrick schoolhouse was constructed. Alas, booms have a tendency to go bust. The school held on for a number of years, but the final bell rang in 1962. Now revitalized, this B&B features three lovely rooms ranging $95–105 per night. Antiques are everywhere, and the feel of being in an old schoolhouse is both pleasant and comforting. A full breakfast is served Saturday and Sunday, with continental breakfast on weekdays. Neither dogs, smoking, children under 14, nor childish, smoking dogs are permitted.

Lakeside Cottages of Joplin (417-781-9230; www.lakesidecottagesof joplin.com). Lakeside Cottages prides itself on being so luxurious and secluded that the proprietors won't give out the physical address until you make a reservation (something Brad Pitt might appreciate if he ever visits his hometown of Springfield). These romantic-getaway cabins (which start at $139.78 per night) include feather bed, fireplace, overstuffed leather love seat, Jacuzzi tub, and thick king-sized towels. The kitchens are modern and well stocked, so you can prepare your own meals whenever you wish. The cottage porches hold a slide-swing chair that faces out over a 6.5-acre lake. Smoking is not permitted inside the cabins (it's okay on the porch; you're even provided with an ashtray), and neither children nor pets are permitted.

⚭ 🐾 **The John Wise Home** (417-627-9657; www.angelfire.com/folk/ thejohnwisehome), 504 S. Byers Ave. Victorian elegance is personified by the John Wise Home, owned and operated by innkeepers Tom and Alice Ward. The first thing you will see are intricate stained-glass windows, all more than a century old. Inside the home, antiques, plants, and a polished, quarter-sawn oak staircase will lend credence to the authenticity and constant care that has been bestowed upon this inn. Three rooms, ranging $85–125 per night, feature such amenities as four-poster bed, private bath, and a Jacuzzi tub. Pets are not allowed, and smoking is expressly prohibited both in rooms and on porches. Children, however, are more than welcome.

Carthage, Mo.
⚭ 🦐 🐾 ❋ **The White Rose Bed & Breakfast** (417-359-9253; www.white rosebed-breakfast.com/), 13001 Journey Rd. When Jim and Jan O'Haro claim that their inn is an Irish estate, there's not a bit of blarney involved. This stately 1900 home, constructed of Carthage marble, resides on a lush 10 acres of maples, oaks, magnolias, and tulips. Lovingly decorated with antiques from the 18th through 20th

centuries, the B&B's Italian marble fireplace, high ceilings, chandeliers, and stone portico will make you wish you could move in permanently. And that's before you even get a taste of either the food or Irish hospitality. Full Irish breakfasts are served, with ingredients both imported and grown in the O'Haros' garden. Those who wish a luxurious gourmet dinner may opt for the full "bed and banquet" treatment, a nice touch all too infrequent in the B&B world. The menu features such delights as salmon pâté and fresh vegetables, French onion soup, Ballycanally chicken in Guinness and honey, home-baked bread, fresh-roasted asparagus, and an exceptional crème brûlée draped in sumptuous strawberries. Though specials are frequently offered, the normal lodging rates at the White Rose are $96 for a room with shared bath, $109 with private bath, and $125 for a suite with Jacuzzi. Breakfast is included in the normal price, but those opting for the bed and banquet option (and it would be a very worthwhile choice) should add another $96 to the total. As expected, there are no facilities for pets, and smoking is not permitted indoors. On the other hand, high tea is served daily at 4 PM.

🦞 🎣 **Grand Avenue Bed and Breakfast** (417-358-7265 or 1-888-380-6786; www.grand-avenue.com), 1615 Grand. Built in 1893, this graceful Victorian mansion is unmistakable due to its huge, wraparound front porch. The interior is an aesthetic masterpiece, with curved plaster walls, antique wainscoting, gas lamps, a large stained-glass window in the sitting room, a library, a miniature upright piano, and period furniture. Four tastefully appointed rooms run from $79 per night, and a variety of corporate and weekend specials are offered. Several times a year the Grand features a **Murder Mystery Weekend**; call ahead for dates and reservations. While the rooms may appear to be turn of the 20th century, they are fully equipped with private bathroom, high-speed Internet connection, a business center, cable TV, VCR, phone, coffee service, and deadbolt lock. Breakfasts are an important part of the Grand; no cold doughnuts or soggy cereal here. The morning meal includes fruit, yogurt, coffee, orange juice, a main entrée, sausage, and bacon. According to local legend, a mine owner named Albert Carmean bought the mansion in 1933 and died of illness just a few months later. It is said that certain guests have noticed a whiff of his trademark cigar smoke from time to time. This is a dubious assertion, as smoking is not permitted inside the home.

GRAND AVENUE BED AND BREAKFAST

Noel, Mo.

WyldeWood Cabin (1-866-547-2591; www.wyldewoodcabin.com), 884 Mount Shira Rd. For those who seek a quiet vacation truly "away from it all," the WyldeWood Cabin, a 70-year-old restored log structure located above the Elk River, provides a great back-to-nature option. A relaxing afternoon on the spacious front porch will take you back to a simpler time, but with the comfort of air-conditioning (have to have it during an Ozark summer), two bedrooms, two foldout couches, two baths, a fully equipped kitchen, an outdoor grill, and a picnic table. The cabin is available year-round (reservations required), and rates begin at $90 per night.

RESORT ∞ 🐿 🐾 ♂ ♿ ❄ **River Ranch Resort** (1-800-951-6121; www.riverranchresort.com), 101 River Dr., Noel, Mo. A large, family-style resort with more than a mile of river-front camping, River Ranch offers tent camping, floating, cabins, RV spots, a store, and a café with a $6.95 Sunday breakfast buffet. The smaller cabins, sleeping four, are a bit reminiscent of the heyday of Route 66. These units are a single room with one full bed and a bunk bed, and rent for $39.95. They share a central rest room and shower. Larger cabins, sleeping up to 10 people, are a bit more in the hotel fashion and include kitchen, bath, and air-conditioning for $169.99 per night. Also available are five-person tepees ($79.99 per night). Tent camping sites start at $10 per night; RV spots, $15. Numerous float trips are available beginning at $18 per adult per day. Your need to bring your own linens and bedding for most of the River Ranch lodging options. If you'd like to bring your pet, you must call ahead first. The resort has had a few problems in the past with folks showing up with large or aggressive dogs, and pets are now permitted (understandably) only at the discretion of the manage-

ment. In other words, your beagle is probably fine, but leave the pit bull in the kennel. River Ranch Resort also has the ability to cater for reunions and weddings.

CANOE OUTFITTERS, CAMPING, AND RVS 🐾 ♂ **Eagle's Nest Campground and Canoe Rentals** (417-475-3326 or 1-800-843-7080; www .4noel.com/eaglesnest), 53 Eagles Nest Lane, Noel, Mo. Situated on 40 acres, Eagle's Nest offers campsites ranging from primitive tent areas to full RV slots with power and water. Camping rates run $6–20 per night. The facility features two beaches on the Elk River, fishing, swimming, a volleyball court, and a store. Tubes, kayaks, and canoes are available for rent, with the latter starting at $27. Children under 5 are admitted free, and dogs are permitted on a leash.

🐾 ♂ ♿ **Shady Beach Campground** (417-475-6483 or 1-800-745-6481; www.shadybeach.com), P.O. Box 473, Noel, Mo. 64854. Catering heavily to the floater, Shady Beach provides canoe, kayak, and six-person rafts. Prices for a two-person float start at $27; primitive tent sites run $6 and up (note that these sites are not marked; this is first come, first served); and any of the 23 RV slots go for $20 and up. Though pets are not allowed in Shady Beach's cabins (they are allowed at campsites), these rustic structures are a good choice, sleeping six people. While they do have electricity, they do not have private baths or showers. Cabin prices are $55 per night double occupancy, with a $6 charge for each additional person. This campground is geared for families, and such noise-makers as boom boxes, ATVs, motor scooters, fireworks, and your Dirty

Harry .44 Magnum are not permitted. Neither are foul language or loud drunks.

☕ ⚓ **Elk River Floats and Wayside Campground** (417-475-3561; www .elkriverfloats.com), P.O. Box 546, Noel, Mo. 64854. With floats on both the Elk River and Big Sugar Creek, Elk River rents canoes, kayaks, and rafts (six and eight person). Canoe prices range from $28 (a 6-mile float with plastic canoe) and up. For those who would prefer to play along the shoreline, paddle boats and tubes are also available. This is another good family spot, and the shallow, slow waters on the banks of the Elk make for an excellent kids' swimming hole. Tent camping (first-come, first-served) sites start at $7, and 98 RV sites (32 of these have sewer service) begin at $22. Aside from its two separate campgrounds (RV and tent), the campground features hot showers, a snack bar and gift shop, firewood, swing sets, and a pleasant gravel beach. Your dog is welcome if he isn't too big and snarly, but he must be kept on a leash.

⚓ ❄ **Big Elk Camp and Canoe** (417-223-4635 or 800-813-0907; www .bigelkcampcanoe.com), 402 S. US 71, Pineville, Mo. Located on the south side of the Elk River bridge. Aside from being a pretty campground, Big Elk is known for being an alcohol-free facility. This makes it an excellent choice for both families and teetotalers. Canoe floats begin at $25 for a 4-mile float; rafts and kayaks are also for rent. Tent camping is $6 per person (leave Fido at home; he's not particularly welcome here), and an electric RV site for two people starts at $25. This operation also features miniature golf, a game room, volleyball, and a tackle and gift shop. Big Elk Camp is open year-round.

☕ ⚓ **Camp Tilden** (1-877-646-1418; www.camptilden.com), 8739 Big Sugar Creek Rd., Pineville, Mo. Situated right on Big Sugar Creek, Camp Tilden offers floats on the Big Sugar, Elk River, and Indian Creek. The cabins are less than 6 years old and contain a screened porch, tiny cooking area, a regular bed and sofa sleeper, and a loft bedroom for the sleeping-bag set. The draw here is location, set in a lovely spot shaded by the trees overlooking the water. Prices for cabin rental begin at $75 per night; tent camping for a group of five is only $15. As with most campgrounds, linens and towels are not provided, so you'd best remember to bring your own. Pets are okay if kept leashed. Six- and 8-mile canoe trips are available, with prices provided upon reservation.

☕ ⚓ ❄ **Big Red Barn RV Park** (417-358-2432 or 1-888-BIG-BARN; www.bigredbarnrvpark.com), 5089 SR 138, Carthage, Mo. One of those mega RV sites (with the advantage of very little highway noise), the Big Red Barn provides 65 level sites, 50 of which feature full hookups. You can rent by the night, week, or month (for $21.90 your space will include 50-amp electric, water, sewer, and 40 channels of cable TV) and find plenty of supplies and ice on-site. There is an adult game room with pool table, central BBQ area, air-conditioned laundry, and Jacuzzi hot tub. Pets are okay as long as both pet and owner behave responsibly. For off-season travelers, the park is open all year long.

☕ ⚓ ♿ **Cubby Bear's RV Park** (417-358-1389 or 1-888-788-7275; www .preciousmoments.com/park/cubbyrv), 4321 Chapel Rd., Carthage, Mo. As part of the Precious Moments Inspiration Park, Cubby Bear's is (as expected) both clean and quiet. There is room here for 70 RVs (prices begin at $17.50 per night), and the facility offers a large swimming pool, water at every site, a dump station, shower and laundry facilities, game rooms, a video arcade, and a picnic area. Of course, upon request, you can grab a shuttle straight to the Precious Moments Chapel and park.

🐾 ✂ ♿ ❋ **Joplin KOA Campground** (417-623-2246 or 1-800-562-5675; www.koakampgrounds.com/where/mo/25106), 4359 SR 43, Joplin, Mo. This RV site offers 18 50-amp sites and can accept vehicles up to 70 feet in length. Tent camping begins at $18 per night, RVs at $26, and cabins at $36. The facility features a store and gift shop, laundry, Wi-Fi access, and a catch-and-release fishing pond.

🐾 ✂ ♿ ❋ **Roaring River State Park** (1-877-422-6766; www.mostateparks.com/roaringriver.htm), Rt. 4, Cassville, Mo. Of the three camping areas at Roaring River, one is open the entire year. The remaining two are open Apr. 1–Feb. 25. Fees are $8 for a basic campsite, $14 for an electric campsite, $15 for a site with electric and water, and $17 for electric, water, and sewer. Pets are okay in Missouri state parks, but they must be kept on a leash or tie-out no longer than 10 feet.

🐾 ✂ ♿ ❋ **Big Sugar Creek State Park** (417-847-2539; www.mostateparks.com/bigsugar.htm), Rt. 2, Cassville, Mo. The same rates apply for Big Sugar Creek as they do for Roaring River State Park. The Missouri state parks reservations number is 1-877-422-6766.

🐾 ✂ ♿ ❋ **Mark Twain National Forest** (www.fs.fed.us/r9/marktwain).

Consisting of more than 1.5 million acres, the Mark Twain is a superb wilderness dotted by rivers, streams, and some of the largest natural springs in America. Broken into nine different ranger districts, the forest includes hundreds of miles of hiking trails, numerous scenic drives, seven congressionally designated wilderness areas, 40 campgrounds (these can be reserved by calling 1-877-444-6777), and thousands of acres of primitive and semiprimitive areas. The Mark Twain is a true playground for hunters, fishermen, hikers, equestrians, and campers.

❋ Where to Eat

EATING OUT ✂ ♿ ❋ ♻ **Kitchen Pass Restaurant and Lounge** (417-451-4700; www.kitchenpass.net/neosho/neoshohotel.html), junction of US 60 and US Bus. 71, Neosho, Mo. Open daily 11–10. Located at the Neosho Inn (adjacent to Neosho's 27-hole golf course), the Kitchen Pass offers a wide and varied menu for breakfast, lunch, and dinner. A blue cheese burger with grilled onions goes for $6.45, while a southern-fried steak sandwich is $6.75. Dinner is a bit of an odd mix here, ranging from stock Chinese dishes to Mexican to Ozark. The cashew chicken is $9.95, the quesadillas are $9.25, and the 8-ounce catfish fillet is $10.25. The lounge features a full bar and occasional live entertainment.

✂ ♿ ♻ **DuParri's Steak, Pasta and Spirits** (417-847-1210; www.duparris.com), SR 112, Cassville, Mo. Open Mon.–Thu. 11–9, Fri. 11–10, and Sat. 4–10. Having opened in 2004 under the ownership of Leigh Ann and Bill DuParri, this restaurant and full lounge combines fine American and Italian food with a casually classy atmosphere. The fireplace in the A-frame dining room is warm and friendly, and the lounge is mellow with big-screen TV, pool table, and the occasional game of Texas Hold 'Em. Menu offerings are a cross between the traditional and the unique. For appetizers, the grilled portobello mushrooms ($6.50) share space with tater skins ($3.59) and hot wings ($5.99). For lunch you can select a great bacon cheeseburger at $5.99 or go for the more eclectic Barbecue Salmon Ranch Salad at $6.50. A number of steaks, seafood, chops, and pastas are available for dinner, but try the grilled portobello cavitelli. These are grilled portobello mushrooms with basil, tomatoes, fresh garlic and shell pasta tossed in olive oil and topped with mozzarella and Parmesan ($9.99). For dessert, chocolate fans will not be disappointed. Elect either the milk chocolate fondue ($6.50) or the brownie ice cream sandwich. At just $2.59, it's vanilla ice cream packed between two brownies and topped with chocolate sauce.

✍ ♿ **Stone's Throw Dinner Theatre** (417-358-7268), 796 S. Stone Lane, Carthage, Mo. For an evening of dinner and a show, check out this relaxed venue in Carthage. Most productions are of the comedy genre, although occasionally a dramatic or children's performance will be offered as well. Call ahead for ticket/meal reservations and prices. The actors for the shows come from the talented Community Theatre of Southwest Missouri.

🍴 ✍ ♿ **Carthage Deli & Ice Cream** (417-358-8820), 301 S. Main St., Carthage, Mo. Mon.–Fri. 7–5, Sat. 8–4. Sometimes you just have to have ice cream. When the urge strikes in Carthage, locals head for this 1950s-style hangout that has been serving the community for more than a quarter century. Aside from old-fashioned malts, shakes, sundaes, sodas, and cones, you can also order smoothies and cappuccino. If you're still feeling a might peckish, the Reuben sandwiches and subs are delicious. Best of all, you'll be hard pressed to find anything here more than $5.

🍴 ✍ ♿ **Lucky J Restaurant and Arena** (417-358-2370; www.luckyj .com), 11664 Fir Rd., Carthage, Mo. Mon.–Sat. 10–4. There's just something nice about watching a cowboy break a bronc while you dive into a steak or burger. In the Lucky J you can do just that, viewing rodeo activities in the adjoining arena through large glass windows. The menu here is traditional and leans heavily toward meat, but the prices are within almost everyone's budget: $6–20. Moreover, a kids' menu in the $3–5 price range is also offered.

✍ ♿ **Shellie's** (417-359-0054), 207 W. 3rd St., Carthage, Mo. Open for lunch Tue.–Sat. 11–3, and for dinner Fri.–Sat. 5–10. I like a place with an open kitchen; you know the cook isn't up to any monkey business. Shellie's is that type of place, a homey restaurant with quite a few offerings not found in your typical Ozark eatery. The Bleu Moon Beef Salad ($8.95) is a green salad with grilled fillet, red onions, tomatoes, and cucumbers topped with blue cheese crumbles. While a standard third-of-a-pound burger is offered at $4.75, a better choice is the apricot-smoked turkey. At $6.50, it features smoked turkey on a hoagie roll topped with apricot mayonnaise, romaine lettuce, tomato, avocado, raisins, and walnuts. Last but not least, the crabcakes here are as good as anything you'll find in Maryland. Two cakes are $13.95, and they arrive topped with a Cajun rémoulade.

❦ ✆ ♿ **Sultan of Smoke** (417-624-2264; www.sultanofsmoke.com), 1218 W. 7th St., Joplin, Mo. Open Mon.–Sat. 11–8. The Sultan of Smoke looks the way a BBQ joint is supposed to look. Your introduction is a redbrick building with a red and white awning. Often, there is a mobile BBQ pit sitting outside. While looks can be deceiving, in this case they aren't. Not only does the Sultan look like it should, the Q tastes like it should. You really can't go wrong here: You can buy smoked brisket, pork, ham, or turkey by the pound ($7.95 per pound, to be exact), and side orders include the drive-in classic "curly fries." The family pack—a slab of ribs, two side orders, rolls, and the Sultan's homemade sauce (which he also bottles and sells)—runs $20. Quite a bargain, but the downside (if something this tasty can have a downside) is that the family pack could easily be scarfed down by two hungry people. That's not a comment on portion size, either; it's a comment on the fact that this is first-rate Q. There are numerous sandwiches at the Sultan, all in the $5 range, with the burned end and Polish sausage sandwiches (both $4.69) being excellent choices.

✆ ♿ **The Red Onion** (417-623-1004), 203 E. 4th St., Joplin, Mo. Located downtown at the corner of 4th and Virginia streets Mon.–Thu. 11–8, Fri.–Sat. 11–9. The one piece of advice you might take to heart if eating here is to bring some spare change. This is a very popular lunch place, and parking can sometimes be a problem around noon. Just drive into the adjacent lot and stick a few

quarters in the meter. The Onion has an extensive lunch and dinner menu featuring appetizers, entrée salads, unique sandwiches, and specialty dinner items. If you're hungry, go for the Blue Moo Sandwich, a thin-sliced rib-eye steak with Monterey Jack, lettuce, tomato, and red onion, served on focaccia bread and topped with blue cheese dressing. For dinner, a much-requested item is the tilapia. This white fish is served with marinated olives, red peppers, and a sauce that has a mild bite. It comes with grilled new potatoes, broccoli, and a butter fondue sauce.

♿ ♟ **Turtleheads** (417-782-4323; www.turtleheads.net), 43rd St. and S. Main St., Joplin, Mo. The slogan is: "No chain, no frills, no sushi." This locally owned raw bar, pub, and live music emporium is not your quiet little restaurant on the corner. But when you're in the mood for oysters on the half shell, some stiff drinks, and loud tunes, it's your first choice in Joplin. With its Polynesian/South Florida chickee hut look, this is obviously a place favored heavily by the college-aged crowd. Raw oysters are $9.95 a dozen, and the étouffée is $12.95. You can order fried gator tail for $7.95, sweet potato fries for $5.50, or a 16-ounce rib-eye steak for $15.95. The kitchen hours are 4–10 PM Tue.–Sat., but Turtleheads bar is open till 1:30 AM. There are more nightly drink specials than you can count.

❦ ✆ ♿ **Timberline Steakhouse and Grill** (417-623-7722; www.timberline steakhouse.com), 2850 S. Rangeline Rd., Joplin, Mo. Mon.–Fri. 4–10 PM, Sat. 11:30–10, Sun. 11:30–9. Not fond of franchises of any sort, I wouldn't ordinarily include Timberline in this book. If you're traveling with the family, though, this is a nice enough spot and offers some very good value for lunch or dinner. There's a wide selection of salads, sandwiches, and entrées here, but for those on a budget, the real deal is the Sun.–Thu. $9.99 specials: your choice of fried chicken, a petite sirloin, or two pork chops, along with side order and salad. The decor is a bit cutesy, but the kids will like the western motif.

🌹 ✒ ♿ **Granny Shaffer's Restaurant** (417-781-1144), 2207 W. 7th St., Joplin, Mo. Open Mon.–Sat. 6 AM–2 PM, Sun. 7–3. Neither over the river nor through the woods, Granny's is located just a couple of blocks east of the Joplin Wal-Mart. Though it serves breakfast all day and offers a number of lunch specials, the real reason to hit Granny Shaffer's is the freshly made pies and baked goodies. A long list of standard pies (chocolate cream, coconut cream, apple, rhubarb, and many more) go for $10 each. Premium pies, such as pecan, blueberry, and blackberry, are $12. For those on special diets there are many sugar-free pies (also $12), and a large blackberry or cherry cobbler is $19.50. The breads and rolls are very tasty as well, with a loaf of banana nut bread costing only $2.49.

🌹 ✒ ♿ **Fat and Happy** (417-626-2002), 5806 N. Main St., Joplin, Mo. The name is appropriate, as Fat and Happy offers a 2-pound hamburger for $14. If you really want it dolled up, for a couple of bucks more you can add five slices of cheese, bacon, lettuce, tomato, or jalapeño. There's also a 1-pound burger for $7.50. Should you seek a more normal-sized meal, you can order anything from a bologna sandwich for $2.95 to authentic Louisiana crawdads for $9.95. An Ozark restaurant is just not worth its salt unless the menu offers catfish, and here the catfish fillets with fries and coleslaw run $6.95. For something different, try the deep-fried frank, a quarter-pound hot dog that has taken a trip into the Fry Daddy.

DINING OUT The Gathering Place (417-627-9657; www.angelfire.com/folk/thejohnwisehome), 504 S. Byers Ave., Joplin, Mo. Located inside the beautiful John Wise Home (an 1890s Victorian bed & breakfast), those seeking an exquisite meal will first be struck by the ambience of the Gathering Place. The antiques, the brass-and-crystal chandelier, the entire atmosphere will transport you back to the late 19th century. The lunch menu holds such offerings as raspberry chipotle chicken ($6.49), a Southwestern steak salad ($7.49), and a miner's pie (much like a shepherd's pie) for $6.49. While the menu is not lengthy, the quality of the entrées more than makes up for limited choice. At $21.95 you will be hard pressed to find a tastier prime rib, and the tilapia ($17.95) is served with a delicious roasted red pepper sauce. Fresh homemade cakes, cream pies, and fruit pies (in-season) will top off the meal. Reservations are requested. Lunch is served Tue.–Sat. 11–2, dinner Thu.–Sat. 5–8. High tea, served 2:30–4:30, features finger sandwiches, scones with lemon curd, and Devonshire cream and jam. The price is $12.

✒ ❋ 🍸 **Givone's Old Miners Inn** (417-525-4332 or 417-525-4400; www.givones.com), 208 Main St., Alba, Mo. Open for dinner Wed.–Sat. 6–9 PM. You would be wise to make your reservations three or four days in advance (around holidays, you'd best call weeks or even months ahead). When I first heard of this restaurant I thought, *What sort of harebrain would open a French restaurant in the boonies of the Ozarks?* That's what I get for thinking, for it turns out Givone's has been in business since 1979 and consistently draws a full house and rave reviews. After a trip here you'll understand why. Founded and operated by Max and Linda Givone, and now operated by Shanen Givone, the Old Miners Inn specializes not just in classic French fare but also in providing the epitome of Old World charm. The tables are covered with linen and illuminated by candles. The service is omnipresent without being pushy or obtrusive. The restaurant seats more than 100 (two dining rooms), something of a little French oasis amid the ridges, valleys, and BBQ emporiums of the Ozarks. Jackets and ties are not required, but keep in mind this is an upscale restaurant. From escargot de Bourgogne to chateaubriand, from smoked salmon to blackberry duck, the Old Miners Inn offers numerous beef, veal, seafood, and chicken entrées. All selections are prepared in either a classic or modern French sauce, and of course a nice selection of wine and cordials is available. For dessert, expect a tableside flambé such as bananas Foster or baked Alaska. Obviously this is not an inexpensive eatery, but you can be assured of getting your money's worth. Entrées run in the $20–40 price range.

✳ **Entertainment**

🎭 ♪ ♿ **Joplin Memorial Hall** (417-623-3254; www.joplinmemorialhall .com), 8th and Joplin streets, Joplin, Mo. With seating for more than 3,000, Joplin's 80-plus-year-old Memorial Hall was created as a tribute to the local men and women who had served in the military. The events held in this venue are legion, not to mention constant. Concerts by nationally known performers, circuses and carnivals, basketball tournaments, boxing and wrestling matches, trade shows, conventions, and opera are just a few of the many possibilities.

LIVE MUSIC ♪ **The Woodshed** (417-358-5620 or 417-359-7426), 311 S. Main, Carthage, Mo. Located in Carthage's Emporium on the Square. Live bluegrass and gospel can be heard every first and third Friday of the month starting at 7:30 PM. Admission is $5.

♪ **Mudflats** (417-358-6808), 2048 Suburban, Carthage, Mo. On the Fridays when live music isn't offered at the Woodshed, you can head to Mudflats. Beginning at 6:30 PM every second and fourth Friday of the month, local and regional players line up to take the stage with country, bluegrass, and gospel music. If you wish to perform, you can sign in at 5:30 PM and are allowed 20 minutes (groups) or 10 minutes (individuals) to serenade the crowd. Admission is free, and this is a smoke- and alcohol-free environment.

THEATER ♪ ♿ **Joplin Little Theater** (417-623-3638), 3008 W. 1st St., Joplin, Mo. Presenting between four and six shows per year, the Little Theater is one of the (if not *the*) oldest operating community theaters in the Midwest. Productions involve local and regional actors and behind-the-scenes crews. Call ahead for show dates, times, and prices.

♪ ♿ **Stained Glass Theatre West** (417-624-1982), 1318 W. 26th St.,

THE LANDMARK 66 DRIVE-IN

Joplin, Mo. The Stained Glass Theatre generally puts on half a dozen productions each year, most centering on a family or Christian theme. Call ahead for show dates, times, and prices.

Also see Stone's Throw Dinner Theatre under *Eating Out*.

DRIVE-IN THEATER ✤ ♿ **66 Drive-In Theatre** (417-359-5959; www .comevisit.com/66drivein), 17231 Old 66 Blvd., Carthage, Mo. A dying breed, the 66 Drive-In is allegedly the last outdoor theater in the United States named for the "Mother Road." It operates Fri.–Sun. nights Apr.–Oct. $5 adults; young children (of car-seat age) are admitted free.

✲ Selective Shopping

Richardson's Candy House (1-800-624-1615; www.candyhouse.net), 454 Redings Mill Rd., Joplin, Mo. Mon.–Sat. 9:30–5:30, Sun. 12:30–5:30. Those with a sweet tooth will find pure Nirvana at Richardson's. In operation since 1970, the Candy House is located in an old rock tavern. All its delights come from family recipes and are made from fresh, natural ingredients. The chocolates are hand dipped, rich beyond belief. This quaint little

shop is the ultimate stop when you are ready to break your diet. Just walk in the door, and you'll gain 5 pounds (and be happy about it).

The Book Barn (417-782-2778; www.vintagestock.com/joplin), 3128 Main St., Joplin, Mo. Whether you need a good book or just some new tunes, the Book Barn in Joplin offers a huge selection. Also on hand are vinyl albums (a million voices born after 1985 just asked "What's that?"), toys, video games, cards, comic books, magazines, and movies.

Courtney's Candles and Creations (1-866-723-6873; www.courtneys candles.com), 2029 Willard, Joplin, Mo. Sure, it's got a huge selection of candles, but what's really nice about this spot (if you're into things that tick and tock) is the large selection of rhythmic, musical clocks. Should you tire of listening to the tunes and telling time, take a deep breath and enjoy the many scented jar candles and fragrance lamps. Ceramics, ornaments, wicker animals, and much more fill the shelves in this fun and attractive store.

The Country Caboose (417-624-3861 or 1-800-371-3861; www.country caboose.com), 1100 N. Prosperity

Rd., Joplin, Mo. The owners call this shop "southwest Missouri's premier gourmet kitchen and gift shop." That may or may not be the case, but I can guarantee it's the premier gourmet kitchen and gift shop located in cabooses and passenger cars resurrected from the Santa Fe, New Jersey Central, and Frisco railroad lines. The Country Caboose is definitely loaded with kitchen accessories, unique cookbooks, and gourmet foods, syrups, coffees, and dip mixes. You'll also find plenty of gifts and delightful home decor items.

The Emporium on the Square (417-358-5620), 311 S. Main St., Carthage, Mo. Six specialty shops are located smack in the middle of town on Carthage's majestic old-time square. For live music there is the Woodshed (see *Entertainment*). The **Mud Puddle** (417-538-5620) is the site of Emporium Square's resident potter and offers handmade creations for either functional or decorative uses. For a bite of lunch or dinner, drop into the **311 Cafe** (417-359-3011) and later check out the collectibles and gifts at **Nutmeg Lane** (417-358-5620). The **Memory Merchants** provide a couple of levels of antiques, primitives, tools, pottery, and a host of hard-to-find items. Last but not least, **Allan's Antiques and Appraisal Service** offers a variety of antiques of the furniture, glass, and book genre.

The Old Cabin Shop (417-358-6720 or 1-800-799-6720; www.oldcabinshop .com), 155 N. Black Powder Lane, Carthage, Mo. Tue.–Fri. 10–7, Sat. 9–5, Sun. 1–5. If you like history and if you like things that go bang, this is your type of place. The shop is the site of the 1830s cabin where the Jasper

County government was formed in 1841. In 1980 the cabin became a retail gun operation, and additions were completed over recent years to better house the business, indoor archery lanes, and a museum featuring Indian artifacts and a fantastic gun collection. Anything involving guns, archery, knives, scopes, or paintball can likely be found under this roof.

Unique Turnings (417-847-2742; www.uniqueturnings.com), Rt. 2, Box 2722, Cassville, Mo. Artist Jerry Crowe takes wood burls (those giant, bulbous growths that pop up on the sides of trees) and—with chain saw, tools, and wood lathe—transforms them into bowls and vases the likes of which you have never seen. Some are left in their natural color, others inlaid with semiprecious stones such as turquoise and lapis. Small wonder Jerry's work is becoming ever more popular in galleries from coast to coast.

✳ Special Events

April **Missouri's Largest Garage Sale**, Neosho, Mo. For those seeking bargains galore, widgets beyond counting, and perhaps even a treasure trove of eight-track tapes, Missouri's Largest Garage Sale should prove satisfying. It happens in Neosho on the first Saturday of every April. More than 400 individual garage sales are put on by local residents, schools, churches, and civic organizations, and bargain hunters arrive by the thousands. If you can't find it here, it probably doesn't exist.

Spring Dogwood Tour (417-451-1925). Neosho is loaded with literally thousands of dogwood (state tree of Missouri) and redbud trees. In early spring the Neosho Chamber of Commerce provides maps to a local driving tour that highlights these gorgeous pink, purple, and white trees, as well as the infinite flowers that bloom all over town. The tour is a bit dependent on weather conditions, but in a normal year prime viewing time will be in early April.

Missouri Southern International Piano Competition (417-625-9755; www.mssu.edu/msipc), 3950 E. Newman Rd., Joplin, Mo. Taking place every 2 years, this competition highlights the talent of 35 pianists under the age of 30. The participants are selected from the best of the best around the world, with $30,000 in prize money and a Carnegie Hall debut at stake. Tickets are $15 for the opening concert and $15 for the gala winners' concert. Held on the campus of Missouri Southern State University in Joplin; the next competition is scheduled for 2008.

June **Carthage Acoustic Music Festival** (417-359-8181; www.visit -carthage.com), Carthage, Mo. Held on the Carthage courthouse square, this one-day festival in June brings out some of the greatest performers you will never hear (unless you're in Carthage). It's free to the public, and the music plays 10–10. Should you wish to join in, just bring your instrument and take part in the open-mike sessions 10–1. Groups are allowed 20 minutes on stage, individuals 10 minutes. The popularity of this event has led to some growth, and you can stroll through various exhibits and look for bargains at the bazaar.

✍ **Airfest Joplin** (417-626-0483; www.airfestjoplin.com), Joplin Regional Airport, Joplin, Mo. $10 adults, $6 kids. You'll see everything from barnstormers to a B-52 flyby at this two-day air show in June. Aside from the acrobatic skills of those magnificent men (and women) in their flying machines, the festival atmosphere is heightened by loads of food, family activities, and a kids' area. This is one place where you would be wise to bring along a camera and—lest your neck get stiff from looking toward the sky—a very comfortable lawn chair. Do note that even though this is an outdoor event, smoking is expressly forbidden. Cigarettes, a stogie, or pipes just don't mix well with extremely flammable, high-performance aircraft fuel.

Festival of the Four States (417-624-4150; www.festivalofthefour states.com or www.joplincc.com), Landreth Park, Joplin, Mo. Celebrating the heartland of America, the Festival of the Four States offers top-notch live entertainment, a BBQ cook-off, an extreme-sports park, an arts and crafts show, rock climbing, a three-on-three basketball tournament, a car and motorcycle display, mechanical bull rides, and a hot-air balloon launch.

July **Newton County Fair** (417-451-1925), Newton County Fairgrounds, Neosho, Mo. Taking place each year in early to mid-July, the Newton County Fair draws visitors from a four-state area. This is a fair of the traditional variety, featuring a full carnival midway, rides, craft booths, livestock exhibits, agricultural displays, music, and (of course) tons of food. The fairgrounds are located just south of Neosho near Crowder College.

George Washington Carver Day Celebration (417-325-4151; www .nps.gov/gwca), 5646 Carver Rd., Diamond, Mo. Though the date varies by year (either late June or early July), the Carver Day Celebration commemorates the Carver National Monument with educational programs, live gospel music, storytelling, nature walks, and numerous exhibits. Admission is free.

Summerfest (417-624-3580), 1730 Byers Ave, Joplin, Mo. $30 at door. Extra charge for workshops. Sponsored by the Ozark Acoustic Music Association and local businesses, the three-day Summerfest takes place at the Byers Avenue United Methodist Church. While the musical arts presented by the aficionados cannot be considered "lost," they do represent the skill and beauty of an earlier time. You may listen to or learn from aficionados on mountain dulcimer, hammered dulcimer, autoharp, psaltry, mandolin, penny whistle, and concertina. And if you've always had a hankerin' to whittle, do not miss the wood-carving workshops.

August **Hillbilly Boogie Skydiving Festival** (1-800-598-5867), Mount Vernon Airport, Mount Vernon, Mo. Personally, I can think of no quicker way to experience coronary vapor lock than by jumping out of a perfectly good airplane. Still, watching others take the leap is fairly interesting. You can do just that (or if you're nuts, you can also jump) at the Hillbilly Boogie Skydiving Festival. Hundreds of jumpers show up for this annual event in early August, falling from the sky both in single and tandem format. Admission is free if you're merely a spectator, but if you seek to go hurtling through the great blue yonder, the fees begin at $20 for registration and $21 for a lift. Heck, they'll even give you a lesson right on the spot

and let you jump. Just remember, the fall isn't what kills you. It's the sudden landing.

All Summer **Gatherin' on the Square** (417-451-1925), Neosho downtown square. At one time almost every small town in the Ozarks had a bandstand on the courthouse grounds, with local musicians and town bands performing for the pleasure of locals and visitors alike. The trend has long passed in most areas, but not in Neosho. During the summer months bluegrass, country, and gospel musicians descend on the square every Thursday evening and fill the air with music. There is no charge for this weekly event. Just drop by, and feel free to bring your guitar or banjo.

September **Carthage Ragtime Music Festival** (417-358-2667; www.powersmuseum.com). At this weekend festival in early September, visitors can enjoy the music of ragtime legend James Scott and other noted composers. A competition for ragtime students 18 and under is held at the Powers Museum on the Saturday of the event. Admission is free.

October ♪ **Apple Butter Makin' Days** (417-466-7654; www.mtvernon chamber.com), Courthouse Square, Mount Vernon, Mo. They cook it in huge copper kettles over open fires, just the way it was done for hundreds of years. No, even though this is the Ozarks, we're not talking moonshine. We're talking apple butter, and the residents of Mount Vernon are crazy about the stuff. This festival, now nearly 40 years old, draws nearly 50,000 people over a three-day weekend in October. As festivals go, it's not only one of the most unusual, but also one of the best. How often do you see a nail-driving competition or turtle race? How often can you take part in apple-biting or apple-pie-eating contests while listening to old-time fiddle music? The entertainment here is geared for kids of every age, from the bubble-gum bubble blow-off to the rope climb to the parade of pets. Nearly 400 craftsmen from around the country will be set up in booths, peddling their wares. There's a gunfight on the square, dramatic skits, and a never-ending procession of country, folk, bluegrass, and Christian musicians. Least you forget the food, be prepared to dive into apple dumplings, caramel apples, funnel cakes, turkey drumsticks, kettle corn, bratwurst, stuffed baked potatoes, and the ever-popular hamburgers and hot dogs.

Barnyard Days (417-451-3399; www.circle-r-festivals.com/barnyard_days.html), 10970 Old Scenic Dr. at the Circle R Ranch, Neosho, Mo. For pure authenticity, one of the best local festivals you will find is Barnyard Days. It's A three-day affair held the first weekend in October, and the Circle R Ranch hosts this event, which places craftsmen from around the country in a natural barnyard setting. The fall colors are spectacular, the crafts (with more than 150 exhibitors) unique. Entertainment is plentiful, with continuous music every day. Also on the agenda are a scarecrow-building contest, a petting zoo, and an antique tractor display. Barnyard Days takes place on Sat.–Sun. 9–6, Mon.

9–4. Circle R Ranch can be found 4 miles north of Neosho off US 71. Just turn west onto Iris Rd. and drive 3.2 miles.

Maple Leaf Festival (417-359-8181; www.visit-carthage.com), Carthage, Mo. The big shindig of the year. For a full week each October the town of Carthage celebrates full tilt with its Maple Leaf Festival. Held both on the historic square and at venues all over town, some of the events include beauty pageants (to crown the Maple Leaf Queen), an old-time bazaar, and wine and beer tasting (this one is $25 at the door). The list of activities is a mile long, with quilt shows, lip-sync competitions, beautiful baby contests, bratwurst cook-offs ($4), an auto show, a marching band extravaganza ($3), a bull-riding rodeo ($8), a dog show, a petting zoo, and a huge parade being just a sample of myriad options.

December **Dickens Christmas Faire and Parade** (417-451-1925), downtown square, Neosho, Mo. Christmas begins in Neosho during the first weekend in December, when the lights come on both at Big Spring Park and at the historic downtown area. The latter is of particular interest, as this little Ozark town begins to take on the presence of Tiny Tim (the Dickens character, not the ukulele-playing tulip man) and Ebenezer Scrooge. Downtown features characters, carolers, horse-drawn carriage rides, food, and craft exhibits.

SPRINGFIELD, MISSOURI

The third largest city in Missouri, with 151,000 residents (nearly 400,000 in the metropolitan area), Springfield has long been known as the "Queen City of the Ozarks." At least, that's how it's inevitably labeled by historians and travel writers. For the locals, it's where you're headed if you're going to town, those times when you find yourself in desperate need of a Sam's Club, sporting events and concerts, great dining and shopping, health care, or even an education. Though the city's population continues to expand at a highly accelerated rate, thanks in part to its beauty and atmosphere but mostly due to the continued explosion of nearby Branson, Springfield has somehow never forgotten its roots. It's the major city of the Ozarks, yet it still manages to feel like a small town.

This aspect of the place can be attributed to the people, who seem to view themselves more as country folk than city folk. You will find Springfieldians a friendly and helpful bunch, proud of their Midwest values, their Ozark heritage, and the fact that their town is utterly up-to-date with the 21st century. Just about the only time you will find a hint of the pretentious is if you watch local news broadcasts, listen too long to the party line from the chamber of commerce, or happen to stumble across one of the myriad eponymous restaurants in town. The more upscale business element of Springfield sometimes tries a bit too hard to distance itself from the stereotype of the Hillbilly. Still, this attempt to appear "cutting edge" could not in any way be construed as disingenuous or even obnoxious. If anything, you'll think that perhaps those creating the public relations image don't realize that the inherent gifts of Springfield are far more attractive and valuable than the urban/media ideals they would emulate. Either way, it's not a big deal. This is a city that, for the most part, truly likes what it is. That's good, for there's plenty to like.

You will find hundreds of restaurants covering virtually all styles and ethnicities. Entertainment runs the gamut from small rock or jazz clubs, to major concerts with nationally known entertainers, to a plethora of collegiate and semipro sporting events. There are a number of major hospitals in Springfield, all state of the art. For families, the vast number of parks, greenways, historic sites, and festivals (not to mention a great zoo) make the city seem almost idyllic.

Shopping is also big in Springfield, as evidenced by Bass Pro Shop's Outdoor World. This massive store (it's the firm's international headquarters) is a marvel to

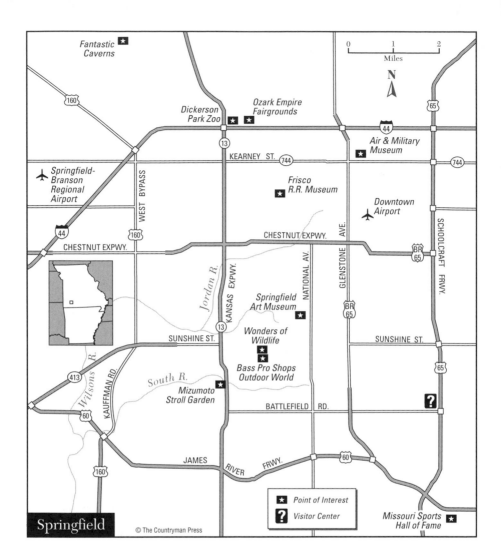

Springfield

© The Countryman Press

behold and succeeds beyond description in promoting (and selling) the romance with the outdoors that is the hallmark of the Ozarks. It's nice, it's classy without hype, and it's also the largest single tourist attraction in the state of Missouri (more than 5 million visitors annually).

All in all, this is just a great town, a community that draws new citizens like a spinster draws cats. Employment is good; housing is reasonably priced. Springfield has an excellent educational system and has birthed more than a few famous native sons. Brad Pitt went to Kickapoo High School, and former attorney general John Ashcroft attended Hillcrest High. Just to prove that the price was right, game-show icon Bob Barker learned his early lessons at Central High. Neither is higher education forgotten. Missouri State University boasts more than 17,000 students, while Ozarks Technical Community College, Drury University, and

Evangel College teach 8,500, 4,600, and 1,800 students, respectively. Then there are Baptist Bible College, Central Bible College, Forest Institute of Professional Psychology, St. John's College of Nursing and Health Sciences, Vatterott College, and Bryan College. Those who believe the Ozarks to be a wholly uneducated locale will quickly have their preconceptions shattered in Springfield.

Founded in 1829 by John Polk Campbell, Springfield was a hotbed of action during the Civil War. Major bloodshed occurred between 1861 and 1863. The largest majority of residents were Southern sympathizers, and during the war itself Republicans were known to keep silent about their pro-Union leanings. After the war the town was the epitome of untamed frontier, with Wild Bill Hickok shooting Dave Tutt (1865) in what is commonly acknowledged as the first "real" shootout of the Old West. Today it is one of those midsized cities that remain something of a secret to the vast majority of Americans.

Perhaps the best description of Springfield is this: It's a nice place to visit . . . but you'll probably want to live here.

AREA CODES Springfield, Mo., and the surrounding area are all covered by the **417** area code.

GUIDANCE The main source of information for Springfield and the surrounding communities is the **Springfield Missouri Convention and Visitor's Bureau** (417-881-5300 or 1-800-678-8767; www.springfieldmo.org), 3315 E. Battlefield or 815 E. St. Louis, Suite 100, Springfield, Mo. Both locations offer a visitors center, plenty of pamphlets, and helpful information. Additional area facts and assistance can be gathered at the **Nixa Area Chamber of Commerce** (417-725-1545; www.nixachamber.com), 105 Sherman Way, Suite 108, Nixa, Mo., and the **Aurora Chamber of Commerce** (417-678-4150; www.auroramochamber .com), 121 E. Olive, Aurora, Mo.

GETTING THERE *By auto:* Springfield can be reached either from the east or the west via I-44, which passes right through the northern section of the city. From north and south US 65 is the most favored route. Other, somewhat more scenic approaches include SR 13 (to the north, a great alternative route now that most of it has recently been four laned) and US 160 to the south.

By air: **Springfield-Branson Regional Airport** (417-869-0300; www.sgf -branson-airport.com), 5000 W. Kearney, Springfield, Mo., is served by American Airlines, American Connection, American Eagle, Northwest Airlink, US Airways, United Express, and Allegiant. The airport offers facilities for buses, vans, rental cars, and hotel and hospitality limousines.

MEDICAL EMERGENCIES **Cox Medical Center North** (417-269-3000; www.cox net.org), 1423 N. Jefferson Ave., Springfield, Mo., and **Cox Medical Center South** (417-269-3000; www.coxnet.org), 3801 S. National Ave., Springfield, Mo., are part of the massive Cox network and include 274 and 562 beds, respectively. **St. John's Regional Health Center** (417-885-2000; www.stjohns.net), 1235 E. Cherokee St., Springfield, Mo., is a 1,016-bed center. All of these hospitals operate satellite clinics in surrounding counties. **Lakeland Regional Hospital** (417-865-5581 or 1-800-432-1210; www.lakelandregional.com), 440 S. Market St., Springfield, Mo., has served Springfield for more than 100 years and includes 133 beds.

✳ Wandering Around

EXPLORING BY CAR Battle of Springfield Driving Tour (417-881-5300 or 1-800-678-8767; www.springfieldmo.org), Tourist Information Center, 3315 E. Battlefield Rd., Springfield, Mo. For Springfield, one of the major battles of the Civil War took place in January 1863. At that time, Union troops defended the town when Confederate forces swarmed in to obtain supplies and secure the Queen City for the Stars and Bars. To memorialize this bloody event, 12 markers chronicling the battle have been placed in strategic, historically accurate locations. For a map detailing this interesting driving tour, contact the Springfield Convention and Visitor's Bureau at the number above.

EXPLORING BY FOOT 🌿 🐾 ♂ ♿ **Galloway Creek Greenway** (417-864-2015; www.ozarkgreenways.org). The trailhead is located at Seminole and Pine streets at the Pershing Middle School in Springfield. Admission is free. Greenways are defined as long stretches of undeveloped areas of natural habitat that generally pass through urban areas. Often following streams or old railroad track, they are often hard-surfaced paths accessible to walkers, runners, bicyclists, in-line skaters, wheelchairs, baby strollers, and old folks on Rascal scooters. The Ozarks Greenways organization has been instrumental in creating six such trails in the Springfield area, with one of the favorites being the Galloway Creek Greenway. The Galloway, designated a National Recreation Trail by the National Park Service, stretches 5 miles from the Pershing Middle School, to Sequiota Park, to its ending at the Springfield Conservation Nature Center. Wandering this way and that under US 60 and US 65, the trail also crosses over the scenic James River Bridge. At the end of this bridge, you will come across a well-tended pet cemetery where many locals have laid their beloved critters to rest. The trail passes through and by a number of Springfield neighborhoods and along Springfield Lake. Best of all, if you get hungry or tired along the way, you can always take a break at the **Galloway Station Restaurant**.

✳ Towns and Villages

Aurora, Mo. Located 33 miles southwest of Springfield, Aurora was one of the original mining centers of the Ozarks. In 1885 some fellows digging a well set off a powder keg and exposed huge chunks of galena ore. After that, the lead boom was on, with rich veins being found one after another. Today Aurora is home to more than 7,000 residents. More importantly for those who can't resist the combination of smoke, spice, and pork, it is also the home of the most excellent Richard's Hawgwild BBQ.

Marionville, Mo. The billboard at the edge of town reads MARIONVILLE WELCOMES YOU. While there's nothing unusual in that, the accompanying photo of a giant white squirrel raises a few eyebrows. You see, Marionville is the White

Squirrel Capital of the United States. Nobody knows how they got there, but a colony of more than 100 pure white squirrels resides in this town of 2,113, located 28 miles southwest of Springfield. The locals feed and protect them, and hunters should beware. Injuring one of the town's beloved albinos results in a $1,000 fine (and you'd likely get a whuppin' from the locals if you were stupid enough to brag about it).

MARIONVILLE TAKES PRIDE IN ITS ALBINO SQUIRREL POPULATION.

Nixa, Mo. Since its founding in the mid-1800s, Nixa has always served as a crossroads of sorts, first for farmers and later for teamsters traveling north from Arkansas. Today the town of 14,000, situated in the prosperous corridor between Branson and Springfield, serves the same purpose. A very pretty place in spring and fall, with its flowering dogwood and vibrant fall colors, Nixa is also home to the legendary Sucker Days festival, held in early May for nearly 50 years. Even the schools officially close on Sucker Days. Residents and thousands of visitors chow down on these nasty-looking, deep-fried bottom feeders (which taste great, by the way) and enjoy live music, a parade, and carnival rides.

Ozark, Mo. The seat of Christian County, Ozark was founded around pioneer John Hoover's gristmill in the 1830s. The town of 10,000 continues to prosper due to its proximity to both Springfield and Branson. The popular Lambert's Cafe (home of the "throwed roll") is found in Ozark and is regionally famous for the staff's propensity to toss fresh-baked biscuits at dining patrons.

Republic, Mo. Another early crossroads town just 14 miles west of Springfield, Republic's nearly 10,000 people are justifiably proud of their pumpkins. On the first Saturday of October, growers from across the region show up for **Pumpkin Daze** to have their giant pumpkins (plus squash and watermelons) weighed and recorded. This effort is part of an international competition (the Great Pumpkin Commonwealth) that awards more than $25,000 in prize money. In 2004 the prizewinning pumpkin from Republic weighed in at 770 pounds, a new Missouri record. We have big pumpkins in these parts (and we're also easily amused).

✳ To See

MUSEUMS ✆ ✎ ♿ **Springfield Art Museum** (417-837-5700; www.ci.springfield .mo.us/egov/art), 1111 E. Brookside Dr., Springfield, Mo. Hours are Tue., Wed., Fri., and Sat. 9–5; Thu. 9–8; and Sun. 1–5. Admission is free. Founded in 1928, the Springfield Art Museum houses more than 8,500 artistic objects covering literally thousands of years of culture. Painting, watercolor, sculpture, and prints are just a start of the collection, and a 329-seat auditorium offers a variety of programs. Past presentations have included a collaboration with the Springfield Opera, with special recitals performed once each week.

✒ ♿ **General Sweeny's Museum** (417-732-1224; www.civilwarmuseum.com), 5228 S. SR ZZ, Republic, Mo. Open Mar.–Oct., Wed.–Sun. 10–5. $4.50 adults, $3.50 ages 5–11. When it came to getting shot, cut, and whittled away, Admiral Nelson didn't have much on General Thomas "Fightin' Tom" Sweeny. Born in 1820 in Ireland and immigrating to the United States at the age of 12, Sweeny first lost his right arm to a musket ball at the storming of Churubusco. In the 1850s he was an Indian fighter in the West. During the Civil War he was in the Battle of Wilson's Creek near Springfield and took another musket ball in the thigh. With the 52nd Illinois at Shiloh, he took numerous bullet wounds and only left the field when forced to by loss of blood. "Fightin' Tom" survived, however, and lived till the age of 72. A linguist of sorts, Fightin' Tom could reportedly curse fluently and with gusto in three languages. The museum that bears his name contains thousands of Civil War artifacts and takes visitors through the War Between the States from beginning to end. From the murderous abolitionists under John Brown, to the Missouri Bushwhackers, to all the conflict's major battles, the museum's displays tell the tales in vivid detail. Rare and unique items, weapons, and flags will take you back in time.

✒ ♿ **Air and Military Museum of the Ozarks** (417-864-7997; www.ammo museum.com), 2305 E. Kearney St., Springfield, Mo. Open year-round, Tue.–Sat. noon–4. $3 adults , $1 ages 6–12. Established in 1989, this museum is dedicated to all those who gave their lives in the defense of American freedoms and liberties. It specializes in the restoration, preservation, and display of military history, and more than 5,000 pieces of memorabilia are exhibited. I'm not just talking bayonets and medals. You can take a simulated flight (while sitting in the cockpit, no less) of a restored Cobra AH-1S military helicopter. This is a great experience for both kids and adults, as you start the engine, take off at 100 knots, and blast away at enemy tanks with a laser-sighted, six-barreled machine gun. Almost equally cool is a GAT-1B Link Trainer Flight Simulator.

Historical Museum for Springfield/Greene County (417-864-1976; www .springfieldhistory.org), 830 Boonville Ave., Springfield, Mo. Admission is free, but a small donation of $3 is appreciated. Located on the third floor of city hall, the museum contains more than 3,000 square feet of exhibit space and features both permanent and rotating exhibits. Historical eras range from prehistoric times, through early settlement, through the Civil War, and up to the 1950s. Two different interpretative videos can be viewed, and a hands-on area for kids offers an Indian grinding stone, Civil War tent, and household items from the pioneer days. Rotating exhibits have included such presentations as the 130-year history of Springfield baseball.

✒ ♿ **Missouri Sports Hall of Fame** (417-889-3100 or 1-800-498-5678; www .mosportshalloffame.com), 3861 Stan Musial Dr., Springfield, Mo. Open year-round, Mon.–Sat. 10–4, Sun. noon–4. $5 adults, $4 seniors, $3 students. A 22,000-square-foot celebration of Missouri sports and the athletes who played them, the museum is loaded with a wide array of sports memorabilia and interactive displays. More than just football, basketball, baseball, and golf, virtually every sport imaginable is represented (including famous Missouri fishermen).

✄ ♿ **The Softball Museum** (417-887-5817), 2141 E. Pythian, Springfield, Mo. Open year-round, Mon.–Fri. 11–5. $2 ages 13 and up, $1 ages 6–12. Springfielders love their baseball and softball, and this museum offers a Hall of Fame commemorating players from both Springfield and the Missouri American Softball Association. Displays trace local accomplishment back to the 1920s. There is even a display featuring softball achievement from Isesaki, Japan, Springfield's sister city.

❦ ✄ ♿ **Aurora Historical Society Museum** (417-678-4150), 121 E. Olive St., Aurora, Mo. Open year-round. Admission is free. A small museum filled with a trove of items from the past, most of which were donated by members of the community, the Aurora museum is located within a 1906 Missouri Pacific Railroad depot.

CULTURAL SITES ❦ ✄ ♿ **Womack Mill** (417-759-2807; www.rootsweb.com/ ~gcmohs/3rd_level/township_08.htm), Main St. and SR 125, Fair Grove, Mo. Open year-round. Tours by appointment. Admission is free. Located roughly 10 miles north of Springfield on US 165, the town of Fair Grove is home to the historic Womack Mill. Built in 1883 and in operation until 1969, the mill was rescued and restored by the Fair Grove Historical and Preservation Society. Today it holds its original burr stones and a nice collection of early-20th-century farm tools and horse-drawn machinery. If you visit the mill on a Wednesday after 4 PM (between late Apr. and late Oct.), you will find a full-scale farmer's market with all sorts of fresh-grown produce and fruit, not to mention BBQ chicken and hamburgers.

❦ ✄ ♿ **Springfield Conservation Nature Center** (417-888-4237; www .conservation.state.mo.us/areas/cnc/springfd/springfd.html), 4600 S. Chrisman, Springfield, Mo. Open daily 8 AM–5 PM. Admission is free. Owned and operated by the Missouri Department of Conservation, this establishment's motto is "A place to enjoy nature's gifts, and to learn about taking care of them." Located within the city limits of Springfield, the center consists of 80 acres of forests, fields, and creeks, with frontage on Lake Springfield. Six hikes are possible on 3 miles of trail, wildlife is prevalent, and a very cool boardwalk crosses the marshy shallows of the lake. However, the inside of the center is just as entertaining and informative as a walk on the grounds. There are classrooms, exhibits, an information desk, a bookshop, and a 150-seat auditorium, and planned events might include a presentation on bears and cougars, a day spent learning primitive living skills, tips on nature photography, classes on wood carving and tree identification, or perhaps even a Halloween party. Missouri has one of the best-funded conservation departments in the nation (for decades a $1/8$¢ sales tax has been earmarked for conservation), and the Conservation Nature Center is a prime example of those funds being put to good use.

❦ ✄ ♿ **Assemblies of God Headquarters** (417-862-2781; www.ag.org/top), 1445 Boonville Ave., Springfield, Mo. Tours are held year-round, Mon.–Fri., at 1:30 and 2:30 PM. Admission is free. A note on local custom here: If you're taking the guided tour of the international headquarters of the Assemblies of God

ASSEMBLIES OF GOD HEADQUARTERS

Church, it is considered in bad taste to ask questions about defrocked AG ministers such as Jimmy Swaggart or Jim Bakker. Even a joke about that duo will be met with roughly the same enthusiasm as screaming "bomb" in a crowded airport. Now that that's out of the way, this is an interesting tour of a religious group boasting 2.6 million members in the United States and 48 million overseas. The headquarters is a massive complex, consisting of 18 buildings spread over 10 city blocks. Part of the facility is the **Gospel Publishing House**. The church paper printed there—*The Pentecostal Evangel*—sizes out at 268,000 copies per week, utilizing enough newsprint to cover 214 miles.

HISTORIC SITES ✍ ♿ **Wilson's Creek National Battlefield** (417-732-2662; www.nps.gov/wicr), 6424 W. FR 182, Republic, Mo. Open year-round 8–5. $3 per person, or $5 per vehicle. Kids under 16 are admitted free. You can nearly hear the guns and smell the smoke at Wilson's Creek, a 1,750-acre battlefield that is little changed since the bloody fight of August 10, 1861. On that day 12,000 Confederates and 5,400 Yankees engaged in fierce combat, resulting in 2,300 deaths in but 5 hours of engagement. The Rebels won the day but lost the war. Today this National Park Service facility features a visitors center, a 13-minute film, a museum, rotating exhibits, and a 5-mile, self-guided auto tour. Easy foot trails lead to the various battle sites.

🌸 ✍ ♿ **Gray/Campbell Farmstead** (417-724-0880), 2400 S. Scenic Ave. in Nathaniel Greene Park, Springfield, Mo. Open Apr.–Sep., 1–4:30. Admission is free. The original home of John Polk Campbell, the nephew and namesake of the fellow who founded Springfield, this historic 1856 residence offers visitors the sight of the detached log kitchen, corncribs, and family cemetery. In-season, tours are given by costumed guides (historical costumes—not Spider-Man or something).

GRAY/CAMPBELL FARMSTEAD

🌸 ✍ ♿ **Wild Bill Hickock Shootout**. Markers are located downtown in Park Central Square at Boonville St. and Park Central. The very first gunfight of the Wild West took place in downtown Springfield in July 1865. Wild Bill Hickock (who had unsuccessfully run for sheriff of Springfield and was a gambler of inveterate proportions) had lost a poker game to his

onetime friend Dave Tutt. Short on funds, Hickock gave Tutt his pocket watch as collateral, telling him not to show it off in public or brag about it. Tutt, of course, embarrassed Hickock by displaying the timepiece all over town. Animosities grew, and eventually Tutt fired a shot at Hickock, barely missing his head. With lightning speed, and from 75 yards away, Wild Bill pulled his pistol and plugged Tutt directly through the heart (it can be assumed he retrieved his watch). If you stand by the plaque on the southwest corner of Park Central Square, you will be walking in Wild Bill's footsteps. If you want to visit Dave Tutt, go to the **Maple Cemetery**.

ZOOS ✪ ♿ **Exotic Animal Paradise** (1-888-578-9898; www.exoticanimalpara dise.com), 124 Jungle Dr., Strafford, Mo. Open year-round, 8 AM–dusk. $11.99 adults, $9.99 seniors, $7.99 ages 3–11. Generally considered one of the finest drive-through animal parks in America, the Exotic Animal Paradise was founded in 1971 by the late Pat Jones (father of Dallas Cowboys owner Jerry Jones). It comprises 9 miles of roads that wind through 400 acres; you'll encounter everything from giraffes, camels, buffalo, and ostriches to tigers, bears, and hundreds of species of birds. The Safari Center offers a snack bar, gift shop, petting area, and rest rooms, and when weather permits the park offers go-carts, paddle boats, and pony and camel rides. The park is just 12 miles east of Springfield on I-44. This is one spot where you don't want to forget the camera.

✪ ♿ **Dickerson Park Zoo** (417-864-1800; www.dickersonparkzoo.org), 3043 N. Fort Ave., Springfield, Mo. Open Apr.–Sep. 9–5, Oct.–Mar. 10–4. $5 adults, $4 seniors, and $3 ages 3–12. For a relatively small city, Springfield's Dickerson Park Zoo is a shining jewel. Exhibits include South America, with Chilean flamingos, squirrel monkeys, toucans, and maned wolves. The Australian area holds red kangaroos, wallabies, and black swans, while the Missouri Habitats display features a boardwalk overlooking black bears, coyotes, bobcats, raccoons, river otter, deer, and turkeys. The popular Africa area includes cheetahs, kudu, cranes and storks, ostriches, giraffes, lions, and Asian elephants. The list goes on and on; you can easily spend a full day or more at Dickerson, viewing more than 500 animals representing 170 species, and never become bored.

✪ ♿ **Wonders of Wildlife Museum and Zooquarium** (417-890-9453 or 1-877-245-9453; www.wondersofwild life.org), 500 W. Sunshine, Springfield, Mo. Open daily from 9 AM; tickets are not sold after 6 PM. $9.95 adults, $8.95 seniors, $5.95 ages 4–11. In this 92,000-square-foot facility, affiliated with both the Smithsonian Institution and the American Association of Zoos and Aquariums, you will

EXOTIC ANIMAL PARADISE

URBAN OASES

With more than 50 public parks within the city limits, Springfield offers ample opportunity to enjoy the great outdoors or take part in sporting activities. For complete info on all parks, sports fields, and golf courses, visit the city's park web site at **www.parkboard.com**. The following is a collection of some of the best Springfield has to offer.

MIZUMOTO STROLL GARDEN

The 6.5-acre **Loren Street Park** (2100 W. Catalpa St.) will appeal to the model-airplane buff, as it includes a model plane pad/landing strip. Loren Street is also planned to be Springfield's first off-leash dog park. The **Chesterfield Family Center and Park** (417-891-1616; 2511 W. Republic Rd.) is more than just a 40-acre expanse of green. This facility holds a family center, fitness center, gym, physical fitness course, playground equipment, and a 2-mile walking trail. Sports fans will love the 127-acre **Cooper Park** (417-837-5817; 2300 E. Pythian) with its five lighted baseball diamonds, 14 outdoor soccer fields, 1.5-mile fitness trail, and concession stands. **Dickerson Park** (417-864-1800; 1400 W. Norton Rd.) is more than just the home of a first-rate zoo; it's also a gorgeous and relaxing public park full of picnic tables, grills, shelters, playground equipment, and a lake. Have your burger while listening to the trumpeting of Asian elephants. At the **Doling Park and Family Center** (417-837-5900; 2600 N. Campbell) a swimming and wading pool shares 40 acres with horseshoe pits, two lighted tennis courts, picnic tables and grills, and a gym. For handball players, **Fassnight Park** (S. Campbell and Meadowmere) is the place to be. In addition to the two lighted handball courts, the park encompasses both swimming and wading pools, a lighted softball field, an outdoor basketball court, and plenty of picnic tables and grills. If you or the kids want to take a spin on your bike, one of the hallmarks of the 41-acre **James Ewing Sports Complex** (Scenic and Bennet streets) is an unlighted BMX track. If Frisbee golf is more to your liking, drop by the **Oak Grove Park and Center** (417-891-1635; 1538 S. Oak Grove).

The **Jordan Valley Park** (735 E. Trafficway) is known for its huge fountain, paved walking trails, and amphitheater featuring concerts and public events. If you seek history, the **Nathaniel Greene Park** (2400 S. Scenic) is an ever-expanding botanical center with more than 20 varieties of plants and the city nursery. Also on this site are the Gray/Campbell Homestead and the Mizumoto Japanese Stroll Garden (below). Not to be forgotten is **Phelps Grove Park** (800 E. Bennett), with its lovely rose and xeriscape gardens, or the 266-acre **Ritter Springs Park** (SR 13 N.), home to the Sac River bike trail, an archery range, horseshoe pits, picnic tables, playground equipment, grills and tables, and a scenic lake.

    ✿ ♿ **Mizumoto Stroll Garden** (417-864-1049; www.parkboard.com), Nathaniel Greene Park, 2400 S. Scenic Ave., Springfield, Mo. Open May–Oct. $3 adults, free for kids. You don't expect to find lovingly tended Japanese gardens in the Ozarks, but such is exactly what you will discover at this elegant 7.5-acre site located within Nathaniel Greene Park, featuring lakes, a teahouse, winding paths, a moon bridge, and much more. The care and expertise that have gone into fashioning this pristine environment are astounding.

    🎭 ✿ ♿ **Jefferson Avenue Footbridge** (417-864-7015; www.parkboard .com), Commercial and Jefferson streets, Springfield, Mo. Open year-round. Admission is free. This century-old, 562-foot bridge is often referred to as Springfield's largest piece of public art. The bridge, fully restored for pedestrian traffic, is a great place to watch the trains that cruise by underfoot (literally inches below your feet). This is a particularly cool spot at night, as the area is well lighted and the train-watching takes on an entirely different tone than during the daylight hours.

THE JEFFERSON AVENUE FOOTBRIDGE

find more than 225 species of animals in live habitats. Interactive electronic displays are prevalent, and the exhibits are outstanding. One area is a treetop, free-flight aviary; another holds river otters and bobcats. Intended to re-create the habitat at the bottom of Table Rock Lake, a 140,000-gallon freshwater aquarium, viewable through huge windows, is the home of bass, gar, catfish, and spoonbills. A 220,000-gallon saltwater aquarium houses sharks, eels, and rays. And of course you will not want to miss the reptile gallery, which at the time of this writing contains the world's oldest and largest albino alligator. Visitors wander the facility on a 1½-hour self-guided tour that will not be soon forgotten.

✳ To Do

FOR FAMILIES Also see *Zoos*, above.

🐾 ✎ ♿ **Archery Quest** (417-863-8060), 2900 E. Pythian St., Springfield, Mo. Open year-round; $6–9 per hour. If you're looking for something different, or if you suddenly become delusional and believe yourself to be William Tell, a trip to Archery Quest is in order. With indoor archery ranges and a "3-D techno hunt" (sort of like virtual-reality-meets-Robin-Hood), you can twang the string and fire the shaft to your heart's content. If the bug really hits you, Archery Quest, of course, sells top-name bows and supplies.

🐾 ✎ ♿ **Andy Dalton Shooting Range & Outdoor Education Center** (417-742-4361; www.conservation.state.mo.us/areas/ranges/a_dalton), Green County Farm Rd. 61, Bois D'Arc, Mo. Open Sep. 14–Apr. 14, Mon.–Thu. 9–4:30, Fri.–Sun. noon–4:30; Apr. 15–Sep. 13, hours are Mon. 9–4:30, Thu. 9–7:30, and Fri.–Sun. noon–4:30. Prices on the rifle/pistol range are $3 per hour per booth. Prices on the skeet range are $3 per person per round of 25 clay birds. Prices for static and 3-D archery ranges are $3 per hour. Featuring a 100-yard baffled rifle/pistol range with 20 covered booths (two of which are handicapped accessible), four trap and skeet fields, and archery facilities, this center is a favorite among local hunters and shooters. A great trip for the entire family, it's the perfect spot when either adults or kids want to practice their shooting skills. The shooting range also offers a training center with indoor classrooms and outdoor pavilion, and it is a leader in providing both gun and hunter safety courses. It is a bit hard to find: Take SR 160 west from Springfield (past the town of Willard but before Ash Grove) and watch for Greene County FR 61. The center will be near a white, stone barn.

🐾 ✎ **Fun Acre** (417-889-1872), 2500 S. Campbell Ave., Springfield, Mo. Open Feb.–Nov. For miniature golf (an 18-hole course) and batting cages, you can't beat the price at Fun Acre. At last check, golf was $2 for adults and $1 for children. If you want to make like Babe Ruth, the batting cage price is a mere 25¢ for seven pitches.

✎ ♿ **IMAX Theater** (417-882-4629; www.bellafilms.com), southwest corner of Sunshine and Campbell streets, Springfield, Mo. Open 10–10. Admission varies but is usually in the $7–9 range. A new facility with giant screens, 3-D viewing, and 12,000 watts of digital sound, this IMAX theater (just like every other IMAX) puts you right in the thick of the presentation. The Springfield IMAX is located on the vast property encompassing Bass Pro Shops Outdoor World and the Wonders of Wildlife Museum and Zooquarium.

✎ ♿ **Jordan Valley Ice Park** (417-866-7444; www.icepark.org), 635 E. Trafficway, Springfield, Mo. Hours vary, but public skating is available for several hours seven days a week. $5.50 adults, $4 kids and seniors. Skate rental is $2.50 per person. Open since 2001, the Ice Park offers public skating and skating lessons for all ages; it's home field for the Missouri State University Ice Bears and the Jordan Valley Figure Skating Club. The complex may also be rented for birthday parties and special events.

GOLF **Oscar Blom Golf Course** (417-833-9962; www.parkboard.org/information/golf/index.html), 1825 E. Norton Rd., Springfield, Mo. For just plain fun, spend an afternoon playing this public, nine-hole, par-27 course. Open year-round (weather permitting), the course is lighted on evenings between May and Nov. Greens fees are $8 for adults for one 9-hole round, $12 for 18 holes. Those 17 and under can play Mon.–Fri. for just $3.

Bill & Payne Stewart Golf Course (417-833-9962; www.parkboard.org/information/golf/index.html), 1825 E. Norton Rd., Springfield, Mo. Situated on a luscious 129 acres, this par-70, 6,162-yard public course is open every day, sunrise to sunset, year-round. Also on the course you will find a driving range, practice greens, and snack bar. Greens fees for 18 holes are $16 on weekdays and $21 on weekends. Cart rental for 18 holes runs $11 per player.

Deer Lake Golf Course (417-865-8888; www.parkboard.org/information/golf/index.html), 5544 W. SR 266, Springfield, Mo. With a par 72, and 7,001 yards in length, Deer Lake features a public 18-hole course, driving range, practice green lessons, and a snack bar. It's open year-round, 6–6 during the warmer months and 7–5 in winter. Greens fees begin at $15 for a round of 18 holes.

Horton Smith Golf Course (417-891-1639; www.parkboard.org/information/golf/index.html), 2409 S. Scenic, Springfield, Mo. Open sunrise to sunset every day except Christmas, Horton Smith is a par-70, 6,312-yard, 18-hole public course. Greens fees are $16 weekdays and $21 weekends for 18 holes. Carts run $11 for 18 holes. Lessons, a driving range, and a snack bar are also found at this nice little course.

Rivercut Golf Course (417-891-1645; www.parkboard.org/information/golf/index.html), 2850 W. Farm Rd. 190, Springfield, Mo. Without doubt the best public course in Springfield, Rivercut was named one of the Top 5 Public Courses in Missouri by *Golf Digest* magazine. A par-72, 7,066-yard course, these prime links offer 18 holes of championship-level golf, a driving range, lessons, club rental, and a snack bar. Open every day except Christmas; greens fees for 18 holes are $32 on weekdays and $38 on weekends.

✳ Wild Places

🐾 ✿ ⚬ **Busiek State Forest and Wildlife Area** (417-895-6880; www .conservation.state.mo.us), 18 miles south of Springfield off US 65. Open year-round. Admission is free. A 2,505-acre wildlife area managed by the Missouri Department of Conservation, Busiek is loaded with trails for hikers, bikers, and the horseback crowd. Mostly forested, with several seasonal and one permanent stream, the area also allows camping, hunting, fishing, and target shooting.

🐾 ✿ ⚬ **Compton Hollow** (417-895-6880; www.conservation.state.mo.us). Located 20 miles east of Springfield. Take the SR B exit south for 5 miles, then travel 1 mile east on Compton Hollow Rd. Open year-round. Admission is free. For fishing, hunting, target shooting, camping, bird-watching, or even some frog-gigging, this 840-acre Missouri Department of Conservation area makes for a relaxing and tranquil day trip. There are several small ponds within the area (you'll see plenty of wildlife), and a rather tough 5.5-mile trail is available for hiking, biking, and horseback riding.

CAVES ⚬ **Crystal Cave** (417-833-9599; www.wcnet.net/adc/crystal_2.htm), 7225 N. Crystal Cave Lane, Springfield, Mo. Open year-round, 9 AM–1 PM. $9 adults, $5 kids. Located 5 miles north of I-44 on SR H (exit 80B), Crystal Cave has been open to the public since 1893. This commercial cave features an 80-minute guided tour, and the owners have strived to keep it in its natural condition (minus the stone steps and handrails, a necessity when traversing a damp cave). There are some unique formations here, most notably the Upside Down Well (an odd cavity that extends 12 feet up in the cave's ceiling) and the conical dome known as the Washington Monument. In the cave you will also see Indian symbols (eons ago this hole in the ground served as a residence) and discover interesting arrowheads and artifacts in the gift shop.

⚬ ♿ **Fantastic Caverns** (417-833-2010; www.fantasticcaverns.com), 4872 N. FR 125, Springfield, Mo. Open year-round except for major holidays. Hours are 8–8 in summer; closing time is 1 to 4 hours earlier in other seasons. $18 adults, $12 ages 6–12. Kids under 6 are admitted free. If you're going to tour a cave, this is the way to do it. Fantastic Caverns is the only ride-through cave in America, with passengers on the 50-minute excursion comfortably seated in jeep-drawn tram cars. This makes the attraction very popular with those who suffer limited mobility, who have small children, or who just don't like the idea of huffing and puffing around in a cave. Discovered in 1862 (a farmer's dog reputedly found it), Fantastic Caverns is still a family-owned business. Deep underground, the tour follows a submerged riverbed and passes by massive formations. Almost everyone visits a cave or two when visiting the Cave State, and given its ease and comfort, this subterranean sojourn is highly recommended.

✴ Lodging

BED & BREAKFASTS

Springfield, Mo.

🗡 ♿ **Virginia Rose Bed & Breakfast** (417-883-0693 or 1-800-345-1412; www.bbonline.com/mo/virginiarose/index.html), 317 E. Glenwood St. A 1906 country Victorian home, this green-roofed inn is notable for its wooded acre located in the heart of Springfield. The "rose" aspect of this establishment is not to be ignored—nor could you. Rose wallpaper is prevalent in many rooms, and the breakfast table is set with collectible Virginia Rose pattern dishes. It's a very well-kept inn that prides itself on hospitality, and one of its drawing points is its location, just a few minutes from the Bass Pro Shops complex. Another is the food. Breakfasts are plentiful, often featuring quiche, fruit, and homemade muffins or biscuits. Rates for any of the four guest rooms (all of which have private bath) start at $65, though a suite of two rooms is available in the $100 range. The parlor includes TV, VCR, books, and games, and all guests are invited to play a tune on the piano. Kids are permitted, though smoking and pets are not.

🗡 **Whispering Oaks** (417-886-5082; www.bbonline.com/mo/plainview/index.html), 2219 W. FR 182. A modern home—something of a ranch-style split level—Whispering Oaks is set on 28 acres away from the hustle and bustle of Springfield proper. Three of the four guest rooms feature king-sized beds, TV, and VCR, and one has a private entrance and deck. The grounds feature two water gardens, and an in-ground pool cuts the heat should you visit during the height of an Ozark summer. Breakfast is quite good here—perhaps strawberry French toast, homemade muffins, and cinnamon coffee. Rates run $80–95, and smoking and pets are not allowed. Kids are permitted, but call first rather than just popping in with your thundering herd.

👓 🗡 ♿ **The Mansion at Elfindale** (417-831-5400 or 1-800-443-0237; www.mansionatelfindale.com), 1701 S. Fort St. Missouri's largest bed & breakfast, the castlelike Elfindale mansion has a long and varied history. It's too bad these walls can't talk. Built between 1890 and 1893 by John O'Day, attorney for the St. Louis–San Francisco Railroad, the original home was constructed by 50 German stonemasons. At 27,000 square feet, and with the raw materials having been quarried on the property itself, Elfindale had 35 rooms and seven baths. Alas, soon after the mansion was completed, O'Day and his wife, Clymena Alice O'Day, were divorced. She received the property as a divorce settlement, a highly unusual event in that time, which signifies John must have been a very bad boy. Clymena built an island in the property's stream (complete with iron and stone pagoda); constructed a lake, boathouse, summerhouse, and greenhouse; and

THE MANSION AT ELFINDALE

WALNUT STREET INN

imported trees from all over America and Europe. Within 6 years she blew through all her money. Though she was offered nearly $300,000 for the property, she sold it to a Catholic order of nuns for $30,000. From 1906 to 1964 Elfindale was the St. d'Chantel Academy for girls. The nuns built a chapel (now used for weddings) and a three-story classroom building. The property was again sold in 1977 to a group of Iranian businessmen for $1,540,000 (it was to be a safe house for the shah of Iran). Springfield's Cornerstone Church acquired the property in 1979 (the shah didn't need it anymore, as he was deposed in that year and dead by 1980) and completed a full restoration in 1990.

Today Elfindale's 13 guest rooms (check out the Art Deco Suite) feature private bath, phone, period antiques, stained glass, and hardwood floors. Some rooms have fireplace. Situated on 13 tree-covered acres, down a love-ly lane, the inn is the epitome of Victorian luxury. Rates range $94–149, and a full breakfast is served in an elegant dining room. Corporate rates are available, and the facility is suitable for banquets, meetings, reunions, and retreats. Also, thanks to the on-site chapel, weddings are a regular occurrence at Elfindale. Event planners are available by calling the main mansion number. Children are welcomed, but smoking is not permitted. Alcohol of any kind is neither served nor allowed on the Elfindale grounds.

⊗ ✐ ⅗ **Walnut Street Inn** (417-864-6346 or 1-800-593-6346; www .walnutstreetinn.com), 900 E. Walnut St. Though it may not have quite the unusual history of Elfindale, the Walnut Street Inn equals (and perhaps surpasses) its competitor in terms of pure class and elegance. Best of all, it accomplishes this task with relaxed and friendly grace. A 12-room establishment (the main house was built in

1894) in the heart of Springfield's Walnut Street Local Historic District (which is included in the National Register of Historic Places), this Queen Anne Victorian, with its hand-painted Corinthian columns, is charm personified. Voted Best Bed and Breakfast in the Ozarks by readers of the *Springfield News-Leader* (4 years in a row!), it features rooms each decorated by a different designer. All include private bath, king or queen bed, two-line phone, and cable TV. Most have Wi-Fi access, private balcony, and stocked beverage bar. The inn also boasts of two parlors with fireplaces, comfortable chairs and chaise lounges, and a large front porch and veranda.

Rooms run $89–169 and are found in the main house, the **1894 Carriage House**, or the **1904 Cottage Inn**. Walnut Street Inn is within walking distance of great restaurants, shops, a health club, theaters, plays, and even Hammons Field. Business rates are available, and the inn does rent for special occasions—it's a popular venue for wedding and family reunions. (The inn's wedding planner, Kristi Ball, can be reached at either 417-880-6689 or 417-535-2244.) Last but not least, ask about weekend packages for honeymoons, birthdays, and anniversaries. As is expected, smoking and pets are not permitted, though kids are okay as long as they're well behaved.

✳ Where to Eat

Springfield is food crazy. There are restaurants on every corner, sometimes two or three on every corner, and they cover the cuisine spectrum. Literally hundreds of options exist, and it seems new establishments open on a weekly basis. As would be expected in the Ozarks, diners, BBQ, burger, buffet, and catfish joints are prevalent. Happily, the overall quality is exceedingly high and the ambience honest and authentic. Then there are the more upscale choices.

Moving beyond frying and smoking, you'll find Mediterranean, French, Italian, Vietnamese, and Thai restaurants. There are Caribbean, Cajun, German, Indian, Japanese, and Korean eateries. There are tearooms and bistros. Also, you'll find a number of high-end places that fly in their fish (flying fish?) three to five times per week. Strangest of all, this town seems to hold more Chinese restaurants per capita than any other locale in America. In fact, there is a vast amount of evidence (from people who have way too much time on their hands and spend years researching Chinese food trivia) that Springfield is the home of cashew chicken. It was created, so the story goes, in the early 1960s by a restaurateur who thought mixing Chinese style with fried chicken would improve his business with grease-addicted Ozarkians.

That's the good news. The other side of the coin is that quite a few Springfield restaurants strive to emulate their big-city cousins, hoping to display the epitome of faddish style. The slightly embarrassing thing is that often what the owners perceive as the cutting edge is 5 or 10 years behind the times. It's a little like thinking tanning beds, leisure suits, Rubik's Cubes, and the DeLorean are the next big things. Eponymous restaurants are the current rage, which is okay for a run-down diner with an EAT sign but sort of silly and pretentious otherwise. Chrome, stainless steel, and odd decor crop up way too frequently in

Springfield. You get the impression that some of the local restaurateurs hope to distance themselves from the Hillbilly image of this part of the world, when in fact what they should do is celebrate their local strengths and specialize in subtle class (for subtle class, examples of folks who do it right, see the listing for either Clary's or Bijan's). Springfield should strive to be uniquely Springfield, not a poor copy of San Francisco or Manhattan.

While space limitations prevent a comprehensive critique of Springfield's huge array of fantastic eats (that would require an entire book), the following are a sample of some of the best. Heck, there's even an eponymous joint or two included. A misdirected attempt at image creation doesn't mean the food isn't swell.

EATING OUT

Springfield, Mo.

🦞 ✒ ♿ **Ziggie's Cafe** (417-833-0900; www.ziggiescafe.com), 2222 S. Campbell St. Open 24 hours a day and nonsmoking. Possessing what seems to be the lengthiest menu in the Western world, Ziggie's now has four locations in and around Springfield. The original Ziggie's, on South Campbell, is the only one open 24 hours a day. Breakfast is the specialty here, available anytime. These folks have any style of omelet you could name, and quite a few you couldn't. Sure, you can have your Denver ($5.45) or Santa Fe ($5.99) or regular country omelet ($5.79), but for a change go for the Greek omelet (at $6.99, it boasts gyro meat, green peppers, onions, mushrooms, tomatoes, and feta cheese). You won't go away hungry here, as all house omelets come with your choice of toast, muffins, biscuits, biscuits and

gravy, or pancakes. For traditionalists, opt for the chicken-fried steak with eggs ($7.99). The lunch and dinner menu at Ziggie's is equally extensive; they should call this place "sandwich world." Choose from burgers, melts, dips, gyros, croissants. If you're really hungry, go for the giant pork tenderloin sandwich deluxe ($8.29). Dinner includes steaks, chicken, seafood, BBQ, Greek, Italian, and Chinese dishes. The most expensive item on the menu is a 24-ounce T-bone for $19.99, with most entrées running in the $8–13 range.

✒ ♿ **1955 Maple Cafe** (417-832-8568), 2253 N. Glenstone. Hours are Mon.–Sat. 5 AM–9 PM, Sun. 5 AM–2:30 PM. This is an alcohol-free restaurant with a nonsmoking section. Appropriate to the name, it was established in 1955 on historic Route 66. The meals have that homemade taste, and you can still get a traditional turkey-and-dressing dinner on Sunday. The menu is relatively simple, though hearty breakfast eaters will enjoy the "Heavyweight" omelet. This $5.45 monster meal consists of three eggs; a choice of ham, bacon, or sausage; hash browns; and two pancakes. Or, for something good and quick, try two biscuits and gravy for just $2.05. The homemade onion rings are very good here ($2.75), and for dinner you can order roast beef, liver and onions, chicken-fried steak, or a pork cutlet for less than $6. A large T-bone with soup or salad, potatoes, and a roll is only $11.50. Traditional sandwiches rule the lunch options, but at $5.10 the chicken-fried steak sandwich will convince you that you're dining like a true Ozarker.

✒ ♿ ♉ **Nonna's Italian American Cafe** (417-831-1222), 306 South Ave.

Open Tue.–Sat. 11–10, Sun.–Mon. 11–9. Nonna's is a nonsmoking establishment with a full bar and wine list. This is a friendly restaurant, well lit and happy. I have to admit that the chefs seem to go a bit garlic crazy here—which is great, since I can't get enough of the stuff, but diners without the same tastes might want to request that the kitchen tone it down a bit. The price for entrées is well within budget. Shrimp primavera is only $6.95, but for an even better deal order the seafood lasagna. At $6.75, this is a fantastic entrée that should fetch a far higher price.

♂ ♿ Casa Rico Mexican Buffet

(417-869-2322), 1700 S. Campbell St. Open Mon.–Sat. 11–4 for lunch, 4–8 for dinner. There is no smoking and no alcohol at Casa Rico. I'll freely admit that the words *Mexican buffet* have always struck me as an oxymoron. They're generally a danger sign that signifies large vats of refried beans, mushy Spanish rice, and burritos stuffed with Tabasco-laced hamburger. That's why Casa Rico is such a pleasant surprise. This is good Mexican food, miles and miles removed from the infinite taco joints that lace the American dining landscape. It's a great place to take the family, as the food is not inordinately spicy (holding close to the theme of authentic Mexican). Better yet, the lunch buffet is just $5.95, and the dinner version $6.95. It's free for kids 3 and under, and $3.95 for kids 4–10. The restaurant's trademark tamales are only served at night, and though they are included in the buffet, you will need to order them from your server. This is a nice touch, as it assures freshness (tamales that sit too long on a steam table end up as a pile of gooey corn husks).

♿ ♼ W. F. Cody's (417-887-8083),

3138 E. Sunshine St. Mon.–Sat. 11 AM–midnight, Sun. 11–10. A second location can be found at 1440 E. Republic Rd. Depending on your take on such things, you may or may not want to bring the kids with you for lunch or dinner. The environment is early American bar (which is not a bad thing—and in this case it's a very good thing), and Cody's permits smoking and features a full liquor selection. This place is an institution in Springfield, the original location in operation for more than three decades, and the reason you come is for the burgers. Yes, there is also plenty of bar food (the wings are good; in the old days they were complimentary, but such is a thing of the past), but the burger is the stuff of myth, the Excalibur of chopped meat. For $6.95 you can get a 1-pound cheeseburger on a giant bun sized to fit. The fixin's come on the side, allowing you to pile on as much lettuce, tomato, and onion as you see fit. I've not sure why the burgers here are so good, but judging by taste, it seems the meat is all very fresh. More than that, I suspect that these are cooked the old-fashioned way, slapped onto a very hot, oiled griddle and then weighted down with the equivalent of a small anvil. Last, it tastes as if the buns are warmed on the same griddle, soaking up just enough burger juice to flavor the bread. Then again, none of this matters. Nobody cares what makes the rainbow; they just enjoy looking at it. At W. F. Cody's, simply order a beer (always cold), order the 1-pounder, and prepare to experience cheeseburger Nirvana.

♠ ♂ ♿ Incredible Pizza Company

(417-887-3030; www.incrediblepizza .com/springfield), 2805 S. Campbell

Ave. Buffet hours Sun.–Thu. 11–9, Fri.–Sat. 11–10. The game room is open till 10 Sun.–Thu., and till 11 on Fri.–Sat. Though this is not the typical restaurant listed in this guide, it makes the cut because of its price, quality, and innumerable opportunities to entertain kids who might well be tired of viewing Civil War battlefields. The original location of franchises that are popping up around the country, Incredible Pizza's fare is much better than you might expect from a buffet pizza establishment. All items are made from scratch, including sauces, and more than 30 different types of pizza are made each day. At a price of just $6.99 for adults (ages 13 and over), $5.99 for seniors and kids 11–12, $4.99 for kids 4–10, and free for kids 3 and under, you can try not only all the pizza you wish, but also a pasta bar, baked potato bar, and 100-item salad bar. There are soups galore, desserts aplenty, and fresh hot cinnamon rolls.

But food is just one aspect of this restaurant; the interior (this is an estimate, but at a minimum it must be 50,000 square feet) includes a Route 66 miniature golf course ($3.25 per person), bumper cars ($2.25 per person), and go-cart races ($4.25 for a

single or $5.25 for a two-seater), with various 10-lap races separated by the age/size of the driver. Last but not least, the Fairground area features more than 100 games of skill, from Skee-Ball to air hockey to all the video options imaginable, and there's a safe funland where the smallest kids can bounce, climb, and basically go wild. As you would assume in a family establishment, no smoking or alcohol is permitted.

🌹 𝄢 **Crosstown Barbecue** (417-862-4646), 1331 E. Division St. Open Mon.–Sat. 11–9. For its size, Springfield possesses a huge array of restaurants. Moreover, I don't know that I've ever come across a single town with so many good BBQ joints. Standing head and shoulders above the crowd is a tough job, though it seems as if the Crosstown achieves such status without breaking a sweat. This is BBQ, pure and simple. A casual place (down to the paper plates), this little slice of smoked pleasure consistently churns out some of the best ribs, hot link sausage, sandwiches, and BBQ platters you'll ever find. A regular-sized smoked beef, pork, ham, or turkey sandwich is $4.99 for the small version and $5.99 for the large (you'd better be hungry—large means *large* at Crosstown). The hot link sandwich is $4.75 or $5.95, and a combo sandwich—your choice of any of the meats—goes for $4.99 or $5.99. If you want to splurge, and it's worth it, go for the $7.75 rib sandwich. A specialty sandwich named "the Bluto" consists of smoked brisket, sausage, and rib meat. It comes with a choice of the Crosstown's homemade coleslaw, potato salad, or baked beans (go for the pit-smoked latter, and don't forget to order some fries, too). A full slab

CROSSTOWN BARBECUE

of ribs is $18.95, and the $12.95 "Big Papa" dinner (brisket, sausage, and ribs) arrives with bread, a choice of two side orders, and sauce on the side. Finally, keep in mind that Crosstown has not forgotten the salad crowd. For $6.95 you can order a chef's salad, but it's hardly suited for vege-terrorists. This plate of greens features smoked ham, turkey, burned ends, and shredded cheese. You gotta love it. If you're in a hurry, Crosstown has a drive-through and sells both family packs and BBQ by the pound.

Pappy's Place (417-866-8744), 943 N. Main Ave. Hours are Mon.–Sat. 11–8:30. Pappy's is not for the claustrophobic. It's a crowded little place that would be just as at home (if not more so) in the 1940s and '50s than the 21st century. The staff is not huge (usually one person), and the surroundings aren't fancy. Why go to Pappy's? A couple of reasons. For starters, a 14-ounce beer is only $2. And to go with that beer, order the smoked pork sandwich at $5.50 (often one of the daily specials). This sucker is big, smoked just right, and tender as a toddler's dreams. Sauce is served on the side (if a place doesn't serve it on the side, it's likely covering something up), and the atmosphere will take you back to a simpler time. This is a smoking establishment and not really set up for the handicapped. Remember to bring cash or a check, as Pappy's doesn't take credit cards.

& Y **Springfield Brewing Company** (417-832-8277; www.springfield brewingco.com), 301 S. Market Ave. Open Mon.–Sat. 11 AM–1 AM, Sun. noon–midnight. While there is a large selection of appetizers, pizza, sandwiches, entrées, and desserts at the Springfield Brewing Company (appetizers start at $3.50, sandwiches and entrées at $6.95), the real reason to come is the beer. This two-story restaurant and pub (with a beer garden on the roof for warm weather) is actually owned by a brewery equipment fabrication firm named the Paul Mueller Company. From this facility, Mueller manufactures and markets its beers to domestic and international markets. Its unfiltered wheat, pale ale, Munich lager, and porter are all local favorites, and there's a constantly changing selection of ales and lagers from around the world. The Brewing Company also offers a full bar. While the downstairs is nonsmoking, the upstairs is suitable both for cigarette and cigar smokers, the latter being accommodated with glass rooms that (personal taste here) are a little too reminiscent of the smokers' cages at the Salt Lake City airport. Nonetheless, live music is offered Wed.–Thu. nights after 10. On Fri.–Sat. live jazz is played 6–9 PM, followed by hot area bands 10–close. Sunday, 7–10 PM, you can usually catch some fine acoustic tunes. The music can be a little loud at times (not terrible, just a bit beyond the auditory pleasure level of old fogies like me)—but then again such is to be expected in one of Springfield's top hangouts.

Aurora, Mo.

♪ & **Richard's Hawgwild BBQ** (417-678-4294), 22 E. Olive St. Hours are Mon.–Sat. 11–9, Sun. 11–3. Nonsmoking and no alcohol. Those who seek the die-hard BBQ experience might be a little disappointed that Richard's doesn't serve beer. Don't let that stop you from dropping in. This is a large place, seating more than

150, that has the typical look of a rustic BBQ joint, complete with place mats shaped like a pig. The fare here is billed as Memphis-style BBQ (as if you couldn't guess that from the Elvis stuff on the walls), which generally is defined as slow-smoked over wood, then pulled apart or diced (sometimes the definition encompasses a semisweet sauce that inevitably includes molasses). Richard's lives up to the Memphis reputation at least in part. The meat has a nice smoky taste, and the pulled pork is very good. Your best bet here is to order the pit plate ($14.99), which comes with ribs, pulled pork, beef, sausage, two side dishes, and bread. It might not be truly authentic Memphis (sorry, but you can only get that in Memphis), but this is some mighty tasty Q.

Marionville, Mo.

🗡 ♿ ❧ **The Bar-B-Q Joint** (417-258-7500), 24322 SR 265. Open Mon.–Fri. 11–8, Fri.–Sat. 11–9, Sun. 11–5. Smoking is not permitted, but beer is sold on the premises. The fact of the matter is, if you get ribs with the meat falling off the bone, they might well not be the real deal. True, you can find ribs that tender if, after smoking, they have been wrapped in foil and cooked for a couple more hours (it's called the Texas Crutch technique). But more likely, ribs with falling meat have been boiled and then grilled. Happily, the meat on the Bar-B-Q Joint's ribs isn't sloughing off. They're tender, and they're smoky (cooked over hickory), and they're just the right texture. While this place is a little hard to find, Q aficionados will find the journey well worth the trip. A rib dinner here runs $10.99, and to add to the perfection, the restaurant's

W & W CAFE

homemade sauce is served on the side. For yet another treat, both the coleslaw and baked beans are made from scratch (or if they're not, I don't care. They're very good). Another sign that the owners know what they are doing is that they make a dandy brisket sandwich. Brisket is hard to smoke, often coming out dry and tough, but the large brisket sandwich at the Bar-B-Q Joint is consistently tender. If you're heading to Marionville to see all the rare white squirrels running around town, you'll want to stop and indulge your appetite at this surprising, off-the-beaten-path smokehouse.

Hurley, Mo.

🗡 ♿ **W & W Cafe** (417-369-6255), 108 E. Main St. Mon.–Sat. 6:30 AM–8 PM, Sun. 11 AM–2 PM. The W & W does not serve alcohol, though it does have a smoking section. Aside from the pretty scenery, there is another reason to drive to the small town of Hurley, 28 miles southwest of Springfield. That would be the W & W Cafe. This is a true small-town diner, but the food is beyond excellent. Simplicity can be magnificent at times, as witnessed by the fact that W & W's menu offers a fried bologna sandwich and Frito pie for less than $3. The folks here even cook their fried chicken in a cast-iron skillet. For urban types who have never tasted food from a country café, the W & W will quickly educate you as to what you've been missing. Best of all—and neglecting to order a slice would be a cardinal sin—try the pie. These are home-baked standards in the vein of pecan, apple, and coconut cream, and just a couple of bucks a slice. It's hard to spend more than $10 per person at the W & W Cafe, unless of course you come for their buffets. The Friday-night seafood version is $14.95, and the well-attended Sunday brunch is $10.95 ($8.95 for seniors). Even at that price it's a bargain.

🦌 🍴 ♿ **Lambert's Cafe** (417-581-7655; www.throwedrolls.com), US 65 between Springfield and Branson. Open 10:30–9 daily. No smoking and no alcohol. One of three locations (the original is in Sikeston, Mo.; another is in Foley, Ala.), Lambert's is frequently featured on national travel shows as "the home of the throwed rolls." For those out of the loop, "throwed rolls" does not refer to a secret dough-making process. It refers to the fact that waiters in Lambert's toss 5-inch fresh-baked rolls at you from across the room (it's more fun than it sounds, okay?). Other than that claim to fame, there are certain factors that should be taken into consideration before you eat here. First off, the portions are huge, coming with side orders, rolls, and "pass arounds." This latter could be anything from fried potatoes and fried okra to macaroni and tomatoes, to black-eyed peas, to sorghum and honey for your throwed roll. Servers patrol the floor with large pots full of these delicious goodies and will heap your plate with as much as you want, as many times as you want. Next, you should expect a wait. Despite the fact that the restaurant seats close to 350 people, it is not unusual to experience an hour's delay in getting a table. This is not because of poor service (in fact, the service is great, and entertaining to boot), but because so many folks like this place. You can kill time looking at the memorabilia or perusing the gift shop. Last, don't expect a calm and quiet dining experience. This is southern cooking on a mammoth scale, with servers who are just as likely to make jokes and sing songs as they are to deliver your meal. Speaking of which, hog jowls and turnip greens go for $10, the fried chicken is $11, and gizzards are $10. Have no fear, though; you can also order very good ribs or BBQ pork steak, a rib eye, catfish, roast beef, or chicken-fried steak. The menu is huge, and Lambert's aims to please. Don't leave without ordering a hubcap-sized cinnamon roll.

Did I say *popular*? Last year Lambert's baked 2,246,400 rolls and served 61,200 pounds of okra. It cooked 110,619 pounds of beef, more than 200,000 pounds of chicken, and nearly 45,000 pounds of catfish.

Ozark, Mo.

👤 🍴 ♿ **Century Buffet** (417-582-2188), 5493 N. 17th St. Open 11–9, seven days a week. You won't find smoking or alcohol at the Century Buffet, but you will find tons of food at a reasonable price. This family-friendly restaurant is right across the street from the semilegendary Lambert's Cafe. If you're seeking passable Chinese food and want to stay within the vacation budget, the Century is unbeatable. The lunch buffet is just $5.49, Mon.–Fri., and $6.49 on the weekends. The dinner buffet is $7.99, and it's tough to find an individual entrée more than $10. Toss in discounts for kids and seniors, and you'll agree that the Century is the deal of the century. That said, low prices mean nothing if the quality is subpar. Happily, this is one buffet that serves good food, not to mention keeping the buffet line free of spills and dried gravy splotches. The fruit and salad bar offers fresh selections (even strawberries at times), and the Chinese buffet line will leave you (a) confused and (b) stuffed. Spring rolls, tiny crab Rangoon, cashew chicken, shrimp, and peanut chicken are really but a tiny sample of the choices. Of course (think about where you are) you'll find American dishes in the vein of catfish and macaroni and cheese. If you so choose—and this is an acquired taste that I never acquired—you can also chow down on fried okra.

DINING OUT

Springfield, Mo.

🍴 ♿ 🍷 **Chardonnay** (417-823-8383), 1620 E. Republic Rd. Open Mon.–Thu. 11–10, Fri.–Sat. 11–11. Reservations are suggested. An elegant yet casual eatery, Chardonnay is a bit reminiscent of what New Orleans looked like before it sank. Full of wrought iron and sporting a fountain, this two-story restaurant offers fine dining, a full lounge (usually with live jazz music on the weekends), and private dining rooms for parties or meetings. For starters, Chardonnay offers a bowl of steak soup (thick and heavy on the rib-eye chunks) for $4 and also boasts a substantial wine list. Though the menu is a collection of steaks, pork, seafood, and pasta, a very good choice is the $21 pork chop. It's thick and juicy (thankfully not overdone), and an interesting potato-turnip au gratin is served on the side. I'm sure this is good, unless you hate turnips. Many Springfield locals like to hit the Chardonnay lounge after work for its calm and mellow atmosphere and (a nice change) music that won't drown out conversation.

🍴 ♿ 🍷 **Metropolitan Grill** (417-889-4951), 2931 E. Battlefield Rd. Hours Mon.–Fri. are 11–2 for lunch and 5–10 for dinner. On weekends, the Metropolitan is open Fri.–Sat. 5–10, Sun. 5–9. Full bar and wine list. This is one of Springfield's top spots for lunch, particularly a midday meal of the business variety. The menu has a tendency to change every 6 months or so, but there are some specialties that are area favorites. For a treat, order the $8.99 flash-fried spinach, and I guarantee you'll never look at Popeye's addiction in quite the same way again. The Siraccia balsamic salmon ($21.99) has enough flavor that it can be enjoyed by those who aren't salmon fanatics, but for an outstanding meal opt to spend the $32.99 and feast on the 8-ounce beef tenderloin with shrimp, scallops, squid, and crab.

🦞 🖋 ♿ ♈ **Fish** (417-886-6200; www .eatatfish.com), 900 E. Battlefield Rd. Mon.–Thu. 11–11, Fri.–Sat. 11–midnight, Sun. 11–9. I'm not crazy about the interior design of Fish. With lots of stainless steel, large windows, wooden chairs and tables, and big blue dots, the look is a bit confusing. That's okay, though, because the price and the quality here make up for the attempt to cross Jacques Cousteau with abstract architecture. Take it from someone who spent a hefty portion of his beach-bum years sucking down oysters, Fish is one of the few places in this part of the world where they do half shell right. The West Coast oysters ($8.99 a half dozen) are fresh, cold, and served on top of a pile of rock salt with a cocktail sauce featuring just enough bite of horseradish. Out of many other appetizers, the fish tacos ($5.99) are almost as good as the ones you find at beachfront stands in Baja. For lunch, you can order a fried grouper sandwich for $6.99 or try some white bean chicken chili for $3.99. House specialties include Mississippi fried catfish and almond-encrusted tilapia at $8.99. There's seafood galore at Fish (hence the name), but carnivores can also obtain their red meat fix via burgundy beef, filet mignon, or a bacon-wrapped chicken breast. For dessert, and worth every bit of the $6.99 price tag, are tempura-fried strawberries with cinnamon sugar and vanilla custard. There are various nightly specials at Fish (sometimes kids eat free, sometimes there are all-you-can-eat deals) as well as a full bar. This place makes a mean vodka martini, but if the restaurant has a drawback, it lies in trying to be a little too New Yorky. You can't emulate New York successfully, and some of their promotions, such as a recent "martini and manicure" night, indicate that the restaurant owners have seen way too many episodes of *Sex and the City*. Such stuff is simply pretentious. Smoking, by the way, is permitted at the Fish bar after 9 PM Mon.–Thu. and after 10 PM Fri.–Sat.

🖋 ♿ ♈ **Bijan's Sea and Grill** (417-831-1480; www.bijans.com), 209 E. Walnut St. Hours are Mon.–Thu. 5–10 PM, Fri.–Sat. 5–11 PM. The **Julieta Cigar and Martini Bar** is open Mon.–Sat. 5 PM–1 AM. Reservations are suggested. Here is the perfect example of a great restaurant that strives to establish its own identity—and succeeds. Others might try to imitate Bijan's, but they will never duplicate its particular style. That would be defined, quite simply, as pure class. From the long bar to the low lights to the comfort of dark wood and leather, Bijan's may well be the best restaurant in Springfield. Fresh seafood is flown in three times a week, and it's impossible to get a bad meal. The wine list is extensive (the restaurant is a four time *Wine Spectator* magazine Award of Excellence winner), and choices run from $17 to $1,400 per bottle. For appetizers, the

FISH RESTAURANT

escargots ($7.50) is a tasty combination of mushrooms and just the right amount of herbs and garlic, and the $9 wood-fired salmon spinach artichoke dip (served with pita chips) is a mouthful in more than name. The most renowned entrée at Bijan's is the Chilean sea bass ($20), which offers a hint of cedar and arrives with a crust of cashews, pecans, and caramelized onions. The tempura lobster ($28) is deep fried and comes with a mango papaya salsa and honey hollandaise. Although this sounds a bit odd, it is complemented by a unique seafood macaroni and cheese. Wood-fired rib-eye steaks, pork chops, and filet mignon are available, but for a true surprise check out the slow-roasted half duckling ($20). It's served with orange hoisin sauce and white chocolate risotto. Dessert is as important as the main dish at Bijan's, and the chocolate lava should receive an Oscar for best finale. It's a flourless chocolate cake with raspberry puree and a frozen peanut butter custard. Also, if you just want to relax and listen to some soft music, you'll enjoy the gorgeous martini and cigar bar with its walk-in humidor.

♠ ✂ ♿ ♉ **Hemingway's Blue Water Cafe** (417-887-5204; www.heming waysbluewatercafe.com), 1935 S. Campbell (fourth floor of Bass Pro Shops). Open Mon.–Sat. 7 AM–9 PM, Sun. 9–5. Breakfast is served 7–10 Mon.–Sat. Sunday brunch is available 9–5. You expect big things from any venture associated with Bass Pro Shops, and Hemingway's doesn't disappoint. It's a casual place that seats more than 350, set off by a 30,000-gallon saltwater fish tank. Many people come to Hemingway's for the

buffets. The breakfast version ($5.89 adults, $2.29 ages 5–10) features the usual suspects of scrambled eggs, bacon, sausage, ham, pancakes, French toast, and biscuits and gravy. However (again, it's the Ozarks), you can also dig into deep-fried catfish, plenty of potatoes, and apple dumplings. The lunch buffet ($7.99 adults, $3.29 kids) offers carved roast beef, ham, or turkey; catfish (surprise, surprise); rice; vegetables; corn bread; soup of the day; a full salad bar; and several desserts. The spectacular dinner buffet ($17.99 adults, $6.79 kids) is loaded with snow crab legs, popcorn shrimp, ham, roast beef, BBQ ribs, clam chowder, vegetables, rice, dessert, and much more.

The restaurant has a full bar and an extensive wine list, and should you choose to forgo the buffet and order off the menu, you will find plenty of options. Nowhere else in Springfield offers alligator tail ($7.49) as an appetizer. If you wish something more traditional, then go for the foot-tall stack of onion rings ($5.19). The fish Reuben ($6.49) is a safe bet for lunch, and the evening entrées make for a delicious cross section of American fare. The coconut chicken is $9.99, and a tasty blackened, rib-eye steak will run you $15.89. A favorite here is the crab and prime rib, a lumberjack-sized rendition of surf and turf priced at $19.99.

✂ ♿ ♉ **Haruno** and **Haruno Next Door** (417-887-0077; www.haruno sushi.com), 3044 S. Fremont Ave. Haruno is open for lunch Mon.–Fri. 11:30–2:30; dinner is served Mon.–Thu. 4:30–10, Fri.–Sat. until 10:30. Haruno Next Door is open Mon.–Sat. 4:30 PM–1:30 AM. I'm not sure exactly what fuels the present American sushi fad, but I'm pretty sure it has more to do with social conformity than it does health. It's the yuppie thing to do at the moment, and the owners of Haruno have provided the rolls of raw fish in a big way. Luckily for those who aren't sushi fans, Haruno also offers an extensive and excellent menu of Japanese appetizers and entrées. The main restaurant (the original space, which opened in 1999) offers such lunch selections as *tonkatsu* (a fried pork cutlet with soup and salad) for $7.95. Shrimp or vegetable tempura is also $7.95. Almost all lunch dishes are less than $10, including the sushi lunch, which consists of one tuna roll, one cucumber roll, and five *nigiri*. For dinner, a large number of appetizers are available, with good choices being the beef sashimi (rare, thin-sliced beef) at $6.50, and *sumai* (shrimp Japanese dumpling) at $4.75. Dinner includes such choices as chicken *katsu* (breaded chicken cutlet with special sauce) for $9.95, and *ton katsu* (deep-fried breaded pork with special sauce) for $10.95. You can also sit at the sushi bar (holds half a dozen people) and watch the chefs chop up the fish (a hobby also enjoyed by those who frequent marinas and bait shops).

Haruno Next Door is the result of an expansion, very modernistic with lots of reflecting stainless steel, and very blue (that's blue as in the color, not blue as in melancholy). It offers a full menu and sushi menu, but also 30 different types of sake and a giant martini list. If your sushi desire hasn't been sated yet, Haruno Next Door features a midnight sushi bar, not to mention live jazz Wed.–Sat. It's something of an odd combination for an Ozark town, granted, but it's also something that seems to draw large numbers of customers night after night.

♂ & ♈ **Clary's American Grill** (417-886-1940; www.clarysrestaurant.com), 3014A E. Sunshine St. Open Mon.–Thu. 5–10 PM, Fri.–Sat. 5–11 PM. Reservations are highly recommended. There are three things you can always count on at Clary's. For starters, no matter what you might order, it will be fresh. The restaurant doesn't skimp when it comes to purchasing or flying in supplies of meat, fish, and vegetables. Fish is flown in five days a week, and there are several nightly specials. Second, you will never get bored. The menu here changes seasonally, and the chefs lack neither creativity nor skill. Third, if you ask anyone in Springfield, chances are they will name Clary's as the best and most elegant restaurant in town. With a full bar and a wine list (selections range $17–175), the restaurant is regarded as having Springfield's best steaks. However, you can just as easily expect French-, Italian-, or Asian-influenced entrées. Put simply, these folks know what they're doing. In addition to the aforementioned fish specials, veal, fowl, or beef specials are also a nightly occurrence. Current favorites here are the sea bass with a lemon dill sauce ($26.99), grouper with wasabi mashed potatoes ($29.99), and a pepper-seared prime fillet in a brandy orange sauce ($38.99). Desserts at Clary's are not to be forgotten, whether that means an ample slice of warm chocolate cake ($6) or the soufflé of the evening ($7.50). For the ultimate, **Clary's Market Kitchen** features a chef's table seating up to a dozen people. Guests can interact with the chef, watch the preparation, and have a great time. Prices for a three-course meal begin at $40 per person.

✒ & ⅄ **Avanzare** (417-567-3463; www.avanzareitaliandining.com), 1908 S. Glenstone Ave. Sun.–Thu. 5–10 PM, Fri.–Sat. 5–11 PM. Smoking is permitted at the bar only. I like Avanzare for its sense of tradition. The tablecloths are white, the bar is black, the menus are bound in leather, and the wait staff are both friendly and knowledgeable. While you can order numerous entrées showcasing the lighter, seafood-oriented fare of northern Italy ("light" in comparison with southern Italy), Avanzare also shows a bit of inventive style. At $24, the filetto portobello features a center-cut fillet topped with sautéed portobello mushrooms in a port wine, veal lemon glaze reduction. Also a fine choice is the pollo balsamico, a chicken breast sautéed in a balsamic vinegar reduction topped with melted Fontina cheese and diced tomatoes. Avanzare offers a good wine list (close to 200 selections), a seasonal menu, and a kids' menu in the $5–10 range.

✒ & ⅄ **Gem of India** (417-881-9558), 211 W. Battlefield. Hours are Sun.–Thu. 11–9, Fri.–Sat. 11–10:30. With every other ethnicity found within the Springfield dining demographic, it was high time that the curry crowd received their due. The Gem of India fills that requirement quite handily. One great thing about this place is the massive offerings of freshly baked Indian breads. For a nice selection (priced at $6.95), order the Gem of India Basket—a combination of onion, broccoli, and *peshawari naan*.

If you're not truly acquainted with Indian food (and I count myself among that caste), just ask; the folks at Gem of India will be happy to assist. There are many veal, chicken, and vegetarian entrées in the $9–13 range, and in the seafood arena you should try the shrimp *saag*. This entrée features jumbo shrimp with spinach, ginger, and garlic and will set you back only $11.95. Another interesting dish, at $10.95, is the lamb *jalfrezi:* tender lamb prepared with tomatoes, green peas, peppers, onion, broccoli, and spices. Tandoori specialties are numerous (cooked in a *tandoor*, or clay oven) and have the benefit of being nonfat. The Gem of India mixed grill—a sampling of chicken tandoori, chicken tikka, *seekh* kebab, and tandoori shrimp masala—is a gastronomic wonderland and priced at $14.95. Combination meals and dinners for four are available, as is a full bar and wonderful desserts. To end your meal, do not pass up the *kheer* ($2.95). This rice pudding cooked in sweet milk with raisins and nuts will make your tongue very happy.

✒ & ⅄ **Agrario** (417-865-4255; www.agrariorestaurant.com), 311 S. Patton Ave. Open for dinner Mon.–Sun. at 5; Sunday brunch 10–3. Another restaurant that contributes to Springfield's multicultural dining scene, Agrario specializes in a Mediterranean taste (basically the style of food you'd find from Spain to North Africa). The owners prefer to buy locally grown products whenever possible and strive to steer clear of any foodstuffs that have been treated with pesticides or dosed up on hormones. The seasonal menu reflects different tastes for different times of year, and the wine list here as been lauded by *Wine Specta-*

tor magazine. For appetizers, those who have had bad chorizo might have their opinions changed by Agrario's house-made version. A little spicy (not too much), it is served with Missouri grapes and Manchego cheese. Salads and soups are both creative and fresh, as are entrées. During the summer of 2005, two excellent options reflecting Agrario culinary skills were Moroccan rubbed elk tenderloin at $32 (and no, this wasn't an elk that was fondled by a Moroccan) and saffron stewed prawns at $19. The latter needs a new name (the word *stewed* is an immediate turnoff), but the finished product overrides the linguistic faux pas. For dessert, try something very different and very good: rosewater and honey crème brûlée at $6.50. The **Bodega** bar at Agrario, with its dark woods, brick walls, and plush seats, is a very relaxing spot, and in a sign of pure class, fresh-squeezed juices are used for mixers whenever possible.

🍴 ♿ 🍸 **Tong's Thai Restaurant** (417-889-5280), 3454 S. Campbell Ave. Open Mon.–Sat. 11–2:30 for lunch, 5–10 for dinner. I have a theory that most people who claim they don't like Thai food have never tasted Thai food (or at least not the real deal). I'll freely admit to have been included in that group until I stumbled upon an incredible little Thai place in Naples, Fla., during the late 1980s. After that, I was hooked. Those who have yet to be initiated into Thai cuisine would likely have a similar experience if they wandered into Tong's. For an appetizer (you can't go wrong here), order the satay ($5.95; chicken marinated in Thai spices and coconut milk, then fried and served on skewers). A traditional favorite here is the Panang shrimp ($12.95; shrimp steamed in Panang curry sauce and served with pasta). A great meal is the Siam beef ($12.95; sliced rib-eye steak marinated in garlic, ginger, pepper, soy sauce, and wine before being stir-fried with onion, green onion, red and green peppers, and carrots). Tong's has a nice wine list and a full bar. As usual with a Thai place (this is true of Indian joints as well), you would be wise to ask your server about the heat quotient of some of these meals. If such is your wish, the chefs will gladly tone down the spice to suit your palate.

Nixa, Mo.

🍴 ♿ 🍸 **Pairings** (417-725-1998; www .pairings-restaurant.com), 381 W. Guin St. Tue.–Sat. 5–10 PM. A Sunday brunch is held 11–2, and dinner is available Sunday night 5–8. Opened in 2005, Pairings is new twist in the Springfield-area dining scene, and it will be interesting to see how it is received. The restaurant has a small lounge, and in addition to the dining room, patrons can enjoy their meal outdoors on a massive deck overlooking the James River. The theme behind Pairings is best exemplified by its "Discovery" menu. For $40 you can create your own five-course meal, with five or six choices available for each course. For another $25, you can choose a glass from one of four or five selections that complement each meal. For example, a first course might be wild boar sausage, sauté of wild mushrooms, a seared tuna loin, or a spinach salad napoleon with Asiago cheese. To accompany these you could choose from one of four different vintages of wine. Again, it's a different concept for this area, and the verdict is still out as to popularity. For those who might not want to dine this way, you are allowed to order à la carte, or order either just a glass or bottle of wine ($6 a glass or $20 per bottle). Reservations are recommended.

✳ Entertainment

✐ ⚴ **Juanita K. Hammons Hall for the Performing Arts** (417-836-7678; www.hammonshall.com), 525 S. John Q. Hammons Pkwy., Springfield, Mo. A 2,200-seat multipurpose performance venue, Hammons Hall is located on the Missouri State University campus near Springfield's historic Walnut Street district. Named in honor of the wife of famed hotel magnate John Q. Hammons (who spearheaded the private funding campaign to build the hall), this facility's events and performances cover the gamut of entertainment. Regular tenants include the **Springfield Symphony** and **Springfield Regional Opera**, but you will find anything from Broadway shows to jazz jams, kids' shows, and chamber groups here. The spot offers only the best; recent performers have included Bonnie Raitt, Jerry Seinfeld, pianist Vassily Primakov, and Clifford the Big Red Dog. Check the Hammons web site for current and upcoming shows.

✐ ⚴ **Springfield Ballet** (417-869-1334; www.springfieldballet.org), 311 E. Walnut St., Springfield, Mo. Founded more than 30 years ago, the Springfield Ballet presents four major dance productions throughout its Sep.–May season. Having recently established its own professional company, which visits schools and community events, the community-supported endeavor continues to expand awareness of the arts through dance. All production performances take place at the Landers Theatre, and tickets are available for individual shows. A season subscription, covering all four presentations, runs $50.

THEATER ✐ ⚴ **Springfield Little Theater at the Landers** (417-869-1334; www.landerstheatre.org), 311 E. Walnut, Springfield, Mo. On average there are nine performances per year (six main-stage performances and three children's shows). Admission price varies but is roughly $20 for adults and $12 for kids. The oldest (1909) and largest civic theater in Missouri, the Landers is on the National Register of Historic Places; John Philip Sousa and Fanny Brice performed on this stage. The season's six plays and musicals are attended by more than 50,000 people.

✐ ⚴ **Vandivort Center Theatre** (417-831-8001; www.vctheatre.com), 305 E. Walnut St., Springfield, Mo. The Vandivort holds 12 main productions per year. Ticket prices vary, but they average $16 for adults and $13 for kids. With performances taking place in the historic 1907 Vandivort Theatre, visitors can expect well-done and professional productions. Past shows have included *Dracula*, *Ruthless*, and *Man of La Mancha*. Given its great value, flexible seating, and impressive talent, the Vandivort has long been a Springfield favorite.

DRIVE-IN THEATER ✐ ⚴ **Sunset Drive-In Theater** (417-678-6609; www.sunsetdriveinaurora.com), E. US Bus. 60, Aurora, Mo. Open Apr.–Sep. Prices vary. This is one place of which it can truly be said "They don't make 'em like this anymore." Opening in 1951, the Sunset holds 325 cars and, due to a lightning storm in 2001, utilizes digital FM for sound (sadly, no more poles with speakers). The concession stand is great, offering entrées such as a Sunset chili burger, ice-cold dill pickles, chili cheese fries, and chicken-fried steak. Of course, there is plenty of popcorn, candy, and Coke as well. This is a trip to the 1950s in the sense that Sunset is not a re-creation. It's the real deal. For the kiddies, there is a playground up front.

SPECTATOR SPORTS 🏟 ⚓ ♿ **Cardinals Double-A minor-league baseball** (417-863-2143), 955 E. Trafficway, Springfield, Mo. The season runs Apr.–Sep. Admission ranges $5–22.50, depending upon seating choice. You will find few small cities that are as baseball crazy as Springfield, but for years the town had trouble attracting a team. Then hotel magnate and Springfield native John Q. Hammons stepped in. In 2004 Hammons not only built a $32 million, 10,000-seat stadium (Hammons Field), but he also convinced the legendary St. Louis Cardinals to buy the El Paso Diablos minor-league team

and move it to Springfield. Cards games at Hammons are a great time in a spectacular setting, and for those on a budget, the price is right. General admission tickets start at $5, though if you're willing to splurge, for $22.50 per person you can have a seat in the **Redbird Roost**, located above the concourse on the third-base line— the view is perfect. Plus, all food and soft drinks are included in the price. This makes the seats worth it, as food at Hammons is excellent. Try the Hammons Hoagie Dog for $6.50 (you'll be stuffed; it weighs half a pound). There's even a **Domino's Pizza** franchise within the stadium. Just place an order from your cell phone, and they'll deliver it to your seat!

⚓ ♿ **Drury University Panthers** (417-873-7265; www.drury.edu), 900 N. Benton Ave., Springfield, Mo. With games held at the Weiser Gym on the Drury University campus, both the Panthers and Lady Panthers have a basketball season that runs Nov.– Mar. Tickets $5–8.

HAMMONS FIELD

Bass Pro Shops Outdoor World (417-887-7334; www.basspro.com or www
.outdoor-world.com), 1935 S. Campbell St., Springfield, Mo. Open 364 days a
year, Mon.–Sat. 7 AM–10 PM, Sun. 9–7. If asked to name the most popular
tourist attraction in Missouri, most people would mention the Gateway Arch
in St. Louis or Silver Dollar City in Branson. They would be wrong. Drawing
more than 5 million visitors per year, Bass Pro Shops Outdoor World in
Springfield wins the title. The original location and international headquarters of what is now the world's largest mail-order sporting goods store,
Springfield's Bass Pro is one of 15 huge retail stores located around the
country. The firm also owns and operates subsidiaries such as Tracker
Boats and the Big Cedar Lodge. Not bad, considering that founder Johnny
Morris only opened his first small store in 1972 with a U-Haul trailer full of
fishing supplies.

The interior of Bass Pro is something to behold. Consisting of more than
300,000 square feet, the store's main lobby boasts a four-story, natural stone
waterfall that empties into a pond stocked with fish and ducks. That's just
the beginning. Shopping areas cover hunting and archery (with indoor
ranges so you can try before you buy), ladies' and men's apparel, wildlife
jewelry, golf gear, every type of sporting equipment and athletic clothing
imaginable, home decor and custom glassware, footwear, the **White River
Fly Shop**, a gargantuan fishing and marine area, camping equipment, and a
40,000-square-foot Tracker Boat and RV showroom. In addition, the complex
offers Hemingway's Blue Water Cafe (see *Dining Out*), a barbershop, an art
gallery, a golf driving range, a taxidermy store, rod and reel repair, and even
a **McDonald's**. Exhibits and seminars are a regular occurrence at Bass Pro
and cover topics from hunting and fishing to fly tying and turkey frying.

✒ ♿ **Missouri State University Bears** (417-836-7878; www.missouri state.edu), 901 S. National Ave., Springfield, Mo. A variety of collegiate events take place at the nearly 20,000-student Missouri State University. Basketball, volleyball, swimming, and diving can be found at the 8,900-seat John Q. Hammons Student Center. The season for both the MSU Bears and the Lady Bears runs Nov.–Mar., and tickets range $9–15 adults, $4.50 ages 12 and under. MSU football games take place at the 16,300-seat Robert W. Plaster Sports Complex (Sep.–Dec.), and admission begins at $10. The MSU Hockey Bears play at the Jordan Valley Ice Park Sep.–Mar., with tickets costing $5 adults, $3 kids.

✳ Selective Shopping

Battlefield Mall (417-883-7777; www.simon.com), 2825 S. Glenstone Ave., Springfield, Mo. Open Mon.–Sat. 10–9, Sun. noon–6. The largest shopping center in southwest Missouri, Battlefield Mall offers more than 150 stores and restaurants. Name brands are prevalent here, in the genre of **Dillard's**, **Famous-Barr**, and **Sears**.

Waverly House Gifts and Gallery (417-882-3445; www.waverlyhouse .com), 2031 S. Waverly Ave., Springfield, Mo. Far more than your stereotypical gift store, Waverly House offers fine art, contemporary American crafts, and a year-round Christmas room. You will find ceramics, wearable art, kaleidoscopes, jewelry, sculpture, stoneware, and turned wood. The Christmas room, in addition to a large supply of unique Santa figurines, contains Christmas decor and ornaments from a variety of different countries.

Battlefield Station Family Hobbies (417-887-5592; www.battlefield station.com), 220 W. Battlefield Rd., Springfield, Mo. Hours are Mon.–Fri. 10–8, Sat. 10–6, Sun. 1–5. If you're a lover of all things train, then you will find a kindred spirit in Larry Levine, owner of Battlefield Station. At this unique shop are both indoor and outdoor model railroads, railroad antiques, gifts, collectibles, and accessories. Names represented include Kato, Lionel, LGB, Thomas the Tank Engine, and many more. Also at Battlefield Station is a huge collection of plastic or die-cast model planes, cars, ships, models, and figures, along with all the paint, tools, and glues required to put them together. Last but not least, this shop is your area HQ for remote-control racing boats, cars, and planes.

Half Price Books (417-889-9042; www.halfpricebooksozarks.com), 1950 S. Glenstone, Springfield, Mo. Open Mon.–Fri. 9–6, Sat. 9–5. With more than 4,000 square feet of space, Half Price Books has upward of 100,000 new and used books for sale. An independent bookseller, its stock includes everything from fiction and romance to westerns, mysteries, audio books, cookbooks, biographies, and much more.

✒ **Ted E. Bear's Toy Factory** (417-823-7883; www.tedebearstoyfactory .com), 1839 E. Independence St., Suite W, Springfield, Mo. Open Mon.–Sat. 10–7, Sun. 1–5. Admission is free, but the final cost of your custom-designed critter can run $9–20. A nice place to take your young kids, Ted E. Bear's lets you create your own teddy bear from scratch. Customers pick out the unstuffed body and then install eyes, stuff it until it feels just right, trim it, brush it, select one of myriad outfits, and then receive an official certificate of adoption. It's reminiscent of the Cabbage Patch doll factory, but without the vegetable motif.

Commercial Street Historic District (417-864-7015). Located on Commercial St., between Washington and Lyon. This six-block federal historic district has been refurbished to resemble a turn-of-the-20th-century railroad town. It's a great place to take a stroll, especially if you are looking for neat little shops offering antiques, art, and a wide range of clothing (some normal, some a bit odd).

Grizzly Industrial (417-887-9191 or 1-800-523-4777; www.grizzly.com), 1815 W. Battlefield Rd., Springfield, Mo. Open Mon.–Sat. 8:30–6. This is the tool man's dream store. The second largest machinery showroom in the world (Grizzly also owns the largest, in Pa.), the Springfield location features 150,000 square feet loaded with literally thousands of tools, accessories, and wood- and metalworking machines. From table saws to planers, from hand tools to power tools, from milling machines to welders, if you can't find it here, chances are it doesn't exist. Also, the store specializes in live demonstrations and has a first-rate cutlery area.

✳ Special Events

February **The Lawn and Garden Show** (417-833-2660; www.ozark empirefair.com.lawnandgarden.html), 3001 N. Grant Ave., Springfield, Mo. Call ahead for exact dates. The three-day Lawn and Garden Show at the Ozark Empire Fairgrounds takes place in mid-February. Hours are generally 10–8 Fri.–Sat., 10–5 on

Sun. Admission is $4, with kids under 12 admitted free. More than 100 exhibitors show up with services and shopping revolving around the latest in lawn and garden equipment and supplies. Pools, ponds, landscaping, grills . . . if you don't find it here, you won't find it.

March **Horsefest** (417-833-2660; www.ozarkempirefair.com.lawnand garden.html), 3001 N. Grant Ave., Springfield, Mo. Call ahead for exact dates. Held on a weekend in mid-March, with hours being 9–5 Fri.–Sun. This fairly new event, held at the Ozark Empire Fairgrounds, is a fun and interesting shindig for both the professional horseman and those who simply like looking at Trigger. Clinics are held to assist owners in training, and a huge trade show features the latest in equine products. You'll see some beautiful horses here, as top breeders arrive en masse to show off their prize animals. Admission for adults is $10 per day (you can add a second or third day for $5); kids are charged $5 (with a second or third day being $2.50). Those under 12 are admitted free.

May **Artsfest on Walnut Street** (417-862-2787). At this open-air celebration on historic Walnut Street in downtown Springfield, hundreds of musicians, artists, artisans, and dancers all gather together to display both their talents and their wares. The event is always held on the first Saturday and Sunday in May, and information as to exact dates and times can be obtained by contacting the Springfield Regional Arts Council at the number above. Admission is $3, with kids 12 and under admitted free.

Sucker Days (417-725-1545), downtown Nixa, Mo. You get the impression that the present city fathers of Nixa don't really like publicizing Sucker Days all that much. Perhaps it strikes them as too "Hillbilly" or something. That's a shame, because this is one of America's most all-time amusing festivals. Taking place for two days in mid-May (even the public schools shut down on Friday), Sucker Days is a festival celebrating the catching and eating of bottom-dwelling fish with odd-shaped mouths. They taste good (really), and more than 15,000 people descend on this suburb of Springfield—just 5 miles south on US 160—to enjoy the giant fish fry, parade, live music, carnival rides, craft booths, and games. The parade starts at 6:30 on Friday night, and the festival kicks into gear 9 AM–8 PM on Saturday. Admission is absolutely free, but a full sucker meal goes for about $6. If you might be wondering how to catch a sucker, it is done by snagging the little devils with a treble hook or jabbing them in the dead of night with a pointy stick. In the old days of this festival (which began nearly 50 years ago), local fishermen would start weeks in advance and sometimes nab as many as 500 suckers per day per person. Should you wish to help in this effort, the town is always on the lookout for volunteer sucker snaggers. Just call the chamber of commerce for further information.

June **Sheep & Wool Days** (417-581-7485), Gray/Campbell Farmstead, Nathaniel Greene Park, 2400 S. Scenic Ave., Springfield, Mo. Held on the second Sunday in June, this one-day, nearly 15-year-old event features a scene from sheep-shearing day on an 1860s farm. You'll see shearing, stock dogs in action, and demonstrations involving the carding and spinning of wool. Admission is free, and there are plenty of games, door prizes, and music.

July–August **Ozark Empire Fair** (417-833-2660; www.ozarkempire fair.com.lawnandgarden.html), 3001 N. Grant Ave., Springfield, Mo. Call ahead for exact dates. Running for 10 days beginning near the end of July, this huge regional fair features a full midway, countless livestock and craft halls, innumerable carnival rides, and major concerts. General admission is $8, with kids 6–12 admitted for $2. Extra charges apply for rides, concerts, food, and drink.

August **Ozark Booster's Club Fall Bull Riding Spectacular** (417-485-7055), Finley River Park, Ozark, Mo. The two-day event generally occurs in late August. Admission is approximately $8 adults, $5 kids, and free for kids under 5. More than 50 professional bull riders travel from all around the country to compete in this $10,000 purse competition. Sanctioned by the North American Bull-riding Association, this particular rodeo also features some of the toughest, meanest bulls in America.

September **Japanese Fall Festival** (417-864-1049; www.parkboard .com), Nathaniel Greene Park, 2400 S. Scenic Ave., Springfield, Mo. Hours are Fri. 10–5, Sat.–Sun. 11–10. $5 adults, $2 children under 12. Taking place at the Mizumoto Stroll Garden in early September, this three-day event includes performers from Japan, music, local artists, Japanese food, and tea ceremonies.

Greater Ozarks Blues Festival
(417-864-6683; www.greaterozarks
bluesfest.com), Springfield, Mo. More
than 10,000 blues lovers flock to this
two-day festival, held the weekend
after Labor Day, to hear nationally
known players, as well as regional and
local musicians (recent headliners
have included the legendary Buddy
Guy). The main stage is at 500 N.
Campbell between Olive St. and
Chestnut Expwy., and music runs
6–11 Friday night and noon–11 Saturday. On Saturday night a blues pub
crawl takes place all over downtown
Springfield, with more than 15 local
bars presenting live blues acts. Ticket
prices range from $20 for Friday
night only to $40 for both days.

Cider Days on Walnut Street (417-
862-2787). An end-of-summer celebration, Cider Days takes place in
mid-September. As with Artsfest,
craftsmen and musicians descend
upon historic Walnut Street to demonstrate their crafts. There are plenty
of booths, not to mention plenty of
locally produced apple cider. For further info, contact the Springfield
Regional Arts Council at the number
above. Admission runs about $3, with
kids 12 and under admitted free.

Steam-O-Rama (417-833-2749;
www.steamorama.com), Farm Rd.
170, east of Republic, Mo., on the
south side of US 60. A four-day event
held in mid-September (call for exact
days, times, and admission), Steam-O-
Rama is sponsored by the Ozark
Steam Engine Association. The 35-
acre show site (half of which is set
aside for camping and parking) displays equipment from days gone by.
The 2005 show featured 400 tractors,
20 steam-driven traction engines,
hundreds of gasoline engines, and
numerous crawlers, garden tractors,
and classic and antique trucks. Both a
full-sized working sawmill and a
thresher are belted to a steam-driven
engines. Also on the site is a large flea
market and vendor booths. An
antique-tractor pull (tractors must be
from 1938 or before) takes place on
Friday night.

October **FarmFest** (417-833-2660;
www.ozarkempirefair.com.lawnand
garden.html), 3001 N. Grant Ave.,
Springfield, Mo. FarmFest generally
falls on the first weekend of October;
call ahead for times, dates, and admission. This is the biggest agricultural
event in the Ozarks, with more than
40,000 farmers and ranchers arriving
from far and wide to view close to
1,000 farm-related exhibits and upward of 500 head of registered livestock. There is machinery both large
and small (as well as old and new),
products for the home, an incredible
number of booths, and numerous
breeds of purebred cattle, goats,
sheep, pigs, and exotic critters.

The Ozark Heritage Region

4

THE ORIGINAL OZARKS

THE OZARK NATIONAL SCENIC
RIVERWAYS

THE ORIGINAL OZARKS

Most who venture into this unique section of southern Missouri, the western side of what is commonly referred to as the Heritage Region of the Ozarks, will eventually realize they are witnessing a number of sudden changes. The land alters: The hills become hillier, and the curved blacktop roads become curvier. The slight aroma of distant wood smoke seems to float on the breeze, a sultry counterpoint to the ghostly fogs that hang low and long in the valleys and hollows. The forests are thick, the rivers are cold, the wildlife is prevalent, and the sounds of chain saws, crows, coyote, and wild turkeys can arise at any given moment.

And more is affected than the five senses. If you linger in this region, you will begin to feel an internal change as well. This is an ancient place, something you will know without being told, something that seeps into your bones. This is a part of the world that I always think of as the Original Ozarks, where geography and culture come together to paint a picture of magical authenticity. With just a little imagination, you can picture the first Scots-Irish settlers of this land as they struggled to make a living from hillside acres that grew little but rocks, moss, and copperhead snakes. You will notice that the accent is a bit more southern here, the attitudes of people more akin to traditional hill dwellers than the farmers or suburban residents who reside in the northern Ozarks. There's a sense of humor here, and, if you're not nosy or pushy or rude, a friendly welcome. This is the part of the Ozarks where language becomes colorful, where a lazy neighbor is "slow as molasses in January," where a difficult decision leaves you "stuck between the devil and the deep blue sea." This is a spot where, on a hot day, you will "sweat like a stuck pig" and the completion of a big meal will leave you "fuller than a tick." Distances are referred to in terms of "as the crow flies," and there is a healthy disrespect for the clock. An appointment will not necessarily be set for a certain time; more likely it will be "oh . . . three o'clock or thereabouts." Those who function without thought or engage in patently stupid behavior will be labeled as "not having the brains God gave a goose."

And strangers who do something silly will inevitably hear the query, "You're not from around here, are ya?"

And on and on and on. Asking directions of locals can (depending on their mood) result in either a monosyllabic grunt or a 20-minute dissertation involving

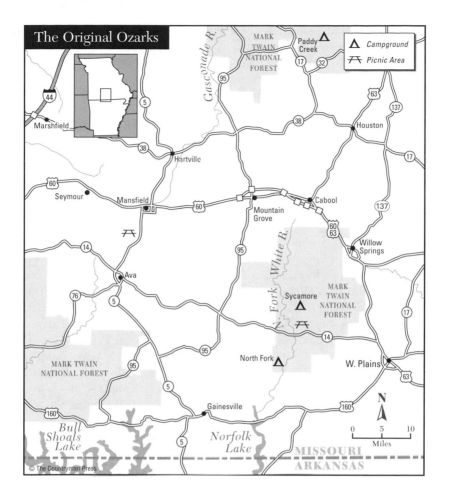

The Original Ozarks

Campground
Picnic Area

stories of third cousins twice removed, busted-up marriages, natural disasters, and local lore. Finally, your question will be answered with a modest, "Just go a couple miles and turn left at the first crossroads."

This is a good part of the world, mostly honest, mostly fun, and mostly gorgeous. Contrary to ignorant representations provided by the media and entertainment elites of the East and West Coasts, it is not wholly populated with toothless inbreds the likes of which would walk out of *Deliverance* or *Ma and Pa Kettle Date Their Cousin*. In many ways it's just as up-to-date as anywhere else. The difference lies in attitude. The Original Ozarks are a slice of heaven on earth that stays just as it wants to stay, despite the best efforts of outside, urban civilization to bring about a politically correct homogenization of culture, belief, and speech.

Modern society has long sought to drag the residents of the Heritage Region of the Ozarks into the 21st century. But this is a headstrong crowd. For the most part this land is populated by rugged individualists who often possess more than their fair share of brains, common sense, well-developed funny bones, and a streak of stubborn independence a mile wide. They like who they are, they're proud of who they are, and "they ain't changin' for nobody."

Yes, modern society has long sought to drag the residents of the Heritage Section of the Ozarks into the 21st century. It is with happiness I can report that modern society has failed miserably.

AREA CODES With the exception of the towns of Licking and Mountain View (whose area code is **573**), the region covered in this chapter lies in the **417** area code.

GUIDANCE Information on area events, sights, and activities is readily available in this region of what is usually considered the traditional heartland of the Ozarks. The **Ava Chamber of Commerce** (417-683-4594; www.avachamber .com), 810 S.W. 13th Ave., Ava, Mo., offers a plethora of advice on such topics as the annual Foxtrotter horse shows and the beautiful Glade Top Trail. For ideas on things to do in the Houston area, home of famed clown Emmett Kelly, contact the **Houston Area Chamber of Commerce** (417-967-2220; http://train .missouri.org/~chamber). The **Mansfield Chamber of Commerce** (417-924-3525) will be happy to provide you with a wealth of details on its most famous resident, the late Laura Ingalls Wilder of *Little House on the Prairie* fame. For those who wish to enjoy the splendor of Bull Shoals Lake, get in touch with the **Theodosia Chamber of Commerce** (www.missourichamber.com/theodosia). The largest town in the region, West Plains, offers both an up-to-date welcome center and two different web sites. **The Ozark Heritage Welcome Center** (417-256-8835 or 1-888-256-8835; www.westplains.net), 2999 Porter Wagoner Blvd., West Plains, Mo., will gladly supply you with all the information you could possibly want. Also, the **Greater West Plains Chamber of Commerce** (417-256-4433; www.wpchamber.com), 401 Jefferson, West Plains, Mo., includes further details on the growing town itself.

Last but not least, for numerous links to events and organizations, check out the **Willow Springs, Mo.**, web site (www.willowspringsmo.com).

GETTING THERE *By auto:* This area, which becomes increasingly rugged as you travel east and south, is roughly bordered on the north by US 60 and on the east by US 63. For a scenic drive along the southern section, US 160 travels all the way from Branson, Mo., to West Plains, Mo.

By air: **Springfield-Branson Regional Airport** (417-869-0300; www.sgf -branson-airport.com), 5000 W. Kearney, Springfield, Mo., is served by American Airlines, American Connection, American Eagle, Northwest Airlink, US Airways, United Express, and Allegiant. The airport offers facilities for buses, vans, rental cars, and hotel and hospitality limousines.

MEDICAL EMERGENCIES **Texas County Memorial Hospital** (417-967-3311; www.tcmh.org), 1333 S. Sam Houston Blvd., Houston, Mo. A not-for-profit, acute care facility with 66 beds, Texas County Memorial is located on the southern edge of Houston along US 63 and SR 17. It features full surgical and obstetrical services, as well as departments for emergency care, X-rays, physical and respiratory therapy, critical care, and cardiac rehabilitation. The hospital covers the health needs of those living in an approximate 40-mile radius of Houston and also provides for outpatient needs.

Ozarks Medical Center (417-256-9111; www.ozarksmedicalcenter.com), 1100 N. Kentucky St., West Plains, Mo. Accredited by the Joint Commission on Accreditation of Health Care Organizations, and with a staff of more than 1,100, the 114-bed, not-for-profit OMC serves a population area of 150,000 residents. The medical staff consists of more than 70 physicians in virtually every specialty imaginable. The complex is certified as a Level III Trauma Center, and emergency services are provided 24/7. Four ambulance services are managed by OMC, and **Air Evac**—a local helicopter ambulance service—utilizes the hospital as its home base. The hospital complex encompasses a 20,000-square-foot surgical center, an urgent care clinic, and a state-of-the-art cancer treatment center; it offers a lengthy menu of rehabilitation services. In house are outpatient imaging services such as MRI, mammography, nuclear medicine, and more. In other words, if you have to get sick in the vicinity of West Plains, this is the place to do it.

✳ Wandering Around

EXPLORING BY CAR **Glade Top Trail** (417-683-4428; www.fs.fed.us/r9/forests/ marktwain/ranger_districts/ava), Ava/Cassville/Willow Springs Ranger District, 1103 S. Jefferson St., Ava, Mo. At a length of 23 miles, winding its way through the Mark Twain National Forest and bordering the Hercules Glade Wilderness Area, the Glade Top Trail is Missouri's only National Scenic Byway. Gorgeous any time of year, the Glade Top takes on special majesty in fall with colors of yellow, deep red, and orange. These colors are present not only on the common oak, walnut, elm, and hickory trees, but also on the brilliant "smoke tree" that's found in very few other Missouri locales. During the third week of October the town of Ava hosts its Flaming Fall Festival in honor of the explosion of color. Spring is almost as grand, as dogwood, redbud, rosebud, serviceberry, and wild fruit trees come to life in vibrant hues. This season is celebrated in Theodosia, Mo., with the **Spring Flowering Tour**.

To access the Glade Top from Ava, Mo., just head south from town on SR 5. If you're wise, you'll watch on the east side of the road for the **Ava/Cassville/ Willow Springs Ranger District Office**. Wheel in there and you can receive not only a map, but also suggestions and advice for places to stop and picnic, take pictures, hike, fish, camp, or hunt. If you miss the ranger station, keep going 8 miles to SR A. Head west for 3.5 miles, take a left onto a gravel road, and follow the signs reading GLADE TOP TRAIL. One of the first things you should come to is a picnic area with a sign offering a general overview of the trip.

During this drive you will often traverse Ozark ridges and view wildlife ranging from deer and turkey to roadrunners and rattlesnakes. Popular stops along the route are the **Caney Lookout Tower** (a 1937 fire observation tower), the **Pinnacle** (where legend has it a somewhat addled old gal spent years digging—

unsuccessfully—for gold), and the **Three Sisters** (a trio of bald limestone knobs). The entire trip does not take long—roughly an hour if you zip through end to end—but such is no fun at all. Just take your time, pack a picnic lunch, and remember to bring plenty of film for the camera.

EXPLORING BY FOOT Wildwood Trail (http://missourichamber.com/theodosia/things_to_do.htm), Theodosia, Mo. If you want a pretty trail that is right in town but makes you feel as if you are in the depths of the wilderness, take a walk on Theodosia's Wildwood Trail. The 4-mile trek, built in large part by the Theodosia Chamber of Commerce and a local Cub Scout pack, will require about 2 hours. It should be noted that the trail, though fairly flat, can get pretty rough in places. If you're either very young or very old (or very clumsy, or out of shape at any age), you should take a bit more than average care. Winding through an oak, hickory, and dogwood forest; topping out on cedar glades; and providing great views of Bull Shoals Lake; this is the sort of trek that requires a camera. The odds are good you will stumble across a bald eagle, white-tailed deer, turkey, or at least an armadillo or two. Also, you will cross a wet-weather stream, view interesting rock formations, and pass a sinkhole.

EXPLORING BY RIVER Bryant Creek is one of those stretches of water beloved by those who detest crowds and love the occasional spell of great fishing. The largely spring-fed Bryant starts in Douglas County and wanders approximately 40 miles through the Mark Twain National Forest before dumping into Norfork Lake in Ozark County. Except during extensive dry spells, almost the entire length is floatable. That said, the most enjoyable and reliable float can be had by putting your canoe in the water south of the town of Vanzant (at the low-water bridge on SR 95). If it's been a wet year, you could encounter some light whitewater on the Bryant, but nothing too serious unless you're in the midst of a full-scale flood (in which case you shouldn't be floating anyway). I've known people who've caught some massive fish out of the Bryant, species of the generalized carp variety, but it also has some great catfish holes. Floaters should note that this is the antithesis of a commercialized float stream; if you see one or two other folks on the water, you can pretty much bet they're locals. If you float far enough on the Bryant, you'll pass a couple of historic mill sites.

Another stream that isn't heavily traveled, **Beaver Creek** is one of the tributaries of the North Fork of the White River. Flowing alongside the Hercules Glades Wilderness Area, it's known primarily for relaxed floating and smallmouth bass fishing. More fun to catch, however (and easier, as they'll strike almost anything), are goggle-eye, a smaller bass hybrid. Like the Bryant, Beaver Creek begins in Douglas County, running roughly 41 miles to Bull Shoals Lake in Taney County. This is a good float for families with kids, as there are plenty of gravel bars along the way that seem custom made for a picnic lunch or wienie roast.

The **Osage Fork of the Gasconade** isn't quite as much of a drunken pretzel as its namesake, the Gasconade, but neither could it be considered straight as a string. This tributary begins in Webster County and travels roughly 60 miles northwest before merging with the Gasconade. A pretty and largely isolated river, the Osage Fork features only a few outfitters. On the other hand, the fishing is excellent (all sorts of bass, bluegill, and catfish), and the generally slow flow of the river offers the chance to enjoy great scenery. Also, plenty of gravel bars allow for overnight camping if you seek a two- or three-day float. At times the water can get a little low in summer—early to late spring is the absolute best time to float this stream, and the redbud trees will make you ooh and ahh. The Osage Fork is largely uncrowded, even on holiday weekends, which makes it a diamond in the rough.

I would call the **James River** pretty much the ultimate beginner's float. Very slow and placid, with absolutely no surprises, it begins in Webster County and meanders to the southwest before emptying into Table Rock Lake. A little more than 60 miles long, the James is a good stream to wet a line. This is another good choice if you're traveling with younger kids, as you're not going to find obstructions or drop-offs that can lead to tipped canoes, wet young'ns, and your cooler floating off downstream.

One of the best-loved rivers in the Ozarks, the **North Fork of the White River** (a tributary of the legendary White River in northwest Arkansas) is highly regarded for having Missouri's largest population of wild rainbow and trophy-sized brown trout. There are 13 miles of officially designated trout water stretching from Norfork Lake back upstream to Rainbow Spring, which churns out 137 million gallons of cold water every day. The river itself begins in Texas County and runs approximately 80 miles to the aforementioned Norfork Lake. The water is cold and clear, and during summer months you can expect plenty of traffic. That should not dissuade you from experiencing the North Fork, though it might lead you to consider floating this river on a weekday rather than the weekend. It's not a fast river, but it does have some low-water bridges and more than a few drops and small waterfalls. None of these is more than a couple of feet, but floaters should still take care and consider a portage, especially in times of higher water. As with everything else, simply exercise a bit of common sense depending on conditions and your individual ability. The worst time to admit that your skills are lacking is when your canoe ends up sideways against a boulder, you're freezing wet, and your camera is at the bottom of the river. Numerous outfitters handle the North Fork, and there are several Forest Service campgrounds along its route. Also check out the River of Life Farm (see *Resorts*) for great accommodations, river advice, and guided trips.

NORTH FORK OF THE WHITE

Ava, Mo. The seat of Douglas County, Ava is strategically located for growth. Less than an hour from both Branson and Springfield, the town's 3,000-plus residents pride themselves on being the site of the world headquarters for the Missouri Foxtrotting Horse Breed Association. Two internationally regarded horse shows are held here each year, celebrating the officially designated state horse of Missouri. Also in or near Ava are the beginning of the stunning Glade Top Trail, the eminently fishable Bryant Creek, and the historic Douglas County Courthouse. One of the best times to visit Ava is in fall, when the trees change color and the town holds its annual Flaming Fall Festival.

Cabool, Mo. You could probably consider Cabool the geographic heart of the Ozarks, rising up from the middle of the Ozark Plateau to elevations in the 1,600-foot range. With 2,168 residents, it is primarily a farming and ranching community that prides itself on traditional values. Although mass communications have propelled all of the Ozarks into the 20th century (and some even into the 21st, believe it or not), spending a bit of time in this town will leave you with the impression that its Ozark roots run deep.

Gainesville, Mo. Four of Gainesville's courthouses have burned down, but the seat of Ozark County, with its nearly 700 residents, just keeps plugging along. Close to Gainesville are six historic mills—Hodgson's, Dawt, Hammon, Zanoni, Topaz, and Rockbridge. Of these, the latter is a must-stop. Now a recreational complex known as the Rainbow Trout and Game Ranch, its owners have utilized several refurbished historical buildings, offer excellent trout fishing, and run a fine restaurant. Also, the third weekend in September brings Gainesville's annual Hootin' and Hollarin' festival.

Houston, Mo. Burned several times during the Civil War, Houston is the county Seat of Texas County, not to mention the hometown of legendary clown Emmett Kelly (who originated the "Weary Willie" character). The first weekend of each May, Houston hosts the Emmett Kelly Clown Festival, which gives everyone an excuse to don greasepaint and squeeze into little tiny cars. Houston is also the locale of the Texas County Memorial Hospital, which is no doubt helpful when once-a-year clowns trip on their giant shoes and require medical assistance.

Mansfield, Mo., is located in Wright County with roughly 1,400 residents. You will rarely hear the name *Mansfield* without also hearing the name *Laura Ingalls Wilder*. The noted author of the *Little House* books fell in love with the Ozarks and wrote all of her books from her cherished Rocky Ridge Farm. Laura's home and museum are visited by fans from all parts of the globe.

Marshfield, Mo. Supposedly possessing the highest elevation on I-44 east of the Rocky Mountains (1,494 feet), this town of nearly 6,000 is located roughly 20 miles east of Springfield. Growing rapidly as something of a bedroom community as Springfield expands, Marshfield is the birthplace of astronomer Edwin P. Hubble, for whom the Hubble Space Telescope was named. Also, fans of blues and folk music might know the old song "Marshfield Tornado" by John W. (Blind) Boone. The tune immortalized the April 18, 1880, tornado that barged through the heart of Marshfield, killing 65 residents and doing $1 million worth of damage.

Theodosia, Mo. If you saw the movie *Million Dollar Baby* with Clint Eastwood and Hilary Swank, then you may recall that Theodosia was trashed as a redneck hole populated by fat folks who lived in trailers with tires on the roof. Theodosia's 240 residents were less than thrilled. The fact of the matter is that Theodosia is situated in an area of incredible beauty. Not only is it the gateway to Bull Shoals Lake (the record bass capital of Missouri), but it's also surrounded by rugged bluffs, creeks, rivers, and deep forests. The scenery witnessed during spring and fall—via redbud, dogwood, oak, and smoke trees—is beyond description. I suppose you could find some fat folks with tires on the roofs of their trailers if you looked hard enough, but you can also find them in New York. Such spottings only prove you're looking for all the wrong things and need to get an attitude adjustment. The Theodosia area is an outdoor paradise.

West Plains, Mo., has experienced some phenomenal growth in recent years. The population of this seat of Howell County now stands at more than 11,000. The Mark Twain National Forest is but a stone's throw away, and within minutes of West Plains are more than 350 miles of floatable water, 63,000 acres of pure wilderness, and more than 100 miles of hiking, biking, and horseback trails. West Plains features the 30,000-square-foot West Plains Civic Center, the Ozarks Medical Center, the Harlin House Museum, and numerous motels, restaurants, and bed & breakfasts. Famous residents include country icon Porter Wagoner (you know, the big-haired boy who introduced the world to the equally big-haired Dolly Parton) and the legendary left-handed Brooklyn Dodgers pitcher Preacher Roe. West Plains was utterly destroyed during the Civil War and didn't really begin to rebuild until the 1870s. In 1928 (and on a Friday the 13th, no less) 50 young adults were killed in West Plains when the Bond Dance Hall exploded. While no cause of the explosion was ever determined, if you ask some of the very old locals (and they're in a talking mood), it's quite possible you'll hear a number of theories.

✳ To See

MUSEUMS 🦌 ✐ ♿ **Calico Cupboard Toy Sewing Machine Museum** (417-934-6330), 116 N. Oak St., Mountain View, Mo. It is guaranteed that you have never encountered more toy sewing machines in one spot than you will here. This little museum has more than 300 of them. Guests should refrain from making bad puns such as "sew what" or singing "Sew long, it's been good, to know ya." Trust me, they've heard 'em all before.

🦌 ✐ **Douglas County Museum and Historical Society** (417-683-5799; www.avachamber.org/tours.htm), 401 E. Washington Ave., Ava, Mo. Open 10–3 on Sat. only, year-round. Admission is free, though donations are appreciated. This stately old white home was purchased and transformed

DOUGLAS COUNTY MUSEUM

into a local historical museum in 1988. Today, along with numerous antiques, the museum concentrates on the history of the Ozarks and the beginnings of Douglas County.

Harlin House Museum (417-256-7801; www.harlinhousemuseum .homestead.com), 405 Worcester St., West Plains, Mo. Open Apr.–Oct. $2 adults, $1 children. Kids under 6 are admitted free. In a bequest, the Harlin House Museum recently received more than 200 original sketches and paintings created by the late Lennis Leonard Broadfoot. The artist, who was born in nearby Shannon County, chronicled the early Ozarks and its resilient, independent characters via his book *Pioneers of the Ozarks*, first published in 1944. In addition to the Broadfoot Collection, the two-floor museum is home to a wide variety of artifacts ranging from farm machinery and war memorabilia to an authentic Ozark moonshine still. Indian artifacts found in Harlin House date from 5000 BC. The photos and historical minutiae devoted to country singer Porter Wagoner are not nearly that old.

Antique Fire Truck and Soda Pop Museum of Missouri (417-469-4589; www.usfirehouse.com), 908 E. US Bus. 60/63, Willow Springs, Mo. Open Apr.–Nov. $5 adults, $3 ages 10–17. If you like to drink soda, you will like this place. It possesses what is arguably the largest collection of soda bottles in the world. If you get tired of gawking at the empty Mountain Dew receptacles, take a look at the museum's large collection of fire trucks. I've really no idea how these two topics were incorporated into one museum, and thus can only say "Welcome to the Ozarks."

Laura Ingalls Wilder Museum and Home (417-924-3626 or 1-877-924-7126; www.lauraingallswilderhome.com), 3068 SR A, Mansfield, Mo. Mar. 1–Dec. 15, the museum and home are open Mon.–Sat. 9–5, Sun. 12:30–5. June–Aug., the facility is open daily 9–5:30. $8 adults, $6 ages 6–18, and $4 for kids under 6. Those over age 65 are admitted free. Fans of Laura Ingalls Wilder's *Little House* books (or even those who liked the TV show of the same name) will love this historic spot in Mansfield, Mo. **Rocky Ridge Farm**, where Laura penned her famous tomes, has been restored with a dedication to authenticity, and in many ways the residence looks just as Laura left it. The talented woman did not even begin to chronicle her life on the prairies until the age of 65 (urged by her daughter Rose Wilder Lane, a noted author, journalist, and world traveler); all her books were composed in this lovely and tranquil Ozarks home.

HARLIN HOUSE MUSEUM

Ava Fine Arts Gallery and Museum (417-261-2919; www.ava chamber.org/tours.htm), 307 E. Washington Ave., Ava, Mo. 65608. Call for

LAURA INGALLS WILDER MUSEUM AND HOME

hours. Admission is free. Interestingly enough, this museum in Ava possesses a collection of English brasses, facsimiles, and rubbings that date from the 14th century.

MONASTERY Assumption Abbey Monastery (417-683-5510; www.assumption abbey.org), SR 5, P.O. Box 1056, Ava, Mo. Located roughly 20 miles southwest of Ava off SR 00 (call for exact directions lest you get lost), the Assumption Abbey has existed in the Ozarks since 1950. The residents are Trappists, more formally known as the Cistercian Orders of the Strict Observance. The atmosphere here, as you would expect, is very peaceful. Those who might come from cities will at first feel a bit disconcerted by the silence, but it will grow on you if given the chance. Guests, both men and women, are welcomed to the abbey and are invited to stay in a simple guest house. Usually no more than six or eight guests are present at any one time, and the goal here is contemplation via an appreciation of the surrounding beauty and silence. If you wish to stay at the abbey, call the main number for a reservation. Also, the order is known around the country for its delicious fruitcakes. You can order one of these delights— which weigh 2 pounds and cost $27—by calling 1-888-738-0117.

✳ To Do

GOLF Oakwood Country Club (417-967-3968), Country Club Dr., Houston, Mo. A nine-hole course located 2 miles from Houston (off SR B in Oakwood Estates), this small facility offers a driving range, lessons, and cart rental. Greens fees run $7 for 9 holes, $11 for 18.

♈ **Theodosia Country Club** (417-273-4877), Country Club Dr., Theodosia, Mo. A nine-hole, par-34 course, the Theodosia Country Club offers a pro shop, lounge, driving range, and cart rental. Open year-round, it's located 0.5 mile east of Theodosia off US 160. Greens fees Mar.–Oct. are $14 for 9 holes, $20 for 18. Fees during the off-season are $10 and $15.

HODGSON MILL

HISTORIC SITES: MISSOURI GRISTMILLS

If you're into taking photos of old gristmills, you have just hit the mother lode. When most of the local mills were built (from the mid-1800s to about the turn of that century), they served a dual purpose. Yes, they ground the grains to provide flour for area families, but they were also a general meeting spot for families and friends who rarely had the opportunity for neighborin' (that would be "socializing" for you non-Ozark types). Taking grain to the mill could sometimes be a several-day event, a time of excitement, music, tall tales, whoppers, lies, and fun. The Civil War (when many mills were burned), the advent of the railroad, and mass production of goods led to the death of the mill lifestyle, but a number of these structures remain in the Missouri Ozarks.

The **Rockbridge Mill**, built in 1868, was once the site of a small village complete with bank and general store. This mill didn't actually close till the

1940s, and it's now restored in detail. Even better, it is the home of the Rainbow Trout and Game Ranch (see *Resorts*). You can get some great photos of this old red mill, catch rainbow trout near the waterfall, and have drinks and a meal. The old bank has been transformed into an antiques store, and the resort has a restaurant that offers excellent food. There are even rooms for rent should you wish to spend the night. To get to Rockbridge, head north of Gainesville on SR 5 until you reach the tiny town of Wasola (more of an eyeblink than a town), then go 4 miles farther until you hit SR N. Take this road 17 miles north and you will eventually come to Rockbridge.

The **Zanoni Mill**, located in Ozark County, was allegedly still grinding grain until 1951. Today the property serves as a B&B (see *Bed & Breakfasts*), and the mill is open for viewing. In front of the Zanoni Mill is a lake, fed by Zanoni Spring, which is a favorite of those staying at the inn. If you wish to see the Zanoni Mill, drive 3 miles west of Sycamore, Mo., on SR 181. Watch on the north side of the road for the sign.

The **Hodgson Mill** is not open to the public, but you can still see the building from a pull-off area along the road. Constructed around 1860 on Bryant Creek, this old red mill was in operation until at least the 1940s and acquired quite a name for putting out stone-ground meal in the area. When the original mill was closed, a new one was built in Gainesville. That operation, which still sells products under the Hodgson Mill name, was then sold to the Siemer Milling Company. To find the original mill, take SR 181 north of Gainesville for about 15 miles. Pass Zanoni; the mill will be on the north side of the road in roughly 4 miles.

The **Dawt Mill** was built in 1887 by Alva Hodgson, the same man who built Hodgson Mill. Though it burned in 1896, it was rebuilt almost immediately and is still open to the public as a resort (see *Resorts*). Inside the mill you can see not only much of the old equipment, but also a gift shop selling everything from bread to T-shirts. This is a popular spot for those canoeing on the North Fork of the White River, and at the on-site store you can rent a campsite or a canoe. Also, a variety of lodging options is available here. Dawt is one of the best mill photo opportunities you will encounter in the Ozarks.

Located approximately 14 miles west of the town of Cabool, the **Topaz Mill** (built in 1895) was also once the center of a community, complete with store, blacksmith, cannery, and post office. Now privately owned (not open to the public), the Topaz Mill can be reached by taking SR 81 south of Cabool to SR 76. Turn right, and then turn left onto SR E (a gravel road). Go straight for roughly 4 miles and you will come to the mill.

&. **West Plains Country Club** (417-256-7197), 1402 Country Club Dr., West Plains, Mo. This semiprivate 18-hole, par-70 course is one of the older links in the area (built in 1926). Open year-round, its fees begin in the $20 range. This is a nice course, with water hazards coming into play on eight different holes.

&. **West Plains Municipal Golf Course** (417-256-9824), 1724 N. Terra St., West Plains, Mo. This 18-hole, par-72, somewhat hilly public course has water hazards on five different holes. Greens fees are $10 for 9 holes, $14 for 18. Cart rental costs $10 and $16.

&. **Willow Springs Municipal Golf Course** (417-469-1214), 123 E. Main St., Willow Springs, Mo. A nine-hole, par-35 course, Willow Springs Municipal charges $10 for 9 holes, $15 for 18. There is a restaurant on site, open weekends 11–4.

✳ Wild Places

Mark Twain National Forest (www.fs.fed.us/r9/marktwain). Consisting of more than 1.5 million acres, the Mark Twain is a superb wilderness dotted by rivers, streams, and some of the largest natural springs in America. Broken into nine different ranger districts, the forest includes hundreds of miles of hiking trails, numerous scenic drives, seven congressionally designated wilderness areas, 40 campgrounds (these can be reserved by calling 1-877-444-6777), and thousands of acres of primitive and semiprimitive areas. The Mark Twain is a true playground for hunters, fishermen, hikers, equestrians, and campers. In this region, two sections of the Mark Twain are under the management of the Ava/Willow Springs District. In the Willow Springs area, you'll find the Devil's Backbone Wilderness Area. The North Fork of the White River and its nine major springs also provide myriad recreational opportunities. Closer to Ava, the Mark Twain features such attractions as the Glade Top Trail, Hercules Glades Wilderness Area, and Caney Mountain Refuge.

Hercules Glades Wilderness (417-683-4428), Ava/Cassville/Willow Springs District Office, 1103 S. Jefferson St., Ava, Mo. Consisting of 12,315 acres, Hercules Glades is located in southwestern Taney County. A combination of steep rocky hills, forests, and open meadows, it is a fairly isolated area that hosts a number of types of wildlife not really found in other parts of the Ozarks. In fact, much of Hercules Glades seems to be out of the Southwest—it's not uncommon to see rattlesnakes, roadrunners, lizards, or tarantulas. On the other hand, it can appear pure Ozarks, with redbud, dogwood, red cedar, oak, and smoke trees, along with plenty of raccoons and white-tailed deer.

Caney Mountain Conservation Area (417-256-7161; www.mdc.mo.gov), Wildlife District Supervisor, Ozark District Office, Box 138, West Plains, Mo. Located 5 miles north of Gainesville on SR 181, Caney Mountain is owned and managed by the Missouri Department of Conservation. A popular spot for squirrel, deer, and turkey hunting, it consists of 7,899 acres and features caves, a headwaters creek, old-growth forests, glades, and savannas. Should you plan on hiking, remember that this is a very steep part of the country (and full of ticks during the warm to hot months). A couple of interesting historic buildings are found here. One is a 1941 log cabin that belonged to Starker Leopold, son of the famous naturalist and writer Aldo Leopold. Starker was the resident biologist for Caney Mountain.

Devil's Backbone Wilderness Area (417-469-3155), Willow Springs Office, Ava/Cassville/Willow Springs District Office, Old Springfield Rd., Willow Springs, Mo. Take SR CC about 15 miles west of its junction with US 63 in West Plains, Mo. This rugged 6,595-acre area, located within the Mark Twain National Forest, is noted for both its trails and its beauty. In spring you can revel in the blooms of oak, hickory, dogwood, and redbud. In fall the oaks, sweet gums, and sugar maples turn the forest all shades of red. The Devil's Backbone is loaded with all sorts of wildlife. Day hiking, backpacking, camping, and horseback riding are all much-loved activities here (take note, however, that both biking and motorized vehicles are prohibited). There are 13 miles of manicured trails, but you can hike anywhere you wish. At the north end of the Devil's Backbone is the **North Fork Recreation Area** (which locals may call Hammon Mill or Hammon Camp)—a great spot for camping or picnics on the North Fork River. You will find a boat launch there, and if you care to take a 0.5-mile hike, have a look at **Blue Spring**, one of the main springs of the North Fork.

LAKES Norfork Lake (870-425-2700; www.swl.usace.army.mil/parks/norfork), Mountain Home Project Office, 324 W. 7th St., Mountain Home, Ark. Only 10 percent of Norfork Lake is located in Missouri (at Gainesville and Tecumseh), with the rest of its 30,000-plus acres stretching to the south in Arkansas. With 550 miles of shoreline, it is a favorite tourist spot, well known for all water sports, camping, and hiking. Fishermen love this lake for its rainbow trout and largemouth bass. Constructed in 1941 by the Army Corps of Engineers—for flood control and hydroelectric power in the Upper White River Basin—Norfork boasts of having one of the largest federal trout hatcheries east of the Rockies. On the Missouri side it's fed by both Bryant Creek and the North Fork. This makes for some fantastic early-spring fishing. During the first part of March, walleye migrate to the north end of the lake. Later on, into April, various species of bass are easily caught here, particularly smallmouths, which migrate down the rivers. Norfork is surrounded by 32,000 acres of public land, with numerous resorts, services, restaurants, marinas, and USACE-managed campsites. Scuba divers from all over the world visit Norfork because of the crystal clarity of the water.

Bull Shoals Lake (573-751-4133, 1-800-877-1234, or 870-425-2700; www .bullshoalslake.org or www.swl.usace.army.mil/parks/bullshoals), Mountain Home Project Office, 324 W. 7th St., Mountain Home, Ark. Another Army Corps project that came about to control flooding in the Upper White River Basin, the 45,000-acre Bull Shoals is nearly 100 miles long. With 1,050 miles of shoreline, Bull Shoals Dam was started in 1947 and completed in 1951. Located 7 miles north of Cotter, Ark., on the White River, it is a major source of hydroelectric power. Most of Bull Shoals Lake can be found in Arkansas, although its northern arms extend into Missouri from Cedar Creek (in the west, south of Branson), through the town of Protem in the middle range, and to Pontiac and Theodosia in the east. The entirety of the lake, on both the Missouri and Arkansas sides, has become increasingly popular with retirees. This migration can be attributed partially to the beauty of the area and the wealth of easily accessible recreation activities. Another factor is that, compared with other lake areas of the country, real estate taxes are low and housing prices are surprisingly affordable.

There are 19 developed parks around Bull Shoals, not to mention countless marinas, boat launches, restaurants, lodges, and resorts. This lake is known far and wide for its largemouth and striped bass fishing, but it is almost as popular with anglers in search of catfish, trout, crappie, and walleye. Divers also flock to Bull Shoals; in some spots it is nearly 200 feet deep, and visibility is in the 25- to 30-foot range.

❋ Lodging

BED & BREAKFASTS ✐ **Victorian Gables** (417-256-7804), 803 Webster St., West Plains, Mo. With two guest rooms, Victorian Gables's rates range $85–115 per night. Amenities include a Victorian pavilion, grill, patio, kitchen, microwave, and TV/VCR with cable. Children are accepted.

✐ **Garden Gate Guest House** (417-256-1199), 119 S. College St., West Plains, Mo. This 1891 Victorian cottage offers a full kitchen, two baths, a fireplace, and laundry facilities. Kids are accepted, and rates run $125–185. Smoking is permitted in a designated area.

Beaver Creek Bed and Breakfast (417-796-2102; www.beavercreek bandb.com), 122 Campbell Ranch Rd., Brownbranch, Mo. Take SR 76

ZANONI MILL INN

from Ava and travel 22 miles to Brownbranch. Turn right onto SR W, and then take a left onto Campbell Ranch Rd.; the B&B is located right across the road from Beaver Canoe Rental. This 1911 Victorian home is close to floating, fishing, and the gorgeous Glade Top Trail. One suite and two guest rooms are offered for $60–100 per night and come with central air, private bath, TV, and VCR. Breakfast is served at 8 AM and offers the usual suspects of fruit, juice, ham, bacon, sausage, biscuits and gravy, hash browns, and pancakes. Smoking is allowed outdoors only, pets are not allowed, and you should inquire about kids.

Zanoni Mill Inn (417-679-4050 or 1-877-679-4050; www.bbim.org/ zanoni), HC 78, Box 1010, Zanoni, Mo. The grandfather of the owner of this bed & breakfast built the actual Zanoni Mill in 1905 (his great-grandparents had settled in the area more than three decades prior). In front of the old mill and beside the remnants of an Ozarks pioneer village now sits this huge Colonial-style home. Located in the midst of a 1,750-acre working ranch, Zanoni is one of those off-the-beaten-path surprises for which everyone searches. There are four guest rooms in the home (two with private bath, two sharing a hall bath) as well as an indoor pool, hot tub, big-screen TV, and game room. Last but not least, the home fronts on a 3-acre lake perfect for fishing, canoeing, or paddle boating. Full breakfasts are served, but pets are not accepted. Smoking is permitted outside, but you need to inquire first if you're traveling with kids. Rates at Zanoni begin at $75 per night for private bath, and $70 for shared. If you're planning on some fishing and floating, this inn puts you close to Bryant Creek, the North Fork River, and Norfork and Bull Shoals lakes.

✧ ㅎ **Aunt Bess's Stoneridge Inn** (417-261-2177; www.stoneridgeinn bedandbreakfast.bravehost.com), HC 79, Box 3000, Dora, Mo. As an item of musical trivia, the tiny town of Dora is best known as the birthplace of legendary R&B artist Steve Cropper (the guitar player in the Blues Brothers Band with Dan Aykroyd and John Belushi). Also worthy of note in town, however, is this fine stone-and-cedar B&B. With its bird and butterfly sanctuary, small springfed lake, and huge screened-in porch (all rooms open onto it), Stoneridge Inn is a prime spot for relaxation in the deep Ozarks. You are close to canoeing and fishing on Bryant Creek or the North Fork and can tour several of the old mills that dot the region. The rates at Stonebridge, which include gourmet meals and tax, begin at $110 per night (the honeymoon suite, which also includes a wine-and-chocolate basket, goes for $130). The food is renowned here, and breakfasts can include such offerings as blackberry soufflé, pancakes, omelets, and sausage. Aunt Bess herself also creates fresh-baked goods, and even

those who are not staying at the inn can call ahead and have a meal served by appointment. The prices are $5.35 for breakfast, $6.35–9 for lunch, and $13.50 for dinner (included in the price of a room for inn guests). There are four guest rooms, all with ceiling fan, queen-sized bed, and private bath. Kids are accepted at Stoneridge, but smoking is permitted outside only. Call to inquire about pets.

Windstone House (417-967-2008; www.bedandbreakfast.com/missouri/ windstone-house-bed-breakfast.html), 539 Cleveland Rd., Houston, Mo. A relatively new home, constructed in 1977 primarily of native stone, Windstone offers three guest rooms (two upstairs and one down). The two-story inn features covered, wraparound porches and a huge balcony on the second floor that is perfect for relaxation, reading, or even breakfast. The home is chock-full of antiques and features three different common areas and a dining room with woodburning fireplace. Double-occupancy rates are $60 per night (single occupancy is $50), and kids over 12 are allowed. Pets cannot stay at Windstone, but smoking is permitted in designated areas.

◯◯ 🌸 ㅎ **The Dickey House** (1-800-450-7444; www.dickeyhouse.com), 331 S. Clay St., Marshfield, Mo. Built between 1910 and 1913, this impressive Greek Revival mansion has been featured in *Time* magazine and has played host to the likes of President George H. W. Bush and Barbara Bush. It's set on 2 acres complete with an aviary full of white turtledoves. Guests can stay in one of the mansion's three guest rooms or in four additional suites located in buildings around the property. All the rooms and suites come equipped with cable TV and VCR, and the suites feature a fireplace, double Jacuzzi, refrigerator, and coffeemaker. Special touches in both the individual rooms and suites have come after much thought, and those staying at Dickey House can expect electric fireplaces in some rooms, four-poster or canopied beds, brass beds, and a plethora of period antiques. In the sunroom you'll find a therapeutic hot tub (57 jets) capable of comfortably holding eight adults. A full breakfast is served each morning (try the caramel French toast), and kids 12 and older are welcomed. Smoking is absolutely not permitted within the rooms or suites; inquire in advance if you are traveling with a pet. Rates at the Dickey House range from $75 for a room to $165 for the largest suite. Weddings are a fairly frequent occurrence here; contact the owners as to prices and details.

∞ ✎ **The Red Oak Inn** (417-767-2444; www.theredoakinn.com), 1046 Red Oak Rd., Fordland, Mo. With five guest rooms, this unusual inn began its life as a 1940s barn. After a renovation by local Amish craftsmen, the barn is now a three-story structure with covered, wraparound porches and sitting areas. The architecture is unique and well done, and plush chairs reside in front of a fireplace in one of the common areas. There are plenty of woods and meadows to explore at the Red Oak, or you might enjoy the gazebo and hot tub. Both a full breakfast and nighttime snack are served. $85–125 per night; kids over 8 are accepted. Smoking is only permitted outside, and the inn does not have accommodations for pets. The Red Oak is also popular for weddings, reunions, and business functions.

∞ ✎ **Born Again Bed and Breakfast** (417-924-4424; www.bbonline.com/mo/bornagain), 107 N. US Bus. 60, Mansfield, Mo. Those who seek lodging with a Christian emphasis will enjoy the Born Again, a 3,200-square-foot, 1881 Victorian located just half a block from the center of Mansfield. The home is furnished with period decor; the two guest rooms (which share a bath) are located on the second story. This inn features a nice stone fireplace and mahogany staircase and is equipped with both central air and heat. The breakfasts are hearty—usually a skillet meal or hotcakes complete with scones, toast, homemade jams and jellies, and juice—and recently a hot tub was installed on a rear deck. Rates begin at $75–85, and various specials are offered throughout the year. This is a smoke-, alcohol-, and drug-free establishment. While children are accepted, it is under the provision that they be supervised (and well behaved) at all times. The owners have a resident cat and dog, and thus no other pets are accepted.

RESORTS ✎ **Bucks and Spurs Guest Ranch** (417-683-2381; www.bucksandspurs.com), HC 71, P.O. Box 163, Ava, Mo. 65608. This dude ranch south of Ava (which has been featured on the NBC *Today* show) offers horseback riding, cattle drives, horse drives, and horse training on 1,000 acres along Beaver Creek. You can swim, fish, canoe, or even go on a turkey hunt. This, while enjoying the beauty of the Ozarks and digging into some hefty meals. Every guest receives personalized attention, and riders are provided with mounts based upon their experience and ability.

FLOATING THE RIVER OF LIFE

River of Life Farm (417-261-7777 or 888-824-2398; www.riveroflife farm.com), Rt. 1, Box 4560, Dora, Mo. You don't have to believe me when I tell you River of Life Farm is one of the coolest resorts in the Ozarks; after all, I've known owner Myron McKee on and off for nearly 20 years and might be biased. But, you should believe the NBC *Today* show, the *Wall Street Journal*, the *St. Louis Post-Dispatch*, *Missouri Life* magazine, and countless smaller publications. It seems everyone who visits this idyllic resort in the heart of the Mark Twain National Forest has nothing but rave reviews. Consisting of 120 acres that have been in Myron's family for three generations, and fronting on the Wild Trout Management Area of the North Fork of the White River, this gated getaway offers the ultimate in lodging, wade fishing, float fishing, canoeing, hunting, hiking, and camping. River of Life is peaceful—the number of guests on-site at any one time is limited— and the scenery is nothing short of spectacular.

Aside from the outdoor glory, one of the main draws of ROLF is the lodging. Myron is a craftsman in every sense of the word, and his "tree-house" lodging options are works of art. Your choices, which rise high into the trees (hence the name), range from the 590-square-foot **Cedar Chest Cabin** and **Tree Top Hideaway Treehouse** (both are $175 per night for two people) to the 1,200-square-foot **Mountain Log Lookout** ($185 per night for two). While this is just a sample, all the choices come with private bath, fireplace, fully equipped kitchen, and queen-sized bed. The only exception is the tiny 100-square-foot **Fisherman's Room**, which rents for $60 per night per person. Canoe and raft rental (with shuttle) begins at $20 per person per day. Guided fly-fishing trips, which include boats, shuttle, and lunch, begin at $225 per day for one person and $275 a day for two. Guided hunting trips or custom-designed trips are also a possibility, and you should contact the resort to discuss pricing. Because of its location, ROLF offers endless hiking opportunities. Also, for those who would prefer to camp under the stars, a campground (the only one in the Ozarks found in the Wild Trout Management Area) features picnic tables, fire pits, hot showers, and bathrooms with running water. Camping fees begin at $8 per night per person ($4 for ages 5– 11), but there is a $20-per-day fishing access fee if you prefer not to rent a canoe. Those considering ROLF need to call ahead for reservations and should note that most lodging choices have minimum-stay requirements.

Lodging at Bucks and Spurs includes several options, including beautiful and large lodges and cabins, but a five-day vacation (per person, double occupancy) runs $965. Rates for one adult would be $580, and a two-day vacation is $395. All vacation packages include meals, lodging, horseback riding, fishing, canoe trips (on the ranch), and any special event. To reach the ranch, head 5 miles south of Ava on SR 5 to SR A. Continue south on SR A for another 5 miles, then turn north onto SR A-422 for 2 miles. Ask about the various discounts when you call for reservations.

✐ ♿ **Golden Hills Trail Rides** (417-457-6222 or 1-800-874-1157; www .goldenhills.com), 19546 Golden Dr., Raymondville, Mo. Open Apr. 1– Nov. 30. With more than 250 miles of trails on 5,100 privately owned acres, Golden Hills offers far more than stunning scenery and trail riding galore. There are horse-and-rider clinics, fishing, hiking, and even a bi-yearly reenactment of a mountain man rendezvous. Capable of hosting 1,100 guests, the facility's lodging options run the gamut from campsites with electricity and water, to bunk-houses, to private rooms with two queen-sized beds. Entertainment can include cowboy bands, hayrides, marshmallow roasts around the campfire, line dancing, mountain biking, and much more. There is a weight room, creeks on the property, and a store. Three hot meals are served daily, and prices range from a low of $200 per week (if you bring your own horse and camp out) to upward of $800 per week if you seek a private room and rent one of the ranch's well-behaved mounts.

✐ ♿ **Turkey Creek Ranch** (417-273-4362; www.turkeycreekranch.com), HC 3, Box 3180, Theodosia, Mo. Owned by the same family for nearly 50 years, this 700-acre resort and working cattle ranch on Bull Shoals Lake was named one of the Top 25 Cottage Resorts by *Midwest Living* magazine. The ranch offers a string of well-trained saddle horses, and trails range all over the property. Open Mar. 1–Nov. 30; $60–190 per night. Accommodations include deluxe cabins with two to five bedrooms, two baths, full kitchen with microwave and range, a master suite, and central air. The standard cottages are slightly smaller, with two to three bedrooms. Both options include a grill; picnic table; screened porch; all pots, pans, and linens; coffeemaker; and TV. Also available are studio-sized "casitas," which sleep two to four people and offer private bath, full kitchen, porch, and picnic area complete with grill and table. Aside from horseback riding, there are plenty of recreational amenities at Turkey Creek. A game room, gift shop, hot tub, indoor pool, tennis courts, basketball, volleyball, and shuffleboard are only the beginning of pastimes that will keep the kids from getting bored. Pets are not accepted.

✐ ♿ **Theodosia Marina-Resort** (417-273-4444; www.tmrbullshoals .net), Lake Rd. 160-25, P.O. Box 390, Theodosia, Mo. 65761. In business since 1952, Theodosia Marina-Resort has grown from a dock, café, and motel to a full-service marina and resort with boat sales and service. On-site you'll find a motel, cottages, lodges, and an RV and camping park. Prices for the motel begin at $45 per night, and the two-bedroom cottages (with complete kitchen, private bath, and TV) begin at $85 per night (check for required minimums pertaining to occupants and reserved nights). If you prefer to rent a lodge, they've a good one here. The 2,000-square-foot log structure includes four bedrooms, two baths with Jacuzzis, complete kitchen with dishwasher, three TVs, a fireplace, and a porch with lake view. Prices start at $225. The season for both the cottages and lodges runs Mar. 1–late Nov. For those who arrive with an RV, sites at the **Fort Cook RV Park** (with water, electric, rest rooms, and hot showers) begin at $20 for two people. As Theodosia Marina is right on Bull Shoals, boat rental is popular. Rental for a fishing boat (a 16-footer with a 50-horse outboard, trolling motor, and depthfinder) is $55 for a half day and $70 for a full day. Pontoon boat rental begins at $35 per hour. Skis, ski vests, life jackets, towropes, and safety gear are all included in the rental charge. Last but not least, the facility also features lighted tennis and basketball courts, an outdoor pool, and a family-style restaurant.

✑ ♿ ⅄ **Dawt Mill** (417-284-3540 or 1-888-884-3540; www.dawtmill.com), HC 1, Box 1090, Tecumseh, Mo. The Dawt Mill, originally built in 1897, is the only remaining gristmill in Ozark County that is still operational. Much more than that, however, the facility for which the mill serves as centerpiece is a full-scale resort. Many folks choose Dawt Mill for canoe rental, as the three trips offered down the North Fork are all very pretty (easy to say, since there's not a single part of the North Fork that isn't gorgeous).

With shuttle service included, the cost of an 18-mile trip for two is $55. Shorter trips, of either 6 or 8 miles, are $39. For those who wish to cast a line, fishing licenses can be purchased at the mill.

Lodging choices here are excellent. The Dinnel log cabin (which is three old cabins hooked together and renovated) has a full kitchen, bathroom, bedrooms, front deck, and air-conditioning and rents from $119 per night. Hodgson House, built in the late 1800s, is divided into four separate units, each of which can comfortably accommodate four people. Prices start at $69 for a standard suite. A modernized cabin in the woods (creatively dubbed the Cabin in the Woods) also can sleep four and costs $60 per night. A recently constructed lodge, the Cotton Gin Inn, offers deluxe or standard suites (two rooms) at $69 and $79, respectively. On the property are also 50 campsites for either RV or tent camping. RV spots with water, electric, and sewer run $36, and tent sites begin at $18. Finally, the resort provides a deli and a full-service restaurant that is open from the end of May through Labor Day.

DAWT MILL

🐾 ⚓ 🍸 **Rainbow Trout and Game Ranch** (417-679-3619; www.rock bridgemo.com), P.O. Box 100, Rockbridge, Mo. 65741. With more than 200,000 fish raised a year in this hatchery, the fishing is always good here at the site of the old Rockbridge Mill (the record is a 16-pound trout). In this idyllic setting in the deep Ozarks, sportsmen can also enjoy guided hunts for upland birds, turkey, and white-tailed deer. Within the 3,000 acres of land that surround this facility, the possibilities are infinite. Also, a sporting clay area and hunter's archery range are of great assistance in sharpening your marksmanship. For lodging, the game ranch features 29 motel rooms as well as five separate guest houses, each having a minimum of three bedrooms and two baths. Prices range from $80 per night for a motel room to $250 per night for one of the houses. Pets are accepted, with a $15-per-night charge in motel rooms and $25–50 per night in the houses. A fine restaurant (see *Dining Out*) is on the property, and in the old mill you'll find the **Grist Mill Club**. Open seasonally (closed in winter), this pub offers a relaxing setting and a great view of the mill's waterfall.

Fishing permits are $5 a day if staying at Rockbridge, and $10 per day if you're just visiting. Because this is a private enterprise, no other license or stamp is needed. You are required to keep any trout you catch (and you can catch a lot), and the cost is $3.65 per pound. As for hunting and shooting, sporting clays run $20 for 50 targets. Guided and nonguided hunt packages are offered for turkey and deer beginning at $525 for a three-day, three-night stay. Other multinight hunting packages run from $595 for three days and two nights to $1,275 for four days and four nights. For the price of $115, you can embark on a guided upland bird hunt (dog provided).

CANOE OUTFITTERS AND CAMPING

🐾 ⚓ **Beaver Canoe Rental** (417-796-2336; www.beavercanoerental .com), 159 SR W, Ava, Mo. This outfitter specializes in floating and fishing on Beaver Creek, a nice little stream featuring decent bass fishing and possessing lots of good gravel bars for picnics. Open Apr.–Oct., Beaver Canoe offers floats starting at $36 per canoe. Shuttle service is provided, and an on-site store carries all the basic provisions. The campground features toilets, hot showers, tent sites, fire pits, and picnic tables and begins at $7 per person per night. Pets are allowed but must be leashed and attended at all times.

🐾 ⚓ ♿ **Boiling Springs Resort and Canoe Rental** (573-674-3488 or 1-800-564-3285; www.boilingsprings resort.com), 15750 SR BB, Licking, Mo. The Big Piney River is a slow-moving body of water, and one that is far from overfished. Such being the case, you can expect to catch plenty of hard-fighting goggle-eye (a smallish bass derivative), smallmouths, and largemouths. Canoe rentals with shuttle begin at $38, and modern cabins (TV, air, bathroom, linens, and full kitchen) begin at $60 per night. Pets are allowed, but they will cost you an extra $20 per night. Tent campsites begin at $6 per night, and RV sites begin at $10 night plus a $6-per-person fee.

🐟 🐾 ⚓ ♿ **North Fork Outfitters** (417-261-2259 or 1-866-261-2259;

www.nfocanoes.com), SR 181 and SR CC W., Dora, Mo. I first became acquainted with this establishment about 20 years ago, when I inadvertently wrapped one of the former owner's (the late Paul Roy) canoes around a rock. I still blame my friend and canoe partner, Wendy Feintech, for not telling me the rock was there. When I found Paul and admitted my idiocy, he just looked at the canoe, shrugged, and said, "Don't worry about it." Thus, even though Roy's Store is now owned by Paul and Linda Francis, I still have a soft spot for the joint. The fact that their slogan is now "The Funnest Outfitter in the Ozarks" does nothing to diminish my attraction. North Fork Outfitters offers a number of different canoe trips on both Bryant Creek and the North Fork. Starting prices range $38.50–42.50. A nice option here is that the business also offers all-inclusive trips beginning at $65 per person ($55 for kids 12 and under). This excursion includes canoe, shuttle, two nights of camping, Friday-night dinner, three meals on Saturday, and Sunday-morning breakfast. That is a great deal.

Additionally, NFO features both RV and tent camping, a motel (rooms start at $59), and cabins ($75–99). The legendary **Roy's Store** carries everything from soup to nuts to fishing licenses, tackle, groceries, gas, and video rental. Also, for a dandy meal (especially breakfast) stop into the Log Cabin restaurant (see *Eating Out*).

Twin Bridges Canoe and Campground (417-256-7507 or 417-256-2726; www.twinbridgescanoe.com), HC 64, Box 230, West Plains, Mo. Located on the North Fork River, Twin Bridges is a multipurpose outfitter offering canoes ($20.50 per person, two-person minimum), rafts ($31 per person with a four-person minimum), kayaks ($30 per person), tandem kayaks ($25 per person), and a variety of camping and lodging options. Both fishing and hunting are first-rate in this stretch of the Ozarks—what with the cold, clear North Fork and the Mark Twain National Forest—and over the years this operation has expanded to ensure that you can pursue those pastimes in comfort. Either owning or leasing 1,200 acres (with 5 miles of riverfront), Twin Bridges has built a number of log homes and cabins right on the river that sleep up to 16 people. A log lodge is capable of sleeping 30. Four separate camping areas are found both on Spring Creek and on the North Fork, as well as another large, wooded site overlooking the river. These tent sites start at $8 per night per person and include picnic tables, grills, hot showers, and bathrooms with running water.

The log homes offered by Twin Bridges offer a good value for larger groups and those who seek more luxury than a tent. Situated on 250 acres, with a mile of riverfront, the homes begin at $135 per night for two people, with $28 for each additional adult, and sleep 16. Cabins begin at $55 per night for two, with $12 for each additional adult. Call for rates on the large trout lodge, as well as for information on minimum stays. Pets are not permitted in either the cabins or lodge. The Twin Bridges facility also features RV hookups, a camp store, and guide services.

For **Bucks and Spurs Guest Ranch**, **River of Life Farm**, and **Dawt Mill**, see *Resorts*.

AVA DRUG SODA FOUNTAIN

✳ Where to Eat

EATING OUT 🏅 ✎ ♿ **Ava Drug Soda Fountain** (417-683-4127), 112 W. Washington St., Ava, Mo. You're going to like this place, located in Ava's local drugstore. This is a true old-fashioned soda fountain. You'll find limeades made from real limes, 1950s prices, banana splits, ice cream, shakes, and all the traditional stools and stainless steel that you either (a) remember or (b) wish you could remember. The menu is simple, and everything tastes wonderful. What you'll find here is an great atmosphere, a happy time, and the sort of sugar buzz that is mandatory from time to time.

🏅 ✎ ♿ **Hillbilly Junction** (417-469-4296), 2364 SR 1270, Willow Springs, Mo. I would be utterly remiss were I not to include the landmark known as Hillbilly Junction, visible on the north side of US 60 as you approach Willow Springs. It's not that the food is that phenomenal (it's just okay . . . but you won't spend more than $5–10), and it's not like there's some sort of spectacular ambience. The reason you have to stop is that you will always regret it if you don't. You see, failing to visit Hillbilly Junction would be a bit like driving through South Dakota and failing to stop at Wall Drug. You do it so you can tell other people you did it, and also to pick up some tourist junk as evidence of your visit. Yes, this is the place to grab a meal (or sometimes hit the buffet) and then purchase stuff you don't need. It's the place for postcards featuring a giant bass in a tiny rowboat with a caption reading THE ONE THAT DIDN'T GET AWAY. It's the place to buy jam, honey, or pork rinds. It's the place where you get your silly-looking felt Hillbilly hat or authentic corncob pipe. It's your prime source for the much-needed Ozark shot glass or the inevitable tiny spoon emblazoned with the Gateway Arch. Look, you have no choice. Just surrender gracefully to the inevitable, pull in, grab a burger, and stock up on bumper stickers.

HILLBILLY JUNCTION

♣ ✎ ♿ **Aunt B and Cajun Jo's** (417-924-8073), 2075 SR B, Mansfield, Mo. Hours are Mon.–Wed. 9–8, Thu.–Sat. 9–9. When you pull up to this restaurant you'll likely wonder what the heck kind of joint it is. The building isn't fancy, and there's not a single window in the place. Still, if you passed the sign featuring an alligator in a chef's hat, then be assured you're in the right place. Walk right on in and you'll find that you've been transported to the swamps of Louisiana. This is a good thing. Some folks might not appreciate the Cajun music or the alligator heads, but unless your taste buds have atrophied, you'll go nuts over the food. There's jambalaya, red beans and rice, gumbo, crab patties (the real deal—not fake crab), catfish, and shrimp. Arrive here hungry because the portions are huge—the pressure-cooker-fried chicken breast weighs in at a pound or more. And of course there's no way you should ever leave Aunt B and Cajun Jo's without having one of the fried pies. These are small, incredibly delicious, and stuffed with a variety of fillings. Prices are reasonable here (especially for what you're getting)—from a low of around $4 to a high of $30. Occasionally there is live bluegrass (generally on Thursday nights); neither smoking nor alcohol is permitted.

✎ ♿ **Cookie's** (417-273-4444; www .tmrbullshoals.net/cookies.html), Lake Rd. 160-25, Theodosia, Mo. Located at the Theodosia Marina-Resort, Cookies is a family restaurant whose menu ranges from hot dogs to filet mignon. There's a full breakfast menu, lunch and dinner specials, Friday- and Saturday-night prime rib specials, and smorgasbords. Breakfast is in the $3–6 range, and a buffet is served Saturday, Sunday, and holidays during the summer season. The catfish lunch is $6.25. Also for lunch, a "steak-n-taters" salad (prime rib and sautéed potatoes with red onions all served over a bed of greens) costs $8.95. A lunch buffet is available on Sunday and holidays in summer. A nice dinner appetizer is the breaded Cajun crawdad tails ($4.95), while a 16-ounce KC strip is $15.95. If you are by chance trying to sample every deep-fried catfish dinner in the Ozarks (which should make your cardiologist even wealthier), the version at Cookie's runs $9.95.

♣ ✎ ♿ **Log Cabin Restaurant** (417-261-2686 or 866-261-2810; www.nfo canoes.com), SR 181 and SR CC W., Dora, Mo. If you're getting ready for a float with North Fork Outfitters in Dora (or just returning from one), you can pass the time with breakfast, a burger, or a meal at the Log Cabin Restaurant. The "hungry hunter" breakfast, at just $4.99, includes three eggs, country-fried potatoes, a ham steak, and two pancakes. There are a variety of other options as well, and Memorial Day–Labor Day a Saturday- and Sunday-morning breakfast buffet ($4.99) is served 7:30–10 AM. Burgers, Philly cheesesteaks, and a pork tenderloin are all in the $4–6 range, and

AUNT B AND CAJUN JO'S

a catfish dinner is $5.95. Daily lunch and dinner specials are available, there's a kids' menu, and during nice weather you can either eat inside or dine outside on the covered deck.

DINING OUT ✐ ♿ ⛾ **Cafe 37** (417-372-0307), 37 Court Square, West Plains, Mo. I never really expected to see a gourmet restaurant in West Plains. Then again, I never expected West Plains to have grown to the degree it has. This restaurant, located in the restored Opera House, involved more than a little thought. The inside is very well done, with a fine antique back bar and copper ceiling. It is in fact this combination of past meeting future that seems to be the hallmark of the contemporary Ozarks. Though the food is first-rate—as is true almost everywhere in this part of the world—the dress is casual. This isn't the most inexpensive place around (plan on $30–50 per person, on average), but you will not go away unhappy. You'll find both a number of standard entrées and also enough unique offerings to keep your curiosity alive. Particularly good is a cumin-lime roast pork tenderloin. Finally, if you're seeking a good lunch place, you just won't beat the blue cheese burger you'll find here. It's a $6 burger that's actually worth $6.

Rainbow Trout and Game Ranch (417-679-3619; www.rockbridgemo .com), SR N, Rd. 142, Rockbridge, Mo. Located at the old Rockbridge Mill, the restaurant of the Rainbow Trout Ranch is open to the public 8–8 year-round (except for Christmas week). It's a great place to get a fine and relaxing meal after a day of fishing, hunting, or simply exploring the ranch's grounds and the old mill.

Breakfast, lunch, and dinner are served. The morning meal ranges from an affordable $3.95 for biscuits and gravy to $7.95 for country-fried steak and eggs (be hungry if you order this). A variety of sandwiches, entrées, appetizers, and salads are offered for lunch. As for dinner, start with some frog legs ($10.95) for an appetizer, and move on to anything from fried chicken ($8.95) to a hefty selection of trout. That's the specialty here, and you can order it amandine, stuffed, broiled, batter fried, or baked. There's also Monterey trout, blackened trout, and lemon-pepper trout. Prices for any of these are $13.95–14.95.

✳ Entertainment
✐ ♿ **Avenue Theatre** (417-256-4420; www.westplains.net/tourism .asp), 307 Washington Ave., West Plains, Mo. Built in 1950 as an art deco movie house, the fully renovated Avenue now plays host to community plays and other local entertainment events. Prices and admission vary depending upon the event.

🐾 ✐ ♿ **West Plains Civic Center** (417-256-8123; www.civiccenter.net), 110 St. Louis Ave., West Plains, Mo. From banquets to basketball games, from pro wrestling to ballet, from gymnasts to Ted Nugent, from gun shows to live theater, you never quite know what you'll find at the West Plains Civic Center. The main exhibit hall/arena here can hold more than 3,500 people, and the smaller theater room seats 450. As expected, admission prices vary with the individual shows.

✐ **West Plains Opera House** (417-256-6666), 37 Court Square, West Plains, Mo. Completely refurbished, this 1886 opera house now plays host to concerts, dancing, and performing arts of all types. Call for information on upcoming events and admissions prices. This is also the home of Cafe 37.

✎ **Yellow House Community Arts Center** (417-256-2433; www.yellow housearts.org), 209 W. Cleveland St., West Plains, Mo. The center is open year-round, but call ahead for performance times and admission prices (generally in the $3–10 range). This 1903 house is now home to a variety of musical performances, speakers, and artistic presentations open to the public. The music is particularly good—everything from bluegrass to Celtic, country, and classical.

SPECTATOR SPORTS West Plains Motor Speedway (417-257-2112; www.westplains-speedway.com), 10603 US 63, West Plains, Mo. Generally considered one of the top three dirt tracks in America, this ⅜-mile oval is open Mar.–Aug. and offers seating for 17,000. Set on 100 acres, with a large campground on-site, the facility includes hot showers, bathrooms, and full concessions. Races include IMCA modifieds, superstocks, hobby stock cars and trucks, and much more. The West Plains Motor Speedway is also home of the **Show-Me 100** and **Show-Me Championship**. Admission prices for the Saturday races are $7 adults, $4 seniors, $2 ages 7–12. Kids 6 and under are admitted free.

✸ Selective Shopping

Memory Lane Antiques (417-683-1063; www.mlava.com), Rt. 1, Box 409, Ava, Mo. Located on the town square at Memory Lane, you'll find just a bit of everything. There's lots of

WEST PLAINS OPERA HOUSE & CAFE 37

glassware (Carnival glass, Depression glass), old books and signs, jewelry, utensils, and even antique fishing plugs and gear. That's not all; there's also usually a wide range of collectible and antique furniture, not to mention dolls, old tools, and pottery.

✸ Special Events

May **Emmett Kelly Clown Festival** (417-967-2220; http://train.missouri .org/~chamber), Houston Area Chamber of Commerce, Houston, Mo. If you suffer from coulrophobia (an intense fear of clowns), then you'd best avoid Houston during the first weekend in May. That would be the time of the annual Emmett Kelly Clown Festival, when clowns of all shapes, sizes, colors, and descriptions descend upon this small town to make weird noises and flop around in greasepaint and such. Dedicated to Houston's favorite son, Emmett Kelly (his Weary Willie character is arguably the world's best-known clown), you'll experience not just clowns and the obligatory clown antics but also a midway, circus acts, myriad booths stocked with crafts and food, face painting, music, balloons, and magicians. You have to wonder, considering the terrifying manner in which he portrays clowns in his books, if Stephen King ever attended this shindig.

June and September **Missouri Foxtrotting Horse Breed Association Show** (417-683-2468; www.mfthba .com), P.O. Box 1027, Ava, Mo. 65608. Riders from around the world love the equine breed known as the Missouri Foxtrotter. Whether used as merely a family horse, for ranch work, or for competition, the Foxtrotter is known for its smooth gait, rhythm, and friendly personality. Located in Ava, the headquarters of the Missouri Foxtrotting Horse Breed Association holds two international shows per year. The **Fall Show and Celebration** (held for a week in early September) and the **Spring Show and Three Year Old Futurity** (held for four days in early June) feature performance horses, trail rides, competition in a long list of different classes, food, drink, and fun. Gate admissions are $5 weekdays, $6 weekends.

July **Douglas County Fair** (417-683-4594; www.avachamber.org/events .htm), 810 S.W. 13th Ave., Ava, Mo. Held for three days in mid-July, this county fair is of the traditional style, with games, music, food, and livestock.

September **Hootin' and Hollarin' Days** (www.bullshoalslake.org/ attractions/hootin.htm). Held on the town square, Gainesville, Mo. Now almost 50 years old, the annual Hootin' and Hollarin' festival in Gainesville takes place the third weekend in September. It's dedicated to preserving the traditions, crafts, skills, and music of the Ozarks, and you'll hear everything from gospel to bluegrass. If your feet are itchy, join in for some line dancing, clog dancing, or square dancing. Wandering around, you'll see folks demonstrating the arts of carving and whittling, blacksmithing, spinning, and much more. There are contests galore. Though they have yet to be sanctioned by the International Olympic Committee, sports such as outhouse racing, hog and husband calling, frog jumping, and turtle racing are old standards. Of course there will be tons of food and craft booths, as well as a parade, queen pageant, chili cook-off, and quilt show.

October **Glade Top Trail Flaming Fall Festival** (417-683-4594; www .avachamber.org/events.htm), 810 S.W. 13th Ave., Ava, Mo. Held the third weekend of every October, when fall colors on the famous Glade Top Trail are at their height, this festival includes live music, square dancing, and an arts and crafts show. On Sunday morning you can enjoy a sausage-and-pancake breakfast. Also on Sunday, a BBQ chicken dinner is held on a peak halfway down the trail at the Caney Tower Forest Service fire lookout.

THE OZARK NATIONAL SCENIC RIVERWAYS

E ven a novice to floating the rivers of the Missouri Ozarks knows the names of the Current River and Jacks Fork. These two legendary waterways, along with 80,000 acres of land that surround their span, make up the Ozark National Scenic Riverways. More than 134 miles in length, the two rivers were federally protected by an act of Congress in 1964. Today they are a beautiful, albeit busy, favorite of canoeists, kayakers, campers, hikers, and fishermen.

The battle to save the Current and Jacks Fork from overdevelopment actually began at the dawn of the 20th century. As was true in most of the Ozarks, hillsides bordering these rivers had been logged nearly to the ground, resulting in a heavy degree of erosion and destruction. Though floaters love to picnic on the many gravel bars they encounter, the truth is that these respites were far from natural. In fact, they were created when gravel and rocks washed down denuded hills into the crystal-clear waters. Tourists began visiting the rivers with enthusiasm, and for many years there was more than a little debate over whether the lands now known as the ONSR should be preserved in a natural state, commercially developed, or (as almost happened) dammed by the Army Corps of Engineers for yet another Ozark hydroelectric facility and lake.

In the 1920s the state of Missouri purchased Big Spring, Montauk, Alley Spring, and Round Spring and designated them as fledgling state parks. In the 1930s the USDA Forest Service (then less than three decades old) began buying up land bordering the rivers and (under the auspices of the Civilian Conservation Corps) planting pine trees and building trails. Also in the 1930s the Army Corps of Engineers, which both then and now seems to erupt in fits of glee at the idea of damming anything larger than a kitchen sink, announced its intent to dam the Current and construct a massive lake. Many Ozarkers, used to a hardscrabble life, weren't terribly opposed to the thought. Jobs were jobs, after all, especially in a rugged land where keeping food on the table was a daily struggle. For other residents, though, the thought of destroying the Current was simply unacceptable. This contingent included Missouri's politicians and newspapers, who took the side of the preservationists.

The battle for the Current was heated to say the least. Few locals, distrustful of the callous attitude of government as shown toward other Ozark communities,

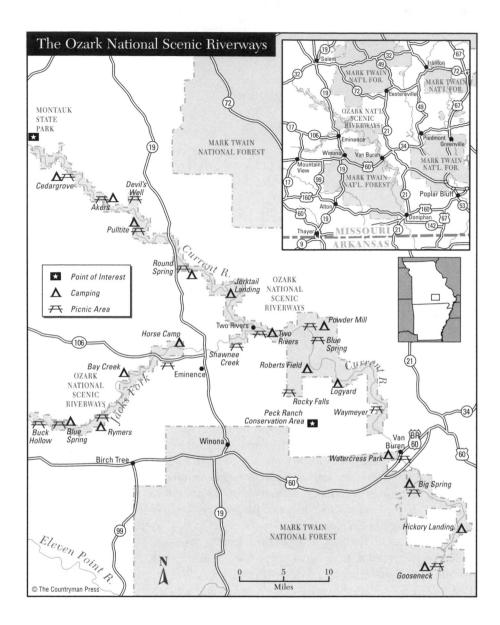

The Ozark National Scenic Riverways

wanted the area under federal control as a national park. Still, the press and the pols won the day, and in 1964 President Lyndon Johnson signed legislation creating the ONSR. In 1972 Tricia Nixon Cox pitched a bouquet of flowers into Big Spring and officially christened the waters. Her father, President Richard Nixon, was apparently too busy to personally attend. Dick was in the process of tending to a water problem of his own, the Watergate scandal that would bring down his administration.

Today the Current and Jacks Fork are a haven for visitors from around the world. The area is home to more than 300 caves, and more than 60 percent of the rivers' flow arrives from uncountable springs (7 huge ones, 51 smaller springs, and infinite tiny jets of subterranean water). Big Spring alone pumps out an astonishing 276 million gallons per day. This is great news for floaters, as the Jacks Fork and Current are floatable year-round. The bad news for floaters is that the popularity of these rivers makes them heavily traveled. More than 60 percent of floaters arrive in summer, and more than half again that number paddle downstream in fall and spring. If you want a quiet and peaceful float, bundle up, bring a thermos of hot coffee, and launch your canoe during winter. You'll probably not see another living soul. (No firm numbers exist on the numbers of disembodied souls you might encounter.)

If you do show up in summer and wish a more tranquil day, you might opt to canoe the Eleven Point River. While designated a Wild and Scenic River, it is not part of the ONSR and thus receives less traffic. There's a trade-off with the Current and Jacks Fork that can be found in many federally protected areas. While a Park Service stewardship preserves and protects the land, the very act of designating a place wilderness or national park draws so many people that the wild aspect becomes something of a memory.

Be that as it may, the streams of the ONSR are still some of the most beautiful in the world. The springs boil without rest, and the caves, bluffs, and wooded glades are reminiscent of the forest primeval. Fishing is good, and wildlife is prevalent—112 species of fish, 196 species of birds, 58 species of mammals, and 25 species of snakes (4 of which have a poisonous disposition) are found in and along the lands of the ONSR. Visitors will also discover quaint and amusing little river towns such as Eminence, Doniphan, and Van Buren. There's plenty of bluegrass, plenty of BBQ, catfish, and trout. For those who choose to look, there are also plenty of hidden respites both on the river and in the woods that will make an incursion into the Ozark National Scenic Riverways a trip to remember.

AREA CODES With a few exceptions on the western border, which remain under the 417 prefix, the Ozark National Scenic Riverways region falls under the **573** area code.

GUIDANCE As you could assume from the title of this chapter, most of the recreational opportunities in this region revolve around the outdoors. Rarely if ever will you find more scenic and enjoyable rivers than when exploring the Ozark National Scenic Riverways. Luckily, there is plenty of information in regard to floating, fishing, and having the time of your life.

For starters, the **National Park Service** web site (www.nps.gov/ozar) offers a great overview of these beautiful waters. Even better, for suggestions, recommendations, and advice beyond what you might anticipate, contact the **Salem Chamber of Commerce** (573-729-6741; www.salemmo.com), 200 S. Main, Salem, Mo. Its tourism packages are both lengthy and informative. For a good look at some of the sites along the Current River, or for a visit to Big Spring, either the **Ripley County Chamber of Commerce** (573-996-2212; www.ripley countymissouri.org), 101 Washington St., Doniphan, Mo., or the **Van Buren Area Chamber of Commerce** (1-800-692-7582; www.vanburen.org), P.O. Box 356, Van Buren, Mo. 72957, will happily send you a list of area sites and services.

One town you don't want to miss in this region is Eminence. It's a beautiful place, not to mention ground zero for those wanting to canoe the Jacks Fork River. Any insight you need into lodging, dining, camping, or canoeing can be gathered for you by the **Eminence Chamber of Commerce** (573-226-3318; www.eminencemo.com), P.O. Box 415, Eminence, Mo. 65466. And then there is Oregon County, which is blessed with such natural wonders as the Irish Wilderness, the Eleven Point River, Grand Gulf State Park, and Greer Spring. The **Thayer Chamber of Commerce** (417-264-7324; www.thayerchamber.com), P.O. Box 14, Thayer, Mo. 65791 and the **Alton Chamber of Commerce** (417-778-6321; http://ortrackm.missouri.org/towns/Alton/alton_index.htm) are your best bets when planning a trek to some of these Ozark treasures. Lastly, if you find yourself in the far southeast corner of this region, check out the **Greater Poplar Bluff Area Chamber of Commerce** (573-785-7761; www.poplarbluff chamber.org), 1111 W. Pine St., Poplar Bluff, Mo.

GETTING THERE *By auto:* As you have no doubt noticed, there are only a few main thoroughfares traversing the Ozarks. In the Ozark National Scenic Riverways region, both US 60 and US 160 stretch the entire distance from east to west. From north to south your best bets are US 63 south from Rolla and US 67 from just south of St. Louis. Now, if you want a pretty drive (not necessarily the fastest, just the nicest), take SR 19 from Salem, through Eminence, and all the way south to the Arkansas border at Thayer.

By air: **Springfield-Branson Regional Airport** (417-869-0300; www.sgf-branson-airport.com), 5000 W. Kearney, Springfield, Mo., is served by American Airlines, American Connection, American Eagle, Northwest Airlink, US Airways, United Express, and Allegiant. The airport offers facilities for buses, vans, rental cars, and hotel and hospitality limousines. Also, **Lambert–St. Louis International Airport** (314-426-8000; www.lambert-stlouis.com) serves a variety of major air carriers with nonstop service to and from many locations. Try to avoid taking I-270 S. between 4–6 PM (weekdays), or you may find yourself in a traffic jam.

MEDICAL EMERGENCIES The med center I'd choose if I became ill in the western part of this region would be the **Ozarks Medical Center** (417-256-9111; www.ozarksmedicalcenter.com), 1100 N. Kentucky St., West Plains, Mo. See "The Original Ozarks" for a full description.

Salem Memorial District Hospital (573-729-6626; www.smdh.net), SR 72 N., Salem, Mo. Should you feel aches and pains in the vicinity of Salem, drop by this 59-bed acute care facility. Services offered include cardiopulmonary, emergency, kidney dialysis, radiology, surgical, and more. A nonprofit, district-owned hospital, Salem Memorial provides care for the residents of Dent, Shannon, Crawford, and Iron counties.

Ripley County Memorial Hospital (573-996-2141), 109 Plum St., Doniphan, Mo., holds 30 beds and offers general medical and surgical care, as well as an emergency department.

Poplar Bluff Regional Medical Center (573-785-7721; www.poplarbluff regional.com), 2620 N. Westwood Blvd., Poplar Bluff, Mo. (north campus), or 621 W. Pine St. (573-686-4111; south campus). This 423-bed facility is the premier regional hospital in the southeastern section of the Ozark National Scenic Riverways region. Accredited by the Joint Commission on Accreditation of Health Care Organizations and Medicare, and a member of both the Missouri Hospital Association and American Hospital Association, it employs more than 100 physicians. Services include emergency, cancer treatment, pulmonary, X-ray and imaging, women's health, mental health, and much more.

John J. Pershing Veterans Administration Medical Center (573-686-4151 or 1-888-557-8262), 1500 N. Westwood, Poplar Bluff, Mo. This center holds 16 acute care and 40 extended care beds and serves 24 counties in southeast Missouri as well as 6 counties in northeast Arkansas.

✳ Wandering Around

EXPLORING BY CAR For pure scenery, you really can't go wrong traveling south on SR 19 from Salem to Eminence. SR 19 was designated a Scenic Highway by the Missouri legislature, and it's so curvy that you can't drive very fast. That's a good thing, because the route is so pretty that you'll want to dawdle, gawk, and occasionally take a short side trip to view various springs, mills, and of course the legendary waterways known as the Current and Jacks Fork rivers. From Salem, head south on SR 19 for approximately 10 miles. The first stopping place for a photo opportunity will be **Standing Rock Bridge**, so named because the rocks look like they are standing on their ends (whether top end or bottom end is yet to be determined). Continue south on SR 19 for another 15 miles and take a right onto SR EE. Follow this road for 4 miles and you'll arrive at **Pulltite Spring**, home of the old **Pulltite Cabin**. After walking around for a time, seeing the spring, and dunking your feet in the Current River, return to SR 19 and head south. In 3 miles you'll cross Sinking Creek Bridge, the point at which Sinking Creek flows into the Current River. Roughly 2 miles farther is the entrance to Round Spring Campground, where (at least between Memorial Day–Labor Day) you can take a tour of **Round Spring Cave**. If you're not into spelunking, enjoy the ride for 20 miles to the south (still on SR 19) and arrive in **Eminence**. This is one of the coolest little towns in the Ozarks, with plenty of things to do and plenty of sites to see. You also may want to turn onto SR 106 and drive east for 6 miles to the mill at **Alley Spring**, probably the most photographed structure in this part of (if not the entire) Ozarks.

EXPLORING BY FOOT **Pine Ridge Trail/Montauk State Park** (573-548-2201 or 573-548-2434; www.mostateparks.com/montauk.htm), RR 5, Box 279, Salem, Mo. What with all the caves, creeks, and springs found within the Ozark National Scenic Riverway, just about any given spot is good for a hike. You'll find one that's a bit more defined, however, at Montauk. The Pine Ridge Trail is not the easiest of treks and can in fact get a bit slick if it's muddy (in other words, wear hiking boots). Remember to take note (as I didn't) that this 1.5-mile trail does not make a full loop, as most trails do. Due to the way the trail winds, you'll have another 0.5 mile (more or less) to walk after completing the trail (assuming you parked at the trailhead by the picnic shelter). The first part of the trail is steep and begins by taking you through the Montauk Upland Forest Natural Area. This is a pretty 40 acres of oak and pine. After that you'll cross a highway and enter a grove of pines that, at least in spring, is loaded with songbirds. You may spy a deer or two, and chances are you'll hear woodpeckers as they jackhammer away at dead trees for insects. Continuing on, you'll come across the highlight of this walk, which is a great view (bring the camera) of Bluff Spring and Montauk Lake. If you're visiting in winter, watch the skies for bald eagles.

EXPLORING BY RIVER The **Current River** is the centerpiece of the Ozark National Scenic Riverways. While not a fast river by any stretch of the imagination, the Current is fed by innumerable springs. This is good for the floaters, and you can be nearly assured of an enjoyable canoe trip year-round. The river has its headwaters in Montauk State Park and travels more than 100 miles southeast into Arkansas. Most floaters, however, prefer the stretches between Montauk and Big Spring, near Van Buren. This is a beautiful river, clean and clear. Thanks to its federal designation, it has been largely protected from commercial disruption. For those seeking caves, deep forests, gushing springs, and a feast of color in both spring and fall, the Current is the preferred choice. That said, the federal designation is a double-edged sword. This is one stretch of water that can become exceptionally busy during the warmer months, with weekends witnessing literal flotillas of canoes. Still, the Current has been and remains the most well-known and popular float stream in the Missouri Ozarks.

HEADWATERS OF THE CURRENT RIVER

A tributary of the Current, and also part of the Ozark National Scenic Riverways, the **Jacks Fork River** has its headwaters in southeast Texas County and flows toward its confluence with the Current near Eminence. The lower sections of the Jacks Fork (below Alley Spring) offer a faster ride than many Ozark streams, with a fair amount of mild whitewater and small waterfalls. This is not the type of whitewater you'd find on a wild and woolly Rocky Mountain raft trip, and for experienced floaters would be considered very tame. In other words, while there is no outrageous danger here, you can receive a happy thrill in spots. This is particularly true in spring, when rains keep the water level high and eliminate the need for long portages around dry spots. Almost everyone loves the Jacks Fork, and almost everyone also manages to take at least half a dozen pictures of Alley Spring.

Designated a Wild and Scenic River, the **Eleven Point** begins near the town of Willow Springs and heads to the southeast in Arkansas. Another river that is fed by innumerable springs, the Eleven Point is floatable year-round (more or less; I'm not saying you might not have to pull your canoe over a gravel bar from time to time). I would rate this river as having a bit more "wild and scenic" quality than either the Current or the Jacks Fork, what with the trees, wildlife, pastures, and tranquil farms that line its banks. As with the Jacks Fork, you will find some mild whitewater on the Eleven Point, which is always nice to break up the day. A slow and tranquil pace is fine and dandy, but there are times where it's nice to feel a few splashes and bump against a few boulders.

✳ Towns and Villages

Doniphan, Mo. Like many towns in the Ozarks, this seat of Ripley County was burned to the ground by Yankees during the Civil War. This is not to imply that said Yankees didn't have reason to be miffed: Not only was Doniphan a hotbed of Southern guerrilla activity, but General Sterling Price and his Rebel troops were moving into the area from Arkansas. It does seem to hint, however, that the "civilized" Union often demonstrated a severe penchant for pyromania and probably just needed to own its feelings and work out deep-seated issues in a safe and nurturing therapeutic environment that would enable closure and healing. (In case you missed it, that last was merely a sarcastic example of the sort of thing that would *never* cross the lips of any Ozarkers worth their salt.) Today, located as always on the Current River, Doniphan is a pretty town that serves as home to the Current River Heritage Museum. Close by is a unique geological formation known as the Narrows—a high, thin ridge that separates the Eleven Point River from Fredrick Creek.

Eminence, Mo. This is another town that rates as one of my top five spots in the Ozarks. Eminence, population 548, was once named both Missouri's Top Outdoor Outpost and one of the 50 Top Outdoor Sports Towns in America by *Sports Afield* magazine. I was a hair away from buying a gorgeous bed & breakfast here in 1999 and have never stopped kicking myself for failure to do so. Surrounded by innumerable springs and caves of jaw-dropping beauty, bisected by the Jack's Fork River, and surrounded by high, forested ridges, Eminence is a center for horseback riding, fishing, floating (the Current River is close by as well), and great fun. You'll be surprised at the shopping available in this seat of Shannon County, and you'll love the B&Bs.

Poplar Bluff, Mo. With nearly 17,000 people, Poplar Bluff is on the southeastern edge of the cultural region that defines the Ozarks. Virtually deserted during the Civil War, it is now home to the Poplar Bluff Regional Medical Center, hosts major entertainment events at the Black River Coliseum, and boasts of the excellent Poplar Bluff Speedway. You'll also find many restaurants, museums, and even a kids' water park in the ever-growing seat of Butler County.

Salem, Mo. There is no false advertising in Salem's claim to being the Gateway to the Ozark Riverways. The town of 4,854, the seat of Dent County, is on the doorstep of Montauk State Park, the Ozark National Scenic Riverways, Indian Trail Conservation Area, and the Mark Twain National Forest. The residents of this Salem never burned any witches; all they did was float the rivers, catch fish, breathe in the amazing scenery, and thank their lucky stars for being able to live in such a picturesque and charming town. While visiting Salem, make sure to drop by both the Dent County Museum and the Bonebrake Center of Nature and History.

Van Buren, Mo. With roughly 900 residents, Van Buren is well known to those who float the Current River. This is known as Big Spring Country, and the natural feature that makes that name possible (pumping out 276 million gallons of water per day) is located just south of town. To see Big Spring is to know that residents of this area have an amazing talent for understatement. Like so many spots in the Ozarks, this small town is ecstatic in the knowledge that it remains a small town. For example, stop in Van Buren between May and October, and there's a good chance you'll enjoy one of the monthly street dances (complete with live music) held on the pavilion behind the stately, old, county courthouse. As we would say in these parts, "You can't beat that with a stick."

✳ To See

MUSEUMS ✐ ⑤ **Epps-Houts Museum** (573-785-2734), 1540 SR 451, Poplar Bluff, Mo. Open year-round; donations are gratefully accepted. This interesting little museum holds paintings, cultural artifacts, and carvings from South Korea, southern Africa, Saudi Arabia, and 10 other countries. Also found in this historic homestead are a huge number of rare cookbooks.

BIG SPRING IN VAN BUREN

🦉 ✐ ⑤ **Moark Regional Railroad Museum** (573-785-4539; http://poplarbluffchamber.org), 303 Moran St., Poplar Bluff, Mo. Hours are Sat.–Sun. 1–4, year-round. Admission is free. If you're into things involving steel rails and iron horses, you'll enjoy this tribute to the choo-choo. Inside are a large number of old photos covering almost every element of railroad life, and a very well-done model-train display. You'll also find tools, lanterns, and even Morse code memorabilia. The Moark, a National Historic Site, is housed in a 1928 Frisco railroad depot.

Poplar Bluff Historical Museum (573-785-2220; http://poplarbluffchamber.org), 1010 N. Main St., Poplar Bluff, Mo. Open year-round, Sun. 2–4. Admission is free. This museum not only centers on the history of Poplar Bluff and Butler County but also takes things a couple of steps further. There are displays devoted to the Boy and Girl Scouts, veterans, and the USDA Forest Service. A nice touch of community pride, there's even a Poplar Bluff Sports Hall of Fame.

BONEBRAKE CENTER OF NATURE AND HISTORY

Bonebrake Center of Nature and History (573-729-3400; www.bonebrake.org), 601 N. Hickory, Salem, Mo. Situated on 12 acres, this property holds a spring-fed pond, stream, natural wetland area, and numerous walking paths. The centerpiece of this living-history museum is a historic home circa 1880, which is still undergoing restoration. Visitors are free to stroll the nature paths at any time, and the home is open for viewing during planned activities. There are minimal charges for various of the programs held on the property.

Dent County Museum (573-729-7267 or 573-729-7374; www.salemmo.com), 400 N. Pershing Ave., Salem, Mo. Open Memorial Day–Oct., Sun. 1–4. Admission is free, but donations are accepted. This 1895 Victorian home features three floors of goodies chronicling the history of the Ozarks. Inside you will find not only period furniture and decor, but also vintage clothing, antiques, glassware, and a huge loom. And if you don't see a trip to Philadelphia in your future, on the back porch of the home is a reproduction of the Liberty Bell.

Current River Heritage Museum (573-996-5298; www.ripleycountymissouri.org), 101 Washington St., Doniphan, Mo. This museum is all about life on the river, both the way it was and the way it is. You'll soon learn the important role played by timber and logging operations along the banks of the Current and see how a life could be built via trapping, hunting, and fishing. Just a block from the museum is a restored 1880s pioneer homestead with log

DENT COUNTY MUSEUM

cabin, barn, and blacksmith shop. The museum is open all year, and there is no admission fee.

🖼 🗝 ♿ **Margaret Harwell Art Museum** (573-686-8002; www.mham.org), 417 N. Main St., Poplar Bluff, Mo. Hours are Tue.–Fri. noon–4, Sat.–Sun. 1–4. Admission is free. Housed in a great old Victorian home, the Harwell Museum offers rotating exhibits for a wide array of local, regional, and national artists. There is a museum gift store on the premises, and by reservation you can arrange a tour.

HISTORIC SITES 🗝 ♿ **Dillard Mill State Historic Site** (573-244-3120; www .mostateparks.com), 142 Dillard Mill Rd., Davisville, Mo. Hard though it may be to believe, this old flour mill is still in working order. Many folks enjoy coming here for a picnic, and tours are readily available. The Dillard Mill is open year-round, with admission prices being a mere $2.50 adults, $1.50 ages 6–12. To find the mill, travel on SR 19 to the town of Cherryville. Turn left onto SR 49, and in 5 miles turn right to stay on SR 49. After 5 more miles, turn onto Dillard Mill Rd. and travel 1 mile.

🖼 🐾 🗝 ♿ **Fort Davidson State Historic Site** (573-546-3454; www.mostate parks.com/ftdavidson.htm), 118 Maple St., Pilot Knob, Mo. The Battle of Pilot Knob was one of the bloodiest Civil War battles of the Ozarks. On September 27, 1864, the South's General Sterling Price, with 12,000 men, attacked the 1,450 men holding Fort Davidson. More than 1,000 Confederate troops died in the assault (Fort Davidson had 9-foot earthen walls and a moat), and the Union forces escaped via a brilliant strategy. Muffling the wheels of their wagons and artillery, the troops snuck out on a stormy night. They also set a time-delay fuse and blew their powder reserves, thus keeping them from Rebel hands. Today this 77-acre site preserves the memory of both the battle and those who gave their lives. Also on-site is a visitors center with exhibits, a diorama of the battle, and an audiovisual presentation. Contrasting the violence of the past with the peace of the present, the grounds now hold a kids' playground and picnic area.

FORT DAVIDSON STATE HISTORIC SITE

✳ **To Do**

FOR FAMILIES 🗝 ♿ **Bo's Hollow** (573-548-2429 or 1-877-313-8744; www.bohollow.com), 22516 Bo's Hollow Lane, Salem, Mo. Any place whose claim to fame is built upon beef jerky, Model A rides, and donkey petting is worth a look. Family created, owned, and operated, Bo's offers a re-created 1930s Ozark village complete with log cabin, outhouse, jail, and the obligatory "lost mine." You'll see Model A Fords in all stages of restoration, and when you tire of that you can pet the donkeys or feed the chickens. The gift shop is loaded with the aforementioned jerky (10 varieties at last count, including one specifically for dogs), and I highly recommend the chipotle version. However, the big draw here is a tour in one of the restored Model A's and a lunch of Ozark BBQ. Hours are Fri.–Sat. 10–4. The price for an hourlong tour is $10 ($5 if you're under 12), or you can take a quick 20-minute spin for $5. Meals are $10 adults, $5 kids. You might want to call ahead and make a reservation if you're traveling with a group.

 ✍ ♿ **Bluff Falls Water Park & Entertainment Center** (573-776-7622; www .blufffalls.com), 2801 Cheshire Blvd., Poplar Bluff, Mo. While the water park section of this facility is only open while weather permits, the dry sections are open year-round (but call ahead for exact days and hours). Built on 12 acres, Bluff Falls includes wave pools, water slides, go-carts, batting cages, miniature golf, an indoor arcade, a gift shop, and all the mandatory food concessions. All-day admission costs $15.89 ($8.89 if you're under 4 feet tall). All-day admission to the dry park is $22.89. Go-carts and miniature golf run $5 each, and batting cage tokens are just $1.

GOLF ✍ ♿ ⛾ **Spring Creek Golf Club** (573-729-3080); Rt. 6, Rolla Rd. off SR J, Salem, Mo. A semiprivate course located at the intersection of SR J and SR 322, Spring Creek is a par-36, nine-hole course open year-round. It's very affordable: Weekday prices are $10 and $15 (9 and 18 holes, respectively); $12 and $17 on weekends. Cart rental runs $10–16. On-site is a clubhouse with TV, pool tables, shuffleboard, sandwiches, and a full bar. Visitors can also take a dip in the swimming pool for $1.50 per person.

Ozark Ridge Golf Course (573-686-8634; http://poplarbluff.org/ozarkridge .html), 3045 Cravens Rd., Poplar Bluff, Mo. This 18-hole championship course features large greens, tree-lined fairways, and a number of tricky bunkers. On-site is a driving range and well-stocked pro shops. Fees with a cart are $16 and $24 weekdays (9 and 18 holes, respectively) and $18 and $27 on weekends and holidays. Walking fees are $11 and $14 during the week, and $13 and $17 on weekends and holidays.

HORSEBACK RIDING 🐾 ✍ **Coldwater Ranch** (573-226-3723; www.coldwater ranch.com), HCR 1, Eminence, Mo. Located just north of Eminence. Turn east on SR 208 (off SR 19) and travel 1.2 miles. For those who wish to experience the Ozark hills and rivers via the back of a horse, Coldwater Ranch offers a variety of camping, lodging, and riding packages. A fully equipped lakeside cabin with two queen-sized beds begins at $110 for two people. For those with larger families, a bunkhouse option, sleeping six, begins at $185. RV and trailer sites (with electric and water) are $15 per night, and if you bring your own horse, stalls are also $15 per night. Dogs and cats are welcomed with prior approval and a $25 nonrefundable deposit. Hourly trail rides start at $30 (horse is provided); longer pack trips (of one to five nights, meals included) start at $200 per person.

✍ **Cross Country Trail Ride** (573-226-3883; www.crosscountrytrailride.com), P.O. Box 15, Eminence, Mo. 65466. If you never travel anywhere without your horse, and if you're a fan of bluegrass, Cross Country Trail Ride offers the best facility in an area known as the Trail Riding Capital of the United States. On SR 19 just 1 mile north of Eminence, on the banks of the Jacks Fork River, the facility offers camping on a 75-acre site, three meals a day, horse shows, major bluegrass and holiday festivals, and all the trail riding you could ever want. While you need to bring your own horse if you want to ride, many people from across America visit this establishment simply to enjoy the Ozarks, the Jacks Fork, and the food. The stunning facilities include a 63,000-square-foot indoor riding arena (open 24 hours a day). Inside the arena you will find a western store, tack store, and restaurant. Nearly 3,000 horse stalls are available for rent at $15 per night, and plenty of hay and oats are available should you forget to bring your own. Basic adult prices to reserve your space as a registered rider begin at $210, and there are separate charges for concert admission. Those who wish to visit CCTR should call ahead for rules and regulations, specifically for state-required vaccination policies (for the horses, not the people).

HUNTING **SayersBrook Bison Ranch and Lodge** (1-888-854-4449; www.sayers brook.com), 11820 Sayersbrook Rd., Potosi, Mo. For the price of $2,500 (two-person minimum) you can stalk the wily buffalo with your weapons of choice, whack it, and haul the big guy home. You will receive guidance from the ranch manager, and—just like the mountain men of old—you bring your own tent and sleep under the stars. Meat processing and taxidermy are not included in the price. However, if you'd like go whole hog (or whole bull, as the case may be), you might opt for SayersBrook's Five Star Trophy Hunt. This package, priced at $7,500 per person (with a two-person minimum), includes three nights in the main lodge, meals prepared by a five-star chef, use of the sporting clay course and machine-gun range, personal guiding by the ranch's owner, the whacking of a buffalo, head mounting and hide tanning by a taxidermist, and all meat processing. If you've got the dough and always wanted a buff head on your wall, this is the trip for you. Those not into the whacking aspect (if you've got a group of 20 or more) can take a basic tour of the ranch ($10 adults, $5 ages 12 and under) or enjoy a tour and delicious buffalo meal (and these folks do great stuff with buffalo). Prices start at around $16 for students and $25 for adults. Finally, if you want an up-close-and-personal tour just for your family, spring for the $100 fee and ranch staff will take you out in one of their Hummers.

✳ Wild Places

The Irish Wilderness (573-996-2153; www.fs.fed.us/r9/forests/marktwain/ ranger_districts/doniphan), Doniphan/Eleven Point Ranger District, 4 Confederate Ridge Rd., Doniphan, Mo. Just before the Civil War, Father John Hogan of St. Louis established a settlement for impoverished Irish immigrants deep in the Ozarks. Unfortunately for Father John and the Irish, the conflict between North and South got in the way. The Irish Wilderness became a haven for thieves and Bushwhackers both Blue and Gray, and the idea of Utopia fell away. To this day it is not known what happened to the immigrants, and more than a few visitors to today's Irish Wilderness will attest that this section of the Mark Twain National

Forest holds an eerie quality. Others will tell you it's chock-full of irritated ghosts with an Emerald Isle brogue and perhaps even an unnatural desire for a box of Lucky Charms. Such is the stuff of myth, but what is known for certain is that this 16,500-acre stretch of forest primeval is loaded with sinkholes, streams, caves, and an abundance of wildlife. It's located in Oregon County on the Eleven Point River. You can reach the Irish Wilderness from Doniphan by traveling 18 miles west on US 160. Turn north onto SR J and drive 7 miles to the Camp Five Pond Trailhead. This is the locale of one of the three trailheads for the White Creek Trail.

Mark Twain National Forest (www.fs.fed.us/r9/forests/marktwain/contact). Consisting of more than 1.5 million acres, the Mark Twain is a superb wilderness dotted with rivers, streams, and some of the largest natural springs in America. Broken into nine different ranger districts, the forest includes hundreds of miles of hiking trails, numerous scenic drives, seven congressionally designated wilderness areas, 40 campgrounds (these can be reserved by calling 1-877-444-6777), and thousands of acres of primitive and semiprimitive areas. Literally hundreds of thousands of acres of the Mark Twain are located in close proximity to the Ozark National Scenic Riverways. For information or maps, contact the following district offices:

Salem District (573-729-6656), 1301 S. Main, Salem, Mo.

Doniphan/Eleven Point District (573-996-2153), 4 Confederate Ridge Rd., Doniphan, Mo.

Poplar Bluff District (573-785-1475), 1420 Maud St., Poplar Bluff, Mo.

Potosi/Fredericktown District (573-438-5427), SR 8 West, Potosi, Mo.

🐾 𝌗 **Indian Trail Conservation Area** (573-368-2225), Department of Conservation, P.O. Box 1128, Rolla, Mo. 65401. This 13,503-acre preserve is located off SR 19 between Salem and Steelville. While primarily forested, it is also the home of a 350-acre warm-water fish hatchery. Hunting can be fairly good here, but there are really no great fishing spots. Primitive camping is permitted, and an area has been set aside for campers and RVs.

𝌗 🐾 **White River Trace Conservation Area** (573-368-2225), Department of Conservation, P.O. Box 1128, Rolla, Mo. 65401. Located 8 miles west of Salem on SR H, this 2,044-acre site permits hunting, fishing, camping (in designated areas), and hiking. Open fires are not allowed. This area was purchased only about 25 years ago, used for an experimental planting of endangered running buffalo clover. White River Trace is a getaway that is not terribly rugged (about 80 percent of the land is open), making it perfect for relaxed camping or picnics.

Roger Pryor Pioneer Backcountry (1-800-334-6946; www.pioneerforest.com), P.O. Box 497, Salem, Mo. 65560. Part of the privately owned Pioneer Forest, this remote 61,000-acre area borders the Current River for 15 miles to the southwest and is located in Shannon and Reynolds counties off SR 19 north of Eminence, Mo. Pioneer Forest was established in 1951 to prove that sustainable and commonsense forest management was possible in the Ozarks, and today the Roger Pryor Backcountry is protected in part via a joint arrangement between the LAD Foundation and the Missouri Department of Natural Resources. Fishing and hunting is permitted by anyone holding a Missouri Department of

Conservation license, 27 miles of fine trails are groomed for hiking, and the camping possibilities are endless.

🐾 🐻 ⚲ ♿ **Peck Ranch Conservation Area** (573-323-4249), SR H, Winona, Mo. Located 8.5 miles west of Winona on SR H, the 23,048-acre Peck Ranch is home to every kind of critter, from pileated woodpeckers to bobcats to black bears, and full of caves, springs, creeks, and sinkholes. There's a great little picnic spot known as Rocky Falls on the back side of Stegall Mountain. While it's not on the ranch proper, it is still on the public lands of the Ozark Trail. The hike is worth it for the chance to watch the waters of Rocky Creek drop 40 feet. Hunting and hiking are very popular here, and there is a special zone set aside specifically for disabled hunters. Primitive camping is permitted in certain areas, but contact the District Ranger's office (at the number above) before dropping in with your tent.

🐻 ⚲ ♿ **Big Spring Conservation Area** (573-323-4236; www.nps.gov/ozar), SR 103, Van Buren, Mo. The first white man to trip across Big Spring was an obscure explorer with the unfortunate name of "Pocahontas" Randolph. That was in 1803, and because of the lack of roads and incredibly rough terrain, few other folks saw this spring until more than 100 years later. Missouri made Big Spring a state park in 1925, and the National Park Service has owned the site since 1971. Located 4 miles south of Van Buren, this is in fact one of the largest springs in the world, pumping out more than 276 million gallons of water each day. The area is open year-round, but campers should know that the water (that would be drinking water, not the spring) is turned off Oct. 30–Apr. 15. Viewing the spring is free, and 123 campsites are suitable for tents. The cost is $12 per night for a regular spot, or $15 per night for one with electricity.

Red Maple Pond Natural Area (573-996-2153), District Ranger, Doniphan/ Eleven Point Ranger District, 1104 Walnut, Doniphan, Mo. This is one of those off-the-beaten-path sights that is worth seeing simply because it's pretty. Consisting of nearly 100 acres located in a portion of the Mark Twain National Forest, this pond/swamp is in fact a strange sort of sinkhole, surrounded by red maple trees and boasting of thick and unusual foliage. To find Red Maple Pond, take US 160 west from Doniphan to SR C. Head north on SR C for a little more than 10 miles and turn right onto FR (Forest Road) 4912. When you reach the top of the hill you'll see a sign.

Greer Spring and Trail (573-785-1475; www.fs.fed.us/r9/forests/marktwain), Poplar Bluff Ranger District, 1420 Maud St., Poplar Bluff, Mo. Jut a tad smaller than Big Spring (located on the Current River), Greer Spring shoots more than 220 million gallons of water per day into the Eleven Point River. This spring is so large, it actually doubles the flow of the Eleven Point. It's located off SR 19, roughly 20 miles north of Thayer. It's a bit of a walk to get back to the spring itself, but it's worth it.

🐻 ⚲ ♿ **Pulltite Spring** (573-323-4236; www.nps.gov/ozar). Located on the Current River, 14 miles north of Eminence off SR EE, the 29-million-gallon-per-day Pulltite Spring got its name from the horse-drawn teams that had to "pull tight" on the reins while traversing a steep hill to the gristmill. Nearby is **Pulltite**

Campground, which is open year-round (though the drinking water is turned off Oct. 30–Apr. 15). There are 55 campsites at Pulltite, but none with electrical or water hookups. The camping fee for a family site is $12 per night.

🐾 ⛺ ♂ ♿ **Alley Spring** (314-323-4236; www.nps.gov/ozar), Ozark Riverways, Van Buren, Mo. Possibly the most photographed spot in the Missouri Ozarks, Alley Spring can be found 5 miles west of Eminence on SR 106. The old red mill still stands proud, and the 81 million gallons of water that flow from the spring each day are typically of a gorgeous turquoise color. You can tour the gristmill Memorial Day–Labor Day, daily 9–4 (there is no charge), and a gift shop offers numerous books and postcards. Though the **Alley Spring Campground** is open year-round and offers 162 campsites at a price of $12 per night, there is no drinking water Oct. 30–Apr. 15. Also at Alley is the restored **Story's Creek Schoolhouse**, which is open May–Dec., Fri.–Sat. 1:30–4:30.

Devil's Well. If you travel south on SR 19 from Salem and then head 6 miles west on SR KK, you will see a sign for DEVIL'S WELL. Make sure you turn left onto this gravel road. What you'll discover is a sinkhole that opens into an underground lake the size of a football field. There's a viewing platform, and when you peer through the natural openings in the rocks you will see this subterranean swimming pool in all its glory.

Cave Spring. Really the only way to see Cave Spring is when you're floating down the Current River. It is located on the river just about halfway between Akers Ferry and the Pulltite Campground, and you can paddle your canoe into it to the very spot where the spring rises. People have long liked to beach their canoes and picnic in this area. Also, if you remembered to bring your tackle, throwing in a line while floating directly over the spring may land you a fish or two.

Akers Ferry. There are no more than a couple of old-time ferry operations still in existence in the United States, and there's only one on the Ozark National Scenic Riverways. To reach it, travel 23 miles south of Salem on SR 19 and head south on SR K (when you're on SR K, make sure you're headed toward the town of Darien—otherwise you'll end up in Montauk State Park). Akers Ferry has been taking cars across the Current River for more than 50 years, and it was the way folks got from here to there when the Ozarks lacked bridges. The ferry is almost always open during daylight hours, and the cost is $4.

ALLEY SPRING MILL

🐾 ⛺ ♂ ♿ **Round Spring** (314-323-4236; www.nps.gov/ozar), Ozark Riverways, Van Buren, Mo. One of the first state parks in Missouri (established in 1932, and then integrated into the Ozark National Scenic Riverways in 1972), Round Spring is located 13 miles north of Eminence on

SR 19. The spring rises up in a basin that was created by the collapse of a cavern roof. Part of this cavern (see *Caves*) is open to the public via National Park Service tours. Pumping 26 million gallons of water per day, Round Springs also offers a campground with 60 sites. As with the other NPS campgrounds on the Current River, the cost is $12 per night. Again, there is no water Oct. 30– Apr. 15.

🐾 🐕 ✎ ♿ **Blue Spring** (314-323-4236; www.nps.gov/ozar), Ozark Riverways, Van Buren, Mo. If you travel 12 miles west of Eminence on SR 106, you will trip across the prettiest spring in the Ozarks. It may not be the biggest (69 million gallons per day), but it is for sure the bluest (hence the name). Arising out of a very deep cave, this spring offers a color that has to be seen to be believed. For those who wish to sit a spell, Blue Spring offers a picnic area.

✎ **Rocky Falls Shut-In**. This seems to be a place that most of the tourists miss, which is a shame seeing as how it's quite an impressive little waterfall. I'm not talking Niagara Falls here. Instead, at Rocky, whitewater comes tumbling down, over, and around ancient stones into one of the best swimming holes you will find. If it's a hot day, this is the place to take the kids. There are picnic areas adjacent to the water, and aside from locals you will normally find Rocky to be relatively uncrowded. You'll find it approximately 9 miles southeast of Eminence on SR NN.

🐾 🐕 ✎ ♿ **Two Rivers** (314-323-4236; www.nps.gov/ozar), Ozark Riverways, Van Buren, Mo. As you could likely guess by its imaginative name, Two Rivers is the spot where two rivers come together. In this case the bodies of water in question are the Jacks Fork and the Current River. You can reach the spot—the site of an old ferry crossing—by traveling 8 miles east of Eminence on SR 106, turning left onto SR V, and then heading 3 miles farther. The pavement will end, and just a short hike downstream is where the ferrymaster used to ply his trade. Also at Two Rivers is a 19-site campground (no water or electric), with spaces renting for $12 per night.

PARKS 🐾 🐕 ✎ ♿ **Montauk State Park** (573-548-2201 or 573-548-2434; www .mostateparks.com/montauk.htm), RR 5, Box 279, Salem, Mo. Sitting on the headwaters of the Current River (about 20 miles southwest of Salem), Montauk Park is noted for its exceptional trout fishing. On the opening day of trout season (Mar. 1–Oct. 31) anglers come from miles around, lining the banks in anticipation of tight lines and ripped lips. The park, acquired in 1926, encompasses 1,353 acres and includes a gristmill, campground, motel, cabins, restaurant, store, and picnic areas. On-site is a fish hatchery (tours are available) managed by the Missouri Department of Conservation. The springs at Montauk pump more than

MONTAUK FISH HATCHERY

43 million gallons of water into the Current River every day, making it prime habitat for rainbow trout.

As at all state campgrounds, a basic campsite costs $7 per night. A campsite with electricity and water is $12 per night. When available, sites with water, sewer, and electricity are $13 per night. Camping is permitted year-round. The **Dorman L. Steelman Lodge** features a store, tackle, restaurant, ice cream, and campsite reservations and registration. The restaurant serves breakfast, lunch, and dinner; there are both motel rooms ($57–61) and cabins ($79–118).

🐾 🏕 🦌 ♿ **Taum Sauk Mountain State Park** (573-546-2450; www.mostateparks .com/taumsauk/trails.htm), HC 1, Box 126, Middlebrook, Mo. At 1,772 feet, Taum Sauk Mountain is the highest point in the state of Missouri. It's one of the oldest points as well, with rocks 1.5 billion years young. This is a stunning park, nearly 7,500 acres in size, and you cannot view sites such as Mina Sauk Falls without a sense of awe. Basic campsites are available ($7 per night), and many visitors choose Taum Sauk for its scenic hiking. A 33-mile stretch of the **Ozark Trail** (which, when completed, will stretch from near St. Louis all the way down to the Ozark Highlands Trail in Arkansas) runs through Taum Sauk, crossing numerous mountains, creeks, and even the east fork of the Black River. Eventually the trail leads into Johnson Shut-Ins State Park, nearly 13 miles to the west. To reach Taum Sauk, at the town of Arcadia turn onto SR CC. In 5 miles you will reach the park entrance.

🐾 ♿ 🦌 **Johnson Shut-Ins State Park** (573-546-2450; www.mostateparks.com/ taumsauk/trails.htm), HC 1, Box 126, Middlebrook, Mo. Johnson Shut-Ins is arguably the most popular state park in the Ozarks, due to the unique scenery, the incredible photo opportunities, and how much fun it is to slip around on smooth boulders coated with a spray of whitewater. The rocks are beyond old, the igneous remainders of ancient lava flows. As the waters of the east fork of the Black River enter this area, they meet the impenetrable rocks and become a maze. The waters twist and turn, leading to chutes and pools. The water knows not where to go, at times seeming to be trapped—hence the name *Shut-Ins*. At 8,549 acres, Shut-Ins hosts what is in fact a natural water slide.

If you're going to visit, I advise you get here early. The park is located approximately 13 miles west of the town of Graniteville on SR N. The day-use area holds only 100 cars—and this is a place nearly everyone seeks to visit. Camping, hiking, and swimming are allowed. The latter (and this is the place that can get crowded) is permitted only in the Shut-Ins area on the east fork of the Black River. To reach it, just take the 0.25-mile paved path that begins at the park office complex. Unlike most state parks in Missouri, pets are not permitted. At the time of this writing the park is temporarily closed, due to a failure of the Taum Sauk reservoir that resulted in a billion gallons of water hitting the Shut-Ins. It should be partially reopened by summer 2006; at this writing, the date of a full reopening is still unknown.

🐾 ♿ 🦌 🦌 **Grand Gulf State Park** (417-264-7600; www.mostateparks.com/ grandgulf.htm), Rt. 3, P.O. Box 3554, Thayer, Mo. 65791. This is the Missouri Ozarks' version of the Grand Canyon. The Gulf is what remains of a cave system

🐾 ⌀ ♿ **Elephant Rocks State Park** (573-546-3454; www.mostateparks
.com/elephantrock.htm), c/o Fort Davidson State Historic Site, P.O. Box 509,
Pilot Knob, Mo. 63663. Sometimes a name can say it all, and such is the
case with Elephant Rocks State Park. These hunks of igneous rock are to
normal boulders what the Sears Tower is to an outhouse. (The biggest rock
in the park is 27 feet high and weighs 680 tons!) The geology behind the Elephant Rocks, too, is one-of-a-kind. The massive stones were not left behind
by glaciers, as glaciers never reached as far south as the St. Francois
Mountains (the range that includes Taum Sauk, Johnson Shut-Ins, and Elephant Rocks). Rather, the Elephant Rocks were formed 1.5 billion years ago,
granite hunks that sheared off as differing joints of volcanic magma cooled
and split. The rocks hid beneath ancient seas and only emerged after countless eons of erosion and uplift. To look at the Elephant Rocks is to look back
at the beginnings of the earth itself.

Though the park consists of only 132 acres, that's more than enough.
Trails wind through this garden of stone, and you will find 30 picnic areas
scattered about. Also, the park offers a **Braille Trail** featuring Braille signs,
a paved and gently sloping surface, railings, and guide ropes. Neither camping nor pets is permitted inside this park. Elephant Rocks is roughly 5 miles
south of the town of Belleview on SR 21.

ELEPHANT ROCKS STATE PARK

that collapsed 10,000 years ago (give or take a year). Nearly 0.75 mile long, a 250-foot natural bridge (a part of the cave that didn't collapse) crosses the huge ravine. A creek drains into Grand Gulf, disappears, and then emerges to the surface 9 miles to the south at Mammoth Springs, Ark. (which spews out 8 or 9 million gallons of water per hour). Consisting of 322 acres, Grand Gulf is laced with trails and overlooks (wheelchair accessible) that allow visitors to peer into the depths without taking a swan dive. To reach the park, head to the northwest on SR 19 at the town of Thayer. Take a right turn onto SR W, and you will head right into Grand Gulf.

LAKES Clearwater Lake (573-223-7777; www.swl.usace.army.mil/parks/clear water), Army Corps of Engineers, Clearwater Project Office, RR 3, P.O. Box 3559-D, Piedmont, Mo. 63957. An Army Corps of Engineers project, Clearwater is a 16,000-acre lake that has retained much of its charm due to its lack of private boat docks. Five campgrounds can be found around the lake (two of those are on the banks of the Black River) and offer nine boat launch ramps, three swimming beaches, and seven playgrounds. In addition, the campsites feature grills, fire pits, tables, showers, and water. The fishing is often very good at Clearwater, particularly if you're after bass and catfish, but boating, skiing, hiking, and hunting (on the surrounding corps-managed lands) are equally popular. If you're looking for a lake that has avoided rampant overdevelopment, this would be your choice.

Shawnee Mac Lakes (573-729-6900; www.salemmo.com), SR 411, Salem, Mo. Located 2 miles east of Salem on SR 411, Shawnee Mac consists of two lakes (one 17 acres, the other 30) sitting amid a total of 256 acres. This state conservation area is a popular spot for fishing (the bass bite particularly well here, though you can get some fair-sized catfish if you fish on the bottom and are patient), boating, camping, and hiking. There aren't any specific hiking trails at Shawnee Mac, but you can wander where you like. Also, the price is right (free), making the area a nice spot for a relaxed family picnic.

Fourche Lake (573-996-2153; www.fs.fed.us/r9/forests/marktwain/ ranger_districts/doniphan), Doniphan/Eleven Point Ranger District, 4 Confederate Ridge Rd., Doniphan, Mo. Located 15 miles west of Doniphan on US 160, and then 2 miles farther on SR V, Fourche is a 40-acre lake perfect for a day of relaxed fishing. Full of bass and catfish, the lake also offers a boat ramp (though only electric motors are allowed). You'll also find picnic sites and rest rooms.

Ripley Lake (573-996-2153; www.fs.fed.us/r9/forests/marktwain/ranger_ districts/doniphan), Doniphan/Eleven Point Ranger District, 4 Confederate Ridge Rd., Doniphan, Mo. Another good bass and catfish hole, the 29-acre Ripley Lake offers a boat ramp and 12 different picnic sites. To reach the lake, head 8 miles west of Doniphan on US 160. Turn north onto SR C and drive 1 mile, eventually turning right onto FR 3240. Ripley Lake is about 1 mile ahead.

CAVES Round Spring Cavern (573-323-4236), Ozark National Scenic Riverways, National Park Service, P.O. Box 490, Van Buren, Mo. 63965. $5 adults, $2 kids. Located on the Current River (roughly 18 miles north of Eminence on

SR 19), this cave is operated by the National Park Service. Lantern-light tours are offered Memorial Day–Labor Day, Fri.–Sun. at 10 AM and 2 PM. Well worth the trip, in that this is a cave that remains largely in its natural state. Keep in mind that this is a first-come, first-served affair, and each tour is limited to 15 people. Arrive early, for no reservations are taken.

✳ Lodging

BED & BREAKFASTS ✿ **Hawkins House** (573-226-5944 or 1-877-875-7050; www.hawkinshaus.com), 210 Main St., Eminence, Mo. Built in 1913, this pretty old home with its covered wraparound porch personifies the laid-back atmosphere that is Eminence. Three guest rooms are offered at $75–125 per night, and a full breakfast is served. Kids are accepted, but pets are not. There is, however, a nearby kennel that can help accommodate the needs of Fido and Spot.

The Old Blue House (573-226-3498; www.oldbluehouse.com), 301 S. Main St., Eminence, Mo. This 1860s home is striking due to the rainbow profusion of trees and flowers that fill the grounds. Magnolia trees, peonies, lilacs, roses, and much more make for a beautiful setting. The home itself, more than a century old, has over the years housed a grocery store, pharmacy, beauty shop, and several retail stores. Three guest rooms feature antiques and cable TV. Rates run $50–57 per night, and the Blue House is within easy walking distance of all the shops of downtown Eminence. A continental breakfast is served (you can have something more substantial for a small fee); neither small kids, smoking, nor pets is permitted.

✿ **Cottage Overnight Lodging** (417-778-7782 or 417-270-0782; www.cottageovernightlodging.com), Rt. 3, P.O. Box 3392, Alton, Mo. 65606. If you happen to be floating the Eleven Point River or exploring the natural wonders in and around Oregon County, this may be your most inexpensive lodging choice. These three cottages in Alton have all the comforts of home (two of them even include a washer and dryer). They're clean, quaint, and comfortable. The rental price is just $35 per night for one person, with $3.50 for each additional guest. Call about kids and pets.

✿ 🐾 ✿ ♿ **Big Spring Lodge and Cabins** (573-323-4423; www.bigspringlodgeandcabins.com), HCR 1, P.O. Box 169, Van Buren, Mo. In Big Spring Park you'll find more than just a huge volume of water. You'll also discover trails, a restaurant, and 14 rustic stone cabins dating from the 1930s. Luckily for the traveler, these great little getaways, built by the Civilian Conservation Corps and on the National Register of Historic Places, are available for rent. Available in a variety of sizes and prices ($55–110 per night), most include a bathroom, shower, bed linens, two-burner electric stove, sink, small fridge, microwave, and coffeemaker. Best of all, your dog is welcomed for only $10 extra per night. The **Big Spring Dining Lodge** is also a must-see. It overlooks the spring itself and is open for business May–Oct.

✿ ♿ **River Birch Lane** (573-729-6965; www.riverbirchlane.us), RR 5, P.O. Box 454, Salem, Mo. 65560. If you want to stay in a hand-hewn stone home, then you'll like River Birch. Situated on 40 acres just outside Salem on SR 616 (best call for directions), the home has been divided into an upper and lower suite with queen-sized bed, kitchen, bath, and porch. Breakfast is served in the owner's home, just a short walk away, where there is also a sitting room with comfortable chairs, a fire, and piano. Kids under 12 stay free at River Birch, and there are several different pricings. A room alone is $60 per night; a room and full breakfast is $75. This B&B is unique in that it offers a package rarely found elsewhere: For a one-night stay you can rent your suite, enjoy dinner prepared by an Italian chef, and receive a massage. The price for two people is $175.

∞ **Plain and Fancy Bed and Breakfast** (573-546-1182; www .plainfancybb.com/index.html), HC 69, Box 2554, Ironton, Mo. A 1908 post-Victorian home, the Plain and Fancy is close to such sites as Elephant Rocks and Taum Sauk state parks, Johnson Shut-Ins, and the Black River. There are nice touches in this home, not the least of which are refurbished original pine and oak floors and a first-floor ceiling of patterned tin. You'll find a hot tub, a wedding gazebo, creek, and patio with fire pit. Two suites are offered at Plain and Fancy. The Red Hat ($115 per night) offers a sitting room, bedroom, private porch, cable TV with DVD, high-speed Internet, king-sized bed, and queen-sized sofa sleeper. Renting the Amish Room ($99) does not mean you are forced to wear black and rise at 4 AM to feed the chickens. You'll find a wealth of fine furniture handmade by the Amish, but you'll also discover the same amenities found in the Red Hat Suite. Plus, I

don't think the Amish provide the plush lounging robes offered by the innkeepers of this establishment (or if they do, it's a well-kept secret). No kids, pets, or smoking. Breakfast is served Mon.–Sat at 9; Sun. at 11 you can enjoy a fine and filling brunch.

RESORTS ✈ ♿ ♟ **Aguila Lodge** (573-226-5665; www.eminencelodge .com), HC 1, Box 17, Eminence, Mo. Right on the banks of the Jacks Fork, on Tom Akers Rd. near Eminence, the Aguila Lodge offers both a motel, cabins, and one particularly nice place on a high river bluff. The motel is open Memorial Day–Labor Day and offers rooms starting at $69 per night. Cabins are very near the river and begin at $114 in-season. Oct.–May, starting rates are $104 per night. The special "Bluff Side" cabin hangs above the Jacks Fork and includes a queen-sized bed, tables and chairs, cable TV, air, shower and Jacuzzi, double sink, full kitchen, and much more. The nightly cost is $200 on weekdays and $250 on weekends. Also at Aguila is the RS Steakhouse (see *Eating Out*) and a popular lounge with full bar.

✈ ♿ **River's Edge** (573-226-3233; www.rivers-edge.com), HCR 1, Box 11, Eminence, Mo. As mentioned earlier, a few years ago I came within a hair of purchasing an Eminence bed & breakfast just downriver from the River's Edge (instead I bought a beer and BBQ joint in the utterly heinous little village of Elk City, Idaho, thus losing much of both my shirt and my sanity but luckily escaping with my life). River's Edge always struck me as having one of the nicest locations in the Ozarks, and many travelers like to come back year after year. A number of lodging options are possible. A large

RIVER'S EDGE RESORT

river cabin (sleeping up to 12) runs from a minimum of $129 per night in the off-season to a minimum of $329 Memorial Day–Labor Day. These cabins are completely equipped and access a private deck looking over the river. Motel rooms overlooking the river are $49–89 per night; suites, $99–199. Smaller cabins, which include stone fireplaces, a great view, and all the electronic video goodies, go for $79–149. Those with kids will appreciate River's Edge, as the folks here neither encourage nor permit crazy or alcoholic behavior. You can drink on the premises if you wish, just don't be stupid about it. Pets are not allowed, and smoking is permitted outside only. This is an establishment strongly dedicated to safe family fun.

Shady Lane Cabins (573-226-3893; www.shadylanecabins.com), P.O. Box 94, Eminence, Mo. 65466. Located right off SR 19 in Eminence, Shady Lane is but 150 yards or so from the banks of the Jacks Fork River. Nine RV sites with sewer, water, and electric run $17 per night. Motel rooms, ranging from one to six beds, cost $35–150 per night. Small cabins begin at $49, and large cabins (with full kitchen and four queen-sized beds) are $89–169. If you've a large family or group and want some privacy, a modern home with barn and horse stalls can be rented (depending on the time of year) for $99–189. Kids are okay, but pets are not permitted in the private home, cabins, or motel rooms (and there's a $100 penalty if you try to sneak one in).

🐾 ✎ ♿ **Reed's Cabins** (573-548-2222; www.reedscabins.com), RR 5, P.O. Box 332, Salem, Mo. 65660. A private enterprise located next door to Montauk State Park, Reed's offers 18 cabins with full kitchens. Prices begin at $65–75 per night, and pets are allowed with a $15-per-night surcharge. On-site are an in-ground swimming pool and store. This latter offers not only a wide supply of grocery items but also a deli, breakfast menu, and all sorts of fishing supplies from the likes of Bass Pro and White River Fly Tackle.

CANOE OUTFITTERS, CAMPING, AND RVS 🐾 ♂ ♿ Akers Ferry Canoe Rental and Campground

(1-800-333-5628; www.currentriver canoe.com). More than 50 years old, this outfitter's operations include not only **Akers Ferry** and **Jason Place Campground** (23 miles south of Salem), but also **Jacks Fork Canoe Rental and Campground** in Eminence. The firm also rents canoes along the Current via **Round Springs Canoe Rental** and **Wild River Canoe Rental**. In other words, this outfitter covers the Current River nearly from start to finish. Canoe rentals begin at $40 per canoe per day, and camping rates start at $6 per night per person. Full RV hookups are available only at the Jacks Fork Campground and begin at $10 per hookup per night. Cabin rentals range $90–110 per night.

♂ **Jadwin Canoe Rental** (573-729-5229 or 1-800-937-4837; www.jadwin canoe.com), RR 1, Jadwin, Mo. Featuring canoes, kayaks, gas, groceries, and a campground, Jadwin (in business since 1966) offers trips ranging from several hours to several days. Rates for a one-day float are in the $40 range. Primitive camping rates are $2.85 per person per night, plus tax. Sites with electric hookups are $3.80 per night per person plus tax. Children 12 and under may stay in the campground free.

For the **Pulltite**, **Alley Spring**, **Round Spring**, and **Two Rivers campgrounds**, see *Wild Places*.

Harvey's Alley Spring Canoe Rental (573-226-3386; www.missouri 2000.net/alleyspring), HC 1, Box 920, Eminence, Mo. Harvey's is located 6 miles west of Eminence on SR 106 (which is less than 0.5 mile from the Alley Spring Campground). With floats on both the Current and Jacks Fork, Harvey's has a fully equipped general store and a number of different rental options. Memorial Day–Labor Day, canoes begin at $30 per day, which includes hauling you and yours both to and from your campsite.

Windy's Canoe and Tube Rental (573-226-3404; www.windyscanoe .com), Eminence, Mo. Just across the street from the River's Edge Resort, Windy's is perhaps the best-known float outfitter in Eminence. This place has been in business for about 40 years, always family owned and operated. The staff here know the rivers, know the best floats, have all the gear you could ever need, and offer floats ranging from 3 hours to 7 days. Canoe and kayak rentals begin at $30 per day. If you'd prefer to go floating down the river on a big rubber inner tube, the cost is only $10. Of course, if you've got the financial wherewithal of Bill Gates, you could go whole hog and rent a canvas-covered tube for $15.

♂ ♿ **Eminence Canoes, Cottages and Camp** (1-800-723-1387 or 1-800-226-5954; www.eminencecanoes cottagescamp.com), P.O. Box 548, Eminence, Mo. Located .75 mile north of Eminence on SR 19, this facility's name succinctly describes its offerings. Canoe and kayak rentals begin at $45 per day, while tube rentals are $12.50. A campsite without extras runs $7 per person per night, while one with water and electric (for a tent) is $10. RV spaces with water, electric, and A/C are $15. The campground does include hot showers, rest rooms, a fire ring, and picnic table. A number of nice cottages can be rented in a price range of $69–263 (based on cottage type and number of guests). Amenities include air-conditioning/gas or electric heating, cable TV, VCR and free movies, bed and bath linens, dinnerware, cookware, coffeemaker and filters, toaster, refrigerator, stove with oven, microwave, and gas barbecue. Neither pets nor smoking are permitted.

Big Spring Canoe and Tube Rental (573-323-4550 or 1-800-567-8701; www.bigspringcanoe.com), P.O. Box 574, Van Buren, Mo. If you'd like to canoe or tube the Current River into the park at Big Spring, this operation offers a number of trips. Rental prices have a tendency to change, so call the 800 number for present prices and availability. On Sycamore St. in downtown Van Buren.

⌀ ♿ **Silver Arrow Canoe Rental** (573-729-5770 or 1-800-333-6040; www.silverarrowcanoe.com), HC 62, Box 164, Salem, Mo. With headquarters roughly 17 miles south of Salem on SR 19, Silver Arrow offers float trips on the Current ranging 8–82 miles. Rates for a single canoe begin at $44 (there's a discount if you rent more than one), and kayaks begin at $25 per day. Campground rates (a basic site) begin at $4 per person per night. A large country cottage, capable of sleeping 10, is also available for rent. The charge for two people begins at $80 per night. The campground's amenities include tables, grills, electric hookups, and hot, pay showers. Best of all, this facility enforces "quiet hours" beginning at 11 PM.

Eleven Point River Canoe Rental (417-778-6497; www.11pointcanoe .com), RR 2, Box 2522, Alton, Mo. The Eleven Point River is usually less crowded than either the Jacks Fork or Current. It's also a bit deeper and offers some great fishing for wild rainbow trout, bass, and a variety of pan-

fish. Eleven Point River Canoe Rental offers canoes starting at $35 per day and kayaks at $25 per day. If you wish (call for a quote on prices), you can also book for a guided fishing trip with experienced river pilots. This outfitter allows camping on its land, but you can also camp on gravel bars and riverbanks all along the Eleven Point.

⌀ **Running River Canoe Rental** (573-858-3371 or 1-800-226-6394; www.runningrivercanoe.com), Salem, Mo. Located on SR 19 about 25 miles south of Salem, Running River specializes in float trips down the Current. Prices begin at $40 a day, and trips can range from 4 hours to 2 or even 3 days. Should you wish to camp, the establishment has a small, private campground with store, rest rooms, and showers. A basic campsite runs $5 per adult per night ($2 for kids). An electric site requires an additional $3, and a full RV spot (water, electric, and sewer) is $25 per night for four people.

✳ **Where to Eat**

EATING OUT 🍴 ⌀ ♿ 🍸 **Gads Hill Pub and Grill** (573-223-3687; www .gads-hill.com), RR 2, Box 2484, Piedmont, Mo. On January 31, 1874, Jesse James and his gang pulled Missouri's first train robbery at Gads Hill. Now you can dine at the site where the James boys laid claim to their future fame. A simple restaurant, big and open with the obligatory pool table found in most Ozark bar and grills, Gads Hill opens Mon.–Tue. at 3 PM and Wed.–Sat. at noon. The prices here are low: For an appetizer, you'll find a plate of fried mushrooms for $3.25 and half a dozen fried chicken livers for $3.50. A quarter-pound burger with fries is only $3.95 (try getting that at McDonald's), and a catfish basket is but $4.95. St. Louis–style pizzas are in the $8 range. Depending on the night, you might find karaoke with a DJ or free pool and darts. This is sort of a friendly neighborhood hangout, and tourists are made to feel very welcome.

✐ ⚲ ☗ **Big Rock Candy Mountain** (417-932-6917 or 1-877-932-4440; www.bigrockcandymtn.com), Jadwin, Mo. Only 8 miles from Montauk State Park and 0.5 mile from the Current River, Big Rock Candy Mountain offers a bar with occasional live entertainment (and this could be anything from a band to local folks pickin' and grinnin'), a simple menu, camping, cabins, and RV hookups. Another very local spot where nobody is a stranger, this is a nice little place to hang out and have a beer after a long day of floating. To reach Big Rock from Salem, go to Jadwin, turn right onto SR ZZ, and drive the 6.5 miles to Cedar Grove. Cross the bridges and turn right onto SR B. Drive 0.5 mile to the top of the hill and you're there.

✐ ⚲ **Cowboy Dean's** (573-226-1201; www.deansbbq.com), 102 Stewarts Landing, Eminence, Mo. If you want to eat real BBQ, you should get it from a cowboy. If you visit Cowboy Dean's, owned by Cowboy Dean Tindall, then your search is over. Dean went into the BBQ biz after the ranch where he worked decided to call it quits. Thus, Dean began putting out fare on the smoker he had built for himself. The rest is history. You can try some armadillo eggs (a jalapeño pepper stuffed with cheddar cheese, wrapped in a beef and pork ball, and smoked on-site) for $2 apiece. Sandwiches here are big and hearty, with brisket, chicken, pork, and beef all go-

ing for $5.50. Platters of ribs, brisket, pork shoulder, or smoked chicken are all $9.50, or you can opt for a 14-ounce rib eye and four jumbo shrimp for $22.50. For the rib lover, a half slab is $10 and a full slab, $20. Dean's has become popular enough that he now ships his BBQ all over America. No matter what you want—ribs, brisket, a combo, or pork—he will send you the meal fully cooked, vacuum sealed, and packed in dry ice. If you wish to have a taste before you actually visit his place, check out the online BBQ store.

✐ ⚲ ☗ **RS Steakhouse** (573-226-5665; www.eminencelodge.com), HC 1, Box 17, Eminence, Mo. Located at the Aguila Lodge in Eminence, the RS specializes in meat, particularly steaks and filet mignon. However, you can also choose plenty of burgers, sandwiches, and Ozark favorites. A 10-ounce filet is $22, while a 16-ounce T-bone is $19. Both the 10-ounce rib eye and New York strip are $17. A cheeseburger and chips will set you back $4.25, and for the vegetarian, an all-you-can-eat salad bar costs $6. You should note, however, that the RS is only open Thu.–Sat. The lounge can be a fairly hopping place in summer, with three pool tables, plenty of music, and a full bar.

✐ ⚲ **Colton's Steak House & Grill** (573-686-3880; www.coltonssteakhouse.com), 2114 N. Westwood, Poplar Bluff, Mo. Colton's is admittedly part of a chain, but it's a small regional chain that offers some good value if you're traveling with the family. For lunch, you can try a fried catfish plate for $6.99, country-fried steak for $6.79, or a bacon cheeseburger for $6.59. For dinner, a variety of steaks range $13.99–21.99, and a pretty standard seafood menu (more catfish, shrimp, salmon, and such) is all in the $9–13 realm. Actually, one of the tastiest things you can order from Colton's menu is the "tumbleweed" appetizer. That's a giant deep-fried blossomed onion served with dipping sauce. It's pretty good (especially for a chain outfit), and the price is $5.99.

✳ Entertainment

✐ ♿ **Black River Coliseum** (573-686-8001; www.blackrivercoliseum .com), 301 S. 5th St., Poplar Bluff, Mo. A new, 115,000-square-foot facility, the Black River Coliseum plays host to major concerts, rodeos, and other sporting events; family and trade shows; and conventions. Encompassing 5,000 concert seats, the building also houses an excellent fitness center. Call ahead or check the web site for information on upcoming events and prices.

LIVE MUSIC 🎤 ✐ **Doniphan's Ozark Jamboree** (573-593-4348), downtown on Washington St., Doniphan, Mo. This is the sort of event that you're always wishing you could find, but never do. Every Friday and Saturday night the Doniphan locals meet up downtown, in a location formerly holding a Ben Franklin store, and make music. Groups are welcomed, or you can pick up the mike yourself and cut loose. You'll hear anything from bluegrass to gospel to classic country. There's no admission fee. All you have to do is be ready to have a good time. Donations would be accepted if you felt so inclined.

🎤 ✐ **Ozark Country Music** (573-729-4811), 202 N. Washington, Salem, Mo. Another authentic venue with tunes performed by the locals. Live

music is performed every Friday night, 7–10, in the Salem City Hall Auditorium. Everyone is welcome to listen or dance, and again, the performers are paid by any donations you might wish to offer.

SPECTATOR SPORTS ✐ ♿ **Poplar Bluff Speedway** (573-785-8989; www.poplarbluffspeedway.com), 1989 Speedway Lane, Poplar Bluff, Mo. $8 adults, $5 ages 6–12. Races are held at this $3/8$-mile, high-banked oval Mar.–Nov. Racing time is generally at 7:30 PM, with gates opening at 4:30. You'll find all the various classes here, everything from late model to super-street, from cruisers and hobby to open-wheel modified.

✳ Special Events

March 1 **Opening day of trout season**, Montauk State Park (573-548-2201 or 573-548-2434; www.mostate parks.com/montauk.htm), RR 5, Box 279, Salem, Mo. March 1 is the day when trout fishermen from all over the state (and parts unknown) descend on Montauk, wait for the bell to ring, and flail the water to a creamy froth as they angle to hook that first trout of the year. It may be more fun to actually watch this event than to take part, as the word *crowded* becomes a vast understatement. Just sit back, take photos, and shake your head in wonder. You've never seen so many people trying so hard to catch the big one.

April **Cross Country Trail Rides Bluegrass Festival** (573-226-3883; www.crosscountrytrailride.com), P.O. Box 15, Eminence, Mo. Drawing thousands of people and featuring big-name pickers, this annual bluegrass festival is an area favorite. Prices vary for the five-day event, but a full-week ticket (including festival admission and camping) runs $100 adults, $40 kids. If you simply want to hear some good tunes, nightly admission is $20 adults, $10 kids. Located 1 mile north of Eminence, off SR 19.

May **Fourche Creek Bluegrass Festival** (573-989-6103). Held on the Fourche Creek Ranch west of Doniphan in mid-May, this local bluegrass festival features a weekend of the best of local and regional players. Call ahead for information on camping and admission.

Upper Current River Pow Wow (573-729-2233; www.westerncherokee nation.org), E. 10th St., Salem, Mo. $2 adults, $1 ages 7–12; free for both seniors and those 6 and under. Taking place on Memorial Day weekend at the old Salem Middle School, the powwow features American Indian arts and crafts, jewelry, food, music, and much more. Of course there will be lots of drumming and dancing, and the event is open to the general public.

Big Spring Arts Crafts and Music Festival (www.semo.net/vanburen). This festival takes place for two days every Memorial Day weekend. While there's plenty of down-home bluegrass and country music, you'll also

see the demonstration of lost arts and pioneer skills.

September **Labor Day Homecoming** (573-996-7980; www.ripley countymissouri.org/index.asp). Held each Labor Day weekend in Doniphan, the affair presents a parade, antique-car show, games, and all types of vendor booths stocked full of arts, crafts, and calories of both the empty and nutritious kind.

October **Current River Days** (www .semo.net/vanburen). Held in Van Buren on the first weekend of every October, Current River Days offers arts and crafts, artists, a beauty pageant, music and dancing, exhibits, a street dance, clogging, square dancing, food, and much more.

Naylor Pioneer Heritage Day (573-399-2285; www.ripleycountymissouri .org/index.asp). Held the first Saturday of each October in downtown Naylor, this local festival offers a themed parade, music, crafts, games, and exhibitions in such pioneer arts as soap making and blacksmithing. You might particularly enjoy the old-time dress contest and the decorated bicycle contest. You'd think there would also be an "old-time decorated bicycle in a dress contest," but perhaps such an oversight merely stems from the fact that no one has suggested the idea.

The Arkansas Ozarks

5

EUREKA SPRINGS AND NORTHWEST
ARKANSAS

THE WHITE AND THE BUFFALO

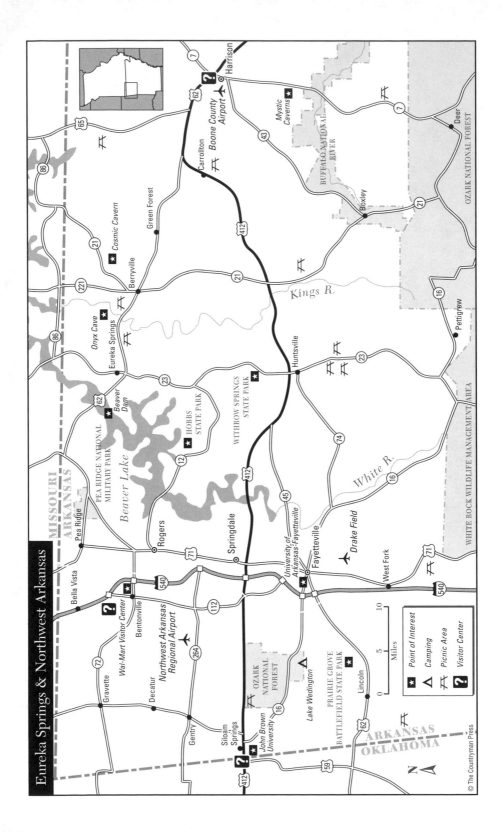

Eureka Springs & Northwest Arkansas

© The Countryman Press

EUREKA SPRINGS AND
NORTHWEST ARKANSAS

The plans of humans often differ from those of fate, with the latter having a tendency to win the day. There are those who, with seemingly zero effort, are rewarded with luck, fame, and riches. On the other hand, there are those who work and struggle for years only to see their well-planned ventures end with a fizzle rather than a boom. The theory applies to lands and regions as well as to individuals. All of us have seen the "unlucky corner" in any given town or city, the spot where business after business is doomed to failure, no matter the quality of its goods or services. Just is prevalent is that little hole-in-the-wall, located far from traveled thoroughfares, a ma-and-pa operation that had the dumb luck to open in a spot that magically draws patrons and visitors from miles around.

Northwest Arkansas enjoys the sort of blessed luck reflected in the latter category. A hard and rugged country, albeit beautiful beyond words, it defies the imagination to think that this isolated region has consistently attracted guests and travelers from around the world. Even before the sunrise of the 20th century, Northwest Arkansas was the playground of the rich and famous. The attraction and accolades continue, in varied forms, to this day.

The first inhabitants of this region were the Bluff Dwellers, prehistoric people who resided in the bluffs and caves prevalent along Northwest Arkansas's many rivers. Later were the Osage, a proud and handsome tribe that was an offshoot of the Sioux. It is said that in 1541 the explorer Hernando de Soto traversed this land, followed by the likes of Marquette and Joliet, and innumerable French fur traders who filled their bellies from the bounty of the White River.

Skipping ahead, by 1856 local residents began to have a sense that the waters boiling from the ground in the Eureka Springs area (long regarded as holy by the Indians) had certain marketing potential. Eureka Springs went from nothing to a boomtown in just a few decades. By the 1890s the "healthful" water of Basin Spring was being shipped all over America (eat your heart out, Perrier), and Eureka Springs boasted of graded, gaslit streets, a municipal water system, modern sewage, stone sidewalks, parks, and even telephone service. Fires devastated the town on several occasions, and just after the turn of the century most buildings were being constructed out of locally quarried stone. The elite of the world came to take the healing water, receive pampering in the spas, enjoy more than

50 hotels (many world class), and engage in a social whirl that rivaled anything found in New York or Boston. There were resorts such as Monte Ne, created by the eccentric silver baron William "Coin" Harvey. Built on 320 acres, Monte Ne was serviced by a railroad that Harvey constructed; at the train depot guests were picked up in gondolas and ferried by water to their rooms in one of two, 320-foot-long log cabins. Though business boomed for some years at Monte Ne, the advent of World War I saw the guest list dwindle. Harvey, deciding civilization was doomed, began construction of a pyramid that would store items from the present and future generations. Alas, he ran out of money, the pyramid was never finished, and when Beaver Lake was built, Monte Ne sank beneath the waves. At the time of this writing (early 2006) a drought has lowered the level of Beaver Lake, and the ruins of Monte Ne have again risen to the surface. Contrary to Harvey's prediction, civilization still exists (more or less), and hundreds of thousands of visitors are expected at Beaver Lake to view the remains of a latter-day Atlantis.

A similar fate befell Eureka Springs. Though it was the hot spot of America for roughly 20 years, the combination of World War I and the Great Depression threw the town into a tailspin. A long fallow period was to follow, but by the 1960s Eureka Springs was beginning a resurgence. Today it has regained much of its past glory, with hotels, restaurants, shows, shopping, and a plethora of social events fueling the town's continuing success.

Just to the west of Eureka Springs, the towns of Fayetteville, Bentonville, Springdale, and Rogers have grown to the point that they seem one vast metropolis. Again, success just seems to ride the coattails of Northwest Arkansas. Bentonville is the birthplace and corporate home of Wal-Mart, the world's largest retailer. Fayetteville is an eclectic, fun, and highly literate town that hosts the University of Arkansas. The entire area is loaded with live music and theater, museums, dining, and shopping of the sort you would not normally expect if you took to heart the media depictions of the state.

The region shows no signs of slowing down. Northwest Arkansas is geared toward the future. This should come as no surprise, as its always been ahead of its time.

AREA CODES The majority of this section of Northwest Arkansas is located in the **479** area code. The exception is to the eastern edge of the area, such as Harrison, which falls under the **870** code.

GUIDANCE Luckily for travelers, the state of Arkansas provides one of the most complete, competent, and helpful tourism departments in the nation. For information on sites and events, contact the **Arkansas Department of Parks and Tourism** (501-682-7777 or 1-800-NATURAL; www.arkansas.com), 1 Capitol Mall, Little Rock, Ark.

When you wish to spend time in one of America's most unique towns, a place named as one of its Dozen Distinctive Destinations by the National Trust for Historic Preservation, make sure to check in with the **Greater Eureka Springs Chamber of Commerce** (479-253-8737; www.eurekasprings.com), 137-B W.

Van Buren St., Eureka Springs, Ark. Also, for information on the town of Rogers (and who could pass up a trip to the Daisy Airgun Museum?), contact the **Rogers/Lowell Area Chamber of Commerce** (479-636-1240; www.rogers lowell.com), 317 W. Walnut St., Rogers, Ark. Yet another Arkansas stop that is increasingly rising in the estimation of national travelers is Fayetteville—a pretty town that not only boasts of great dining, music, and nightlife, but is also home of the University of Arkansas. Details on things to do and places to see can be obtained from the **Fayetteville Chamber of Commerce** (479-521-1710; www .fayettevillear.com), 123 W. Mountain St., Fayetteville, Ark. Or, if you particularly seek live music and concert information, just dash on over to **www.fayette villetourism.com**.

If you are thinking of Wal-Mart, then you're thinking of Bentonville, the hometown and global headquarters of the world's largest retailer. At the **Bentonville/ Bella Vista Chamber of Commerce** (479-273-2841; www.bentonvillebellavista chamber.com), 202 E. Central St., Bentonville, Ark., you'll find there's much more going on than low prices. Just down the road a piece is Springdale, defined quite admirably by the **Springdale Chamber of Commerce** (479-872-2222; www.springdale.com), 202 W. Emma Ave., Springdale, Ark. Last but not least, on the far eastern side of this district you will discover the quaint little town of Harrison. The **Harrison Convention and Visitor's Bureau** (1-888-283-2163; www.harrisonarkansas.org), P.O. Box 940, Harrison, Ark. 72601, can tell you everything you wish to know. Or, drop by the **Harrison Chamber of Commerce** at 621 E. Rush St. in Harrison.

GETTING THERE *By auto:* From the north, US 71 enters Arkansas from Missouri, and at Bentonville transforms into I-540. This major thoroughfare continues to travel south though Washington County (Springdale and Fayetteville) until it joins I-40. US 62 will take you on a drive from the western part of this region to the southeast, passing through Eureka Springs and Berryville until joining with US 65, which traverses Harrison as it continues on its journey to the south.

By air: Travel by air becomes simpler for Ozark visitors as they travel into Arkansas. **Northwest Arkansas Regional Airport** (479-205-1000; www.nwara.com), 1 Airport Blvd., Bentonville, Ark., is a relatively new airport (completed in 1998) serviced by American Eagle, Continental Express, Delta, Northwest Airlink, US Airways Express, and United. For even more flight opportunities, albeit requiring a bit more travel by auto, you can fly to or from the **Little Rock National Airport** (501-372-3439; www.lrn-airport.com), 1 Airport Dr., Little Rock, Ark. This facility is serviced by American Eagle, Continental Airlines, Delta, Delta Connection, Frontier Airlines, Northwest, Northwest Airlink, Southwest, and US Airways. At the far southwest edge of this region, **Fort Smith Regional Airport** (479-452-7000; www.fortsmithairport.com), 6700 McKennon Blvd., Fort Smith, Ark., is serviced by American Eagle and Northwest Airlink.

MEDICAL EMERGENCIES **Northwest Medical Center of Benton County** (479-553-1000; www.northwesthealth.com/nmcb.cfm), 3000 Medical Center Pkwy., Bentonville, Ark. Part of the **Northwest Health** group, this hospital is one of the most modern in the Ozarks. Services include emergency care, surgery, neurosurgery, cardiac care, senior services, imaging, women's care, and obstetrics. Just to the south in Springdale, Northwest Health also operates the **Northwest Medical Center of Washington County** (479-751-5711; www.northwest health.com/nmcw.cfm), 609 W. Maple Ave., Springdale, Ark. Serving Washington County for more than five decades, the facility offers cardiac care, emergency services, surgery, neonatal ICU, cancer care, and senior health services.

Mercy Health Center/St. Mary's Hospital (479-936-2905; www.mercyhealth nwa.smhs.com/stmarys/default.asp), 1200 W. Walnut St., Rogers, Ark. This 165-bed, not-for-profit health center features emergency care and a full menu of services ranging from cancer treatment and diagnostic imaging to outpatient care and a sleep disorder center.

Siloam Springs Memorial Hospital (479-524-4141; www.ssmh.us/home.htm), 205 E. Jefferson St., Siloam Springs, Ark., is a 73-bed not-for-profit acute care facility known for its primary care, internal medicine, surgical and obstetrical services, emergency care, and both in- and outpatient clinics.

The Regency Hospital group operates facilities both in Springdale and Fayetteville. **Regency Hospital of NW Arkansas** (479-713-7000; www.regency hospital.com), 1125 N. College Ave., Fayetteville, Ark., is a 25-bed long-term acute care hospital located within Washington Regional Medical Center. **Regency Hospital of Springdale** (479-757-2600; www.regencyhospital.com), 609 W. Maple Ave., Springdale, Ark., is also a 25-bed acute care facility, located within the Northwest Medical Center of Washington County.

North Arkansas Regional Health Center (870-365-2000; www.narmc.com), 620 N. Willow St., Harrison, Ark., is a 174-bed hospital that employs a staff of more than 600. In operation for more than 50 years, this hospital also handles any ailment you could imagine.

Other area hospitals include the **Carroll Regional Medical Center** in Berryville and the **Eureka Springs Hospital** in Eureka Springs.

✳ Wandering Around

EXPLORING BY CAR **Boston Mountains Scenic Loop**. For many years US 71 was the only route through the Boston Mountains. This hallowed road, which travels from Louisiana to Iowa, takes on the attributes of a pretzel when it reaches Northwest Arkansas. It travels between I-40 to the south and Fayetteville to the north, and travelers could at one time count on twists, turns, hills, valleys, and a disconcerting amount of traffic. Take it from one who had occasion to travel this road while pulling a very large U-Haul trailer behind a very small Toyota (overheating and in first gear all the way): In its glory days US 71 was not for the faint of heart.

Today, though, while the twists, turns, hills, and valleys remain, traffic on US 71 is light-years away from the white-knuckle journey of days past. The main route through the Bostons is now I-540, which speeds along just a short distance to the west. The construction of that superhighway makes US 71 the perfect leisurely drive through the highest, and some of the most scenic, stretches of the Arkansas Ozarks. This is 42 miles of sheer beauty, and you'll find plenty of places to pull off, gawk at the scenery, and shoot photos.

The Boston Mountain Loop shows off just how rugged this section of the Ozarks really is. Here, the mountains feel like mountains. To the south, just off I-40, the trip begins in the town of Alma. Drive north and you'll pass through the hamlets of Winslow and Mountainburg, experiencing jaw-dropping vistas, numerous farms, and the obligatory tiny motels common to small-town America. In Mountainburg, make sure to stop at the **Ozark Mountain Smokehouse**. For about 60 years this place has been offering cured and smoked meats, homemade jams, jellies, pickles, and relish; it even has a "make-your-own-sandwich" bar. Throughout the trip you should keep your eyes peeled for more than few off-the-beaten-path cafés, diners, gift shops, and antiques stores. Or just take your time and enjoy the views, rivers, creeks, and forests. Either way, you'll win.

EXPLORING BY FOOT Devil's Den Self-Guided Trail (479-761-3325 or 1-800-264-2417; www.arkansasstatepark.com/devilsden), 11333 W. SR 74, West Fork, Ark. Located in **Devil's Den State Park**, this 1.5-mile trail can be a little strenuous in spots, but it will also provide a bird's-eye view of two fracture caves (the Devil's Den and the Devil's Icebox). Along the walk, which requires a couple of hours minimum, you'll come across numerous springs, waterfalls (in spring, at any rate), and animals and plants galore. Be certain that you haven't forgotten a few good flashlights if you plan to do a little cave exploring, and prepare to get dirty. Also, if you are in the caves, watch your step. There are plenty of cracks and fissures custom made for unwary feet and ankles. The trailheads for this hike are just behind the Devil's Den State Park Visitor's Center, and by the SR 170 bridge at Lee Creek.

EXPLORING BY TROLLEY ❀ ✦ ♿ **Eureka Springs Transit System** (479-253-9572; www.eurekatrolley.org), 137A W. Van Buren, Eureka Springs, Ark. Eureka Springs is a pain to walk, as there probably isn't a single flat spot in town. Here you only have two choices, up or down. Driving isn't much better; the streets wind this way and that, and it's easy to get lost. Luckily, the local transit system can solve all your problems. No smoke-belching buses here. Instead, you can explore the town via trolley car. The cars run all over town, are wheelchair accessible, and have seat belts and shoulder straps. Schedules are Jan.–Feb., Thu.–Mon. 10–4; Mar.–Apr., daily 9–5; May–Oct., Sun.–Thu. 9–5 and Fri.–Sat. 9–8; Nov., Thu.–Mon. 9–5; Dec., Thu.–Mon. 10–4. Rates are just $4 for an adult's all-day pass, while a kid's pass (ages 7–11) is $1. A two-day pass is $6, and a one-ride pass is $2. You can also take a narrated trolley tour through the Eureka Springs Historic District at a cost of $9 adults, $4 kids under 12.

THE EUREKA SPRINGS TROLLEY

EXPLORING BY RIVER Although the best portions of the best Arkansas Ozark rivers are covered in the next chapter, Northwest Arkansas does offer some opportunities for floating and fishing. The **West Fork of the Upper White River** starts south of Fayetteville (near Winslow), runs north through Fayetteville to Beaver Lake, then heads into Missouri to Table Rock Lake. From there it drops into Bull Shoals Lake and finally emerges as the famous **White River**, renowned for monster trout and land scams masterminded by an impeached president. While the West Fork isn't really a great floating river, it is floatable year-round. It offers few services, however, and you're probably going to need to bring your own canoe and shuttle yourself back and forth (there are a lot of campgrounds close by, but at the time of this writing there were none on the river itself). If such doesn't bother you, this could be a peaceful little float largely absent of canoe traffic.

A more popular floating creek (when it's floatable—and during many dry summers it's not) is **War Eagle Creek**. This is the stretch of water to take if you're visiting in winter. The scenery is gorgeous, and at times you'll even come across a few rapids. War Eagle's headwaters are in the Ozark National Forest, and it flows in a generally northwestern direction through Winthrow State Park and on to Beaver Lake. If you're planning to both canoe and camp, Winthrow is a good place to stop. It offers a couple of dozen campsites, rest rooms, water, showers, electric hookups, and canoe rental.

The most popular body of water for canoeists and fishermen in Northwest Arkansas is the **Kings River**. Formed in the Boston Mountains of Madison

WAR EAGLE CREEK

County, the river flows more or less north, eventually joining with the White River, crossing the Missouri border, and dumping into Table Rock Lake. Roughly 90 miles from start to finish, the Kings is superb for both floating and fishing. Canoeists will encounter the occasional rapid, and deep pools make for some excellent bass and catfishing. The cats can get large, but the smallmouth bass population is the real draw. Don't think you'll only catch dinky fish here; it's not that unusual to take a lunker from the Kings. The best time to float this river—depending of course on rainfall—is spring. That's also the best time to view the scenery, as the deep forests and bluffs that line the Kings are a sight to behold. A number of outfitters offer trips on the Kings River; you'll likely find the best choices in the Eureka Springs and Berryville areas.

✳ Towns and Villages

Bentonville, Ark. On Bentonville's downtown square you will find a large statue of a Confederate soldier. Perhaps, though, the statue should be of Sam Walton, founder of Wal-Mart. This is the home of the world's largest retailer, and the Wal-Mart Visitor's Center still resides in what was once old Sam's original Bentonville Variety Store. One of the fastest-growing towns in Arkansas (increasing in population from nearly 20,000 in 2000 to nearly 30,000 in 2006), Bentonville also boasts beautiful old mansions and is just southwest of the Pea Ridge National Military Park. In September you won't want to miss the annual **Harvest Music Festival**, and in June the sky fills with color during the Ozark Balloon Fest.

Eureka Springs, Ark. Sometimes known as Little Switzerland, from the mid-1800s on Eureka Springs was renowned for its "healing" waters. It's also renowned for being quirky, fun, and one of the steepest, hilliest towns in existence, loaded with fine Victorian architecture, hotels, spas, restaurants, antiques, and much more. Just a few of the attractions here are the Turpentine Creek Wildlife Refuge (home to 110 lions, tigers, leopards, and cougars), Opera in the Ozarks, and the seven-story sculpture *Christ of the Ozarks*. An open-air trolley will show you the entire town (this is either a walking or trolley town; driving is

not suggested), and thousands of people from around the world show up to see the outdoor theater presentation of *The Great Passion Play*. Because the area is less than an hour south of Branson, Mo., many visitors make sure to spend time in both places.

Fayetteville, Ark. There's no reason to worry if, when in Fayetteville, you happen to see folks walking around wearing plastic hog snouts. It's likely just football season, and the crowds are preparing for yet another Arkansas Razorbacks game. Fayetteville, with nearly 65,000 residents, is home of the University of Arkansas. It was

BENTONVILLE'S CONFEDERATE WAR MEMORIAL

also home to former president Bill Clinton and his wife (you can take a tour of the small home where they were married) and is the site of the very hip Dickson Street, loaded with shops, restaurants, and live music. Devil's Den State Park is near Fayetteville, and for good fishing or floating it's hard to beat the White River.

Harrison, Ark. Just over the Missouri border (in fact, less than 70 miles south of Springfield, Mo.), Harrison is the seat of Boone County. Home to more than 12,000 residents, the site now occupied by Harrison was once home to a large Osage Indian village. That is, it was home to the Osage until around 1816. In that year the Cherokee tried to move in, and the Ozarks witnessed a full-fledged Indian war that lasted until both tribes were shipped off to Oklahoma. Harrison is a growing town that offers a host of activities and events both for locals and visitors. Two worth checking out are the Crawdad Days Music Festival in May and the Annual Bluegrass Festival in August.

Rogers, Ark. It's probably not fair to say that what Wal-Mart is to Bentonville, the Daisy BB Gun Factory was to Rogers. After all, only Daisy's corporate offices and museum remain in town (the factory is now in an underground facility near Neosho, Mo.). Nevertheless, I have fond memories of both Daisy BB Guns (as in the famous movie *A Christmas Story*, where lead character Ralphie Parker is repeatedly warned, "You'll put your eye out!") and touring the Daisy factory when I was a kid (they gave away packets of free BBs). Rogers, with nearly 40,000 residents, is just minutes from the 30,000-acre Beaver Lake. It also has one of the coolest main streets in the country (2004 winner of the Great American Main Street Award). Last but not least, Rogers is the closest sizable town to the massive War Eagle and Applegate craft festivals. These two events, combined with other craft festivals, draw more than a quarter million visitors per year to the region.

Siloam Springs, Ark. Founded as a health resort in the 1880s, Siloam Springs is now an ever-growing town of nearly 14,000. A truly great event in Siloam is the annual **Dogwood Festival**, held the last weekend of every April. The party attracts more than 30,000 people, and you will not only view dogwood trees in full bloom but also enjoy mountains of food and a wide variety of music. For a drive on the wild side, take a tour through the Wild Wilderness Safari, or just hop the state line into West Siloam Springs, Okla., and try your luck at the Cherokee Casino. Both the casino and restaurant are open 24 hours a day and offer live blackjack and more than 500 electronic gaming machines.

A EUREKA SPRINGS STREET SCENE

Springdale, Ark. Seeing as how it's the home of Tyson Foods, people in Springdale probably don't care if you label their town a "fowl place." Okay, bad puns notwithstanding, this progressive small city of 62,000 is home to more than 75 manufacturers, top-notch health care, and award-winning schools. Springdale is very close to Beaver Lake, and while in town you can hop on the Arkansas & Missouri Railroad for an up-close-and-personal tour of the Ozark hills. Also, because this is a town that loves its poultry, you won't want to miss **FeatherFest**, held every spring. It could be safely argued that nobody knows how to have a wing cook-off as well as the natives of Springdale.

✳ To See

MUSEUMS ◯◯ 🐾 ✐ ♿ **1875 Peel Mansion Museum & Heritage Gardens** (479-273-9664; www.peelmansion.org), 400 S. Walton Blvd., Bentonville, Ark. Tue.–Sat. 10–4. $3 adults, $1 ages 6–12. The home of a number of Benton County historical societies, the Peel Mansion is an 1875 Italianate structure built in 1875 by Confederate colonel Samuel West Peel. Authentic from top to bottom and loaded with period antiques, this living museum is the site of many events, tours, and Civil War reenactments. The elaborate gardens feature roses, perennials, and native plants in keeping with the original 19th-century design. The gift shop and gatehouse of the mansion are found in the **Andy Lynch log cabin**, moved from a location near the original Battle of Pea Ridge to the Peel grounds. The mansion and grounds can be rented for private events and weddings.

🐾 ✐ ♿ **Carroll County Heritage Center** (870-423-6312; www.rootsweb.com/~arcchs), 403 Berryville Public Square, Berryville, Ark. Open Apr.–Oct., Mon.–Fri. 9–4, Sat. 10–1. Nov.–Mar., it's open Mon.–Fri. 9–4, Sat. 10–1. $2 adults, $1 kids. I tend to believe that the moonshine still is an almost integral part of any Ozark museum worth its salt. The CCHC has one, thus proving without doubt that it's a fine place. Located on the west side of the Berryville public square in the former courthouse, the center contains a wealth of artifacts from the early days of the county. Aside from the aforementioned still, another interesting item is the old-time funeral parlor (probably handy for those who imbibed too heavily from the still).

🐾 ✐ ♿ **Saunders Museum** (870-423-2563; www.berryvillear.com/history.htm), 113 Madison, Berryville, Ark. Apr. 15–Dec. 30, Mon.–Sat. 10:30–7. $3 adults, $1.50 ages 6–12. If you like old guns, you'll like the Saunders Museum. They've a bunch of them here, the collection of the late Colonel D. B. Saunders, not to mention knives, antiques, and a variety of Victorian artifacts. You'll discover that the firearms are definitely not of the generic style, as some in the collection belonged to the likes of Wild Bill Hickock, Pancho Villa, and the notorious Jesse James.

SAUNDERS MUSEUM

⌀ ⅄ **Abundant Memories Heritage Village** (479-253-6764 www.abundant memories.com), 2434 SR 23 N., Eureka Springs, Ark. Open May–Oct., daily 9:30–3:30. Historama shows are held at 10:30 AM. $8.50 adults, $3.50–4.50 kids. The re-creation of American history is the genre of Abundant Memories. The grounds contain 25 buildings loaded to the gills with antiques and artifacts. The most popular stop in the village is the **Historama Show**, a live rendition of American history performed on five stages.

⌀ ⅄ **Frog Fantasies Museum and Gift Shop** (479-253-7227; www.frog fantasies.com), 151 Spring St., Eureka Springs, Ark. It's a fact that you can draw more flies with honey than you can with vinegar. It's also a fact that you can draw more frogs with flies than you can with vinegar. This is why vinegar has low self-esteem; its uses are quite limited. At any rate, you'll find here a 7,000-piece collection of amphibians, created from every material under the sun. There is also a gift shop where you can pick up things froggy. After a tour in this establishment, you may have the urge to hit the closest restaurant and order frog legs.

⌀ ⅄ **Aviation Cadet Museum** (1-800-643-4972; www.aviationcadet.com), 542 CR 2073, Eureka Springs, Ark. Wed.–Sat. 10–5. $12 adults, $7 ages 5–12. Located at Silver Wings Field, this museum honors the fliers and support staff who have protected America's skies. All branches of service, including the U.S. Army Air Corps, Air Force, Navy, Marines, and Coast Guard, are represented. The permanent displays include not only a wealth of historic information but also an F-105 and an F-100.

⌀ **Eureka Springs Historical Museum** (479-253-9417; www.eshm.org), 95 S. Main St., Eureka Springs, Ark. The architecture of the **Calif House**, site of the Eureka Springs Historical Museum, is a perfect example of the classic homes to be found in this amazing little town. The structure was built in 1889 as a private residence, and since 1971 it has played host to the museum that celebrates the town (which, with its 62 separate springs, was at one time was America's premier Victorian health spa town). There are three floors of artifacts to be viewed, as well as hands-on exhibits and a historic log cabin. The ESHM is open all year, Mon.–Sat. 9–4 and Sun. 11–4. Dec.–Feb., the facility is closed on Mon. Admission and tours vary, but in a good way. A self-guided tour is $5 adults, $2.50 kids. A tour by a costumed guide is $8 per person with a minimum of eight people (reservations required). Finally, those who are really into their history can be led through the museum and around Eureka spots of note by local historian Sondra Torchia. The cost is $17.50 per person, and reservations are necessary.

⌀ ⅄ **Arkansas Air Museum** (479-521-4947; www.arkairmuseum.org), S. School Ave. and US 71, Fayetteville, Ark. Mon.–Fri. 11–4:30, Sat. 10–4:30, Sun. 11–4:30. $4 adults, $2.50 ages 6–12. A recommended stop by the History Channel, this museum features racing planes from the 1920s and '30s, as well as an early airliner and everything from Vietnam-era helicopters to navy fighters. The displays rotate on a regular basis, as almost all of these craft are fully restored and are flown to different parts of the country from time to time. The museum also features engines, engineering, and a history of Arkansas aviation. Best of all, show up in mid-June around Father's Day for Airfest, a fantastic air show.

Clinton House Museum (1-877-245-6445; www.clintonhousemuseum .com), 930 California Dr., Fayetteville, Ark. Generally open Tue.–Sat. 9–4. Not only was this the first home of former president Bill Clinton and wife Senator Hillary Clinton, but the couple were also married right in the living room. Inside, you'll find memorabilia of Bill Clinton's campaigns, a replica of Hillary's wedding dress, items on loan from the Clinton Museum in Little Rock, and of course a gift shop. For those with a hankering for all things Clinton, this is a must-stop. That said, it should be noted that the gift shop does not include any photos of Monica Lewinsky, Gennifer Flowers, or any of Bill's other girlfriends.

Headquarters House Museum and Garden (479-521-2970; www .washcohistoricalsociety.org), 118 E. Dickson St., Fayetteville, Ark. It's a mystery how this 1853 Greek Revival home survived the Civil War. The Battle of Fayetteville took place (literally) on its front yard, and both Union and Confederate troops used it at one time or another as a headquarters. While the museum office and gift shop are open Sat. 10–noon, you need to call ahead for exact hours of tours and prices. These vary, and a guided tour of both Headquarters House and other historic Fayetteville locales ranges from 35 minutes to 2 hours, costing $7–27 per person.

Arkansas Country Doctor Museum (479-824-4307; www.drmuseum .net), 107 N. Starr Ave., Lincoln, Ark. Wed.–Sat. 1–4 PM. Admission is free, but they'll happily accept a donation. There are allegedly but two country doctor museums in America; this is one. Opening in 1994, this museum served as both a home and clinic to three different Lincoln doctors 1936–1973; it's now both a tribute to country doctors everywhere and a historical record of the times. You'll see medical instruments, an antique horse and buggy, a vintage car, and loads of Ozarkian medical paraphernalia.

Daisy Airgun Museum (479-986-6873; www.daisymuseum.com), 202 W. Walnut St., Rogers, Ark. Tue.–Sat. 10–5. $2 adults; kids 16 and under are admitted free. What started out in Michigan as the Plymouth Iron Windmill Co. would become the best-known BB gun manufacturer in the world. Daisy, founded in 1895, has sold what was for countless Americans their very first shooting iron. It's perhaps most famous for the Red Ryder model. Though the company left Rogers in the 1990s (guns are now assembled in an underground plant at Neosho, Mo.), both the corporate offices and museum are still located here. In the museum you will not only find the long and interesting history of Daisy, but also a collection of airguns that, believe it or not, date from the late 1600s. Of course there is a Daisy gift shop, where you can pick up a few

DAISY AIRGUN MUSEUM

memories of your journey into BB gun history (and you don't even have to worry about putting an eye out).

♦ ✐ & **Rogers Historical Museum** (479-621-1154; www.rogersarkansas.com/museum), 322 S. 2nd St., Rogers, Ark. Open May–Oct., Mon.–Fri. 10–4. Admission is free. One of the best-respected museums in the state of Arkansas, the Rogers Historical Museum offers a tour of the **1895 Hawkins House**, re-created with authenticity to demonstrate how the average family lived at the turn of the last century. The 1st Street exhibit is a true-to-life rendition of an 1880s bank, barbershop, and general store of the late 1800s in downtown Rogers. The Attic, a favorite with kids, features a replica of a Victorian-era attic; nonadults are allowed to try on old clothes, play with books and toys, crank an old phone, and type on a manual typewriter. The museum is loaded with countless items and offers a rotating selection of new and interesting presentations and exhibits.

♦ ✐ & **Shiloh Museum of Ozark History** (479-750-8165; www.springdale.com/shiloh), 118 W. Johnson Ave., Springdale, Ark. Mon.–Sat. 10–5. Admission is free. This 21,000-square-foot facility, with beautiful grounds and six historical buildings, holds more than 100,000 pieces and more than 400,000 photographs. You can wander for literally days in this place and still not see everything. There is a huge collection of Indian and prehistoric artifacts; eight other collections include everything from World War I items to household objects, furniture, tools, and much more. Just a few of the permanent exhibits are Native American, Pioneer, Folkways, and Serving Our Country. This museum tells the entire story of the Arkansas Ozark region.

CULTURAL SITES ♦ ✐ & **Wal-Mart Visitor's Center** (479-273-1329; www.walmartstores.com), 105 N. Main St., Bentonville, Ark. You probably shouldn't go through Bentonville without stopping at old Sam Walton's original five-and-dime. This humble building serves as a museum for the world's largest retailer and offers a history of the firm. Admission is free.

THE ORIGINAL WAL-MART

✐ & **Blue Spring Heritage Center** (479-253-9244; www.bluespringheritage.com), US 62 W., Eureka Springs, Ark. Mar. 15–Thanksgiving, 9–6. $7.25 adults, $4 ages 10–17. Focusing heavily on modern impressions of the Indian culture, this heritage center offers a historic film, interactive classes, trails, an old mill site, and the remnants of a Bluff Dweller's cave. Used by the Osage Indians as a trading post, Blue Spring was also a stop for Cherokee forced to march the Trail of Tears in 1839. The spring itself, with its deep blue lagoon, pumps out 38 million gallons of water per day.

⚲ ✍ ♿ **Arts Center of the Ozarks**
(479-751-5441; www.artscenterofthe
ozarks.org), 214 S. Main St., Springdale, Ark. A complete center for both
the performing and visual arts, this
center features classes, plays, an art
gallery, and numerous musical events.
The hours of the gallery itself are
8:30–5 during the school year, 9–5 in
summer, and 9–3 on Sat. For prices
and times of performances, contact
the box office.

🌿 ✍ ♿ *Christ of the Ozarks* (1-866-
566-3565; www.greatpassionplay.com),

CHRIST OF THE OZARKS

935 Passion Play Rd., Eureka Springs,
Ark. Located on the site of *The Great Passion Play* (the most attended outdoor
drama in the country). Visitors who take their religion literally may well assume
from this statue that Jesus was really tall and really white. The huge sculpture
of Christ, standing atop Magnetic Mountain, is more than 250 feet tall, weighs
more than 2 million pounds, and was constructed of 24 layers of white mortar
applied on a steel frame. Remarkably, sculptor Emmet Sullivan (who assisted
in the creation of Mount Rushmore) fashioned the statue completely by hand.
Christ of the Ozarks is open for viewing 24 hours a day, and admission is free.

HISTORIC SITES ∞ ✍ ♿ **Queen Anne Mansion** (479-253-8825 or 1-800-626-
7466; www.queenannemansion.com), 115 W. Van Buren St., Eureka Springs, Ark.
This huge home, originally located in Carthage, Mo., was built in 1891. Apparently needing a change of locale, it was moved, piece by piece over a 2-year
period ending in 1985, to Eureka Springs. Featured in *Southern Living* magazine, the mansion boasts nearly $500,000 worth of antiques and is listed on the
National Register of Historic Places. It's more than just a tourist site; you can
also stay in one of the seven guest rooms, throw a party, or have your wedding
here. Call the proprietors for rates and detailed information.

🌿 ✍ **Quigley's Castle** (479-253-8311; www.quigleyscastle.com), SR 23 S., Eureka
Springs, Ark. Open for tours Apr. 1–Oct. 31, 8:30–5; closed Sun. and Thu. $5.50
adults; ages 14 and under are admitted free. When Ozarkers take a notion to
involve themselves in a project, they at times get carried away. This is the case
with the home of the late Elise Quigley, whose love of rocks and flowers became
a lifelong passion that was integrated into her dream home. The home, built in
1943 and on the National Register of Historic Places, features a perennial garden with more than 400 varieties of flowers, garden paths, bird baths, and tropi-
cal plants (the latter being inside the home, with some species stretching to the
second story). A native of Italy, Elise Fiovanti married Albert Quigley during the
Depression. He promised her a dream home and, good to his word, built the 32-
window home with timber cut from their own property. It's a great story, and a
labor of love you won't want to miss.

⬭ 🐾 ✏ ♿ **Thorncrown Chapel** (479-253-7401; www.thorncrown.com), 12968 US 62 W., Eureka Springs, Ark. According to architect E. Fay Jones, the style of the Thorncrown Chapel is "Ozark Gothic." With more than 6,000 square feet of glass and 425 windows, the chapel was constructed from all-organic materials and rises 48 feet high. As inspiration, Jones chose the St.-Chappelle in Paris, and his design won the 1981 American Institute of Architecture National Honor Award. Thorncrown ranked fourth on the AIA's list of the Top 10 Buildings of the 20th Century. A nondenominational chapel, Thorncrown is the premier location for weddings in Eureka Springs, and in fact has attracted happy couples from around the world. Also on the site is the **Thorncrown Worship Center** (also designed by Jones), which seats 300 and features a 75-foot glass steeple and a 50-foot-tall window. Thorncrown Chapel is open Apr.–Nov., 9–5; Mar–Dec., 11–4. Closed Jan.–Feb. Sunday services are held Apr.–Oct., 9–11 AM. From October through the third week in December a single service is held at 11 AM. There is no charge to tour the chapel and grounds, though donations are accepted. For information on wedding packages, call the Thorncrown directly at the number above.

🐾 ✏ **War Eagle Mill** (479-789-5343; www.wareaglemill.com), 11045 War Eagle Rd., Rogers, Ark. Mar.–Dec., daily 8:30–5; open weekends only Jan.–Feb. Located on the War Eagle River, the reconstructed mill is actually the fourth such structure to be built on the same spot. The first mill, dating from the 1830s, was washed out in a flood. The second mill, which went up in 1848, was burned by a Confederate general to prevent the Yankees from taking it. The third mill came to be in 1873, and a century later it was completely refurbished by the new owners. Today the 18-foot undershot waterwheel is the only operating type of its kind in the United States. The stone buhr grinders are still milling today, and more than 25 varieties of organically grown grains, conrmeals, flours, and buckwheats are offered for sale. The mill is also loaded with crafts, and the gift shop features such items as graniteware dishes, kitchen items, knives, jams and jellies, and literally hundreds of other items. This is also the site of the renowned War Eagle antiques and craft show in early May, and close to the War Eagle Mill arts and crafts fair. Last but not least, the mill is also home to the **Bean Palace Restaurant**, open for breakfast, lunch, and teatime.

WAR EAGLE MILL

Beaver Bridge. Located north of Eureka Springs on SR 187 is a 1949 suspension bridge (still in use) that

you won't believe exists. Crossing the White River, Beaver Bridge is 554 feet in
total length, with a main span of 312 feet. The bridge is only open to one-way
traffic and has a weight limit of 10 tons. Bring the camera.

ZOOS ✍ ♿ **Turpentine Creek Exotic Wildlife Refuge** (479-253-5841; www
.turpentinecreek.org), 239 Turpentine Creek Lane, Eureka Springs, Ark. Open
9–6 (5 during Daylight Saving Time) every day but Christmas. $15 adults, $10
kids and seniors. This refuge, dedicated to saving neglected or mistreated big
cats and other critters, contains more than 100 lions, tigers, and leopards, not
to mention bears, monkeys, deer, and birds. At this facility you can not only view
the cats, but also sleep with them. This is not meant to imply that the animals
are of limited virtue, but rather to inform that the refuge is also the site of the
Call of the Wild Bed and Breakfast.

✍ ♿ **Wild Wilderness Drive-Thru Safari** (479-736-8383), 20923 Safari Rd.,
Gentry, Ark. Hours are 8 AM–dusk daily. $7 adults, $6 kids. During the nearly
6-mile drive through this park you will encounter rhinos, hippos, giraffes, alligators, bears, and leopards. Situated on more than 200 acres, more than 100
species either roam about freely or are contained behind high fences. In addition there are foot trails (no worries, they don't go into big-carnivore country)
and a petting zoo.

✳ To Do

FOR FAMILIES Also see *Zoos*, above.

∞ ✍ ♿ ***Belle of the Ozarks*** (479-253-6200 or 1-800-552-3803; www.estc.net/
belle), 354 CR 146, Eureka Springs, Ark. Cruising May–Oct. at 11 AM, 1 PM, and
3 PM (as well as a 6 PM evening cruise Memorial Day–Labor Day), the *Belle* sets
sail every day but Wed. $17 adults, $7.50 for kids under 12 .Travelers are taken
on a 1¼-hour tour of Beaver Lake covering 60 miles of shoreline. The captain of
the *Belle* narrates the excursion, pointing out such sites as a Bluff Dweller burial
ground, Whitney Mountain, Whitehouse Bluffs, and Beaver Dam. If you choose,
and have a willing partner, you can even hold your wedding on the *Belle*.

✍ ♿ **Dinosaur World** (501-253-8113; www.billyhill.com/dinosaurworld), 8608
SR 187, Eureka Springs, Ark. Open Mar.–Dec. 9–6, and open seven days a week
in summer. $4 adults, $3.50 seniors, $2.50 ages 4–12. It may not be Jurassic
Park, but it's the next best thing. Where else but Eureka Springs could you trip
across a 65-acre park full of 90 giant prehistoric reptiles and a four-story King
Kong? Right next to Beaver Dam, at this park you can wander amid the dinosaur
replicas, enjoy a picnic by the lake, or cast your line for a few fish. If you want to
wean your kids from the horrors of Barney, bring them here. After Dinosaur
World the purple menace may well lose his oddly hypnotic and larger-than-life
appeal. The park includes a gift shop.

✍ **Eureka Springs Ghost Tours** (479-253-6800; www.eureka-springs-ghost
.com), 75 Prospect Ave., Eureka Springs, Ark. There is something about Eureka
Springs that is a tad reminiscent of Savannah, Ga., or New Orleans. For those
who want to search for spooks and sprites, this ghost tour may just part the

curtain to "the other side." The company, which is located in Suite 212 of the historic **Crescent Hotel**, offers a couple of different tours. The first is a tour of the Crescent itself, constructed in 1886 and regarded as Eureka's finest lodging by 19th-century Victorians. You'll learn history, but also hear tales of the mysterious "Lady in the Garden" and travel below the hotel to what was once an early cancer hospital. Tours begin at 8 PM and cost $17.50 adults, $7 kids. Another tour winds its way through the eerie and historic **Eureka Springs Cemetery**. You'll hear all the folklore, have a look at the elaborate monuments, and ponder the questions of mortality. $15 adults, $7 ages 9 and under; tours are held May–Oct., Fri.–Sat. at 8 PM. It should be noted that children under 16 are not allowed on these tours unless accompanied by an adult.

✦ ♿ **Arkansas & Missouri Railroad** (479-751-8600 or 1-800-687-8600; www .arkmorr.com), 306 E. Emma St., Springdale, Ark. If you'd like to see the Ozarks the way travelers viewed them 100 years ago, climb aboard for this railway excursion. You'll enjoy riding in fully restored passenger cars with inlaid mahogany interiors, and the crew of the train will offer tidbits of info and trivia on the region. The Arkansas & Missouri features several different round trips (you depart and arrive back at your original depot by 4:30 PM) from Springdale to Van Buren (a 134-mile jaunt with a 2½-hour stopover for dining and shopping), Van Buren to Winslow (a 70-mile trip with great scenery and passing through the Winslow Tunnel), and Fort Smith to Winslow (a 3-hour tour with historic narration). You can ride in coach, an upgrade, or first class; the two latter options provide either lunch or snack bar and a souvenir photo. Departure times vary, and regular schedules are May–Dec., with a variety of specialty holiday rides at other times of year. Prices range from $15 for kids to $65 for adults.

✦ ♿ **Eureka Springs & North Arkansas Railway** (479-253-9263; www .esnrailway.com), 299 Main St., Eureka Springs, Ark. Open for regular excursions Apr.–Oct., the ESNA takes you back in time as you explore the Ozark hills from a 1940s diesel choo-choo. Not only can you ride this locomotive and listen to a historical presentation by the conductor, but you can also view a wealth of railroad artifacts and memorabilia. Excellent dinner service is available on the Eurekan Dining Car (see *Eating Out*). The trains take a 4.5-mile trek through the hills surrounding Eureka Springs and are available Tue.–Sat. at 10:30 AM, noon, 2 PM, and 4 PM. $10 adults, $5 ages 4–10.

THE ESNA RAILROAD

🔊 ✦ ♿ **World's Largest Wind Chime** (479-253-5288), 381 SR 23 S., Eureka Springs, Ark. Erected by artist Ranaga Farbiarz in the parking lot of the **Celestial Windz Harmonic Bizaar**, this chime is roughly 32 feet long. The deepest-toned tube is 20 feet long, and the shortest, higher-pitched tube is 14 feet. The giant chime (and without doubt your neighbors would love you if you placed it a few feet from their bedroom window) is free for public viewing.

GOLF Golfing in Bella Vista, Ark. If you're truly a golf nut and plan to retire in Arkansas, you would be wise to check out Bella Vista. This place might not be for everyone, in that it's a master-planned, unincorporated community of nearly 17,000 (which means lots of owner association rules). However, the golf courses here are excellent. The community's 18-hole courses include the **Bella Vista Country Club**, the **Kingswood**, the **Berksdsale**, the **Highlands**, the **Scotsdale**, and the **DogWood Hills**. Nine-hole courses are the **Brittany** and the **Branchwood**. Now, this is all well and good if you're a member or resident, but it appears that visitors to the area need to be sanctioned guests to play. For further information, you'll need to call 479-855-8172 and discuss rates and times with the powers that be.

☙ **Razorback Park Golf Course** (479-443-5862), 2514 W. Lori Dr., Fayetteville, Ark. An excellent value open to the public, this 18-hole course in Fayetteville is open year-round. Best of all, greens fees are less than $15.

☙ **Stonebridge Meadows Golf Club** (479-571-3673; www.stonebridge meadows.com), 3495 E. Goff Farms Rd., Fayetteville, Ark. Rated as one of the top 10 golf courses in the state by *Golf Digest* magazine, Stonebridge Meadows is an 18-hole public course with a 13-acre practice area and clubhouse with snack bar. It's a good value: The greens fees cover everything (including cart, tees, and range balls). Rates are $32 weekdays and $42 on weekends. Be prepared to hit long, for there are two 520-yard holes on this course. Stonebridge Meadows is open year-round, seven days a week.

The Creeks Golf Course (479-248-1000; www.realark.com/creeks), 1599 S. Main St., SR 112 S., Cave Springs, Ark. An 18-hole course convenient to both Springdale and Bentonville, the Creeks offers a full round of Mon.–Fri. golf for $20 per round (or $33.60 with cart). Play on the weekends and the price is $25.75 (or $39.80 with cart).

Big Sugar Golf Club (479-451-9550; www.bigsugargolfclub.com), 12122 E. Sugar Creek Rd., Pea Ridge, Ark. Open every day except Mon., this 18-hole championship course is part of the Big Sugar residential community. However, the course is open to the public. Fees for 18 holes and a full cart are $30 on weekdays and $34 on weekends. Also located within this pretty 165 acres is a practice range, putting green, pro shop, and food and beverage area.

☙ **Prairie Creek Country Club** (479-925-2114; www.realark.com/pc), SR 12 E. and Country Club Rd., Rogers, Ark. A bargain of a course, Prairie Creek was rated the fourth best public course in Arkansas in 1996 by *Golf Digest*. Over the years more accolades have followed from the likes of *USA Today* and the *Arkansas Democrat-Gazette*. An 18-hole course, the upper 9 of this course traverse the top of a ridge, while the bottom 9 wind through a valley. An all-day greens fee (as many holes as you'd like to play) is $16 on weekdays and $18 on weekends. Cart rates are $20 for 18 holes, but walking is also allowed. Prairie Creek is open all year.

🐾 ✐ ♿ 🐾 **Ozark National Forest** (479-968-2354; www.fs.fed.us/oonf/ozark). With 1.2 million acres, the Ozark National Forest offers literally anything the outdoorsperson could desire. From hiking, biking, and horseback riding to floating, kayaking, picnicking, and camping, this sprawling and rugged forest is a cavalcade of bluffs, mountains, rivers, and trees. The sections that lie within the region covered in this chapter begin roughly 25 miles south of Fayetteville off I-540. You can camp basically anywhere in the ONF for free (if you don't mind roughing it). If you choose one of the established campgrounds that has a day-use area (and they are prevalent), the fee is generally $3 per car. Some areas offer cabins (historic) that generally run in the $30–100 per night range. Note that, if you're visiting in summer, Arkansas is noted for its ticks, chiggers, and snakes. Also, for campers and hikers, the black bear population is on the increase. Occasionally a traveler will stumble across one of these critters in the woods (it's rare—bears are shy by nature—but it does happen from time to time), and the old maxim regarding "an ounce of prevention" is a dandy policy to keep in mind. It's not a bad idea to carry pepper spray. Also, the tactic sometimes applied to grizzly bears (falling down and playing dead) does not work on black bears. They'll just think you're supper. Make plenty of noise, wave your arms, and try not to lose control of bodily functions while you look for a tree to climb.

Baker Prairie. Found within the city limits of Harrison, Baker Prairie is a 71-acre area co-managed by The Nature Conservancy and the Arkansas Natural Heritage Commission. Integrated in the Arkansas System of Natural Areas in 1991, this open field is a wonder of wildflowers and native grasses. It is, in fact, all that's left of this region's much-vaunted tallgrass prairie. Bring your camera, particularly in spring and summer. Such beauties as Indian paintbrush, shooting star, and pale purple cornflower are just a sample of the flora that abounds on this natural palette.

Pivot Rock and **Natural Bridge** (479-253-8860), 1708 Pivot Rd., Eureka Springs, Ark. Found right in Eureka Springs, back in the trees via a three-block walking trail, is Pivot Rock. This is one of those odd, natural geological formations that become the hallmark of many a family photo or visitors center postcard. If you're into odd rocks, take the short stroll and snap a picture or two. Let's just say the rock is unusually top heavy.

PARKS 🐾 🐾 ✐ ♿ **Withrow Springs State Park** (479-559-2593; www.arkansas stateparks.com/withrowsprings), 33424 SR 23, Huntsville, Ark. Located about 5 miles north of Huntsville, this 732-acre park is best known for the waters that spill out of a small cave at the base of a steep bluff. The spring, named for Richard Withrow (who established the area's first gristmill on the site in 1832), spills into a deep and pretty pond. This is a peaceful place, with War Eagle Creek flowing along, heavy forests, and the aforementioned protective bluffs. Many folks enjoy tossing a line for catfish, bluegill, and bass at Withrow, but you can also take a canoe float, swim, hike, play a game of tennis, enjoy baseball and softball fields, or make like Robin Hood on the crossbow range. Camping at Withrow is facilitated by 30 nearly new sites with water, 50-amp electric, and sewer hookups ($25.50 per night). There are four different tent sites ($9), 16 sites with electricity and water ($15.50 per night), and five sites with electricity and water for tents only ($13 per night). The campgrounds also offers a bath-house that is handicapped accessible.

🐾 ✂ ♿ **Pea Ridge National Military Park** (479-451-8122; www.nps.gov/peri), US 62 E., Pea Ridge, Ark. Set on 4,300 acres, Pea Ridge pays tribute to the strategically critical 1862 Civil War battle that forced Missouri to remain in the Union. On March 7–8 of that year, 16,000 Confederates battled 10,250 Union troops, unsuccessfully, and the course of the War Between the States was changed forever. A complete visitors center is at the park entry and features both an interesting museum and a movie titled *Thunder in the Ozarks*. Later, you can embark on a 7-mile, 10-stop, self-guided driving tour that will show the progress of the battle and the various events that transpired during those two days of blood and bullets. Also in the park is a hiking trail and backcountry horse trail. Pea Ridge is open year-round, daily 8–5. visitors center hours are Mon.– Fri. 9:30–4, Sat.–Sun. 8–5. Entrance fees are $3 per person for those ages 17–61 (or $5 maximum per vehicle).

🐾 🐾 ✂ ♿ **Prairie Grove Battlefield State Park** (479-846-2990; www .arkansasstateparks.com/prairiegrovebattlefield), 506 E. Douglas, Prairie Grove, Ark. The year 1862 was a nasty one in Arkansas, and on December 7, 2,700 sol-diers lost their lives at the Battle of Prairie Grove. Revered by Confederate vet-erans and their families for decades after the battle, the site became a state park in 1971. Today, thanks to additional purchases of land, more than 750 acres of the original battlefield have been preserved. This has led to Prairie Grove being recognized as one of the best-preserved Civil War battlefields in America. Com-ing here, you walk the ridges and valleys that witnessed the worst of the carnage, stroll along the 1-mile **Battlefield Trail**, or take a 6.5-mile driving tour. If you show up in December of an even-numbered year, you will witness one of the best battle reenactments known to humankind. Also on the site is a museum, a pre–Civil War Ozark village, and plenty of picnic tables. Admission to the park is free, but if you wish to explore the museum and take a self-guided tour of the buildings, the charge is $2.75 adults, $1.75 ages 6–12. Even better, opt for the museum and guided tour, which is only $4.50 adults, $2.50 kids.

🐾 🐾 ✂ ♿ **Devil's Den State Park** (479-761-3325 or 1-800-264-2417; www .arkansasstatepark.com/devilsden), 11333 W. SR 74, West Fork, Ark. At 2,500 acres, Devil's Den is known for its scenery, rustic cabins, and 8-acre lake. You'll find plenty of campsites as well as hiking, biking, and horse trails, not to mention a park café, store, and swimming pool. The stone cabins, built in the 1930s by the Civilian Conservation Corps, have all been modernized and come with full kitchen, heating and air-conditioning, and stone fireplace. Options and rates range from a studio cabin at $95 per night to a three-bedroom, two-bath version at $170 per night. There are 97 campsites in the park, and they run the gamut from primitive tent sites ($8) to spots with electric and water ($17.50). If you brought along a horse, a campsite for you and Trigger is $13. If playing in the water is your specialty, you can rent canoes, kayaks, pedal boats, and water bikes. For fishing, just make sure you have obtained an Arkansas license. Caving is very popular at Devil's Den (hence the name), and **Devil's Den Cave** is a 550-foot-long sandstone hole in the wall. Make sure to bring a flashlight lest you bonk your head in the dark. More than 20 miles of well-marked horse-riding trails traverse the Lee Creek Valley, in which Devil's Den is situated. If you're in good shape, the 15-mile **Butterfield Hiking Trail** should provide all the ambulatory amusement your legs and stand. Just remember that, just as in the Missouri Ozarks, the ticks and bugs can get pretty vicious in spring and summer.

✿ 🐾 ✎ ♿ **Hobbs State Park–Conservation Area** (479-789-2380; www .arkansasstateparks.com/hobbsstateparkconservationarea), 21392 E. SR 12, Rogers, Ark. Comprising 11,964 acres (along the south shore of 28,370-acre Beaver Lake), Hobbs is located roughly 10 miles east of Rogers on SR 12 and always undergoing further development. Visitors to this park will discover a number of hiking trails, a 17-mile multiuse trail, a public shooting range, and seasonal hunting. One of the best trails is the ADA-accessible **Van Winkle**, a 0.5-mile trek that passes under SR 12 via a large tunnel and leads hikers to the site of the historic Van Winkle lumber mill and home. More visitor services are in the planning stages at Hobbs—in the future expect cabins, more trails, and a 17,000-square-foot visitors center.

LAKES ✎ ✿ ♿ 🐾 **Beaver Lake** (479-636-1210; www.swl.usace.army.mil/parks/ beaver), 2260 N. 2nd St., Rogers, Ark. With 28,370 acres and 487 acres of shoreline, Beaver Lake (the headwaters of the White River) is one of the most popular recreation areas in Northwest Arkansas. Spring and fall are particularly gorgeous, as the area is loaded with redbud and dogwood trees. Fall is equally as colorful, offering a cornucopia of colors. Add in a plethora of limestone bluffs, caves, and the endless water-sports opportunities, and you have the makings of a perfect getaway. Managed by the Army Corps of Engineers, Beaver was completed in 1966. The corps has provided 12 developed parks featuring 650 individual campsites, available (with electricity) for $16 per night. The campgrounds are modern, with paved roads, fresh water, showers, rest rooms, dump stations, and fire rings. Within seven of the parks are full-service marinas with gas, groceries, guides, and boat rental. Numerous private outfitters of all sorts surround Beaver Lake, and the body of water is known for some fine bass fishing. However, those who want a real thrill should try and hook some of the monster catfish and hideously ugly spoonbill that inhabit the depths.

BEAVER LAKE DAM

✿ ✎ 🐾 **Lake Leatherwood** (479-253-2866), 532 Spring St., Eureka Springs, Ark. A spring-fed body of water, the 85-acre Lake Leatherwood lies within the midst of the 1,600-acre Lake Leatherwood Park. Trails for hiking and mountain biking abound, and the lake itself is popular with local fishermen. Keep your eyes open, and you are likely to spy plenty of herons, wild turkeys, and bald eagles.

CAVES ✍ **Cosmic Cavern** (870-749-2298; www.cosmiccavern.com), 6386 SR 21 N., Berryville, Ark. Contrary to popular belief, the blind trout found in the subterranean lakes at Cosmic Cavern do not wear dark glasses or utilize the assistance of Seeing Eye bass. Still, both the sight-impaired fish and the cave itself are worth a look. This is the site of Arkansas's largest underground lake (in fact, there are two lakes), and the 1¼-hour tour leads through a number of rooms and across a rock bridge. You can even pan for gems in an authentic sluice if you wish, and to keep everything requires only a $5.50 surcharge. As a rule the cave is open at 9 AM daily Mar.–Jan., with closing time around 5 PM depending on the time of year. Jan. 1–Mar. 3, Cosmic Caverns is closed except for weekends and by appointment. Tour fees are $11.98 adults, $6.50 ages 5–12.

✍ 🐾 **War Eagle Cavern on Beaver Lake** (479-789-2909; www.wareagle cavern.com), 21494 Cavern Dr., Rogers, Ark. When you see the entrance to this cave, located in a box canyon, you will feel you are about to descend to the farthest depths of the earth. Open since 1978, War Eagle Cavern remains a very natural cave, and a wide, smooth walkway follows a creek that runs inside this subterranean attraction. If you're wondering about the difficulty of the trek, a person of average condition will have no problems. Plus, you will encounter no stairs. The guided public tour takes about an hour (roughly 0.5 mile). Tours leave on the hour and half hour, and if your dog is on a leash, he can come along, too. $9.75 adults, $5.25 ages 4–11. A more extensive journey, the Spelunker Tour, requires a couple of hours and heads much deeper into the cave. This excursion is by reservation only and has a few restrictions. First off, you must be at least 4 feet tall and have a minimum group of four people. You'll see all sorts of strange formations and literally thousands and thousands of bats. Oh, lest you think this is a clean tour, please be advised that you will get both wet and muddy. Spelunkers must sign a release, wear appropriate clothes (jeans, a jacket, gloves, knee pads, and hiking shoes), and carry a couple of flashlights. The Spelunker Tour runs $29.95 per person and is only available July–Nov., as a colony of 75,000 bats hibernates in the deep cavern Nov.–Mar.; they're normally busy caring for their young until July 1.

✍ **Old Spanish Treasure Cave** (479-787-6508; www.spanish-treasure-cave.com), 14290 N. SR 59, Sulphur Springs, Ark. As the story goes (and keep in mind that most Ozark stories should be taken with portions of salt ranging from a grain to a pound), about 300 years back Spanish conquistadores buried a $40 million treasure in this cave. Now, there *have* been a few helmets, coins, and pieces of armor found in this cavern, so who knows? The only certain fact is that more than a few people spent years looking for the booty, and it's yet to turn up. The Spanish Treasure Cave offers several tours, but for the best look, you should opt for the Adventure Tour. You'll be guided deep into the earth (at $30 per person) and need to bring along your gloves, boots, hard hat, and three flashlights. And yes, you will get dirty. The cave is open 9–5 in Mar. (closed Wed.–Thu.) and daily 9–6 in Apr.–May. Hours are extended to 9–7 June–Sep.

𝓢 **Mystic Caverns** (870-743-1739 or 1-888-743-1739; www.mysticcaverns.com), SR 7 S., Harrison, Ark. Mar.–Dec., 9–5. $11.95 adults, $5.95 kids. Although it's had many names over the years, Mystic Caverns was once a part of the often maligned, now defunct amusement park known as Dogpatch USA. Now, I happened to like Dogpatch USA when I was a kid (good rides and amusing Lil' Abner characters running to and fro), and thus can only state that detractors of the site were seriously humor impaired. Sadly, Dogpatch overestimated the draw of a Hillbilly-based funland and is now grown up in weeds. On the bright side, though, Mystic Caverns is still going strong. In fact, a tour of the cavern actually takes you into two separate caves. Mystic Caverns itself has all the normal formations you expect in a show cave, but the large **Crystal Dome Caverns** (discovered 100 years after Mystic) really do live up to their billing. You'll see an eight-story dome and some great crystal formations. It's a pretty place, a tad better than your average hole in the ground.

✳ Lodging

BED & BREAKFASTS There are so many lodging options in Eureka Springs—hotels, motels, luxury log cabins, and B&Bs—that space limitations do not allow an adequate description of all. For an excellent list, you should check out the **Alliance of Better Bed and Breakfasts** web site (www.allianceofbetterbandbs.com). Also, for a complete list of accommodations, go to the state of Arkansas's Eureka Springs lodging site (www .arkansas.com/attractions/ald_search_ lodging/r/Ozarks/city/Eureka+Springs). As you will see, the possibilities are nearly endless.

𝓢 **Beaver Town Inn and General Store** (1-888-819-0221; www.beaver towninn.com), 102 SR 187, Beaver, Ark. Located at the foot of the Beaver Bridge, the Beaver Town Inn offers five different rooms and suites located above the Beaver Town General Store. This is a beautiful place, a local hangout since the day it was built as a trading post in 1901. Now completely restored and refurbished, this native limestone inn's rooms run $80–120 per night. Just about 10 minutes from Eureka Springs, this is a nice choice

for those who wish to tour Eureka during the day and escape to some peace and quiet in the evening. Non-smoking rooms are available, and kids are okay.

𝓢 **11 Singleton House** (479-253-9111 or 1-800-833-3394; www.single tonhouse.com), 11 Singleton St., Eureka Springs, Ark. There's just something about this place that reminds me of the Hansel and Gretel gingerbread house. With its beautiful gardens, and a location tucked back into a hill just a block from the Eureka Springs Historic District, the 1890 Victorian is colorful, fun, and loaded with antiques and trails. Five guest rooms each feature a private bath, with one option further providing a Jacuzzi for two and a treetop balcony. Some rooms include two beds, and one will sleep up to five. Amenities include cable TV, air-conditioning, rockers on the porch, hot tea and cocoa, and a gourmet breakfast. Also on the property, if you wish more privacy, is the **Gardener's Cottage**, with fireplace, whirlpool tub, and full kitchen. Rates for the guest rooms range $69–125; the Gardener's Cot-

LUXURIOUS BOMB SHELTERS

⊙ ✿ ♿ **Beckham Creek Cave Haven** (888-371-2283: www.ozarkcave.com), HC 72, west on SR 327 from Parthenon, Ark. For what may be the strangest and most luxurious lodging in the entire Ozarks, you need to go underground. This cave house, residing amid a 530-acre estate, was originally built by the co-founder of the Celestial Seasonings Tea Company. Apparently, after viewing the 1980s end-of-the-world movie *The Day After*, the gentleman decided to build himself a little post-apocalyptic haven in Arkansas. When the end of the world failed to appear on schedule, his wife insisted he sell it. The present owners now allow travelers the chance to spend a night or a week in a lodging that's been featured on *Lifestyles of the Rich and Famous*, Home and Garden TV, *NBC Nightly News*, *People* magazine, *National Geographic*, *Four States Living*, and *The Barefoot Traveler*.

Though the chopper pad, blast-proof concrete walls, and private water system fed by an underground spring still exist, such is just the beginning. The great room alone measures 2,000 square feet, and there's a huge window that allows light in from outdoors. You might need this if you want to watch the satellite TV or enjoy the professional sound system. The kitchen is of chef quality, coming with all appliances and utensils, and between the kitchen and great room is a long bar with stools and a breakfast nook. Upstairs is a game room and recreation area with pool table and gaming table. Five bedrooms each feature a private bath, and each is themed (in the vein of presidential or honeymoon suites). Lest you suffer discomfort, central air and heat, as well as humidifiers, will keep you both cozy and dry. Beckham Creek Cave Haven can accommodate parties from 2 to 20 at one time, and there is a two-night minimum. Rates for two people begin at $450 per night. Weddings and family reunions are encouraged.

tage, $125–145. Pets and smoking indoors are not permitted, but kids are okay if they are housebroken and well behaved.

✿ ♿ **Call of the Wild Bed and Breakfast** (479-253-5841; www.turpentinecreek.org/b&b.htm), 239 Turpentine Creek Lane, Eureka Springs, Ark. The proprietors refer to this establishment on the Turpentine Creek Wildlife Refuge not as "bed and breakfast," but rather as "bed and big cats." There are several lodging options, all unique. The first is the Tree House, which sleeps two to four and is modeled after similar lodgings in Africa. Yes, you'll be able to see the big cats (as in *lions and tigers*) right from your window. The Tree House has a kitchen, bath with shower, refrigerator, microwave, double futon on the main floor, and loft with two double-futon pallets. You'll receive a continental breakfast and have unlimited admission to the refuge during daylight hours. The cost per night for two is $125. Other accommodations include two Call of the Wild Suites at $100 per night. Last but not least, an RV park is located outside the main compound and offers 10 spaces with either 30- or 50-amp service. Rates are $25 per day.

The Benton Place (479-253-7602 or 1-866-253-7602; www.eureka-usa.com/benton), 32 Benton St., Eureka Springs, Ark. With three Victorian suites ranging $125–145 per night, the Benton Place is known for its beautiful rooms, rock formations, gazebo, and intimate atmosphere. Two of the suites include a full kitchen, and all three offer such amenities as microwave, cable TV, in-house massage by appointment, private dining area, breakfast, and Jacuzzi for two. This establishment is geared for couples only, and a smoking area is provided. According to the *2004 Book of Lists* (published by *Inn Traveler* magazine), Benton place ranks as the sixth most intimate inn in America.

✍ ♿ **Johnson House** (479-756-1095; www.innsite.com/inns/A000413.html), 5371 S. 48th St., Johnson, Ark. This two-story home was built in 1882 by one Jacob Q. Johnson. Constructed of brick and featuring impressive 12-foot ceilings and 8-foot windows (not to mention an elaborate spiral staircase), the home is loaded with antiques. Quite a few of these are apparently heirlooms of the Johnson family. Three guest rooms, all with private bath, are priced at $65–85 per night. The nearly 2-acre grounds offer games such as horseshoes and croquet, and a full breakfast will start your day off on the right note. The little town of Johnson is located about halfway between Springdale and Fayetteville

and is convenient to the nightlife and shopping of both. Pets are forbidden, but kids are okay with prior approval. A designated smoking area is provided, and the home is partially handicapped accessible.

◎ ♿ **Maguire House Bed and Breakfast** (501-442-2122; http://members.aol.com/maguirebnb), 19154 SR 74, Elkins, Ark. Loaded with history, Maguire House is an antebellum home located just a few miles west of Fayetteville on SR 74. Built by state representative Hosea Maguire in the late 1800s, this inn is what a B&B should be. It's comfortable, in the sense that both the first glance—that of an old, white, family home—and the comfortable interior seem livable. Too many B&Bs make the mistake of feeling like a museum or art gallery, as if you shouldn't sit on the priceless antiques. Not this one. Set on more than 4 acres, Maguire House offers four bedrooms and two bathrooms upstairs. Guests are free to wander the orchard, check out the vegetable garden, watch the chickens, or just kick back in the parlor or gazebo. One great draw of this establishment is the food: Eggs are fresh from the resident hens, and the bread is homemade. Fruits and vegetables come straight from the orchard or garden. If your idea of breakfast is ham, fried potatoes, a three-cheese omelet, and lots of toast and homemade jam, this is the spot for you. Rates for two people are $65 per night, and small weddings are encouraged. Leave the pup at home, check on bringing kids, and smoke only in the designated areas.

♿ **Apple Crest Inn Bed and Breakfast** (479-736-8201 or 1-888-APPLE-US; www.bbonline.com/ar/

applecrest), 12758 S. SR 59, Gentry, Ark. With its brown roof, splashes of blue trim, huge chimney, turrets, and gables, the Apple Crest looks a bit like a gingerbread house that's been hitting the gym. Situated on 5 acres, this Victorian home and carriage house has its own claim to history, having first been deeded by President Rutherford B. Hayes. With nightly prices ranging $100–185, in 2005 Apple Crest was voted Best Bed and Breakfast in Northwest Arkansas by the readers of *Citiscapes* magazine. Five guest rooms are decorated with antiques and collectible items, and guests are met with chocolate truffles. There's a hot tub outdoors, a gourmet breakfast, and plenty of books, games, and TV in the common room. One room is handicapped accessible, but there is no smoking inside the home. As usual, it is wise to check with the innkeepers before you show up with a minivan full of children.

RESORTS ◯◯ ♂ ⭤ Hotel Seville

(870-741-2321 or 1-866-660-7136, www.hotelseville.com), 302 N. Main St., Harrison, Ark. By the time the Hotel Seville opened in 1929, total costs had topped the $150,000 mark (that was a truckload of greenbacks during the Great Depression). Now on the National Register of Historic Places, this "Spanish Castle of the Ozarks" was once the site of some of the swankiest affairs imaginable. You can just imagine the pomp and pageantry when you view the grand staircase, no doubt the site of many an impressive entrance. With its traditional Spanish Revival architecture, the hotel now provides the European plan in bed & breakfast style. All 12 suites offer a private bath and cable TV, as well as coffeemaker, kitchen-

ette, and refrigerator. Room rates include breakfast and range $55–120 per night. Within walking distance of the historic Harrison Square, the Seville permits neither pets nor smoking. This is a popular spot for weddings, and you should contact the hotel directly for prices and packages.

🦆 ♂ ⭤ **Lost Spur Crooked Creek Cabins** (870-743-SPUR or 1-800-774-2414; www.lostspur.com), 8148 Lost Spur Rd. Harrison, Ark. If you've come to Arkansas for some smallmouth bass fishing, Lost Spur can offer you a fine creek, nice cabins, and the chance to do some hiking as well. While the cabins aren't spectacularly fancy, they do offer TV, VCR, Jacuzzi, woodstove, fireplace, and air-conditioning. Weekday rates for two are $85, with the price rising to $95 on weekends. Cabins can comfortably sleep four, and the cost for additional guests is just $9.50 per night.

Palace Hotel and Bathhouse (479-253-7474; www.palacehotelbathhouse .com/palace.html), 135 Spring St., Eureka Springs, Ark. In operation since 1901 and on the National Register of Historic Places, the Palace was at one time considered one of the premier spots in Eureka Springs. At the turn of the 20th century this was the location where the rich and famous arrived to partake of the "healing" waters. Today the Palace still offers its famous spa to visitors, as well as eight guest suites. Each one features king-sized bed, double-sized tub, wet bar, refrigerator, cable TV, and Wi-Fi access. Victorian antiques are everywhere, and a continental breakfast is delivered to your room each morning. Rates are $140–165 per night, and all suites are nonsmoking. If you're here for the spa treatment, you will be met

PALACE HOTEL AND BATHHOUSE

by an attendant who will take you to your private bath. Or perhaps you would enjoy a eucalyptus steam in a traditional wooden-barrel steam cabinet? The services are many and include mineral bath ($15), eucalyptus steam treatment ($12), mask-clay treatment ($12), half-hour massage ($40), or full-hour massage ($60). Or you can receive all of the above for $63 ($79 with the full-hour massage).

 **1905 Basin Park Hotel** (479-253-7837 or 1-877-643-4972; www.basinpark.com), 12 Spring St., Eureka Springs, Ark. Located in the heart of Eureka Springs, the Basin Park offers 61 rooms (some smoking, some nonsmoking) with a variety of different suites ranging $89–219 per night. This is a very historic place, having at one time hosted the likes of Pretty Boy Floyd. *Ripley's Believe It or Not* has also profiled the Basin Park, as every room in the multistory building is at ground-floor level. This is because (a) the hotel was built into the side of a mountain, and (b) Eureka Springs lies more vertical than it does horizontal. While staying in the

Basin Park, you can also enjoy the Balcony Restaurant (see *Eating Out*) and a variety of spa services.

Grand Central Hotel (479-253-6756 or 1-800-344-6050; www.grandcentralresort.com), 37 N. Main St., Eureka Springs, Ark. With 14 suites ranging $119–219 per night, the Grand Central is on the National Register of Historic Places. This establishment has been totally renovated and features very high ceilings, some great oak woodwork, and English antiques. Within the hotel is the **Grande Taverne**, noted for its excellent food, complete lounge, and extensive wine list. A trip to Eureka Springs just wouldn't be complete without a trip to the spa, and the Grand Central can provide you with the full treatment. Massage, reflexology, paraffin dips, facial wraps, and a variety of other pampering services are available. Prices for services range from $40 for a half-hour massage to $200 for a package.

The Crescent Hotel and Spa (1-877-342-9766; www.crescent -hotel.com), 75 Prospect Ave., Eureka Springs, Ark. When constructed in the late 1800s at a price of nearly $300,000, the Crescent was regarded as one of the most luxurious hotels in the United States. Today its 71 rooms are still something special. Spa services (generally $40–200) are readily available at the **New Moon Day Spa and Salon**, and the Crystal Dining Room (see *Dining Out*) offers breakfast, lunch, dinner, and Sunday brunch. For pure relaxation, Dr. Baker's Lounge offers a full bar, big-screen TV, and live entertainment on weekends. Suites at the Crescent come in a variety of styles and with varying amenities: $129–279 per night.

🦫 🐾 🗡 ♿ **Fairwinds Mountain Cottages** (479-253-9465 or 1-800-242-3128; www.fairwindsmountain.com), 637 CR 111, Eureka Springs, Ark. With their stone fireplaces, vaulted ceilings, full kitchens, and antiques (not to mention being within 2 miles of both Beaver Dam and the White River), the cabins at Fairwinds are probably the nicest you will find in this area. All 10 cabins have TV and VCR, stereo, a covered porch with swing and rocking chairs, and a charcoal grill. They're set on 80 acres; you can fish in the stocked pond (with a floating dock) or head on down to the river. Other activities include hiking, horseshoes, badminton, and volleyball. And pets are accepted. Prices (for a two-night stay) range $272–338.

♿ **Cabin Fever Resort** (479-253-5635, 479-253-2848, or 1-877-993-3837; www.cabinfeverresort.net), 15695 SR 187, Eureka Springs, Ark. Situated in the solitude of the hills, and just about 15 minutes from downtown Eureka Springs, Cabin Fever provides well-outfitted log cabins that are barely 5 years old. All of the cabins (five at present) feature full kitchen, microwave, coffeemaker, Jacuzzi for two, grill, TV and VCR, full bath, and beautiful deck. This is a peaceful resort, but that's what you'd expect from an operation that remembered to include a porch swing with each cabin. $99–199 per night; smoking is allowed outside only. Kids over 14 are okay, but pets are not permitted.

Sugar Ridge Resort (479-253-5548 or 1-800-TOP-VIEW; www.eureka-net.com/sugarridge), 1216 Dam Site Rd., Eureka Springs, Ark. With luxury log cabins geared for adults only, Sugar Ridge lies on 20 acres overlooking Beaver Lake and the Damsite Park. Better yet, for the fisherman, the great trout angling available from the White River is only 1.5 miles away. All the cabins come with TV, VCR, fully equipped kitchen, native stone fireplace, and 16-jet Jacuzzi. Throw in a private deck looking out over the lake. Neither pets nor kids are allowed. $135–225.

War Eagle Cavern Lodge (479-789-2909; www.wareaglecavern.com), 21494 Cavern Dr., Rogers, Ark. Located close to both War Eagle Cavern and the War Eagle Trading Post, this elaborate cabin offers something noteworthy for those seeking to get away from it all: There's no phone, no satellite, and no cable. What the lodge *does* have is the capability of sleeping four adults, a very cool deck at the treetop level, a full kitchenette, and a private bath. Pets aren't accepted, and the going rate is $125 per night.

CANOE OUTFITTERS, CAMPING, AND RVS 🗡 ♿ **Spider Creek Resort on the White River** (479-253-9241 or 1-800-272-6034; www.spidercreek .com), 8179 SR 187, Eureka Springs, Ark. Spider Creek offers the great fishing of the White River, not to

THE HISTORIC CRESCENT HOTEL

mention 16 furnished cabins and houses with cable TV, Jacuzzi, and kitchenettes. $70–200 per night; no charge for kids under 10. Float rental is very affordable here. Canoes and kayaks start at $20, rafts at $50, and flat-bottomed Jon boats at $45.

✔ **Riverside Resort and Canoes** (870-423-3116; www.riversideresort andcanoes.com), 3031 US 62 W., Eureka Springs, Ark. People rave (and justifiably so) about the trout fishing on the White River. Less often heard, however, is the fact that small-mouth bass fishing on the Kings River is also excellent. Riverside Resort, just 5 miles from Eureka Springs, offers seven cabins, some of which have fireplace, Jacuzzi, or hot tub. In all you can count on cable TV, a kitchen, and a grill on the deck. Pets are not accepted, and you should call for current prices. The resort offers both canoe rental and shuttle service (fishing guides are available as well) for the entire Kings River. Trips range in length from 4.5 miles to overnight, and rental starts at $35 a day.

For **Withrow State Park**, **Devil's Den State Park**, **Beaver Lake**, and **Ozark National Forest**, see *Wild Places*.

🐾 ✔ **Kings River Outfitters** (479-253-8954; www.kingsriveroutfitters .com), Eureka Springs, Ark. In business for more than a decade, Kings River Outfitters was named the 2001 Conservation Outfitter of the Year by the Arkansas Stream Team (part of the Arkansas Fish and Game Commission). Located 8 miles southeast of Eureka Springs off SR 221, the firm rents canoes and kayaks, provides shuttle service, and has guides available for hire. The majority of canoes and kayaks rent for $38 per

day, but a few larger 20-foot canoes (some with three seats) can be had for $45. Also on the property is a primitive campground (your dog is welcomed as long as he doesn't act up, bite, or spend all night baying at the moon); camping is $4 per person.

✔ **Kings River Retreat** (479-253-2346 or 1-866-253-2346; www.kings riverretreat.com), 8190 SR 221 S., Eureka Springs, Ark. Situated on 30 acres, with 1,600 feet of Kings River frontage, Kings River Retreat offers cabins and cabin suites that can comfortably sleep from two to nine adults. The cabins themselves are warm and welcoming, with solid pine interiors and amenities that can include (depending upon which cabin you rent) handmade cedar beds, Jacuzzi, kitchenette, and fireplace. All face the river and mountain bluffs, assuring a good view no matter what time of year you happen to arrive. The cabins are nonsmoking, and no pets are allowed. Call this establishment directly for latest prices. Also on-site is a primitive campground (your pet is welcomed there if it's well behaved): $7 per adult per night, $5 ages 2–12.

✳ Where to Eat
EATING OUT

Eureka Springs, Ark.
✔ ♿ 🍷 **Balcony Bar and Restaurant** (479-253-7837 or 1-800-643-4972; www.restauranteur.com/balcony), 12 Spring St. Open Mon.–Thu. 11–9, Fri.–Sat. 11–11, and Sun. 11–5. Located in the historic 1905 Basin Park Hotel, the Balcony is a relaxed establishment offering a full bar, alfresco dining overlooking downtown Eureka Springs, and frequent live music. The restaurant offers a good list of appe-

tizers, including seafood-stuffed mushrooms ($6.50) and jalapeño-and-onion straws ($5.95). This latter dish is a combination of onions and spicy peppers, battered and deep fried. Salads, soups, and a variety of burgers fill out much of the menu. For dinner, entrées include Ozark smoked chicken (at $16.99 you get half a smoked chicken topped with a Jack Daniels molasses glaze), a $10.95 chicken-fried pork loin fritter, or the ever-present 12-ounce rib-eye steak for $18.95.

🦞 ✂ ⚙ ♿ 🍸 **Forest Hill Restaurant** (479-253-2422 or 1-888-253-1907; www.foresthillrestaurant.com), 3016 E. Van Buren. For those with a large appetite or who wish to feed the family without totally breaking the bank, a good choice is Forest Hill. The breakfast buffet runs $5.75, while the lunch version is $7.50. Of course you can also order off the menu, and lunch finds the Ozark standards of chicken-fried steak for $6.95, deep-fried catfish for $7.50, a wide variety of sandwiches in the $5 range, and personal-sized pizzas cooked in a wood-burning oven for less than $7. A Sunday brunch buffet takes place every week at this restaurant, and the nightly dinner buffet costs $9.50. Evening menu favorites include a rib-eye steak for $19.95 or (once again) catfish and hush puppies for $9.95. Forest Hill also features beer, wine, and mixed drinks.

✂ 🍸 **Rogue's Manor at Sweet Spring** (479-253-4911 or 1-800-250-5827; www.roguesmanor.com), 124 Spring St. Located at the very cool Rogue's Manor bed & breakfast, the Rogue's Manor restaurant offers casual fare in a fun, yet classy, environment. While one of the most popular entrées has a very boring name, you'll

want to give it a try. The seafood casserole ($23.95) is a mesh of scallops, shrimp, and salmon; sautéed in white wine, sherry, and herbs; baked in hollandaise sauce; and topped with Swiss cheese. You may also partake of smoked prime rib ($24.95) and a number of pasta, chicken, and vegetarian entrées. For relaxing either before or after dinner, the **Hideaway Lounge**, with its deep leather chairs, offers a fine spot for a drink or three. You can even order one of its special hand-rolled cigars.

✂ ♿ 🍸 **Sparky's Roadhouse Café** (479-253-6001; www.sparkys.net), 147 E. Van Buren. The food at Sparky's is simple and casual, but the real reason to come is the beer. You can choose from a selection of nearly 100 imports, domestics, microbrews, and imports. If you prefer your alcohol from grapes, there is plenty of wine, as well as a full bar. This is just a fun little place, with indoor seating and a huge outdoor deck (nice in summer months). Plenty of appetizers are on the menu, such as the Picasso Platter. This selection, at $8.50, consists of fresh goat cheese, tomatoes, cucumbers, red onions, olive tapenade, and pita bread. Or you can go for standards such as nachos ($6.95) or the excellent Vidalia onion rings ($4.95). You may choose from a host of burgers and sandwiches in the $5–8 range. One of the best is the bistro burger. At $8.50, this half-pound patty is topped with Brie, grilled ham, and sautéed mushrooms. For an extra $3 (and you can do this with any burger), Sparky's will double the meat. There's nothing like a 1-pound burger for a light midday snack. Entrées more in the dinner vein include chile-rubbed salmon for $14.95 and a filet mignon dinner for $17.95.

🦗 ♿ **AQ Chicken House** (479-751-4633; www.aqchicken.com), 707 Sanders Ave., Springdale, Ark. Also, **AQ Chicken House** (479-443-7555; www.aq chicken.com), 1925 N. College Ave., Fayetteville, Ark. With its two locations, this 50-year-old chicken house serves almost a million customers per year. That's a lot of bird, even for the state that is home to Tyson chicken, and there's enough evidence to form a decent argument that AQ is the most popular restaurant in Arkansas. At least in part (if not mostly), such a reputation stems from the fact that the fried chicken is prepared much the same as it was back in 1947: pan fried in a cast-iron skillet. Start your meal at AQ with an order of pickle q's. In short, these are dill pickles that have been battered and dunked in a deep fryer. I'd seen these on a menu years ago at the Atomic Cafe in Atomic City, Idaho (out in the middle of the desert), but AQ fried dills are far better. The menu also includes a number of sandwiches, and while I'm sure they're all good, you really come here for the chicken. The original, pan-fried meal, which arrives with three pieces and two side orders, is $8.39. I'm talking chicken like you would have at Grandma's house on Sunday. If fried food doesn't set with you, you can order it charbroiled or barbecued. The best deal here is the all-you-can-eat chicken buffet. For $10.99 you can eat chicken till you grow feathers and receive two side orders and a plate of spaghetti besides. This is the epitome of the Ozarks meal.

But AQ has branched out to more than chicken. Catfish from the White River prepared southern-style (fried), grilled, with lemon-pepper, or charbroiled is available for less than $9. And don't forget the hickory-smoked BBQ ribs, lunch and blue plate specials, a kids' menu, and the specialty combo platters. On the latter you can pick three entrées (chicken or catfish in any style, ribs, you name it) and a couple of sides for $12.99. Restaurants like the AQ just aren't that common anymore; if you're within 100 miles, it's worth the extra drive.

✍ & ⅋ **The Eurekan Dining Car** (479-253-9623 or 479-253-9777; www.esnarailway.com), 299 N. Main St. A service provided by the Eureka Springs & North Arkansas Railway, the Eurekan Dining Car wanders the hills and serves scrumptious dinners Apr.–Oct. The trip departs at 5 PM and requires roughly 1½ hours. The dinner menu consists of either a baked chicken breast, prime rib, or rainbow trout amandine (all $35) and comes with soup, salad, rice pilaf, and flaming baked Alaska. Wine and champagne are available, and the price includes both your train fare and meal. Almost all ages are permitted on the train, with the proviso that you be older than 5. May–Oct., a lunch train departs at noon and requires 1 hour. The cost is $22 adults, $11 kids under 8, and the meal consists of either beef stroganoff, chicken salad with fresh fruit, or a hot deli croissant. Accompanying your lunch are beverages, dessert, and homemade bread.

DINING OUT ✍ ⅋ **James at the Mill** (479-443-1400; www.jamesatthemill .com), 3906 Great House Springs, Johnson, Ark. Mon.–Fri. 11–2 and 5:30–10, Sat. just 5:30–10. Located at the **Inn at the Mill** (a four-star Clarion Hotel), James at the Mill has pioneered a unique dining style known as Ozark Plateau Cuisine via the creative mind of chef Miles James. In 2000 this restaurant was named one of the 10 Best Restaurants in the United States by the *Nation's Restaurant News*. Also, this eatery is inevitably voted Best Overall Restaurant in Arkansas by the *Arkansas Times*. It's the sort of establishment where the food is not only delicious but also a work of art on a plate. For lunch, you

might try a cream of asparagus and blue lump crab soup for $10. Or, for a novel twist on an Ozark favorite, order the chicken-fried steak with black beans, cilantro rice, lime aioli, scallions, and red pepper ($8). A number of other great salads, sandwiches, soups, and daily specials are also available. In the evening order the appetizer known as the homemade andouille sausage corn dog, which arrives with Johnson Valley mustard, salsa fresca, and whipped potatoes ($8). There are no mistakes to be had with the dinner entrées, but perhaps the all-time favorite is the hickory-grilled, bone-in rib eye for $36. It comes with Southwestern black beans, crispy cumin onion rings, salsa fresca, and grilled corn on the cob. Desserts run $7 (with options such as pecan pie with chocolate Jack Daniels ice cream, or Tahitian vanilla cheesecake flan). While at James at the Mill you'll also encounter a number of specialty coffees, espresso, and teas. The restaurant offers a full bar, and the wine list here is phenomenal, garnering a 2004 Award of Excellence from *Wine Spectator* magazine. If you choose, you can even book a private dining room for two in the 60-degree wine cellar (and yes, blankets are provided).

Eureka Springs, Ark.

✍ & ⅋ **Crystal Dining Room** (479-253-9766; www.restauranteur.com/ crystal), 75 Prospect Ave. Mon.–Sat. 7–10 for breakfast, 11–2 for lunch, and 5–9 for dinner. Sundays offer a popular brunch. As with most fine restaurants in the Ozarks, the surroundings can be elegant—but you need not feel compelled to dress the part. With its hardwood floors, white tablecloths, and chandeliers, the Crystal is located within the famous 1886

Crescent Hotel and Spa. The restaurant offers a full bar and extensive selection of wines, and **Dr. Baker's Lounge** provides a relaxed setting for those who wish to view the big screen, enjoy some appetizers, and occasionally hear live music during the summer season. Breakfast tends to run in the $8–10 range; one offering too seldom found in eateries is a traditional grilled corned beef hash with farm-fresh eggs ($8.95). Delicious appetizers for lunch, at a cost of $6.95, are the portobello fries (the tasty mushrooms are cut into strips and deep fried) at a cost of $6.95. Or go for the Ozark trout cakes, a nice Arkansas twist on Maryland crabcakes that goes for $7.95. An array of sandwiches, salads, entrées, and pastas are also available for lunch. The dinner choices cover the spectrum of beef, pork, fowl, and seafood. A filet mignon with Stilton blue cheese is $32, while a cornmeal-encrusted trout will set you back $17. Twin lobster tails with drawn butter are $42, and the grilled chicken with prosciutto pasta is $16. If you're in search of excellent service and fine (yet casual) dining in Eureka Springs, it's hard to go wrong with the Crystal.

✐ ☍ Gaskins Cabin Steak House

(479-253-5466; www.gaskinscabin .com), 2883 SR 23 N. Open Wed.– Sun. 5–9 PM. This restaurant isn't huge, seating just over 50 people. This just goes to show that quantity is not nearly as important as quality. An interesting setting, Gaskins resides in a historic log cabin built in 1864 by an early settler (and bear hunter) named John Gaskins. It is in fact the oldest standing structure in Carroll County, Ark. A relaxing and homey place, with

its big fireplace burning whenever the mercury drops, this establishment is well regarded for its steaks and prime rib. It also has an extensive wine list and serves a variety of domestic and imported beers. For $9.95 the escargots appetizer is a good buy, and the renowned beef is all acquired via Omaha Angus Steak company. A boneless rib eye goes for $24.95, and the combination of a porterhouse boneless strip and fillet is $32.95. The cornmeal-crusted rainbow trout costs $16.95. The prices may seem a bit high at times, but steak lovers who wish to splurge will be graciously thanked by their taste buds.

✐ ☍ ☍ Autumn Breeze Restaurant

(479-253-7734; www.autumnbreeze restaurant.com), 190 Huntsville Rd. Mon.–Sat. 5–9 PM. A nonsmoking establishment, Autumn Breeze has been hailed by *Wine Spectator* magazine as having "one of the most outstanding wine lists in the world." Chef and co-owner Richard Bloch is a graduate of the Culinary Institute of America, and his dishes have received rave reviews since the opening of this restaurant in 1993. This is a restaurant that believes in the importance of the fine details, and such care is reflected not just in the food, but also in the knowledgeable staff and intimate surroundings. There are a number of appetizers, but the coconut beer-battered shrimp ($5.95) is a far cry from the coconut shrimp now a staple at any number of chain restaurants. The veal Olympic is something special, at $15.95 a combination of veal medallions and jumbo shrimp in a brandy lobster sauce. You'll also find a 12-ounce lobster tail for $29.95, and a pound of king crab legs for the same price. The list goes on and on, from rack of lamb for $23.95 to Chinese-style baby back ribs at $12.95, to a 13-ounce prime rib for $19.95. For a finishing touch, don't forget the chef's specialty, a chocolate soufflé that, at $5.50, will send you into chocolate Nirvana.

✍ ₺ ♈ **DeVito's** (479-253-6807; www.eureka-springs-usa.com/devito), 5 Center St. Open 4–9 every night but Wed. DeVito's not only was voted Best Italian Restaurant in Arkansas by readers of the *Arkansas Times*, but it has also been praised by the likes of the *New York Times*. In this very special eatery, in operation since 1956, all the sauces, meatballs, Italian sausage, and bread are made from scratch. The trout that are DeVito's claim to fame are raised on the nearby family trout farm. For appetizers, the traditional toasted ravioli ($6) or the trout fingers ($8) will provide a teaser for the meal yet to come. Many regulars come back time and again simply for the spaghetti and meatballs ($12), but equally popular are such time-tested entrées as a ravioli dinner ($15), chicken Parmesan ($16), eggplant Parmesan ($14), and veal Piccata ($20). There are a wide variety of trout offerings less than $20 (such as pesto trout Parmesan, lemon trout, char-grilled trout, and trout Italiano). DeVito's offers beer and wine.

✍ ₺ ♈ **Bavarian Inn** (479-253-8128; www.eureka-net.com/bavarian), 325 W. Van Buren. Open daily 9–5, the Bavarian Inn is something you would not expect in the Ozarks, an authentic Czech-German establishment serving both European and American favorites. Apparently the style and quality of entrées has been a hit, as the Bavarian has been written up in publications ranging from *Southern Living* and the *Arkansas Democrat-Gazette* to the *New York Times*. Dinners arrive with soup, salad, and a renowned basket of homemade rye bread. Better-known dishes such as sauerbraten ($12.95), Wiener schnitzel, and Jäger schnitzel (both $13.95) are available, as is Hassen-pfeffer, a delicious roasted rabbit with potato pancake ($16.95). Selections with a more American appeal include steak Madagascar at $19.95 and a fillet of salmon at $14.95. A children's menu is available, and you do not want to miss the desserts at the Bavarian. For a treat, and low priced at $4.95, order the chocolate coconut rum roll.

✍ ₺ ♈ **Cottage Inn** (479-253-5282; http://cottageinneurekaspgs.com), 450 W. Van Buren. Open Thu.–Sun. 5–9 PM (seasonally; the restaurant generally opens in spring and closes for season in early Dec.). Cottage Inn offers yet another style of fare not common to the Ozarks. In this case, the taste is Mediterranean. Guests with a hankerin' for the culinary stylings of Greece, Spain, France, and Italy, not to mention a large selection of wines, will not be disappointed. The menu changes here from time to time, but particularly noteworthy entrées have been in the genre of a French country duck trio. This is a combination of roast duck confit, duck breast, and duck sausage served with seared fresh apple slices ($18). Straying a bit farther afield, this establishment has also been known to offer such delights as spicy Thai shrimp ($19) and roast rack of lamb ($34).

✳ Entertainment

LIVE MUSIC 🎻 ♿ **Opera in the Ozarks at Inspiration Point** (479-253-8595; www.opera.org), 16311 US 62 W., Eureka Springs, Ark. For all those who suffer from geographic snobbery, yes, we do have opera in the Ozarks. And no, it's not necessarily of the Grand Ol' variety. True, we generally do prefer bluegrass, blues, and country, but we are equal-opportunity providers when it comes to music. Therefore, no matter if your taste is Rossini, Verdi, or Puccini, you can catch a performance at Opera of the Ozarks. For curtain times and prices, call the box office.

🎻 ♿ **North Arkansas Symphony** (479-521-4166; www.nasymphony.org), 605 Dickson St., Fayetteville, Ark. Performing for more than 50 years, the extremely talented North Arkansas Symphony performs on average once per month at the Walton Arts Center. From music of the movies to the classics, you can't help but enjoy the selections provided by these fine instrumentalists. The shows generally start at 7:30 PM, and tickets run $28–36. Call the box office for exact nights and times.

OZARK MOUNTAIN HOE-DOWN

🎻 ♿ **Ozark Mountain Hoe-Down** (479-253-7725 or 1-800-458-2113; www.hoedown.net), Eureka Springs, Ark. Shows are presented every night but Tue., Mar.–Dec. Performances are offered every night July–Oct. $18.50 adults, $11.50 kids. If you just didn't get enough of Branson, you can see a Branson-style show in Eureka Springs. The Hoe-Down is your expected fare of country, western, pop, and corn-fed comedy (i.e., guys in overalls and gals with a couple of blacked-out teeth).

🎵 **Little O' Opry** (479-839-2992), 271 Campbell Ave., West Fork, Ark. This is not a fancy little theater, but it's the real deal. There seems to be a house band, but regulars and locals take the stage as well and join in with the jam. These are people who can play, who probably grew up with one hand on a banjo, guitar, or walking bass. Best of all, during the intermission you can chow down on cake and cookies and see if you won a door prize. At last check admission was $6. Call for times.

Pickin' in the Park, Frisco Park, 300 S. 1st St., Rogers, Ark. Among the nice things about the Ozarks, and there are many, are the community get-togethers you'll find on the town squares. It's a part of American life absent from many locales, but to which we hold more tightly than a snapping turtle with a headache. In Rogers's Frisco Park, every Saturday evening May–Oct., you can join the 500 or so folks who will show up with lawn chairs, picnic dinners, and maybe even a banjo, mandolin, guitar, washboard, or harmonica. Anyone can play. and anyone can attend. As you stroll around you'll see various groups and soloists picking out tunes, some jams growing ever larger as other musicians arrive and join in. It's a great time, and it's free. This little shindig is better than anything that costs cash money. It's more fun, and the music is great. The only requirement is that you play acoustic music; no electrics or amps are permitted. Also, leave the booze at home; it's not permitted.

THEATER AND MORE *✆ ♿ The Great Passion Play* (479-253-9200; www.greatpassionplay.com), 935 Passion Play Rd., Eureka Springs, Ark. One of the best-known spectacles in the region, *The Great Passion Play* has been viewed by more than 7 million people in the last four decades. It is, in fact, the world's number one most attended outdoor dramatic presentation. Chronicling the last 7 days of Jesus Christ, the epic is held in a 4,100-seat outdoor amphitheater, involves 200 actors and a plethora of exotic animals, and runs for 2 hours. Performances take place from the last Fri. in Apr. through the last Sat. in Oct., every day but Sun. and Wed. Showtimes vary, but as a general rule you can count on an 8:30 PM curtain in all months but Sep.–Oct. (at which time the performance begins at 7:30 PM). $23.25 adults, $10 kids, includes a trip through the park's **Bible Museum** and **Sacred Arts Center**. Package prices are available for various other sites and activities at the facility, not the least of which is the **Passion Play All-You-Can-Eat Buffet**. In the Ozarks it's not unusual to see bumper stickers reading WHAT WOULD JESUS DO? At least at this attraction, the answer would seem to be that he would enjoy a large salad bar, meat and chicken entrées, vegetables, and a big, whoppin' dessert bar. Now, that's a last supper.

*✆ ♿ **Rogers Little Theater*** (479-631-8988; www.rogerslittletheater.com), 116 S. 2nd St., Rogers, Ark. With performances held in the lovely and historic Victory Theater, which offered 750 seats upon its grand opening in 1927, the Rogers Little Theater offers a wide variety of concerts, plays, dinner theater, and performances for kids. To learn about presentations, times, and admission fees, call the box office.

*✆ ♿ **Sager Creek Arts Center*** (479-524-4000; www.sagercreekartscenter.com), 301 E. Twin Springs Rd., Siloam Springs, Ark. Located just across from the pretty Twin Springs Park in Siloam Springs, the Sager Creek Arts Center was incorporated in 1984 and is housed in a former Methodist church sanctuary. A large variety of events are featured. Community theater, musicals, dinner theater, art workshops, exhibits and competitions, concerts of every type, and many workshops are all part of the yearly agenda. For information, dates, times, and ticket prices on performances, call the center directly.

*✆ ♿ **Walton Arts Center*** (479-443-5600; www.waltonartscenter.org), 495 Dickson St., Fayetteville, Ark. Featuring major name performances, classes,

THE GREAT PASSION PLAY

plays, and visual presentations, the Walton Arts Center holds two theaters, a multipurpose room, an art gallery, and an amphitheater. Call ahead for tickets, times, and the various entertainment du jour, but you can expect anything from jazz and symphony concerts to opera, musicals, and touring Broadway shows.

Also see **Arts Center of the Ozarks** under *Cultural Sites*.

✳ Selective Shopping

Eureka Springs Downtown Historic District (1-866-947-4387; www .eurekasprings.org), Spring St., Eureka Springs, Ark. The shopping, dining, and lodging center of Eureka Springs, the historic district's main landmark is the 1886 Crescent Hotel. Just hop the trolley to downtown and start wandering; you're bound to find something you like. If not, then you should seriously consider checking into a rehab center for some attitude adjustment.

Kaleidokites (479-253-6596; www .kaleidokites.com), 1C Spring St., Eureka Springs, Ark. This store is reputed to have the largest collection of handmade kaleidoscopes in a four-state region. One look at the place, and you can assume the claim to fame is true. Better yet, it also stocks a large selection of kites, cards, and gifts.

Sweet's Fudge Kitchen (479-253-5810; www.sweetsfudgekitchen.com), 36 Spring St., Eureka Springs, Ark. In business since 1959, Sweet's makes all its chocolates from scratch, hand dipping in small batches to assure freshness. However, chocolate alone does not a candy store make. This one also carries an extensive variety of homemade fudge and many different flavors of saltwater taffy. Candies,

licorice, turtles, nut clusters . . . the spectrum of sugar is covered at Sweet's. Even if you end up with a stomachache from overconsumption, you could well find yourself saying, "Thank you, sir, may I have another?"

White River Tobacco Company (479-253-5350), 99 Spring St., Eureka Springs, Ark. It's probably not politically correct to be plugging a tobacco emporium in this day and age, which should give you an insight into the workings of the typical Ozark mind. We'd endorse such an establishment just to be contrary, even if an awfully large percentage of us didn't love our tobacco (which we do; I personally smoke a corncob pipe). At White River you'll find not only a large selection of fine-tasting tobaccos but also a nice selection of pipes and cigars. Smoke 'em if ya got 'em.

Mountain Handcrafts Company (479-253-4965 or 1-888-353-4965; www.mountainhandcrafts.com), 2058 E. Van Buren, Eureka Springs, Ark. Open only three days a week (Fri.– Sun. 10–5), this is truly a specialty store. The focus of this establishment is the primitive art of rug hooking. The shop carries literally walls of fabric (wools and burlaps, to name a couple), hoops, stands, kits, frames, and all the other odds and ends rug hookers crave.

Dickson Street Bookshop (479-442-8182), 325 W. Dickson St., Fayetteville, Ark. The Dickson Street Bookshop has been around forever and a day, and you could spend almost that much time leafing through the 100,000-plus volumes in stock. If you're a fan of the written word, you have just found the mother lode of rare volumes, antique books, and out-of-print volumes.

✳ Special Events

Also see Towns and Villages.
February **Chocolate Lovers Festival** (479-253-7888; www.eurekachoc fest.org), Best Western Inn of the Ozarks, US 62 W., Eureka Springs, Ark. Taking place on Valentine's Day weekend, this orthodontist's dream festival features chocolate sculpting, a chocolate fountain, numerous chocolate competitions, entertainment, and an all-day chocolate feast. $10 adults, $5 ages 12 and under. My guess is you could probably raise the price to $100, and the 12-and-under crowd would still come.

April **Carving in the Ozarks** (479-253-2080; www.carvingintheozarks .com), Eureka Springs, Ark. Donatello and Michelangelo were okay, but you just wonder what those ol' boys could have accomplished if some wise soul had placed a chain saw in their hands. A reasonable facsimile of the answer to such a question can be found in late April at Carving in the Ozarks. Chain saw carvers from all over America show up to transform chunks of wood into bears and eagles and such. Admission is free, and after the carving is done all the pieces are auctioned, with proceeds benefiting the Make A Wish Foundation. Call for the location of the event.

Ozark UFO Conference (479-354-2558; www.ozarkufo.com), Best Western Inn of the Ozarks, US 62 W., Eureka Springs, Ark. If you've really been missing *The X Files*, you can likely sate your need for things extraterrestrial at this little green man shindig in Eureka Springs. You'll come across three days' worth of speakers, audiovisual presentations, discussions, and (I assume) a few abductees who have come into contact with Elvis, Bigfoot, Mr. Spock, and nasty probing devices. Admission at the door is $50 for all three days.

May–October **Pickin' in the Park** (479-636-8204; www.mainstreetrogers .com), Frisco Park, Rogers, Ark. For the best in bluegrass, country, and gospel, just drop by Rogers's Frisco Park any Saturday evening between May and the end of October. Folks show up from all over with their guitars, banjos, basses, and dulcimers to pick the tunes and jam with whoever feels the urge. Or you can simply bring a lawn chair and listen. There is no alcohol allowed, and if you wish to do a bit of pickin' of your own, then keep in mind that this is strictly an acoustic gig.

May **War Eagle Fair** (see *October*).

Applegate Farm Spring Fair (1-888-404-7478; www.oleapplegateplace .com), 1807 S.W. 2nd St. (Applegate Farm), and 211 S.E. Walton Blvd., Bentonville, Ark. This is yet another of the giant crafts fairs so prevalent in Northwest Arkansas. In fact, this one is so big that the spring version requires two locations. You'll find more than 500 of the finest craftsmen from around the nation displaying and selling their wares, and there are also plenty of music and concessions. Taking place in early May, the fair at Applegate Farm runs Fri.–Sat. 8–6, Sun. 8–4. $2 adults; kids 12 and under are admitted free. Hours at the Clarion Convention Center are Fri.–Sat. 9–8, Sun. 9–3. Admission is free.

Crawdad Days Music Festival (870-741-2659), Harrison, Ark. The mid-May Crawdad Days take place on the Main Street Square and Lake Harrison. The main entrée of the day is music, music, and more music. However, once your feet take to bouncing, you can enjoy food, a cardboard boat race, volleyball, basketball, and (for the more enthusiastic among you) a 5K race. It should go without saying that one of the highlights of the event is a crawdad boil. Admission is free.

June ✈ **Ozark Balloon Festival** (479-273-2841; www.ozarkballoon fest.com), 1901 S.E. J St., Boooooooooooooentonville, Ark. Parking for this event is at the Bentonville High School on J Street, and shuttles transport visitors to the actual event site. There is no charge for the shuttles, but gate fees are $2 per person. At this two-day festival in early June, the sky will fill with hot-air balloons. If you tire of looking up, you'll find plenty of food and activities to keep you and the kids occupied.

✈ **Airfest** (479-521-4947; www.ark airmuseum.com), 4290 S. School Ave., Drake Field, Fayetteville, Ark. Taking place at the Arkansas Air Museum, Airfest is held in mid-June. A truly different type of air show, this one is modeled after the traveling, barnstorming extravaganzas of the 1920s. There are always abundant high-altitude examples of derring-do demonstrated by pilots in both the oldest and newest heavier-than-air craft. In addition, look for jet flyovers, food, exhibits, concessions, and lots of planned events for kids. $10 adults, $5 ages 6–12.

Mudtown Days (479-770-0023; www .lowellarkansas.com), McClure Park, Lowell, Ark. For more than 30 years the annual Mudtown Days festival has

AIRFEST TAKES PLACE AT DRAKE FIELD.

taken place over Memorial Day weekend. You'll find a parade, fireworks, softball and baseball tournaments, lawn mower and wheelbarrow races, and an infinite amount of food and music. The commemoration of Lowell (originally named Mudtown given how many stagecoaches seemed to get stuck here) even includes a Civil War reenactment and a tractor pulling contest (for you coastal folks, that would be where tractors pull heavy weights, not where people try to pull tractors).

Rusty Wheels Spring Show (see *October*).

August **Frisco Festival** (479-936-5487; www.friscofestival.com), downtown Rogers, Ark. Taking place on the last weekend of August, the two-day Frisco Festival is a celebration of the now defunct Frisco Railroad. There's a chili cook-off and a very elaborate cardboard train race. There's live music, rides galore, not to mention a chicken BBQ, an old-fashioned ice cream social, and a pancake breakfast. Admission is free (in that you can wander all over the place), but specific events, shows, and amusements may charge a fee.

Annual Bluegrass Festival, Harrison, Ark. Taking place in mid-August at the Harrison Fairgrounds, this is the oldest three-day bluegrass festival in the state of Arkansas. There are jam sessions galore, stage performances, and endless gospel and bluegrass. Of course no bluegrass festival would be complete without a wide selection of food. Camping is available, and alcohol is not permitted on the fairgrounds. $9 Thu., $10 Fri.–Sat. Or you can purchase a three-day pass for $24.

September **Bikes, Blues and BBQ** (1-800-766-4626; www.bikesbluesand bbq.org), Fayetteville, Ark. This biker rally is quickly becoming one of the most popular in the United States, drawing more than 250,000 people and 75,000 bikes on the last weekend in September. You'll see 15 or more free bands (music from country to rock to blues to jazz), and the food found along Fayetteville's eclectic Dickson Street could keep you occupied for hours. Still, you might not want to gorge yourself too much . . . at least not until after the BBQ cook-off is over. And as you no doubt suspected, no bike rally is complete without a variety of "biker babe" competitions.

October **War Eagle Fair** (479-789-5398; www.wareaglefair.com), 11036 High Sky Inn Rd., Rogers, Ark. Taking place both in mid-October and in early May, the War Eagle Fair dates from 1954 and showcases the very best of arts, crafts, and handmade items (you won't find mass-produced trash here) at hundreds and hundreds of vendor booths. Both admission and parking are free, and of course there is plenty of food available. Gates open at 8 AM and close at 5 PM on Thu.–Sat. during the event. On Sun. the gates close at 4 PM. For the finest products from weavers, woodworkers, painters, sculptors, stained-glass artists, and much more, War Eagle is the best-known craft fair in Northwest Arkansas.

Applegate Farm Autumn Fair (1-888-404-7478; www.oleapplegate place.com), 1807 S.W. 2nd St. (Applegate Farm), and 211 S.E. Walton Blvd., Bentonville, Ark. (See *May* for more details.) Hours of this fall event, taking place in mid-October, are Wed.–Sat. 8–6, Sun. 8–5. These hours are for the Applegate Farm location of the fair, and admission is $3. The second location, the Clarion Convention Center, is open Wed.–Sat. 9–8, Sun. 9–3; free.

Rusty Wheels Tractor Show (870-743-1511; www.rustywheels.com), Harrison, Ark. For the finest in old tractors, old engines, and old guys who really like old tractors and old engines, don't miss this show. It's held on the second weekend of October (and the second weekend of June) at the tractor club's showground 6 miles south of Harrison on US 65. Hours of the show are 6 AM–7 PM, and you can stock up on good country food such as biscuits and gravy.

THE WHITE AND THE BUFFALO

As I wrote this chapter, several Ozarkian friends suggested that perhaps I shouldn't heavily broadcast the majesty and charm that exudes from this region. They do not want it to change, to become overpopulated, to alter in form, style, or grace, by a single iota. They love the quiet peace found in secret places not commonly frequented by visitors or tourists. They revel in the sheer beauty of locales that still look and feel like centuries past. In good conscience I could of course never fully abide by such a request; after all, this guide is meant to serve as a complete road map to the reader. It is meant to lift the veil and reveal the indescribable magic that is the Ozarks.

On the other hand, in some simple way my friends are inadvertently granted their wish. The truth is, neither words nor pictures can do justice to the intangible allure of the White and Buffalo rivers. You have to see it, taste it, touch it, hear it. Only then can you honestly discover what makes the locals cherish this area so deeply. You have to float the rivers or walk their banks. You have to breathe deep the crisp air as you gaze at towering bluffs. You have to stroll the forest, allowing the silence to permeate your soul. You need to feel the primeval tug of that trout on the line, watch the bass leap, regress to a more primitive state of mind as an elk pushes its way through briars and limbs. To know it, to really know it, the icy chill of spring-born whitewater must splash on your face, carrying you away to the nesting ground of dreams unborn.

And it's not just about the great outdoors. Yes, the fishing in the White, the Buffalo, and the Little Red rivers is excellent. Streams that produce world-record trout are not something at which one scoffs (a 40-pound, 4-ounce brown was taken from the Little Red in 1992). Bull Shoals, Norfork, and Greers Ferry lakes offer visitor and native alike a water wonderland. Being Army Corps of Engineers projects, these huge bodies of water are surrounded by the type of wooded campsites that make lodging under the stars a pure pleasure. In the populated havens along their borders you will find restaurants, museums, bed & breakfasts, and entertainment galore.

But still there is more. This is an area that virtually dispels unhappiness; it is not tolerant of brooding minds or downturned lips. Just *try* to keep your toe from tapping when you visit Mountain View, the Folk Music Capital of the World. When you hear the joyous strains of banjo, bass, fiddle, and guitar at

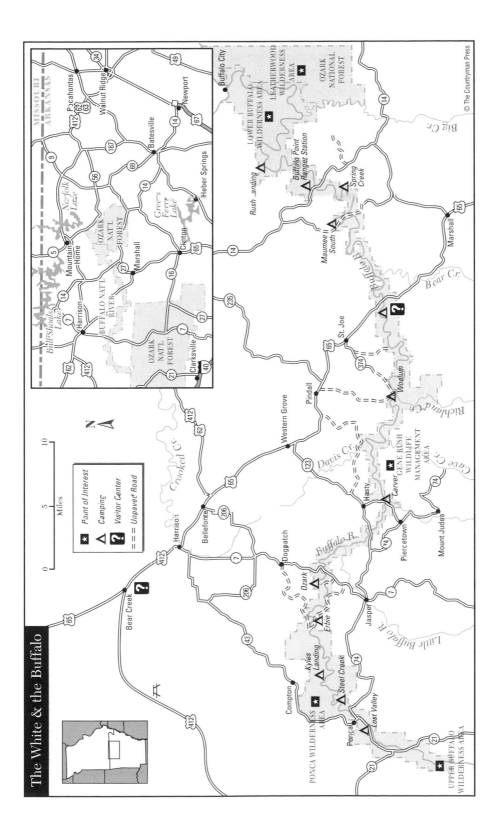

The White & the Buffalo

every turn, when you see musicians jamming for the pure fun of it on the town square, the smile will rise to your face unbidden. You might go to Heber Springs and watch the World Championship Cardboard Boat Races, just another of the countless festivals that illustrate the endless humor of the Ozarks and its people. You will begin to understand the type of personality that has perfected the art of self-amusement, that has mastered the ability to create laughter from thin air.

Some things just have to be seen to be believed. Some things just have to be felt. Some places are like that, too. They're rare as hen's teeth, granted, but they do exist.

This is one of those places.

AREA CODES This region of Arkansas wanders a bit, containing all three of the state's area codes. The vast majority of the towns here utilize the **870** code. Near Greers Ferry Lake and Heber Springs, the code is **501**. Should you happen to drop by Clinton, Ark., for the annual Chuckwagon Races, remember that the code is **479**.

GUIDANCE While you won't want to misplace the invaluable, multipurpose resource put out by the **Arkansas Department of Parks and Tourism** (501-682-7777 or 1-800-NATURAL; www.arkansas.com), 1 Capitol Mall, Little Rock, Ark., another fantastic general vacation site can be found under the name of **Ozark Mountain Region** (1-800-544-6867; www.ozarkmountainregion.com), P.O. Box 194, Lakeview, Ark. 72642.

When traveling near Batesville, Ark., hints and tips are available from both the **Batesville Area Chamber of Commerce** (870-793-2378; www.mybatesville .org), 409 Vine, Batesville, Ark., 75201, and the **Ozark Gateway Tourist Council** (870-793-9316 or 1-800-264-0316; www.ozarkgateway.com), 1652 White Dr., P.O. Box 4049, Batesville, Ark. 75201.

In the southern part of the region, details on the many recreation opportunities available in the Greers Ferry Lake district can be found at the **Greers Ferry Lake & Little Red River Association** (501-745-6101; www.greersferrylake .org), P.O. Box 1170, Fairfield Bay, Ark. 72088, or the **Fairfield Bay Area Chamber of Commerce** (501-884-3324 or 1-888-244-4386; www.ffbchamber .org), P.O. Box 1159, Fairfield Bay, Ark. 72088. Also at Greers Ferry, check out the **Heber Springs Area Chamber of Commerce** (501-362-2444 or 1-800-774-3237; www.heber-springs.com), 1001 W. Main, Heber Springs, Ark. 72543.

Two other chambers of note are the **Jasper–Newton County Chamber of Commerce** (870-446-2455 or 1-800-670-7792; www.theozarkmountains.com), 204 N. Spring St., Jasper, Ark., and the **Clinton Chamber of Commerce** (501-745-6500; www.clintonchamber.com), P.O. Box 52, Clinton, Ark. 72031. The former is a prime source for those who wish to float the Buffalo National River, while the latter will provide the detail you need to enjoy the National Championship Chuckwagon Races.

For more fun on the water, a rundown of activities in and around Bull Shoals and Norfork lakes (as well as the White River and Buffalo National River) are as close as the **Mountain Home Chamber of Commerce** (870-425-5111 or

1-800-822-3536; www.enjoymountainhome.com), P.O. Box 488, Mountain Home, Ark. 72654. Another "mountain" town that should not be missed is Mountain View, Ark., home to the amazing Ozark Folk Center State Park. Find out more via the **Mountain View Chamber of Commerce** (870-269-8068 or 1-888-679-2859; www.ozarkgetaways.com), 107 N. Peabody Ave., Mountain View, Ark.

GETTING THERE On the eastern side of this region, US 65 is your quickest route to the general vicinity of both the Buffalo National River and Greers Ferry Lake. More to the west, US 63 crosses the Missouri-Arkansas border at Thayer, Mo., and runs south through Batesville. Traversing the northern edge of the section is best accomplished on US 62. For a more scenic excursion and a slower pace, opt for SR 5, SR 9, and SR 14.

By air: Once again, your best bet for travel in the northern section of the Arkansas Ozarks is **Northwest Arkansas Regional Airport** (479-205-1000; www.nwara.com), 1 Airport Blvd., Bentonville, Ark. This is a relatively new airport (completed in 1998) serviced by American Eagle, Continental Express, Delta, Northwest Airlink, US Airways Express, and United. For even more flight opportunities (and approximately an hour away from Greers Ferry Lake), you can fly to or from the **Little Rock National Airport** (501-372-3439; www.lrn-airport.com), 1 Airport Dr., Little Rock, Ark. This facility is serviced by American Eagle, Continental Airlines, Delta, Delta Connection, Frontier Airlines, Northwest, Northwest Airlink, Southwest, and US Airways.

MEDICAL EMERGENCIES The Buffalo River country has several large hospitals that can handle any medical needs or emergencies. Also keep in mind that many small towns have local hospitals or medical clinics. In Batesville you will find the **White River Medical Center** (870-793-1200; www.wrmc.com), 1710 Harrison St., Batesville, Ark. This regional hospital offers 180 beds and 80 physicians, covering the gamut of services. The **Ozark Health Center** in Clinton (501-745-7000; www.myozarkhealth.com), US 65 S., Clinton, Ark., moved into a brand-new facility in 2004. Services at Ozark Health include 24-hour emergency care, surgery, labs, radiology, respiratory, and outpatient care. Considering that Clinton hosts the Chuckwagon Races, which inevitably result in some nasty accidents, you can presume that the emergency room docs here know their stuff.

Should you suffer injury or illness while playing around on Greers Ferry Lake or the Little Red River, you would be well served to drive on down to the **White County Medical Center** in Searcy (501-268-6121; www.wcmc.org), 3214 E. Race Ave., Searcy, Ark. This 245-bed acute care hospital boasts of more than 1,000 employees and better than 100 physicians. It's a state-of-the-art health center, handling virtually every procedure and nearly every test you could ever require. A much smaller hospital, **Stone County Medical Center** (870-269-4361; www.wrmc.com), SR 14 E., Mountain View, Ark., is a 25-bed critical access facility offering emergency room service, surgery, diagnostic imaging, respiratory, rehab, and lab work. Last but not least, the **Baxter Regional Medical Center** in Mountain Home (870-508-1000; www.baxterregional.com), 624 Hospital Dr., Mountain Home, Ark., is a 268-bed hospital with 90 physicians on staff. As a large regional facility, Baxter Regional's menu of services is as long as your arm (which the folks here will happily fix if you break it).

✳ Wandering Around

EXPLORING BY CAR **Sylamore Scenic Byway** (479-964-7200; www.fs.fed.us/ oonf/ozark/recreation/byways.htm), Ozark–St. Francis National Forests, 605 W. Main, Russellville, Ark. If you head south on SR 5 at Calico Rock, Ark., you will be traveling on the 26.5-mile Sylamore Scenic Byway. This is a particularly gorgeous drive in fall, what with all the changing colors of the oak-hickory forest, but you will also experience high limestone cliffs and a number of panoramic vistas. Continuing on your route through the Ozark National Forest, turn west onto SR 14 (at the town of Allison) and then north onto FR 1110. This road takes you to **Blanchard Springs Caverns**, and you really have to see this hole in the ground to appreciate why it has attracted millions of visitors since 1973. Blanchard is a living cave, still in formation, and the Forest Service offers both mild and difficult tours. You can also fish in Mirror Lake (where the spring emerges) or take a short walk to a glorious waterfall. From Blanchard, you may continue on FR 1110 back to SR 14, or you can just stay a while. Camping is available at not only Blanchard Springs but also the nearby Gunner Pool and the Barkshed recreational area.

EXPLORING BY FOOT ♿ **Mossy Bluff Trail** (501-362-2416; www.swl.usace.army .mil/parks/greersferry), 700 Heber Springs Rd. N., Heber Springs, Ark. Located at Greers Ferry Lake, Mossy Bluff is a 1.6-mile trail that wanders up a wooded bluff and looks down upon both Greers Ferry Dam and the Little Red River. Along the way you will spy Balanced Rock, which should be arrested for breaking the laws of gravity, the Double Tree (sort of an interdeciduous marriage— two healthy trees of differing species that have somehow grown together), and the Weeping Rocks. This last is a bluff face that often seems be shedding tears, as groundwater percolates through the earth and emerges through tiny cracks in the stone. For those who are either handicapped or less than ambulatory, the 660-foot **Buckeye Trail** is wheelchair accessible and offers picnic tables and some pretty views. Trailheads for both Mossy Creek and Buckeye can be found at the William Carl Garner Visitor Center.

EXPLORING BY RIVER **Buffalo National River** (870-439-2502 or 870-741-5443; www.nps.gov/buff), Harrison, Ark. The Buffalo was the first river in America to receive the title "National," achieving that designation via a 1972 act of Congress. Beginning in the Boston Mountains to the west, the Buffalo is nearly 150 miles in length and features limestone bluffs in excess of 500 feet high, whitewater, tranquil floating, horseback and hiking trails, wilderness areas, gravel and sandbars, and infinite opportunities to take photos of wildlife (including a growing elk population). Smallmouth bass are the fish of choice along this river (although you may catch any of about 50 different species), and more than 135 miles are floatable. Throughout the area you will find plenty of outfitters, and camping is available year-round at most of the access points. Better yet, because this area is under the jurisdiction of the National Park Service, you can set up your primitive campsite anywhere along the length of the Buffalo. For those who might want to learn more of the river before embarking, stop by the **Tyler Bend Visitor's Center** (near Marshall, Ark., just off US 65).

This is seriously one of the most beautiful rivers in America, and both the middle and lower sections can be floated by anyone who can tell the difference between a canoe and a calliope. In other words, it's mellow from midpoint all the way to the spot where it joins the White River. There are any number of little towns close by to these sections, so both access and acquisition of supplies are a breeze.

The upper sections of the river are a somewhat different story. The Buffalo's upper reaches feature a number of whitewater rapids of varying difficulty; you'd be wise to know your level of expertise before putting paddle to stream. On the other hand, should you float the Upper Buffalo, you can pull your canoe to the bank, take a 1-mile walk, and visit Hemmed-In Hollow. This box canyon features a 200-foot waterfall, the highest in the heartland.

There is one other section of the Buffalo, but it should be reserved solely for aficionados of whitewater. Found in the headwaters section between the towns of Boxley and Fallsville, in this area the Buffalo is in fact known locally as the Hailstone River. You'll encounter whitewater in the Class III range, not to mention boulders, undercut banks and ledges, twists, turns, and drops. Again, not for the faint of heart, and not recommended for any but the most proficient.

White River (870-425-2700 or 1-800-364-4263; www.agfc.com/fishing_ol.html). When discussing the White River below Bull Shoals Dam, you're discussing the quest for monster trout. Yes, the scenery is gorgeous, and there are resorts and access points aplenty. But the 90-mile stretch of river downstream from Bull Shoals (basically to the town of Guion, a little blip of a place in Izard County) has produced brown trout more than 30 pounds and rainbows more than 19. The fish are fat and plentiful for a couple of reasons. First, the discharge from the Bull Shoals hydro plant comes from the cold water deep in the lake. It's just the right temperature for trout. Second, Arkansas Game and Fish annually dumps untold thousands of trout in the river. This combination of factors makes for the type of angling experiences that are the stuff of dreams. True, you may not catch a 33-pound brown, but trout in the 5-to-10-pound range are extremely common (and people catch a few 20-pounders nearly every year). Oh, and there is also the possibility of catching cutthroat and brook trout.

BULL SHOALS DAM

As a general rule, most folks like to float fish the White in a Jon boat (a flat-bottomed aluminum craft—one

of which can be seen at the side of almost any house in the Ozarks) with a fairly small outboard, comfy chairs, and a well-stocked cooler. While fly-fishing is extremely popular, Ozarkers aren't picky about bait. Crawdads are very popular, but then so are worms, corn, and marshmallows. This might offend the sensibilities of fishing purists, but then again, your garden-variety Ozarker has never really cared too much about such politically correct nonsense. We fish with what they're biting on, be it a Woolly Bugger fly, a Bass Buster Beetle Spin, or a fat ol' nightcrawler. Fishing is about catching fish, after all, not what the neighbors think of your equipment.

The beauty of the White River, with its high bluffs and deep forests, cannot be overstated. However, again, it is the fishing that draws the crowds. That, and the White River Monster.

Indeed. From Guion south, the White starts warming up, and you will catch your regular river fish. But near the town of Newport, locals have reported seeing a 30-foot, spiny-backed, snaky sort of critter for the past 100 years. They call him "Whitey," and he supposedly bellows and (when not swimming) walks the muddy banks on three-toed feet. A fellow snapped a good picture of Whitey in the early 1970s, and in 1973 the Arkansas State Legislature created the White River Monster Refuge next to Jacksonport State Park. The resolution put in the record by the legislators deemed it a crime to "molest, kill, trample, or harm the White River Monster while he is in the retreat."

I've said it before and I'll say it again: If you want to be amused, you'd best learn to amuse yourself. Ozarkers are real good at that.

Little Red River (501-362-9067; www.swl.usace.army.mil/parks/greersferry/visitorscenter.htm), 700 Heber Springs Rd. N., Heber Springs, Ark. The Little Red begins its trek around the town of Scotland, Ark., and meanders to the west until dumping into Greers Ferry Lake. It is below Greers Ferry Dam where things start to get interesting. Stocking of trout in the Little Red began in 1966, and the downstream good-fishin' stretch of 35 miles has since become a favorite of those seeking browns, rainbows, and cutthroats. Just how popular is this river?

MAMMOTH SPRING

In 1992 the late "Rip" Collins pulled a 40-pound, 4-ounce brown from the river, setting a new world record (incredibly, he caught the monster on ultralight tackle). You'll find numerous outfitters, access points, marinas, and camping along the Little Red, and at Greers Ferry's **Carl Garner/Army Corps of Engineers Visitor's Center** you can hike trails overlooking the river and find more specific details.

Below the dam, the Little Red's flow is dependent upon the release of waters from the hydro plant. The river may be lower or higher, but it's floatable at all times. If you want a river that has fast sections (and not a lot of boulders and snags), this is a great choice. The scenery is classic, and as a basic rule, the farther you get from the dam, the more placid the waters become. Of course, the farther downstream you go, the greater the risk that the water is low. No matter. The fishing is fine, and you can't beat the surroundings.

Spring River (870-856-3210 or 870-625-7364), Hardy, Ark. The fact of that matter is that some folks prefer a natural spring over those that are aided or assisted by human-made dams. I personally don't see the difference—water is just water after you're a few miles downstream—but in deference to the purists, the Spring River is about as natural as they get. The massive Mammoth Spring, which pumps out more than 9 million gallons of 58-degree water per hour, is the fountain from which the Spring springs. Trout fishing is good, fly-fishermen love it here, and the floating is superb. Outfitters abound, and canoe rental is always right around the corner. Floaters will not be disappointed in the least by the high bluffs or the forests that line the banks of the Spring. One nice thing about this river is that its waters are clear as glass (and cold—just get splashed by the guy in the front of the canoe if you don't believe me). The Spring is all sorts of gorgeous, and you'll want to bring your camera for shots of wildlife and the occasional (small) whitewater waterfall.

✳ Towns and Villages

Batesville, Ark., is the second oldest city in Arkansas, ceded to the United States by a 1808 treaty. Trading outposts appeared on the White River around 1810. Today the "City of Hospitality" lives up to its name by throwing one of the best pig-smoking festivals in the country. The last weekend in March witnesses the Ozark Hawg Barbecue Championship, which not only fills the air with the aroma of hickory-smoked pig but also draws nationally known country music stars. The town of 10,000 is also known for Lyon College, home of the annual Arkansas Scottish Festival and the renowned Old Independence Regional Museum.

Clinton, Ark. Located on the Little Red River, and just a stone's throw from Greers Ferry Lake, this seat of Van Buren County holds an annual event that cannot be duplicated anywhere in America. Though the National Championship Chuckwagon Races began as just an excuse for a Labor Day party among a few friends, they didn't stay that way for long. Today more than 20,000 people show up to watch not only chuckwagon racing but also bronc fanning and a "Snowy River Race." And yes, just like the movie of the same name, that latter event involves downhill runs and a dive into the river. This town of 2,300 does it right.

Fairfield Bay, Ark. A new town by any standard of dating, Fairfield Bay can be found on the western shoreline of Greers Ferry Lake. Established in 1966 as something of a retirement village, Fairfield is called home by approximately 3,000 full-time residents. One of the many reasons visitors stop here is for golf, with the famous Mountain Ranch (usually named the Top Public Course in Arkansas by *Golf Digest* magazine) and challenging Indian Hills golf courses. Also in Fairfield Bay are activities such as trail riding, cruises, camping, and fishing.

Hardy, Ark. With only 600 residents, Hardy may not be the biggest town around. It is, however, loaded with things to do. Mammoth Springs is located just a few miles north, and the river it feeds (the Spring) offers year-round floating and excellent fishing for rainbow trout. In the warmer south fork of the river, you can try your luck for bass, walleye, or even a muskie. Originally settled in the late 1800s, and a getaway for the wealthy of Memphis during the Roaring '20s, Hardy's downtown of today is full of quaint shops offering the wares of local artisans. In addition, you can check out three museums, enjoy summer musical shows and festivals, and stay in a number of bed & breakfasts.

Heber Springs, Ark. The seat of Cleburne County, Heber Springs is regarded as the epicenter of activity for both the 31,000-acre Greers Ferry Lake and the Little Red River. Originally known as Sugar Loaf, the town today boasts nearly 7,000 residents. Since 1963 particularly, when the lake was completed, Heber Springs has drawn visitors from around the country for a variety of water-sports, fishing, and resort opportunities. Even better for anglers, the Little Red holds the distinction of being the site where the world's largest brown trout (40 pounds, 4 ounces) was landed in 1992. Greers Ferry Lake also holds the world angling record for walleye and hybrid striped bass. In Heber you'll find a wealth of places to dine, stay, and shop, not to mention the annual World Championship Cardboard Boat Races.

Jasper, Ark. This is a small but gorgeous area, and the 500 residents of Jasper are nestled in the midst of lands protected and owned by either the state or federal government. The most popular spot to float on the Buffalo National River is just north of Jasper (a 25-mile section between the towns of Ponca and Pruitt); it offers huge bluffs, campgrounds, and the highest waterfall in the heartland (Hemmed-In Hollow). Each June, Jasper plays host to the Buffalo River Elk Festival. This shindig honors the large-racked herbivores that are making a comeback in the region, not the folks who join a fraternal organization and have a secret handshake.

Mountain Home, Ark. This town of 12,000 is virtually surrounded by the 22,000-acre Norfork Lake and the 45,000-acre Bull Shoals Lake. Just a few miles south of Mountain Home, the Buffalo National River flows into the White. If this information doesn't give you a good impression of what goes on in these parts, then it might be helpful to add that the state-record striped bass taken from Bull Shoals weighed in at 53 pounds. In the White River brown trout of more than 30 pounds and rainbows topping 19 pounds have been landed on rod and reel. Canoeing, camping, and water sports of all sorts rule the day in Mountain Home, not to mention the glorious beauty of Bull Shoals–White River State Park. Restaurants, resorts, golf courses, and historic venues are plentiful. You could easily spend a couple of weeks around Mountain Home and not even come close to being bored.

Mountain View, Ark. This town of 3,000, seat of Stone County, is widely known as the Folk Music Capital of the World. Such a lofty claim can easily be backed up should you happen to drop by the Ozark Folk Center. This state park, really the only one of its kind, has as its mission the task of preserving the traditional music, crafts, heritage, and traditions of the Ozarks. In Mountain View you will find a plethora of music festivals, such as the Arkansas Folk Festival in April and the Mountain View Bluegrass Festival in both March and November. Then again, you could also attend the **Arkansas Bean Fest** and the **Great Championship Outhouse Races** on the last weekend of October. During the warmer months you'll find all sorts of folks pickin' and grinnin' on the town square, and if you tire of the music, there's always the phenomenal fishing on the White River. Indeed, it's a little place, but during some of its festivals the town population may expand to upward of 100,000.

Pocahontas, Ark. It is only fitting that a woman named Cinderella was involved in the naming of Pocahontas. Dr. Ransom Bettis, father of the aforementioned glass-slipper girl, is listed as the first settler in the area that would later become the Randolph County seat. Thomas Drew married young Cindy, and, apparently fond of lyrical names, Drew and Bettis joined forces to found Pocahontas. It is good they focused on the female protagonist of the Pocahontas tale, as a town named Captain John Smithburg would be less than pleasing to the ear. At any rate, this town of nearly 7,000 souls is the site of Old Davidsonville State Park (Davidsonville having been the oldest settlement in Arkansas). Good fishing and floating abound here, and in fact there are five streams (the Fourche, Current, Eleven Point, Black, and Spring) that can keep any worm-drowner occupied for days.

✳ To See

MUSEUMS 🐾 ✐ ♿ **Mark Martin Museum** (870-793-4461 or 1-800-566-5561; www.markmartinmuseum.com), 1601 Batesville Blvd., Batesville, Ark. NASCAR fans will be well acquainted with the name Mark Martin. During his long racing career Martin has racked up an impressive number of wins (he's started in more than 500 Nextel Cup races, and in 2002 alone won the Coca-Cola 600 and brought home more than $5 million in prize money). Now, at his brand-new Ford/Mercury dealership in Batesville, Martin has created a museum dedicated to his legendary career and the sport of racing. You'll see the Batesville native's Viagra/Coca-Cola car, his 1990 Folgers Thunderbird, and the 2005 IROC car that he drove to his fifth championship. For racing fans, this is a must-see. The museum is just opening at the time of this writing, so call ahead for hours.

🐾 ✐ ♿ **Old Independence Regional Museum** (870-793-2121; www.oirm.org), 380 S. 9th St., Batesville, Ark. Hours for the Old Independence are Tue.–Sat. 9–4:30, Sun. after 1:30. $3 adults, $2 for those over 55, and $1 for kids over the age of 6. Housed in an impressive 1936 WPA structure constructed of locally quarried sandstone, the Old Independence is on the National Register of Historic Places. Open since its restoration in 1998, the museum is a living legacy to the 12 counties that were at one time part of the huge Independence County (Baxter, Cleburne, Fulton, Independence, Izard, Jackson, Marion, Poinsett, Sharp, Stone, White, and Woodruff). Exhibits date from the days of the Shawnee Indians to more modern times.

🐾 ✐ **Van Buren County Historical Society Museum** (501-745-4066; www.gozarks.com/pride/vbcmuseum/index.htm), 1123 3rd St., Clinton, Ark. Tracing the history of Van Buren County, with a priority placed on family histories and displays, the Van Buren County Museum is open weekdays 10–4. There is no admission fee.

❦ ✍ **Log Cabin Museum** (501-884-4899), 335 Snead Dr., Fairfield Bay, Ark. Admission is free, and hours are Mon. 2–5, Tue.–Sat. 1–4. For a look at how Arkansawyers lived in the 19th century, drop by this 1850 log cabin, which was dismantled, moved to its present site, and re-created in painstaking detail. All items found within the cabin would have been used in a home of the 1880s.

❦ ✍ **Veteran's Military Museum** (870-856-4133 or 870-856-3677), 738 Main St., Hardy, Ark. Admission is just $1, and hours are Sat. 10–5, Sun. 11–5. There are thousands of items crammed into this little museum, memorabilia ranging from the Revolutionary War to the Gulf War, including a nice selection of the virtually indestructible Willys Jeeps.

✍ ♿ **Vintage Motorcar Museum** (870-856-4884), 301 W. Main S., Hardy, Ark. Open daily; $6 adults, $3 for kids under 12. This private collection features 50 autos ranging from a 1908 Sears Runabout to a 1981 DeLorean (gotta love that stainless steel and those gull-wing doors). Some of the exhibits are a little odd (car jacks?), but all in all this is a pretty amusing place.

❦ ✍ ♿ **Hilary Jones Wildlife Museum & Elk Information Center** (870-446-6180; www.arkansaselkcenter.com), SR 7 Byway N., Jasper, Ark. With a free admission price, and open daily 9–7, this museum is named for Newton County native Hilary Jones. Mr. Jones made a repopulated Arkansas elk herd his main priority when he was on the Arkansas Game and Fish Commission, and in fact the herd itself bears his name. This museum features elk information, aquariums, and a plethora of information on rivers, hunting, fishing, and outdoor recreation. A gift shop features carved wooden toys and all sorts of interesting geegaws and gimcracks fashioned from elk antlers.

❦ ✍ ♿ **Olmstead Museum** (501-362-2422; www.olmstead.cc), 108 S. 4th St., Heber Springs, Ark. Open weekdays. Sometimes it's a good thing to be able to say that business is dead. The Olmstead Museum, found in the Olmstead Funeral Home, traces the history of the postmortem biz. Established in 1896, this is the oldest business in town, and it's on the National Register of Historic Places. You will find the obligatory horse-drawn hearse, funeral artifacts, and many photos of early Heber Springs. As you'll soon discover, people are dying to come to the Ozarks.

E. Bob Jackson Memorial Museum of Funeral Service (870-523-5822), 1900 Malcolm Ave., Newport, Ark. Just in case you didn't get enough funeral fun and inhumation hijinks while you were back in Heber Springs, the E. Bob Jackson Memorial Museum of Funeral Service can help you top off your tanks. On hand is yet another 19th-century, horse-drawn death wagon, as well as a chapel and all sorts of memorabilia.

CULTURAL SITES ❦ ✍ ♿ **Batesville Confederate Monument** (870-793-2378), 192 E. Main St. (Independence County Courthouse), Batesville, Ark. Maybe the South won't rise again, but the soldiers of the Confederacy are never truly forgotten in Batesville. On the lawn of the courthouse square you will find the Batesville Confederate Memorial, a remembrance of the local men and units that served in the War Between the States.

◎ ✐ ⭑ **Top O' the Ozarks Tower** (870-445-4302; www.topotheozarks.com), Tower Road off SR 178 (2 miles west of Bull Shoals Dam), Bull Shoals, Ark. Open seasonally every day (usually from mid-March till December), this 180-foot tower on top of Bull Mountain permits a view of more than 50 miles on a clear day. The panorama of Bull Shoals Lake and the White River is very nice as well. The tower is elevator equipped (you don't have to walk the entire 240 steps, but you do have to walk some to reach the uppermost deck) and has been the site of 34 weddings since 1964.

◎ ♞ ✐ **Mountain Village 1890** (870-445-7177 or 1-800-445-7177; www.1890 village.com/index.htm), 1011 C. S. Woods Blvd., Bull Shoals, Ark. Open Mar. 15–May 15, Wed.–Sun. 10–5; May 15–Labor Day, daily 9–6; Labor Day–Oct. 31, Thu.–Mon. 10–5; and Nov. 1–Dec. 1, Fri.–Sun. 10–4. $10 adults, $6 children. Mountain Village 1890 (located next to Bull Shoals Caverns) is a collection of 11 authentic houses and businesses that have been restored to 1890s perfection. There's a jail, blacksmith and coffin shop, church, doctor's office, general store, and much more. Around the re-created village you'll see plenty of livestock (ducks, rabbits, and miniature horses and donkeys), and of course you don't want to miss the Ozark moonshine still. This one is the real deal, discovered in Bull Shoals Cavern in 1958, and it allegedly belonged to a ridge runner named Manfred Long. Should you wish to get hitched among stills and miniature donkeys, the church at Mountain Village 1890 is available for the service (as is the Crystal Altar Room in Bull Shoals Cavern).

♞ ✐ ⭑ **Cotter Rainbow Bridge** (870-435-2663; www.cotterarkansas.com/bridge.htm), US 62-B, Cotter, Ark. Spanning the White River at the little town of Cotter is the famous Rainbow Arch Bridge. One of the most photographed bridges in the Ozarks, this one was built in 1930 and is listed on the National

THE MUCH-PHOTOGRAPHED RAINBOW ARCH BRIDGE

Register of Historic Places. The old bridge was getting to be in sad shape, and in 2002 the Arkansas Highway Department began an extensive renovation. Work was completed in 2004 (to the tune of $6 million), so now you won't feel you are going to plunge into the river when you drive across the thing.

✿ ✐ **Indian Rock House** (501-884-4899), 337 Snead Dr., Fairfield Bay, Ark. Okay, kids, it's unsubstantiated-rumor time again. The Indian Rock House, a sandstone grotto residing under a hillside on Fairfield Bay's Indian Hills Golf Course, was for certain the home of Bluff Dweller Natives. A more dubious story that consistently makes the rounds is that at this site, in 1542, Hernando de Soto met with Indians while searching for the Fountain of Youth. My bet is that he probably met with Jerry Lee Lewis, Bigfoot, Judge Crater, and the ghost of Jim Morrison while he was there, too. At any rate, the grotto is sort of cool, if you're into grottoes, and is conveniently located close to the Log Cabin Museum.

✿ ✐ ♿ **Greers Ferry National Fish Hatchery** (501-362-3615; www.fws .gov/greersferry), 349 Hatchery Rd., Heber Springs, Ark. Established in 1965 by the U.S. Fish and Wildlife Service, the Greers Ferry Hatchery breeds and stocks more than 220,000 pounds of trout each year, placing them to a large degree in the very cold tailwaters of dams such as Greers Ferry (just in case you wondered, 220,000 pounds of trout translates to more than 1,225,000 fish). More than 50,000 visitors tour this facility each year, and a visitors center features an aquarium and guided tours. The hatchery is open every day 7–3, and admission is free.

✿ ✐ ♿ **William Carl Garner Visitor Center** (501-362-9067; www.swl.usace .army.mil/parks/greersferry/visitorscenter.htm), 7000 Heber Springs Rd. N., Heber Springs, Ark. Admission is free, and hours (though they do vary) are generally Apr., Mon.–Thu. 10–6; May–Sep., daily 10–6; and Oct., Mon.–Thu. 10–6. The center is usually closed Nov.–Mar. The official Army Corps visitors center for Greers Ferry Lake, the Garner Center offers general information on the lake and dam, an exhibit area and auditorium, an audiovisual presentation on the Little Red River region, and a replica of the 40-pound, 4-ounce, world-record brown trout caught by Rip Collins in the Little Red in 1992.

✿ ✐ ♿ **Old Mill** (870-269-5337), 308 W. Main St., Mountain View, Ark. This old mill, aptly named "Old Mill," was in operation 1914–1969. A large-scale restoration was undertaken in 1983, and today visitors may view the original equipment and peruse photos and memorabilia from the very cool town (Folk Music Capital of the World) of Mountain View.

WOLF HOUSE

Wolf House (870-425-2755; www .baxtercounty.org/wolf.html), SR 5, Norfork, Ark. The oldest house in Arkansas (built sometime between 1809 and 1825), the Wolf House resides in its original location at the confluence of the White and Big North Fork rivers. Owned by the city of Norfork and staffed by volunteers, the renovated old home is full of nearly 500 items dating from the 18th and 19th centuries. The 1870 "hanging mousetrap" and "glass parlor flytrap" indicate that keeping up with pesky and pestilent vermin was a full-time job in years past (now we just worry about computer spam, politicians, and the supplicants of political correctness . . . somehow the vermin of then seems preferable to the vermin of now). For a step back in history, this is the place. Call ahead for hours and fee information.

HISTORIC SITE **Natural Bridge** (501-745-2357), Clinton, Ark. Just travel 4 miles north of Clinton on US 65 and you will find a natural 100-foot sandstone bridge. The Natural Bridge took millions of years to form, and in fact was often used as a bridge by the pioneers. Near the site is a small museum and gift shop, open mid-Mar.–late Oct.

ELEPHANTS ♂ ♿ **Riddle's Elephant and Wildlife Sanctuary** (501-589-3291; www.elephantsanctuary.org), Greenbrier, Ark. I've always wondered if an elephant with skin problems has to visit a pachydermatologist. No matter, if you want to see elephants up close and personal, you must absolutely visit Riddle's. Granted, this 330-acre preserve is just a tad outside of the Ozark borders (a few miles north of the town of Conway off US 65), but it's also just different enough that a few miles shouldn't prevent inclusion in this book. This sanctuary, founded in 1990, houses and cares for all breeds of elephants obtained from zoos, circuses, and even private owners. You can visit the sanctuary on the first Saturday of every month 11–3. Admission is $5. If you're really, really into elephants, the sanctuary offers numerous "Elephant Experience Weekends." From Friday night till Sunday you'll take part in feeding, watering, bathing, toenail trimming, and (one imagines) filling up the peanut trough. The price is $700 (you must be 18 or older) and includes all meals (the human type) and lodging in a dorm.

✴ To Do

FISHING ♞ ♂ ♿ **Collins Creek** (501-362-2416 or 1-877-470-3309; www.swl .usace.army.mil/parks/greersferry/hiking.htm). Located off SR 25, Heber Springs, Ark. Near the Greers Ferry Fish Hatchery and adjacent to Greers Ferry Dam, this seasonal stream was converted to a year-round trout fishery by the Arkansas Game and Fish Commission. Named for the late Rip Collins (who caught the world's largest brown trout from the Little Red River), the project required the building of a cold-water supply line from the base of the dam to the creek and took 8 years to complete. Now the creek is home to rainbow and brook trout and includes three special fishing platforms for the handicapped. This is a catch-and-release-only stream, and kids under 16 may fish anywhere for free. Adults (who have licenses) are permitted to fish the lower stretches when accompanied by a kid under 16.

GOLF ♞ ⛳ **The Course at Eagle Mountain** (870-612-8000; www.thecourse ateaglemountain.com), 800 Gap Rd., Batesville, Ark. This relatively new course in Batesville is an 18-hole, 7,009-yard semiprivate challenge complete with pro shop, bar, and grill. Greens fees for 18 holes are $45 (which includes a cart and range balls) Fri.–Sun. and $35 Tue.–Thu., Apr. 1–Oct. 31. Rates are $10 cheaper in the off-season. Nine-hole fees are $25 Fri.–Sun. and $20 Tue.–Thu., Apr. 1–Oct. 31 (and $5 less off-season).

🦅 ⅋ **Cooper's Hawk Golf Course** (870-368-3280; www.coopershawkgolf.com), SR 69 Spur, Melbourne, Ark. Another recently built facility, this 18-hole, 7,011-yard public course features a fully stocked pro shop, full bar and grill, and very affordable rates. With cart included, greens fees for 18 holes are $25 Mon.–Thu. and $30 Fri.–Sat.

🦅 ✐ ♿ ⅋ **Mountain Ranch Golf Club** (501-884-3400; www.mountainranch golf.com), 820 Lost Creek Pkwy., Fairfield Bay, Ark. The awards are many for this course. The *Arkansas Democrat-Gazette* gives it a number one ranking, and *Golf Digest* says it's the best public course in the state. Both that renowned authority and *Golf Week* magazine place Mountain Ranch as one of the top 500 courses in the nation. This very challenging par-72, 18-hole layout features a well-stocked pro shop, practice range, and clinics by PGA experts. Also on-site, for after your round, is **Bogie's** restaurant. There are various fees at Mountain Ranch, depending on whether you have purchased a golfing package. However, for the general public, rates run $49 with cart included. That is a phenomenal deal for a course of this quality.

🦅 ✐ ♿ **Tannebaum Golf Resort** (501-362-5577 or 1-866-876-8269; www .tannenbaum.com), 5 Kustin Dr., Drasco, Ark. This golfing community/resort offers another par-72, 18-hole course rated highly by *Golf Digest*. The joy or the curse here, depending upon your perspective and golf proficiency, are the wide changes in elevation from hole to hole and tee to green. The facility also offers a driving range, putting and chipping green, and practice bunker. Also, if you tire of golf, you are always close to the incredible fishing of Greers Ferry Lake and the Little Red River. Greens fees, Mon.–Thu., are $39 from 10 to 2 and $30 from 2 to closing. Fees Fri.–Sun. are $49 from 10 to 2, $35 from 2 on.

✐ ♿ ⅋ **Big Creek Golf and Country Club** (870-425-8815; www.bigcreekgolf .com), 452 Country Club Dr., Mountain Home, Ark. Seeing as how *Golf Digest* gave Big Creek five out of five stars and in 2001 called it "the best new course in America," the magazine obviously thinks it's a doozie of a place to play. Sitting on 200 acres, the 7,320-yard, 18-hole course features a three-tiered driving range, practice putting and chipping greens, and a practice bunker. Also on-site is a well-regarded restaurant with a full bar. Summer rates for the general public are $60 on weekdays and $70 on weekends, Apr. 1–Oct. 29. This includes a cart rental; winter rates are lower. You can't wear blue jeans or tank tops on this course, and the management will be right unhappy if you try to tote along your own cooler of Budweiser.

TRAIL RIDES ✐ ♿ **Horseshoe Canyon Guest Ranch** (501-791-2679 or 1-800-480-9635; www.goher.com), SR 74 W., Jasper, Ark. An all-inclusive 350-acre dude ranch located 7.5 miles west of Jasper, Horseshoe Canyon is high in the sky at 2,100 feet. Offering a horsy type of vacation for the entire family, it charges a single rate that covers cabin, meals, maid service, kids' programs, canoeing, horseback riding, rock climbing, and any other ranch activities. Summer rates begin at $185 per night adults, $145 ages 8–16, and $95 ages 3–7. During summer there is a three-night minimum stay; in fall and spring (when rates are lower), a two-night minimum. This is an interesting ranch featuring knowledgeable staff and a herd of very well-trained horses. Rides generally last from 1½ to 4 hours (primarily in the morning and afternoons), and any number of social gatherings take place after dinner. The ranch offers satellite Internet access for guests, but pets are not accepted. Also, should you wish a swallow of hooch while sitting around the campground, you'll need to bring your own. Newton County, where Horseshoe Canyon ranch is located, is drier than an Amish jokebook.

✳ Wild Places

✎ ☸ ✐ ᇰ **Ozark National Forest, Sylamore District** (870-269-3228; www .fs.fed.us/oonf/ozark), 609 Sylamore Ave., Mountain View, Ark. Part of the 1.2-million-acre Ozark National Forest, the 133,000-acre Sylamore District consists of deep forests and beautiful streams, bluffs, meadows, and rivers. It also holds such treasures as Blanchard Springs Caverns. There are campgrounds set up at such places as Blanchard, but since this is national forest, you can also pitch your tent almost anywhere. Hiking, hunting, fishing, and horseback riding are all equally popular in the Sylamore District. If you're really into hiking, a 31-mile stretch of the Ozark Highlands Trail travels close to SR 342 north of Mountain View.

For the **Buffalo National River** and the **White River**, see *Exploring by River*.

PARKS ✎ ☸ ✐ ᇰ **Bull Shoals–White River State Park** (870-431-5521; www .arkansasstateparks.com/bullshoalswhiteriver), 129 Bull Shoals Park, Lakeview, Ark. Consisting of 45,440 acres of water straddling the Missouri-Arkansas border, Bull Shoals Lake and the White River offer one of the greatest combinations for water sports and monster-trout fishing in the United States. The Bull Shoals–White River State Park, at 732 acres, is located at the spot where Bull Shoals Dam crosses the White River. The park (established in 1955) in fact stretches along the banks of the White; over the years it has become one of the most popular fishing/camping destinations in Arkansas. Featuring 105 campsites along the river, the park offers interpretive programs Apr.–Jan., picnic areas, playgrounds, trails, and a marina. The latest addition to Bull Shoals–White River (scheduled to open in spring 2006) is a $4.5 million, nearly 16,000-square-foot visitors center. The center, to be named after longtime Arkansas resort owner Jim Gaston, will include interpretive exhibits, a theater, gift shop, and exhibit hall. Campsites run from $9 per night for a primitive tent spot to $75 per night for "Rent-A-RV" units. At the marina/dock, 20-foot Jon boats with a 15-horse motor begin at $40 per day plus fuel, and kayak rental begins at $25 per day (or $8 per hour). Rental of a canoe or kayak with haul-back services is $40 per day. Those wishing an interpretive tour by water might opt for a Jon boat float trip ($15 per hour), an interpretive barge tour ($6 per person for adults, $3 kids), or an interpretive kayak or canoe trip ($15 adults, $7.50 kids).

🦫 🐾 🐟 ♿ **Mammoth Spring State Park** (870-625-7364 or 870-625-7382; www.arkansasstateparks.com/mammothspring), SR 9 and US 63 N., Mammoth Spring, Ark. Spewing out 9 million gallons of water per hour, Mammoth Spring forms a 10-acre lake and serves as the headwaters of the Spring River. You can't actually see this spring (it's 80 feet under the lake), so you'll just have to trust me that it's there. However, this park features much more than simply its giant natural spigot. A tourist information center offers exhibits, basic services, and a gift shop, and a walking trail leads to a restored 1886 Frisco railroad depot. The

🦫 🐾 🐟 ♿ **Ozark Folk Center State Park** (870-269-3851 or 870-269-3871; www .ozarkfolkcenter.com), SR 382 Spur (1 mile north of Mountain View). Turn left onto Jimmy Driftwood Pkwy. (which is also SR 382). It dead-ends at the Folk Center parking lot. Let's put it this way: If you can visit only one place in the Arkansas Ozarks, this should be it. In a word, the Ozark Folk Center State Park is amazing, not to mention one-of-a-kind. An 80-acre complex within the 640-acre park is dedicated to preserving the old Ozark heritage through traditional music, dance, pioneer skills, stories, and native crafts. More than anything else, it is this park that makes Mountain View the Folk Music Capital of the World. In the park's **Crafts Village** (open Apr. 15–Sep. 31, Wed.–Sat. 10–5, and Tue.–Sun. 10–5 in Oct.) you'll find a plethora of local artisans demonstrating the art of the old homestead and creating Ozark crafts. During this same season, the park's 1,025-seat music theater offers Wed.–Sat. concerts at 7:30 PM (Tue.–Sun. concerts in Oct.) and frequent Sunday gospel sings. There's a gift shop (open Apr. 1–Dec. 17) offering everything from corn husk brooms, pottery, and oak baskets to knives, quilts, and real fruit preserves. You may stay in the park's 60-room **Dry Creek Lodge** or enjoy a uniquely southern Ozark meal (no possum, though) at the **Skillet Restaurant**. The lodge is open year-round, but the restaurant is only open Apr. 15–Oct. 29, 7 AM–8 PM. You'll find a smokehouse, herb garden, tram service, and music, music, and more music. It seems everywhere you venture in this park you will trip across musicians playing either solo or in groups; strumming fiddles, dobros, and dulcimers; picking at guitars, banjos, bass, and autoharp.

In addition, the Ozark Folk Center holds a celebrity concert series every season (call or check the park's web site for details and prices), along with myriad classes, workshops, and festivals. Workshops cover the gamut from using medicinal herbs and botanicals to learning pottery techniques and playing the dulcimer. And this is but a tiny sample.

Admission fees to the Crafts Village or music auditorium alone are $9 adults, $6 ages 6–12. A combination admission for both the Crafts Village and music auditorium is $15.50 adults, $8.25 kids. Tickets for the celebrity concert series vary by performer.

depot and its grounds not only hold a caboose and historical artifacts, but are also near the remains of an early mill and hydroelectric plant. Picnic tables and a playground, set amid large oak trees, overlook the lake. The Depot Museum and Caboose is closed to the public on Mon., but on other days the admission fee is $2.50 adults, $1.50 ages 6–12. Both pedal boats and single kayaks can be rented for $6 per hour, and a tandem kayak is $8 per hour. You should note that there is no camping at Mammoth Springs.

Jacksonport State Park (870-523-2143; www.arkansasstateparks .com/jacksonport), 205 Avenue St., Newport, Ark. Marking the border of the Delta and the Ozarks is Newport, Ark., home of Jacksonport State Park. Via the steamboat trade, Jacksonport was a busy and rollicking place in the 1800s. During the Civil War, the area was nearly always in a tug-of-war between the Gray and Blue, and at one time or another it was occupied by both sides. Today the park features the old 1872 **Courthouse Museum** and a restored stern-wheel paddleboat, the *Mary Woods No. 2*. Also on the site are picnic tables, a playground, a swimming beach on the White River, and 20 campsites with water and 50-amp electric service. Campsite fees run from $13 per day for a tent site to $18 per day for a site with water and power. Admission to either the Courthouse Museum or the *Mary Woods No. 2* is $3 adults, $1.50 ages 6–12 (or you can by a combination ticket for $5 adults, $2.75 kids).

Old Davidsonville State Park (870-892-4708; www.arkansasstate parks.com/olddavidsonville), 7953 SR 166 S., Pocahontas, Ark. Near the town of Pocahontas, Davidsonville was the site of the first post office, courthouse, and land office in Arkansas. This town is so old that, by the 1830s, it was already approaching ghost status. Today the 180-acre park contains trails, exhibits, picnic tables, and interpretive tours, but the real reason most folks come to Old Davidsonville is to fish. The park is bordered by the Black River, holds a 12-acre fishing lake (handicapped accessible in places), and rents fishing boats, pedal boats, and canoes. Of the 49 campsites, 23 offer water and electric ($15.50 per night), 25 are tent sites ($9), and 1 offers water and 50-amp service ($18.50). A 14-foot fishing boat (human powered) is just $10 per day, and either a canoe or pedal boat is $5 per hour. A canoe trip with hauling included is $25. There is also the chance to take an interpretive/historical canoe trip ($35 per canoe) or an interpretive tour by foot of the old Davidsonville townsite ($6 adults, $3 kids).

LAKES Greers Ferry Lake (501-362-9067; www.swl.usace.army.mil/ parks/greersferry or www.greersferry lake.org), 700 Heber Springs Rd. N., Heber Springs, Ark. Consisting of nearly 40,000 acres of water surface, Greers Ferry Dam was dedicated in 1963 by President John Kennedy; in fact, this was Kennedy's last dedication before his assassination in Dallas.

Old Davidsonville State Park
First U.S. Post Office established in Arkansas
1817

Around the lake you'll find 18 Army Corps of Engineers campgrounds, not to mention nearly infinite private campgrounds, B&Bs, hotels and motels, marinas, restaurants, and entertainment. Because of the mild winter climate, this area is becoming increasingly popular as a retirement spot. This translates to mean that some of the more passive types of recreation—such as golf, fishing, shopping, and eating—are catered to heavily by local businesses. The Little Red River, below the dam, is renowned for its monster trout, and (as if I haven't mentioned it enough in this chapter) the 40-pound, 4-once brown caught by Rip Collins still holds the world title.

Norfork Lake (870-425-2700 or 1-877-444-6777; www.norfork.com or www.swl .usace.army.mil/parks/norfork/index.htm), Mountain Home, Ark. I was straddling a sailboard about half a mile out on Norfork Lake (I never have learned how to tack correctly; sailing is an evil sport) when a freak storm dropped rain, lightning, and 50 mph winds on my head. My old friend Edward T. Boys was stuck out there as well, graciously trying to help fix the twisted rudder on my board. As I recall, with lightning blasting all around us, Ed and I were forced to lie flat in the water and hold on to those stupid hunks of plastic polymer for near an hour. Bobbing and freezing, I finally looked at him and said, "Well, here's another fine mess I've gotten us into." Ed and I have inadvertently gotten each other practically killed, deafened, humiliated, or maimed a few hundred times over the course of our lives (driving, sailing, blowing things up, accidentally dropping cars on each other), but that's another story.

Finally a brave soul in a motorized Jon boat cruised out through the crashing waves, tossed us a rope, and saved Ed and me from hypothermia and/or becoming popcorn salesmen at the Pearly Gates. It was a highly embarrassing situation, and I'm glad we survived, as dying via an inability to paddle a modified surfboard on a normally placid lake is simply pathetic.

That said, in no way, shape, or form do I blame such a mishap on Norfork Lake itself. With its 550 miles of shoreline and 22,000 surface acres of water, this is one of the most popular weekend spots in the Ozarks. Created in 1944 by the Army Corps, a dam (built for both flood control and hydropower) crosses the North Fork River a few miles from the little town of Norfork (where the North Fork joins with the White River). Around the lake you will find 19 developed parks either managed or subbed out by the corps, and camping is nearly as popular as fishing and boating. The numerous commercial docks offer guides, boats, and equipment of all sorts, and there are a plethora of lodging and dining options. Norfork Lake is loaded with catfish, bass, walleye, bluegill, and crappie, and it's not terribly uncommon for someone to catch a 30-pound striped bass. The North Fork River below the dam once provided the world-record brown trout. Moreover, because of the lake's water clarity, scuba is a hot ticket. Last but not least, the 25,000 acres of corps land around the lake allow for great hiking.

Bull Shoals Lake (870-425-2700; www.swl.usace.army.mil/parks/bullshoals), Mountain Home, Ark. Featuring 45,000 acres of surface water, and surrounded by 60,000 acres of Army Corps of Engineers land, Bull Shoals has been a haven for vacationers and retirees since the 1950s. The White River was dammed for both flood control and hydropower in the late 1940s (the dam itself is about 7 miles north of Cotter, Ark.), and the fishery below Bull Shoals has long been known for containing some of the largest trout in the United States. Within the lake itself, though, the usual suspects of fish (catfish, bass, walleye, and all sorts of panfish) are plentiful for the talented (or just patient) angler. Between the corps, the state of Arkansas, and local entities, there are 19 separate parks around Bull Shoals. In total these hold more than 20 boat ramps, 11 campgrounds, 13 picnic shelters, 11 marinas, and much more. As you would imagine, private enterprises such as lodges, resorts, motels, restaurants, and bed & breakfasts are more than plentiful. With little or no effort you can locate any number of places that will sell or rent you boats and equipment, provide guides, or meet any other need you might imagine.

CAVES ∞ 🐟 ♪ **Bull Shoals Caverns** (870-445-7177 or 1-800-445-7177; www .bullshoalscaverns.com), 1011 C. S. Woods Blvd., Bull Shoals, Ark. Open Mar. 15–May 15, Wed.–Sun. 10–5; May 16–Labor Day, daily 9–6; Early Sept.–Oct. 31, Thu.–Mon. 10–5; and Nov. 1–Dec. 1, Fri.–Sun. 10–4. $10 adults, $6 children. If you are in the dark about the personality of your spouse-to-be, it might be appropriate to get hitched in the Crystal Altar Room deep within Bull Shoals Caverns. Then again, for something less permanent (and in some cases less rocky), you might just want to tour the sights to be found in this living cave. Owned by the same folks who own the Mountain Village 1890, the cave features such geological nifties as a rotunda, cave drapes, stalactite and stalagmite gardens, soda straws, and boxwork. By the way, at the time of this writing (March 2006) you can purchase both the cave and the Mountain Village 1890 for your very own. It comes with 11 acres, 13 buildings stocked with antique furnishings, a 19-hole miniature golf course, and a 2,000-square-foot gift shop. The price is a mere $495,000. Just call the main cavern numbers if you want to own your own cave and village.

🐟 ♪ ♿ **Blanchard Springs Caverns & Recreation Area** (870-757-2211 or 1-888-757-2246; www.fs.fed.us/oonf/ozark/recreation/caverns.html), SR 14 W., Mountain View, Ark. Caves administered by the USDA Forest Service often feature much better tours and sights than their commercial counterparts. This scenario is especially evident at Blanchard Springs Caverns, one of the most interesting holes in the ground you'll ever discover. A three-level cave (two levels are open for guided tours), Blanchard offers several options for exploring. The Dripstone Trail Tour requires about an hour and is accessible to strollers and wheelchairs (if you have helpers with some muscle). Tours leave frequently; $10 adults, $5 ages 6–15. The price is the same for the Discovery Trail Tour, although this path is more arduous

BLANCHARD SPRINGS CAVERNS

(there are 700 steps), so you need to be in decent shape. The Discovery Trail Tour is only available between Memorial Day and Labor Day. Lastly, if you really want to get down and dirty (with emphasis on both—literally), take the Wild Cave Tour. About 4 hours long and requiring reservations, this trip takes you through parts of the cave's undeveloped middle level. You need to be in good shape, as there is much climbing and crawling involved. Also, kids under 10 are not allowed, and parents must accompany kids 10–12. The price for the Wild Cave Tour is $65 per person.

🐚 ✐ **Hurricane River Cave** (870-429-6200 or 1-800-245-2282; www.hurricane rivercave.com), US 65 S., Pindall, Ark. Located north of Conway off US 65 (or about an hour due south of Branson, Mo.), the cave's tour follows an ancient subterranean riverbed. Of course the usual stalactites, stalagmites, columns, and soda straws are both evident and prevalent. One interesting aspect of Hurricane River is that it's been a prime spot for skeletons. Saber-toothed tigers, prehistoric bears, and a complete Indian skeleton have been found within this hole. No surprise on the latter bones, as those who share space with lions and bears tend to have a shortened life span. There's a neat waterfall at the entrance to this cave, and the grounds are quite pretty. Hurricane River is open Mar. 1–Oct. 31; tours take about 45 minutes and cover roughly 1 mile. There aren't a lot of steps (fewer than 40 total), so you don't need to be an Olympic athlete to wander about under the ground. $8.50 adults, $4.50 ages 5–12. In addition, a Wild Cave Tour—which includes a boat ride on an underground river, followed by climbing and crawling—is available. This option is by reservation only and limited to parties of six with everyone above the age of 12. Call for pricing.

✳ Lodging

The number of inns, resorts, B&Bs, and cabins located in this section of the Ozarks is truly astounding. Catering to the millions who visit the White and Little Red rivers, as well as Bull Shoals, Norfork, and Greers Ferry lakes, innkeepers offer accommodations to suit every taste, style, and thickness of wallet. Should you wish to peruse further than the recommended establishments listed here, I suggest you check out the web site provided by the **Bed and Breakfast Association of Arkansas** (www.bedandbreakfastarkansas.com). This site will provide you with further possibilities (as well as some dandy recipes) and more than a few photos of individual guest rooms.

BED & BREAKFASTS ⬤⬤ **Ashley House Bed & Breakfast** (870-368-4577 or 870-368-7455; www.ashley house.net), 618 E. Main St., Melbourne, Ark. Reputed to be the oldest home in Melbourne, the Ashley House was transformed via a 1999 renovation from antiques store to B&B. The home's original flagstones nicely set off the front porch and white picket fence, and Ashley's seven guest rooms are loaded with antiques. Four of these rooms feature king-sized beds, three have queens, and there are also two private guest cottages on the property. All rooms have a private bath and, in a bow to technology, wireless Internet. Located within close proximity to both the Cooper's Hawk Golf

Course and the White River, Ashley House also handles wedding, meetings, and conferences, and it offers both antiques and original artwork for sale. $50–100 per night; call to inquire about kids and pets.

The Cedars Bed and Breakfast (870-297-4197 or 1-800-233-2777; www.thecedarsbnb.com), Old Dolph Rd., Calico Rock, Ark. For a stay in the country, it would be hard to beat the setting or hospitality of the Cedars. You can stay in any of the three guest rooms in the Big House ($74–84) or opt for one of two private cabins ($74–125). This is a well-designed establishment, set in a 240-acre stretch of woods, and the entertainment found in the great room of the Big House will no doubt keep you amused. There's an entertainment center and pool table, or you might want to play a tune on the piano or try out the antique pump organ. The Cedars also offers a pool and sunroom, and a full breakfast comes with your stay at the Big House. The cabins feature a continental breakfast. You'll enjoy blackberry cobblers and blueberry muffins made from berries picked right on the property. Call ahead for info on kids and pets.

☙ **River View Hotel Bed & Breakfast** (870-297-8208; www.ozarks riverview.com), 100 Rodman, Calico Rock, Ark. With a view of the White River, and on the National Register of Historic Places, this 1923 hotel is a simple sort of place for those who wish to get away from it all. Nice touches that help accomplish this goal are rooms without telephones (which may cause a nervous breakdown for those who can't live without their BlackBerry), cotton sheets dried on a clothesline, and a spacious front porch with a swing looking down at the White. All rooms have private bath. Breakfast is a big deal here, featuring everything from biscuits and gravy to eggs laid by the hotel's chickens. There are TVs in all the rooms, but note that some of them are old black-and-white critters. Kids are welcomed here, and though you can smoke outside, don't puff in your room. The River View gives you a bit of the feel of being in the 1950s, and the rates for any of the eight rooms range $65–75.

☙ **The White River Inn Bed & Breakfast** (870-430-2233; www .thewhiteriverinn.com), 924 CR 174, Cotter, Ark. The White River Inn offers more than a touch of luxury for those vacationing on the White River. Three individual guest suites feature 14-foot ceilings, custom-made Mission furniture, fireplace, and Jacuzzi. You'll sleep under 600-thread-count sheets and hand-fashioned quilts. In addition, for a kicked-back evening you can enjoy satellite TV and wireless Internet. In the lodge's great room you may relax on overstuffed leather couches and chairs, watch the big screen, or play any number of board games. A wall of 8-foot windows looks down upon the White River Valley, which makes this room also a wonderful spot to enjoy a leisurely breakfast of locally picked berries, cereals, sausage or bacon, juices, coffee, and homemade biscuits. There is also a trophy room with mounted big game from around the globe, and an outdoor hot tub. Rates at White River Inn are $225 per night, or $860 per night if you'd care to rent the entire lodge. This facility is

more than happy to set you up with fishing guides and spa services, but smoking and pets are not permitted. Kids under 15 are okay, if well behaved, at the owner's discretion.

⊕ 🐾 🐕 ✿ ♿ **Biggers Bed & Breakfast** (870-856-4718; www.biggers bnb.com), 20 Bluff Rd., Hardy, Ark. Looking down on the Spring River, Biggers B&B is often the choice for weddings, honeymoons, anniversaries, and (of course) fishermen. On-site is an outdoor pool and hot tub, and the facility prides itself upon arranging such services as fishing guides, massages, and spa treatments. Three luxury suites include king-sized bed, gas fireplace, two-person hot tub, microwave, refrigerator, coffeemaker, digital cable TV, private bath, and wireless Internet. Five guest rooms in the main house offer similar amenities. Rates at Biggers range $70–175 per night, and both pets and kids are welcomed (there is a $25 charge for pets kept in the room). Smoking is not permitted. Breakfast is included in your room price, and on the property is the well-regarded **Bluff Steak House**, open Thu.–Sat. evenings.

⊕ ✿ **Olde Stonehouse Bed & Breakfast** (870-856-2983 or 1-800-514-2983; www.oldestonehouse.com), 108 W. Main St., Hardy, Ark. A classic stone home built in 1924, the Olde Stonehouse is listed on the National Register of Historic Places. This inn has been serving guests since 1992 and offers six guest rooms and two suites (the latter in a 1905 home located a few blocks from the main house). The rooms here are fairly typical for a B&B—Victorian furnishings, clean and relatively simple—but the suites provide something a bit above and beyond. For instance, the Rose

Suite includes a sitting room, a bedroom with a black cast-iron king-sized bed, cable TV, a VCR, a microwave, a miniature refrigerator, and a 5-foot-diameter jetted whirlpool spa. While a number of packages are offered at the Olde Stonehouse (everything from fishing or golf to weddings and murder mystery weekends), regular rates are $69 for a guest room and $119 for a suite. Kids are welcomed, but smoking and pets are not.

⊕ ♿ ♈ **Abbe House Inn & Sports Resort** (501-250-2223 or 1-877-250-2223; www.abbehouse.com), 3144 Riverbend, Heber Springs, Ark. You will find no shortage of space in this 12,000-square-foot home. A home of the "Tara" genre, it features giant white columns and three verandas totaling 1,700 square feet. It comes as little surprise that Abbe House was voted 2005's number one B&B for outdoor sports enthusiasts by *Inn Traveler* magazine. Situated on 12 meticulously cared-for acres, this inn also backs onto the Lost Creek Golf Course and is close to the Little Red River, Fairfield Bay, and Greers Ferry Lake. Each of 11 guest rooms features a queen-sized bed and whirlpool bath and includes a true southern breakfast served family-style. For those who wish dinner on the premises, the Louisiana-born owners can provide delicious entrées in the $15–25 range. Also, beer and wine are available with your meal. Rates for individual rooms run $65–95 per night, but a variety of packages are offered. One very good option is a guided fishing trip (for two) on the Little Red River. All tackle and equipment is provided, as are accommodations and breakfast, lunch, and dinner. The cost is $400 plus tax, and the only thing that isn't guaranteed is that you'll catch fish. Also, the Abbe House is well known for its weddings. Full or partial planning is available, and price quotes are happily provided.

☞ **Anderson House Inn Bed & Breakfast** (501-362-5266 or 1-800-264-5279; www.yourinn.com), 201 E. Main St., Heber Springs, Ark. With 15 guest rooms, Anderson House is another establishment that is in the heart of fishing Utopia. All rooms have queen-sized bed and private bath, while a great room offers a big-screen TV, stone fireplace, plenty of books, and comfortable lounging couches. You can relax on the front porch overlooking Spring Park (which has walking and jogging paths, as well as tennis courts) or enjoy a breakfast of fresh fruit, scones, pancakes, muffins, or omelets. Room rates are $60–70 per night (add $10 if you wish breakfast included), and packages for fishing and romantic getaways are prevalent. Kids are okay, but dogs will have to find their own accommodations. Use of the devil weed (that would be tobacco, for you city folks) is relegated to the porches and balconies.

☙ ☞ **Barn on the Buffalo** (870-446-6121; www.barnonthebuffalo.com), SR 74 E., Jasper, Ark. After observing some of my more eccentric housekeeping habits (so the dog has his own couch—big deal), visitors have occasionally been moved to comment, "Boy . . . you musta been born in a barn." Seeing as how I've seen some pretty spiffy barns in my life, such criticisms don't rile me a whit. A perfect example of fine barn living would be the Barn on the Buffalo. Located near Jasper, Ark., the peaceful haven on 8.5 acres is located just 300 feet from the Little Buffalo River. Walking trails, beaver dams, fishing, swimming, and canoeing are just out your door. The Barn itself, fully renovated, features hand-painted floors, complete kitchen, full bath, air-conditioning, TV and VCR with movies, and three bedrooms. It sleeps seven and includes all utensils, dishes, and linens. The best part of the Barn is its affordability. You can rent just one bedroom for $75 per night, or all three for $125 a weekend. Call to inquire about dogs, smoking, and the best places to fish.

☙ ☞ ♿ **Enchanted Hideaway Bed & Breakfast** (870-428-5440; www.enchantedhideaway.net), 1.25 miles off SR 7 on CR 23 (Smith Mountain Rd.), Jasper, Ark. Talk about a great-looking home: This large new residence in the woods (bordering the Ozark National Forest) was built from hand-peeled logs and has shining wood floors, and upon arrival you'll feel as if you've discovered a secret cabin in the forest. This is the place for those who love nature, as wildlife is everywhere and not necessarily shy. All rooms have private bath, ceiling fan, central heat and air, TV, VCR, movies, refrigerator, coffeemaker, and clock radio. Breakfast is standard with a room rental, and rates are $60 per night for a downstairs room (two rooms, both handicapped accessible) and $65 if you stay in one of the three rooms on the second floor. There's the smell of wood smoke in the air, coming from the cozy fire in the great room, and a library full of good books is at your disposal. Of course the big draw here is your proximity to the breathtaking Buffalo River. However, you're also close to such hot spots as Eureka Springs, Ark., and only about 60 miles south of Branson, Mo. Kids are welcomed, and you can smoke outside, but leave your dog, cat, badger, kangaroo, raccoon, aardvark, or ferret at home.

Country Oaks Bed & Breakfast (870-269-2704 or 1-800-455-2704; www.countryoaksbb.com), 17221 SR 9, Mountain View, Ark. It's pretty hard to go wrong in Mountain View; all that music floating around in the air just makes a body feel perky and bright. And you certainly won't go wrong if you stay in the Country Oaks. Situated on 69 acres, a newly built, Victorian-style farmhouse holds five guest rooms, while a separate carriage house holds three more. On the property is a 7-acre lake, noted for producing bass as large as 10 pounds, and you'll greet the morning with a full breakfast. As is consistent with many B&Bs in this region, the unspoken theme here is simplicity and fun. Relax on the porch or one of the many benches scattered about the property. Play horseshoes, read a book, or take a walk. Rates run $65–105, and neither pets nor kids under 12 are permitted. A dog and a cat or two do reside here, so if you want canine companionship, the house hound will likely be glad to oblige. Smoking is outside only, and since this is a dry county, you'll either have to bring your own firewater or learn how to build a still.

✍ **Wildflower Bed & Breakfast on the Square** (870-269-4383 or 1-800-591-4879; www.wildflowerbb.com), 100 Washington St., Mountain View, Ark. In summer some of the greatest bluegrass and folk musicians imaginable congregate on the town square and play till their fingers wear out. For those of a musical bent, the Wildflower's location cannot be beat—it's located right on that same square, so you can pick, grin, sing, or just listen to your heart's content. Of course you're also close to some great fishing, hiking, and shopping. This inn, built in 1918 and on the National Register of Historic Places, features rooms with king- or queen-sized bed, cable TV and a CD player, private bath, phone with dataport, ceiling fans, central heat and air, bathrobes, fresh cookies, and a huge breakfast. $85–125 per night. Kids are okay, but pets are not. Also, Wildflower is pretty strict about its no-smoking policy. Get caught smoking inside the building, and you'll have a $200 cleaning fee added to your credit card.

✍ **Inn at Mountain View, 1886** (870-269-4200 or 1-800-535-1301; www.innatmountainview.com), 307 Washington, Mountain View, Ark. Okay, here's a secret. If you want to stay on the square in Mountain View, you will not find anyone more hospitable than the innkeepers (Scott and Shay Pool) at the Inn at Mountain View. Aside from being nice folks, they're liable to pull out the banjo or fiddle at any time. In my book this rates as a prime reason to reserve a room. Built in 1886 (hence the name) and on the National Register of Historic Places, the inn offers 10 guest rooms and two cottages. Frankly, there's not a square inch of this place that could be described as anything other than friendly and charming. Rates run $78–140 per night, with the $140 Garden Suite including a Jacuzzi for two, fireplace, shower, kitchenette, lace curtains, and antique Victrola. Amenities in the other rooms are private bath, king- or queen-sized bed, central heat and air, ceiling fan, cable

INN AT MOUNTAIN VIEW, 1886

TV, VCR, and wireless Internet. The common room holds a pool table, PlayStation 2, Gamecube, video library, books, and popcorn. In the backyard are water gardens, and you stay (literally) right next to the fire rings and square where all the local musicians gather for acoustic jams. What is *really* cool about this inn (especially to a blues-harp playing Hillbilly like me, who also enjoys pickin' the strings whenever possible) is that should you fail to bring your musical instrument the innkeepers will loan you a banjo, fiddle, guitar, or dobro. Now, that's hospitality. And don't forget breakfast. It can include thick smoked bacon, scrambled eggs cooked with cream and butter, hash browns, biscuits and sausage gravy, mini waffles, fruit compote, juices, and homemade pecan syrup.

These folks win the prize hands-down. Put it this way: If your grandma was/is inordinately cool, her house would be just like the Inn at Mountain View.

RESORTS ⊗ ✿ **Esta's White River Retreat** (808-324-8637 or 808-324-0174; www.estaswhiteriverretreat.com), 280 Sloan Lane, Locust Grove, Ark. Relaxing and off the beaten path (about half an hour from either Mountain View or Batesville), Esta's offers eight log-and-cedar cabins with stunning views of the White River. The grounds themselves feature a pool, "swimming hole," and sports field with volleyball, basketball, and horseshoes. A two-night stay is required, and for the price of $115 you will stay in a river-view cabin with Jacuzzi, enjoy a full breakfast, and have access to the pool, boat ramp, and sports field. For $10 more (per person, per day) you may order a gourmet picnic basket lunch. Several different packages are offered, one being a canoe trip down the White. For an additional $25.50 to your room charge, you can rent a two-person canoe with all the equipment, a prepared picnic basket lunch, and transportation of both yourself and the canoe. Esta's can also provide full wedding services, and those interested in nuptials on the White should call for a quote. This is another spot that is located in a dry county, so if you want a drink (and don't want to have to drive 40 miles), it is advised that you BYOB.

🔫 🐾 ✂ ⓖ **Bull Mountain Resort** (870-445-5971 or 1-800-530-5647; www.bullmountain-resort.com), 2224 Central Blvd., Bull Shoals, Ark. Your pet is welcomed here for an additional $35 fee (with approval), $25 of which will be returned if the room doesn't need excessive cleaning. In addition to liking the pups, Bull Mountain offers 10 one- and two-bedroom cottages with heat and air-conditioning, cable TV, coffeemaker, microwave, linens, and dishes. You're close to Bull Shoals Lake; for those evenings when you wish to stay in, the facility features a pool, fire pits, horseshoes, and volleyball. $60–90 per night; $360–540 per week. Please note that smoking is not permitted inside the cottages.

✂ ⓖ **Calico Rock Cabin** (901-299-4952; www.bbonline.com/ar/crcabins), 500 Calico St., Calico Rock, Ark. If you seek a little more privacy than you'll find at the resorts or B&Bs, this cabin—sitting on a high bluff above the White River—offers it in spades. You'll love the view, the glowing wood interior, and the stone fireplace. The cabin offers a full kitchen with dishwasher and microwave, wraparound deck, gas grill, Jacuzzi, and all linens and towels. The price is $150 per night for a couple ($20 for each additional person), and neither smoking nor pets is allowed. While the phone works for local calls (free), you will need to bring a calling card if you wish to contact anyone long distance.

🔫 ✂ **Rainbow Bridge Lodge** (870-435-6666; www.rainbowbridgelodge.com), 2nd St. and McLean Ave., Cotter, Ark. Located in downtown Cotter on the second story of a historic building, this 3,400-square-foot space comes with a full kitchen and cable TV and offers access to a dock, pier, and boat launch. Cotter is at the heart of great trout fishing in the White River, and you can find plenty of outfitters, guides, and equipment rental. The entire lodge can be rented for $225 per night (10 people . . . a great deal), or any of five rooms can be rented singly for $45–85.

🔫 🐾 ✂ ⓖ **Sportsman's Resort on the White River** (870-453-2424 or 1-800-626-3474; www.sportsmans-resort.com), 458 Marion County Rd. 7004, Flippin, Ark. A well-known resort on the White River, Sportsman's offers 22 cabins located on 5.5 park-pretty acres. All the cabins (newly renovated in 2003) come with kitchens, satellite TV, microwave, coffeemaker, cookware, and utensils. Daily maid service is available for a small additional fee. Conveniently, a small grocery store on the premises carries almost every staple you will need. Should you prefer not to cook at all, the resort's casual little café is open for breakfast and dinner (closed at lunch, but box meals are available for picnics or fishing trips). Cabin rentals range from $89 per night for an efficiency to $329 for a chalet that sleeps 12 and boasts a 48-foot outdoor deck. Amenities include a playground for the kids, basketball court, and horseshoe area, but in truth most people are here for the fishing. Rental boats—20-foot Jon boats with motors—are available for $89 per day, or you can opt to hire an experienced guide. $179 per day for one person, $109 per person per day for two people, or $99 per person per day for three. The cost encompasses the guide, boat, motor, fuel, a box lunch, soft drinks, hooks and sinker, and fish cleaning. If you want the guide to bring bait, add $6 a person.

Sportsman's is one of the few places around that are truly dog-friendly, something exemplified by the fact that it doesn't charge an extra fee for Rover. This is a very gracious gesture, as dog owners know how hard it is to find accommodations that will (a) accept a pet at all and (b) not charge you an exorbitant extra fee for hypothetical damages. That said, it is the responsibility of Rover's owner to not abuse the pet policy this establishment offers (i.e., don't screw it up for the rest of us). Keep pup off the bed, and don't let him trash the joint.

🐾 🏕 ✿ 🚱 **Gaston's White River Resort & Restaurant** (870-431-5202; www.gastons.com), 1777 River Rd., Lakeview, Ark. Without doubt the best-known resort on the White River, Gaston's has been serving customers since 1958. What started as six cottages and six boats on a 20-acre plot is now 400 acres, 2 miles of riverfront property, and 79 cottages that cover the spectrum from an economy model with two beds to a two-story lodge with 10 bedrooms. There's an airstrip on the property for those who wish to fly in, more than 70 rental boats, a very nice restaurant, club, gift shop, tennis court, playground, game room, swimming pool, and nature trails. And if you're looking for a ringing endorsement, Gaston's has been written up by (take a deep breath here), the *Arkansas Times*, *Better Homes and Gardens*,

Woman's Day, *Midwest Living*, *Outside* magazine, *Southern Living*, *Field & Stream*, and many other publications. There is no additional fee for bringing your pets, but the resort does ask that they not have fleas and that they do stay on a leash if outdoors.

Cottage amenities include cable TV, phone, voice mail, and high-speed Internet. A two-bed unit with a bath (more of a hotel room) is $90 per night for two people. The standard cottage, which comes with king-sized and double bed, bath, and kitchen, is $115. Two-bedroom cottages are $132–193, and prices go up from there. Four-bedroom cottages are $322–635, and the 10-bedroom River Villa rents for $1,050 per night (sleeps 20 people). A two-person guided float trip (18 miles) is $270 per day and is best for those who want to sightsee and just do a little bit of fishing. Serious anglers will want to opt for a local trip, which covers far fewer miles and is intended to help you hook a lunker. The price for a full day is $230 for two people, or $270 with lunch. Note that you need to bring your own equipment, bait, and fishing license. You can also rent boats, fishing tackle, rods, and reels at the dock. Gaston's calls itself "America's Number One Trout Fishing Resort." Judging by its longevity and repeat business, more than a few folks agree.

CANOE OUTFITTERS, CAMPING, AND RVS ✿ 🏕 🚱 **Sylamore Creek Camp & Cabins** (870-585-2198 or 1-877-475-4223; www.sylamorecreek .com), 214 Sylamore Creek Rd., Mountain View, Ark. Located on Sylamore Creek on the site of an old Indian village, and with the White

River just a few hundred yards downstream, this facility is but 5 miles north of Mountain View. Fishing and swimming are at your disposal—there is a boat ramp on the creek—and cabins, tent sites, and RV spaces are available. A "lodge"-style camp store carries all sorts of groceries, drinks, ice, and fishing supplies. Though off-season rates are less expensive, Mar. 1–Nov. 1 cabins cost $65–120 per night or $350–680 weekly. Kids under 12 stay free, and all the cabins are nonsmoking. RV sites come with water, electric, picnic table, grill, and fire rings. For basic water and electric the price is $15 per night, $90 per week. A full hookup is $18 a night, $108 per week. If you'd like cable TV, there's an additional fee of $2 per night, $7 per week. Wireless Internet is also available. Last but not least, both primitive tent sites and those with services are available. A site with electric and water is $15 per night, $90 per week, and a primitive site goes from $10 per night or $60 per week. Pets on a leash are permitted.

🐾 🏕 ✎ ♿ **Bull Shoals–White River State Park** (870-431-5521; www .arkansasstateparks.com/bullshoals whiteriver), 129 Bull Shoals Park, Lakeview, Ark. (See *Parks*.) To make reservations, either call the number above or make online reservations at www.accessarkansasparks.com/pages/ adpt_reslist.htm.

🐾 🏕 ✎ ♿ **Jacksonport State Park** (870-523-2143; www.arkansasstate parks.com/jacksonport), 205 Avenue St., Newport, Ark. (See *Parks*.) To make reservations, either call the number above or make online reservations at www.accessarkansasparks .com/pages/adpt_reslist.htm.

Old Davidsonville State Park (870-892-4708; www.arkansasstateparks .com/olddavidsonville), 7953 SR 166 S., Pocahontas, Ark. (See *Parks*.) To make reservations, either call the number above or make online reservations at www.accessarkansasparks .com/pages/adpt_reslist.htm.

Greers Ferry Lake (501-362-9067; www.swl.usace.army.mil/parks/greers ferry or www.greersferrylake.org), 700 Heber Springs Rd. N., Heber Springs, Ark. The Army Corps of Engineers manages 13 campgrounds around Greers Ferry containing more than 1,200 individual campsites. Most are open Apr./May–Oct./Nov., though the John F. Kennedy Park (which also offers access to the Little Red River) is open year-round. Campsites are free at the Mill Creek campground, while other areas (depending on water and electric availability) run $10–18. Spots may be reserved. Either contact the number above or visit www.reserve usa.com.

Bull Shoals Lake (870-425-2700; www.swl.usace.army.mil/parks/bull shoals), Mountain Home, Ark. At Bull Shoals, 12 campgrounds containing 500 individual sites are managed by the Corps of Engineers. The range is from primitive tent clearings to spots with both water and electric. The campgrounds are open Apr.–Oct., but call ahead; exact dates vary. Campground fees are $12–16. Spots may be reserved. Either contact the number above or visit www.reserveusa.com.

Norfork Lake (870-425-2700 or 1-877-444-6777; www.norfork.com or www.swl.usace.army.mil/parks/ norfork/index.htm), Mountain Home, Ark. At Norfork the Army Corps manages eight campgrounds with 467 individual sites, as well as four primitive camping areas. As a rule the campgrounds are open Apr.–Sep., with prices $9–16 per night. Spots may be reserved. Either contact the number above or visit www.reserveusa.com.

Ozark National Forest, Sylamore District (870-269-3228; www.fs.fed.us/oonf/ozark), 609 Sylamore Ave., Mountain View, Ark. You may camp almost anywhere for free in the Ozark National Forest, as long as you don't mind not having any services. There are a number of day-use areas in the forest—which include swimming beaches, boat ramps, and more—and most of these have a $3-per-vehicle, per-day fee. For maps, brochures, or information, you might want to stop by the Sylamore Ranger Station on SR 14 N. in Mountain View, Ark.

Buffalo National River (870-439-2502 or 870-741-5443; www.nps.gov/buff), Harrison, Ark. Camping opportunities are plentiful along the Buffalo National River. There are 13 separate campgrounds, with the Maumme South, Mount Hersey, Spring Creek, and Woolum sites being free and open year-round. These sites are of a more primitive nature (as is the Carver site, which charges a fee) and are available on a first-come, first-served basis. Also, these sites are not handicapped accessible. The popular Buffalo Point campground offers both tent sites and drive-in sites with water and 20- or 30-amp service. To play it safe, you should reserve a site here by calling 1-877-444-6777 or by checking out www.reserveusa.com. This campground offers 83 drive-in sites, 20 walk-in sites, and is handicapped accessible in spots. Fees vary; call or visit the reservation web site

for details. Campgrounds of a more modern variety, but that charge a fee Apr.–Oct. (they are open and free the rest of the year), are the Erbie, Kyles Landing, Lost Valley, Ozark, Steel Creek, and Tyler Bend sites. Some offer drive-in services, tent camping, or both. Most offer a few handicapped-accessible sites. Tent sites average $10 per day; drive-in sites, $17.

✳ Where to Eat

EATING OUT ♨ ♿ ✎ ☷ **Josie's at the Lockhouse** (870-793-7000 or 870-926-9670; www.josiessteakhouse.com), 50 Riverbank Dr., Batesville, Ark. Open for lunch Tue.–Fri. 11–2, for dinner Thu.–Sat. 4–11. Reservations are recommended for dinner. A family restaurant, Josie's is a big and airy establishment that overlooks the White River. The restaurant moved to this location in 2004, after many years in Waldenburg, Ark. Not only can you get a great steak or catfish fillet, but if so inclined you can also take the stage during frequent open-mike and karaoke nights. On weekends, more times than not, you'll find live music. For lunch, grab the "Loaded Fries" appetizer. Yeah, they're french fries, but for the $6.95 price tag you get a pile of them. Plus, they're covered with three different cheeses, bacon, and chives (could these be Arkansas-style nachos? It sure seems that way). Char-grilled burgers fall into the $8 range, or you can opt for pasta, salads, or the fully obligatory catfish. A whole cat, served with fries, hush puppies, and coleslaw, is a mere $8.95. The evening meal becomes a tad snazzier, with appetizers such as coconut shrimp ($8.95) and shrimp-stuffed portobello mushrooms ($12.95). Josie's is known for Angus steaks, and prices range from steak on a stick at $18.95 to a 6-ounce fillet at $21.95 (the 16-ounce rib eye and the 14-ounce New York strip are $21.95 as well). Of course you can also order a 7-ounce lobster for $24.95 or (again) a catfish fillet for $12.95. Wine is available by either the glass or bottle, and there's a decent selection of beer by the bottle.

🍴 🚗 ♿ **Sodie's Fountain & Grill** (870-453-7632 or 870-453-2218; www.sodies.com), 109 N. 1st St., Flippin, Ark. It goes without saying that any restaurant that features large seating capacity (I'd estimate about 150 in this case) and a gift shop is gearing heavily for tourists. That's not a bad thing as long as the food is decent, and Sodie's definitely gets a ranking of more than decent. Okay, you can get breakfast, lunch, or dinner (a fairly standard menu), but that's not why I'm recommending you stop. The reason to come to Sodie's is for its reasonable facsimile of an old-fashioned drugstore soda fountain. The shakes and malts are hand dipped; the ever-trustworthy banana splits and sundaes are made while you watch. More than that, you have to like a place that fixes you a lime or cherry Coke by squirting (or "jerking"—hence the name *soda jerk*) a dollop of flavoring into your cola. It's a nice touch. In Flippin you're right on top of some pretty fine fishing holes—the White and the Buffalo rivers, to name two. Better yet, in case you didn't know, this town was pretty much ground zero for Bill and Hillary Clinton's infamous Whitewater land-development fiasco. I couldn't tell you if the famous political power couple ever ate at Sodie's, and thus I will refrain from expounding on the ironic, hypothetical interplay that might have transpired when a soda jerk meets the other kind.

🚗 ♿ 🍷 **Gaston's White River Restaurant** (870-431-5202, ext. 206; www.gastons.com), 1777 River Rd., Lakeview, Ark. Open daily from mid-Feb. till Thanksgiving weekend for breakfast, lunch, and dinner. Dec.–mid-Feb., the restaurant is open Fri. night–Sun. Brunch is served every Sunday year-round. Judging by the number of the contraptions hanging from the ceiling, somebody at Gaston's likes bicycles. Then again, they also enjoy old-timey photos, farm tools, and antiques. Gaston's Resort itself has been around for nearly five decades, and the restaurant features not only locally famous trout dishes but also a full bar and wine list. Breakfast includes the usual suspects of eggs, omelets, pancakes, and French toast, with a steak-and-eggs meal (arriving with hash browns, toast, or biscuits) setting you back $10.50. For lunch, you can pig out on a half rack of ribs for $18, chicken-fried steak for $11.50, or the catfish fillet for $16. For $10.50 you can bring in your own catch, and the kitchen will prepare it either broiled or fried. Most sandwiches are in the $8–10 range. Dinner offers a host of appetizers (again, running at or around $10), and a full rack of hickory-smoked ribs for $25. A variety of trout dishes (of the amandine and hollandaise genre) are priced in the $21–23 ballpark, and a filet mignon is $34. Numerous seafood entrées are on the menu, and half a fried chicken costs $18.

🍴 🚗 ♿ **Fred's Fish House** (870-625-7551), 207 Main St. (off US 63), Mammoth Spring, Ark. Sometimes less is more—more or less. Thus, the only thing you need to know about

Fred's Fish House is that it's often cited as serving the best catfish in Arkansas. I'd say such a statement is partially incorrect; Fred's serves up the best catfish in the Western world. The cooks use cornmeal batter (not too heavy and not too light), and your meal arrives with hush puppies, cole-slaw, and pickled green tomatoes. If ordering the all-you-can-eat deal, don't fill up too quickly on french fries or the puppies. Pace yourself and concentrate on the catfish. Best of all, it's tough to spend much more than $10–12 at Fred's.

DINING OUT ✎ & ♈ **178 Club Restaurant** (870-445-4949; www.178 club.com), SR 178 W., Bull Shoals, Ark. Open Tue.–Sat. 11–5 for lunch, 5–10 for dinner. There's a Sun. buffet 9:30–1, and Sun. dinner is served noon–9. In business since 1980, this well-known eatery at Bull Shoals has a menu that is roughly the size of the Reader's Digest condensed version of *War and Peace*. If you can't find something you like at 178, then you'd best just cook at home. Dinner appetizers include oysters on the half shell for $9.89 a dozen, escargots for $7.99, or gator bites (just what it sounds like) for $6.89. The seafood menu covers the gamut from tilapia to grouper to crawdad étouffée, but in keeping with the in-depth catfish reports featured throughout the other chapters of this book, please note that 178's fillet, either fried, broiled, or blackened, is $14.29. For a better deal, and more novelty, the seafood platter offers shrimp, scallops, catfish, and frog legs for $19.99. Steaks are in the $15–22 range, and chicken entrées run $11–17. Moving into the pork arena, you can grab a full rack of ribs for $22.99. If you want your sauce on the side

(and who the heck doesn't), tell your server when ordering. Burgers, salads, desserts, and a large kids' menu round out the evening meal. Plus, there is a full bar, wine list, and beer. Among the salads, sandwiches, and entrées found on the lunch menu, few items exceed $10.

✎ & ♈ **Café Klaser** (501-206-0688; www.cafeklaser.com), SR 110 E. (across from the Swinging Bridge Resort), Heber Springs, Ark. Hours in summer are Mon.–Wed. 4:30–8:30, Thu.–Sun. 11–8:30. On Fri.–Sat. nights the restaurant is open till 10. Located right on the Little Red River, Café Klaser has a signature dish that everyone should try at least once. The crawdad-stuffed tenderloin, available in 4 ounce, 8-ounce, and 12-ounce varieties, is that fine fillet of beef stuffed with crawdads and rice. The cost, from small to large, is $9.95, $15.95, or $18.95. Other than that, you will find a number of Cajun-style dishes here, as well as plenty of sea-food and steak. Frog legs are $12.95, and the catfish fillet is $8.95. Another specialty is the shrimp moutarde at $11.95, or you can have the tried-and-true 16-ounce rib-eye steak for $17.95. You'll find plenty of salads and burgers, and (happily) Café Klaser does offer the legendary oyster po'boy sandwich. It's $5.95, as is the equally delicious catfish po'boy. The exterior of the café is a bit disconcerting—basically a very large green and white steel building. Don't let that stop you in the least. The inside is nice, and the food is terrific. Liquor laws in Arkansas can be a bit dicey, but Café Klaser has a private club license, so you can get a beer or a drink. The law states that all members of the club (and their guests) can have a nip, and thus a year's membership is only $10. It's a silly law that makes no sense, but then again an awful lot of laws are like that.

✳ Entertainment

✿ ✎ Ozark Heritage Arts Center & Museum (870-447-2500), 410 Oak St., Leslie, Ark. You might not think the old stone gym in Leslie (a 1938 WPA-built structure) would hold a 400-seat theater. As we say in the Ozarks, "That's what ya get for thinkin'." The auditorium features everything from local performers to an open-mike night on Friday. And there's not only a theater in the facility but also an art gallery, a museum full of artifacts from the Leslie of yesteryear, and all sorts of interesting remnants that came from what was once the world's largest whiskey barrel factory. This place is amazingly gorgeous

JIMMY DRIFTWOOD BARN

inside; definitely worth a stop for nifty sights and good music. Hours change in winter and summer, so call ahead for both this information and various admissions.

LIVE MUSIC ✿ ✎ ♿ **John Taylor's Laid Back Pickin'** (870-269-9597; www.taylorstradition.com), 16484 SR 9 S., Mountain View, Ark. The present John Taylor carries on the Mountain View music tradition pioneered by his father and grandfather. This music show of long-standing reputation features not only the old tunes of the Ozarks but a number of newer pieces as well. Dancing is also part of the show, and visitors are invited to kick up their heels (but not during the gospel numbers—that would be viewed as rude in these parts). This is a family show, and everyone is welcomed. While there is no set admission price, donations are expected (this can be whatever you think is fair and can afford). This is good mountain music the way it ought to be, and well worth any price you're willing to pay. Apr.–Oct., all shows begin at 7:30 on Mon., Tue., Fri., and Sat. Weekend shows only are held in late Feb. and Mar.

✿ ✎ ♿ **Jimmy Driftwood Barn** (870-269-8042), 19775 SR 5 N., Mountain View, Ark. If you aren't immediately acquainted with the name of the late Jimmy Driftwood, he was the man who wrote the classic tune "Battle of New Orleans." In fact, he wrote it 18 years before it became famous, as a way for his high school history students to remember that the fight took place during the War of 1812. Driftwood is an Arkansas icon for his prolific recordings and compositions, and his barn is still a hot spot for music. Stop by at 7 PM Fri.–Sun. and you'll catch incredibly talented local musicians playing county, gospel, and bluegrass. Call ahead for information on special events and prices.

🌹 ✒ ♿ **Mountain View Folklore Society** (870-269-8215; www.mtnview folkloresociety.com), 224 Franklin St., Mountain View, Ark. At 6 PM every Sat. drop by this Franklin Street address to hear local musicians playing traditional Ozark tunes. In summer bring a lawn chair, look at the stars, and watch the performers as they take the stage in front of the courthouse. There is no admission fee, but donations are always welcomed if you feel like pitching a few bucks in the hat.

THEATER 🌹 ✒ ♿ **The Imperial Dinner Theatre** (870-892-0030 or 1-888-515-8218; www.imperialdinner theatre.com), 1401 SR 304 E., Pocahontas, Ark. When it opened in 1941, the Imperial was one of those grand old movie houses that featured nickel flicks, neon marquee, and that newfangled air-conditioning. The theater closed in the mid-1970s and sat empty for two decades. Renovated in the 1990s by volunteers, the Imperial now features live plays and musical presentations (along with full meals) approximately every other month. Dinners always include salad, entrée, dessert, and beverage, with the price for the meal and the show $19.95 adults, $17.95 students. On Fri.–Sat. dinner is served at 6:30 and showtime is 7:30. For Sunday matinees, the meal is served at 1 PM and showtime is at 2.

SPECTATOR SPORTS ✒ **Batesville Speedway** (870-251-1200; www .batesvillespeedway.com), 5090 Heber Springs Rd., Locust Grove, Ark. A

³⁄₈-mile, red-clay oval track, the Batesville Speedway features stock cars, modifieds, sprint cars, and even demolition derbies. For Fri. and Sat. races the gates generally open at 5:30. Grandstand seating is $10 for adults, with kids 11 and under admitted free.

✒ ♿ **North Central Arkansas Speedway** (870-449-5277 or 870-453-8450; www.northcentralarspeed way.com), US 62, Flippin, Ark. Located 4 miles west of Flippin on US 62, this speedway features a ³⁄₈-mile dirt track, with races every Fri. night. You'll see hobby stock cars and trucks, modifieds, pure stock and cruisers, mini stocks, and go-carts. The racing season runs mid-Mar.–Sep., with gates opening at 6 PM and racing beginning at 8 PM. Call for prices of the various races.

✳ Selective Shopping

Serenity Farm Bread (870-447-2211; www.serenityfarmbread.com), Leslie, Ark. Mon.–Fri. 8–5, Sat. 9–4, Sun. 9–3. For some of the best sourdough bread you'll ever taste, stop by one of Serenity Farm's two locations in Leslie (that's about 50 miles south of Harrison, Ark.). The first location is in the old Farmer's Bank Building; the second is about 0.5 mile south of town in a 100-year-old Sears "kit" house. This operation uses only certified-organic flours, unrefined sea salt, filtered water, and natural sourdough starter.

The Dulcimer Shoppe (870-269-4313; www.mcspaddendulcimers .com), 104 Sylamore Ave., Mountain View, Ark. Mon.–Sat. 9–5. The dulcimer is one of those instruments that is incredibly easy to play—and much harder to master. The craftsmen at the Dulcimer Shoppe have nearly 150

THE DULCIMER SHOPPE

years' combined experience in hand building these instruments and will have you up and strumming in no time.

Stone County Ironworks (870-269-4766 or 1-800-380-4766; www.stone iron.com), 408 Ironworks Dr., Mountain View, Ark. This place calls itself "America's Blacksmith Shop," which is not bad considering that the operation began in 1979 in an abandoned gas station. For beds, furniture, garden accessories, or virtually anything else forged and crafted from iron, this is the place.

✴ Special Events

Also see Towns and Villages.
March **Ozark Hawg BBQ Championship** (870-793-2378; www.my batesville.org/recreation.php), 409 Vine St., Batesville, Ark. BBQ fans will want to be in Batesville during the last weekend in March. The Ozark Hawg Championship, held at Batesville's Riverside Park on the White River, brings in pitmasters from around the nation. This is a sanctioned BBQ event (yes, there is a competition BBQ tour), and winners in the various categories are invited to the legendary Memphis in May BBQ cook-off. In addition to great food, you'll hear great music; in years past, entertainers such as Trace Adkins and Jon Randall have been on hand.

Bluegrass Music Show (870-448-3665), Van Buren County Fairgrounds, Marshall, Ark. This mid-March show features numerous bands guaranteed to keep your toes tapping. $8 per day.

Main Street Hardy Spring Gun & Knife Show (870-856-3571; http://oldhardytown.net), Hardy, Ark. Held in late March in the old Hardy gym (there's also a fall show in November), this is the place to be if you like things that go bang. There's plenty of buying, selling, and trading of both old and new guns, but you'll also find knives of every shape, size, and description, Civil War memorabilia, and a variety or doodads, geegaws, gimcracks, and novelties. The show takes place Sat. 9–5, Sun. 10–4. $3 adults; kids under 12 are admitted free.

Mountain View Bluegrass Festival (1-888-679-2859; www.mountainview-bluegrass.com), Mountain View, Ark. One of the many productions hosted at the Ozark Folk Center State Park, this three-day event in early March features not only a plethora of great bands and solo artists but also an infinite number of impromptu jams. A three-day pass is $40, with tickets for individual days falling in the $12–18 range.

Ozark Folk School (870-269-3851; www.ozarkfolkcenter.com), P.O. Box 500, Mountain View, Ark. Held for five days in mid-March, the Ozark Folk School affords you the opportunity to learn all the stuff your humorless, grammar-obsessed high school teachers ignored. You can take workshops in blacksmithing, stained glass, pottery, or quilting. You can learn how to make lye soap, cook on a wood-stove, or grow and tend an herb garden. You'll pick and grin as you attend workshops on mountain dulcimer, banjo, fiddle, or ukulele, and tone your voice on Ozark folk songs. Craft workshop fees run $225, and music workshop fees are $325. As a rule, you can take only one class during the week (since classes are given at the same time). If you wish to stay on site, check out the various lodging and meal programs. The Ozark Folk School is found at Ozark Park Center State Park, located 1 mile north of Mountain View on Spur Rd. 389 (which is off SR 5, SR 9, and SR 14).

April **Arkansas Folk Festival** (870-269-8068 or 1-888-679-2859), Mountain View, Ark. It would be something of a letdown if the Folk Music Capital of the World didn't have a folk festival. Fear not, for it takes place over three days in mid-April. Bring an instrument if you play; if you don't, just grab yourself some spoons, kazoo, or tambourine. People will be jamming all over town, particularly on the town square. In addition to nonstop music, you will enjoy a parade, arts, crafts, and food vendors, and a variety of games and competitions.

Arkansas Scottish Festival (870-698-4382; www.lyon.edu/webdata/groups/shp/asf/festival06), 2300 Highland Rd., Lyon College, Batesville, Ark. Taking place for two days in late April, this festival celebrates the Scottish roots of Lyon College with piping, dancing, a parade of clans, and a traditional feast. There are also Scottish athletic events, most of which seem to revolve around tossing oddly shaped objects. A two-day pass is $16 adults, $10 ages 17 and under.

June **Hardy Homesteaders Day** (870-966-3644), Loburg City Park, Hardy, Ark. For one day in mid-June, Hardy celebrates the past with wagon rides, quilting and spinning demonstrations, blacksmithing, corn grinding, mule jumping, turtle races, and much more. Admission is free, though there are some minimal charges for food and drink.

Buffalo River Elk Festival (870-446-2455; www.theozarkmountains.com), Jasper, Ark. Taking place on the town square for two days in late June, this free event draws more than 100 artists, vendors, and artisans. The kids can take part in the fishing derby, and everyone loves the Dutch oven cook-off and horseshoe tournament. Live entertainment is a given. These are the Arkansas Ozarks, after all.

Arkansas Fiddler's Contest (870-447-2500; www.ohac.info), Ozark Heritage Arts Center, Leslie, Ark. Aficionados of the fiddle descend on Leslie to compete in junior and senior divisions, as well as an open competition, for one day in late June. The winner is pretty much regarded as the best fiddle player in Arkansas (at least till next year). $7 adults, $5 kids and seniors.

July ☞ **World Championship Cardboard Boat Races** (501-362-2444; www.heber-springs.com), Heber Springs, Ark. If you always wanted to be a boatbuilder but lacked the time, knowledge, or funds, you can still sate your latent desire by entering the World Championship Cardboard Boat Races in Heber Springs. It's held on a single day at the end of July, and you can shoot for being the "pride of the fleet" (unless your boat happens to sink in spectacular fashion, in which case you receive the Titanic Award). In addition to the boat races, kids can take part in a sand-sculpting contest and dig for buried treasure. You won't want to miss the World Championship Watermelon Eating Contest, and at the end of the festival the Cardboard Boat Demolition Derby is a flat-out riot. For admission and parking you won't spend more than about $5.

August **White River Water Carnival** (870-793-2378; www.mybatesville.org), Riverside Park, Batesville, Ark. It's not the oldest festival in Arkansas (that would be the Yellville Turkey Trot), but it is the oldest Arkansas festival on the water. The White River Carnival, nearly 70 years old, takes place for two days on the first weekend in August. You can expect a car and motorcycle show; arts, crafts, and food vendors; a huge parade; and the White River beauty pageant. As always, prepare yourself for great music.

September **National Championship Chuckwagon Races** (501-745-8407; http://chuckwagonraces.com), 2848 Shake Rag Rd., Clinton, Ark. Taking place Fri.–Sun. on every Labor Day weekend, the Chuckwagon Races make a NASCAR event seem as tame as a game of Yahtzee. With a variety of races, this extravaganza's prime focus involves folks driving their carts and chuckwagons at full tilt around an oval track. It has to be seen to be believed, and there are plenty of ambulances on hand in case somebody flips, tips, or crashes. More than 20,000 people show up for the races, and if you want

a motel room in Clinton, you'd best call months in advance. The ranch where the races are held does offer camping, and reservations (yes, you'll need them if you want a spot) are accepted after July 5. Call 501-745-5250 or 501-745-8407 to reserve your spot. More than just races, the spectacle also includes clinics, concerts, BBQ, horse and mule sales, a barn dance, a trade show, and even a non-denominational church service. If you tire of the chuckwagon races themselves, which is virtually impossible, you can also watch a Snowy River Race. This flat-out horse race is straight out of the famous scene from the movie *Man from Snowy River*. Admission to the races is $20 Fri.–Sat. and $10 on Sun.

White River Days (870-431-5521), Bull Shoals–White River State Park, 129 Bull Shoals Park, Lakeview, Ark. This Labor Day weekend event celebrates the history and majesty of the White River. Admission is free, but there is a charge if you wish to take either a lake or river cruise.

October **Turkey Trot** (870-449-4676; www.yellville.com/turkeytrot.html), Yellville Area Chamber of Commerce, P.O. Box 369, downtown Yellville, Ark. The oldest festival in Arkansas, the Turkey Trot has been held in mid-October every year since 1946. You'll hear turkey callers from all over America, watch the turkey parade, eat a turkey dinner, and enjoy innumerable food booths, vendor stands, live bands, and contests. There's even a turkey trot beauty pageant.

INDEX

Continued on next page

Continued from previous page

S

Sager Creek Arts Center, 325
Salem, Mo.: about, 268;
chamber of commerce,
263–64; music, 24. *See also*
Ozark National Scenic
Riverways
Salem Memorial District
Hospital, 264
Salem Plateau, 14
Salem Ranger District, 273
Sand Spring Resort, 108
Saunders Museum, 299
scenic drives: Branson, Mo.,
39–40; Eureka Springs and
Northwest Arkansas,
294–95; Lake of the Ozarks,
123; Original Ozarks area,
237–38; Ozark Mining
Region, 30, 167; Ozark
National Scenic Riverways,
265; Route 66 Country,
89–90; Springfield, Mo.,
200; White and Buffalo
Rivers area, 334
Scheffer's Lounge, 113
Schifferdecker Memorial Golf
Course, 180
Schifferdecker Park, 177
seasonal and special events,
17–26; Branson, Mo.,
82–83; Eureka Springs and
Northwest Arkansas, 297,
299, 324, 327–29; Lake of
the Ozarks, 144–47; Origi-
nal Ozarks area, 237,
259–60; Osage Lakes Dis-
trict, 151, 160; Ozark Min-
ing Region, 193–96; Ozark
National Scenic Riverways,
286–87; Route 66 Country,
109, 117–18; Springfield,
Mo., 230–32; Springfield,
Mo. area, 201; White and
Buffalo Rivers area, 339,
364–66
Seasons Ridge golf course, 130
Seasons Ridge grill, 139
Serenity Farm Bread, 363
Shack, The, 58
Shady Beach Campground,
185–86
Shady Lane Cabins, 282
Shawnee Mac Lakes, 279
Sheep & Wool Days, 231
Shellie's, 188–89
Shepherd Hills Factory
Outlet, 117

Shepherd of the Hills, 45–47
Shepherd of the Hills Out-
door Drama, 75
Shepherd of the Hills Trout
Hatchery, 40
Shiloh Museum of Ozark
History, 302
Shoji Tabuchi Show, The,
76–77
shopping: Branson, Mo.,
79–81; Eureka Springs and
Northwest Arkansas, 295,
326; Lake of the Ozarks,
144; Original Ozarks area,
259; Osage Lakes District,
156, 158; Ozark Mining
Region, 192–93; Ozark
National Scenic Riverways,
286; Route 66 Country,
116–17; Springfield, Mo.,
229–30; White and Buffalo
Rivers area, 363–64
Showboat *Branson Belle,*
75–76
Showcase Jubilee, 63
Show-Me 100/Show-Me
Championship, 259
Siegfried & Roy Present Dar-
ren Romea: The Voice of
Magic, 76–77
Siloam Springs, Ark.: about,
298; Dogwood Festival, 19.
See also Eureka Springs and
Northwest Arkansas
Siloam Springs Memorial
Hospital, 294
Silver Arrow Canoe Rental,
284
Silver Dollar City, 46–47
Simon Bolívar statue, 153–54
66 Drive-In Theater, 192
Skaggs Community Health
Center, 39
Skelton, Red: A Tribute to by
Tom Mullica, 74–75
Slice of Pie, A, 26, 111
Smoke on the Mountain,
77–78
snakes, 30
Snyder, Robert, 132–33
Sodie's Fountain & Grill, 360
Softball Museum, The, 203
Soleil, 139
Sons of the Pioneers, 47
Southwest Missouri Ozarks.
See Ozark Mining Region;
Springfield, Mo.
Spa Chateau, 55–56

Sparky's Roadhouse Café,
319
spas, 139
Spa Shiki, 139
specialty shops. *See* shopping
spectator sports: Original
Ozarks area, 259; Route 66
Country, 116; Springfield,
Mo., 227–29; White and
Buffalo Rivers area, 363
Spider Creek Resort on the
White River, 317–18
Spirit of the Dance, 78
Spiva Center for the Arts, 174
Sportman's Resort on the
White River, 356–57
Spring Branch Trail, 102
Spring Creek Golf Club, 271
Springdale, Ark.: about,
298–99; catfish house, 19;
chamber of commerce, 293;
sightseeing highlights, 15.
See also Eureka Springs and
Northwest Arkansas
Spring Dogwood Tour, 193–94
Springfield, Mo.: about,
197–99; area code, 199;
BBQ, 18; cultural sites,
203–4; Dickerson Park Zoo,
31; entertainment, shows,
226–27; family entertain-
ment, 208–9; getting to,
199; golf, 209–10; hiking
and walking trails, 200;
historic homes and sites,
204–5; lodging, 211–13;
map, 198; medical emer-
gencies, hospitals, 199–200;
museums, 201–3; parks,
206–7; restaurants and
eateries, 200, 213–26;
seasonal and special events,
230–32; shopping, 229–30;
sightseeing highlight, 15;
spectator sports, 227–29;
towns and villages near to,
200; visitor information,
199; wild places, 210; Wonders of Wildlife Museum
and Zooquarium, 30–31;
zoos, 205–8
Springfield Art Museum, 201
Springfield Ballet, 226
Springfield-Branson Regional
Airport, 38, 89, 122, 150,
166, 199, 236, 264
Springfield Brewing Com-
pany, 217

Continued on next page